D1230111

# THE VICHY REGIME
1940–44

# THE VICHY REGIME 1940-44

BY

ROBERT ARON

*In Collaboration with*

GEORGETTE ELGEY

*Translated by*

HUMPHREY HARE

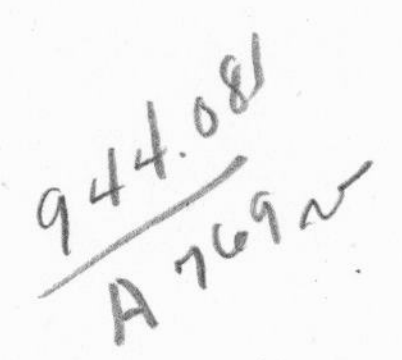

PUTNAM
42 GREAT RUSSELL STREET
LONDON MCMLVIII

Histoire de Vichy 1940–44 *first published in France* 1955
The Vichy Regime 1940–44, *abridged by the author, first published in Great Britain* 1958

*Made and Printed in Great Britain
at the Pitman Press, Bath, for the publishers
Putnam & Co. Ltd.,* 42 *Great Russell Street, London W.C.*1.

# CONTENTS

## THE END OF THE THIRD REPUBLIC



## VICHY, THE FIRST PERIOD
(10th July 1940–9th February 1941)



## VICHY, THE SECOND PERIOD
(9th February 1941–18th April 1942)

# THE VICHY REGIME
1940–44

# The End of the Third Republic

## CHAPTER 1

# CANGÉ

(12th–13th June, 1940)

IN the early evening of Wednesday, 12th June, 1940, a general officer in service dress was led by two door-keepers from the Élysée to the drawing-room of the Château of Cangé on the Cher, where the President of the Republic had taken refuge before the enemy advance. Twenty-three ministers of Paul Reynaud's Government were gathered about the Head of the State. Weygand, the Commander-in-Chief, had come to inform the Council that an armistice was necessary.

Appointed Commander-in-Chief of the French Armies on the 19th May, 1940, Weygand, on his arrival at the Grand Quartier Général, had had to face a military situation which had already become desperate. After nine months of "phoney war", in which operations had remained stagnant, only ten days had elapsed since the beginning of the German offensive on the 10th May, 1940. The front had been pierced in two places, in Belgium near Namur, and in France near Sedan. On the 25th May, at a War Council held under the chairmanship of the President, Albert Lebrun, General Weygand, without concealing the gravity of the situation, had still been talking of fighting to the end in order to defend the honour of the flag. But successive reverses on the Meuse and in the Nord, the British retreat in Flanders and the capitulation of the Belgian army on the 28th May soon dashed all hopes of re-establishing a junction between the armies of the Nord, surrounded about Dunkirk, and the rest of the army. In a memorandum, dated 29th May, 1940, Weygand informed the Government of the increasing gravity of the situation.

The battle of the Somme, the ultimate effort to contain the advance of the Wehrmacht with forces only a third the size of the enemy's, began on the 5th June, 1940: it was lost on the 10th. On that date, Weygand informed the Government in writing that the decisive disruption of the French front was imminent.

On the 11th June, 1940, a Supreme Inter-Allied Council was held at Briare, where Generals Weygand and Georges explained the situation to the French and British ministers: all available forces had been thrown into the battle. During the course of the meeting, Weygand offered his resignation, declaring that he would be happy to serve under anyone who could re-establish the situation.

On the 12th June, 1940, the front was pierced in numerous places and the German armour advanced deep into the Basse-Seine and Champagne: Rouen, Elbeuf, Villers-Cotterêts were occupied. Italy entered the war and compelled France to face her with the last intact divisions. The battle of France was lost. For the first time, at Cangé, Weygand did not hesitate to describe the situation as it was: he demanded that the Government should face the consequences of the greatest disaster the French armies had ever suffered: since the 10th May, there had been a hundred thousand killed. In his opinion, an armistice was now inevitable.

The horizon about the Château of Cangé seemed blocked by a stampede of the whole population.

On that day, when France had become a prey to feverish panic, who were these twenty-three men whom destiny had gathered in Council to decide the country's fate? Their precedence and their places at the Council table were no longer subject to protocol. Like the refugees who, a few yards away from the drawing-room in which the Council was meeting, were preparing to eat at some corner of a field or sleep in some wood, the ministers, representing a scattered population, sat face to face, haphazardly, in two rows. Lebrun was in the centre. Next to him was Paul Reynaud, the President of the Council. Opposite them were Marshal Pétain and MM. Chautemps and Mandel.

Here, to begin with, were the survivors from an earlier period, the ministers of the 21st March, the date on which Paul Reynaud had replaced Daladier: some of them represented an ultimate concession to the Radical majority that had supported the previous government, others an opposite concession to the Right which, with Laval, had put it in a minority: thus Chautemps, Campinchi and Queuille balanced, in accordance with relative parliamentary strengths, Pomaret, Louis Rollin and Laurent-Eynac. Moreover, since the 21st March, two Socialists had been co-opted, Sérol and Georges Monnet, in order to increase the Government's support from the Left, whose weakness had become apparent on the first vote of confidence which had been successful only by a majority of one. There was one technician, Raoul Dautry, a specialist in armaments. And there was one Independent, Mandel, who had been Clemenceau's right hand man at the time of the allied victory in 1918.

On the 10th May, when the German offensive began, Louis Marin, President of the Fédération Républicaine, and Ybarnegaray, of the Croix de Feu, were brought into the Government in order to introduce a conservative element which had been absent since the Front Populaire. On the 18th May, after the first disasters, Paul Reynaud called in the heroes of the last war. Marshal Pétain, the victor of Verdun, became Vice-President of the Council, while Foch's chief-of-staff, Weygand, one of the architects of victory, replaced General Gamelin at the head of the French armies. On the same day, Mandel, who under Clemenceau in 1917 had rounded up the defeatists, moved from the Colonies to a more important ministry, that of the Interior.

Paul Reynaud declared enthusiastically: "From now on Marshal Pétain is at my side as Minister of State and Vice-President of the Council, devoting his wisdom and his strength to the service of the Country." The Assembly was equally enthusiastic: on the 21st May, the whole Senate rose to its feet to salute the victor of Verdun and give him a prolonged ovation.

Nevertheless, the arrival of Pétain and the promotion of Weygand did not strengthen the Government's cohesion for long. Reynaud might well affirm that "there is total agreement between Marshal Pétain, General Weygand and myself upon the conduct of the war," but discord was nevertheless latent.

Reynaud would not admit that France could be defeated. "We shall fight in front of Paris, we shall fight behind Paris, we shall make a stand in one of our provinces, and if we are driven from it, we shall go to North Africa and, if need be, to one of our American possessions." For Pétain, after the 18th May, the war was virtually lost. As he left, on that date, his Embassy in Madrid, the Marshal was already convinced that his role in the Government would not be so much the conduct of the war as the conclusion, if possible, of an acceptable peace. Weygand was less pessimistic: he thought, on taking up the command, that however unfavourable the situation might be it could be ameliorated, but he was not prepared *a priori*, however painful it might be, to discard the possibility of being compelled to ask for an armistice.

On the 5th June, before the last battle on the line of the Somme and the Aisne, Paul Reynaud, over and above the few politicians of whom he made Excellencies, Yvon Delbos, Rivière, Chichery, Pernot, summoned experts who were not parliamentarians: he selected as Under-Secretary of State for War a young acting Brigadier-General, who had foreseen the shape of modern war and who, in command of one of the armoured divisions, had achieved on the Aisne one of the few French victories: this was General de Gaulle who, alone of members of the Government, was not at Cangé: he was on a mission in London. Reynaud appointed Bouthillier, an expert, to the Ministry of Finance, Prouvost, editor of *Paris-Soir*, to the Ministry of Information, and to the Under-Secretaryship at the Foreign Office, Paul Baudouin, an ex-director of the Bank of Indo-China who, in that capacity, had had dealings with Ciano and, it was believed, might by his presence in the Government prevent Italy's entry into the war: thus was completed a team which had certainly never expected to have to decide so suddenly upon an armistice.

Faced with these disasters, Weygand was an army chief who was no spinner of words and knew what he wanted. He stated precisely the reasons for demanding an armistice. The military reasons in the first place: the troops were harassed, disorganised and incapable of fighting; the officers and men were exhausted and dropping with sleep; the horses were dying of fatigue, at least those who had escaped the enemy tanks and planes; and the unhappy divisions were reduced to two or three battalions with but two or three 75's for artillery. Weygand concluded: "It is still an army, but I hold it at arm's length. You want to go on to the end: you have now reached the end." He then gave the civilian reasons: only a cessation of hostilities could enable some minimum order and cohesion to be maintained: "The country cannot be allowed to go completely adrift: a few troops must be preserved in order to maintain public order which may be seriously endangered in the very near future. . . . If the war continues, the troops will be cut to pieces, there will be a rout and chaos. . . ." And Weygand repeated several times that an urgent decision was necessary: "If an armistice is not asked for without delay, the armies will fall into the same disorder as have local communities and refugees. From that moment an armistice will be pointless because the harm will already have been done."

Amid the stupor that weighed over the Council, Paul Reynaud endeavoured to oppose the General's military reasons with political arguments. He pointed out the difference between Nazi Germany and the Germany which had attacked France in previous wars: "You take Hitler for another William I, the old gentleman who seized Alsace-Lorraine from us, and that was all there was to it: but Hitler is Ghengis Khan." What limits would there be to the demands of this chief of a barbarian horde if an armistice were asked for? He also invoked the agreements with Great Britain which forbade France to make a separate peace. It was a valid political argument, but it did not impress Weygand in face of the report he had made on the condition of the troops. Paul Reynaud continued in moving tones: "Gentlemen, we shall retreat into the redoubt of Brittany. When we can no longer defend ourselves, we shall be obliged to embark in a cruiser. We shall embark amid falling bombs. And if some of us are killed, so much the better. It will prove that we only left the soil of our country when there was no alternative open to us."

Mandel, Marin, Monnet, Dautry and Laurent-Eynac tried amid the hubbub to support Paul Reynaud's opinion. Pétain, in a few words, gave his support to Weygand: "I am," he said, "of the same opinion as the military commanders, who alone are in a position to judge." Prouvost suggested that negotiations for peace should be put in hand at once. Pomaret created a break in the discussion by asking the Commander-in-Chief if he were also proposing an armistice with Italy. Weygand replied, "I admit that I have not as yet considered the point." But, on the intervention of Campinchi, Minister of Marine, Weygand gave the order to carry out the intended bombing of Genoa and told his orderly officer, Captain Gasser, to telephone the Admiralty.

Amid the noisy breaking up of the meeting, Reynaud, who was to meet the British Prime Minister the following afternoon, was heard to say to Chautemps: "I shall ask Churchill." What was he going to ask him? Was it his advice concerning an eventual armistice or was it to invite him to attend the next Council of Ministers to discuss the matter with the French Government? The majority of ministers adopted the second hypothesis.

Thus, late in the evening, the first Council of Cangé came to an end. During the night and the following morning, two

Ministers exerted themselves in persuading their colleagues that an armistice must be signed: these two were Baudouin and Bouthillier, who canvassed unceasingly.

After the Council, Baudouin accompanied Paul Reynaud to his Château de Chissey in order to try to persuade him that an armistice was necessary. Madame de Portes, the President's Egeria, who had already had dinner, watched them with an anxious expression, while General de Gaulle, who had returned from London a few hours earlier, obstinately argued in favour of his idea of continuing resistance in Brittany. Baudouin, having dined, was invited by Paul Reynaud to sleep at the château, which gave him an opportunity the following morning of lecturing him once more upon the uselessness of continuing the struggle. He then left, and was joined by Bouthillier who was also showing great zeal in favour of an armistice. Within a short time, or as short a time as the crowded roads allowed, the Minister of Finance visited Dautry, then Marin, two "resisters" whom he lectured. Then he visited Marshal Pétain before rejoining Paul Reynaud at Cangé.

The Council of the 12th June had been horrified and, for the most part, surprised. That of the 13th June marked the beginning of the ministerial crisis, the rupture of the apparent unity of the Government.

The meeting had been summoned for five o'clock in the evening, but it began an hour late, the President of the Council having been delayed at Tours, where he met Churchill, Halifax, Beaverbrook, Cadogan and Spears. During the course of this Supreme Inter-Allied Council, Reynaud asked Churchill what the British attitude would be if France laid down her arms. The two Prime Ministers agreed to send a joint and pressing appeal to Roosevelt.

When at last the Ministers met at six o'clock, it could be felt at once that opinions had hardened since the day before. The atmosphere was glacial.

Paul Reynaud began by giving the Council a report of the conversations at Tours: ". . . Gentlemen, the reason for my late arrival is that I have been seeing Mr. Churchill as arranged; but the latter did not think it proper for the minister of a foreign country to take part in a meeting of a Council of Ministers, even of a friendly power." And Reynaud went on without his usual assurance. He seemed hopeful that the telegram which the two Prime Ministers had decided to send to Roosevelt would be favourably received; he informed them, but without emphasis, of the reply Churchill had made when asked what attitude Great Britain would adopt if France were to conclude a separate armistice: "Whatever happens, England will fight on till the defeat of Hitler. . . . there will be no reproaches or recriminations against France . . . the cause of France will always remain dear to her and . . . England will restore her to her power and dignity." Comprehensive, even generous words, but which could not be interpreted either as accepting or rejecting the proposal to demand an armistice which, however, Reynaud said he had told Churchill had been decided against by the Council of the day before.

These last words, no doubt uttered for the purpose of deferring the debate, had the contrary effect. They provoked two interventions. Chautemps indicated his surprise that Reynaud had not brought Winston Churchill to Cangé, in spite of the promise he had made him the night before. Then Bouthillier spoke. Disregarding the custom that Ministers should speak extempore, he drew from his pocket a tendentious note which declared, in contradiction of Reynaud's words, that the Council of the day before had approved an armistice. The shock was so unexpected that it even roused M. Lebrun, who exclaimed: "How can you say that yesterday's Council of Ministers decided in favour of an armistice? . . ."

It was now the old Marshal's turn to intervene in the debate. Inconvenienced by the fading light, he went to a window embrasure also to read a note, which stated that an armistice could no longer be avoided.

". . . The Government's duty, whatever happens, is to remain in the country, or no longer to be recognised as such. To deprive France of her natural defenders in a time of general confusion is to deliver her to the enemy. This is to kill the soul of France, and thereby render her renaissance impossible.

"The regeneration of France must be brought about by our staying on the spot rather than by the reconquest of our land by allied guns in such conditions and with such delay as it is impossible to foresee.

"I am, therefore, of the opinion that we should not leave the soil of France and that we should accept whatever suffering may be imposed on our country and her sons. The renaissance of France will be the fruit of this suffering. . . .

"As far as I am concerned, I declare that, outside the Government if it must be so, I refuse to leave Metropolitan France. I shall remain among the people of France to share their sufferings and their misfortunes."

And Pétain concluded: "In my view, an armistice is the necessary condition for the perpetuation of France eternal."

The taking up of so decisive a position was not without its effect on the Ministers. Ybarnegaray stood morally to attention: "Since Marshal Pétain and General Weygand show us our duty, we have but to obey. I am a soldier, and I support the opinion of the military chiefs."

Not all those present had a similar conception of discipline. Reynaud stated categorically that this solution was dishonourable. Campinchi, Monnet, Marin, Dautry and Rio stated the arguments against an armistice. Weygand replied with some vehemence. He pointed out the desperate situation of the troops. Further, he announced the news of a Communist rising in Paris and of the installation of a provisional government at the Élysée under Maurice Thorez. One of his orderly officers, Captain Gasser, had brought him the news in the Council. Mandel immediately went out of the room, got Langeron, the Prefect of Police, on the telephone, and informed the Council that the news was false. What he did not know, what no one could know in Cangé with its lack of communications, was that the rumour had a certain foundation: the radio "Komintern" had given the French Communists a formal order "not to leave Paris, whatever happens, and to publish *l'Humanité* legally as soon as the German troops enter the city, and thus face them with the accomplished fact." Weygand declared that France could only be saved by a government which remained on metropolitan soil. "What authority over France do Ministers think they will be able to preserve when they have quitted Metropolitan France? How long will they be away? The time it will take American factories to produce the necessary aeroplanes and tanks to allow them to reconquer it? That will take several years, and do they imagine that anyone will remember them? Moreover, how do they expect to reconquer France? By bombing our towns and our countrymen? It's an absurd and horrible programme."

In his anger against these chatterers who refused to listen to his arguments, Weygand turned to invective: "If I had been Minister, I should not have wanted the Government to leave Paris at the approach of the invader, but rather remain like those Roman senators, who sat in their curule chairs as the Gauls entered Rome . . . but the geese only saved the Capitol once." This historical reference did nothing to pacify the atmosphere. And when one of the Ministers remarked that the departure of the Government for North Africa was a political question and outside the province of the military command and exceeded the General's competence, the latter went out banging the door behind him: "I have had enough of these fire-eaters who want to go on fighting and dash off abroad." "I," he concluded, declaring a similar intention to Pétain, "shall not leave the soil of France, even if they put my legs in irons."

The Council had resolved nothing: no decision had been taken. But, more serious and more decisive than any resolution they could have adopted, the meeting of Ministers had perpetuated an irreparable rupture in the Government's unity, which, in this catastrophic hour, presaged a profound and fatal dissension among Frenchmen. This disagreement over the choice which lay before them constituted the first episode in the drama that was to follow.

On the 14th, the Government's flight was renewed. Once more Ministers were confronted with the spectacle of a whole people in confusion, in material, intellectual and moral chaos.

At such a time of disaster, if one stopped and thought for a moment, it could be only to be disquieted that France, as her only resource, had but an old man, laden with glory and years, who still remembered having learned his catechism from a chaplain who had been a veteran of the Grand Army.

CHAPTER 2

# BORDEAUX

(14th–29th June, 1940)

THERE were machine-guns manned by German soldiers all round the Arc de Triomphe in Paris. From each of the stone posts, which surrounded the monument, a machine-gun covered one of the avenues which terminate at the Étoile. It had become a defensive position, reinforced by an armoured car, parked under the Arc itself near the grave of the Unknown Soldier, and by four pieces of artillery, trained on the entrances to the Avenues Foch, Victor-Hugo, Marceau and the Champs-Élysées. Since morning, mobile loud-speakers had been going to and fro in every district in Paris, announcing Hitler's victory and enjoining the rare inhabitants remaining in the city to lay down their arms and stay at home. It was across a dead city, its streets and avenues deserted, that a General, surrounded by his staff, marched to the foot of the Arc de Triomphe, saluted the tomb of the Unknown Soldier and, before taking the salute of the march-past of the conquerors, ordered a flag bearing the swastika to be hoisted on the monument, where it flew during the first thirteen hours of the Occupation only to appear there no more.

On this day of the 14th June, 1940, France no longer had a capital. While the occupying troops billeted themselves in the empty palaces, which had contained the Ministries, the Chamber or the Senate, the Presidents and Ministers, driven out by the invasion, had left the châteaux of Touraine. By way of departmental roads, or by National Road 10, cleared on their behalf of the traffic jams of the exodus by contingents of police, they drove towards Bordeaux, where awaited them the memories of previous invasions and previous retreats: 1871, 1914, 1940. Three times in less than three quarters of a century, retreating governments had installed themselves on the banks of the Garonne. And General Lafont, commanding the 18th Military

District, who, towards five o'clock in the evening, crossed the Pont de Pierre to meet the Government convoy, might have evoked the ghost of Monsieur Thiers or that of Raymond Poincaré, both of whom had also been received by the city.

On the other side of the river, on the outskirts of the town, he saluted the President of the Republic, then the President of the Senate. Marshal Pétain, whose personal friend he was, made him get into his car; and the two men conversed during the short journey to the Préfecture.

The Marshal, Vice-President of the Council, confirmed his decision not to leave the soil of Metropolitan France whatever might happen, whether he were still a member of the Government or not. Accepting in advance all the risks of his mission, he had decided to ask for an armistice and dedicate all his efforts towards the restoration of the country.

At eighty-four, he was one of the two surviving victorious Marshals of the Great War, the other being Franchet d'Esperey. When, two years later, he heard of the other's death, his obituary valediction was: "From now on I shall no longer be called Marshal Pétain, but *the* Marshal." In fact, from 1940, his popularity so eclipsed the other great leader that he was "the Marshal".

The country was almost unanimous in regarding him as its only hope and was to place its trust in him in the days of its greatest ordeal.

The early part of his military career gave no inkling of such a destiny. In 1914, on the eve of the Great War, Philippe Pétain, a Colonel commanding a regiment of Infantry at Arras, was on the point of retiring from the army without having achieved a general's stars. Born at Cauchy-la-Tour, in the Pas-de-Calais, on the 24th April, 1856, and therefore approaching sixty years of age, his outstanding success first as a pupil and then as an instructor at the École de Guerre had not sufficed to assure his promotion to the higher ranks, which seemed to go by right to most officers who had passed the staff course. His career, later admitted General Laure, his official biographer, "was very ordinary, almost below the average."

It may have been that Colonel Pétain had the reputation of being too independently minded. When the General Staff extolled the tactics of the continuous offensive, Colonel Pétain, almost alone in his opinion, obstinately clung to his faith in defensive tactics and a war of position. This doctrine was a manifestation of his natural prudence, and was in accordance with the lessons he drew from the recent Russo-Japanese war, in which trenches and field fortifications had re-appeared. And he clung obstinately to his opinion.

Conscious of his own worth, Pétain always refused to make such concessions as might have helped his advancement in his profession. Even when addressing his superiors, he never minced his words. A short while before the war, the General directing the manoeuvres in which his regiment was taking part, assembled the senior officers to discuss the operations. He admonished them in these terms: "In a war it is a mistake to have a preconceived idea. The situation must be judged objectively according to the terrain, the state of the forces engaged, the information available concerning the enemy, but certainly with no *a priori* ideas. It is clear that you have all acted in accordance with a preconceived idea which has turned out to be wrong. Colonel Pétain alone certainly had no such idea, for he correctly executed the manoeuvre. I shall ask him to explain his plan to us." Colonel Pétain, thus cited as an example to the others, came forward, saluted his superior and, standing impeccably to attention, said, in the middle of a religious hush: "Gentlemen, I had a preconceived idea." Recounting the incident at a later date, the Marshal was to comment: "Clearly, I was not destined to become a general."

For the stars to appear and multiply upon his sleeves, it needed the exceptional circumstances of the First World War. That war, the shape of which he had foreseen, and for which he had never hesitated to say how ill-prepared the General Staff was, brought him the promotion that had passed him by in peace.

When in command of a brigade, he distinguished himself at Guise, one of the few victorious episodes in that first disastrous month in which the allied armies retreated from Belgium almost to Paris before the miracle of the Marne.

Promoted general at last, he commanded successively the 6th Division, then the XXXIIIrd Army Corps, at the time of the Artois offensive when, for the first time, artillery preparation opened the way for the infantry and minimised their losses; finally, he commanded the Second Army with which, in September 1915, he took part in the battle of Champagne, which failed to pierce the enemy front.

In these successive commands, Pétain won victory after victory by remaining faithful to the ideas he had professed before the war and which had impeded his promotion. He never mounted an attack without being certain of its success.

Pétain never cared for hazardous adventures: above all he was careful of his men's lives. To repeat Paul Valéry's comment: "He had discovered that fire kills." Inspecting a regiment which had been decimated in an heroic action, Pétain profoundly moved the officers and men with these simple words: "You went into the assault singing the *Marseillaise*: it was magnificent. But next time you will not need to sing the *Marseillaise*. There will be a sufficient number of guns to ensure your attack's success."

His prudence and concern to spare lives explain, and were the foundation of, the climax of his military career.

This climax was manifest in two separate events in which Pétain revealed himself as a great servant of his country. In February, 1916, as an Army Commander, he had to withstand the Crown Prince's attacks on Verdun: a defensive battle which suited both his tactics and his temperament; and in which his humanity was evident once again. From the steps of his headquarters at Souilly, he watched reinforcements going up to the line and, when a few days later, he saw these young soldiers, weary, bewildered and distressed, return from the inferno, he gave expression to his grief. In June, 1917, the victor of Verdun, Supreme Commander designate of the French Army, restored the morale of the troops which had been shattered by a hazardous offensive. He made no speeches and imposed the minimum of sanctions, but employed limited and practical measures which proved effective within the formations under his command: regular leave, better food, more frequent rest periods. When he visited regiments that had mutinied, he did precisely the opposite to that which the men feared. Instead of punishing the guilty, he awarded decorations to those who had behaved well. He assembled the generals, the officers and the men, blaming such commanders as deserved it, and asked the simple soldiers themselves to designate those of their comrades who had earned the Croix de Guerre. In August and October, 1917, at Verdun and at La Malmaison, two limited offensives, mounted with an exceptional concentration of material, gave the army the opportunity to win victories without much risk or heavy losses, and restored confidence.

The following year, he reached his apogee. In command of the French Army during the decisive victories, promoted Marshal of France, issuing the last *communiqué* of the Great War, he seemed nevertheless inhibited by the very qualities which had earned him his extraordinary success. Foch had been preferred to him as Commander-in-Chief of the Allied Armies; and, in that position, was set over even Pétain, the Commander of the French Army. But Foch, who believed in the offensive and the war of manoeuvre, and who indeed seems to have had greater military genius, was not in agreement with Pétain upon the method of conducting the final stages of the war. There was at least one occasion where the two commanders disagreed and where the facts show Foch, rather than Pétain, to have been right. This was on the 18th July, 1918, the decisive turning point of the war. After the halting of the last German offensive of the 15th July, in Champagne, Foch ordered Mangin's Army to make a surprise counter-attack from the Forest of Villers-Cotterêts. On the 17th July, the eve of D Day, Foch learnt that Pétain had taken it on himself to send a counter-order; the operation seemed to him premature; he was not calculating on an offensive before the spring of 1919. Foch imposed his will; and on the 18th July, Mangin, falling upon the enemy, threw him into disorder and compelled him to begin a retreat which, less than four months later, obliged him to capitulate.

It was owing to his prudence that Pétain so often incurred the reproach of being pessimistic, "negative" or even, as some were to say later, "defeatist". Clemenceau, Poincaré and General Sir Henry Wilson had already noted this trait in his character. Even Joffre, giving this criticism a retroactive validity, went so far as to dispute his merit at Verdun: on two occasions he should have been prevented from evacuating the right bank of the Meuse. The credit for the victory was due more to his subordinate, Nivelle, to which Pétain was to reply: "I do not know who won the battle of Verdun: but I do know that, if it had been lost, it is I who would have lost it."

But this merely cast the faintest of shadows across the brilliance of the picture; victory was then too recent; the part which the French armies commanded by Pétain had played in it was too great in November, 1918, for Pétain not to take his place in history, his glory unassailable.

It had taken the second-lieutenant nearly forty years from the moment he left Saint-Cyr to become a colonel; four years had sufficed for him to rise from colonel to marshal. Paul Valéry, receiving him into the Académie Française, was to say: "You are the only one among our leaders who, beginning the war in command of six thousand men, have finished it at the head of three million combatants." Was there not perhaps something too exalting in such a change of rhythm?

A period of extraordinary plenitude now began for Marshal Pétain. Circumstances had proved him right, had raised him to the level of his own conception of himself.

His popularity was more universally recognised than that of any of the other holders of his fabulous rank. Every section of opinion gave him equal admiration, since he was reputed to be at once the most republican of conservative generals and the most conservative of republican generals. For both the Left and the Right, he was the incarnation of the humane commander, sparing of his soldiers' lives.

The period after the war was fertile in new experiences: the experience of married life, in particular, which set the seal on a relationship that had already long endured. He married at the age of sixty-five. And was later to think even this premature: "I had been waiting twenty years. I should have waited another ten!"

Pétain never tried to precipitate or forestall events. He delighted in saying that he had never asked for anything, but that people always came to him. In 1926, it was he who was called on to suppress Abd-el-Krim's revolt in Morocco. In 1934, after the February riots, his membership seemed indispensable to the Gaston Doumergue Government, which was to pursue a policy of reform and general pacification. In 1938, Daladier had need of his prestige to re-establish diplomatic relations with Franco, and asked him to be the first French Ambassador to Madrid. And, finally, in May 1940, Reynaud had recourse to him.

While his sympathies were certainly towards the Right and he had little sympathy with the Parliaments of those days, Pétain took care not to be compromised by the clumsy, improvised conspiracies to which conservative circles were so addicted in the years that preceded the war.

All those of the Right, who wished to regenerate the political life of the country, had Pétain in mind as the embodiment of a State which would be free of the demagogue and of disorder.

He knew it; and did not object to pamphlets, inspired from within his own circle, demanding power on his behalf: for instance, Gustave Hervé's pamphlet, *C'est Pétain qu'il nous faut!*, composed under the influence of Alibert, in which, even as early as 1935, were adumbrated the authoritarian measures which the Marshal's government would put into effect at Vichy in 1940.

Before these anticipations, which were to be realised in the future, Pétain remained impassive and unperturbed, but himself never gave any sign of agreement or connivance.

Pétain never schemed during this period, when so many others, including Marshal Franchet d'Esperey, failed to hide their sympathies with certain secret conspiracies. Nor did he ever put himself forward as a candidate for any position whatever. In 1939, when Albert Lebrun's first term of seven years came to an end, the Marshal refused to be a candidate for the Presidency of the Republic, which he had once described, thinking of MacMahon, as "suitable for defeated Marshals".

Among various other projects were those of Pierre Laval. For a long time past, this professional politician had accounted the Marshal a necessary figurehead to preside over, without obstructing, a government of which he himself would be the leading spirit. Expert at pulling strings, he sought to rally a diversity of political leaders to Pétain and to bring him to power by the normal parliamentary processes. Already, in 1932, Laval was campaigning for Pétain as President of the Republic. The Marshal published a disavowal in the newspapers. In the course of a secret conversation, with an agent of General Franco, in April 1937, Laval affirmed that, at the fall of Léon Blum's government, "the salvation of France rested in a Pétain government and that the Marshal was determined to accept that responsibility"—an assertion there was nothing to confirm. Finally, in September 1939, Laval proposed to the Marshal through an intermediary, Commandant Loustaunau-Lacau, to get rid of Daladier and form a government in which he, Laval, would "rid him of all rival candidates". Pétain, so it appears, did not pursue the matter.

His innate prudence, therefore, prevented him either putting himself forward as a candidate or playing the part of a conspirator. In either case, by entering the lists too soon, would he not have been tempting fate and compromising those sympathies he knew so well how to preserve in every political party, even in those which in his heart he disapproved of the most?

Pierre Cot, a young Radical, using the same words with which, fifteen years later, he was to praise Maurice Thorez, asserted that Pétain was the only man capable of saving France. Léon Blum, when he heard that Pétain had been appointed Ambassador to Madrid, complained that this was doing Franco too much honour. And the Marshal, himself, took care of Republican circles: did he not regularly attend the Paul-Hervieu luncheon which was frequented by Radicals?

His manner became more and more that of a spiritual leader expressing himself in moral terms and attaching particular importance to educational problems: he, himself, had no children.

In 1934, when Doumergue summoned him to join the Government, it was only reluctantly that he accepted the Ministry of War: he had set his heart on the Ministry of Education.

In asserting itself, Pétain's moral conscience failed to reduce his pessimism. He consistently believed in the regenerative virtues of suffering.

Prudence, patience, faith in his mission, a sometimes rather narrow morality, such were the apparent characteristics that Pétain, as Head of the State, was to inherit from Pétain the soldier, Pétain the minister, and Pétain the ambassador. There were other less obvious characteristics which contributed to his complex personality.

In the first place, his cunning and his taste for underhand methods are surprising in the supreme position to which he was soon to accede.

On the 5th February, 1940, he wrote to General Gamelin a letter of congratulation on, and entire approbation of, his methods of conducting the war.

At the same period, contradicting himself, he held the following conversation with an intimate friend: "Gamelin is incapable of conducting this war." "Have you said this to Daladier?" "No, let him get out of his own difficulties."

Another shadow cast across the brilliant portrait: Pétain's ingratitude sharpened as he grew older. He was never to hesitate to sacrifice one of his collaborators, even the oldest and most devoted. "Between Laval and Pétain," wrote Maurice Martin du Gard, "there is competition in ingratitude." A competition, whose rules, as far as he was concerned, the Marshal defined thus: "I sacrifice nobody: but no one is indispensable to me, the best among them will come back to me improved by absence."

From these unworthy measures put to the service of great designs, from these apparent blemishes on a shining shield, some have diagnosed the effects of senility.

Undoubtedly, in 1940, Pétain had moments of great intellectual acuity and remarkable presence of mind. From time to time he made rejoinders with such speed and precision that they proved his intellectual faculties to be in full vigour: nevertheless, even his most intimate and devoted friends were compelled to recognise that, at eighty-four years of age, there were moments when his brain did not function well. His orderly officer, Captain Bonhomme, who devoted a veritable cult to him, admitted in a private conversation: "He is very, very old. His thought is no longer geared to action."

Another of his intimate friends has told us that one could always "succeed by wearing him down" and, by taking time, make him sign a document which, in the first instance, he had laid aside, at least when it did not concern some essential matter. Finally, it often happened, or at least appeared to do so, that through weariness he agreed with the last speaker, thus contradicting himself.

His intelligence, subject as it was to eclipses, owed to his great age the fact that it was often congealed in retrograde ideas. Already, before the war, Pétain had committed mistakes in prognosticating the shape that the future conflict would take, imagining that it would be very similar to that of 1914–1918. In 1934, as Minister for War, in the Gaston Doumergue government, he declared before the Senate Army Commission that it was supererogatory to fortify the precise sector through which the Germans advanced in 1940: "Beyond Montmédy are the Ardennes forests. They are impenetrable if certain special dispositions are made. In consequence, we consider this to be an impassable zone. Naturally, the borders of the forest on the enemy side will be protected. Blockhouses will be built. But as this front will have no depth, the enemy will not be able to deploy. If they did so, they would be caught as they came out. We thus do not look upon this sector as dangerous."

In 1938, in a preface to a book by General Chouvineau, he discounted the effectiveness of tanks: "The small numbers of these weapons restrict the front on which they can attack, the time necessary to the development of their effective action can be used by the defence for bringing up reserves."

The country paid no heed to these limitations of age, these failures of will-power and this sclerosis of thought, but anxiously placed its hopes on Pétain. His physical health, his vigour, surprised all who saw him: at eighty-four, he had the strength of a man of sixty and could still walk five or six kilometres without fatigue.

When Pétain spoke of France Eternal, it seemed as if he made no distinction between the country and himself, as if, almost, they were one. To an attaché at the Portuguese Embassy at Vichy, he was to say sententiously: "Nations must learn to speak to each other in the language of Heaven and not that of this world."

Such he wished to be—and such perhaps he was—for the majority of the people of France when, a legendary figure, he made his entry into Bordeaux on the 14th June, 1940.

The town in which his destiny and that of France was to be played out was in considerable turmoil.

The President of the Republic, Ministers and Ministries installed themselves as best they might in two provisional but governmental buildings, the normal seats or offices for the transmission of power: ministerial meetings were held in the Bordeaux Préfecture in the Rue Vital-Carles. Reynaud took up his abode in the headquarters of the 18th Military District. Mandel was at the Préfecture, which he turned into a meeting place for the adversaries of the armistice. The President of the Chamber, Herriot, the President of the Senate, Jeanneney, both hostile to an armistice, never left the office of the Minister of the Interior. There they met Campinchi, Monnet and President Léon Blum, whom Mandel, anxious to have the support of his authority, had summoned by telephone on the Government's arrival. Mandel had also warned Senator Lémery whom he knew to be hostile to Germany and to have influence with Marshal Pétain.

Thus, little by little, the politicians gathered. Having made their way there as best they could, there were soon two hundred members of Parliament in Bordeaux, and they held their meetings in a school in the Cours Anatole-France. Journalists and business men thronged the steps of the theatre or the neighbourhood of the Préfecture. Marquet, the Mayor of Bordeaux, billeted the arrivals in accordance with the political esteem in which he held them. The privileged were placed among the well-known vineyards in the surrounding districts, such as Bergery—the only deputy to have voted against the war subsidies on 2nd September, 1939—the others in less agreeable localities, the "warmongers", for instance, whom he placed near the station, where their sleep was disturbed by their fear of bombs. Léon Blum, suspect—already!—on two counts, his hostile attitude towards an armistice and the fact that he was a Jew, had all doors closed against him—both hotel-keepers and private individuals showed no enthusiasm to entertain so compromising a personality—until a deputy, Audeguil, took him in.

Finally, creating a following about himself which was soon to oppose that of Mandel, Pierre Laval, who had also arrived on the 14th June, was constantly to be seen in the lobbies of the Bordeaux Mairie, through which every deputy and senator in search of a lodging had to pass. His demeanour was authoritative, he behaved as a leader, he attracted members of Parliament to himself and lectured them. Often, wishing to speak to one of them out of the hubbub of the ante-chamber, he would take him by the arm and lead him into a little office opposite that of Marquet. There, without worrying about the presence of the Mayor's Chef de Cabinet and his two secretaries, the ex-President of the Council lashed the Reynaud Government which was, according to him, incapable of taking the decision that had now become imperative.

On the morning of the 15th June, summoned by an urgent telegram from Pétain (which was somewhat irregular, since the Government had not even been informed),[1] Weygand arrived in Bordeaux.

Thus, in spite of a certain amount of improvisation and confusion, everything was more or less ready for the continuance of the drama. The stake in this decisive game was whether an armistice should be asked for or not. Officially, the game was being played out between three men, whose opinions were opposed to each other. On the one hand, was the President of the Council, Paul Reynaud, who supported a continuation of the

[1] There was another significant anomaly: the telegram told Weygand to go to the private house of Baudouin, one of the Ministers who shared the Marshal's views.

struggle. On the other, his Vice-President of the Council, Marshal Pétain, and the Commander-in-Chief, Weygand, were determined to achieve a cessation of hostilities by negotiation. In this crucial debate, both camps maintained that they alone were inspired by the true interests of the nation. It was merely that each side had a different conception of what course would serve the country best.

Paul Reynaud, in his desire not to sign an armistice, was not unaware of the fact that the campaign of France was lost. This is proved by the telegram which, during the night of the 13th–14th June, he sent to President Roosevelt, imploring him to bring America into the war. France was incapable of saving herself; her condition was desperate. If America did not intervene, "you will see France sink like a drowning man and disappear with one last look towards the land of Liberty, from whence he awaits salvation."

France, according to Reynaud, even if moving towards the abyss, could not sign an armistice: this seemed to him both contrary to the national honour—France was bound to England by the Agreement of the 28th March which forbade her to treat separately—and against her interests, since, in his opinion, the war was only beginning and, sooner or later, the Nazis would be defeated.

The solution he envisaged consisted in the first place in accepting the consequences of the disaster by making the French army surrender, as the Dutch and Belgian armies had done, the solution of the "Brittany redoubt" having been abandoned, because it was unrealisable in the chaotic state of the French Forces. The surrender would be purely a military act, which would not bind the Government. The latter, in order that France should remain in the war beside her allies, would abandon metropolitan soil either for North Africa, to which it would transfer such troops as were still in condition to fight and had escaped the surrender, or even for one of the American possessions. In either case, France would preserve control of her Empire and of her Fleet, which would continue to fight at the side of the British.

In the other camp, Pétain's and Weygand's position was irreconcilable with Paul Reynaud's: they both wished to sign an armistice for reasons which, however, were not altogether identical. Pétain produced two arguments: one was the supposed bad faith of the British, the other was the only too real brutality of the invaders, against which he wished to protect the people of France. Weygand alleged more typically military motives.

Weygand supported the armistice as being the lesser evil because it would save the honour of the French Army. Surrender, he told Reynaud on the 15th June, would cover the colours with opprobrium and dishonour the Army. Was it to suffer that shame that Paul Reynaud had recalled him from Syria to take the command in a campaign, which from its very beginning had been compromised by the errors of successive governments during the last twenty years?

This conflict between Reynaud on the one hand, Pétain and Weygand on the other, was to be resolved during the two first days the Government spent in Bordeaux. Constitutionally, Reynaud should have won: he was President of the Council, while Pétain was only Vice-President of the Council. It was Reynaud who had appointed the Commander-in-Chief: if the military power were to oppose the civil power, why should he not replace him? Moreover, he had on his side, as we shall see, the majority of members of Parliament—or at least those who were officially supposed to represent it.

In fact, things turned out differently. When, on the 15th June at 4.15 in the afternoon, the first Council of Ministers in Bordeaux opened, Reynaud had already virtually lost the contest.

Doubtless, the Presidents of the Assemblies, Jeanneney, President of the Senate, and Herriot, President of the Chamber of Deputies, supported Paul Reynaud. And, in theory, they represented the nation. But, in fact, they no longer represented any real power, only depreciated titles and absent Assemblies. When Vincent Auriol suggested to Herriot that Parliament should be convoked, the latter cried, "Good God! What on earth for? What a pretty spectacle they would afford the country!"

On the other hand, before the meeting of the Council of Ministers, Reynaud had been subjected to damaging pressure, against which he was powerless. He had not the necessary authority with the nation to dismiss the three great military leaders.

In the morning, Pétain, supported by Alibert, his chief civilian assistant, told Reynaud that, if an armistice were not asked for, he would immediately resign. All that Reynaud could obtain was a few hours' grace: the threat remained.

Weygand produced new arguments, some of which were unforeseen, in support of his refusal to surrender. When Reynaud adduced the example of Queen Wilhelmina of Holland, whose army had laid down its arms while she went into exile in order to continue the war, Weygand exclaimed: "What analogy can there be between a monarch and the head of one of these ephemeral governments, of which the Third Republic has already had more than a hundred in the seventy years of its existence? Once out of France, Paul Reynaud will be replaced and forgotten!"

Moreover, there was a third threat which there had been no reason to foresee. Paul Reynaud had just learnt that Admiral Darlan, Commander-in-Chief of the Fleet, had suddenly defected. Even the day before, apparently determined to resist, he had said to Edouard Herriot: "Is it true, President, that . . . Pétain and Weygand wish to conclude an armistice? If this is the case, and make no mistake about it, I shall leave with the Fleet." But now, in the presence of Paul Reynaud, he adopted a contrary attitude: "The proposal, made by General de Gaulle a fortnight ago, of transferring seven hundred and eighty thousand men to North Africa is absurd."

It was, therefore, in the worst possible circumstances that Reynaud opened the Council of Ministers at 4.15. His resistance sapped by his collaborators, blocked by the opposition of the military leaders, without parliamentary support, he could still delay the event but could no longer evade it.

And yet, constitutionally, Reynaud still had a theoretical advantage. It is now known that out of the twenty-four Ministers a majority of fourteen supported a continuation of the war and a departure for Africa.

But what did those Ministers represent in face of the victor of Verdun and the great military leaders? Even Georges Mandel, once Clemenceau's lieutenant, might forcefully elaborate the future possibilities which made it ill-advised to sign an armistice, yet his influence was nugatory. "The incompetence of our military leaders has lost us the Battle of France, but our country is not finally defeated. . . . I believe in the superiority of the forces of the democracies. It is mere folly to declare ourselves beaten when we may be able to win by continuing the war with our allies." Hypotheses which required four years in which to prove themselves true. In opposition to them, Weygand and Darlan, summoned at the beginning of the Council, described the immediate situation: the Maginot Line was surrounded, the Germans were crossing the Rhine, Normandy was occupied and the disaster was, if possible, increasing hour by hour. Having made their report, the two Service chiefs left the Council Chamber for a neighbouring room.

In the Council Chamber, Reynaud, realising the effect the disastrous military report had produced on the Ministers, and still refusing to ask for an armistice, was making a new effort for surrender. The Council appeared to agree: Pétain, either from fatigue or tactics, pretended also to be in agreement and accepted to become the Government's messenger to the Commander-in-Chief in order to try to convince him. He went to join him in the neighbouring room. His absence lasted a quarter of an hour: when he returned, it appeared that his mission had had the opposite effect to that envisaged. Pétain had not succeeded in persuading Weygand: but Weygand had confirmed the Marshal in the idea that surrender would be dishonouring, and that it was the Government's duty to ask for an armistice.

It was at this point that two members of the Government, experienced members of Parliament accustomed to political bargaining, of whom one, Chautemps, as Vice-President of the Council and Vice-President of the Radical Party, enjoyed great authority, suggested the compromise on which the future of France was to depend.

Frossard spoke first and indicated a possible issue from the impasse. "Since," he said, "the Marshal and ten Ministers refuse to leave France and envisage an armistice, while the President of the Council and fourteen Ministers are prepared to leave Metropolitan soil without signing an armistice, the only conceivable hypothesis which could restore agreement between them would be if the conditions of the armistice were so dishonourable that neither one side nor the other could consent to them. . . . And it is impossible that they should not be so."

Frossard did not carry his reasoning to its logical conclusion which would indeed have made Hitler the saviour of French unity. But Chautemps, more expert, more subtle and a better tactician, stated with authority that the conditions of an armistice would undoubtedly be unacceptable, and that, once they were known, public opinion could not but approve the departure of the Government and the continuation of the war: his conclusion was therefore not to ask for an armistice, but to discover what the eventual conditions of an armistice would be. This was a compromise which did not resolve the disagreement of Ministers among themselves, but allowed of its being concealed. It attracted both the supporters and adversaries of an armistice: the first were sure that, once the conditions were known, an armistice could not be accepted; the others felt that, once the question as to conditions had been lodged, an armistice would no longer be able to be avoided. As for Reynaud, he managed to obtain that the Government would make no decision on Chautemps' proposal before they knew President Roosevelt's answer to the appeal sent forty-eight hours earlier.

During that day of the 15th June, the determination of both Paul Reynaud and Lebrun had been shaken by Pétain and Weygand. The next day, events seemed to have concerted to give them the final blow.

Four signals, coming from Washington, London and from the armies, addressed either to Lebrun or Reynaud, determined the form of the drama.

The first, expected since the day before, was Roosevelt's reply to the appeal sent him by Winston Churchill and Reynaud. The American President confirmed (a fact, which Reynaud must have known) that he was constitutionally unable to declare war on the mere demand of two European Ministers. But as long as the French continued to fight for democracy and their independence, the United States would do all that was in its power to help them. Between "throw into the balance the weight of the power of America", as Reynaud had asked, and these imprecise promises, there was a considerable gap. "I know," Roosevelt said, "that you will not interpret this declaration as implying military intervention. Only Congress can enter into such engagements."

This official telegram was communicated to the Ministers.

The second and third telegrams were the most important of all because, apart from their immediate effect on Paul Reynaud, they were not without influence on the attack, made a fortnight later, by the Royal Navy on the French Fleet at Mers-el-Kebir. Coming from London, and transmitted by the British Ambassador, Sir Ronald Campbell, they were as follows.

"From Viscount Halifax to Sir Ronald Campbell, 16th June,

13.30 hours. Please give M. Paul Reynaud the following message which has been approved by the Cabinet: Mr. Churchill to M. Reynaud, 16th June, 1940, 12.35 p.m.

"Our Agreement forbidding separate negotiations, whether for armistice or peace, was made with the French Republic and not with any particular French administration or statesmen. It therefore involves the honour of France. Nevertheless, *provided, but only provided, that the French Fleet is sailed forthwith for British harbours pending negotiations*, His Majesty's Government give their full consent to an enquiry by the French Government to ascertain the terms of an armistice for France. His Majesty's Government, being resolved to continue the war, wholly exclude themselves from all part in the above mentioned enquiry concerning an armistice."

The third telegram, which arrived two hours later, confirmed and added precision to the stipulations contained in the second.

"From Viscount Halifax to Sir Ronald Campbell, 16th June, 3.45 p.m.

"You should inform M. Reynaud as follows:

"We expect to be consulted as soon as any armistice terms are received. This is necessary not merely in virtue of treaty forbidding separate peace or armistice, but also in view of vital consequences of any armistice to ourselves, having regard especially to the fact that British troops are fighting with the French Army. You should impress on the French Government that in stipulating for removal of French Fleet to British ports we have in mind French interests as well as our own, and are convinced that it will strengthen the hands of the French Government in any armistice discussion if they can show that the French Navy is out of reach of the German Forces. As regards the French Air Force, we assume that every effort will be made to fly it to North Africa, unless indeed the French Government would prefer to send it to this country. . . ."

The French President of the Council could not look favourably on these two communications. Whichever policy was to be pursued, once information had been obtained concerning the German conditions, whether an armistice was to be asked for or the war continued, the transfer of the Fleet to England would weaken the French position. In the first case, France would no longer hold its principal trump card in the eventual negotiations, moreover, if the armistice were signed, it was inconceivable that French ships, handed over to a still belligerent power, should risk battle or be suspected of being able to do so after Franco-German hostilities had come to an end. In the second case, if France continued to fight, the concentration, even provisionally, of French ships in English ports, left North Africa open to attack by the Italian Fleet.

Besides, these two telegrams, containing unacceptable suggestions, reached Bordeaux in circumstances which prevented their being placed before the Council of Ministers. The Council, on this fateful day of 16th June, met twice: at 11 o'clock in the morning and again in the afternoon at 4 o'clock. Halifax's telegrams were communicated to Reynaud in the interval between the two meetings; and were withdrawn by Campbell before the opening of the second Council of Ministers. The reason for their withdrawal, so soon after the Ambassador had received his instructions, was that during the interval between the receipt of the second British communication and the second Council meeting, Campbell had received an order from Churchill to cancel both telegrams. They were replaced by a sensational offer of indissoluble union between France and Great Britain, of which Reynaud was informed by telephone from London by General de Gaulle. Put forward without enthusiasm by Churchill, on the suggestion of two Frenchmen, members of the Economic Mission in London, MM. Pleven and Jean Monnet, and General de Gaulle, as well as by Lord Vansittart, the offer implied the immediate setting-up of a single government and a single parliament for the duration of hostilities, and conferred a double citizenship on all members of the condominium thus formed in defeat. If, in England, Churchill was somewhat sceptical of such an improvised plan, in France, only Reynaud, Mandel, Marin, Dautry, Rio and Georges Monnet supported it; the greater part of the Ministers agreed with the opinion of Ybarnegaray, Chautemps and Pétain, who accused England of wishing to debase France to the position of a dominion.

Thus, owing to the circumstances, Paul Reynaud was unable to make an official statement about the two telegrams concerning the eventuality of a French armistice. They therefore received no answer, neither negative nor positive. The silence with which they were received could, after the rejection of indissoluble union, be interpreted in London as a refusal to accept them, or as an indication that the policy concerning the future of the French Fleet had not yet been formulated.

The fourth telegram, transmitted, to be precise, by telephone, sent by General Georges and addressed to Weygand, who handed it to Lebrun, was as follows: "17 hours.—Situation deteriorating. In the East, northern outskirts of Dijon and Saône front reached by the enemy. In the centre, numerous armoured columns in the neighbourhood of La Charité, threatening G.A.3 with envelopment. Forest of Fontainebleau occupied. Grave supply situation for retreating troops and civil population. Movement difficult owing to blocked roads and bombing of railway lines and bridges. Essential decision should be made soonest. Signed: General Georges."

This desperate appeal from Weygand's immediate subordinate in command of the French Army was not transmitted to the Ministers, but contributed to the weakening of Albert Lebrun's determination before the decisive Council, which was held at 4.20 p.m., and which was to be the last of Reynaud's Government.

The atmosphere of the Council was stormy: there was a violent altercation between Mandel and Chautemps. Tempers flared. Mandel said that the Council was divided into two parties, "the brave and the cowards, those who want to fight and those who do not want to"; Chautemps replied, with no less violence: "There are here only Frenchmen equally conscious of the great distress in which these military reverses have placed France, and who desire to find the best means of saving her. I have no lesson to learn from M. Mandel."

After the rejection of the offer of indissoluble union, a majority was found to adopt Chautemps' proposal. Reynaud pointed out the consequences: "Monsieur le Président de la République, you will recognise that I no longer have a majority in the Government: I have therefore no alternative but to hand you my resignation." Albert Lebrun replied: "My dear Président du Conseil, I will not accept your resignation. You alone control the destiny of France. I ask that the meeting be closed." Lebrun and Reynaud agreed to summon the members of the Government at 10 p.m. for another Council of Ministers.

Reynaud's resignation, which had been thus only narrowly avoided, nevertheless took place in the interval, during a meeting of four people, the President of the Republic, the Presidents of both Chambers and the President of the Council. Reynaud showed himself resolute in his refusal to agree to Chautemps' solution. Lebrun, playing the constitutional game, tried to bring him over to this policy approved by the majority. When asked who should be Reynaud's eventual successor, Jeanneney and Herriot said that Reynaud should continue: but the latter advised the President of the Republic to call on Pétain.

Lebrun agreed to send for Pétain. It was an appointment which, as he himself said, gave him "a happy surprise", for the Marshal drew from his pocket a list of ministers which he had ready prepared. "I was not accustomed," wrote Lebrun in his memoirs, "to such speed, for I remember, not without some bitterness, the extraordinarily difficult processes of forming governments over which I had presided during my term at the Élysée." And more ingenuously still, Albert Lebrun recounted at Pétain's trial that "amid the great sorrow of the time, he had at least had one small alleviation: for whereas the formation of a government often lasted for three or four hours, Pétain had one ready on the spot. . . ."

When, at 10 p.m. the Ministers returned to the Préfecture, it was to learn that they were out of office: "Messieurs," said Albert Lebrun, ". . . forgive my not having been able to warn you not to come. I have been unable to make M. Paul Reynaud change his mind and he has refused to withdraw his resignation. In consequence, the Council will not take place, but I would ask you to remain within call. A new Government will be formed under Marshal Pétain. A certain number among you will be summoned by the new President of the Council to become his colleagues. But let the others stay too. I should like us all, this evening, to be united in our sorrow."

At 10 o'clock, the Government was formed, comprising sixteen Ministers and two Under-Secretaries of State of which eleven had formed part of the previous Government. Among those left out was de Gaulle. Among those newly appointed were General Weygand, to National Defence, General Colson to the Ministry of War, Admiral Darlan to the Ministry of Marine and Frémicourt, First President of the Court of Cassation, to the Ministry of Justice—the last was only to learn of his appointment on the radio the following morning. Alibert was Under-Secretary of State to the Presidency of the Council. Rivaud, whom Pétain had also known for a long time, went to the

Ministry of Education; Robert Schuman was Under-Secretary of State for Refugees.

Pierre Laval refused to become a member of the Government because Pétain, at the urgent request of Weygand and Charles-Roux, Secretary-General at the Ministry of Foreign Affairs, refused to give him the Ministry of Foreign Affairs, the only portfolio which he considered worthy of himself. He did not want the Seals. Nevertheless, eight days later, he joined the Government in the capacity of Minister of State, though he did indeed perform the functions of Vice-President of the Council.

At 11 o'clock, Léon Blum gave his consent to the entry of the Socialists, Rivière and Février, into the new coalition. And at midnight, after a short Council of Ministers, held amid considerable tumult, Baudouin, Minister for Foreign Affairs, as a delegate of a Government presided over by Pétain, Marshal of France, one of the victors of the previous war, departed to ask the Germans, through Lequerica as intermediary, what the conditions of an armistice would be.

In the new Government, which had been thus improvised, many of the Ministers would play little more than an episodic part or would be quickly replaced. On the other hand, two men, one of whom was not yet a member of it and the other of whom, at the start, only occupied a post of secondary importance, were to become, first behind the scenes, but soon openly, the real power in it. Their influence was to found a new regime, whose nature they alone had thought out, and concerning which the Marshal had not as yet made any announcement. These men were Alibert and Laval.

Raphaël Alibert, who was the real author at the start of the internal policies of Vichy and a defender of all the arbitrary measures promulgated during its first six months, was the evil genius of the National Revolution. "I liked Alibert very much," said the Marshal later, "but he gave me very bad advice."

Was anything else to be expected from a man who, excelling in theory, had consistently suffered failure in practice? The course in Constitutional Law, which he professed at the École des Sciences Politiques, was something of a masterpiece; but it did not prevent its author from multiplying blunders throughout his career. He resigned from the Conseil d'État, thirteen years after his appointment, and when he was already Maître des Requêtes.

Wishing to devote himself to business and to politics, he became simultaneously a director of several companies controlled by the Mercier group and one of the controllers of the Redressement Français, financed by capital from the same source. He was equally unsuccessful in both cases owing to his incompetence; and none of the businesses with which he was successively associated thought much of his qualities, nor did the electors of Pithiviers, who twice refused to elect him as a moderate candidate.

No doubt the reason for these failures was his temperament. Here is the unpublished diagnosis made by Doctor Ménétrel, the private medical attendant to the Marshal: "Alibert suffers from megalomania with a certain tendency towards mental disequilibrium, characterised by periods of excitement alternating with periods of mental depression."

It is certain that Alibert's behaviour was not always completely normal: on the day in January, 1941, when Pétain dismissed him from the Government, he was seen walking past the Hôtel du Parc, the seat of the Government, shaking his fist at the sky and removing his files in a baby-carriage.

His was a frenzy which led to insane ambition: "I shall leave here either dead or as dictator," he said at the beginning of his period of power. When he replaced President Frémicourt as Minister of Justice, he declared that he would undoubtedly remain Keeper of the Seals for at least fifty years: having been born in 1887, he was then fifty-three years of age!

It was this anachronistic and abnormal personage whom Lémery, his intimate friend, to whom he had been Chef de Cabinet in 1917, had presented to Marshal Pétain long before the war. The Marshal, impressed by his dogmatic manner and attracted by his assurance, made him his political "preceptor".

From that moment, Alibert had lived in the hope that his pupil would one day achieve power: his constitutional projects were centred round the old man. And at Bordeaux, feeling that the hour had come, he employed every means at his disposal to bring this about, at the risk of losing all.

Pierre Laval was an altogether different type. He achieved power with startling faults and yet with singular qualities. His vulgarity repelled, but his magnetism attracted. His temperament was that of an Auvergnat countryman. He was born on the 28th June, 1883, at Châteldon, his father being an inn-keeper. It has been suggested that there was Spanish or Oriental blood in his veins. He had led the rough and healthy life of a country boy. When the young Pierre was fifteen, he was seduced by his schoolmaster's wife, who was attracted by the intelligence her husband so much appreciated. Intellectually, he rebelled early; his naïve anti-clericalism, so common among countrymen, began, as it did for Proudhon, as the result of an incident which took place during a procession in which, as a boy of twelve, he carried the Cross and received a box on the ear from a nun for deliberately stamping in a couple of puddles. "My ecclesiastical career finished early," he said later. Hard on animals, he had no hesitation in persuading a stubborn horse to obey him by lighting a truss of straw beneath its stomach. He had the same hardness towards men and delighted in fighting; his skull bore to the end of his life the marks of blows exchanged with his comrades.

As he grew older and more mature, he succeeded in disciplining his tendency to violence. But it was never altogether exorcised. At the beginning of his political career, it was this tendency which made him turn instinctively to the extreme Left; during the 1914–1918 war, he was a militant pacifist. Called to the Paris bar at twenty-four years of age, Laval was, seven years later, elected Socialist Deputy for Aubervilliers, a constituency he selected because of its considerable Auvergnat population. He was successively its Mayor and its Senator, first as a Socialist, then as an Independent, owing allegiance to no political party; ultimately, he turned to the Right wing. But this made no difference: "I used," he said in 1944, "to have a sure criterion for judging politicians; the good ones, those who were worth anything, were those who had never changed their constituencies, even if they had changed their political affiliations." More complacently, at the Socialist Congress at Tours, when he had left the S.F.I.O., he expressed his contempt for political parties: "From now on, I shall no longer submit to the rule of a party. It is fallacious. I shall only listen to that interior voice which never deceives me."

His confidence in himself enabled him to take, on his own, decisions, however unpopular, which he considered right. He was prepared to defy all pressure from public opinion and was, indeed, afraid of nothing when he was sure of being right. Whether, as in 1935, in a pre-election period, when such rashness could only play into his opponent's hands, he recommended a policy of deflation by reducing wages or, on the 2nd September,

1939, alone among the Senators, he voted against the war subsidies, it was always with the same contempt for his adversaries, the same harsh temper which animated and isolated him. He thus acquired a certain stature, though he was rarely honest in the means he chose to achieve his ends.

It had become a commonplace to say that Laval was dishonest: Léon Blum accused him of it to his face, when speaking in the Chamber on the 27th December, 1935, during the course of the debate on the Italo-Abyssinian war: "You have acted in world affairs as we have seen you act in smaller matters. You have tried at once to give and to retain. You have tried to draw benefits from numerous opposing policies; you have contradicted your words by your actions and your actions by your words. You have altered everything for the worse, by machination, intrigue and double-dealing. The deplorable fact is that, insensible to the power of great and objective events, you have reduced everything to the level of your minor jobberies. And by your jobbery, you have created formidable consequences." The last phrase is similar to a judgment of the Marshal's: "What is so discouraging about M. Laval, is his ignorance of spiritual values." This pitiless verdict is also a diagnosis and, perhaps, an explanation.

What Léon Blum condemned in his political actions, was what Vincent Auriol had already pointed out in the early days of Laval's professional and parliamentary career. For he had said wittily: "Whether you spell his name backwards or forwards, he will always be Laval." Laval had made himself the advocate for a certain legal project which was likely to gain for the young barrister, as he then was, "the grateful sympathy of certain magistrates who aspired to promotion".

Another example of his cunning: Laval, when a schoolmaster at the beginning of his career, called together seven of his colleagues, bought a rubber stamp with the inscription: "General Society of Schoolmasters of France and the Colonies", and demanded an interview with Doumergue, the Minister of Education. Before the interview, he persuaded one of his colleagues to play the part of confidential witness. The Minister would undoubtedly ask how many members the Society numbered. Laval would reply, "Eight hundred." His acolyte was to interrupt shyly: "So far we have only seven hundred and eighty seven." The interview proceeded as foreseen. And the Minister, impressed by such frankness, put his faith in the Society which, in fact, had but eight members. He awarded Pierre Laval appreciable benefits for schoolmasters: a minimum salary of 45 Frs. a month and one night off per week.

How did Laval rise from those 45 Frs. a month to the considerable fortune of the 57 millions, equivalent to a million pounds today, which he possessed in 1945, according to an official estimate given at his trial?

In the first place, owing to his undeniable qualities as a man of business, in which he was both competent and intuitive, knowing how to buy businesses that were in difficulties for a song and sell them again at a large profit, when he had put them on their feet; also from the opportunities that his political position opened to him. Thus, in 1928, he acquired for 400,000 Frs. the private station of Radio-Lyon, which he ran himself, an activity which his political associations could not but facilitate; in 1943, when he was in power, which was clearly no disadvantage, he was offered 55 millions for it. The same thing occurred over the Sergental waters from a spring at Châteldon, which he asserted were the most radio-active in France. For this eminent quality to be recognised, the spring had to wait for its political representative to be in power. Finally, *Le Moniteur*, the newspaper of Clermont-Ferrand, had, when Laval bought it in 1927, an extremely old-fashioned printing-press. Laval re-organised it so well that in 1940, when he was Vice-President of the Council, he was able to discover that it was the only press in France capable of printing ration-books.

Such proceedings, which were common practice in certain political circles, and in which Laval was certainly no innovator, nevertheless did not exclude a certain sincerity and even, towards the end of his life, a certain elevation of feeling.

In the first place, there was sincerity in his permanent loyalty to his country origins. "I cannot live, if I cannot tread the earth, the furrows, every evening and if I cannot gossip with peasants, with people from my home."

He was equally sincere in his feelings as a Frenchman. He had a sort of physical attachment to the soil of his native land, which was neither ineffective nor without grandeur. On the 9th November, 1943, Laval spoke to the Mayors of Cantal, apparently with heart-felt sincerity: "If Russia wishes to be Communist, that is her business, but let her keep her Communism to herself.

"If Germany wishes to be National Socialist, that is her business, but let her keep her National Socialism to herself. . . .

". . . I have but one ambition, one aim, towards which I strive almost as if I were walking in my sleep, it is that of endeavouring to do all I can to save our country by reducing her sufferings each day, of endeavouring to assure that the land which belongs to the fathers shall be inherited by their children and that it shall always be called the land of France." But in the nightmares of the sleep-walker, all was not so innocent. There were to be found all the hatreds that had filled his politician's heart with gall. Hatred for the Radicals who, in 1935, had caused his Government to fall and ruined his policy; hatred against the Chamber of the Front Populaire which had placed him in a minority: "It spewed me out, I shall spew it out in my turn." And, finally, hatred, which was no virtue in a statesman, against England, which had thwarted his policy of reconciliation with Italy.

These hatreds grew out of the illusions, the megalomania and the personal myths to which Laval's career, from inn-keeper's son to the pinnacle of power, had given rise.

Had he not been received by all the great ones of the earth in the same year, by Roosevelt and by Stalin, by Mussolini and by the Pope? After this last audience, he made an ingenuous and indeed touching avowal, but how revealing it is of the psychology of the self-made man! For once without the eternal cigarette between his lips, he said, "Oh, if Mama could see me now!" It was rather like Napoleon, at his coronation, saying to his brother Joseph: "If only our Father could see us!" Intoxicated by his success, he asserted that he had dominated Roosevelt as he had dominated Stalin. Moreover, he announced that the marriage of his daughter with a descendant of La Fayette had made him more popular in the United States than Roosevelt himself. His down-to-earth realism began to take on a certain quality of exaltation. Was he not, from his lowly birth, his Socialist origins, his magnetism and his courage, the man who should be to France what Mussolini and Hitler were to Italy and Germany? And this France, even defeated, weakened, mutilated as she was, did he not see her, in his more bombastic moments, playing, thanks to himself, a leading role in a Latin Europe, which was to be re-constituted and of which she would be the guiding hand?

Thus Pierre Laval visualised himself playing an exalted part, without however ceasing from jobbery. He no longer had the clogs of Châteldon on his feet, nor his native earth beneath them. He had become a papal count, or something approaching it, an unhoped-for destiny for the little choir-boy who had broken up the procession. From that moment, sure of the direction in which he was going and in which he was leading France, no trickery or sharp practice mattered. He uttered such phrases as seemed to him useful to the end he had in view, phrases so provocative that they could never be effaced; and, in the end, perhaps, he paid more for his words than for the facts they covered: "I hope for a Germany victory without which Bolshevism will shortly be dominant everywhere."

Laval's last fight, in 1944, against the ultimate demands of a Germany so soon to be defeated, and which was to drag him down with her, is like that of a captain who is the last to leave his ship: it matters little, at such a moment, whether he is captain of a pirate vessel or a man-of-war: he deserves the respect of his crew.

Nothing, in the first hours of Pétain's Government, presaged the entry of such combatants into the lists. To read the announcement which, on the 17th June, made public the change of government, one might have thought that it was merely a question of a simple ministerial crisis, similar to those the Third Republic had known in the past.

"In the present grave circumstances, the Council of Ministers, on the proposal of M. Paul Reynaud, President of the Council, has decided that the Government of France should be vested in a high personage, who has the unanimous respect of the Nation.

"As a result, M. Paul Reynaud has placed the resignation of the members of the cabinet in the hands of the President of the Republic, and M. Lebrun has accepted their resignations while respecting the patriotism which determined them, and has immediately called upon Marshal Pétain, who has accepted the duty of forming a new Government.

"The President of the Republic has rendered thanks to Marshal Pétain who, in assuming the heaviest responsibility which has ever been laid upon the shoulders of a French statesman, manifests once again his devotion to the Fatherland."

But, on that very day, two events occurred which were significant of a radical change in French policy.

The first was the arrest, ordered by Alibert, of Georges Mandel, who, twenty-four hours earlier, had still been Minister of the Interior. It marked the re-appearance of a despotism to which, during the succeeding years, the instigators were themselves to become victims.

The second, was the Marshal's first appeal to the country, whose hasty delivery marked both Pétain's hurry to proclaim his policy and his contempt for the democratic usages which had previously been in force. Delivered without the Ministers being informed, before even the conditions of the armistice were known, it placed the Government, the High Command and the country to all intents and purposes face to face with an accomplished fact: the end of hostilities.

At mid-day on the 17th June, the Chapon Fin restaurant in Bordeaux was crowded; pleasure at having found a table in this famous restaurant, perhaps also the relief of knowing that an armistice had been asked for immediately by the Pétain ministry, contributed to create an extraordinarily animated atmosphere.

In the middle of luncheon, a commissaire of Police, sent by Alibert, who had been a Minister for twelve hours, came to arrest Georges Mandel. The reason, or the pretext, was an anonymous letter accusing Mandel and General Buhrer, the Director of Colonial Troops, of having assembled arms for the purpose of assassinating the Ministers. The news of the arrest spread like wild fire through Bordeaux. It soon reached Lebrun who, at 2 o'clock, sent for Alibert to give an explanation. The latter could do no more than produce vague accusations. He alleged that an unknown journalist had denounced Mandel. Lebrun advised him to make a more detailed enquiry and sent him away.

Ultimately, Mandel was freed. The President of the Council expressed his regrets. But Mandel demanded an apology in writing; and since the first draft seemed to him unacceptable, he demanded and obtained from the Marshal, in the presence of Pomaret and Frossard, a letter written on his own terms. Then Mandel proceeded to give his views on the incident: "I have the greatest respect for you, Monsieur le Maréchal. . . . My arrest has no importance in itself, but it is serious because it shows that you are in the hands of people who are capable of making you commit such appalling errors at such a tragic moment in our history. Nothing could be more disquieting."

At the very moment that Mandel was being arrested, the Marshal was delivering his first message to the country: the second sign of the change in policy determined on by the new Government.

"Frenchmen,

"Summoned by the President of the Republic, I assume from today the leadership of the Government of France. Assured of the affection of our wonderful army, which is fighting with a heroism worthy of its long military traditions against an enemy superior in numbers and in arms, assured that, by its magnificent resistance, it has fulfilled its obligations towards our allies, assured of the spirit of the Anciens Combattants whom I had the honour of commanding, assured of the confidence of the whole population, I give myself to France in order to mitigate her disasters.

"In these sad hours, I think of the unhappy refugees who, in the utmost destitution, are crowding along our roads. I wish to express to them my compassion and my solicitude. It is with a sad heart that I tell you today that we must stop fighting.

"I have this night approached the enemy and asked him if he is prepared to negotiate with us, as between soldiers and after the battle has been fought in all honour, means of putting an end to hostilities.

"Let all Frenchmen gather loyally during these hard trials in support of the Government over which I preside, and let them turn a deaf ear to their anguish and listen only to their faith in the destiny of our Fatherland."

This appeal, heard by the troops, either directly or re-transmitted by the Germans, caused the last of them to lay down their arms.

The Germans spread it to every sector where the French were still fighting. In some places they did so by pamphlets printed both in French and in Alsatian.

During the afternoon of the 17th, General Georges informed General Weygand that the troops were now refusing to fight by whole regiments, since they had taken literally the Marshal's phrase: "We must stop fighting."

Weygand and Baudouin tried in vain to take action. The first by issuing an order of the day to the army saying that, as long as no armistice had been signed, resistance must continue; the second by reducing the force of the Marshal's words in the version given to the press. "We must stop fighting" was replaced by "We must endeavour to stop fighting." In both cases it was wasted effort.[1]

On the 18th June, the campaign of France came to an end. At the Council of Ministers, which began at 11 o'clock, Weygand, promoted to Minister of National Defence forty-eight hours earlier, presented the last report on the military situation: resistance was everywhere at an end; in the West, the Loire had been crossed by the Wehrmacht which was advancing southwards; in the East, the Haute-Saône was occupied—our troops had been routed: "It is what I feared," the General concluded, "we have been much to blame for our delay in asking for an armistice."

While waiting for the German conditions, which arrived on the 21st June, the Government had no longer need to discuss the problem of an armistice.

They were unanimous in deciding to break off negotiations and continue the war if the Germans made any demands upon the Empire or the Fleet. Against this eventuality, the Service Ministers took a whole series of measures: General Colson ordered the troops still fighting in Metropolitan France to hold their positions; all anti-tank weapons, arms and munitions, still available in the military districts, were to be concentrated at Bordeaux in order to be transferred to North Africa. Admiral Darlan, for his part, issued an order of the day to the Fleet: "The war continues relentlessly."

And that very day, the *Jean-Bart*, a battle-cruiser of 35,000 tons, which had not yet put to sea, succeeded in leaving the shipyards of the Loire at Saint-Nazaire, thus escaping the Germans. At Brest, the *Richelieu* managed to do the same. Finally, General Pujo gave similar orders to the Air Force: approximately nine hundred aeroplanes capable of crossing the Mediterranean were to concentrate in North Africa. The only question which the Government, in the meantime, still had to decide, was whether it should leave for North Africa or remain in Metropolitan France—a question whose urgency was apparent, since the

[1] A few units, surrounded in the Maginot Line, alone continued to fight. They surrendered only on a direct order from the Government ten days after the armistice had been signed.

Wehrmacht's advance towards Bordeaux would soon deprive it of all freedom of choice. Moreover, those who wished to depart and those who opposed departure were, during the next three days, owing to the confusion and lack of information which then reigned in Bordeaux, to become involved in a whole series of obscure intrigues.

Lebrun supported departure with all his authority: even if the Nazi conditions were not unacceptable, the Government would have the advantage of negotiating freely from beyond the reach of the enemy's troops.

Pétain, as far as he was concerned, would not contemplate leaving Metropolitan France. He did not openly oppose the transference of governmental power, but he himself, in all circumstances, would remain to protect the people of France.

Divided between the President of the Republic and the Marshal, the Government arrived at no decision. Members of Parliament discussed matters uneasily around it, while leaders in the Empire bombarded it with telegrams expressing their willingness to resist.

In despair, the Ministers decided that the question should be fought out by the Head of the State and the Head of the Government at a meeting with the Presidents of the two Chambers.

The four Presidents met in the afternoon: Lebrun, Jeanneney and Herriot were firmly in favour of departure. Pétain declared that his duty was "to remain with the people". Nevertheless, on a suggestion of Edouard Herriot and Jeanneney, he was prepared to accept a division of the Government: a minority of Ministers would remain with him in France, while the greater number would depart for Africa with the President of the Republic, the Presidents of both Chambers and such members of both Assemblies as wished to go. The Vice-President of the Council, Chautemps, would become head of the African section and would receive from the Marshal delegated powers permitting him to govern on the other side of the Mediterranean. Agreement having been reached, embarkation was arranged for the late afternoon of the following day, the 19th June.

During the course of a semi-official meeting of deputies, held the same day in the Anatole-France school, presided over by the Questeur Barthe, a minority declared themselves determined to remain in France.

The majority, somewhat disquieted, sent a delegation, headed by Barthe, to sound out Pétain's intentions. The President of the Council cajoled them and re-assured them: "You can be assured that as far as I am concerned, you are risking nothing. . . . But it is a joy to me that you come to me in the name of Parliament; Parliament is necessary. . . . I know well what services Parliament rendered when I was in the Government. I found in Parliament a great devotion to the public cause and, if you had not come to me, bringing me the adherence of Parliament, I could not undertake my task. I desire the collaboration of Parliament. Tell your colleagues so, you know how loyal I am. . . . I have always been loyal." Barthe then told his colleagues that they could leave for North Africa without anxiety.

These were the resolutions of the 18th June at Bordeaux. If they took first place in the minds of the politicians assembled on the bank of the Gironde, there was another voice raised that day in London, which would count for much in the future—that of General de Gaulle. It was an appeal which had as yet no political tendency: the ex-Under-Secretary for War in Reynaud's Government was only concerned with recruiting soldiers and technicians in order to maintain a French force in the war side by side with France's allies. The General justified the design, which then seemed so hazardous, thus:

"The leaders who, for many years, have been at the head of the French armies, have formed a Government.

"This Government, alleging that our armies have been defeated, has started negotiations with the enemy to stop the war.

"Indeed, we have been, we are, overwhelmed by the mechanical forces of the enemy both on the ground and in the air.

"It is the quantity of tanks and aeroplanes as well as the tactics of the Germans which, much more than their numbers, have surprised our leaders and led them to the situation in which they are today.

"But has the last word been said? Has all hope gone? Is defeat final? No!

"Believe me, and I tell you I know what I am talking about, when I say that France is not lost. The same methods which have defeated us may well one day bring us victory.

"For France does not stand alone. She is not alone. She has a vast Empire behind her. She can make a solid block with the

British Empire, which has command of the seas and continues the struggle. She can, like England, make limitless use of the huge industrial resources of the United States.

"This war is not confined to the unhappy territory of our land. This war is not determined by the outcome of the battle of France. This war is a world war. All the mistakes, all the delays, all the sufferings do not alter the fact that there are, in the world, all the necessary means for destroying our enemies one day. Overwhelmed today by mechanised forces, we can conquer in the future by superior mechanised forces. The fate of the world depends on it.

"I, General de Gaulle, at present in London, invite French officers and soldiers who are in British territory or who may find themselves there, either with or without their arms, I invite engineers and technicians of armament works who are in British territory or may find themselves there, to get into touch with me.

"Whatever may happen, the flame of French resistance must not go out and will not go out.

"Tomorrow, I shall speak, as I have done today, on the radio from London."

These prophetic words were scarcely heard at the time, in spite of the great number of people who, later on, pretended to have heard them. The majority of Pétain's ministers knew nothing of them.

At 6.30 in the morning of the 19th June, Lequerica, the Spanish Ambassador, wakened Baudouin, the Minister of Foreign Affairs, to inform him that the Germans agreed to open armistice negotiations.

At 8.30, Baudouin transmitted the news to the Marshal, then to Lebrun. At 10.30 the names of the plenipotentiaries were communicated to the Spanish Ambassador. Weygand, who in the first instance was considered for the leadership of the delegation, and who had not thought himself in a position to refuse this sacrificial mission, was finally set aside: could Marshal Foch's Chief-of-Staff be submitted to such humiliation? Chautemps, also considered, was also set aside: to send a Vice-President of the Council to meet the Germans would be to do them too much honour. In the end, General Huntziger led the French delegation, which comprised a diplomatist, the Ambassador Léon Noël, a sailor, Vice-Admiral Le Luc, an army officer, General Parisot, an airman, General Bergeret, and Rochat, Deputy-Director of Political Affairs in the Ministry of Foreign Affairs.

On that day, when the possibility of an armistice seemed to be becoming more certain, the departure for North Africa appeared to take second place. The Council of Ministers, which assembled at 9 o'clock, had been informed of the decisions arrived at the day before at the meeting of the four Presidents. It had agreed that the Government should be divided into two sections, of which one would leave at once in order to avoid being made prisoner by the Germans. It had even decided that Lebrun should embark in the late afternoon from a Mediterranean port and that, at some hour still to be arranged, the members of Parliament should leave Bordeaux in the *Massillia*.

But, while the Council was preparing its own exodus, it was at the same time, through Lequerica as intermediary, making a *démarche* with the Germans, which might allow of some delay. On the strength of the first favourable reply from the Nazis, the Government asked the Spanish Ambassador to obtain from the Wehrmacht a suspension of the German advance on Bordeaux during the negotiations. At first the German High Command would not listen to the proposal, but later it gave the required promise.

This hope of a breathing-space seemed to diminish the urgency of the decision which had been taken in the morning. Besides, the Government that day had its time occupied by a more urgent matter: three important Englishmen, Alexander, First Lord of the Admiralty, Sir Dudley Pound, First Sea Lord, and Lord Lloyd, Colonial Secretary, had arrived by air to spend the day in Bordeaux in order to obtain an assurance that the French Fleet would in no circumstances be handed over to the Germans.

In the morning they were received by the Marshal and by Admiral Darlan. In the afternoon they saw Baudouin. All three solemnly gave the promise asked of them. In the evening the Englishmen returned to London completely satisfied.

During the night of the 19th–20th June, German aircraft bombed Bordeaux for the first time: it was thus that the Nazis kept their promise. In the meantime it was learnt that, far from stopping their advance, the Wehrmacht was approaching by forced marches.

And on the morning of the 20th June, Lebrun, who, accompanied by Marquet, Mayor of Bordeaux, had gone to salute the dead of the night before and visit the wounded, exercised his authority to insist on the departure. At the Council of Ministers, which met at 10 o'clock, he was categorical: the embarkation must take place that day.

The departure was irrevocable: the preparations were hurried on.

The members of Parliament were to leave from Bordeaux. Herriot, summoning the two Questeurs of the Chamber, ordered Perfetti to accompany the Assembly and Barthe to remain in France to defend the interests of Parliament.

From then on, it was a case of orders and counter-orders in the confused atmosphere which preceded the departure of the members of Parliament. At 11 o'clock, a few deputies held an excited meeting in the Cours Anatole-France, though it was adjourned to await instructions. At 11.45, Perfetti arrived and announced that the Council of Ministers had just decided on the immediate departure of members of Parliament with the Government. Half an hour after mid-day, Herriot telephoned Barthe that only the Government was to go to Port-Vendres, and that the members of the Assemblies would sail from Verdon in the *Massillia*: Léon Blum and Jeanneney, misinformed, were already on the road to Port-Vendres. On their arrival at Toulouse, they received orders to return to Bordeaux.

In the meantime a note arrived from Admiral Darlan, confirming that, on the order of the Government, the deputies and senators would embark that very day in the *Massillia*. He informed them that the transport, which was to take them from Bordeaux to the ship, would leave the town at 5.30 p.m.

At 2 p.m., Frossard went to the Cours Anatole-France to announce officially to the members of Parliament the departure for North Africa. He found only a few of them in session. It was perhaps at the same time that a delegation of members of Parliament, who were hostile to the departure for North Africa, was received by Pétain, with Laval at its head. The Marshal congratulated them upon their desire to remain in France as, two days before, he had approved the Barthe delegation's desire to leave Metropolitan soil.

At 2.30 p.m., Barthe confirmed the news to an Assembly which was scarcely more heavily attended.

The transport for Verdon, where the *Massillia* lay at anchor, left Bordeaux punctually, conveying only thirty-one members of Parliament; a large number, whom it had been impossible to warn, were unaware of the embarkation. A few, who did know about it, changed their minds at the last moment.

The sailing of the *Massillia* was delayed by a whole series of incidents: the sailors, showing considerable hostility towards certain members of Parliament whom they reproached with abandoning France, refused to work the ship. Campinchi, using his authority—a week earlier he had been Minister of Marine—harangued the mutineers and succeeded in pacifying them.

While the members of Parliament, on board the *Massillia*, were waiting to leave France in order to join the President of the Republic in North Africa, a meeting of their colleagues, who had remained in Bordeaux, was already accusing them of treason: they had, however, embarked as the result of an official order and by virtue of an arrangement which was valid not only for themselves, but also for the Government.

But the Government was not conforming to its own orders. Lebrun and certain Ministers ought, indeed, to have been at Port-Vendres, the first stage of their journey to Africa, at the same time as the members of Parliament were embarking in the *Massillia*. In fact, while the latter were embarking, the former were still in Bordeaux, where a conspiracy had been unexpectedly improvised at the last moment to retain them.

The chief conspirator that day was Alibert who, in order to achieve his ends, was prepared to stop at nothing, not even lies and deceit. Two years later, Alibert recounted the details of his manoeuvres to the deputy Fernand-Laurent as follows:

"I made Pétain—and I have no need to blush for it, because I thought that in acting as I did I was serving my country—I made Pétain by a lie and a piece of duplicity.

"On Thursday, 20th June, I received an urgent telephone call from the President of the Republic who insisted on speaking to me personally. His bags were packed, he was due to embark at Port-Vendres for Algeria. He wanted to know at once the exact hour of departure: 'I am told,' he said in concern over the telephone, 'that the Germans have crossed the Loire between Nantes and Tours. Pray ask the Marshal what he has decided and let me know as soon as possible. . . .' I replied," went on Alibert, "respectfully but evasively, and went to see the Marshal. It was 3 o'clock in the afternoon; the Marshal was alone in his office: 'Oh, it's you, Alibert,' he said, 'you've come just at the right moment. I must go and see "him" (Lebrun). You will accompany me.'

". . . We went out and together walked the few yards to the Préfet's House and went to M. Lebrun's office. He was alone with M. Camille Chautemps.

"The Marshal sat down without saying a word.

" 'M. le Président de la République,' said Chautemps, 'in order to make certain, I should like to repeat to you your instructions. We are in complete agreement, are we not? As Vice-Président of the Council, I shall leave immediately for Algiers and there take over the leadership of the Government. I shall convoke such Senators and Deputies as have been able to follow us and we shall take all proper measures for pursuing the war in the Empire. Monsieur le Maréchal Pétain will remain on the soil of France to assure by his prestige the protection of the population and the country's material wealth to the utmost possible extent. You, Monsieur le Président de la République, will leave without delay. We are in complete agreement?'

" 'We are in complete agreement, my dear Président,' replied M. Albert Lebrun. 'My luggage is ready.'

"The Marshal confined himself to an inclination of the head in sign of assent.

"We were about to get to our feet," went on Alibert, "everything was arranged, the departure was to take place at once. The Government of France would shortly be in Algiers. Pétain would never have been head of the state.

"It was at that moment that I decided to tell a lie: 'Monsieur le Président de la République,' I said, taking the plunge, 'I must inform you of an extremely important piece of news. I received it at the very moment we were leaving to come here, and I have not even had time to make it known to Monsieur le Maréchal Pétain. It is news, however, whose nature will, I think, influence your decisions. It is not true that the Germans have crossed the Loire. The High Command, on the contrary, has informed us that our troops are holding well and that the river has not been crossed at any point.'

" 'That is very important information,' the Marshal intervened.

"Lebrun was clearly somewhat abashed and hesitant. I pursued my advantage.

" 'Do you not think, Monsieur le Président de la République,' I said, 'that, the urgency being less great, we might adjourn making a definite decision till tomorrow morning?'

" 'It would certainly be wiser,' the Marshal supported me.

" 'This is a last minute delay,' said M. Albert Lebrun unhappily, 'but I remain ready to leave. Send me the reports the moment you receive them, I can count on you, can I not?'

"Chautemps said nothing. I exchanged a rapid glance with the Marshal. We rose to our feet. We had won.

"That was the lie," Alibert concluded; "but it was only the first rubber: it was necessary to win the second. This was my piece of duplicity.

"When we had returned to the Préfecture, I was bombarded with telephone calls from Jeanneney, Herriot and Campinchi, who all asked me whether the order for departure had been finally given. 'We must put an end to this once and for all,' I decided. I took the Marshal's private writing-paper, I dictated to my secretary an order to each Minister to remain in his house till 8 o'clock the following morning, while awaiting instructions, and on no pretext whatever to leave the town before receiving them. I took the Marshal's seal. I sealed the orders and signed them. Without this piece of duplicity, Pétain would never have been head of the state."

At 12.30 p.m. on the 21st June, the ship in which thirty deputies and one senator were embarked, set sail for Casablanca. Among the passengers were Mandel, Campinchi, Jean-Zay, Mendès-France and Daladier.

It was also on the 21st June that Pierre Laval began to take a hand in the game, having decided to torpedo once and for all the proposed departure to Africa which Alibert had succeeded in delaying the day before and towards which Pétain now no longer concealed his hostility: "If he (Lebrun) insists on leaving, I shall have him arrested!"

At this date Laval had as yet no other right to intervene but his position as a deputy. However, he was to make no use of the attributes of power; his methods were very different from those of the Garde des Sceaux: they were purely personal. He used no deceit, he took the bull by the horns.

Accompanied by Marquet, Piétri, Bonnet, Portmann, Sérol, Bergery, Landry, Dommange, Crutel and Barthe, whose duties compelled his presence against his will, he stormed the door of Lebrun's office.

"They came in like a whirlwind," wrote the latter in his memoirs, "without having their names entered in the book, as is the custom. I was confronted with a lot of hysterical men, who had lost control of themselves. They were all gesticulating and talking at the same time." Laval, almost at once, succeeded in imposing silence on the shouting crowd by the mere force of his own vehemence; and turned his invective on Lebrun: "More than a hundred members of Parliament, Senators and Deputies, have just met: they have appointed a delegation which I am charged with introducing to you.

". . . You will not leave, you must not leave. We will not accept that the Government should continue from Africa by this almost fraudulent subterfuge a war which is admittedly hopeless. Are you going to pursue a policy which has already been condemned, the policy of Reynaud and Churchill, which favours a departure for Africa? . . ."

Lebrun, his face haggard, listened without interrupting. Laval raised his tone still further: "I do not recognise your right to do so on any pretext or subterfuge whatever. You should no longer listen to the counsel of those who have led the country to the abyss. Why have you followed them?" Lebrun, thus personally attacked, tried "by a piece of cold reasoning, which might have appeared callous" to overawe his frantic visitors. He replied without raising his voice: "My constitutional duty obliged me to do so." The reply did not satisfy Laval, who went on: "And as for Jeanneney who has done us so much harm, I hate him, I hate him, I hate him!" "Don't talk so loud," suggested Lebrun, "the more you shout, the less I can hear what you say." But Laval, now launched, paid no heed: "Your duty now is to save all that can be saved of the country. And it is not by leaving France that you can serve her." "But how," asked the President, "can the Government of France remain sovereign and free in a land occupied by the enemy where it is exposed to the risk of being made prisoner?" Dommange now took up the argument: "If you abandon forty million French people, the population itself will constitute the true government of France. And we shall be of it, for we shall never leave France." Their violence was becoming threatening, almost blackmailing. Laval emphasised this: "If you leave the soil of France, you will never set foot on it again. . . . Yes, when it is known that you chose as the hour of departure the very hour in which our country was sunk in the greatest distress, there will be but one word on every lip: desertion. . . . Perhaps an even graver word: treason. . . . If you wish to leave, it is your right to do so, but you can only leave as a private individual. Hand in your resignation."

The President of the Republic listened to this diatribe sitting in his chair behind his desk, his hands clasped, his eyes fixed on the ground, while he merely reiterated: "You don't know the Germans. . . . You don't know the Germans. . . ."

During the evening after this improbable scene, the French delegation at Rethondes communicated the armistice terms to the Government. Compared to the conditions which might have followed upon the total collapse of the army, compared also to the attitude taken by Germany towards the other conquered nations, Poland, Belgium and Holland, they appeared almost moderate. They did not contain the only two clauses against which Pétain would have been adamant: the surrender of the Fleet, which was forbidden by the solemn agreement of the 19th June entered into by the Marshal and Admiral Darlan with Alexander, First Lord of the Admiralty, or the occupation of the Empire, even temporarily, by German or Italian troops. The negotiations began. All plans for departure were set aside. The whole Government devoted itself to the armistice negotiations.

To begin with Hitler tried not to take too much advantage of his victory. During the course of an interview which he had had with Mussolini on the 18th June, he had endeavoured to moderate the Italian demands. The Duce, having joined the victor's camp but eight days before, wished to profit by his success *in extremis*: his claims on France provided for the occupation of all the territory east of the Rhône, Corsica, Tunisia, the Somali Coast and numerous strategic points in Metropolitan France and the Empire, among which were Algiers, Oran and Casablanca. They also provided for the handing over of the Fleet and the Air Force.

If Hitler opposed these demands until the conclusion of peace and himself abstained from formulating similar ones, it was not, one may well suppose, out of sympathy for France. But he feared, if he pushed France too far, that she might be incited to refuse an armistice and set up a government on British soil. Above all, he feared that, if the French Fleet joined the British, the united Navies would be able to develop the convoy system to a very considerable degree and assure military and commercial contact between England, the Commonwealth and the United States. As regards the Fleet, therefore, it was wiser not to be too precipitate; perhaps one day the French would scuttle it themselves—and that would be the best solution.

The day after the terms had been fixed in principle, the French delegation left Bordeaux at 2.30 p.m. to meet the Germans.

Having entered the German lines at about 10 p.m., the French delegation spent the whole night being taken from the neighbourhood of Amboise to Vendôme, where they waited a long time in a street before being received by General von Typpelskirch and until the cars, which were to take them on, arrived. Once beyond the Loire, they saw hundreds of abandoned military vehicles in the ditches, a witness to the French collapse; they saw German troops marching down the road, the men looking fresh, well-fed and disciplined, as if the regiments were merely leaving barracks to go on manoeuvres. Reaching Paris, which most of them had only left ten days before, they found it fallen to the state of being no more than a milestone on the road followed by the invading armies across France. The Place de la Concorde was a roundabout covered with German signposts.

After seventeen hours of travelling without rest or food, the French delegates were received during the morning at the Hôtel du Royal-Monceau; at 3.30 p.m., they arrived at the clearing of Rethondes, where the armistice had been signed in 1918; the Führer's guard, dressed in black uniforms, did them the honours in front of the 1918 monument which was covered with a Nazi flag. They were shown into the armistice railway coach, which, twenty years earlier, had heard Foch say to the conquered Germans: "I will read to you the conditions drawn up by the Allied Governments." Today, the ultimatum was the same, but it had changed sides. On the entry of the French delegates, Hitler, Goering, Hess, Roeder, Ribbentrop and their staffs stood up with raised arms. Their faces registered no emotion. General Keitel, the commander of the victorious army, read an address in the name of the Führer. Hitler gave the Frenchmen the text of the armistice terms, which had been drawn up in a hurry by the conquerors during the night; the rapidity of their victory had prevented their preparing it at leisure. He then left, having effaced the shame that had obsessed every German heart for twenty years.

The ceremony over, the negotiations began. Keitel was insolent and brutal. He refused to allow the French delegation to communicate by radio with its Government; he authorised them to telephone if it were strictly necessary; Schmidt, the German interpreter, listened to every communication. Keitel also refused a cessation of hostilities till the armistice was signed.

It was a *diktat*. The French delegates retired into the tent provided for them in order to study the text of the terms. They were annoyed, during these dramatic moments, by a German who entered the tent out of curiosity and wished to photograph them. Bergeret threw him out. The forest, moreover, which Foch had chosen as the scene of negotiations because of its loneliness and in order to protect the vanquished from indiscreet attentions, was now filled with an immense crowd of Germans, massed round the door of the railway coach, spread out among the brushwood, armed with cameras and ciné-cameras. The French were unable to move without being photographed at point-blank range. Even in the railway coach itself, photographers had been present at the preliminary session over which the Chancellor had presided.

At 6 p.m., the French delegates, having read the text, took their places round the table once more; Keitel had been replaced by General Jodl, calm, courteous, but just as intransigent: he was not there to discuss, merely to give any necessary explanations.

He confirmed the more essential points: the maintenance of a free zone in France, consisting of some two-fifths of the total territory, and over which the French Government would have complete sovereignty; should the French Government prefer to return to Paris, the Germans were prepared to study the conditions in which it might do so.

While in 1918 the armistice had included a clause concerning the handing over of one hundred and sixty submarines and the internment of the rest of the German Fleet, this time Article 8 made no claim on the French Fleet.

"The French Fleet—with the exception of that part of it which is to be left at the disposal of the French Government for safeguarding its interests in the Colonial Empire—shall be concentrated in ports to be determined and shall be demobilised and disarmed under the control of Germany or Italy respectively.

"The nomination of these ports shall be based upon the home ports of the ships in peace time. The German Government solemnly declare to the French Government that it has no intention of using during the war, for its own purposes, the French Fleet stationed in ports under German control, except for such ships as may be necessary for surveillance of the coasts and for mine-sweeping.

"Moreover, it declares solemnly and formally that it has no intention of formulating claims to the French Fleet on the conclusion of peace. Except for that part of the French Fleet to be determined which shall be appropriated to the safeguarding of French interests in the Colonial Empire, all French warships now outside French territorial waters shall be recalled to France."

The Wehrmacht would not interfere in the administration of the occupied territory, Article 3 indicating merely collaboration between the French and German authorities. The French authorities might freely perform their functions "so long as they did not oppose the exigencies of German operations". For the rest, there were merely the customary clauses in documents of this nature: the conquered would pay the costs of the occupying troops (the strange interpretation put upon this clause was not as yet foreseen). All armed forces were to be disarmed except those necessary to the maintenance of order. With regard to the Air Force, which the Germans had originally demanded should be handed over, Bergeret, objecting that it was as dishonourable for an airman to hand over his machine as it was for a sailor to hand over his ship, obtained that it should merely be disarmed.

All this, though hard, was normal and contained nothing contrary to honour. Nevertheless, Pétain's Government, to whom, at 10.30 p.m. during the night of the 21st–22nd June, Huntziger transmitted the German conditions by telephone, protested against three clauses and, during a Council of Ministers held on the 22nd at 8 a.m., suggested amendments.

The clauses the French Government considered unacceptable were the following:

Article 17, forbidding "all transfer of stocks and articles of an economic nature" from one zone to another, which implied that the line of demarcation was not purely a military delimitation.

Article 19, which Keitel made a condition *sine qua non* and which demanded the handing over of all German nationals in

French territory who might be designated by the Government of the Reich.

Article 23, which made the Convention of armistice effective only on the signature of a similar document with the Italian Government.

But Huntziger at Rethondes obtained but little in the way of modifications. The first point remained unchanged. On the second point, which was dishonourable, Huntziger clashed with Keitel's categorical refusal. The German ultimately confined himself to giving a verbal assurance that the only German refugees whom the Reich would demand were those who had been guilty of incitement to war. The third point provoked the only emotional scene marking the negotiations.

Article 23 would have allowed the Italians to re-open the terms agreed in the Franco-German armistice: Huntziger could not accept it: "Italy has declared war on us, but she has not made war on us. . . . If we are faced in Rome with unacceptable demands, the whole edifice of our Convention with Germany will fall to the ground. . . . You can trample on us, you can do us more harm than you have already done, and we will bear it, but we shall not sign and will regain our freedom of action: our Fleet is intact and our Air Force is intact. Come what may, France has seen other disasters! France considers her honour more important than her life!"

On the 22nd June, at 6.34 p.m., Keitel handed the French delegation an ultimatum. The last moment for signing the armistice was fixed at 7.30 p.m. Having consulted Weygand, Huntziger had no alternative but to do so. The signature was followed by reciprocal assurances of trust and esteem. Huntziger said to Keitel: "General, you are a soldier and you know what a severe ordeal it is for a soldier to do what I have just done. We French soldiers must not have occasion in the future to repent having taken the action I have."

The German Generals were moved: Jodl had tears in his eyes. Keitel replied: "It is honourable in a conqueror to honour the conquered," and he invited the members of both delegations to rise to their feet for a moment in memory of the dead.

The following day, Sunday the 23rd June, the French delegation left for Rome where their reception did not confirm the fears Huntziger had formulated.

The Italians seemed almost to be apologising for gathering the fruits of a victory others had won. Count Ciano, Minister of Foreign Affairs, shook Ambassador Noël's hand warmly and lengthily. General Badoglio, who presided over the negotiations, considerably mitigated the original text. There was to be no question of occupying French territory, except (a clause inserted merely for the look of the thing) such territory as had been conquered by the Fascist troops. The clause concerning the handing over of political refugees was suppressed in the Franco-Italian document. Italian military control over French territories, particularly in North Africa and Syria, would be reduced to a minimum. The Convention was signed at 7.15 p.m. Badoglio then informed the French that, certain of agreement, he had, forty minutes earlier, advised the German Government on his own initiative that the negotiations had succeeded. This was in order to put an end to hostilities that much sooner. And, indeed, hostilities ceased in the night of the 24th–25th June at 12.35 a.m. instead of 1.15 a.m., which would have corresponded to the six hours' delay foreseen in the armistice convention with Germany.

The armistice negotiations at Rethondes took place in constant touch with Bordeaux. And there, while the negotiations were in process, another drama was in preparation which was soon to come to a head between France and England. During the night of the 21st–22nd June, when the conditions for an armistice had just been communicated, a tragic misunderstanding arose between the French Government and the British Ambassador, Sir Ronald Campbell.

The cause of the misunderstanding was the fate of the French Fleet. On this point, the French and English positions had differed since the 16th June. On that date, Campbell handed Paul Reynaud two telegrams from Churchill asking that the French ships should be despatched to English ports: a demand which Paul Reynaud, as we have seen, had to refuse.[1] On the 18th, after Pétain had replaced Reynaud, Campbell presented the telegrams once more to Charles-Roux, who understood from his conversation with Campbell that it was simply a matter of their being communicated to the new Minister for information. But, in fact, in Sir Ronald Campbell's eyes, it was an official notification; England would accept no other solution than the despatching of the French Fleet to British ports.

[1] Cf. *supra*, p. 28.

The point of view of the French Government, on the other hand, was that the Fleet's security was sufficiently assured in a North African port or in the free zone. Moreover, the undertaking entered into on the 19th June by Pétain and Darlan not to hand over any ship whatever to the Germans or Italians should, in the view of the French Ministers, have spared the English all further anxiety.[1]

These misunderstandings explain the British Ambassador's impatience to know the German conditions, of which he was supposed to be informed as soon as they arrived.

The actors in this imbroglio were Sir Ronald Campbell, the British Ambassador, Paul Baudouin, the new Minister for Foreign Affairs in Pétain's Government, and Charles-Roux, Secretary-General to that Ministry. The question on which their evidence differs and which still remains today in suspense, is whether, during the course of that night, the French Government kept their promise to the British of communicating the conditions of the armistice *as soon as they were received* or not. Sir Ronald Campbell asserts that the promise was not kept, and that he had to insist repeatedly in order to get knowledge of the terms even eleven hours after the French Government had received them. He deduces from this that Baudouin was a "knave" who was not to be trusted. It was in this conviction that he returned to London on the evening of the 22nd and, transmitting it to Churchill, doubtless influenced the latter in his decision to attack the French Fleet at Mers-el-Kebir. Baudouin, on the other hand, asserts that he kept his promise, and drawing an extremely tendentious portrait of Sir Ronald as a self-satisfied egoist, he throws the whole responsibility for the incident on to the Ambassador. Charles-Roux, a high official, manifestly makes every effort not to give his Minister the lie: nevertheless, his record of events corroborates in several places Sir Ronald's thesis, leaving in doubt however one point, which one may make an attempt to explain.

Here then is the time-table of the events of that night and of the following day. Uncontested in outline, it is however in the detail that the discrepancies between Campbell's and Baudouin's accounts lie.

[1] The English would have been completely reassured had they known of the secret order for scuttling in case of aggression which Darlan had sent to the ships under his command on the 20th June (cf. *infra*, p. 74, the text of the Admiral's secret instructions), but they were clearly not able to divine their existence.

At 10.30 p.m. on the 21st, General Huntziger, telephoning from Rethondes, transmitted the German terms.

A meeting was immediately held at the Préfecture in the Rue Vital-Carles, at which Pétain, Bouthillier, Baudouin, Alibert, Charles-Roux and General Weygand were present.

After the meeting, Charles-Roux had a few moments' conversation with Campbell.

At 1 o'clock in the morning, there was a full meeting of the Council of Ministers at which Charles-Roux, naturally, was not qualified to be present.

At 3 o'clock the Council came to an end.

At 8 a.m. on the 22nd June, there was a meeting in the Rue Vital-Carles, attended by Weygand, Darlan, Bouthillier and Baudouin, to consider the modifications the French Government would ask of the Germans.

At 9.15 a.m., General Weygand telephoned the proposed alterations to General Huntziger at Rethondes.

Paul Baudouin told Charles-Roux to inform Campbell of the amendments asked for by the French and of the German replies. The two diplomatists had an interview.

That evening, when Huntziger had signed the armistice convention at Rethondes, Campbell decided to return to London.

This is the time-table about which there is no disagreement. Where do the differences lie within it? According to Baudouin, as soon as the armistice conditions reached him at 10.30 p.m., he told Charles-Roux to maintain contact with Sir Ronald Campbell and to inform him of them. He believed, therefore, that this had been done, particularly since at midnight, when he came out of the meeting in the Rue Vital-Carles, Charles-Roux had met the Ambassador, who was waiting in a neighbouring room, and had had several minutes' conversation with him.

Moreover, during the Council, which was held between 1 and 3 a.m., Sir Ronald Campbell had, according to Baudouin, sent in to the Minister, while in session, the following note: "I have no doubt that the Council is aware of the insidious character of the condition concerning the Fleet. No reliance can be placed on the word of the Germans: they have never kept their promises. Forgive my emphasising what I am sure has not escaped your notice. My anxiety must be my excuse!"

From this note, Baudouin concluded that Charles-Roux had

communicated, at least verbally, the armistice conditions to Campbell.

At 3 a.m., when the Council was over, Baudouin ran into Campbell who was still on sentry-go. The Ambassador vehemently complained that the French Minister "had kept him waiting". Baudouin, harassed, irritated by the Englishman's insistence, states that he then gave Sir Ronald Campbell a written text of the armistice conditions. Then, curtly cutting short the conversation, he informed Sir Ronald Campbell that, after some hours' work during the night, he would receive him first, at 7.30 a.m., at the beginning of his next day's work.

At 7.30, Campbell did not appear. The Ambassador, having mistaken the meeting-place, and thinking that Baudouin had affronted him, had gone to complain to Pétain. And it was on arriving at the Rue Vital-Carles at 8 o'clock that Baudouin learned from the Marshal of Sir Ronald Campbell's anger. As the meeting was about to take place, the Minister had not the time to receive the diplomatist.

This is Baudouin's story. Essentially, it rests on two points, the first being the misunderstanding as to the meeting-place for the morning with Sir Ronald Campbell, and it is clearly impossible to know whether it really happened and what the reasons for it were: no witness can be summoned except Baudouin and Campbell themselves and their evidence differs. Second, the remitting by Baudouin to Campbell, during the night of the 21st at 3 a.m., a written text of the armistice conditions, which the Ambassador denies: on the second point, Charles-Roux confirms Campbell's denials, and states that the document was only handed to the Ambassador in the afternoon of the 22nd.

This unwilling refutation of his Minister's assertions by the Secretary-General rests on two points. In the first place, Charles-Roux states that during his conversation with the British Ambassador at 3 o'clock in the morning, when the Council of Ministers broke up, "M. Paul Baudouin, arguing that the deliberations had not come to a close, had refused to part with the text of the Convention, the first consideration of which, according to him, was due to the French Government". Furthermore, Charles-Roux states that it was only during the morning of the 22nd, after 9.15 a.m., and not during the preceding night at 10.30 p.m., that Paul Baudouin ordered him to have a conversation with Campbell which had nothing to do with the communication of the armistice conditions:

"I was in process of recording my ideas about the brief negotiations at Rethondes when M. Paul Baudouin said to me:

" 'You will receive today the British Ambassador and you will communicate to him the amendments we are asking for and the German replies.' "

It was, moreover, on the same occasion that Baudouin told him, thus giving himself the lie, that he had only just sent the armistice terms to the Ambassador.

It is therefore probable that the ex-Minister's recollections of that hideous night are not always in accordance with the facts, and that Campbell is right in asserting that the armistice conditions were not communicated to him, even verbally, as soon as received, but with a delay of more than half a day. It was a failure to keep a promise and was sufficient to justify the Ambassador's mistrust, if not the extreme conclusions that the head of his Government was later to draw from it.

There is, however, one point which remains in doubt. If Campbell really had no knowledge of the armistice proposals before the morning of the 22nd, how was it that, during the Council of Ministers of the preceding night, he sent Baudouin a note formulating his anxieties concerning one of the stipulations which, if one is to believe Charles-Roux and himself, had not yet been communicated to him?

There are two possible answers to this: the first, which makes sense of the facts, seems however to be unlikely in face of the precision of Charles-Roux' evidence and the disciplined attitude he has not ceased to show towards his Minister: Charles-Roux, during the course of his brief conversation with the Ambassador, after the meeting at the Préfecture, might have told Campbell unofficially the text of the clause which affected him the most and to which he would most certainly have directed his first question: what would be the fate of the Fleet? It is, however, a hypothesis which one hesitates to retain, because it would have been an indiscretion and a professional error on the part of Charles-Roux of which nothing in his customary behaviour permits one to believe him capable.

There is another possibility. Baudouin, whom we have seen to be in error over the time-table of these days, may have made the same mistake over Sir Ronald Campbell's note. It may not have been handed to him during the Council that night but in the afternoon during the course of another Ministerial meeting, after Charles-Roux had officially communicated the armistice conditions to the British diplomatist: Campbell's note, indeed, bears for date and hour merely the "23rd June, 1.30."—which may well mean either the morning or the afternoon.

If this is the case, the whole business becomes clear and can be explained by an error of Baudouin's memory, which is perfectly comprehensible in such tragic circumstances.

However that may be, one fact is certain: Campbell had reason, apparent if not real, likely if not true, to suspect the sincerity of the French Government on a point which was vital to the future of his country. He wrongly supposed that the French Government had entered into secret engagements which had not been communicated to him: a misunderstanding from which he immediately drew certain conclusions and terminated his mission.

At 11.30 that same night, Campbell knocked at the door of Baudouin's lodging. The Minister awoke, put on a dressing-gown, and went to open the door himself: it was to hear Campbell's announcement that he was leaving for London, in conformity with his Government's orders not to allow himself to be made prisoner in any circumstances: since the port of Bordeaux was to be included in the zone occupied by the Germans, the destroyer, which was to take him back to London, could wait no longer.

Thus, every event, whether brought about by Laval and Alibert or not, tended to the same result. In spite of the opposition of the majority of members of Parliament and Ministers, in spite of the hostility of Presidents Lebrun, Jeanneney and Herriot, the Government remained in France, the armistice was signed with Germany and Italy, and a rupture created with the British.

It was then, in a situation which had been utterly transformed in less than forty-eight hours by the arrival of the armistice conditions and the negotiations which followed, that Laval, on the 23rd June, entered the Government. It was a decisive fact which confirmed the reversal of French policy and crystallised about a man of the first rank the tendencies which until then had been expressed only confusedly by the enemies of the regime.

In summoning him, with Marquet, to the Cabinet, as Minister of State, and appointing him four days later, on his own authority, Vice-President of the Council, while confiding to Marquet the Ministry of the Interior, the Marshal had recourse to the only politician whom events seemed to have shown to be right; and this did not surprise him. In 1934, Doumergue had recommended Laval to him as follows: "The Republic is rotten; they no longer have anyone except that man!" A judgment which had ever since remained firmly established in the Marshal's mind.

The Marshal was not unaware both of Pierre Laval's redoubtable qualities and his faults. "But," he said to those who feared the outcome, to Charles-Roux and Baudouin, "Laval's intrigues will be less dangerous if he is in the Government than if he creates an opposition outside it." One thing was sure, within the Government Laval would succeed in winning a second trick: after the liquidation of the war against Germany, which came to an end on the 25th June, he would achieve the liquidation of the regime: an operation whose final act was to be played in the National Assembly on the 10th July, when Laval took the leading part.

Laval's accession to power was accompanied by numerous signs which foreshadowed a change of regime. In his appeal to the nation on the 25th June, on the occasion of the armistice, the Marshal announced: "A new order is about to begin. . . . I urge you in the first place to an intellectual and moral regeneration. Frenchmen, you will accomplish this and you will see, I promise you, a new France arise from your fervour."

There was another indication, still more significant: Laval's return to the Government coincided with the first measures taken against members of Parliament. He himself lodged against Mandel, accused of having begun negotiations with the British, an indictment for plotting against the safety of the State: nor did he do anything to oppose the steps that were being taken against the passengers in the *Massillia*.

On the 23rd June, at 11 o'clock, Darlan, who had himself signed the order for their departure, wrote a letter to Barthe accusing those who were at that moment sailing towards Africa and were due to arrive at Casablanca on the following day. On the 25th June, Prouvost, the Minister of Information, went further in his newspaper, *Paris-Soir*, in which a violent attack appeared. The Questeurs of the Senate and the Chamber, Manceau and Barthe, demanded an audience with Pétain, whom they saw in the late afternoon in the presence of Alibert. Alibert stated in the first instance that the members of Parliament had sailed at their own risk. Then, when Barthe told him of the order signed by Darlan on the 19th June at 7 p.m., his expression changed: "I knew nothing about these orders," he said. Pétain read Darlan's order and blamed Prouvost: "I look on the *Massillia* affair as finished and done with." The same day, Pétain confided to the deputy, Fernand-Laurent: "I dare not put the members of Parliament against me at this moment, I may have need of them." But it is certain that Pétain's statements on this subject did not prevent the attacks continuing; they resulted on the 18th July in sanctions against those members of Parliament who had sailed in the ship. Thus, with Laval's return to power, the atmosphere became one of political change though its precise form was not yet established.

Laval and Alibert were alone in contemplating a veritable *coup d'état*. Alibert pressed his convictions concerning internal policy. A monarchist of the Action Française, he wished to destroy the Republican regime and eliminate its members: that was his whole ambition. Laval, on the other hand, was also aware of the decisive events which were taking place in the outside world. He was certain that Germany would win the war during the next few weeks, that England would be defeated and that the whole of Europe would be subjected to German domination. In that eventuality, it was necessary to adapt France, as quickly as possible, to the new German order: it was the only chance of crossing over from the camp of the vanquished to that of the potential conquerors. It was the only chance of preventing England, soon to be defeated in her turn or to negotiate an ineffective peace, from coming to an understanding with Germany at the expense of France. That was why he envisaged at this period a reversal of alliances; and why he wished to make an end of the Republic which he looked on as an obstacle to his efforts to align French policy with that of her conquerors. Laval and Alibert, on the 25th June, 1940, were almost alone in their desire to destroy the Republican regime.

Baudouin and Bouthillier were content to confer upon the Marshal full provisional powers, limited to the period anterior to ultimate peace. The fact that this procedure had but lately been employed by Léon Blum and Daladier would tend to remove all scruples.

The Marshal was equally hostile to the Third Republic. In his view, France's defeat was not due to military causes alone; it had become inevitable owing to the decadence of the country's institutions and political personalities. The contempt he had for the President of the Republic, Albert Lebrun, is revealing: Pétain it has been noted, never referred to him by his name, or by his title of "President": at the most, he consented, his lips pursed, to allow him the pronoun "he".

On the 11th June, Pétain had maintained to Darlan the necessity of renewing the country's institutions, without however revealing as yet that he was prepared to take the initiative. On the 14th June, it was Baudouin's turn to hear him declare that the attitude of the Government was craven and ignoble.

Having said this much, and repeated it on several occasions to his intimates, Pétain had not at this date put forward the measures for the reorganisation he considered so indispensable. For the moment, the Marshal was still hesitating to follow Laval. He was more inclined, out of prudence, and because he feared a repulse, to limit himself to dismissing the Chambers and forming a new and more homogeneous government. As for reforming the constitution, that could be considered later, after returning to Paris, a free Paris. He asked Bouthillier to find some means of allowing him to govern legally and constitutionally without having to submit to the incessant control of Parliament.

Against this indecisive attitude, which was typical of the Marshal, Laval was to bring to bear all the influence he could exercise on him.

Nothing had however been decided when the Government left Bordeaux on the 29th June for Clermont-Ferrand, following a road which, for over thirty kilometres, was guarded by the Germans. Between Montpont and Mussidan, the official convoy slowed down to pass a road-block as high as a man; it marked the frontier between the occupied and unoccupied zones.

At the very moment the Government were leaving Bordeaux, a German Colonel ordered the French flag to be struck on the Hôtel de Ville. Marquet, the Mayor of Bordeaux and Minister of the Interior, succeeded in getting the order cancelled. The tricolour remained. Yet, at half mast for the last four days as a sign of mourning, it no longer floated free.

The armistice, whose signing was the Government's first act, has not ceased to divide opinion. It is one of the main subjects of disagreement concerning Pétain's policy.

According to the supporters of the armistice, the cessation of hostilities, militarily inevitable, was also a fortunate decision. Here are their principal arguments: they consider in the first place that the army in Africa, deprived of arms, was incapable of resisting the Germans on its own. They assert, furthermore, that in the long run, the signature of the convention of Rethondes turned out to be favourable to the allies. They maintain that there is no doubt that, if hostilities had not come to an end, Hitler would have obtained Franco's support for an invasion of North Africa, concerning which, since the 17th June, 1940, the Spaniards had already formulated conditions. Thus, the armistice not only preserved French Africa from German occupation but permitted the Allied landings in November, 1942—a decisive operation for the eventual Allied victory. The opponents of the armistice, on the other hand, are not lacking in arguments.

The continuation of the war in North Africa was, if they are to be believed, possible. If not, how is it to be explained that all the Governor-Generals of the colonies, Le Beau at Algiers, Peyrouton at Tunis, Noguès in Morocco, Cayla in French West Africa, Boisson in French Equatorial Africa, Puaux and General Mittelhauser in the Levant, Brunot in the Cameroons, Coppet in Madagascar, Annet in Dahomey and Catroux in Indo-China began by spontaneously declaring themselves in favour of prolonging the war and only became resigned to the armistice on Pétain's formal order?

For them, the invasion of North Africa by the Germans, even assisted by the Spanish, was an absurd hypothesis, which took no account of the existence of an impregnable fortress at Gibraltar, nor of the absolute control of the seas which the Royal Navy could have maintained with the assistance of the French Fleet.

They therefore considered the armistice as responsible for prolonging the war: without it, Great Britain, supported by the French Empire and Fleet, would have been victorious sooner.

It is an argument which it is impossible to resolve, and in which it is no business of this book to take sides, the object of these pages being not to re-write history on the basis of a hypothesis, which did not eventuate, but to recount the facts as they were in reality.

Pétain and his Ministers having opted for the armistice, it is necessary to determine and understand the motives which led to their decision.

The over-riding reason was the unanimous conviction of the Government that a German victory was imminent. From this point of view, the armistice, at that time, does not lack arguments in its favour. At the time, it seemed to constitute a lesser evil.

It undeniably brought in its train an almost physical relief to those who were obsessed by the spectacle of a routed army and a whole population crowding along the roads. Compared to the fate which the other victims of Hitler had suffered, Czechoslovakia, Poland, even Holland and Belgium, that which the armistice imposed on France seemed relatively almost enviable: had France not got a Government and an administration which, in accordance with the stipulations made at Rethondes, could not have their independence limited? Had not France a free zone in which her sovereignty remained unimpaired? She preserved in Metropolitan France an army of one hundred thousand men, without taking into account such units as were destined for the defence of the Empire. Moreover, the Fleet and Empire remained intact.

These considerations appeared to enable defeated France to play the classic role of the conquered, which is gradually to nibble away at their conqueror's victory and thereby effect their own rehabilitation. Pétain had always looked on the 11th November, 1918, the day on which the Allies accorded the defeated Germans an armistice, as a day of evil omen and mourning. The fact that the Nazis, in this new armistice, had imitated their error, gave him hope that the mourning would change sides and that Germany would one day deplore her forbearance when she saw France also recovering herself. Thus the supporters of the armistice expected an early peace and a slow effort towards the reconstruction of France, while the opponents of the armistice foresaw a longer war which, through victory, would bring about a sudden recovery of the country: this was the position taken up by General de Gaulle in his first announcements which were in response to the first broadcasts of Marshal Pétain. They were both playing for time, but in opposite directions.

The man of Bordeaux and the man of London from that moment took up irreconcilable historical points of view.

For Philippe Pétain the war was over. The war which, in his view, was but a third episode in seventy years of Franco-German conflict: 1914 had been a resumption of 1870, 1939–1940 was in its turn a resumption of 1914. The military defeat having occurred, it was only by a slow and patient series of negotiations with the victor and by a reorganisation on the part of the defeated that the latter could hope to recover; the first duty of a Head of the Government was to protect the French who had remained in France.

For Charles de Gaulle, on the other hand, the war was only beginning. A war of a different nature and of a different period from all previous wars. A war on a world scale, in which France, who had lost the first battle, might with her allies and her Empire be present at the final victory.

There was a further difference between the two points of view, the two men and the two camps between which, until our day, all Frenchmen have been divided: they imply two opposed emotional attitudes, two different conceptions of honour.

Those who, before de Gaulle, with de Gaulle, or after him, opposed the armistice, embodied a whole French tradition which, from Corneille to Péguy, has always refused to consider itself beaten or accept defeat. In Foch's phrase, "One is never defeated till one admits defeat." All the prophecies upon which, in his first appeals, de Gaulle based his decision to resist, are in fact but expositions of such an act of faith: all the arguments, both sensible and prudent, by which, in his speeches to the people of France, Pétain supported his decision to ask for an armistice, were also but the exegesis of a different principle.

The honour of which Marshal Pétain spoke was the honour of a government which has succeeded in maintaining the basis of its independence and is protecting the population: in a word *civic* honour. But the honour evoked by General de Gaulle was *military* honour because for a soldier to admit defeat is always an infamous act.

## CHAPTER 3

# VICHY

## (1st–10th July, 1940)

THE signing of the armistice marked the end of the military phase: Laval and Alibert were now to draw political inferences from it which seemed unassailable: the destruction of the Third Republic, which had been responsible for the defeat, and its replacement by an authoritarian regime, would now allow France to conduct peace negotiations and pursue a policy of rehabilitation.

The operation, according to their plan, was to be effected in two stages. In the first place it was necessary to persuade the Government and the President of the Republic to convoke the National Assembly, composed of the Chamber of Deputies and the Senate, who were alone qualified, in consonance with the laws of 1875, to alter the constitution; then obtain from the Assembly the delegation of its constitutional powers to Marshal Pétain.

The Government convoy, chased out of Bordeaux by the German occupation, arrived at Clermont-Ferrand on the 29th June towards the end of the afternoon. All the ministerial offices crowded into the Préfecture, while their departments bivouacked in villas scattered about the various spas: it often took a Minister three quarters of an hour to drive over mountain roads to his department.

It was on the morning of Sunday, 30th June, that the question first officially arose, during the course of a ministerial Council limited to Pétain, Alibert, Laval, Baudouin and Bouthillier, of altering the regime. The five Ministers were, however, far from being unanimous on what decisions to take.

Bouthillier was hostile to the extreme solution of abolishing the Republic: he suggested to the Marshal the possibility of "governing without being harassed by Parliament", which corresponded to the wishes expressed by Pétain himself: it would be sufficient to defer a new meeting of the Chambers until the 15th January, 1941.

This interpretation of Article 1 of the Constitutional Law of the 16th July, 1875,[1] would, according to Bouthillier, allow of suspending Parliament without implying the suppression of the Republican regime. Pétain declared that he was prepared to accept this temporary expedient. Was the Republic on the point of being saved?

It was threatened again in the afternoon. During the course of another meeting, Laval and Alibert, unmasking their batteries, put forward a proposal which would have suppressed it: that of convoking, as soon as possible, the Deputies and Senators to the National Assembly and making them vote a motion authorising the Marshal, President of the Council, to promulgate a new Constitutional Law. In a word, it was a question of destroying the regime.

To both Bouthillier and Baudouin this plan seemed insane: how could a majority of both Chambers be persuaded to commit suicide?

To begin with Pétain also opposed Laval: it was impossible, the Marshal declared, to reform the constitution in present circumstances.

Laval then ran riot; he would accept no delay, tolerate no hesitation. Defeated France must provide herself with a regime which would permit her to negotiate with Nazi Germany when the imminent moment for making peace should arrive. There must be no shuffling, no delays: the choice must be made at once. If not, France would be outstripped by events, as she had been for months and years. Laval felt certain of being able to persuade the Assemblies to commit hara-kiri. His conviction was so impressive and so catching, that he silenced all objections and ended almost by shaking the Marshal himself. Nevertheless, before yielding, Pétain dug himself in behind one last obstacle: what Laval desired could not be done without the consent of the President of the Republic. Here, then, was Albert Lebrun being put forward as the last bastion of the regime! Laval proposed to take him by assault: "I guarantee to obtain Albert Lebrun's full agreement to his own disappearance," he asserted; then,

[1] This article stipulates in fact that "the Senate and the Chamber of Deputies shall meet each year on the second Tuesday in January, unless previously convoked by the President of the Republic."

without waiting for the Marshal's consent, he jumped into his car and was driven to Royat, where the President was staying, and came back an hour later saying: "Well, Monsieur le Maréchal, it's done." "Then, you may try to do the rest," replied Pétain, who looked with admiration on the author of an offensive so quickly determined on and so promptly realised.

In the afternoon of the 1st July the Government made another journey: it left Clermont-Ferrand for Vichy.

The Ministries took up their quarters in the requisitioned hotels: the Ministry of National Defence in the Hôtel Thermal, the Ministry of Marine at the Helder, a second-rate hotel, the Ministries of Justice and Finance at the Carlton, the Diplomatic Corps at the Ambassadeurs (a predestined name, said a high functionary with facile irony). The Quai d'Orsay crowded into two storeys of the Hôtel du Parc, where lived also Marshal Pétain and President Laval, who had to enter Vichy on foot, his motor-car having broken down a kilometre from the town: was this an omen? As for President Albert Lebrun, he had shut himself up and become invisible within the Pavillon Sévigné.

The members of Parliament had to report to the Hôtel Majestic: they were to be seen arriving by night through the blackout, electric torches in their hands, to enquire of the Questeurs for the lodgings which had been or, indeed, frequently had not been, arranged for them. At Bordeaux, they had numbered two hundred. They were soon to be three times as many at Vichy, summoned by the press and by the radio, thanks to foreign stations, both Swiss and Spanish, for the French wave-lengths had been suppressed by the armistice convention.

It was not only politicians who swarmed about the Government. An improbable fauna haunted Vichy at the beginning of July, 1940: journalists, adventurers in search of unexpected preferment, electoral agents who feared that they would henceforth be deprived of their livings, recipients of secret funds who were anxious that their salaries should be continued, financiers on the watch for opportunities, industrialists fearing the cancellation of their Government contracts, writers in search of new material.

The hotels were crowded, the Mairie bursting at the seams. People slept where they could, on straw, at the Concours Hippique and elsewhere.

Bars and restaurants were overflowing with rumours, speculations, and false information.

The great pleasure of this idle crowd was to invade the hall of the Hôtel du Parc and watch for Laval, who would pass through with an air of assurance, or for the Marshal, whose dignity and bearing were in contrast to the surrounding confusion.

"There was not silence," recalls Pierre Nicolle, who witnessed one of these appearances, "there was whispering." Everyone's attention was irresistibly fixed on the end of the big drawing-room which gave on to the private dining-room. At every table, men and women rose respectfully to their feet. A man had appeared, surrounded by two or three people. That man was Marshal Pétain.

"Wearing a lounge suit, his head held high, he advanced slowly with that peculiar gait which seemed to carry him so majestically. His blue eyes took in the whole room, while he affably acknowledged with an inclination of the head or that gesture of the hand, which was his alone, the deferential salutations that greeted him. From time to time he stopped to exchange a few words here and there, ask a question, smile, and then he withdrew. . . ."

A vision of history which, for the moment, reassured those who saw it without however dissipating the atmosphere of anguish that reigned over the whole country on the morrow of defeat. More than a quarter of the population of France had been dispersed: eight million civilians had been driven from their homes by the exodus, while about half the army was prisoner.

The armistice had not been signed for a week, before the conquerors were infringing it. Their violations accumulated. On the 26th June, they had transgressed for the first time the convention, which had only come into force the day before, by improperly occupying the Fort de l'Ecluse near the Swiss frontier.

Contrary to their other undertakings in the agreement of Rethondes, they carved France into two impenetrable zones. From the end of June onwards, it appeared that the demarcation line established by the conquerors on the periphery of the occupied zone, was not only a military line as had been laid down in the armistice: it had become a frontier which impeded the movement of individuals, goods and securities and which subjected telegraphic, telephonic and postal communications between the two zones to the control of the occupying power.

To the north and the east there were even more serious violations: the frontier provinces were detached from France. The northern departments became a forbidden zone and a dependency of the Brussels military administration; the departments of Alsace-Lorraine were virtually annexed.

At 12.20 p.m. on the 19th June, 1940, the Swastika flag was hoisted on the pinnacle of the cathedral of Strasbourg. Hitler arrived a week later, on the anniversary of the Treaty of Versailles.

He visited the sanctuary, was much moved and, on coming out, while being cheered by a crowd of German soldiers, asked: "What do you think? Should we restore this jewel to the French?" The unanimous reply was: "No, never!" After that, the administrative annexation of Alsace-Lorraine by Germany began immediately.

The reports which began reaching Vichy after the disaster indicated the paralysis or disappearance of the French administration. In Seine-et-Oise, all public relief had shut down for lack of funds: the Germans were setting up National Socialist organisations, often financed with the French money they had seized on arrival. In the Marne, there was no food, water or gas: Frenchmen were standing, hands outstretched, begging from the conquerors. In the villages, the administration was controlled by the non-commissioned officers of the occupying army.

In the Yonne, the Préfet had seen the heads of every administrative service depart: at Auxerre, the lunatics from the asylum, abandoned by the doctors, had got loose. There was no one to look after the children in the orphanage. Furthermore, there was not a penny of public funds left anywhere: municipalities were issuing their own currencies.

There was general anarchy and administrative insolvency: the Germans exploited it. On the walls of towns and villages a poster appeared showing a Frenchwoman with two children. The legend ran: "Abandoned population, put your trust in the German soldier."

Sometimes, the occupying army was not content with propaganda: it fomented "autonomist" movements.

On the pretext that the Bretons constituted a racial minority, the Germans endeavoured to make Brittany independent.

On the 3rd July at Pontivy, a National Breton Council, composed of four people in the pay of the Nazis, organised a great congress to proclaim the separation of Brittany from France. Three hundred Breton prisoners, carefully selected on the advice of the "autonomist" leaders, were given their liberty on the occasion of this solemn act. The best hotels were requisitioned for them, they were given a present of a civilian suit, an honorarium and a thousand pamphlets printed in Germany.

Paper, clothes and money were wasted! An enormous counter-demonstration, in which—with what ingratitude!—the prisoners participated, created a panic among the members of the congress, and obliged the leading autonomist, Debauvais, to ask the occupying troops for protection. While the Bishop of Quimper, Mgr Duparc, had a warning read from the pulpit which effectually put an end to the movement: Brittany remained French.

What did the population feel in this appalling catastrophe? The majority remained faithful to the Marshal; a small number left to join General de Gaulle. The two camps, equally convinced that they were serving France, began to accuse each other mutually of treason.

In addition to so much that was disastrous, Vichy suddenly received, on the 3rd July, news of the most dread ordeal which could have assailed France: the action taken by the Royal Navy against the French ships at anchor in the roads of Mers-el-Kebir.

The attack by the British Fleet on the 3rd July against French ships at Mers-el-Kebir was stigmatised by Admiral Darlan as the greatest error in British policy.

To the British Government, however, it seemed a necessity: Churchill was convinced that the promise given by Hitler to respect the French Fleet was worth no more than any other of the Führer's promises. The misunderstanding between Baudouin and Campbell, moreover, engendered in him suspicions of the good faith of the French Government.

Operation "Catapult" was planned immediately on Campbell's leaving France and might have been foreseen by the French Government.

Admiral Odendhal, head of the French Naval Mission in London, had telegraphed Darlan on the 24th June that "the English fear that our Fleet, once disarmed, will be used against them." At the same time, he informed the Admiral of the Fleet that all French ships, whether merchant ships or warships, at that time in British ports, had been prevented from sailing.

Another warning came from the French Embassy in Washington. The French journalist, Pertinax, published an article in the *Baltimore Sun* prophesying some desperate action by the British Navy against the French. Finally, the British and American Governments continually reproached the French for not having sent their Fleet to Great Britain before asking for an armistice.

All these were premonitory signs, which were not taken seriously enough by the French Government because it seemed inconceivable that the British should not have confidence in the solemn promise given by the Marshal and confirmed by the orders of Admiral Darlan.

On the 20th June, realising that an armistice was bound shortly to be concluded, Darlan had sent all Admirals and Préfets of Maritime departments instructions covering the possibility that the Admiral of the Fleet might be prevented from exercising his authority. The message finished thus: "Whatever orders may be received, no warship must be handed over to the enemy intact."

And on the 24th June, 1940, at 12.45 p.m., Darlan, using the naval secret code for the last time, sent to the same Admirals and Préfets these irrevocable instructions.

"I am taking advantage of the last messages that I can transmit in code in order to inform you of my thought on this subject: these orders remain valid, whatever contradictory orders you may receive hereafter, even if signed by me.

"1. The ships which have been demobilised must remain French and under the French flag, reduced crews must be French, and they must remain in either Metropolitan or Colonial French ports.

"2. Secret preparations for scuttling must be made so that, if the enemy or an ex-ally seize a ship by force, they will be unable to make use of it.

"3. If the Armistice Commission, whose duty it is to interpet the position, should decide otherwise than in paragraph 1, all warships, upon this decision being put into effect, will, without further orders, set sail for the United States or be scuttled, if there is no other means of denying them to the enemy. In no circumstances will they be left intact in enemy hands.

"4. Such ships as take refuge in foreign ports must not be used in warlike operations against Germany or Italy without orders from the Commanders-in-Chief of the French Naval Forces.

"5. In no circumstances will the orders of any foreign admiralty be obeyed."

These last secret instructions, issued before the armistice, prove the good faith of the French, and in the eyes of French sailors rendered the attack at Mers-el-Kebir still more unjustifiable.

The French Atlantic Squadron, called "Raid Force", comprised about a fifth of the French Fleet: four cruisers, of which two were modern battle-cruisers: the *Dunkerque*, flying the flag of Admiral Gensoul, the *Strasbourg*, and two older ones: the *Provence* and the *Bretagne*; six destroyers (*Volga*, *Mogador*, *Terrible*, *Lynx*, *Tigre* and *Kersaint*) were all in the roads of Mers-el-Kebir under the direct orders of Admiral Gensoul; one aircraft carrier, *Commandant-Teste*, four torpedo boats, a few despatch boats and four submarines, under the command of Admiral Jarry, Naval Commander at Oran, were lying between Mers-el-Kebir and Oran.

The greater part of the squadron, in which the demobilisation of the crews had begun the day before, were in an unfavourable defensive position: the four cruisers and the aircraft carrier, *Commandant-Teste*, were anchored too close to each other to be able to use their guns while a rocky spur, closing the entry to the harbour on the north, prevented reply being made to the guns of the British ships. The latter were in no danger as long as the French ships remained in the harbour.

During the night of the 2nd–3rd July, "Force H" of the Royal Navy, infinitely stronger than the French squadron, appeared off Mers-el-Kebir.

It began operations by laying magnetic mines in the only practicable channel between the nets: the French ships were therefore trapped, and had no chance of taking counter-measures.

At 07.05, Greenwich time, the British destroyer, *Foxhound*, was detached from "Force H" with Captain Holland on board. He was the bearer of an ultimatum to Admiral Gensoul, and sailed up to the entrance to the harbour.

At the same time, Admiral Somerville sent a first signal to Gensoul, announcing the despatch of a plenipotentiary:

"I am sending Captain Holland to confer with you. The Royal Navy hopes that the proposals he will make you will allow of the valiant and glorious French Navy joining forces with us. In that case, your ships will always remain yours, and no one need have any anxiety for the future. The British Fleet is lying off Oran ready to greet you."

To Holland's demand for a personal interview, Admiral Gensoul replied: "I shall not receive Captain Holland under threat." He sent Lieutenant de Vaisseau Dufay, whom he knew to be on friendly terms with the British officer, on board the *Foxhound*. The latter handed over the sealed letter, containing the British demands, and a few minutes later it was handed to Gensoul.

After protestations of friendship for France and a repetition of the conditions laid down by the British Government at the opening of the armistice negotiations, the document contained the following ultimatum:

"His Majesty's Government have instructed me to demand that the French Fleet now at Mers-el-Kebir and Oran shall act in accordance with one of the following alternatives:

"(*a*) Sail with us and continue to fight for victory against the Germans and the Italians

"(*b*) Sail with reduced crews under our control to a British port. The reduced crews will be repatriated at the earliest moment.

"If either of these courses is adopted by you, we will restore your ships to France at the conclusion of the war or pay full compensation, if they are damaged meanwhile.

"(*c*) Alternatively, if you feel bound to stipulate that your ships should not be used against the Germans or Italians unless these break the armistice, then sail them with us with reduced crews to some French port in the West Indies—Martinique, for instance—where they can be demilitarised to our satisfaction, or perhaps be entrusted to the United States and remain safe until the end of the war. The crews being repatriated.

"If you refuse these fair offers, I must, with profound regret, require you to sink your ships within six hours.

"Finally, failing the above, I have the orders of His Majesty's Government to use whatever force may be necessary to prevent your ships falling into German or Italian hands."

Faced with this ultimatum, the French Admiral ordered his ships to prepare for battle and to re-light their fires, orders which were enthusiastically received by the crews who were persuaded that it was a question of resuming hostilities side by side with the British Fleet.

He sent the French Admiralty a signal informing them of the British ultimatum:

"A British force composed of three battleships, one aircraft-carrier, cruisers and destroyers, before Oran, have sent me an ultimatum: 'Sink your ships within six hours or we shall use force.' My reply has been: 'French ships will reply to force with force.' "

A succinct but very incomplete report, which omitted, in particular, to inform the Admiralty that the British had proposed another alternative: the sailing of the French ships to a French port in the Antilles.

To this incomplete and hasty signal, the French Admiralty could give no other reply than an order to resist. Would they have done otherwise if Gensoul had informed them of the third alternative put forward by the British? It must be doubted: sailing for a French base in the Antilles was contrary to the armistice conditions, which specified that the ships must remain in their peace-time home ports. Barely eight days after the signature of the convention of Rethondes, the French Government could not be the first to take the initiative of transgressing one of its most important clauses.

Captain Holland, representing Admiral Somerville, and Lieutenant de Vaisseau Dufay, representing Admiral Gensoul, did all they could, their mutual friendship adding zeal to their efforts, to prevent the irreparable outcome, but their breathless discussions, their hasty comings and goings between the two Fleets were without result.

Holland vainly tried to persuade his French opposite number that the British note was not an ultimatum, but "the expression of a hope".

Gensoul finally consented to see him at five minutes past three in the afternoon, and suggested the possibility of a compromise. He informed Holland of Darlan's secret order of the 24th June, which laid it down that, in the case of the armistice clauses not being respected by the Germans, the ships should, without further orders, either sail for the United States or be scuttled. These were definite instructions to which Gensoul added his personal word of honour that, if any German threat to the security of his ships should arise, he would take them either to Martinique or the United States, but freely and without being subject to the threat of force.

At this point, Holland saw a possibility of preventing the tragedy; he signalled Somerville:

"Admiral Gensoul says that his crews are to be reduced and that, if he is threatened, he will sail to Martinique or the United States. It is not exactly what we have asked, but I cannot get any closer to it!"

If the negotiations had depended entirely on Somerville, further conversations might well have reduced their differences which were now limited to a single point: Gensoul agreed to do, in the event of a German threat, what the British ultimatum demanded that he should do at once. But Somerville was no longer free to negotiate: London was harassing him with imperative telegrams enjoining him to make an end before nightfall.

Holland was still on board the *Dunkerque* with Gensoul when, at 4.30 p.m., the latter received a signal from Somerville which he showed the British officer:

"Unless one of my proposals is accepted by 5.30,[1] I shall be compelled to sink your ships."

Holland turned pale and rose to his feet, finding nothing more to say. Conducted to the accommodation ladder with appropriate honours, he was back in the English Fleet by 4.50 p.m.

At 4.57 p.m. the first salvo hit the French ships.

Caught in a trap, shelled at point blank range by the English guns without being able to reply, the French Fleet was destroyed in thirteen minutes. At 5.10 p.m., Gensoul signalled: "All my ships are disabled: I ask you to cease fire."

Only the *Strasbourg*, which succeeded in breaking away from her anchors and driving through the British shells and magnetic mine-field, and the destroyers *Volga*, *Terrible* and *Tigre*, were able to escape the trap and reach Toulon the following day.

The *Dunkerque* ran aground. The *Bretagne* blew up and capsized. The *Provence* ran aground. Of the big ships, only the *Commandant-Teste* remained unscathed in the harbour.

The dead were buried on the 5th July.

The following morning, as a result of a rash message sent in clear by Admiral Esteva, according to which the damage to the

[1] British Summer-time.

*Dunkerque* was only slight, three waves of torpedo-carrying aircraft endeavoured to finish off the battle-cruiser; they sank a tug, the *Esterel*, and a trawler, the *Terre-Neuve*, which were alongside her; they made a hole in the side of the ship and killed or wounded four officers and one hundred and fifty men.

The total French casualties caused by the two British attacks amounted to one thousand, two hundred and ninety-seven killed or missing, and three hundred and fifty-one wounded.

This action, lacking in grandeur as it was, provoked public opinion to an unanimous reaction: the French press in the free zone, though far from favourable to Germany, did not conceal its anger and scorn. Some newspapers even went so far as to write in carefully measured terms that "Mers-el-Kebir has restored to France her liberty of action."

Mers-el-Kebir was, moreover, not an isolated attack, but formed part of a number of measures taken by the British against the French Fleet: on the very day of the attack, the British seized without warning the French warships in Portsmouth, Plymouth and Southampton, interning their officers and crews in far from honourable conditions. The same treatment was meted out to the French merchant ships calling in British ports. The French Fleet in Alexandria was blocked in that port: a personal agreement between Admiral Cunningham and Admiral Godfroy alone enabled him to evade the fate suffered at Mers-el-Kebir. Finally, on the 8th July, the battle-cruiser *Richelieu* was bombarded at Dakar, where she had taken refuge, by British ships and aircraft.

These hostile acts gave rise to political consequences which might have been irreparable.

On the 3rd July, the French Chargé d'Affaires in London, M. Roger Cambon, received orders to protest to the British Government: "It is with stupefaction that we have learned of this act of aggression which would be unjustified in any circumstances, but which is the more so since North Africa will not be subject to occupation. I pray you to protest immediately and formally to the British Government, and to await further instructions which I shall send you tomorrow."

The next day, 4th July, at 10 a.m., there was a Council of Ministers which might have been fatal to Anglo-French relations. It had been preceded at 6.30, by a limited meeting between the Marshal, Laval, Darlan and Baudouin. The Admiral informed the Head of the Government and the two Ministers of the instructions he had issued on his own initiative the day before to what remained of the French Forces in the Mediterranean. A squadron of cruisers, based on Algiers, had passed south of the Balearics during the night; the *Strasbourg*, which had escaped from Mers-el-Kebir, had been ordered to join it, in order to make a surprise attack on the British Fleet which was returning to Gibraltar. Darlan was envisaging hostilities against Great Britain, so furious was he at the attack: "I have been betrayed by my brothers-in-arms. They have not believed in the promise I gave them."

Baudouin reacted immediately: "But," he cried, "that means war with England!" Laval replied: "We have decided to reply to yesterday's attack by making an attack ourselves." Baudouin turned to the Marshal and adjured him to suspend all military measures that might lead to irreparable consequences. Since the President of the Council agreed with the opinion of the Minister for Foreign Affairs, the latter suggested, as a lesser evil, "making official the breaking off of diplomatic relations which has existed in fact between England and ourselves since the departure of Sir Ronald Campbell and the whole staff of the British Embassy."

The Council of Ministers, which was held between 10 and 1 o'clock at the Pavillon Sévigné, supported the position taken up by Baudouin and the Marshal, which did not prevent Laval, in the afternoon, saying to the Brazilian Ambassador: "We are not declaring war, but we shall reply with a hostile act to the hostile acts committed by England." An inflammatory statement which immediately went the rounds of the Diplomatic Corps.

To nip the danger in the bud, Baudouin summoned the representatives of the French and foreign press at 9.30 p.m. He read them a statement which, while announcing the "stupefaction and indignation" of the Government in face of the British attitude, nevertheless concluded with great moderation and refuted Pierre Laval's intentions:

"To this ill-judged act of hostility, the Government has replied with no act of hostility on its side. It remains calm, watching the development of a situation which it has done nothing to bring about, anxious merely to defend, by every means that remains in its power and by such political action as it may deem necessary, the honour and interests of France."

If the Council of Ministers on the 4th July avoided the major danger of an immediate opening of hostilities against the British Fleet, other decisions had been taken which created certain risks for the future. Darlan had, indeed, persuaded the Council to adopt in principle several naval and military measures: the stopping and searching of British merchant ships by French warships, the escorting of French merchant ships by warships with orders to open fire immediately in case of a British menace, and the bombing of Gibraltar by aircraft. Darlan went so far as to propose a military expedition against one of the British African colonies and a Franco-Italian naval operation to break the blockade holding the French warships in Alexandria.

The Ministry for Foreign Affairs called in their lawyers to demonstrate that such measures would immediately create a state of war. They succeeded in limiting reprisals to a symbolic bombing of Gibraltar: on the 5th and 6th July, two raids, each of three aeroplanes, dropped bombs in the sea.

Another consequence of Mers-el-Kebir was that, owing to the resistance the French had put up against the British, the Germans allowed them certain facilities for re-arming.

Mers-el-Kebir made it easier for Pierre Laval to put an end to the Republic, which was now reproached with having founded its whole foreign policy on an alliance with a nation which had attacked defenceless French ships.

Mers-el-Kebir was not the only question raised in the Council of Ministers on the 4th July: the drama constituted the background against which a plan of the first importance, prepared several days before, was now revealed.

To his colleagues who, for the most part, were quite unprepared for anything of the kind and were taken aback with surprise, Pierre Laval, Vice-President of the Council, read the draft of a parliamentary bill he had prepared in collaboration with Alibert. It was to be presented to the National Assembly on the 10th July, and its provisions did no less than abolish the Republican Constitution of 1875.

"The National Assembly confers all powers upon the Government of the Republic under the signature and authority of Marshal Pétain, President of the Council, to promulgate by one or more acts the new Constitution of the French State.

"This Constitution will guarantee the rights of Labour, Family and Country. It will be ratified by the Assemblies it will create."

Having come to the end of this brief announcement, Laval, without giving the Ministers, or even President Lebrun, time to make any remark immediately left the Council: "Forgive my not giving you the opportunity of opening discussions on this subject: sixty Senators await me, to whom I must explain matters."

When, a few minutes later, Laval began his speech in the Hall of the Medical Societies, where the Senate was provisionally meeting, it was to acquit himself of his duties in curiously cavalier fashion. Instead of giving explanations to the sixty Senators present for their being summoned to Vichy, he proceeded to assault them with a couple of hammer-blows.

"The Government," Laval began, "has decided not to declare war on England." There was stupefaction among his audience to whom the eventuality of a conflict between the two countries had never occurred. Laval took advantage of it to make a second point.

"Parliament," he announced with similar matter-of-factness, as if this too were a perfectly obvious matter, "must be dissolved. The Constitution must be reformed. It must fall into line with the totalitarian states. The formation of labour camps must be envisaged. If Parliament does not consent to them, Germany will impose these measures upon us with, as an immediate consequence, the occupation of the whole of France."

The threat fell like a bomb upon the stunned Assembly; no one said a word.

It was with this two-fold act of audacity, that Pierre Laval inaugurated, on the 4th July, the great adventure of his political career; he had six days, from the 4th to 10th July, to convince the seven hundred members of the two Assemblies that they must vote the deposition of the Republic and their own abdication: he went about it, in the first place, by holding semi-official information meetings which, between the 4th and 8th July, members of Parliament, as they arrived in Vichy, attended. Later, he held official meetings on the 9th and 10th July.

During these six days Laval multiplied his attacks, and the documents published by the Commission of Enquiry now allow of their detailed reconstruction.

Laval felt at home with the tragedy which he boasted he was one of the only people to have foreseen, and which he alone, so he said, could have prevented if he had been listened to. His forcefulness was impressive, his belief in his own infallibility almost contagious: had not the drama of Mers-el-Kebir only yesterday proved him right in the Anglophobia which he had manifested for such a long time past?

Moreover—and it was a tactical advantage this brilliant practitioner of oratory and conspiracy did not fail to exploit—he spoke in the name of the Marshal, in the name of the only personality whom every member of Parliament, however loyal to the Republic he might be, considered indispensable to the salvation of the country.

In opposition to him, the senators and deputies had no one upon whom they could lean: "They are overwhelmed and wander through the corridors of the Casino or the hall of the Medical Societies like souls in torment." They had no party policy, no leaders to guide them. The Socialists sought despairingly for Léon Blum. But he was not to be found: even the Director of the Sûreté Générale, M. Didkowski, who wished to leave a card at his hotel, could not discover where he was staying. Paul Reynaud, a leader by right, who had been detained by a motor-car accident in which Madame de Portes was killed, only put in an appearance on the day of the National Assembly. Herriot had not yet taken possession again of his presidential chair. Daladier, Campinchi, Delbos and Jean-Zay were on board the *Massillia*.

On the other hand, Laval was in control of a reduced, though active, minority of coming men, all those who, since Bordeaux, and some even long before that, had diagnosed the shipwreck of the regime and had prepared for its successor. Among them were representatives of every party: a Radical, Jean Montigny, the future historiographer of the National Assembly, appointed by Pierre Laval; a man of the extreme Right, Xavier Vallat, who had been seriously wounded in the 1914–1918 war; a man of the Left, a founder with Adrien Marquet of Neo-Socialism, Marcel Déat, who owed his notoriety to an article published in *Oeuvre*, in which he refused to go to war over Poland and "die for Danzig": his political friends went with him, Château, Garnier, Deschizeaux, Lafarge and Chasseigne; an Independent, Gaston Bergery, who, for the first time in his life, the centre of a Parliamentary group which included Piétri, Georges Bonnet, Portmann, Cayrel, Dommange and Temple, was preparing a doctrinal manifesto which he had been contemplating for several years.

For Laval and his supporters the game was far from being won on that first day. The reception given his explosive speech on the 4th July was not of very good augury; the silence which followed on it did not imply acquiescence, but was rather a manifestation of the Senators' stupefaction at such an unexpected offensive.

On Friday, 5th July, Pierre Laval's position was no stronger. Opposition was being organised in the Senate.

In the early hours of the morning, Jean Taurines, Senator for the Rhône, and hero of the 1914–1918 war, summoned the ex-Servicemen among the senators. There were twenty-five of them who, scandalised by the violence shown by Laval the day before, decided to defeat him. It was a question of winning over the majority of members of Parliament to a proposal which, while granting the Marshal the full powers that were necessary, would yet not abolish the Republican regime.

The ex-Servicemen voted unanimously the following motion: "The ex-Servicemen among the Senators meeting at Vichy on Friday, 5th July, under the chairmanship of M. Jean Taurines, first Vice-President, salute with pride and emotion their venerated leader, Marshal Pétain, who, in these tragic times, has made the gift of his person to his country.

"They place their trust in him to re-organise the national strength, galvanise the energies of the people and prepare the moral ground upon which a France worthy of their sacrifices may be re-built under the legal constitution of the Republic."

It was a motion which was to be presented to the President of the Council with an explanation of why Laval's proposals were unacceptable. If the Marshal accepted the motion passed by his comrades of the Great War, Laval and Alibert would clearly be forced to abandon their policy.

For these members of Parliament, whom all Vichy knew by hearsay to be hostile to Laval, the first difficulty consisted in seeing the Marshal. Taurines telephoned the Hôtel du Parc at 3 p.m., to ask for an audience with Pétain. On the other end of the line, the Under-Secretary of State to the President of the Council, Alibert, promised to let him know during the course of the evening the time of the audience. When, having heard nothing, Taurines telephoned him again at 9 o'clock, Alibert had, of course, "gone out", leaving no message.

While behind the scenes, Alibert was doing his best to block the Senator ex-Servicemen, his ally, Laval, was confronting new obstacles: he was now going to "explain himself" to the deputies.

The atmosphere in the Casino was less confused than it had been the day before in the Hall of the Medical Societies. The eighty deputies, who took part in the session, had been warned by their colleagues in the Senate. Laval, therefore, would not have the advantage of surprise.

Laval, sitting on the front bench, wearing his eternal white tie, listened to a succession of speakers who were also, to all intents and purposes, adversaries.

Marcel Héraud, Independent Deputy for Paris, opened fire: "If the Republic has lost one war, has it not also won another? Our misfortunes should therefore be attributed more to men than to the Republican regime."

Then Georges Monnet, an S.F.I.O. deputy, a personal friend of Léon Blum, asked Laval a most embarrassing question from the third bench: "You ask us to close our ranks behind Marshal Pétain. We are prepared to do so. But there is one point about which we are concerned and to which we require an answer. What would happen if Marshal Pétain, having been invested with power, should suffer an accident?"

After this brief intervention, an unidentified voice was heard to enquire: "Have we got a quorum?" In other words, was the number of Deputies and Senators present at the National Assembly sufficient to make a vote legal? Finally, Chasseigne, an old Socialist Deputy, who had been wounded in the last war and now leaned upon a stick, uttered his complete support of Laval in a hollow voice. All parties must be liquidated. Parliament had but one duty: to place itself in Marshal Pétain's hands.

Laval was no longer going to play the part of a Republican in order to answer the speakers; those times were over. Disdaining to go to the rostrum, merely rising in his place and taking a few steps forward into the hall, he abandoned his insinuating "Auvergnat" (as some said) tones, which he but lately used to carry conviction. He launched himself brutally into the offensive and gave his innate violence free rein. Marcel Héraud was the first to feel its weight: "You have made a speech, a fine speech . . . Do you imagine that we have still time to listen to speeches? You are wrong: speeches are done with. We are not here for you to make speeches nor are we here to listen to them. We have to rebuild France."

And rebuild it according to his own ideas: "We must destroy all that is. Then, the destruction accomplished, we must create something that will be entirely different from what has been, from what is. There are only two alternatives: either you accept what we demand, and align yourselves with the German and Italian constitutions, or Hitler will impose it on you." And praising Chasseigne for having announced the end of all political parties he went on: "From now on . . . there will be but one party, the party of all Frenchmen, a national party which will provide the framework for national activity."

Laval was even more aggressive and violent in the presence of the deputies than he had been the day before in the presence of the members of the Senate. He was also more explicit and, in order to justify his extremism, he re-edited the history of the last years in his own fashion.

England was the prime cause of all the trouble: he blamed England for having forced him out of office: "I had, by sustained efforts, committed France to the only policy in which she could find safety. I had succeeded in developing close relations with Mussolini. Moreover, I had persuaded Austria to accept an *entente* with the successor states. The Chancellor of Austria was coming to Paris. . . . I had also achieved an understanding between Yugoslavia and Italy. The Yugoslav Minister for Foreign Affairs was to come to Paris to arrange matters. But the day before he was to leave Belgrade, the British Ambassador in that city, Mr. Neville Henderson, made a *démarche* to the Yugoslav Government and all my efforts were ruined."

The drama of Mers-el-Kebir gave Laval the opportunity of concluding in these terms his diatribe against England:

"France has never had and never will have a more bitter enemy than Great Britain. All our history proves it. We have been but a plaything in British hands and have been used to assure her own protection. Today, we are at the bottom of the abyss to which Britain has led us. France has the right to maintain for herself and her Empire an army of only one hundred thousand men. That is the tragic reality of our country's circumstances."

Having dealt with France's old ally, he now turned the violence of his invective against the Republic:

"We have been living through years in which it seemed of no importance to say of a man that he was a thief, a swindler, a pimp, or even a murderer. But, if one said of him: 'He is a Fascist,' then one had said the worst of him that was possible! Today, we are paying for the fetishism which has chained us to democracy and delivered us up to the worst excesses of capitalism, while all about us Europe was creating a new world without us, a world founded on new principles."

The effect of this diatribe on the deputies was similar to the effect created on the senators the day before: the silence about Laval was sombre and hostile. The speaker then changed his tone: it was as if he had suddenly realised that he was not alone. His impassioned monologue became a plea for the defence. Addressing himself to Georges Monnet, his tone became courteous, flattering even:

"Monsieur Monnet, you have asked a question which it was necessary to ask and that I am surprised to have not heard asked before. You are right. One must foresee the circumstances in which accidents might deprive us of Marshal Pétain. We have considered them: and this is what is proposed: what we demand is that, through the National Assembly, Marshal Pétain be invested with complete constitutional power. From the day on which these powers are conferred on him, the Marshal will proceed, not by laws or decrees, but by 'Acts'. By the terms of the first act, he will confer upon himself all the rights at present exercised by the President of the Republic, Parliament, the President of the Council and the Ministers. Then, by a second act, he will nominate the person who, in the event of his being prevented from exercising power, will exercise it in his place."

When the session had come to an end on this more pacific note, Laval endeavoured by private conversations in the lobbies to seduce and convince those whom he might have offended.

Even Héraud, whom he had vehemently attacked in public, was now a recipient of his confidences.

"Hitler and Mussolini," he was good enough to explain to him, "exist: we must take up a position between them; you know that I get on very well with Mussolini. By playing one off against the other, I may be able to achieve something, but in order to do that, I must be in power. Your criticisms have no basis in fact. Leave it to me, I am working in the interests of France."

On the following day, 6th July, during the information meetings attended by deputies and senators, Laval made further points.

In the Senate, he obtained the support of one of the members of the Assembly whose prestige was great among his colleagues. Léon Blum, a member of the Academy, a man of letters, and a great advocate, succeeded in a paradoxical speech in rendering homage to the Republic, while sounding its death knell.

In the Chamber of Deputies, Laval acquired the adherence of two members—a much more spectacular reinforcement than the limited support of Bérard—which made a sensation in Parliamentary circles. Two deputies, one of the Left, a Socialist, the friend of Léon Blum, Spinasse, the other of the extreme Right, Xavier Vallat, were at one in publicly expressing their desire for a new political order:

"Parliament," said Spinasse, "must take the blame upon its shoulders for the faults of all. This crucifixion is necessary in order that the country shall not lapse into violence and anarchy. Our duty is to give the Government an opportunity of carrying out a bloodless revolution. If the authority of Marshal Pétain makes this task possible, then the gift he has made of himself to us will not have been in vain. Our decision must be without appeal: it must pledge France decisively. We must make the break without any thought of returning to the past. The past was filled with illusion and, if the horizons of the world seemed to conform to them, it was but a mirage. We have believed in individual liberty and in the independence of man. These were but anticipations of a future which was not within our reach. We must have a new faith built upon new values. . . ."

To this speech, which gripped the assembly, Xavier Vallat responded in these terms: "I rejoice at the fact that all the parties will soon be united in one national group in which the disagreements that we persisted in fomenting among ourselves will be effaced.

"Men have been corrupted by institutions: the institutions must be changed. But men have also corrupted the institutions: men must also be changed that France may revive."

These various declarations which foreshadowed, according to

some, a single party and, according to others, a national coalition, were all equally playing Laval's game.

But, at the actual moment when these unexpected acolytes were grouping themselves about Laval in the Hall of the Casino, outside Parliament the audience which Alibert had vainly tried to prevent was taking place. Thanks to Captain Bonhomme, the Marshal's orderly officer and a personal friend of one of the group of ex-Servicemen, the latter succeeded at last in piercing the defences that had been erected about Pétain.

At 6.15 p.m., the Head of the Government received a delegation consisting of Taurines, Paul-Boncour, Jacquy and Chaumié. It had taken twenty-six hours for a group of members of Parliament, who were ex-Servicemen, and whose only fault was that they were hostile to Laval's policy, to obtain an audience with their old chief of Verdun days.

Confronted with the delegation, the only one he received during this period, the Marshal appears to have been at once very natural and extremely clever. He allowed his authority to appear, not in order to dominate the delegation, but rather to show its members that it was at their service and at the service of the country.

The political role circumstances had forced upon him did not, he implied, conform to his true ambitions. Once peace was concluded, the Marshal would go into retirement and live at Antibes. In the meantime, he wished to be spared the incessant difficulties that arose because of Lebrun's existence, the opposition and untimely intrigues in which the Assemblies were so constantly involved.

He had no intention of playing the despot. When one of his visitors declared himself ready to confer upon him a similar dictatorship to that which ancient Rome had several times conferred in her hours of extreme peril, the Marshal replied good-humouredly that he was no Caesar and had no wish to be one.

The Senators might be reassured: Pétain had no thought of eliminating Parliament; he intended "to act openly": and when the powers had been conferred on him, "he would submit the new constitutional proposals successively, as they were drawn up, to Parliamentary committees."

At these words, the delegation manifested considerable relief. And Paul-Boncour suggested the "suspension of the constitution until the signing of peace, Marshal Pétain, head of the executive power, to have full powers to take by decree such measures as he might deem necessary and, at the same time, establish in collaboration with the Assemblies the basis for a new constitution."

Pétain agreed: "That is an important proposal; send me a memorandum." On this the audience came to an end. The ex-Servicemen went off considerably relieved. As for Pétain, he had nothing more to fear: if Laval won, his power would be absolute, if the senators won, he would be able to govern without being harassed by Parliament.

Whatever happened, he was playing a winning game.

Sunday, 7th July, marked the turning point in Laval's offensive. On that day, his chances seemed imperilled: two facts seemed to foreshadow his losing the game.

On the one hand, the menace of the ex-Servicemen seemed to become actual: neither trickery nor violence would succeed in quieting them.

On the other hand, an ex-President of the Council, Pierre-Etienne Flandin, who enjoyed an authority comparable to that of Laval, took up his position against constitutional reform and rallied to his views the majority of deputies. The opposition against Laval had at last found a leader.

These two events happened almost simultaneously during the course of the afternoon.

At 3 p.m., the group of ex-Servicemen Senators unanimously adopted with the exception of two votes (one hostile and one abstention) the counter-proposal, put forward by Paul-Boncour, which conformed to the conversations held with the Marshal.

"The National Assembly has decided as follows:

"1. The application of the constitutional laws of the 24th–25th February and 16th July, 1875, are suspended until the conclusion of peace;

"2. Monsieur le Maréchal Pétain has all powers to take, by decrees having the force of law, such measures as are necessary for the keeping of order, the maintenance of life, the re-establishment of the country and the liberation of the territory;

"3. The National Assembly confides to Monsieur le Maréchal Pétain the mission of preparing, in collaboration with its competent committees, the new constitution which will be submitted to the nation as soon as circumstances permit a free vote."

Laval, warned of the danger, made an effort to parry it. At a meeting of the Senate he made another speech, intended to cajole his opponents.

On the 4th July he had announced the suppression of Parliament; today, he allowed it to be understood that Parliament might perhaps preserve some of its prerogatives. Certain members of Parliament would be appointed legislators in the new regime; others might even hold executive positions. It might even be that the Senate—to whom he was speaking—would be, in the absence of the other Chamber, kept in being.

Finally, taking every precaution not to give umbrage, he allowed it to be understood that the members of the Assemblies would preserve the material advantages attached to their mandate, even if they no longer exercised it.

These kind words and generous intentions were without effect on his colleagues. Paul-Boncour replied to Pierre Laval with energy: "This is beside the point. What we have to determine is whether we are prepared to resign into the hands of one man, whoever he may be, the constitutional power which belongs to the nation alone."

A few hours after this rebuke was addressed to Laval, two of the ex-Service Senators, Taurines and Jacquy, obtained another interview with the Marshal, once more through the goodwill of Captain Bonhomme. They brought him the text of the counter-proposal.

Pétain, having declared that, as drawn up, it was in conformity with the conversations of the day before, said: "I accept your counter-proposal, but now it is necessary to convince M. Laval, who, as you know, is the Government's advocate on this question."

At 8.30, Taurines and Jacquy were on the storey below, where were Laval's offices. The Vice-President of the Council once more changed his tone. He refused categorically to accept the proposals and tried to shake his adversaries by threats.

"If your counter-proposal is carried, I shall resign and you will then have General Weygand as dictator."

"Monsieur le Président," replied Taurines, "during your so-called semi-official meetings in the Senate, held to achieve the reform of the constitution of 1875, you have already produced the spectre of the Germans. Tonight, you produce that of General Weygand. Whom will you find tomorrow?

"I warn you that the ex-Servicemen will put forward and discuss the proposals they have drawn up and they have a right to intervene in a debate which concerns the destiny of France whom they saved in the 1914–1918 war."

This, on the 7th July, was Laval's first setback: the senators refused to yield. There was a second setback in preparation for that very afternoon at the meeting of the deputies. Pierre-Etienne Flandin, who had arrived at Vichy the day before from his department of Yonne, rose to oppose Laval.

Flandin, ex-President of the Council, and several times a Minister under the Third Republic, had the peculiarity of being profoundly attached to Republican institutions, both from family tradition and from a taste for Liberalism, without, however, being *a priori* animated by any particular hostility towards dictatorships: with a somewhat spectacular gesture, which was received with mixed feelings, he had, in 1938, after Munich, simultaneously sent telegrams of congratulation to both Chamberlain and Hitler.

When, at about 4 p.m., he went to the rostrum, the deputies, who crowded in to listen to him, were still wondering whether he was also going to support an alignment with Nazism. But from the very first words of a most moving speech, he put an end to speculation: "I have come from Yonne, and have spent these last weeks in contact with the German authorities. I believe us to be running a mortal danger. If the Government does not immediately take action, we shall witness the complete nazification of our people. They lack everything . . . the French authorities have fled.

"There is no longer a single representative of the French Government, while the German military authorities are making every effort to assure the distribution of food and organise relief. . . . This German propaganda is effective. People who are hungry tend to follow those who give them food."

Then Pierre-Etienne Flandin, supported by the almost unanimous applause of the deputies, continued with an attack upon the Government, expressing openly what most of those present thought but had not the courage to say.

"When there is so much to do, what is the Government doing? Nothing at all! It has summoned us here, but for what purpose? Is it to ask our help in whatever action it proposes to take for the administration of occupied France, for the despatch and distribution of food, for relief, for the organisation of the country? . . . Not at all! Merely for the purpose of modifying or changing the constitution.

"This seems incredible to those who, like myself, know the urgency of the work to be performed, because, like me, they see, hear and ascertain the facts.

"Change the constitution? . . . What for? What need is there to change institutions which we may be blamed above all for not having respected?"

Surprised by so much assurance, and by hearing a language to which they had become unaccustomed, those present, having at last found an opposition leader, burst into applause. Breathless applause, which was transformed into surprise, when the speaker formulated with precision a policy which was opposed to the proposals of Pierre Laval: "In fine, what does the Government want and what do we want? That Marshal Pétain should be placed at our head in order to negotiate with the Germans and lend his name and his prestige to the re-organisation of France.

"But what necessity is there to change the constitution? Here we are assembled, senators and deputies. The President of the Republic is also in Vichy. The National Assembly is convoked.

"What could be simpler, in the circumstances, than to ask the President of the Republic to resign and to nominate Marshal Pétain in his place. Thus we should achieve the desired result while respecting the constitution."

Theoretically, Flandin's plan had great advantages.

It left the constitution of 1875 in being.

It limited the operation to replacing Lebrun by the Marshal and to voting full powers to the Marshal until the conclusion of a treaty of peace.[1]

It maintained the Assemblies which would have an important part to play in case of a vacancy in the executive (the Marshal's death for instance).

But, though impeccable in principle, the proposal nevertheless had the serious drawback of being impossible of realisation without the consent of three people as difficult to bring into accord as the Marshal, Albert Lebrun and Laval. To win over these three Presidents to the views of a fourth, was to square a

[1] The constitutional laws of 1875 do not forbid a President of the Republic to be at the same time President of the Council.

circle, whose centre Flandin was to seek successively among the diverse Government cliques in Vichy.

To begin with, he approached Laval. The latter was mellifluous: there was nothing that he would like better than to please Flandin by adopting his proposal. But it was the Marshal's decision: Pétain held to the original proposal. No one could persuade him out of it.

Flandin, as he walked up the steps to the Marshal's office, was expecting a refusal. But he was in for a surprise: Pétain agreed with him, as a few hours earlier he had agreed with the ex-Servicemen. But he once again did not forget to specify that it was Laval who was conducting the negotiations. Who was to be believed? Flandin, preparing to leave, asked the Marshal for his authorisation to inform Pierre Laval of his agreement. Not only did Pétain acquiesce, but he sent a message to the Vice-President of the Council asking him to grant Flandin another interview.

Here was Flandin hurrying downstairs again, now full of hope. But once again he was to be disappointed and astonished: "The Marshal has given you his assent," said Laval, "but he gives it to everyone; and you would be making a mistake to rely on it, because he immediately forgets all about it. But I will support your proposal if you bring me Lebrun's resignation."

This was to ensnare Flandin in his own plan.

At 6.30 p.m., the few loiterers outside the Pavillon Sévigné saw the ex-Radical Minister, Mistler, busily engaged in putting on a pair of wash-leather gloves. He was, with Candace, one of the two members of Parliament who were to accompany Flandin to the President of the Republic. Accoutred in accordance with etiquette, he passed through the door and joined the two other deputies within.

Albert Lebrun, as always, received them courteously, but did not appear particularly delighted with the proposal they made him. "I really do not see," he said to Flandin, "why I should resign. The situation is perfectly clear: the Chambers have taken cognisance of a Governmental proposal. They do not approve it. They throw it out. I appoint a new Government: it's perfectly simple." Did Lebrun really believe that he was still capable of appointing another Government?

He did not, however, formally refuse to resign. Before taking a definite decision, he intended to consult the Presidents of the Senate and of the Chamber of Deputies.

Thus, by the end of this day which might have been fatal to Laval, the number of Presidents who had to be persuaded to adopt Flandin's proposals had increased from three to five. Flandin included, the squaring of the circle had become hexagonal.

On the 8th July, Laval resumed the offensive along the whole front, neutralising his opponents, galvanising his supporters, and successively bringing into play every trick he had up his sleeve.

Against the ex-Service Senators it was guile, for he made use of a lie to "do them down", to use Vincent Auriol's expression. At the Council of Ministers, which was held in the morning, Rivière, a Socialist Minister, supported Taurines' proposal and demanded that it should be presented to the National Assembly as a Government proposal. Laval authoritatively interrupted: "I have just," he said, "been holding a conversation with the Senatorial group of ex-Servicemen. I have calmed them all down. They have withdrawn their counter-proposal. Rivière's suggestion is therefore no longer relevant." Taken at a disadvantage Rivière insisted no further. Two days later he learned from Auriol that this was a lie.

Laval did not even find it necessary to adopt so cynical an attitude to Flandin. Having involved him in the labyrinth of a Presidential consultation, he merely had to leave him to exhaust and lose himself. Flandin, abiding by the rules of the classical parliamentary game, at a moment when Parliament was of no account, awaited Lebrun's answer all day. The latter, equally correct, consulted Jeanneney and Herriot, who do not appear to have encouraged him to relinquish his post. At the Council of Ministers, he docilely appended his signature to Pierre Laval's proposal which thereby became the Government's proposal. And when, during the course of the day, he received Flandin once again, it was only to explain his attitude in somewhat surprising terms: "I really have no guarantee that Republican Institutions under your proposal would be safeguarded." Did he really believe that Pierre Laval would preserve them any better?

With his two principal opponents eliminated or rendered impotent, Laval could speak in the Assemblies to his heart's content, for it was necessary at once to calm their apprehensions and to assure their votes.

He went successively to the Chamber and the Senate.

At the beginning of these sessions, he read to the members of Parliament for the first time the draft of the bill which would be submitted to the vote of the National Assembly, and explained the reasons which had led up to it. The bill was drawn up thus, we have seen it:

"The National Assembly confers all powers on the Government of the Republic, under the signature and authority of Marshal Pétain, President of the Council, to the effect that he may promulgate by one or more acts the new constitution of the French State. This constitution must guarantee the rights of Labour, the Family and the Country.

"It will be ratified by the Assemblies which it creates."

The explanation of the reasons for the bill gave no guarantee concerning the use which would be made of the powers conferred by its text. Would the new regime still be republican? Or would it be totalitarian? Nothing in its wording enabled members of Parliament to decide. It said merely that it would "open the doors of the future" (what future did it mean?), that it would allow "a national representation" to subsist (but in what form? and how would it be recruited?), that it would reconcile authority with a respect for the essential liberties (without detailing which those liberties were). Moreover, it would increase the birth-rate and protect the family, which can be done equally well in a democracy as under an authoritarian regime. It would reduce the state to the role of a controller and arbitrator: the only phrase which seemed out of keeping with totalitarian ideals. On the other hand, it would restore France to her vocation of agriculture, while integrating her with the continental system of production and exchange, and would create a professional organisation in a corporative form to associate employers and employees with the economic life of the country, which was indicative of an alignment with Fascist economy.

In order to understand what this explanation of the motives for the bill really signified, the members of Parliament needed to be six months older and know the consequences which the National Revolution would deduce from such principles.

Was Pierre Laval aware of these uncertainties? Sitting on the stage, leaning forward towards the auditorium, he invited the members to a friendly discussion. But, in truth, the latter had nothing very new to say during the hour it lasted.

Laval reiterated the justification of the armistice, his attacks against England, and the reasons for an alignment with Germany and Italy which, alone, could save France.

On only two points did he say anything new, while dealing tactfully at once with the dictatorial goat and the parliamentary lamb, or rather confusing the issue between the two to such an extent that it became incomprehensible.

"Parliamentary democracy has lost the War. It must disappear and give place to a hierarchical authoritarian regime, national and social." But that regime would not be a dictatorship: a surprising statement which the speaker did not comment upon very luminously: "It is not a question of dictatorship but, on the contrary, a question of preserving the predominance of the civil power. If the Assemblies do not understand their duty, let them beware of a military *coup d'état*. I warn you, we are being watched!"

To whichever regime people may have thought they were tending, after these contradictory statements Laval led the country: one thing only appeared certain, that he would hold the first place in it and that the civil power was himself.

This speech, in which nothing was lacking except the information the Assembly desired, was received with an hysterical ovation from Laval's supporters. The others—the majority—tried vainly to reply. There was a furious clamour against them which made all intervention physically impossible.

The opposition appeared to be checkmated.

On the evening of this last day of informative sessions before the public meetings, the last Council of Ministers of the Third Republic was held. Let us leave it to Albert Lebrun, who presided, to evoke its oppressive atmosphere.

". . . We must all feel how useless a discussion would be, because we know from the events of the last few days that the dice are cast. For myself, I feel, in presiding over this Council, which will be the last, a profound sadness."

There was however one member in opposition, the Garde des Sceaux, Frémicourt, who refused to append his signature to the draft constitutional law permitting Pierre Laval to abolish the Republic.

On the following day the official meetings began. On the 9th July, there were separate meetings of the two Assemblies (in the morning the Chamber of Deputies, in the afternoon the Senate). They both were to vote on the Bill which declared that the constitutional laws must be revised. On the 10th July there were two plenary meetings of the National Assembly, one private in the morning, the other public in the afternoon; they were to decide on the proposals for reform put forward by Pierre Laval in the name of the Government.

In the theatre of the Grand Casino, for this unique performance of an important play, notices recalled the names of the halls, alas distant and occupied by the enemy, of the two Paris palaces.

The members, on entering, were surprised to discover that their seats were arranged in accordance with their length of membership, rather than by party or political affiliation: they therefore were deprived of the neighbourhood and support of their accustomed factions.

Moreover, most of them were considerably confused. All the senators and deputies, with practically only two exceptions—Pierre Laval and Gaston Bergery—had voted, nine months before, for subsidies for the war, thus bearing part of the responsibility for the beginning of the disaster. Besides, most of them had never ceased calling themselves Republicans, opposing the dictatorships and affirming that France was fighting for liberty. Attitudes of yesterday which, opposed to the realities of today after the German victory and the shattering of the regime, tended to give some of them a bad conscience.

From this arose that psychosis of fear which hung over the Assembly; it seized on every excuse, was nourished by every rumour, and promoted every surrender.

Léon Blum described it in masterly fashion: "For two days I watched men debasing themselves, becoming corrupt beneath one's eyes, as if they had been plunged into a bath of poison. They were possessed by fear: the fear of Doriot's gangs in the streets, the fear of Weygand's soldiers at Clermont-Ferrand, the fear of the Germans who were at Moulins. . . . It was a human swamp in which one saw, I repeat, beneath one's very eyes, the courage and integrity one had known in certain men dissolve, corrode and disappear."

In this atmosphere, the great Republican leaders, with Flandin as almost the only exception, seemed either to have been annihilated or to be playing what they knew to be a losing game.

Two of them, Edouard Herriot and Paul Reynaud, still tried to fight, but only over points of detail which could have no influence on the outcome. Others, Léon Blum, Jeanneney, remained silent or deliberately avoided taking up any definite position.

Herriot contented himself with defending the members of of Parliament who had sailed in the *Massillia*. His intervention in the session of the 10th July showed clearly that he no longer believed in the survival of the regime: "I am," he said, "or I was, President of the Chamber of Deputies, and until the end, whatever that may be, I will fulfil my duty, preferring integrity of speech to masterly silence." But Herriot limited his duty to asserting that the "traitors of the *Massillia*" "had been furnished with proper embarkation permits and that the *Massillia* had been chartered and placed at their disposal by the Government."

This was also true of Paul Reynaud whose very presence at Vichy at this period was in itself an act of courage. But he did not attend the Assembly.

Léon Blum, personally attacked during the morning of 10th July by Laval who, from the rostrum, reproached him with having, in 1936, subordinated his foreign policy to party interest, remained silent. Doubtless any intervention on his part would have aroused the clamour of Pierre Laval's supporters and he would not, in any event, have been allowed to make himself heard.

Jeanneney, in these circumstances, played a somewhat equivocal part. As President of the National Assembly, he had promised, on the 9th July, to call on Vincent Badie, a Radical Deputy, to speak on the following day in support of a motion, known as the Motion of the Twenty-Seven,[1] which was in opposition to Laval's proposals. When the moment came, Jeanneney, as we shall see, allowed himself to be circumvented by Bouisson, one of Laval's supporters.

This default clearly played into Laval's hands.

The few dozen members of Parliament who, at Bordeaux, had already abandoned the sinking ship of the regime and had wanted an armistice, now became more and more sure of themselves, more and more imperious, as the others weakened from hour to hour; among them were the following who, drawn from various parties, had, as we have seen, played their part in the preparatory sessions: Déat and Marquet, Montigny, Spinasse, Scapini and Xavier Vallat, Mistler, Tixier-Vignancour and

[1] Cf., *infra*, p. 105 for the text of this motion.

Ybarnegaray. A heterogeneous team, but a young and enthusiastic one, who felt that their hour had come and were to a great extent animated by the "realistic" desire to save all that could still be saved from the disaster.

Conversations in ante-rooms or speeches in public were all grist to the mill.

Léon Blum, who, for many reasons, was one of the first to be aimed at, was laid open to attacks by members of his own party. "Just as well," said certain Socialists who found his influence embarrassing, "we shall have done with Blum." In the corridors and ante-rooms odd incidents revealed the curiously troubled state of affairs. Ybarnegaray, a deputy of the Right, encountering Vincent Auriol, S.F.I.O., endeavoured to protect this political adversary towards whom he felt a personal friendship. When the Socialist Deputy told him that he proposed voting against the motion for constitutional reform: "Good God," cried the former, taking his hands in his, "I beseech you, don't do that . . . you know my friendship for you . . . don't do that!" And Doriot, attacking Marx Dormoy, whom he had never forgiven for dismissing him from the position of Mayor of Saint-Denis, cried: "We'll have your hide, do you hear, Dormoy, and it won't be long now!"

In such an ambience, Laval showed himself at his most forceful: he was indeed the master of the hour. Imperturbable, omnipresent and omniscient, pulling the strings of these disarticulated puppets, of these parties in chaos, presenting the extraordinary spectacle of a man who has identified himself with a situation, who is dominating it, the only conductor of a tumultuous orchestra, he was at the height of his powers, in full possession of his exceptional abilities, at once adamant on the goal he had set himself to achieve, and both subtle and cunning in the means he used to lead others to it. He was to be seen in every group, at every conference. He neglected no means of bringing members of Parliament over to his side.

In the first place, he struck the chord of patriotism: was not the destiny of France at this moment in the balance? And in order to demonstrate the urgency of the decision, he did not shrink from announcing that he had news from a sure source that England was secretly negotiating peace "in order to beat us to the post and conclude it at our expense". He even went so far as to pretend that his intentions were to strengthen the Republic.

To those whom such patriotic considerations were insufficient to convince, Laval laid siege in other ways. To some, he extended the prospects of important posts in the new regime: "You have many admirable qualities, we may well have need of you. We shall have to appoint Regional Prefects. You are most certainly qualified for such a position. Potut and others will be appointed. I ask you, therefore, to consider the matter." This was actually said, in his name, to Vincent Badie by Adrien Marquet.

To others, he used threats. Senator de Moustier, Director of the Charbonnages du Nord, was called to order by Laval: "Take care! If you won't give full powers to Pétain, if you persist in your attitude, all your profits will be taken from you and you'll regret it."

The Republic was still in existence on the 9th July.

Article 8 of the Law of the 25th February, 1875, laid it down that:

"The Chambers shall have the right, by separate resolutions, taken in each by a majority of votes, either spontaneously, or on the demand of the President of the Republic, to declare that there is need for a revision of the laws of the Constitution."

It was by virtue of this clause that the members of the two Assemblies, during separate sessions, held at 9.30 a.m. in the case of the Chamber of Deputies and at 4 p.m. in the case of the Senate, were presented with a motion of which the single clause was as follows:

"The Chamber of Deputies (or the Senate) declares that there is need for a revision of the laws of the Constitution."

This motion was adopted almost unanimously: there were 3 votes cast against it in the Chamber out of 398, and one in the Senate out of 230.[1] Even those who, the following day, were to oppose the Government Bill, voted for the preliminary motions which, according to them, did not imply the disappearance of the Third Republic. Some of them even saw the opportunity, so long awaited, of reforming it.

Moreover, whatever their party loyalties might be, the members of Parliament as a whole were completely at one in their support of Pétain.

At 9.30 a.m., the first meeting, that of the Chamber of Deputies,

[1] These were two S.F.I.O., deputies, Biondi and Léon Roche, and one Radical Socialist, Margaine. The Senator was the Marquis de Chambrun.

began in the Hall of the Grand Casino with the customary ceremonial. There were Gardes Mobiles on the approaches. . . . At the gate, officials of the Assembly inspected the cards. . . . A wide, well-designed flight of steps led up to the door of the building. One entered a great hall, humming with conversation. At the end, on the left, was the cloakroom. Not far from it, and set back a little, was an office in which the voting papers were distributed: each deputy received five white voting papers for "yes" and five blue ones for "no". At the appointed hour, President Herriot entered the hall and crossed it with the usual ceremony. The three hundred and ninety-eight deputies went into the session, there were not enough of them to fill the stalls which had been designed for an audience of seven hundred. The President and the secretaries took their places on the stage with the officials. The public occupied the boxes and the seats in the balcony. To all appearance it was an ordinary opening session of Parliament.

President Herriot made the usual speech in memory of the three deputies who had died on the field of battle since the previous session. Then, announcing the object of the meeting, he rendered homage to the Marshal and proclaimed his support of a revision of the constitution. He made an emotional appeal to the Chamber to vote unanimously in favour of the motion before it.

"About the person of Monsieur le Maréchal Pétain, in the veneration that his name inspires in us all, our nation is gathered in its distress. Let us be careful not to disturb the harmony which has been established under his authority.

"We must reform ourselves, make a Republic we have allowed to become too easy-going more austere, though the principles on which it is founded maintain all their virtue. We must remake France, and the outcome of this labour depends on the example of wisdom we are able to set."

There are two important points to be noted in this speech, which otherwise was pretty banal: complete adherence to Pétain, which was on the following day, 10th July, to be of advantage to Laval, who was officially designated by the Marshal as his mouthpiece. And the assertion that the Republican principles maintained all their virtue. In this conviction, Herriot, in spite of the "loud and prolonged applause from every bench", would only be supported on the following day by a small majority of his auditors.

After Herriot's speech, there was an incident, quickly repressed, which marked the impatience of Laval's supporters.

The President of the Chamber of Deputies announced, in conformity with the rules, that the draft Bill must be referred to the Commission of Universal Suffrage. An hour later, the Commission having sat in accordance with the regulations, Mistler presented his report and expressed the wish, in imitation of Edouard Herriot, that "the immense efforts for the re-construction of the country," which were necessary to assure the future of France, should be made "in accordance with the Republican system and its laws".

In the afternoon, the meeting of the Senate was held in similar conditions.

Jeanneney, who presided in the same hall, paraphrased Edouard Herriot: he also rendered homage to the Marshal, but was more reticent in speaking of Republican principles:

"I assure Monsieur le Maréchal Pétain of our veneration and of the great debt he is owed for this new gift of his person.

"He knows what my feelings towards him are, which now date back over many years. We know the nobility of his spirit. It has brought us days of glory. May it have the effect in these days of terrible trial of guarding us whenever necessary against all discord. . . .

"To work! Let us forge a new spirit for our country, that there may be a resurgence of creative force and faith, that our country may grow strong, and that finally, by the authority of moral values, authority itself may be re-established."

Conventional eloquence which played into Laval's hands. M. Boivin-Champeaux, spokesman for the Legislative Commission of the Senate, playing the same role as Mistler had done in the morning, read a report which was full of respect for the Republic. He began by stating that the procedure followed for reforming the Constitution "is legal and in order: it conforms with precedent, with but this difference that the previous revisions of 1879, 1884, and 1926, were only partial revisions whereas, today, we must envisage a total remoulding of our institutions."

He went on to say that on that day, the 9th July, it was not yet a question "of going to the root of the matter", but merely "of deciding on the principle of revision", about which everyone was agreed. The details would be discussed on the following day.

"It is not without sorrow," declared Boivin-Champeaux, with some courage, "that we shall say goodbye to the Constitution of 1875. It made France a free country, a country in which one could breathe freely, a country in which one felt oneself to be at once strong and happy.

"It is dying less by reason of its own imperfections than by the fault of the men who were charged with assuring its safety and its working.

"One may even wonder if it is is not dying because it was not more strictly applied."

The meetings of the two Assemblies on the 9th July were merely preliminary. It was on the 10th July that decisive action was to be taken in accordance with procedure proposed to the Assemblies by Laval.

In the morning a private meeting of the National Assembly was to be held during which the Government motion was to be discussed. In the afternoon, there was to be a public meeting at which the vote would be taken: Laval hoped without a debate.

On the morning of the 10th July, when the Deputies and Senators entered the hall of the Casino, it had already been carefully inspected by the officials of the Assemblies, in order to make sure that no gate-crasher attended the sitting, which was reserved for members of Parliament alone. A Questeur had examined the boxes to make sure that they were empty: at the entrance to the hall there was a triple row of Gardes Mobiles standing shoulder to shoulder, their bayonets fixed, forbidding entry to all representatives of the Press and public opinion.

Within these closed doors, Laval was to endeavour to persuade the members to vote that afternoon, and without discussion, the delegation of their constitutional powers to the Marshal, by virtue of a Bill which had been printed and distributed to the members.

Four alternative motions were expected on the morning of the 10th July: that of Flandin, who having failed to obtain President Lebrun's agreement, had given up all hope of preserving the Republican regime in accordance with his own views.

That of the ex-Servicemen Senators who, in spite of Laval's opposition, were insisting on putting to the vote their counter-proposal which corresponded indeed to the views of the majority of members. It differed from the Government motion on two points: the new constitution would be prepared with the assistance of the Parliamentary commissions and would be ratified by the nation.

A third motion, equally hostile to Laval's proposal, had been drafted on the 8th July by the Radical Deputy, Vincent Badie, and signed by twenty-seven members (six senators, and twenty-one deputies).

"The undersigned members of Parliament believe that it is essential to grant Marshal Pétain, who in these grave hours represents so perfectly the traditional French virtues, all essential powers for the safety of the state and for the achievement of peace.

"But they refuse to vote for a motion which would ineluctably bring about the disappearance of the Republican regime.

"The undersigned proclaim that they remain more than ever attached to the democratic liberties in whose defence the best sons of our country have given their lives."

The fourth possible motion was that of Bergery. He had drawn up a declaration, signed by twenty-seven members and supported by fifty-one more. It endeavoured to impose a doctrinal form upon Laval's policy, which neither he nor Alibert were prepared to allow anyone to do but themselves. Having stigmatised the impotence of the recent Republican governments, it envisaged an authoritarian anti-Capitalist and National regime to achieve the independence of France and the rehabilitation of the country. In foreign policy, it foreshadowed, in agreement with Laval, the integration of France with the new European order.

On the morning of the 10th July, Pierre Laval wished to clear the ground in order that there should be no debate during the afternoon sitting and an almost unanimous demonstration in his favour. The first essential was to disarm the opposition of the ex-Service Senators, theirs being the only alternative which could have any chance of success, and which Taurines proposed once more at the beginning of the sitting.

Ignoring the two points of difference, indeed asserting that the ideas of the ex-Servicemen coincided with his own, Pierre Laval, full of deference towards his gallant adversaries, declared that, to avoid all misapprehension, he was prepared to modify the Bill.

For the first version which stated that "the constitution will be ratified by the Assemblies it has created," Laval agreed to substitute the formula: "The constitution will be ratified by the nation and applied by the Assemblies it will have created."

A substitution which only corresponded upon one point to the reservations of the ex-Servicemen. There was no guarantee concerning the Republic, nor even any allusion to the means by which the ratification by the country would operate; when pressed on this point, Laval replied that he was in no position to make a statement on the subject at the moment but that the proper authorities would later be consulted on this important matter.

Senator Dormann, who had been wounded in the 1914–1918 war, and was a member of the group of ex-Service Senators, then thanked Laval.

And Laval, feeling that his opponents were weakening, struck the blow which was to decide the outcome of the battle. He addressed the Assembly in a good-humoured, homely tone as follows:

"I shall remain seated," he said, "so that the debate may have a more informal character and provoke fewer interruptions.

"I spoke a little while ago to inform you of the new text of the motion which the Marshal has accepted; and, to avoid all misunderstanding, I now wish to give those observations the Marshal's authority by reading you a letter which he sent me on the 7th July, 1940:

"Monsieur le Président,

"The motion on the constitution, tabled by the Government over which I preside, will come up for debate on Tuesday and Wednesday, 9th and 10th July before the Assemblies. As it is difficult for me to take part in the sittings, I ask you to represent me. The passing of the motion which the Government is submitting to the National Assembly seems to me necessary to assure the safety of our country.

"Please accept, my dear Président, the expression of my most cordial sentiments."

This was a weighty argument before an Assembly in which there was almost no one who did not place their confidence in the Marshal: indeed, the letter was to all intents and purposes a blank cheque made out in favour of Pierre Laval. From that moment, the latter knew that the game was won. Neglecting the only real opposition which could have impeded him, and which he had succeeded in neutralising with a partial concession, he proceeded, during the course of an extraordinary speech which took up half the sitting, to deal, in his own words, with the "real dispute".

At this decisive moment in his political career, Laval said crudely, almost with provocation, words which, by their very excess, were to astound the Assembly.

"You may be re-assured, I am going to make a declaration. We have no intention of declaring war on England. (*Some excitement.*)

"But there is one thing I must say: it is that we have every intention, whenever we can, to give blow for blow." (*Some applause. Interruptions.*)

It was an odd way of "re-assuring" an Assembly which was for the greater part loyal to the allies. Similarly, he expressed himself with arrogance on another tendentious subject:

"There are some who say that the motion tabled by the Government is a deathblow to the Parliamentary regime.

"Never! I wish to emphasise this. (*Murmurs.*) Why? Because it is a deathblow, not only to the Parliamentary regime, but to everything that has existed but must no longer continue to do so."

And then, with all the passion at his command, with all his venom, Laval reinforced his indictment of the practices of Parliament before the war with anecdotes of events in which he had been involved and with the emotions he had felt.

He demonstrated that the Popular Front Government had refused, from political prejudice, an Italian proposal which would have been favourable to France. Léon Blum, thus attacked, remained silent.

He quoted Daladier's reply on the occasion of his explaining to him that the interests of France demanded that, like England, she should have a Consul-General to represent her with the Spanish Nationalists during the Civil War: "You are quite right, but if I did what you ask, I should lose eighty votes in the Chamber."

He cleverly introduced other and perhaps more honourable incidents: Goering for instance, at Cracow, at the funeral of Marshal Pilsudski, standing to attention in the presence of Marshal Pétain.

He struck blow after blow in order to destroy all misconceptions: "Make no mistake, we are now living under a dictatorship.... The Chambers will necessarily have reduced powers..."

and: "We shall accept no amendments, your duty will be to vote for or against so that the result may be clear before the country and before the world."

It was difficult to be more categorical; it was also difficult to be more moving than was Laval when he allowed his anguish expression: "Do you not feel that disaster has fallen upon France? Do you not feel the sorrow and the pain?"; when he expressed, in an aberrant form no doubt, his lawless but indubitable love for France: "Did I say that one cannot save France by leaving her soil? I maintain it. That is why the Government is determined, whatever may happen, not to let France become Nazified.

". . . . We will not allow our fellow-countrymen to be subjected to the humiliation of voting under the control of the German army."

His speech was continuously interrupted, which gave him the opportunity of attacking the Assembly; it was a speech in which argument followed upon argument, illustration upon illustration; assailed by a paroxysm of emotion and conviction, it was certainly one of those moments in which Laval was at his least cautious: certain of victory, certain of being right, he was like some force of nature breaking in waves upon an assembly of politicians who were able to do no more than repeat unimpassioned, commonplace, if sensible, arguments.

In face of his speech, what weight could his opponents, whose motions he had not even deigned to take into consideration, carry? What weight could his ally, Bergery, carry with his doctrinaire proposal, even? Laval persuaded him not to intervene in the debate by promising that the text of his motion would be published in the Press: a promise that was not kept.

Vincent Badie was persuaded by Jeanneney that his motion would be discussed during the course of the afternoon. He was also to be disappointed by being given no opportunity to speak.

After Laval, Flandin alone was given the opportunity of going to the rostrum and making a long speech which, though elevated in thought and of a curious emotional significance, in practice supported Laval to the hilt.

The speaker expressed in moving terms his love for France and the sorrow inspired in him by the state of the country. He wished that its traditions might be preserved.

While listening to Flandin, a wave of Republican emotion passed over the Assembly.

He seemed to be attracting some agreement. But, much to everyone's surprise, instead of using the effect he had made, as he had done three days before, to oppose Laval, he devoted it to his service and even to the defence of the motion which previously he had condemned.

The fact was that, during the last three days, circumstances had altered: Flandin had failed in his attempt to replace Lebrun by the Marshal. He thought that nothing now could stop Laval; by joining the majority, he hoped still to be able to exercise some influence. He, therefore, asked the Assembly to vote in favour of the Government motion and to give Laval the necessary authority to negotiate with the conquerors.

"I think we must learn all the lessons of the defeat and of the war, that we must realise that it is not sufficient to laugh at, mock or criticise the regimes which fought it, or disapproved it, but that we must examine them profoundly, learn to know their strength, make use of them, assimilate them, adopt them. But nothing could be worse . . ."

A voice: "Long Live France!"

". . . than a servile copy of institutions from which perhaps we should acquire only what was mediocre or bad, and from which we should not, on the other hand, assimilate what they have of strength. We must acquire their strength, but eliminate their weaknesses and, if the phrase is not exaggerated, the sort of contempt for human individuality with which they are imbued. (*Applause.*)

"This, you must acknowledge, we have no right to introduce into our new institutions, because human respect is a sacred legacy that has come down to us from our fathers and which we must hand on intact to our sons. If France is of account in the world, she is so because of her genius which did not come to birth yesterday, will not be born tomorrow, but derives from the long centuries, generation upon generation, that have fashioned her very soul and shaped her land.

"In the very freedom of our towns and villages there is something to delight everyone who sets his foot upon the soil of France. (*Applause.*) The soil of France must remain the soil of France, and if you wish to acquire and deserve the esteem of those with whom you will soon be treating (*Renewed applause*), you must show yourselves, with all the faults ascribed to us indeed, conscious of that pride in liberty that we must preserve in our hearts though suppressing, certainly, the freedom of propaganda that has so much weakened the state, yet without ever doing injury to that freedom of thought that has been the glory of France. (*Applause.*)

"It is in the name of these profound emotions concerning the spirit of France that I beseech my colleagues to yield to those who, like myself and so many others, will be returning tomorrow to the occupied region, there to be for days and weeks under the constant, hidden threat of the foreign occupation, so that we may all feel that, having fulfilled our duty here, we are leaving to the Government of France, which will take our place, our country free and strong. (*Applause.*)

"Long Live France!"

From the rostrum, Pierre Laval thanked Flandin "with profound emotion". He accepted, without alteration, the conclusions of "his friend", Pierre-Etienne Flandin.

Before the meeting drew to a close, having triumphed over all opposition, he said one more word which impressed the members:

"Do you know what lies behind everything I have said? Do you know the real reason for our tabling this motion? It is because, and remember this, think it over before coming to the public session, it is because we wish to achieve the best possible peace for France."

If the public session, which took place in the afternoon, had not had for result the suppression of the Republic, it would have had but little to distinguish it from the preceding debates: it was neither one of the more dramatic, nor one of the more shameful. Parliamentary usages were observed, at least to the same extent that they had been for many years past in the Chamber of Deputies. It seemed that Parliament would itself effortlessly beget the authoritarian regime which was to replace it. Laval's behaviour was very different from that of the morning.

The session fell into three parts in accordance with the agenda and the drama moved towards its close, almost without a single unexpected incident.

Determination of procedure and agenda.

Appointment of a Commission to report on the Government Bill.

Voting on the Bill and closure of the session.

The first part, instead of beginning at 2 p.m., in accordance with the time-table, was considerably delayed: was this, some members wondered, in order to limit the time for debate? Jeanneney, the President of the Senate, presided by right over the National Assembly. He read the Government proposal, which had been modified since the morning in accordance with Laval's promise. The new text, which had been typed, was not distributed to members.

"The National Assembly confers all powers on the Government of the Republic, under the signature and authority of Marshal Pétain, President of the Council, to promulgate by one or more acts, the new Constitution of the French State.

"This Constitution will guarantee the rights of Labour, Family and Country. It will be ratified by the nation and applied by the Assemblies it will have created."

Jeanneney then called upon Herriot, President of the Chamber of Deputies, to make an announcement concerning the members who had embarked in the *Massillia* and had been prevented from returning to Metropolitan France in time for the Assembly.

Herriot read a telegram from Algiers protesting against the calumny to which his colleagues were victims. The speaker declared to a largely hostile Assembly, that the incriminated members had only embarked upon precise instructions from the Government: if they had not disembarked again, when a counter-order had been issued, it was because they had never received it. Their journey to North Africa was therefore perfectly legal.

Pierre Laval took note of this declaration which should have put a term to the campaign of lies. But he also immediately minimised its effect by contrasting the attitude of the travellers with that of the politicians who, like the Marshal and himself, had refused to quit French soil.

Herriot's intervention was the only occasion on which the opposition, even timidly and partially, had an opportunity of expressing itself.

The procedure, which had been adopted on Laval's insistence, was to limit the Assembly to a ratification of the Government Bill without any real debate.

It concluded two new resolutions which guaranteed the Government's success by a large majority.

In the first place, Fernand Bouisson, an ex-President of the Chamber, asked for a vote giving priority to the Government measure. No counter-proposal could then be submitted, unless Laval's motion was first set aside.

Then, in order that the official motion should be passed by a comfortable majority, M. Mireaux, Senator for Hautes-Pyrénnées and editor of *Le Temps*, which had been the official organ of the Third Republic, hoping perhaps to see his paper play a similar role in the new regime, submitted an amendment to the Constitutional Law of the 25th February, 1875, which concerned debates in the National Assembly: he proposed that the majority should not be calculated in accordance with the legal number of seats in the two Assemblies, but on the basis of the number of members who were actually present at the sitting. They amounted to six hundred and sixty-six.

In the first case, the absolute majority, taking into account the absent members and the Communists, who had been deprived of exercising their mandate since 1939, would have been four hundred and sixty-seven votes. In the second, it was reduced to about three hundred and thirty.

Pierre Laval intervened to support the motion, which was adopted.

The ground having thus been prepared, the agenda provided for a suspension of the sitting and a meeting of a special commission, made up of the Legislative Commission of the Senate, and the Commission of Universal Suffrage of the Chamber. M. de Courtois was appointed its President, Boivin-Champeaux its spokesman.

Laval, who appeared before the Commission, side-stepped all questions with such assurance that no one dared press them.

When Senator Giacobbi asked him how the Constitution was to be ratified by the nation, Laval replied by talking of a preparatory Commission on which would sit by right the Presidents of the Commissions of Finance, of the Senate and of the Chamber, as well as those of the Constitutional Commissions of the two Assemblies. Was that an answer to the question? When pressed as to what form the referendum would take, he declared that he did not wish "to anticipate the results of decisions which had not yet been taken".

And similarly, when another member of the Commission, Masse, was concerned to know if the new Constitution would respect the liberty of the subject, Laval replied with a flaming nationalist tirade, which had nothing to do with the question: "If you mean by the liberty of the subject, the rights of all strangers and foreigners . . . I am prepared to state, for example, that no one will be able to become a deputy, unless he has been French for several generations. This will be our way—I have understood your implications, have I not?—of pursuing a racial policy . . ."

Finally, Marx Dormoy referred to an extremely controversial subject: on whose authority would peace or war be decided? Laval replied aggressively:

"M. Dormoy is alluding to necessary counter-measures, if I understand him, to the bombing of Dakar.[1]

"You don't suppose that we are going to hamper ourselves with procedure when it is a question of returning blow for blow. Having been unable to fire on His Majesty's ships, if we can find some other means of replying, we shall take it, with or without your permission."

In spite of Laval's evasions and his violence, the Commission obtained three assurances.

In the first place, a confirmation of the amendment already granted, by which the Constitution would be "ratified by the nation and applied by the Assemblies which it will have created".

The second was perhaps the most important. After Laval's reply to Dormoy, the Commission insisted upon an amendment forbidding the Head of State "to declare war without the previous assent of the Legislative Assemblies". Laval accepted this amendment, and in the event it was respected.

The third assurance arose out of the natural anxiety of members of Parliament not to put an immediate term to the activities of the two Chambers. Pierre Laval promised that these should continue to exist "until the Assemblies foreshadowed by the Constitutional Law of the 10th July, 1940, shall be formed."

The results of the Commission's work were therefore not entirely negative: few conquered regimes, abolished by defeat, have obtained such promises from their successors.

But, towards the end of the meeting, Laval regained his advantage, but with such good humour and discretion, it is true,

[1] On the 8th July the British had bombarded the battle-cruiser, *Richelieu*, which had taken refuge in Dakar., cf., p. 79.

that practically none of the members present were aware of his trickery.

He declared incidentally that the Marshal, once charged with promulgating a new Constitution, would also assume legislative power. And Laval, as if this were the most natural thing in the world, asked Boivin-Champeaux to insert this phrase in his report to the National Assembly.

This extraordinary demand raised no objections. Laval, with a sly but well directed blow, had immeasurably extended the range of his constitutional proposals. Instead of merely conferring upon the Marshal constituent power, by assent of the Commission was added "without restriction to the full exercise of executive and legislative powers".

Thus, by this ultimate concession, the vote of the Assembly was to give the Marshal the rights of an absolute monarch.

From now on, whether the new Constitution were promulgated or not, whether it were ratified or not, Pétain could do exactly as he liked while boasting of the assent of the National Assembly.

It was really a brilliant piece of work on Laval's part to have used the Commission to destroy still further the powers of the Assemblies when, in fact, its duty was to bring precision to their debates and perhaps give them due warning.

While Laval was completing his manoeuvre before the Commission, his supporters were playing their part in the lobbies.

When the sitting was resumed, and Boivin-Champeaux read his report, it was apparent that there was no one left to oppose the motion.

Part of the Assembly seemed to be struck dumb; while the other part seemed to wish to get it over and done with as soon as possible, while manifesting its anger against the last supporters of the regime which was so soon to be abolished.

Vincent Badie, the only member except for Margaine, who wished to speak, as he had been promised he might by President Jeanneney, was prevented from doing so. This is how he reported the incident:

"The moment had arrived to vote. It was at that moment that I rose in the middle of the hall to ask to be called upon to speak ... There were cries, shouts and exclamations.

"I went up on to the stage. I looked at President Jeanneney, I made to read my speech. I was seized by two or three of my colleagues. I saw one of them coming towards me at a furious rate: it was an ex-President of the Council, Fernand Bouisson; his face was scarlet.

"Fernand Bouisson seized hold of my coat, shook me, and tried to make me leave the stage. I don't need to tell you how pale I was. My heart was beating fast; nevertheless, I remained master of myself and said to Bouisson: 'I will not permit you to do this! Let go of me, or I shall push you away.' Bouisson let go of me and hurriedly regained his seat. While this incident was taking place, President Jeanneney put the Constitutional motion to the vote without calling upon me to speak.

"President Jeanneney did not therefore keep his promise."

There was only one formality still to be observed: the vote itself. Its result, which was favourable by five hundred and sixty-nine votes to eighty with seventeen abstentions, was greeted with a brief speech from Laval in which he thanked members in the name of the Marshal and of France, by many shouts of "Long Live France!", and by one isolated cry from Marcel Astier, Senator for the Ardèche, "Long Live the Republic, all the same!"

This vote marked the triumph of Pierre Laval, the destruction of the Republic and the advent of a new regime which was to be that of Vichy. These results were obtained moreover, and this must be emphasised, by perfectly legal means.

The summoning and meeting of the National Assembly had been carried out with perfect legality: the number of members present was large enough for the Assemblies to be really representative; the absence of the Communist members, which could be objected to, was not due to any action taken by the Pétain Government, but to a previous disqualification, dating from 1939, at a time when there was no threat to the Republic.

A similar legality attended the vote on the resolution of the 10th July, 1940. The necessary constitutional majority was largely surpassed.

But there is another question which must be asked: was the vote a free one or was it obtained under threat? The question is not as simple as it appears: physically, no doubt, there was nothing to limit the freedom of the voters: contingents of police and the army protected the Assembly from all external attack. Within, the conduct of the sitting and the attempts at obstruction did not surpass in violence those to which the Assemblies are frequently subjected to today. But morally, besides the fear psychosis instilled by Laval, there was a grave threat weighing over the majority of deputies. A long-term threat perhaps, but one that they felt to be ineluctable.

They knew that a change of regime was in process of coming about and that the new regime would be a dictatorship: and none could disregard the treatment the supporters of Hitler and the Fascist regime had reserved for their defeated opponents. By opposing the masters of tomorrow, were they to place themselves among their victims? This, to many of them, seemed the fatal, if distant, result of the vote they were to take. From this arose those incidents in the lobbies that have been related, and which played on members' fears.

The 10th July saw a free vote taken in an atmosphere of great distress; for each member of the opposition freedom depended on his own courage. Moreover, the allegation that the vote of the members of the Assembly was not a free one is contradicted by the fact that eighty senators and deputies voted publicly against the Government measure.

Before finishing with the National Assembly, it remains to decide whether it could legally delegate to the Marshal the power of revising the Constitution which resided in itself by virtue of Section 6 of the Constitutional Law of the 25th February, 1875. Upon this point, the lawyers are not in agreement. But they are at one in stating that this irregularity, if it was one, was much less grave and much less obvious than that which resulted from another delegation of power which had been continuously practised by Parliament since 1935: the powers of legislating by decree granted to the Government by the Chambers.

On the 14th July, four days after the vote had been taken in the National Assembly, the national holiday was celebrated. At Vichy, before the monument to the dead, in the presence of the Marshal, who on that day donned his Verdun uniform, a few hundred soldiers, their faces still marked by defeat, paid homage to the hundred thousand of the newly dead and the two millions of prisoners. In London, an almost similar number of volunteers, who had decided to continue the struggle, marched, to the cheers of a foreign crowd, past the Cenotaph which did not commemorate the French dead. The soldiers in London, even as they performed the same rite, were already suspicious of those at Vichy. Where on this day were the echoes of all the words uttered to celebrate the 14th July, 1939, the hundred and fiftieth anniversary of the first victorious day of the French Revolution?

Only a single year had elapsed: France was divided in soul, territory, and in the minds of her children.

This was the true drama of Vichy, which began on the 10th July, 1940.

# Vichy, the First Period

(10th July, 1940–9th February, 1941)

## CHAPTER 1

# THE BIRTH OF A REGIME

THE Marshal of France, who had been charged by the National Assembly with the duty of restoring, both morally and materially, a country three-fifths occupied by the enemy and still at war, had at his disposal in Vichy an organisation which neither facilitated his task nor that of his Government.

Lodged on the third storey of the Hôtel du Parc, Pétain's whole accommodation consisted of a bedroom and an office.

Next door to the Marshal lived his immediate staff, in particular his orderly officer, Captain Bonhomme.

The Ministry of Foreign Affairs occupied the first storey of the hotel. Laval had taken the second for the Vice-Presidency of the Council: an excellent strategic situation which allowed him to keep an eye on the comings and goings between the makeshift Quai d'Orsay and the makeshift Élysée. Indeed, Baudouin, the Minister for Foreign Affairs, was soon to be somewhat embarrassed by seeing his lines of communication with the Marshal thus threatened.

Bouthillier, with the Ministry of Finance, was installed on his own in the Carlton.

In this improvised governmental city the hotels did not lend themselves either to the dignity of power or to the secrecy of deliberations of state. Why had the Government's choice landed on Vichy? From July 1940 onwards this problem was the subject of much speculation.

In fact, the Government, in July 1940, had only selected Vichy as a temporary capital and had intended to make but a short stay: had not the Germans at Rethondes given a verbal promise to allow the Government to return very shortly to Paris?

In spite of its somewhat precarious establishment, the new regime was soon almost universally recognised. Thirty-two foreign governments—not the least of which were the Vatican, the U.S.S.R. and the United States—maintained there the representatives who had previously been accredited to the Élysée.

Hardly anyone disputed its legality: the President of the Republic himself left Vichy amid almost total indifference, without even feeling the necessity for resigning. The principal magistrate of the Republic confirmed that the vote of the National Assembly was in conformity with the laws of the Republic.

France suddenly believed it saw in Pétain the incarnation of that miracle which Paul Reynaud had so desperately invoked in one of his final speeches: was not gratitude due to the Marshal for having put an end to an unpopular war? His majestic bearing, and his simplicity, impressed all who saw him.

At this time the Marshal enjoyed a popularity such as had been given to no one for a very long time. During his first journeys in the free zone, the ringing of bells from cathedrals and churches greeted the arrival of the "providential old man". All along the line by which his train travelled, peasants waited in the hope of catching sight of him through the carriage window. When he walked in towns and mingled with the crowd, women held their babies out to him that he might touch them. Here, taken from official reports, is such a scene, producing a somewhat naïve effect. At Toulouse, in November, 1940: "Walking slowly, accompanied by six members of his suite and by the Prefect, the Marshal made the grand tour. Would he halt? Everyone wanted to hold him for an instant immobile in his field of vision and to hear him speak. Only one person was to have that honour: a child of four years old who, raised in his mother's arms, clapped his little hands." A few moments later, the Prefect of Toulouse, sitting beside the Marshal, started at the sight of a woman throwing herself before the motor car and taking advantage of the halt to try and touch the Head of the State's hand. He turned towards the Marshal, with the intention of making excuses for the hysterical woman. The Marshal had seen nothing: he was asleep . . . "without however losing his dignity or his sovereign bearing." This detail, nevertheless, did not appear in the official report.

Innumerable requests for an audience arrived from all corners of the free zone, emanating from every class of society. The few who were admitted revived a custom which had long been abolished: they brought "offerings in accordance with the ceremonial of the monarchy". The Marshal liked these little presents: it pleased him that peasants from the Puy-de-Dôme or from Gers, that artisans from Thiers or Aubusson, master-smiths and lace-makers should offer him in homage the works of their skilled hands.

This somewhat ingenuous cult was no surprise to the Marshal. Once more, Pétain had seen events play into his hands without his having to force them; once more, circumstances had proved him right without his having to make any effort or concession.

Supported more than ever by his self-confidence, he had become, in his own eyes, the centre of the new regime and he was to organise the Government's work according to his own principles and convenience. Even his deafness played its part in his organisation of the State. On the 25th June, he confided to the Deputy, Fernand-Laurent: "In Paul Reynaud's Government, there were more than twenty of us, I couldn't hear what was going on. Today, we are not more than a dozen, which is already much better; soon I shall reduce our numbers to five or six and that will be perfect." His deafness therefore co-operated with his military training to make him desire a hierarchical and concentrated organisation of power. "What is necessary," he said, "is that I should be able to give orders to three men who will give them to fifteen who will give them to a hundred, and so on . . . the pyramid of power!"

On the 12th July, a law limiting the number of portfolios to fifteen: twelve ministers, whose holders bore the titles of the Ministries of State[1] and three Secretariats of State corresponding to the three divisions of National Defence.

This figure being still too high, Pétain immediately divided the members of the Government, whether Ministers or Secretaries of State, into two categories.

The first category, who had full powers—Baudouin, Bouthillier, Alibert, Laval, Darlan, Weygand—attended, at eleven o'clock

[1] Vice-President of the Council: Pierre Laval. Justice: Raphaël Alibert. Interior: Adrien Marquet. Foreign Affairs: Paul Baudouin. Finance: Yves Bouthillier. National Defence: General Weygand. Education and Fine Arts: Émile Mireaux. Family and Youth: Jean Ybarnegaray. Agriculture and Food: Pierre Caziot. Production and Labour: René Belin. Communications: François Piétri. Colonies: Henri Lémery.

every morning, a limited Council which dealt mainly with relations with the German and Italian Armistice Commissions.

The other category only attended full meetings—two or three a week—called Councils of Ministers. These were, in reality, more meetings for information than real governmental discussions.

On the 6th September, there was a re-modelling of the Government which marked an important date in the history of Vichy.

Weygand, removed from the Government, was given the essential post of Pro-Consul in North Africa.

Anti-parliamentarianism was openly manifested by the elimination from the Government, always with the exception of Pierre Laval, of the last five members of Parliament who still had a place in it, whatever their personal qualifications may have been, Lémery, Marquet, Mireaux, Piétri and Ybarnegaray.

The third and last process of governmental re-organisation, on the 6th September, was that the structure of the Government became still more concentrated. From now on, a new differentiation was created between the Ministers,[1] whose number was fixed at nine, and the five Secretaries of State;[2] the first took charge of the key departments, while the Secretaries of State were subordinated to the Ministries with which they seemed to have the greatest affinity: Communications to Finance, Colonies to Foreign Affairs, Air to Marine, Education to Justice, Food to Agriculture.

These already somewhat arbitrary juxtapositions were carried a stage further in January, 1941, when Education was subordinated to the Ministry for War: the historian of ancient Rome, Carcopino, promoted Grand Master of the University, never became accustomed to having General Huntziger as his superior.

Apart from Pierre Laval, the Ministers were more like head clerks, as Louis XIV's were, than ministers in the modern sense.

[1] Vice-President of the Council: Pierre Laval. Justice: Raphaël Alibert. Interior: Marcel Peyrouton. Foreign Affairs: Paul Baudouin. Finance: Yves Bouthillier. Agriculture and Food: Pierre Caziot. Production and Labour: René Belin. War: General Huntziger. Marine: Admiral Darlan.

[2] Communications: Berthelot. Colonies: Admiral Platon. Air: General Bergeret. Education: Georges Ripert. Food: Jean Achard.

In the Council of Ministers, discipline was strict.

"There are no more discussions in the Council," said the Head of the State magisterially, "everyone merely gives his opinion in turn."

Only Weygand and Laval had the authority and mettle to depart from time to time from the agenda. They could both discuss and even argue angrily.

As far as the Marshal was concerned, the Ministers were to limit themselves to carrying out his orders, and had no business to know the whole of his thought.

It happened that after one of the Council Meetings, Pétain sent for a Minister, handed him a Law drawn up by one of his personal advisers and said simply: "Here, sign this, it must be sent to the *Journal Officiel.*"

This was how Pétain appointed Ministers: on the 6th September, 1940, in an interview with Peyrouton, he told him that he was Minister of the Interior. When Peyrouton protested that he felt himself unable to accept, Pétain cut him short with: "That's quite enough, we are at war, your only duty is to obey. If someone were to tell me tomorrow to wash the dishes, I should wash them. Go and sit down in your place."

He used the same method when dismissing Ministers.

On the 12th July, the day on which Act No. 1 of the Constitution was promulgated making him Head of the State, Pétain upset all the Republican traditions: he announced the first list of Ministers to the Cabinet in the following terms:

"You will have learned from my broadcast last night that my new Government consists of only twelve Ministers. There are, therefore, at least six Ministers among you who will have to go. I thank you for your loyal collaboration. You will learn from the *Journal Officiel* tomorrow who the members of my new Cabinet are. I thank you." And on that, the Marshal rose and left the meeting.

To new customs were added new men.

Pétain's collaborators and Ministers were for the most part well-known men of the Right. Several of them had been the victims of the Popular Front. Bouthillier and Peyrouton had been dismissed for having failed to conceal their sympathies with the Right or the Centre. Similarly with du Moulin de Labarthète. Dr. Ménétrel had played a militant part in the organisations of the extreme Right, which had come into existence on the 6th February, 1934. Baudouin, if he had not taken up so precise a position, had nevertheless published in the *Revue de Paris*, on the 1st February, 1938, an article on political doctrine in which, though he condemned them, he pointed out the efficiency of the totalitarian regimes.

René Belin, alone, was of the Left: Pétain and Laval deluded themselves that his presence would prevent the Government being stigmatised as of the Right.

Six members of this team were to play fundamental parts: Baudouin, Bouthillier, Belin, Peyrouton, Caziot and Chevalier. There were only four who knew anything of parliamentary methods: Baudouin, Bouthillier, Belin and Peyrouton.

Paul Baudouin belonged to an extremely wealthy upper middle-class family. When still quite young, he had been on intimate terms with the ex-President of the Council, Roubier; he had travelled all over Europe with his mother and had even been received by the Empress Eugénie. During the 1914–1918 war, he had been in the Air Force and distinguished himself, while later he passed brilliantly out of the École Polytéchnique and equally brilliantly into the Ministry of Finance; with this enviable success to his credit, he was on the staff of several ministers. At forty, he became Director General of the Bank of Indo-China, which gave him the opportunity to play, on several occasions, the part of unofficial ambassador from the French Government to Mussolini and Ciano on matters of colonial finance.

Under-Secretary of State for Foreign Affairs at Bordeaux and at Vichy, his political outlook appears somewhat complex. Privately doing all he could to renew diplomatic relations with England, he succeeded officially in widening the breach by being too subtle. While he asserted in all good faith that he was profoundly Anglophile, he succeeded in making himself as much disliked by the English as he was hated by the Germans.

Yves Bouthillier, who was Minister of Finance from the beginning of Pétain's Government until April, 1942, did not correspond to the classical conception of a Treasury official. There were in particular two characteristics which distinguished him from most of his colleagues. He had a taste for general ideas and a sense of history, which made him one of the theoreticians of Pétainism, and indeed the Minister to whom the Marshal himself was most inclined to listen. He was not afraid of opposing big business: he was the originator of the laws against Joint Stock Companies and Trusts promulgated by the Vichy Government. And from then on was subject to the vindictiveness of certain capitalist circles without, however, having been able to conciliate the masses, whose indifference disappointed him.

In contrast to these two Treasury officials, promoted to key Ministries, was the syndicalist Belin, their living antithesis, both in his life and in his personality. René Belin began life at the age of eleven as an office boy. At fourteen he got a job in the P.T.T. as an auxiliary telegraph boy: the lowliest position in the whole French administration. Placed on the establishment at fifteen, he earned 33 Frs. 33 centimes a month, 6,000 Frs. of French money today. After the war, he devoted all his evenings to study and, by immense labour, succeeded in passing all the examinations of the P.T.T. and rising from grade to grade. At thirty, he was sixth on the list for the position of manager. A militant Trades Unionist, he had the courage to organise a strike of the P.T.T. at Lyon with the same gusto with which he threw himself into the preparation of his professional future. But he had to pay the price and, summoned before a disciplinary committee, was dismissed from the administration.

But the Trades Unions took care of him. In 1935, at the age of thirty-five, he was appointed Deputy Secretary-General to the Confédération Générale du Travail. But, determined to preserve the independence of the Trades Unions, condemning the politicisation of workmen's organisations, he attacked the entry of the Communists into the C.G.T. In October, 1938, he founded the weekly newspaper, *Syndicats*, the organ of resistance to the totalitarian pressure exercised by the extreme Left. In June, 1940, he resigned from the office of the Confédération. A Trades Unionist out of work, he was, a month later, summoned by the Marshal and somewhat reluctantly joined the Government.

Baudouin, Bouthillier and Belin, if they were not members of Parliament, had at least a certain practical experience of politics.

So had Peyrouton. A son-in-law of the Minister Malvy, Marcel Peyrouton was one of those high officials who were completely Republican so long as the Republic lasted; he had made his career in the Colonial Service.

Dismissed in 1936, by the Popular Front, from the position of Secretary-General in Tunisia and Morocco, he obtained in compensation the Ambassadorship to the Argentine Republic. In May, 1940, he was in Tunisia again as Resident-General and from there opposed the armistice. This did not, however, prevent his being promoted, on the 27th July, Secretary-General to the Ministry of the Interior under Marquet whom he replaced on the 6th September.

His career as a high Republican official having led him to Vichy, he was responsible, as Minister of the Interior, for putting the anti-Republican measures into practice: "Public opinion," he said, seeing the mote in other people's eyes but not the beam in his own, "no longer wants to see servants of the old regime in the seats of power."

Next to this man, who had been vaccinated by political circles and upon whom the vaccine had taken, were two of the principle Ministers of Vichy, pure technicians, who had to all intents and purposes never breathed the air of political circles.

Pierre Caziot, Minister of Agriculture, came from ancient country stock at Sancerrois. As an agricultural engineer, he had a passion for the soil. Not only did he know it in theory, but he also had practical experience. The author of well-known works on agriculture, he liked to recall that his family property at Veilly-sur-Sauldre had an extent of seventy-seven acres and had belonged to his family for between five and six hundred years; he was also proud of the fact that his mother had worn, until the day of her death, the Berrichonne headdress. He was also an expert in real estate concerning which no one contested his authority. At the Palais de Justice, it was said that anyone who had an assessment of Caziot against him, had lost his case in advance. He was one of the few Ministers who exercised any influence on the Marshal, whom he revered, and of whom he said: "He is a peasant like me."

And here, finally, was the most pure-hearted of them all, the Platonic philosopher, astonished to find himself promoted to govern the Republic, an intellectual strayed into politics, the Dean Jacques Chevalier, who was Dean of the Faculty of Letters at Grenoble. He was a well-known philosopher and had been Henri Bergson's favourite disciple. Having passed his examinations in philosophy at the age of twenty-one, after a period at Oxford, where he had made friends with Lord Halifax, he became Dean at the age of thirty-eight. Profoundly hostile to Germany's tendencies towards hegemony, he had the very great courage, during his period in power, never to compromise on this point of doctrine. The unofficial intermediary between Pétain and Churchill, he was attacked by the Paris press for his attitude at the time of Henri Bergson's death: it was thanks to him that the Vichy Government was represented at the funeral of the great Jewish philosopher.

But Chevalier, in his candour and his lack of political experience, was not always sufficiently conscious of realities. When students at Grenoble demonstrated in favour of General de Gaulle, Chevalier from a desire to keep order, and not grasping the difference between such a manifestation and an ordinary students' row, called in the authorities. At this moment the authorities were represented by the Militia, that is to say by men hand in glove with the Gestapo. Chevalier was unperturbed, or rather did not realise what had occurred, and thus, casually, without meaning to, he handed over to the enemy some of his young fellow-countrymen whom, in other circumstances, he ceaselessly protected from the Nazis. Indeed, the administration of the Faculty had become in part, thanks to him, a manufactory of false papers for the purpose of saving students from being sent to work in Germany.

The formation of the Government coincided with the period when, under the influence of Admiral Darlan, the greater part of the more important posts in the administration were being confided, little by little, to admirals. Admiral Esteva became Resident-General in Tunisia, Admiral Abrial was Governor-General of Algeria, Admiral Decoux of Indo-China, Admiral Robert of Martinique, Admiral Auphan was placed in charge of the Merchant Marine and Admiral Fernet of the General Secretariat of the Presidency of the Council . . . Cardinal Liénart was reported, no doubt apocryphally, to have said: "I wonder if, after my death, they'll find another available admiral to take my position."

Admiral Platon, on the 6th September, 1940, was made Minister for the Colonies, a post for which his only qualification was a recent and rapid inspection of the North African ports.

This ex-Professor from the École Supérieure de la Marine, an austere Protestant, believed that the salvation of France lay in total collaboration with the Reich.

The Marshal had also to recruit new men to complete his staff.

The Marshal's staff consisted of four distinct sections: the Civil Office, whose chief was Henri du Moulin de Labarthète; the Military Office which, within six months, had two different chiefs, Generals Brécard and Laure; the Secretariat-General to the Presidency of the Council under Vice-Admiral Jean Fernet; and the Personal Secretariat whose chief was young Dr. Bernard Ménétrel, personal physician to the Marshal.

Besides these, there were a few people without clearly defined status among Pétain's intimates: Captain Bonhomme, his orderly officer; the writer, René Gillouin who, at the beginning, was his personal secretary; the airman, René Fonck, an ace of the first world war, who, on several occasions, was his liaison officer with Marshal Goering. And finally, one of the Ministers, Raphaël Alibert, who, alone of the members of the Government, took all his meals at the Marshal's table. The members of the Marshal's *entourage* were not recruited, like the Ministers, for their competence, but rather for the personal references they were in a position to produce.

The Marshal did not know very many people; he was mistrustful. And in the choice of his personal assistants, he had recourse almost exclusively to his few contacts. The opinion of an old friend, the memory he had preserved of some A.D.C. whom he had met during the course of his long career, or some family recommendation would determine his selection.

Henri du Moulin de Labarthète had been Financial Attaché when Pétain was Ambassador in Madrid. Commandant de Gorostarzu, of the Military Office, had also been a member of the Embassy Staff. General Brécard was a friend of the Marshal and of Alibert: they had both known him long before the war. While Alibert, at that time the great recruiter of the personnel of the regime, had recommended to the Marshal Admiral Fernet, whose brother, André Fernet, who had been killed during the First World War, he had known, and René Gillouin, whose action he had approved at the time of the National Formations of the 6th February, 1934. General Laure had been one of the Marshal's staff officers for many years and Captain Bonhomme had similarly been his orderly officer for a long period. As for Dr. Ménétrel, Pétain made him his personal physician because he had been a particular friend of his father, Médecin-Major Ménétrel.

Admiral Fernet, head of the Secretariat-General to the Presidency of the Council, was one of the most solid and stable influences on the Marshal's staff. Utterly devoted to his chief, without other ambition than to serve him well, he brought to the atmosphere of Vichy an element of balance and sound sense.

Henri du Moulin de Labarthète was certainly less loyal, his personality consisting of a number of facets. There was a certain casualness about him which, sometimes, bordered on ingratitude. All his patrons were successively subjected to its effects. Chéron, the first, had helped his career before the war, which no doubt provoked du Moulin to attack him with sarcasm when Reynaud, in his turn, became his patron: "What will du Moulin say about me when he no longer has need of my protection?" joked Paul Reynaud, who had no suspicions of such an eventuality. Then came the war and the armistice: Reynaud was imprisoned, du Moulin in power. The prophecy came true: Reynaud's old protégé criticised his fallen protector. He took the same attitude towards Pétain who, however, preferred him to all his other collaborators.

This instability did not prevent his supporting the Head of the State, in particular when he resisted the Germans.

Counter-balancing du Moulin was René Gillouin, the secretary. At Bordeaux, the Marshal, on the advice of Alibert, had abruptly summoned to his *entourage* this essayist of the extreme Right, who had been a Municipal Councillor of Paris on the 6th February. The *entourage* of the Vice-President of the Council cordially disliked him: "He is an agent of the Intelligence Service, and he says that the President goes in for table-turning, practises sorcery and says the black Mass. Those are the kinds of people that the Old Man has about him!" In 1942 Gillouin fled before the Germans and took refuge in Switzerland.

Beside these film-stars, General Brécard seemed to fulfil a useful function, whatever his personal merits and his political aims. Protocol and precedence obsessed him.

Devoted, always in the background, having lived all his life in the Marshal's shadow, Laure spent his time in sending him manuscript notes on policy; he admitted himself that Pétain seldom read them. The scandalmongers of Vichy said that his return from captivity was the only positive result of the meeting at Montoire. Laure was to be the Marshal's official historiographer though the latter had no hesitation in dismissing him, together with du Moulin, in April 1942, on the demand of Laval.

Captain Bonhomme had also never left the Marshal's wake; he had a real adoration for his master. Pétain looked upon him rather like a housekeeper and treated him with a certain freedom of manner.

Bernard Ménétrel, the physician and head of the private office, soon became the spoilt child to whom nothing was refused. In any case, what is certain, is that Ménétrel, unceasingly at the Marshal's elbow, was the necessary intermediary through whom certain Ministers could make contact with the Head of the State; he had a finger in every pie and organised about the old man a sort of narrow-meshed filter through which he only allowed those who suited him to pass.

Sometimes, Pétain tried to escape this constant supervision. Ménétrel was notoriously and fiercely anti-Semitic and Pétain, having decided to bring his influence to bear on Xavier Vallat, Commissioner for Jewish Affairs, in favour of certain Jews, hid the matter from his doctor and asked Madame Gillouin to be his intermediary. Another example was in 1942, when Pétain received a member of the Resistance and, before allowing him to speak, went to the door, looked through the key-hole, and said: "Bernard is not there. So fire away: how's the Resistance going? Is there anything you need?"

In 1940, Ménétrel had to begin with few political pretensions: he merely enjoyed being in power. Later on, however, he took himself more seriously. We shall see that from November, 1942, onwards he played an anti-German role.

The Marshal's intimates constituted at once the general-staff of an old man who bore upon his shoulders heavier responsibilities than anyone in the whole history of France, and also a court of a sort of Principality of Gerolstein, astray in a world of cataclysm.

This anomalous, improvised team, which sometimes sank beneath the weight of its task, and was sometimes in restless motion about the Marshal, had one feeling which it shared in common with its chief: hostility towards Pierre Laval, Vice-President of the Council.

Besides the fact that he was a member of Parliament—the only one, after September, to remain in power—Pierre Laval fulfilled to an extraordinary degree all the political and human conditions which the Marshal most disliked.

Laval made no effort to conceal his contempt for the National Revolution, while Pétain, his Ministers and his staff attached a great importance to it.

Towards his colleagues in the Government, he showed even less respect. On occasion, if one of them happened to ask him a question, he was likely to be snubbed with a "Don't bother me, I know my business and what I have to do!"

Even towards Pétain, Laval showed but little more deference. The Marshal, for him, was a "soldier", which, when he said it, had a purely pejorative implication. Moreover, he wrongly believed him to be totally incapacitated by his age, and did not hesitate to say to anyone who was prepared to listen, that the Marshal was merely useful to him as a figurehead and had none but a decorative function. He allowed his entourage to treat the Head of the State most irreverently as an old booby.

The success Laval had achieved on the 10th July, in the name of the Marshal, had been so brilliant that he considered himself personally invested with power by the National Assembly.

There was an irreducible lack of accord between the two men, which was exaggerated by the actual physical repulsion Pétain felt for Laval.

Laval was often untidily dressed, his appearance uncared for, a cigarette stub always hanging from the corner of his mouth. It was perhaps in reaction to the formal conventionality of Pétain's entourage and of the Ministers, that Laval at Vichy accentuated his apparent vulgarity.

Everything about Laval was calculated to offend the Marshal.

However, Pétain could not but admire him. He could never forget that in 1934, Doumergue had said to him of Laval: "He is the last politician we have." Laval's triumphant success on the 10th July had persuaded the Marshal that Doumergue was right.

And, in the regime which was in process of creation, Laval was for the Marshal not only a scandalous object whose vulgarity horrified him, but a man whose political sense impressed him.

Thus the Marshal and his Vice-President of the Council constituted an inharmonious team which sometimes tolerated each other, and sometimes were in enmity: the unceasing peripeteia in the relations between the two men was one of the most serious of the internal disasters that afflicted Vichy.

CHAPTER 2

# FRANCE DURING THE PERIOD OF THE TWO ZONES

DURING the three months which followed on the armistice, the conflict in Europe had been limited to an Anglo-German duel. But the Battle of Britain, a sort of aerial Verdun, which the British won in August 1940, constituted the decisive episode of the war.

When the Battle of Britain came to an end on the 31st October, three hundred and seventy-five pilots of the R.A.F. had been killed and three hundred and fifty-six wounded. The civilian population had suffered 14,281 dead, and 10,325 wounded. The Luftwaffe, however, had lost for certain 2,375 aircraft, without counting those which had not returned to base or those which, having returned, were no longer usable.

The invasion had not taken place: it had been postponed till the spring.

Hardly had the Battle of Britain come to an end, than a number of other countries were preparing to intervene in the Anglo-German duel. Hitler, from November onwards, was contemplating attacking Russia, but he had to delay his offensive in order to help Italy which, on the 26th October, had attacked Greece but was unable to bring the campaign to a successful conclusion.

At this period various alliances were in process of formation. On the 27th September, 1940, a Tripartite Pact was signed in Berlin between Germany, Italy and Japan, providing for a new European order to be set up by the two former, and a new Asiatic order by the last. The three countries pledged themselves over the next ten years to give mutual political, economic and military assistance in the case of any one of them being attacked by another power. Successively, and with an identical ceremonial, Hungary, Rumania, Slovakia, Bulgaria, Yugoslavia and Croatia gave adherence to the pact, which was completed by the conclusion of a treaty of friendship and non-aggression at Ankara between Bulgaria and Turkey and a similar agreement between Germany and Turkey.

On the side of the democracies, another coalition was in process of slower formation. The President of the United States, Roosevelt, had to await his re-election on the 5th November (449 votes against the 82 for Wilkie, the Republican candidate) in order to begin the campaign to sway public opinion towards official intervention by the U.S.A. at Great Britain's side: it was only on the 9th March, 1941, that the American Senate voted, by sixty votes to thirty-one, the Lend-Lease law which authorised the lending and hiring of war material to all nations whose defence seemed vital to the interests of the United States. But, by November, it was clear to which camp American power was bringing aid. A new continent was preparing to take part in the conflict.

In the middle of global war, France thought herself to be protected, particularly in the free zone.

With the return of the refugees, life seemed to become normal once more; after the agonies of the exodus and the destruction caused by battle, the public services began functioning regularly again.

Soon the theatres were switching on their footlights. The last to close down, L'Oeuvre, which had had, on the 10th June, 1940, to refund the single member of its audience, was the first to re-open, on the 11th July, for a revival of *Juliette*, a comedy by Jean Bassons. The National Theatres: the Opéra, the Opéra-Comique, the Comédie-Française and the Odéon, in which the occupying authorities were particularly interested, had to change their managers, in so far as these were considered undesirable, place some hundreds of free seats at the disposal of the Wehrmacht every day, reserve the stage-boxes of the Head of the State for the Nazi dignitaries, and, finally, submit their programmes to censorship. In spite of all this, everything began again as in the good old times: on the 22nd August, the Opéra-Comique gave *Carmen*, on the 24th the Opéra gave *The Damnation of Faust* and, on the 15th September, the Odéon revived *l'Arlésienne*.

The Feldgrau crowded into the music-halls to receive their first lessons in aesthetics from the spectacle of practically naked chorus girls. The Palace opened on the 6th July, followed by the Concert Mayol, the Folies-Bergère, the Lido and the Casino de Paris, enjoying summer audiences which the managers of these establishments could not have foreseen were to be so numerous or so wealthy. *Amours de Paris*, *Voilà Paris!* and *Folies d'un Soir*, spectacular reviews, shared the favours of the tourists in uniform.

One of the characteristics of this period which was most remarked and commented on was what was called the Nazis' "Korrektion".

It is certain that at the start the brutality of the occupying forces was hardly perceptible to the occupied. On the contrary, many anecdotes stand witness to the Nazis' courtesy.

A German officer, meeting a pupil of a free school, dressed in school clothes, congratulated him and exhorted him to be worthy of his uniform. A French Air Force General, who had been wounded and had taken refuge in an occupied village, was presented with his respects by the commander of a German unit. The wife of a Parisian doctor, who was a refugee in Britanny, attended all alone the six o'clock Mass in a church. She was suddenly aware of the unusual sound of boots in the sanctuary. "Good God," thought the worshipper, who had read stories of German atrocities in Poland, "they're going to enter the church, kill Monsieur le Curé, and kill me." The following day, at the same service, there was, indeed, a green uniform in the church: a German soldier was serving the Mass.

Every day, the Germans paraded in the Champs Élysées.

Here is a description of the scene given by a diplomatist, Acevedo.

"From afar, one heard the shrill sound of fifes to which the rolling of drums succeeded. Armed motor-cyclists preceded and followed the parade, turning quickly from side to side, clearing the street, obliging vehicles to stop and park themselves along the pavements.

"Then followed the parade, a band at its head, fifes, cymbals, drums, preceded by a Drum-Major; then a gap, then an officer on horseback, his sword drawn; then the colours with a colour party; then the company, in threes, ranks closed, according to the German practice, marching at attention with fabulous precision. The German civilians and soldiers on the pavement stood rigidly to attention, their arms raised. The French continued walking, their hearts heavy, pretending not to see."

All over the French capital there were flags bearing the swastika.

At all important cross-roads there were signposts erected for the German military lorries.

The whole of the district of the Avenue Kléber was reserved for the military staffs of the occupying forces. Wooden barriers prevented all access. The Élysée, for a period of eight days, was transformed into a prisoners' camp. More permanently, the Grand Palais became a garage: it contained 1,200 military vehicles. The Cercle Interallié, in the Rue du Faubourg Saint-Honoré, was turned into a Casino for German officers. The Écoles Polytéchnique and Normale became barracks. The Luxembourg sheltered the general staff of the Luftwaffe, and Goering took up his residence there in great luxury. There were German soldiers' clubs in cafés-restaurants in every district of Paris. There were cinemas reserved for German soldiers: the Marignan, the Rex, the Paris. There were theatres reserved for German soldiers: the Empire, in the Avenue de Wagram, and the Palais de Chaillot.

The names of the streets had also to conform to the instructions of the new masters. All streets, which by their names seemed to betray the Jewish influence of Republican France, were replaced by the name of some notorious anti-Semite: Péreire thus lost his boulevard which was given to Edouard Drumont.

In the occupied zone the clocks had to conform to Central European time.

The differences of time and the midnight curfew created curious consequences.

Such, for instance, as the first midnight Mass held during the occupation at the Madeleine in Paris: the observance of the Nazi rules which, even on this holy day, allowed of no exception, obliged it to be held during the afternoon in full daylight. And the faithful, as they came out, saw German troops marching along the boulevards to the tune of the *Horst Wessel Lied.*

Even the University was compelled to adapt itself.

The beginning of the new term in the schools, for all that it took place in the same buildings and according to the same time-tables, nevertheless made the scholars both in the secondary and primary schools feel from the very start that something had changed: certain masters had disappeared or been sacked without reference to their professional qualifications. The school books had been censored, particularly in the occupied zone: everything that was not "purely Arian" had been pitilessly removed. The *Lorelei* of Heine, a Jewish poet, was soon stigmatised as the work of an "*unbekannte Dichter*": and soon this "*lied*" by an unknown poet was removed from the school books.

At the Palais de Justice, the judges were compelled to sit in judgment on cases hitherto unknown in the annals of the French courts, among others those of slanderous denunciations of Frenchmen by Frenchmen to the Germans.

There were other public buildings which necessarily suffered enemy infiltration: the prisons. In the occupied zone, they now had German sections side by side with the French sections.

In those prisons which remained entirely French, there was a strange mixture of prisoners, most revealing of the period. Guillain des Bénouville, imprisoned, in 1940, as a Gaullist in a prison in Algiers, was surprised to hear the cell opposite resounding to the *Horst Wessel Lied*: the prisoner was a German ex-member of the Foreign Legion, arrested for spying in favour of the Third Reich, and was now "giving himself heart and soul to singing the hymn of Nazi Youth".

The presence of the Nazis imperceptibly created networks which in the end were to encompass without their realising it the existence of all Frenchmen: the German Intelligence Service, the Abwehr, which was part of the German General Staff with its three sub-divisions: military and economic intelligence; sabotage and fifth-column; military security and counter-espionage; the police, whose general headquarters, the R.S.H.A., (Reichssicherheitshauptampt), in July, 1940, had its representative in France, the Sturnbamführer Boemelburg, with a deputy called Knochen, began to take measures against the Jews and the Freemasons.

There was a second German network of tragic notoriety, the Gestapo, which was organised in six sections: Section 1: purely administrative. Section 2: supervision of the French police. Section 3: control of the economic life of the country. Section 4: control and repression of anti-German activities. Section 5: capture and arrest of suspects, escaped prisoners of war and German deserters. This section demanded the collaboration of the French police. Section 6: Intelligence.

Let us continue to examine the ramifications of the German networks: there was the "Propaganda Abteilung", the official organ for Nazi propaganda in France and a sub-division of the Ministry of Information and Propaganda of the Reich.

It had jurisdiction over the whole of occupied France, except for Alsace-Lorraine, which had been annexed, and the departments of the Nord and the Pas-de-Calais which came under the "Propaganda Abteilung" of Belgium. It also had jurisidiction over the Channel Islands, which were the only British territory occupied by the Nazis.

From October, 1940, in Paris and from February, 1941, onwards in the provinces, Propaganda Abteilung organised "civilian propaganda columns" composed of trustworthy people, recruited by the secret police, whose duty it was to create waves of propaganda to influence public opinion.

The first wave of propaganda against England began in October, 1940.

In the second half of the same month, an anti-Jewish programme was launched to be followed by action against the Freemasons and the Gaullists.

Very soon began the propaganda for recruiting French workmen to work in Germany. And in July, 1941, the propaganda turned naturally against the U.S.S.R.

The first care of the German administration was to create parties or political movements which would be at their disposal. In July, 1940, Achenbach, Councillor to the German Embassy, as yet doubtless ill-informed, financed and advertised on all the walls of Paris the Maître du Feu party, invented by a half-wit called Costantini. A windfall for the printers, this grotesque episode ended by being laughed out of court. The Maître du Feu, who signed his editorials Prometheus in his newspaper *La Tempête*, disappeared amid ridicule. The lesson was not entirely lost on the occupying power who was soon to foment movements and finance publications less fantastic in character.

Furthermore, the Germans encouraged the black market. On the orders of Goering, German purchasing companies were founded in December 1940, whose purpose was to acquire, at no matter what price, undeclared commodities. The first of these, the Roges, had numerous employees.

Where did the money come from? The description of one of these companies for organised pillage, the Otto Office, leaves one in no doubt: "The payments were made in new thousand franc notes, made up into bundles of one hundred thousand francs with bands giving their origin, and taken from bags sealed with lead seals bearing the stamp of the Bank of France." It was therefore the money paid over for the cost of the occupation by the Bank of France, which permitted the Reich to be so generous for the German black market.

Against these official or semi-official networks, set up by the Nazis in France, the still embryonic network of the Resistance movements was beginning to take form. 1940–1941 was merely the beginning of them. It was still the period of initial effervescence and spontaneous creation. From the summer of 1940, soldiers had begun grouping themselves about a regular officer, Captain Henri Frenay, who seems to have been one of the first to take up the fight again after the signing of the armistice. He created the movement Libertés, and issued a typewritten newspaper which he edited at Lyon with Berthie Albrecht.

Another movement, Libération, the successor to an earlier organisation, Dernière Colonne, was founded at Clermont-Ferrand by Emmanuel d'Astier de la Vigerie, General Corniglion-Molinier and Professor Cavaillès, who were joined by elements of the Socialist party and the two central Trades Unions, the C.G.T. and the C.F.T.C.

At Lyon, which soon became the capital of the Resistance in the free zone, appeared also a movement called France-Liberté, which soon changed its name to Franc-Tireur. Also at Lyon, France d'Abord began recruiting from military and intellectual circles. There were also Le Coq Enchainé among Radical Freemasons and the Groupe du Témoignage Chrétien, founded by Father Chaillet, which was to find its principal supporters among the Jesuits of Fourvière.

At Toulouse, Libérer et Fédérer, of Socialist origin, proposed giving to France and her Empire a federal structure.

At Marseille, some Socialists were preparing another movement which was to become La France au Combat.

At this period, the Communist party was not as yet taking an active part against the occupying power.

At the time of the entry of the German troops into Paris, a Soviet radio transmission gave the Paris militants the following order: "Do not leave Paris, whatever happens; publish *l'Humanité* legally as soon as the German troops enter the city, and thus face them with the accomplished fact."

In accordance with these instructions, Maurice Tréand, a member of the Central Committee of the party, and the officer in charge of the formation of cells, returned to Paris from Lille, where he had learned that the daily Communist newspaper, *La Voix du Peuple*, was appearing in Brussels with the authorisation of the occupying power. Why should the same thing not be true for *l'Humanité* in Paris? He ordered two of the party militants, Mme. Ginollin and Mme. Schrodt, to get in touch with the Kommandantur. On the 18th June, these two emissaries had an interview with Leutenant Weber, the press officer, who stated his approval and even asked that *l'Humanité* should appear as soon as possible.

As soon as the editing was under way, Mme. Ginollin warned the pre-war printer of *l'Humanité*, M. Dangon, and gave him a sum of 50,000 Frs. on account. On the evening of the 20th, Mme. Ginollin, accompanied by Mme. Schrodt met Tréand near the métro station of Saint-Martin, and gave him the copy for the first number. But at that moment, 10.30 p.m., a round-up by the French police arrested the three militants. On them was found incontrovertible evidence of an intent to publish *l'Humanité*; and, by virtue of the decrees of August and September, 1939, which had suspended *l'Humanité* and prohibited the Communist party, the French authorities charged them and sent them to prison on the 22nd June. Three days later, on the 25th, they were freed owing to the intervention of the German authorities.

The very day of their release from prison, Maurice Tréand, with the assistance of another member of the Central Committee, Jean Catelas and a lawyer, who was a member of the party, Robert Foissin, sent a letter to the Nazi Councillor of State, Turner:

"We alone took up a position against the war, and asked for peace at a time when there was some danger in doing so . . . *L'Humanité*, published by us, would set itself the task of pursuing a policy of European pacification and of defending the conclusion of a pact of friendship between Germany and Russia, thus creating conditions for a lasting peace."

This letter, handed to Turner on the 27th June, was transmitted by him to the Military Governor of Paris. But, finally, the negotiations failed, perhaps because of intervention by the Vichy Government.

On the 1st July a first secret number of *l'Humanité* appeared. And until June, 1941, when Germany declared war against Russia, it never ceased demanding the authorisation to publish legally. In certain cases it incited French workmen to fraternise with German soldiers.

The food ration was barely sufficient to keep the French alive:

| | | |
|---|---|---|
| Bread: | 250 grammes per day. | (Approx. 9 oz.) |
| Meat: | 180 grammes per week. | ( ,, $6\frac{1}{2}$ oz.) |
| Fat: | 15 grammes per day. | ( ,, $\frac{1}{2}$ oz.) |
| Cheese: | 40 grammes per week. | ( ,, $1\frac{1}{2}$ oz.) |
| Sugar: | 500 grammes per month. | ( ,, $17\frac{1}{2}$ oz.) |

This ration, if it had not been augmented for many by numerous necessary frauds, would have led to the slow death of the entire population. 1,700 calories corresponded, according to the Germans themselves, to "a process of slow famine leading to death"; 3,000 to 3,500 calories are necessary for a man leading a sedentary life, 4,500 for manual workers. From September, 1940, the daily ration for French adults was reduced to 1,800.

During the course of the winter, the black market became organised: 350 Frs for a metre of cloth, 100 Frs for a meal without coupons, comprising a plate of meat and some cheese, inaccessible luxuries to the average salary which was about 1,000 Frs a month.

Ill-nourished bodies suffer cruelly from the cold. In the winter of 1940–1941, one of the most severe that France had known for many years, the fuel ration was barely sufficient to allow of a family slightly and intermittently heating one room for a few weeks: eleven degrees centigrade was considered luxury.

There were, however, certain people who continued their normal life unchanged. Maurice Rostand, in an ode written in November, 1940, did not abandon his usual manner.

Sacha Guitry surpassed himself. In order to show the Germans that he was not afraid of them, he put on at the Madeleine a play evoking the French monarchy, *Le Bien-Aimé*, in which appears the whole of Louis XV's court and which by implication was certainly worth the Führer's.

Besides these masterpieces, with which all world wars enrich literature or encumber school books, there appeared a new psychological characteristic in most people due to the occupation.

Emotions were no longer straightforward: they were nearly all doubled by some complementary or contradictory feeling.

Gregarious docility was complemented by anarchic revolt: the same man who, at Bordeaux station, would happily show his identity card to a Nazi policeman, murmuring: "One now feels that one really is governed," would protest against the regulations imposed on him by the period, and would endeavour to circumvent them: he would admire priests who, beneath their soutanes, concealed provisions which, later on, became with some of them false documents and clandestine newspapers. He himself, in secret, would listen to broadcasts from London: 9.15 p.m. was the hour at which his evening recreation consisted of bellicose words: *The French speaking to the French.* It was a mixture of vanity and masochism. During the first months of the occupation, the more courageous recalled all the historical examples of conquered peoples who, by their cleverness, had learned to dominate their conquerors. "*Graecia capta ferum victorem vixit*", a quotation more or less adapted to the circumstances. At the same time, overwhelmed by a feeling of sin, public opinion, for the greater part, was in accord, at least to start with, with those repeated acts of contrition made by the Marshal in his *Messages*: "It is my sin, it is my very great sin", confessed the average Frenchman who, in his nostalgia for the facilities of the past, asked indeed no better than to fall once more into error.

There was also a mixture of patriotic revolt and resignation. The revolt of so many of the young who defied the occupying power with spontaneous gestures. On the 11th November, 1940, the anniversary of the other armistice, a procession of students tried to reach the Étoile in order to place a tricolour wreath on the tomb of the Unknown Soldier in the name of General de Gaulle. Stopped by a phalanx of French police, the disrupted procession flowed back onto the German police, who opened fire: there were several dead and numerous wounded.

During this first period of the occupation, many people were very confused as to where their duty lay. Many French families, brought up to respect the law, were much troubled when they suddenly saw their children become the prey of tribunals and gaols. This was the problem of conscience which worried Henri Frenay's mother when she first learned that her son was fighting against the established authorities. The police said to her: "France is unhappy and the Marshal wishes to save her: he wishes to rebuild the great Christian nation of the past. And your son is preaching revolt and civil war." The widow of a professional soldier, and profoundly religious, she could not help being concerned at this information; and she wrote these terrible words to her son: "You are committing treason, Henri, and I ask myself the appalling question as to whether I should not tell where you are, for you are doing wrong."

The most patriotic Frenchmen were beginning to wonder where their duty lay.

CHAPTER 3

# THE NATIONAL REVOLUTION—DOCTRINE

IN internal policy, the ambition of the Vichy Government, at least until 1942, was to transform radically both institutions and morals.

Most of Pétain's Ministers and collaborators, who took part in the National Revolution, came from the upper middle classes.[1]

The majority belonged to the Right, many even to the extreme Right. Ardent patriots, they were pained by the decline of France for which they held the Republic responsible.

Certainly most of them disapproved of totalitarian principles: they had no thought of aligning France to the dictatorships. But they had hoped to find, within the French tradition, an efficiency comparable to that of the inhuman regimes which were threatening the peace of the world.

The war supervened. A truce, and the basic duty of showing a common front, suspended their opposition to a regime which, for the moment, seemed to them to be identified with France. But the defeat revived their old animosities: they made the Republic responsible for the collapse of the armies and wished to bring about a National Revolution—the only example in France in recent times of a revolution which had no popular origin.

The National Revolution was principally inspired by two tendencies: one, which dated from before the 1914 war, was Nationalism, the other, which came to birth ten years later, was "Personalism".

The influence of Nationalism reached the Marshal from two sources: on the one hand through an article concerned with military problems, and on the other through a political movement,

[1] With exception of René Belin. Cf., *supra*, p. 127.

the Action Française, of whose members his *entourage* at Vichy was largely composed.

When in 1891, there appeared in the *Revue des Deux Mondes*, under the title "The Social Role of the Officer in National Service", an unsigned article, which was known however to have been written by a young cavalry captain, there was something of a revolution in Nationalist and military circles. Soon published as a pamphlet, under the name of its author, Lyautey, it exalted the officer's independence of big business and political influence; it demonstrated the educative part he could play to the benefit of the thousands of recruits whom compulsory National Service brought each year from the school to the barracks. Furthermore, it extolled the simple hierarchical principles which assured discipline in the army.

During the early 1900's, the Action Française had among its members a whole team of writers who were endeavouring to give new meaning to the policy of the Right. Charles Maurras, Jacques Bainville, Léon Daudet and, later, Henri Massis criticised the Republican regime, which they considered both incapable of sustaining the authority of the State and of guaranteeing the true liberties of the nation.

They supported the idea of an hereditary king who would be above private interests and political parties. They also demanded decentralisation of power which, by giving the provinces and the professions back their autonomy, would allow the French to guarantee their own liberties instead of delegating their protection to an irresponsible parliament. From this resulted two principles of the Action Française: the decentralisation of the administration; and corporatism in the economic life of the country, that is to say the professions would organise and administer themselves without falling either into liberal anarchy or into the power of the State. This was also expressed in the famous distinction established by Charles Maurras between the "real country" on the one hand, which must be restored and which would be composed of natural communities, and the "legal country" on the other, which, in a Republican regime, needed to have both its impotence palliated and its abuses suppressed.

The State thus would become the protector of the nation against exterior or interior enemies: among the latter everything and everyone who was not of pure French stock or of pure French tradition—at least if the Action Française was to be believed—all foreigners, all recently naturalised Frenchmen, Freemasons, Jews and sometimes even Protestants—were all to be registered or removed from public employment.

Before England, Germany had been and remained France's enemy No. 1, not only for political reasons, but also for ideological ones, Maurras having consecrated a great deal of his work to the refutation of the German philosophy. The access of Hitler to power had not diminished this hostility, on the contrary indeed—totalitarianism seemed to Maurras a natural perversion of democracy.

Maurras, moreover, during the war, counted on neither of the sides engaged, neither on England, nor on Germany, to assure the future of France. His watchword, "France alone", shows him to have been anxious to the point of unreality concerning the autonomy of French politics.

Under the occupation, the sectarianism of the Action Française led to grave misunderstandings: Maurras, walled up in his deafness, isolated in his convictions, committed excesses of language whose consequences he failed to recognise. When, in 1943, he incriminated by name in his newspaper Frenchmen who were Gaullists, Freemasons or Jews, he acted under the sinister illusion that the French Government was still independent and alone in the exercise of justice on French territory. He did not realise that in naming Frenchmen to the Government, he was at the same time naming them to the occupying power. Maurras has been accused of intelligence with the enemy because, in his articles, he exposed Frenchmen to Hitler's repressive measures. In reality, what Maurras can be reproached with is not having had any understanding of the enemy, of not having grasped the fact that the enemy was there (and this for a politician was almost as grave a fault) and might gather, unknown to the author, information which was not intended for him.

"Personalism", formulated by a younger generation during the 1930's, had no such crystallisation as that represented by the Action Française in the case of the Nationalist tendency: it was not susceptible of systematisation.

Thus Personalism appeared in Christian papers of the Left, such as *Esprit*, edited by Emmanuel Mounier, in Catholic reviews of the Right, such as the *Revue Française* or the *Revue du Siécle*, edited by Jean de Fabrègues and Thierry Maulnier; it was also to be found in a review which had readers in all circles, the

*Ordre Nouveau*, edited by Arnaud Dandieu, under the significant motto: "Neither Right, nor Left".

Personalism had the same policy as the Action Française had originally; like it, like indeed most revolutionary movements, including Marxism in its first stages, it proposed to return to the realities and restore their initiative to the natural communities.

It was born of a period when men were becoming more and more aware that their personal liberties were being compromised by collective pressure; in economic matters, the great industries, either in the form of private or state-owned trusts were proletarianising the workers. In political matters, the totalitarian state, of recent appearance, was enslaving its citizens. The world had thus changed a lot in thirty years: a period in which Nationlism flourished was bound to react against excessive individualism. The period in which Personalism had come to birth had to defend itself against the various forms of collectivism and State control.

Personalism therefore asserted that the human individual was of supreme value and that the guarantee of his liberties should prevail over reasons of State; it was hostile to all suspensions of the law and to all discriminatory measures. Nationalism condemned the democratic rights of man and of the citizen as proceeding from an outmoded liberalism; Personalism recognised their human values, but endeavoured to restore them and adapt them in accordance with a new political system, in which no man could assure his independence merely by his own efforts.

On this basis it was not anti-democratic, nor fundamentally anti-Republican as was Nationalism. Democracy assuredly still corresponded to popular aspirations; Personalism merely demanded that it should be reformed in order to escape from the pressure of trusts, political parties, or the still more redoubtable pressure of the totalitarian states. To bring this about there would have to be a correspondingly new organisation of power, divided among the various levels, national or regional, on which the real life of the country took place, and in conformity with the old Republican tradition. That is to say that the nation is not itself the ultimate value, it is merely one of the levels of political life: nor indeed is the State the motivating power of all the activity of the country: it is a useful auxiliary in the service of the country's liberties, which implies that it should function with precision, but should never be dominant.

At the beginning of the new regime, there were a great number of followers of Maurras at Vichy, besides Alibert himself. Henri Massis, one of Maurras' intimate adherents and also one of the most powerful writers in the movement, was charged with elaborating the doctrine of youth and was not unaware of the risks of undertaking a National Revolution in such critical circumstances.

There were also at Vichy a number of less strict and less bigoted followers of Maurras, such as du Moulin de Labarthète, René Gillouin and Admiral Fernet, who at the beginning were all part of the Marshal's staff and frequently assisted in the writing of his Messages, as well as many others who, without being actually attached to the movement or aware of its precise thought, had been subjected to the contagion of its principles. Amid the shipwreck of other ideologies, Maurrasian dogmas came to their minds. Many had not even read Maurras' books. Many, if they had read them, would not have understood their implications; but everyone realised that here was a coherent and dominant system of thought.

Maurras, himself, was not one of the Marshal's intimates. In four years, he only came to Vichy four times.

The only direct intervention that Maurras seems to have made in Vichy politics was *in extremis* in 1944, when he gave his opinion, a somewhat severe one, on the last constitutional project put forward by the Marshal.

Pétain, himself, in spite of the sympathy which he always showed towards his colleague in the Académie Française, not being a doctrinaire himself, could not be a Maurrasian in any precise sense of that term—no more than he showed himself to be a Personalist. He did not follow the Action Française to the extremes of its thought, nor Maurras in his polemical excesses. The old writer, a prisoner of his own proud independence, isolated by his deafness and by the adoration of his *entourage*, made many mistakes that Pétain knew how to avoid. His Anglophobia became excessive, while the Marshal never broke with Great Britain but, on the other hand, multiplied unofficial contacts.

The Personalists were less numerous at Vichy than the Maurrasians.

The inspirers of the movement for the most part remained absent from the provisional capital. Neither the editorial staff of *Esprit*, nor that of the *Ordre Nouveau*, compromised in general with the movement's hostility towards the regime which had signed the armistice. But their policies had affected readers and sympathisers of whom some were to be found in the neighbourhood of the Hôtel du Parc.

Moreover, three men who, before the war, had been more or less allied to Personalist circles, were to exercise an episodic but undoubted influence upon the elaboration of the doctrine of the National Revolution: a syndicalist, René Belin, Minister of Production; a deputy, who had never played the parliamentary game, Gaston Bergery, whom the Marshal made successively one of his "*missi dominici*" and one of his ambassadors; and an engineer, Robert Loustau, whom Baudouin selected as head of his personal office in the Ministry for Foreign Affairs, but whose preoccupations were more economic and social.

All three had, before the war, made a name for themselves as independents or sharp-shooters in Trades Union political life. René Belin, as Deputy Secretary-General to the C.G.T., where he had fought against the politicisation of the workers' organisations, and as editor of the weekly, *Syndicats*, which had a similar political tendency. He therefore represented a minority of French Trades Unionism, less opportunist than Jouhaux, and less sectarian than the Communists. Gaston Bergery, as founder and National Secretary of an embryonic movement, Frontisme, of which he was the sole representative in Parliament, had reached his apogee on the day that party voted alone and unanimously in the Chamber against war subsidies. He was also director of the Independent weekly, *La Flèche*, whose policy was to save France from foreign influences and from the power of financial interests. Robert Loustau, a mining engineer, was interested in social questions and economic doctrines and owed his political outlook to the *Ordre Nouveau*.

In July, 1940, these men, Nationalists or Personalists, felt that the moment had come for a break with the past.

Pétain himself was not, in the beginning, a partisan of the National Revolution. He would have been content, as we have seen, to govern within the framework of the Republican regime on condition that the Parliamentary Assemblies were dismissed.

The very word Revolution shocked him. He said that, rather than use "a word that we do not know", he would have preferred

French Recovery as in the time of Ernest Mercier, or National Resurgence.

But the influence of his *entourage* and of his advisers led him little by little to adopt a new motto: "Work, Family, Country," and to accept the expression "National Revolution".

The National Revolution had nothing comparable to what the *Declaration of Human Rights* was to Liberal thought, the *Communist Manifesto* to Marxism or *Mein Kampf* to National Socialism. Instead, it had a number of short texts, often drawn up under the pressure of events by the Marshal, the Head of the State, and addressed to the population. Their character smacks more of a conversation with the nation than of a magisterial or doctrinal thesis. They are *Words to the French People.*

During the first period of the National Revolution, the Marshal addressed the nation some twenty times. At the start, in the days which immediately preceded or followed the termination of hostilities, short announcements followed rapidly on each other: four appeals in eight days between the 17th and 25th June. It was a question of explaining to the French the reasons for the armistice and of outlining a plan of reconstruction. On the 17th June, for the first time, the Marshal, as soon as he had been appointed President of the Council, presented himself to the nation as the man destined to ask for an armistice "with honour" and then to re-establish the future of France.

On the 20th June, he explained the causes of the defeat, military, political but moral also: the spirit of pleasure had prevailed over the spirit of sacrifice.

On the 23rd June, the Marshal, without glossing over France's misfortunes, declared his confidence in the future.

"It may happen that one of our peasants sees his harvest devastated by hail. He does not despair of the next harvest. He tills the same land with the same faith in order to grow future corn."

Finally, on the 25th June, the day on which the armistice came into force, Pétain evoked the "new order" which was beginning, the "intellectual and moral recovery" which must be accomplished: "I hate the lies which have done you so much harm. But the earth does not lie . . ." the Marshal concluded, uniting two themes that he was ceaselessly to reiterate: a return to reality and a return to the land which, according to him, expressed and symbolised it.

On the 11th July, explaining the confidence which the country had placed in him, commenting on the drama of Mers-el-Kebir, he elaborated his first proposals and drew up a complete plan for the reconstruction of France. He stated his hope of bringing the Government back to Paris, his anxiety to avoid the double errors of Socialism and Capitalism, his desire to promote new and eternal values of Work, Family and Country, and to make new plans for the Government and the administration.

Soon the main lines of the new policy and of the structural reform were laid down. On the 11th October, he delivered the first of his important Messages in which he dealt in turn with all the problems of the Government, foreign policy, internal policy, economic policy. On the 13th and 14th November, he made two statements to journalists on the incidence of the reorganisation of the State. On the 18th November, he spoke on economic affairs. It was an elaborate plan of construction which will be described later on.

He similarly dealt with educational reform and social policy in two articles in the *Revue des deux Mondes*, on the 15th August and the 15th September. While the *Revue Universelle*, on the 1st January, 1941, under the title of "Individualism and the Nation", outlined the philosophy of the new regime.

Thus, little by little, day by day, in speech or by the written word, by talks on the wireless or in speeches made directly to an audience, the National Revolution took shape.

What part did Pétain take in drawing up these speeches and articles? Was he their only author, or did he call upon collaborators?

The Marshal was no creator or innovator; he was, rather, an amalgamator.

He knew how to impose his own style on drafts prepared by others, select ideas from those put forward by others and formulate a synthesis in accordance with his own temperament.

Pétain employed these methods for his Messages as Head of the State. The first draft of the Message of the 20th June, was made by an officer, Commandant Minart, who was only a temporary member of Pétain's *entourage*. Among the Marshal's collaborators, Bouthillier was soon one of the most frequent. Then the team grew bigger. René Gillouin drafted the texts of the 13th August, 1940, and the 13th July, 1941. Bergery that of the 11th October, 1940. Robert Loustau the Saint-Étienne Message of the 1st March, 1941. Henri Massis drew up the Messages aimed at the youth of the country. Du Moulin de Labarthète those of Christmas, 1940, and the Feast of Joan of Arc in 1941. And on many other occasions General Laure, Admiral Fernet or Caziot undertook this duty.

Thus, Pétain made an amalgam of such ideas about him as seemed to him new and valuable. Once the definitive text had been established, he claimed that he was its only author. When, in 1942, an individual whom Pétain knew well through family connexions was going on a secret mission to Portugal for La France Combattante, the Marshal asked him to enquire of Salazar what he thought of them and added this categorical assertion: "I've read his. They aren't as good as mine."

It was a claim to authorship that was not only justified by the part Pétain took in their composition. The texts bear witness to two characteristics that were peculiarly his own: the humane tone in which he expressed himself and the philosophy which seemed to arise out of it.

As he himself said, the Marshal spoke sometimes with the voice of a father, sometimes with that of a leader. And the *Words to the French People* benefited by this new tone in the relationship between a Head of the State and the nation. They were far removed from Hitler's frenzy, Mussolini's emphasis and as far from the verbosity so frequent among parliamentary orators.

"You have suffered. You will have more to suffer yet. Many among you will not recover your trade or your house. Your life will be hard. I shall not endeavour to soothe you with false words. I hate the lies which have done you so much harm. But the earth does not lie. It remains your recourse. It is the Fatherland itself. A field lying fallow, is a portion of France dying. Fallow land that is sewn again, is a portion of France reborn."

"Life is not neutral; it consists in taking sides boldly. No neutrality is possible between truth and falsehood, between good and evil, between health and sickness, between order and disorder, between France and anti-France."

It is true that occasionally the style loses something of its simplicity and acquires a certain demagogic tendency.

"Think upon these maxims: 'Pleasure lowers, joy elevates; pleasure weakens, joy gives strength' . . . 'May the springtime of our youth soon expand into the springtime of renascent France'.

"I keep all promises, even those of others . . ."

According to Pétain, the doctrine of the National Revolution presented a dual character. Spiritually, it claimed to derive from Christian civilisation. Politically, it was a reaction against the democratic concepts of the Third Republic.

Pétain himself, if he was a believer, certainly did not practise his religion: it was not until 1945, when he was in prison, that he renewed the habit of taking Holy Communion. But he always respected the teaching of the Church and the social role the Church played. It was one of the principal points that differentiated his policy from that of National Socialism. The official annotator of *Words to the French People*, Gabriel-Louis Jaray, wrote that for two centuries there had been a struggle between religion and materialism, "between those who, believing in the natural goodness of man, deify the forces of nature and those who, battling against the evil tendencies of man, wish to dominate them by subjecting them to Christian law."

It was in this sense that Pétain insisted on the importance of "the simple rules" which "have in all times been the basis of the life, the health and the prosperity of nations."

In the first place, respect for the family and the child:

"Rejuvenated France is determined that the child shall fill your hearts with the hope that vivifies and not with the fear that withers. It will give you back the confidence you have lost in the child's education and future.

"The families of France remain the depositories of a long and honourable past. Their duty is to maintain across the generations the ancient virtues that make a people strong.

"Family discipline will be safeguarded."

He affirmed the priority of work which, alone, could recover and consolidate the country:

"One of the great inventions of Christianity was to teach man to accept freely the necessity of work and to confer a spiritual value on the most humble labour. We aspire with all our soul to restore this value, which is ultimately based on a sense of duty and a respect for human individuality."

Labour must be protected against "international capitalism and international socialism" which have exploited and degraded it . . . For our misled society money, too often the servant and instrument of falsehood, was a means of domination . . . "In renascent France, money will be but the wages of effort."

Above all, it was necessary to return to those forms of labour which had always been considered the most pure and the most authentic; the Marshal incessantly extolled a return to the land, he praised the handicrafts, in which individual ability has greater opportunity than in great industries and in which the worker remains free in his professional life.

It was a somewhat archaic and paternalistic conception: it showed, however, that for Pétain true freedom was not exclusively an attribute of political democracy. The latter might give the appearance of it: the reality lay elsewhere.

Finally, it was necessary to control man without oppressing him, to allow him to expand in natural communities without crushing him beneath the power of the State. From this arose the definition Pétain gave of the new regime:

"National in foreign policy, hierarchical in internal policy, economically co-ordinated and controlled and, above all, social in spirit."

The National Revolution therefore presented itself as an authoritarian regime which was not a dictatorship, a corporative regime which was not totalitarian, and a libertarian regime which was not anarchic.

The solutions advocated by the National Revolution varied according to whether it was a question of economic or political structures. In the first case, it extolled "corporatism", that is to say the organisation of professional freedoms; in the second, the multiplication of the representatives of the central power and the extension of their functions.

The "corporatism" of the National Revolution consisted, as do all "corporatisms", in organising the activities of the various branches of industry and trade and the professions. But, while the totalitarian "corporatism" of Fascism in Italy or of National Socialism in Germany subjected by this means professional life to the exclusive direction of the State, the French "corporatism" of the National Revolution proposed that each profession should organise and govern itself freely. It was still no doubt a controlled economy, but not controlled by the State, "auto-controlled" rather. Professional organisations, in principle, chose their own leaders, drew up their own rules and, when needed, their own plans; each leader was on the level suited to him and freely took such decisions as did not exceed his competence. In theory, the State had only to intervene to arbitrate in certain disputes and bring production plans into harmony with the general interest.

On the other hand, in political and administrative life, all power emanated from the State: nothing would be done except by the State or by its delegates. It was a question of achieving a "revolution from the top" which "would descend step by step to the very basis of the State and the nation". Government consisted, therefore, in transmitting the orders of the central authoritarian power to the various existing levels, and eventually creating new ones. Over the heads of Prefects and sub-Prefects, it was desired to superimpose Governors; departments were to be grouped into provinces or regions.

Each Prefect or Governor would have a Council whose members he would select himself in agreement with the central power; and this Council would have no more than advisory powers.

"For cities and townships, I should feel inclined to make an act of authority as I already have done in the case of certain towns, but on the other hand we shall extend the authority of the Mayors. You must, however, expect the Mayors to be nominated by the Government."

An almost dictatorial attitude which precisely differentiated the political doctrine of the National Revolution from its economic doctrine. In these two cases, the National Revolution pursued courses which were practically totally opposed. On the one hand favouring freedom and on the other centralisation in the State. In its early days, it appeared, in its principles, to be a hybrid resulting from contradictory tendencies, which perhaps corresponded to the diversity of its sources of inspiration.

But, in spite of its contradictions and its failures, the theoretical importance of the National Revolution must not be underestimated. No one can take up any true position outside Stalinism, Fascism or Liberalism, without having first considered the Vichy experiment, with all its merits and all its faults, with all its truths and all its fallacies.

But now we must consider an essential question: was the

doctrine of the National Revolution entirely French or was it, due to the circumstances, subject to National Socialist influences?

Its sources, as we have seen, were French.

"The new order," said the Marshal in his Message of the 11th October, "must not be a servile imitation of foreign experiments; certain of these experiments are sensible and fine, but every nation must develop a regime adapted to its climate and its genius. The new order is a French necessity."

National Socialism was basically anti-Christian, not only because of the Semitic origins of Christian thought, but because it contrasted Christianity, "the religion of weakness", with the Germanic virtues. In the second place, National Socialism was centralised in the State. This is particularly evident in the conception of a "corporatism" subjected to the central power and in which producers have no longer any opportunity of defending their autonomy, but are reduced to being no more than State servants of production. There was, therefore, an utter incompatibility of principle between the National Revolution and National Socialism.

Obvious though this may be, the Marshal, in an article published by the *Revue des deux Mondes*, on the 15th September, 1940, nevertheless emphasised the analogies between his doctrine and that of National Socialism. A comparison in which he did not show any very precise knowledge of Nazism; rather the contrary!

This single reference to National Socialist ideology occurred at a period when the Marshal desired a meeting with Hitler. Indeed, his sincerity must be doubted.

Nevertheless, the last phrase supports the principal argument of those who deny the French character of the National Revolution, for it is indeed certain that, intentionally or not, the National Revolution contributed to the integration of France with the new European order founded by the Third Reich.

When Pétain, extolling a return to the land, defined France's vocation as being primarily agricultural, his first aim was undoubtedly to encourage the moral renascence of France; but, at the same time, his policy had its place in the plan of European reconstruction which the Führer wished to realise. Heavy industry the key to economic power and the essential element in all political and military power, was to be reserved to Germany or subjected to her control. The secondary or satellite countries, in whose ranks her defeat had placed France, were to content themselves with producing the foodstuffs for Nazified Europe.

The doctrine of the National Revolution appears therefore as a French conception adapted in one important point to a period of German predominance.

This ambiguity risked compromising the Vichy policies. Would French originality be preserved or would the Nazi influence turn out to be the stronger?

CHAPTER 4

# THE NATIONAL REVOLUTION—REALISATIONS

THE Marshal's Government had, in principle, no need to account to anyone. There were no more parliamentary debates, no more votes that could restrict its action. Even the Commissions of the Assemblies which, on the 10th July, Laval had left with the hope that they would be recalled, were not consulted.

Freed of all control, the Ministers made laws at a speed which had not been known for a very long time . . . "The *Journal Officiel* of the 19th September alone contained not less than 45 laws and 27 decrees."

"No period in our history, since the Consulate, had seen so great a re-organisation," a contemporary asserted.

What were to be the results of this Revolution of the Right, a unique experiment in France?

During the course of the first six months, there were three facts which were incontestably apparent: the country had been restored to order, the Rights of Man had been abolished, and a new order had been instituted.

The first was merely a matter of administrative and practical organisation: the other two, by contrast, corresponded to a political upheaval.

### *The Restoration of Order in the Country*

It was a considerable task to re-establish more or less normal life in a nation which had succumbed to paralysis, whose population was dispersed and whose whole economy had been adapted to war production and then brutally interrupted.

In order to deal with the most pressing matters, the new regime, during the month which followed its inauguration by the National Assembly, took provisional measures: a moratorium on payments, cancellation of Government contracts for national defence, compensated by initial loans to businesses in difficulty, laws concerning food-stuffs tending on the one hand to diminish consumption (ration cards) and on the other to allow of importations into Metropolitan France of colonial produce, thanks to advances by the Treasury and insurances against war risks for the importers.

At the same time, the Government attacked two problems which had attained unique proportions: that of the refugees, who numbered 3,800,000; and that of the unemployed, whose numbers, immediately following on the armistice, could not even be estimated: it was clear however that a million and a half workmen, who had been employed in armament factories, would now be workless, without counting the factories which had either been dispersed or shut down.

Within three months, a gigantic counter-exodus involved the return home of all displaced persons, except for 300,000 who either could or would not return to the occupied zone.

By the same date, the unemployed were in process of being re-absorbed: a measure of extreme urgency permitted each Préfecture to obtain the necessary credits for putting major works in hand: a telephone call to the Ministry of Finance, indicating the nature of the work, the number of workmen it would employ and its cost, was sufficient for permission to go ahead without further formalities.

By this means, 6,000 schemes in connection with the railways or the roads were put in hand. Canals and harbours were re-opened, two-thirds of the network of electric power began functioning again. By the end of the year, the total number of unemployed was less than 900,000.

Thus were the ruins cleared and the victims provisionally relieved. It was now necessary to organise the labour market on a durable basis.

Those engaged in "black labour", that is to say paid work over and above the legally permitted number of hours, were tracked down by obliging all self-employed persons to register in the trade or commercial lists.

The quota of foreign labour, suspended during hostilities, was restored.

Women were removed from employment, at least those whose husbands were already supporting the household. This had a double advantage: to provide more jobs and keep wives in their homes, which was in conformity with Vichy's family policy. The State made grants to young married couples, who on their side promised to devote themselves to their families.

Finally, the working week was limited to less than forty hours, a commission was set up to deal with unemployment and unemployment benefits were increased.

Such were the practical advantages of an authoritarian regime. Its disadvantages were as follows:

*The Abolition of the Rights of Man*

"We, Marshal of France, Head of the French State . . . the Council of Ministers being in agreement, DECREE . . ." These words, drawn up by the Government of a defeated country, which was three-fifths occupied by the enemy, preceded, from the 11th July, 1940, all Pétain's legislative decisions: after seventy years of a Parliamentary Republic they strike one as somewhat surprising.

The three first constitutional acts, signed on the day following the National Assembly, and promulgated in the *Journal Officiel* of the 12th July, implied indeed a radical change of regime.

Drawn up secretly by Laval and Alibert even before the sitting of the Assembly, safe from all German interference, according to plans conceived long before by Pétain's "preceptor", these documents form one of the shortest and most brutal pieces of constitutional machinery of which French history can furnish an example.

By Constitutional Act No. 1, which consisted of five lines, Pétain abrogated the Presidency of the Republic and declared that he "assumed the functions of the Head of the French State".

By Constitutional Act No. 2, the rights and prerogatives of the Head of the State were defined in ten paragraphs. He acquired "full governmental powers", and the power of appointing and dismissing "Ministers and Secretaries of State who are responsible only to him". "He exercises legislative power in the Council of Ministers" until the formation of new Assemblies and, after their formation, "in case of external tension or serious internal crisis". "He promulgates the laws and assures their being put into execution." "He has the right of appointment to all civil and military posts, for which the law has not laid down some other method of nomination." "He is invested with control of the armed forces", "with the right of reprieve and amnesty", "the right to negotiate and ratify treaties", "and may declare a state of siege".

There was only one reservation, which corresponded to the pledges given on the 10th July: "He cannot declare war without previous assent from the Legislative Assemblies."

This constitutional law gave Pétain greater powers than those of the ancient Kings of France.

Constitutional Act No. 3 dealt with the future of Parliament. In conformity with the promise given by Laval on the 10th July in Pétain's name, Clause 1 left the Senate and the Chamber of Deputies in being, "until the formation of the Assemblies laid down by the Constitutional Law of the 10th July, 1940", but Clause 2 circumvented the promise made to the National Assembly by placing Parliament in recess:

"The Senate and the Chamber of Deputies are adjourned until further orders.

"In future they may only meet on being convoked by the Head of the State."

Constitutional Act No. 4, signed immediately after the 12th July, and promulgated in the *Journal Officiel* on the 23rd July, dealt with the provisional structure of the new French State. It dealt with the questions of the deputy and successor to the Head of the State; it re-established the "*delphinat*", a dignity abolished in France since the Ancien Régime, and whose first incumbent was to be Pierre Laval.

This was a constitutional arrangement which did not fail to provoke considerable astonishment: "I would never have expected," said Weygand, "that a marriage between a Marshal of France and the Republic could produce Pierre Laval for offspring." But, rather than a marriage, was not this in reality a divorce between Pétain and the Republic?

A fortnight later, there was a fifth Constitutional Act, signed on 30th July and promulgated on the 31st July in the *Journal Officiel*, inaugurating an institution which was to allow the new Head of the State to bring his Republican predecessors to trial:

"A Supreme Court of Justice is created whose organisation, competence and procedure will be laid down by law."

This was an explicit document which made political repression subject to the Marshal's pleasure. Justice was also subject to his authority.

Constitutional Act No. 6, of the 1st December, 1940, published in the *Journal Officiel* of the 4th December, 1940, authorised the Marshal to pronounce the disqualification of members of Parliament:

"In accordance with the Constitutional Law of the 19th July, 1940.

"When there is occasion to disqualify a Deputy or a Senator, this disqualification will be confirmed by decree made on the recommendation of the Garde des Sceaux, Minister Secretary of State for Justice, and of the Minister Secretary of State for the Interior."

Long before the promulgation of this last Act, the Republic was already dead. In most public buildings, the democratic formula "Liberty, Equality, Fraternity" had been replaced by "Work, Family, Country", a device due to the collaboration of Alibert with a certain Doublet, who, having founded before the war a Committee for the Family, suggested the second word.

Seven days after the vote of the National Assembly there began a series of discriminatory measures which in fact resulted in the abolition of the Rights of Man as defined by the Declaration of 1789.

This new legislation re-introduced two offences which had long been off the statute book, the offence of subversive opinion and the offence of belonging to subversive organisations, the latter permitting an innocent man, if he belonged to some organisation which was considered detrimental, to be prosecuted; it also made these laws retroactive.

These discriminatory measures, which upset the traditional idea of the law, followed quickly upon each other during the first months.

In July, they made it possible that, by simple ministerial decree, all magistrates, functionaries, civil or military personnel could be relieved of their posts; they closed all public employment to people born of a foreign father; they enjoined the revision of all naturalisations granted since 1927; they announced that all persons who had left French Metropolitan territory for abroad between 10th May and 30th June, 1940, were disqualified from holding French nationality; and they created a Supreme Court of Justice to try the Ministers and ex-Ministers of the Third Republic who were "accused of having committed crimes or misdemeanours in the exercise or on the occasion of their functions or who had betrayed their responsibilities".

In August, all secret associations were forbidden; all civil servants had to take an oath that they did not belong to any forbidden organisation.

This law of the 13th August was aimed in particular at Freemasonry.

In September there was a law which allowed, on a mere prefectorial decision, the arrest of all persons deemed "dangerous" to National Defence or Public Security. The law also set up a Court-Martial for the purpose of trying, as a matter of urgency, the followers of de Gaulle.

In October there was a law concerning the status of Jews, which prohibited them from holding most public posts and positions of control in the Press and in industry; there were also laws authorising the internment of foreign Jews and withdrawing the status of French citizenship from Algerian Jews. There was also a law suspending General Councils and Councils of Arrondissements.

In November, a new law authorised the Ministry of the Interior to announce the dismissal from office of General Councillors, Councillors of Arrondissements and Municipal Councillors.

These discriminatory measures formed one of the most completely repressive series of laws that France had ever known: from then on, there was no single person in France, whatever his associations or his personal status, who might not become subject to administrative sanctions. There were certain categories of Frenchmen who, *a priori*, were excluded from the protection of the laws. There was now no longer any elected political assembly which was not subject to the decisions of the Government. The Republican regime was dead.

The majority of these discriminatory measures, inspired by the nationalist and anti-Republican principles of the National Revolution, did not provoke much argument in the Council of Ministers; they appeared to an authoritarian Government as normal, indeed indispensable, measures against those supposedly responsible for the decadence of France.

Two of them however did give rise to discussion, either among Ministers, or between the Government and the German authorities: the law of the 13th August concerning secret associations, and that of the 3rd October concerning the Jews.

At the beginning of July, the question of Freemasonry was raised by Alibert and the Maurrasians among the Marshal's *entourage*, who imputed to the Freemasons all the misfortunes, old and new, to which France had been subject. After 1918, so they declared, an international conspiracy among Freemasons had sabotaged the victory and constrained France to accept Wilson's Fourteen Points.

Twenty years later, Freemasonry had clearly been responsible for the incoherence of French foreign policy. How else could the fact be explained, if not by some occult intervention by Freemasons, so it was asserted at Vichy, that France had tolerated, in March 1938, without protest, the annexation of a Catholic country such as Austria while risking war over the annexation of Czechoslovakia whose President, Bènès, was a Freemason?

And on the 13th August, Alibert proposed to the Council of Ministers that the principal Lodges should be dissolved: "the Grand Orient, the Grand Lodge and the Human Rights."

But each party had its own scapegoats: for those of the Right it was the Lodges, for those of the Left The Two Hundred Families and the Trusts. The Minister of Production, René Belin, a man of the Left, blamed the latter and demanded that they should be dissolved at the same time as the Masonic organisations.

When he was asked what secret societies besides the Lodges should, in his view, be suppressed, he replied: "For example the Comité des Forges and the Comité des Houillères, who have long been taking secret action, notably in the Press." These words, no doubt, created a certain amount of stupefaction in the Council: M. Mireaux, then Secretary of State at the Ministry of Education and director of *Le Temps* newspaper, who had good reason to know of the activities of the Trusts in relation to the Press, was present at the Council and said not a word. After some rather embarrassed controversy, the Marshal, pointing a finger at his Trades Union Minister, said magisterially: "M. Belin is right."

And the law of the 13th October, 1940, without mentioning Freemasonry by name, announced the dissolution of "all associations or groups whose activities take place, even partially, in clandestine or secret ways".

The measures against the Jews were among those which stirred public opinion the most, both in France and abroad.

It is, therefore, all the more important to specify precisely their origin and their significance.

An anti-Semitism based on Nationalism had, particularly since the Dreyfus Affair, very deep roots in the restricted circles of the extreme Right without however, having ever affected the rest of the population.

The defeat, blamed by a considerable section of public opinion on the misdeeds of the Popular Front and of the Minister, Léon Blum, increased, after June 1940, its propagation among the public, but in a form very different from Nazi anti-Semitism.

While Nazi anti-Semitism was racial and took into sole consideration, in its definition of a Jew, the race of an individual's grandparents, French anti-Semitism, represented by the Action Française among others, tended in its origins to be inspired by religious and national considerations.

Xavier Vallat, first Commissaire for Jewish Questions at Vichy, during his trial in the High Court, tenaciously defined his position, which was also that of Alibert.

In the first place, from the religious point of view, it was not, according to him, desirable that members of a minority cult should exercise an influence in Christian countries.

From the Nationalist point of view, Xavier Vallat declared moreover that, *a priori*, the Jew was an unassimilable and disruptive element in the French community: he proclaimed his "wish to defend the French organism from the microbe which was producing in it a fatal anaemia".

In practice he allowed, if not exceptions, at least ameliorations, to this generalisation. Careful to take into account the French qualifications of certain categories of Jews, he distinguished between the old Jewish families of Alsatian origin, whom he was prepared to admit where "sufficiently assimilated"—those Jewish families who had arrived in France after the Third Republic and who had many ex-Servicemen of the 1914–1918 war among their number—and the mass of Central European Jews, who had emigrated during the last twenty years from Poland, Austria, Czechoslovakia and above all Rumania, "a category which it is impossible to consider as being French." Tending thus to reduce the Jewish problem to the particular case of foreigners residing in France who had not yet been assimilated, he declared that ex-Servicemen, who had "received the baptism of blood", were to be exempted from most of the discriminatory measures.

His doctrine, shocking and sectarian as it was, was nevertheless strikingly different from that of the Nazis: "There is no question of imitating the legislation of any totalitarian regime: it is merely in pursuance of an anti-Jewish tradition in the State, for which precedents can be found, not only in the past history of our country but in that of Christianity."

If the anti-Jewish laws had been inspired merely by French anti-Semitism, they would have had to take into account, in order to define who would be subject to them, two criteria only, both of which have nothing to do with racialism: that of religion and that of nationality.

The elaboration of the French Jewish statute began at the beginning of October, 1940, when Alibert took into association a young auditor of accounts to the Council of State in order to draw up the anti-Semitic measures.

On the 27th August, a law appeared in the Press which annulled Daladier's decree of the 21st April, 1939, which punished slander and libel "towards a group of people who belong by origin to a particular race or a particular religion". This abrogation was put forward as a return to the liberty of the Press: a surprising consideration for the period. In fact, it was a method of assuring to the Government the support of the Press for the proposed measures.

During the course of this period of preparation, a new circumstance supervened. Violating the Hague Convention, which forbade the occupying power to legislate, the German military authorities, on the 27th September, promulgated in the occupied zone an ordinance concerning measures to be taken against the Jews.

It defined as Jews those persons who belonged to the Jewish religion or had more than two Jewish grandparents.

It forbade Jews who had left the occupied zone to return there. It obliged Jews to register at the Sous-Préfectures; it compelled all businesses, whose proprietor or manager was Jewish, to exhibit a placard drawn up in German and French announcing that the business was Jewish.

Two days before the promulgation of the ordinance, the French Government had protested to the German authorities in Paris, as is evidenced by an unpublished note addressed to them by Baudouin:

"General de la Laurencie informs us that he has been advised by the liaison officer of the chief of the German Military Administration that certain measures are very shortly to be taken against the Israelites. According to the Colonel's statement . . . these measures will give effect to the four following points:

"1. No Israelite will be permitted by the German authorities to pass from the free zone into the occupied zone.

"2. The Israelites at this moment residing in the occupied zone will be permitted to remain there. They will, however, be compelled to report to the police under conditions not as yet precisely specified.

"3. Business houses and shops belonging to Israelites will receive a special placard, to be clearly displayed, indicating that their proprietors are non-Aryan.

"4. All businesses belonging to Israelites who have not yet returned to the occupied territory are to be placed in the hands of a manager.

"Without going into the details of the problems thus raised by the occupying authorities, I am to inform you that the decision taken by the General seems to call for the following observations:

"The measures which the German Administration propose to apply go further than the exercise of the rights granted to the occupying power in their totality: they tend to create in one portion of French territory a regime affecting a minority and by unilateral action on the part of the German Authorities in a realm which is subject to the French Authorities alone. They destroy the administrative unity of France, a unity which, indeed, was recognised by the Armistice Convention.

"There is another point to which I must also animadvert. In applying the measures in question, upon what basis do the German Authorities propose to establish the discriminatory regime they have in mind? Racial characteristics and the terminology of names are often uncertain criteria. As for the religious basis, it is difficult to invoke this in France where individuals are not compelled officially to declare the religion to which they belong and where birth certificates do not mention the religion to which the parents have belonged. This uncertainty creates a danger of precipitating regrettable incidents."

This unpublished note is extremely revealing of the initial attitude of the French Government towards the Jewish question: it considered Jewish legislation necessary, but did not wish to let the initiative in this matter pass to the Germans.

A few days later, the Government discussed the problem.

And on the 18th October, in the *Journal Officiel*, appeared the first Jewish Statute, dated 3rd October.[1]

French anti-Semitism manifested itself, in conformity with its principles, in two kinds of measures: in the first place, it excluded Jews from public employment, with a few exceptions in favour of ex-Servicemen who were authorised to remain in subaltern appointments. They were forbidden all employment in journalism, films, theatre and radio. That is to say, they were denied professions in which they might exercise authority or influence. Nevertheless, industry, agriculture and commerce remained accessible to them in the southern zone, while the German measures, in the occupied zone, compelled the Aryanisation of all businesses belonging to Israelites.[2]

German anti-Semitism, however, marked an important desideratum in the definition of a Jew. But the statute of the 18th October[3] reproduced and even went beyond, in one particular, the German definition as it is to be found in the decree of the 27th September, 1940, promulgated in the occupied zone. This defined as Jews not only those who belonged or had belonged to the Jewish religion, but those who had more than two Jewish grandparents. It was therefore the ethnic origin which was more important than the personal circumstances of those it affected; owing to this bias, the racial criterion eclipsed all other forms of discrimination, whether religious or national.

On the 8th October, 1940, Abetz, German Ambassador in Paris, informed Ribbentrop that he had heard from Peyrouton of the measures which the forthcoming Jewish Statute would contain. He noted with satisfaction that the French law would consider as Jewish anyone having more than two Jewish grandparents, "exactly as in Germany," he added.

In the French law, as in German law, a Catholic priest of Jewish origin did not cease to be a Jew. While a Jew coming from a family which had been French for generations was still not considered to be wholly French.

[1] Cf., *supra*, p. 164.

[2] The second Jewish Statute of the 2nd June, 1941, and a subsidiary law of the 20th July, extended the spoliations practised in the northern zone to the southern one.

[3] The French law went further than the German in the matter of defining a Jew by taking into consideration the race of the husband or wife: a man or woman having but two Jewish grandparents was considered a Jew if married to a Jew.

In thus adopting the German definition, French law appeared more severe than that of many satellite countries of the Third Reich.

The adoption by the Vichy Government of racial measures, which had never previously existed in France and had been inaugurated by the Nazis, appeared to many as "a proof of a loss of independence".

It was to arouse much anxiety, as is evidenced by a brief note sent by Léon Blum, at the time interned by Vichy, to Ambassador Scapini who was responsible for the protection of French prisoners of war.

The ex-President of the Council, having just learned of the Jewish Statute, expressed but one anxiety: it was that in the prison camps in Germany, the French officers and soldiers, who had become subject to anti-Semitic measures, would be separated from their comrades and placed in special camps. That a distinction should be made in the presence of the enemy between Frenchmen who had all fought equally for their country seemed to him intolerable.

The measures taken by the Marshal's Government against the statesmen of the Third Republic passed through many phases.

On Pétain's suggestion, the Government decided to lease a château in the neighbourhood of Vichy, which could be used as a place of forced residence for the ex-Ministers.

At the beginning of September, the Château de Chazeron was selected and, on the 3rd September, a law formulated solely for the future beneficiaries of this "protective hospitality" authorised administrative internment.

About the 5th September, Reynaud, Gamelin and Daladier were taken to Chazeron. On the 9th September, Mandel joined them there in a very bad state of health.

On the 15th September, it was Léon Blum's turn; on the 19th that of Guy La Chambre, ex-Minister for Air, who had come back from America in order to stand his trial in France. On the 25th, Vincent Auriol, Marx Dormoy, Salomon Grumbach and Jules Moch were imprisoned, on the 27th, Schrameck, ex-Minister of the Interior; on the 30th, Pomaret, even though he had been a Minister in Pétain's Cabinet from the 17th June to the 10th July: he was accused of having, since that date, said things which were lacking in respect to the Head of the State. Since Marius

Moutet, ex-Minister for the Colonies in the Popular Front Government could not be found, his son Jacques, a Paris lawyer, was taken to Chazeron in his stead.

The same severity was shown towards the Jews. The consequences of the Jewish Statute did not all become manifest before 1941. But, from the end of 1940 onwards, the Garde des Sceaux, Alibert, concerned himself with the strict application of racial legislation.

Towards the conspicuous followers of General de Gaulle, the Government showed no greater indulgence.

The law of the 23rd July, 1940, which deprived civilians who had left national soil between 10th May and 30th June of French nationality and condemned to death members of the Services who had been guilty of the same crime, permitting in every case confiscation of property, produced some spectacular victims. Among them were Pierre Cot, Baron Édouard de Rothschild, Philippe, Henri, Robert and Maurice de Rothschild, René Clair, Vera Korène, a member of the Comédie-Française, Alexis Léger, ex-Secretary General to the Ministry of Foreign Affairs, General de Gaulle, General Catroux, General Legentilhomme and Colonel de Larminat.

General de Gaulle, himself, having been summoned to surrender to military justice, was condemned to death in his absence on the 2nd August, 1940, by the Military Tribunal of Clermont-Ferrand. In the margin of the judgment pronounced against the leader of Free France, of whom he said however: "He is a serpent whom I have nourished in my bosom," Pétain wrote: ". . . It is evident that this judgment by default can but be one of principle. It has never been my intention to put it into effect . . ."

The Court of Gannat, created on the 24th September, devoted itself to trying Gaullists. In January, 1941, on the demand of Alibert, it tried General Catroux, Colonel Brosset and Captain Robert. The first two were condemned to death in their absence, the third was acquitted.

Moreover, the Court of Gannat, which functioned till October 1941, on which date it was suppressed, only convicted twenty people, all in their absence.

The Law of the 22nd July, which was concerned with the revision of naturalisations, was at first applied far from rigorously. The commission set up by Alibert, instead of de-naturalising eighty per cent. as was required, only announced a total of three per cent. in the first six months, and Alibert had to sign but 442 decrees.

As for the civil servants, there are no official statistics to establish the number of victims of the law of the 17th July. However, in searching the *Journal Officiel* for decrees of dismissal the following approximate figures for 1940 can be obtained:

| | | |
|---|---|---|
| Ministry of Finance | 686 | |
| Ministry of War | 435 | (Civilian personnel) |
| Ministry of Justice | 285 | |
| Ministry of Interior | 335 | |
| Ministry of Education | 137 | |
| Ministry of Marine | 125 | |
| Ministry of Agriculture | 89 | |
| Ministry of Foreign Affairs | 35 | |
| Ministry for Colonies | 99 | |
| Ministry of Production | 56 | |

Among the "purged" the vast majority were among the higher ranks. Thus the Prefectorial administration had almost half its senior ranks dismissed: 49 Préfets, 58 Sous-Préfets and Secretary-Generals. Among the personnel of the Ministry for Foreign Affairs who were dismissed were a considerable number of Ambassadors.

For the principal Ministries an approximate total can be arrived at of 2,282 Civil Servants of all grades who were affected by this despotic law.

This figure, somewhat inaccurate though it may be, nevertheless gives the proportion of three in a thousand Civil Servants dismissed in six months.

By absolute standards of value, this number of innocent victims was scandalous in a country which, less than fifty years before, at the time of the Dreyfus case, had become impassioned over the fate of one man. Relatively, however, the number of these victims confirm that at the beginning, though the repressive measures were harsh, they were limited in scope.

So far as elected councils and municipal servants were concerned, the case was much the same: the suspension of 163 Municipal Councils is recorded, among which were those of the big towns: the Council of Paris and the General Council of the Seine were suppressed and their powers conferred respectively upon the Prefect of the Seine and the Prefect of Police; that of Marseille (presided over by M. Tasso, Senator and Mayor); those of Lyon, (presided over by Édouard Herriot, Deputy and Mayor), of Toulouse, Vienne, and Montluçon (presided over by Marx Dormoy) were deprived of their powers in September.

But, in the less important localities (and France has approximately 36,000 townships), the Government dismissed only 56 Mayors and 13 Deputy Mayors, mostly for reasons which at any time would have entailed their dismissal, such as embezzlement or criminal convictions. A Mayor in the Jura was dismissed for having asked the German authorities to include his village in the occupied zone.

Thus, it is possible to conclude that the Vichy Government applied the discriminatory laws without excessive severity when dealing with minor offences.

On the other hand, when dealing with the personalities of the Third Republic, with the Jews and Freemasons, it manifested a total despotism.

### *Vichy's New Order*

The National Revolution had not for sole ambition the creation of a new political structure or of the reformation of institutions: it also wished, and perhaps principally wished, to affect morals and transform man himself.

The idea of a sterling Frenchman, of a new man arising by Government decree and by the will of the prince, was a somewhat idyllic and paternalistic conception: nevertheless, the National Revolution neglected nothing that might conduce to his appearance by formulating a comprehensive system of measures which were to accompany him, stage by stage, through life from the cradle to his coming legally of age.

The school teachers, whose duty it was to form this *homo nationalis*, were to mould him, not only with their knowledge, but also with their loyalty and their morality. There would no longer be teachers such as the Right and the Marshal himself had denounced for their subversive outlook and for their responsibility for the defeat. They knew that, if they did not keep loyal to the regime and the virtues it encouraged, nothing could protect them from the appropriate sanctions.

The school must be right-thinking: it must also think correctly, its intellectual tone must be on a level with its moral tone. Teachers from now on must have passed through secondary education and have taken the first part of the *baccalauréat*. The standard of their teaching would be improved: the fledgling *homo nationalis* would profit by it from the start.

He would also benefit, if he profited by secondary education, from being obliged to learn Greek and Latin. He would be taught civics: "His duty towards the State and the general interest, respect for the law, the meaning and dignity of the idea of service, his duty towards his country and national and patriotic pride."

Finally, he would be told about God, which would do no harm: God whom the Republican school had made into the "Great Absent" would thus return to the curriculum.

"*Mens sana*", or "*sacra*", "*in corpore sano*", physical education would give the child as much bodily strength as mental strength: "Ten hours a week in primary education, nine hours in secondary education shall be devoted to activities in the open air: games and physical education, outings, excursions, singing, manual labour . . ."

As soon as the child left the primary school, another school received him and perfected the moulding of his character, the youth camps, in which he spent eight months.

And thus, when the child was grown up, he would be in the bosom of the new Order, a conscientious and organised citizen.

The Guardian State would protect his family and professional life.

Pétain's first object was to keep the woman in the home and this led him to propose Government measures benefiting the girl who became engaged, the mother and the father of a family . . .

The *virgo nationalis* would receive a grant from the State if she promised not to take any paid job. The *mater nationalis*, after her third child, would have the advantage of a *carte de priorité*, while her husband would have the right of working overtime at his trade and, if he inherited money, to financial allowances which might amount to an exemption from tax.

He was also protected against the vice of alcoholism which ruins so many homes. The privilege of distilling was suppressed and certain detrimental beverages, such as absinthe, were forbidden.

Finally, if the individual wished to divorce, he would find more difficulty in doing so, and then only in grave and limited circumstances.

Moral health, physical health, family health . . . these were the personal benefits that, whether he liked it or not, the new man was to acquire under the National Revolution. And now he had to earn his living.

If he were a peasant, he was lucky! He benefited by all the measures which encouraged the return to, or the remaining on, the land: a re-organisation of the conditions of labour, re-distribution of abandoned land, and the repairing of his house. His trade was organised by an autonomist agricultural corporation in which big finance was no longer the dominant influence, and in which the State intervened only for purposes of control and co-ordination . . . in principle, of course.

If he were a labourer—there had to be some—he would have the advantage of a theoretically similar organisation, that of the Comités d'Organisation, which only the misfortunes of the times obliged to adopt a certain authoritarian appearance and to employ despotic methods.

If by any chance he were a doctor, he registered with the Conseil de l'Ordre, which maintained discipline in the profession and represented it with the Government.

If his natural eloquence had made of him a lawyer, he was rejoiced to see his profession re-organised by two measures, one of which implied a prohibition of all political action and the other of which altered the necessary professional qualifications.

If he were a merchant seaman or a docker, he would exercise his talents in a trade which had been re-organised by the Government.

Preached at as an adolescent, honoured as the father of a family, organised as a worker, the new man might also be an ex-Serviceman, disciplined and respected, who could join the French Legion of Combatants, by taking an oath which was in conformity with the ideals of the regime:

"I swear to continue serving France honourably in peace as I have served her under arms.

"I swear to devote all my strength to the country, the family, and to work. I promise to give friendly and mutual aid to my comrades of both wars, and to remain faithful to the memory of those who fell on the field of honour. I freely accept the discipline of the Legion in everything that I may be ordered to do for the realisation of this ideal."

And with all this, what was to become of his political life? It appeared to be extremely reduced. The new order was hierarchical. Elections were abandoned, except in very limited cases.

No more voting, clearly. As far as local assemblies were concerned, the General Council and District Councils were suppressed and their functions handed over to the Prefects.

As for the Municipal Councils, if he lived in a township of at least 2,000 inhabitants, he still voted for the election of the Mayor and his Councillors. But in other cases, he had to leave to the Préfecture or the Government the duty of appointing his aediles.

At this birth of a new order, there were four important institutions, whose geneses are worth recounting in detail, in order to establish the political circumstances in which the National Revolution took place.

These are the Legion of Combatants, the Youth Camps, the Comités d'Organisation and the Agricultural Corporation.

The Legion of Combatants was intended by the Marshal to spread the principles of the National Revolution throughout the country and to maintain contact between the Government and the best elements in the nation, in these circumstances the ex-Servicemen. In origin, the Legion had nothing totalitarian about it. It was content to inherit the social ideals of the ex-Servicemen's associations which had existed before the war. The Law of 29th August, 1940, which brought it into being, laid it down that it would be confined to unifying the various movements which already existed. Xavier Vallat, who created it, stated, as Secretary-General of the ex-Servicemen, that it was in accordance with the wish formulated in 1936 in a book, *Vers l'action combattante*, in which the soldiers of the 1914–1918 war had claimed the honour of fulfilling a civic role.

The Legion had also the aim of maintaining a military spirit among the soldiers disarmed by the armistice.

This para-military function of the Legion caused it to be forbidden in the northern zone by the Germans. (Ordinance of 23rd August, published September, 1940.)

In order to circumvent the prohibition, Xavier Vallat charged Pierre Héricourt and Heurteaux to open a secret office of the Legion in Paris. To this end, he gave the first the title of Directeur de Cabinet and the second the title of Chargé de Mission. The Marshal approved this secret action and handed Xavier Vallat

500,000 Frs. in cash for the Legion in the occupied zone; later on, he supported from his own civil list the resistance movement "Hector", organised by Heurteaux under the cover of the Legion.

Thus, originally, the Legion was essentially a patriotic and civic organisation.

But there was one circumstance which predisposed it to become totalitarian and play the part of an instrument of the central power, as it might be a single party. Its directors were not elected, as had been the case before the war with the ex-Servicemen's associations. Its chairman, appointed by the Marshal, himself nominated the presidents of local and departmental sections.

The problem of youth came to the fore at the armistice: in the first place it was a question of re-grouping the recruits of the 1940 class, who had been mobilised in the month of June and whose military life had consisted only of disaster.

For their benefit, the Law of the 30th July, 1940, created the Youth Camps, in which they were grouped for six months under the command of General de la Porte du Theil; on the 18th January, 1941, when this first stage was over, a new Law determined that all young Frenchmen of the age of twenty years in the free zone would be called up to these camps for eight months.

The avowed object of the Camps was to take in hand demoralised youth and prepare it for the tasks of the immediate future. But General de la Porte du Theil had another object; in complete agreement with the general staff of the army, he wished to maintain recruiting in the southern zone and camouflage reservists in a post-Youth Camp Association; thus, if the day came when hostilities were resumed, the Army Command would have at its disposal, over and above the army permitted by the armistice, a mass of disciplined and organised men, provided with transport, rations and arms hidden in secret depots.

But the material conditions in the Youth Camps became more and more harsh. General de la Porte du Theil was eventually to deplore that some of them gave the impression of being concentration camps.

In professional and economic matters, the new order was to be *co-ordinated and controlled.*

In practice, a distinction must be made between industry and commerce on the one hand, and agriculture on the other.

Contrary to its principles, the National Revolution inaugurated State direction over industry.

The Law of the 16th August, 1940, which created provisional Comités d'Organisation, completely subjected industry and commerce to the Government.

It established a Comité d'Organisation for every branch, giving it powers over every business within that branch whether it formed part of a Trust or was independent. Its composition and its activities were subject to the State; its directors could not be appointed without the agreement of the Minister of Production and Labour. Its decisions had to be ratified by him. Its competence extended over all professional matters: the census of businesses, production programmes, raw materials, salaries, hours and conditions of work, the price of products, etc.

Later, as we shall see, the State went even further towards direction and itself took decisions without consulting the Comités.

This inconsistency with the doctrine of the National Revolution is explained by the necessity to withstand the pressure of the occupying power.

The Law of the 16th August was, according to Bouthillier, "a law required by the circumstances". "Hastily conceived", added René Belin in an unpublished report. Considered and drawn up in forty-eight hours, 9th–10th August, 1940, by a committee of five people sitting almost continuously in the Minister's office, promulgated seven days after work on it had begun, its essential aim was to protect the industry of the northern zone against the pressure of the occupying power by interposing between the managers of isolated businesses and the German demands the screen of the French State.

The Law of the 18th September, 1940, concerning joint stock companies, which was due to Bouthillier, the Minister of Finance, took a "workman's pick" to one of the essential arrangements of modern capitalism: the personal irresponsibility of the directors of joint stock companies.

From then on the president of a board of administration was in the same position as a merchant, personally responsible for the management of the business before the law and his shareholders.

Furthermore, in order to prevent certain private interests dominating too large a proportion of the economic life of the country, pluralism was limited: no one could hold more than two presidencies of boards of administration. No one might be a member of more than eight such boards of businesses registered in France. This number was reduced to two for persons over seventy years old.

Finally, on the 9th November, 1940, three decrees, made under the Law of the 16th August, simultaneously dissolved centralised organisations whether of employers or Trades Unions:

"The Comité Central des Houillères de France, the Comité des Forges de France, the Confédération Générale du Patronat Français (C.G.P.F.), the Confédération Française des Travailleurs Chrétiens, (C.F.T.C.), the Confédération Générale du Travail (C.G.T.), the Confédération des Syndicats Professionnels Français (C.S.P.F.) are suppressed."

In fact, the directors of the Trusts preserved in most cases their influence. Was it not laid down that the State would choose the heads of the Comités d'Organisation among those "who were experienced in industry . . . owing to their previous positions and by their experience in management"?

On the other hand, agriculture was subject to a professional reorganisation which conformed to the doctrines of Vichy, that is to say, corporative and not centralised in the State.

The Law of the 2nd December, 1940, concerning the corporative organisation of agriculture inaugurated the Agricultural Corporation, the first proposal for which had been put forward by Caziot long before the advent of the totalitarian regimes.

Contrary to what had been done in industry, where the central organisations of Trades Unions and employers had been dissolved for political reasons, none of the organisations which had already been set up by the peasants to protect their interests was suppressed. Co-operative associations, mutual benefit associations, specialised organisations representing one or another form of production, all preserved their powers, some on a local level, others on a national scale. They merely took their place in a unifying structure which respected their autonomy.

The Assembly of Regional Delegates created a National Corporative Council and elected a permanent committee of ten members who were to administer the Corporation.

These diverse organisations no longer limited themselves, as had the agricultural associations before 1940, to representing and protecting their interests. They now had legal powers to "promote and administer the common interests of peasant families in the moral, social and economic spheres".

In principle, there was no control over the local committee: it chose its own chairman as it pleased. The nominations of the regional delegate and of the standing committee were submitted for ratification to the Minister of Agriculture, though he took no part in the elections. The Government Commissioners, who were allowed to attend local regional or national meetings, were limited to transmitting to the Minister for endorsement the regulations or decisions formulated by the meeting; they did not intervene in discussions. In all these cases, the State did not direct: it co-ordinated and controlled.

Thus, as opposed to the Fascist or National Socialist corporation, the French corporation was, in theory at least, an autonomist institution.

Vichy's military policy does not raise, properly speaking, any problem of doctrine. It corresponds to the instinctive reaction which every conquered government, whether of the Right or the Left, hierarchical or republican, manifests after defeat: to restore as soon as possible to the nation that essential attribute of sovereignty which is the army.

Paragraph 4 of the Convention of Armistice reduced the role of the French army to the maintenance of order; its effectives in Metropolitan France, stationed in the southern zone alone, were fixed at 100,000 men, of which 4,000 were officers, and divided into eight divisions. Their weapons included no mortars, heavy machine guns, or anti-tank guns. There was no motorised transport. For artillery, they had nothing but the 75 of the 1897 model. Their reserves of ammunition were so reduced that they would allow of no more than a brief action against rioters. All troop movements involving more than a battalion were subject to previous authorisation by the Germans.

Precisely ten days after the ceremony at Rethondes, there began a considerable clandestine effort to increase the number of effectives and augment armaments and war materials. The majority of the French military leaders wished thus to make preparations for a resumption of hostilities against Germany; for certain Ministers who helped them the existence of a real army seemed to be above all an essential attribute of French sovereignty.

On the 5th or 6th July, General Colson, Minister for War, sent a letter in his own hand to the commanders of the eight Regions of the southern zone telling them to conceal the material which the armistice demanded should be delivered up. In August 1940, a secret order of General Weygand, who had replaced Colson, similarly forbade the surrender of anti-tank guns.

At the same time, the leading commanders of the army made numerous personal contacts with officers in order to give them verbal instructions since written orders might fall into the hands of the Armistice Commission. In August, 1940, General Verneau, Chief of the General Staff, held a meeting at the Hôtel des Bains which was attended by eighty staff officers; he said in substance: "The war is not over . . . France is undergoing but one ordeal the more, but we are a country of invincible hope . . . Keep in contact with me." Words which strangely recalled General de Gaulle's speech made at the same period.

But words said in secret were not all, measures were taken and actions performed.

One of the first cares of the General Staff was to keep out of German clutches the motorised vehicles which the armistice enjoined France to deliver up. An officer of the General Staff, Commandant Mollard, was detailed in July to conceal them. Shortly afterwards, on the 20th October, 1940, General Picquendar took command of an organisation which was formed independently of the Government and the High Command, in order that they might not be compromised if it came to light.

The concealing of vehicles and certain motorised weapons was dealt with in two ways: the first consisted in hiding them in special depots where trusted teams assured their maintenance.

The other procedure was less hazardous: it consisted in creating civilian transport companies, the XV Companies, created by Commandant Mollard, which bore that name because the first of them, "Les Rapides du Littoral", was created in September, 1940, in the territory of the XVth Region. They received, as free loans, trucks, cars and military tractors, on the understanding that they would maintain them in good condition and above all be ready, at six hours' notice, to transport troops according to necessity.

During the winter of 1940–1941, more than 35,000 cars, 11,000 trucks and 500 tractors were concealed from the occupying power, without counting a huge quantity of spare parts and batteries . . .

Other companies, which on the face of it looked equally commercial, provided for the secret manufacture of armoured cars from American bull-dozers; by the end of the summer of 1942, 225 of these machines were in process of completion; it had necessitated the production of turrets and armoured plate in factories unbeknown to the Armistice Commission.

At the same time, during the winter of 1940–1941, 65,000 rifles, 9,500 infantry automatic weapons, 200 mortars, 55 guns of 75 mm., 18 of 47 mm., 90 of 25 mm., were hidden in villages and maintained by pseudo-smiths or garage-keepers who were, in fact, members of the armed Forces.

There was another clandestine contravention of the armistice conditions: the military intelligence services continued their work; they furnished the allies with much valuable information. At Lyon, a centre of tactical studies was created under the command of General Baurès; the selected officers who took part in it invented a formula of "mixed detachments of all arms", a mobile and autonomist formation, an idea the Americans took up under the name of "combat groups", and which was to give proof of its value in 1944.

A secret mobilisation plan, which provided for the increase of the number of usable divisions from 8 to 24, was elaborated by a "demographic" department, attached to the Ministry of Finance. Its central headquarters was established at Lyon, under the Command of the Controller General of the Army, Carmille, who, arrested by the Germans, was to be deported and die. His offices, camouflaged as statistical, were the centre for all the demobilisation papers used after the armistice, which allowed of a new mobilisation being prepared. The decree organising it appeared in the *Journal Officiel* of the 29th November, 1940; and on the 25th December, the Paris press, playing its usual role of informer, drew the attention of the Germans to this somewhat suspicious organisation: "What is its significance?" wrote Déat in *l'Oeuvre*. "Is it an ingenious method of replacing the recruiting offices? Is it a military or civilian organisation?"

Some of the civilian Ministers helped in this business of camouflage. On the demand of General Huntziger, Peyrouton, Minister of the Interior, created a supplementary Police Force, the Groupes de Protection, which made it possible to keep supernumerary officers and non-commissioned officers on the active list. The Minister of Agriculture, Caziot, made his

Forestry services conceal material of war. The Minister of Finance, Bouthillier, spread military finance among the budgets of the civilian Ministries or those of the African possessions.

Nothing had been laid down in the Armistice Convention concerning the Army of Africa. For the purpose of maintaining it and building up a sufficient force, the French Government made use of two procedures. On the one hand, official negotiations between the French Directorate of Armistice Services in the Ministry of War and the Italian Armistice Commission at Turin; on the other hand, secret action taken on the spot by the French military authorities.

After Mers-el-Kebir, which proved to the Axis that the French would resist the attacks of their ancient allies, conversations opened at Turin. At the beginning of September, the Italian Armistice Commission proposed that the effectives of the French Army in Africa should be fixed at a total of 30,000 men, excluding all supplementary troops.

Laborious negotiations succeeded in transforming the situation to the extent that, in September 1941, there were 111,555 men serving with the colours in North Africa, of whom 4,213 were officers, and in French West Africa, 56,500 of whom 1,100 were officers.

Besides these official negotiations conducted within the terms of the armistice conditions, the French staff, under the leadership of General Weygand, carried out a considerable work of camouflage in North Africa.

During the four months which followed the armistice, great quantities of arms and munitions were screened from the control of the Armistice Commissions: 55,000 rifles, 1,500 machine guns, 210 mortars, 82 guns of 75 mm., 5 tanks, 23 armoured cars, 72 flame-throwers . . .

Stocks of metal, which could be used in the manufacture of armaments, were concealed from the Italian investigators; while national transport companies took 6,000 vehicles into stock. The secret manufacture of armoured vehicles and signalling material was undertaken by Naval workshops.

Moreover, an excess of 60,000 men was maintained with the Colours on the pretext of reinforcing the police, labour gangs, Goums, or the units guarding depots.

The combined effect of these various operations allowed the reconstruction of a military force which was sufficient to withstand the first shock of the German forces in Tunisia in November, 1942.

It is difficult, at the end of the first six months, to make out a balance sheet for the National Revolution.

The administration had accomplished an enormous work in the restoration of order in the country. But the discriminatory laws, which followed so rapidly upon each other, stain the whole of the Government's record. As for the reforms made to the structure of the Government, they were as yet far from having fulfilled their objects or rallied public opinion to their support.

Taken as a whole, they conformed to the Government's doctrine: but on one point they were in opposition to it: as far as the Comités d'Organisation were concerned the exigencies of the occupying power obliged the Government to inaugurate State direction.

Thus, owing to German pressure and the sectarianism of some of its promoters, the National Revolution, from its very beginning, showed certain deviations from its own doctrines.

## CHAPTER 5

# FROM THE NATIONAL ASSEMBLY TO MONTOIRE

(10th July 1940—24th October 1940)

IN July, 1940, practically no one at Vichy believed for a moment that the armistice would last several years: no one doubted that a German victory was near at hand. In the opinion of the majority there was, therefore, not a moment to lose if a few months hence, at the Peace Conference, France were to defend her independence, her territory and her Empire.

However, though they were all agreed about the shortness of the time at their disposal, the principal personages at Vichy, Pétain, Weygand and Laval, wished to pursue different policies.

For Weygand, the situation was perfectly simple: France had been obliged to ask the Reich for an armistice, but the Reich remained nevertheless France's enemy. The General's duty was, therefore, whatever the Nazi pressure, to hold rigorously to the armistice conditions, execute its ineluctable stipulations but oppose every violation of its clauses, every extension or political encroachment. . . .

"The Armistice, nothing but the Armistice."

And "the English remain allies of France," continually asserted the General, who could not conceive that France should break her word.

For Pierre Laval, old revolutionary as he was, this conception was out of date. In his opinion, the decline of the bourgeois world—of which the defeat of France was a signal manifestation—demanded radical change.

His historical role, rising as he had from the people like the Führer, sprung from Socialism like the Duce, was to accomplish this revolution in France. By doing this, by placing France at the side of the conqueror, not only politically but ideologically, he was convinced that he was giving her the only real chance of salvation.

In such circumstances, France's engagements towards England, who would have no part to play in the new Europe, were of but little importance. Besides, had not England first broken the alliance by attacking France so disloyally at Mers-el-Kebir?

To Weygand and Laval, both equally intransigent, though in opposite ways, the Marshal offered a striking contrast.

Having never read *Mein Kampf*, knowing nothing, to begin with at least, of the spirit of totalitarianism, he believed the solution was to conduct a policy similar to that of the Germany of Weimar after the other war. Finesse, in the manner of Stresemann, by negotiating simultaneously with both the Germans and the British, seemed to him the best way of assuring France's future whatever might eventuate.

And it was not only Stresemann's example which haunted the Marshal and his Ministers. Had not Prussia, after Jena, crushed by an intractable conqueror, used cunning to rise again and take her place once more among the victorious states? Why should not France in 1940 do as much?

At Vichy, this became an obsession.

But the French Government was at the mercy of an all-powerful totalitarian regime which, for the last seven years, had been accustomed to destroy all internal resistance and, for the last four, to surmount every external obstacle.

One problem, which arose immediately after the armistice, and which was in fact never resolved, was the return of the Government to Paris. For the Vichy Ministers, persuaded that France could not be governed except from her capital, this became a fixed idea. The principle having been accepted at Rethondes, the Germans henceforward continuously opposed its realisation.

The first Nazi exactions began even before the armistice by a series of ordinances issued during the invasion "in the interest of the occupied territories."[1] Occupation money, the Reichkreditkassenmark, was put into authorised circulation. On the 20th May, its exchange value was fixed at 20 Frs. instead of 16 Frs., the legal rate of the Mark before the war. Thus the

[1] This formula, which preceded the majority of Nazi ordinances, referred hypocritically to the Hague Convention: this, in Article 43, authorises an occupying power "to take all measures within its power to re-establish and assure, in so far as is possible, public order and the life of the population, while respecting, unless absolutely prevented from doing so, the laws in force in the country."

Germans were able to buy at ridiculously low prices, with sham money, all they wanted in France.

Then followed the requisitioning of all raw materials in occupied territory, and the appointment of managers to all businesses which were not "working normally": as the exodus was in full swing, how many businesses were likely to be? On the 23rd May, "in order to re-establish public order" the German army replaced the tax-collectors, who had in the circumstances disappeared, and set about collecting the taxes itself. An attention which must have been particularly appreciated by the French tax-payers who had remained at home.

On the 20th June, by a new ordinance, the Germans killed two birds with one stone: by forbidding all increases in salaries and prices, it encouraged social unrest and facilitated the activities of the Nazi "slavers", who were already endeavouring to recruit volunteers to work beyond the Rhine.

Finally, on the same day, in order to make it possible for "the German Army to guarantee to the inhabitants full personal security and the safeguarding of their property", the French administration was placed in its entirety under the control of the Wehrmacht.

"The administration of the State, the districts, the police and the schools will continue to function. They will thus remain in the service of their own population. The heads and directors will be responsible to the occupying authority for the loyal functioning of these services. Persons in public employment will continue to receive their salaries and wages."

One might have thought that the armistice would have abrogated all these measures taken during the course of operations. On the contrary, it increased them. The Convention of Rethondes, hurriedly drawn up, contained many loose statements which favoured Nazi dishonesty.

Article 19 laid it down that all armament factories, machines and stocks should be handed over to the Germans: but as, since 1939, practically the whole of French industry had been working on armaments, it was only too easy for the Germans to pretend that the armistice authorised them to lay their hands on an immense proportion of French factories: 540 machines were thus transferred across the Rhine during the first three months of the occupation.

Article 17 subordinated to German authorisation all transference of raw materials or products from the occupied territories to the free zone or abroad: a clause which allowed of a complete stoppage of economic life if the French Government should displease the Germans too much.

There were Nazi sentries on the factory doors. In the offices there were "commissaries" assisted by technicians to replace French staffs, if the latter were not docile.

The key iron and steel industry was subject to the extent of 85 per cent. to Nazi control or simply annexed.[1]

The motor-car factories of the Paris region were left free, though under German control, to recommence their peacetime production: but Germany appropriated the war material in process of production.

In the meantime, the Germans were doing considerable plundering: twenty merchant ships were requisitioned at Bordeaux for military use. At the Joliot-Curie Radium Institute, German scientists demanded to be informed of all the work in progress and forbade all future production without their endorsement. The premises of the Messageries Hachette were requisitioned, the occupying authorities creating there a newspaper co-operative while expropriating the French proprietors.

Nor did they hesitate, in spite of the stipulations of Rethondes, to infringe the integrity of French territory.

In Alsace-Lorraine, Germanisation went on apace: the French administration was suppressed. The property of the political parties, the Masonic lodges and the Jews was handed over to the

[1] At the beginning of July, 1940, the German administration divided the French iron and steel industry into six categories.

Category 1: Moselle: where the Nazis merely seized it, placing their own managing personnel in every factory and refusing to permit the return of the French staff: this was annexation.

Category 2: Meurthe-et-Moselle: where the factories were taken over by the German authorities and put under the control of Hermann Roechling. German commissaries replaced the management: the French staffs and personnel were retained.

Category 3: The factories of Meurthe-et-Moselle Nord, the Longwy group, were left legally in the hands of their proprietors: but they were nevertheless controlled by a German commissary who took up residence at Longwy.

Category 4: the factories of the Nord and the Pas-de-Calais were left under the control of their proprietors, but were economically attached to the German authorities in Brussels through their delegation at Lille.

Category 5: the other factories in the occupied zone constituted the group called "Centre-Ouest"; with the exception of the Creusot and Imphy works, naturally the most important, their management was left in French hands.

Category 6: the factories in the free zone, which formed the group "Centre-Midi", remained independent.

Nazi organisations. On the 16th July, certain inhabitants of Alsace-Lorraine, too well known for their patriotism, French "from the interior", who had been residing in these three departments since the 11th November 1918, with North Africans to the total number of 22,000, were expelled to the free zone: they were given half an hour to leave with 125 lb. of luggage and 2,000 Frs. per person: the first sad episode in the Calvary of the population of the East.

Another form of action taken against the unity of the country was that the line of demarcation, laid down by Article 2 of the Armistice Convention, was transformed by the Germans into a veritable frontier.

The line was so drawn that, if it were used as a water-tight partition, it would bring about the death of France.

Indeed, neither of the two zones could live cut off from the other.

In the occupied zone there was little wine, no oil or soap. There was insufficient smaller livestock, pigs, rabbits and poultry to begin re-stocking the devastated areas. It needed hay from Limousin and from the Crau, feeding stuffs, manufactured in the Marseille region, and artificial manures from Toulouse.

The free zone, on the other hand, lacked wheat, sugar, potatoes, vegetable seeds, oats and coal. Its industrial resources were to all intents and purposes insignificant.

Most unexpected details demonstrate at once the consequences of the separation of the two zones. The only nail factory for horse-shoes was in the northern zone at Delair (Seine-Inférieure): all the cart-horses in the southern zone were quickly rendered useless: this in itself was sufficient to create a danger of famine.

Moreover, the postal services were interrupted between the two zones. 'Ausweis', which gave permission to cross the line, were practically suppressed. Only a few political or economic collaborators with the Germans were provided with them. Apart from Pierre Laval, the French Ministers were continually refused them.

At the beginning of July, General Stülpnagel, talking to General Huntziger, thought it witty to sum up the situation thus: "This line is a bit we have put in the horse's mouth. If France bucks we shall tighten the curb chain. We shall loosen it in proportion as France behaves well." Thus was a sinister threat put into cavalier terms!

There was another form of pressure to which Pétain was particularly sensitive: the presence in Germany of a million and a half prisoners of war who were at the mercy of the goodwill of the occupying power.

Thus, the French Government was subjected to an economic and political pressure greater than any it had known in its history.

After a number of official protests transmitted to Wiesbaden[1] had remained without effect, Pierre Laval decided to negotiate directly with the Nazi leaders, without passing through the official channels of either Wiesbaden or Paris.

The Vice-President of the Council was convinced that he could shortly achieve a success on the international level as startling as that of the 10th July in the National Assembly.

It did not matter that German pressure should have increased during the first months after the armistice: he needed only to talk with the Germans to "arrange everything". This was a vague formula which, however, in his mind included not only establishing enduring collaboration between Germany and France and the suppression of the line of demarcation, but also the putting of an end to certain attacks made by *Radio-Paris* against the Vichy Government, and which exasperated Laval all the more for the fact that he himself was not spared.

But there still remained the problem of "talking with the Germans", and Pierre Laval knew none of the Nazi leaders personally, except possibly Marshal Goering, with whom he had had a long conversation at Cracow, in 1935, at the time of the funeral of Marshal Pilsudski. Goering, being a soldier, did not seem to him to have the necessary qualifications for a diplomatic interview.

A certain Otto Abetz, Counsellor to the German Embassy in Paris, had just been appointed the delegate of the Ministry of Foreign Affairs to the Headquarters of the Military Occupation of France. He had arrived in Paris eight days before: was he perhaps the man whom Laval needed?

Abetz, an ex-drawing master in a secondary school, had always been a somewhat romantic champion of Franco-German reconciliation.

[1] The German Armistice Commission presided over by General von Stülpnagel had first taken up its quarters at Wiesbaden. The French Delegation, comprised of 39 soldiers and 27 civilians (almost a Ministry), under the leadership of General Huntziger, joined it there on the 29th June. Its role was "to receive executive orders from the Nazi organisation."

While taking part in a Franco-German Youth Congress at Rethel, in 1931, Abetz met two young people who were profoundly to affect his life: Jean Luchaire, the organiser of the Congress with whom he made friends, and his secretary, a young Frenchwoman, whom he married.

At that time both Abetz and Luchaire were still zealous democrats who looked upon the beginnings of Nazism with horror: "made obdurate and appalled by the memory of the war," Abetz publicly declared, "we all, young Germans and young Frenchmen, desire that in future force shall not triumph over right. We wish all nations and all classes to have justice, that their right to determine their own future shall be respected, and that their liberty shall never be subjected to constraint."

When the Congress was over, Abetz came to Paris; he frequented literary and political drawing-rooms, listened to the new movements which were preparing for action, noted, catalogued and made appreciations of this figure and that. Soon, his methodical work made of him the German who knew France best and, indeed, better in some ways than many Frenchmen.

In 1937, when Abetz joined the Nazis, he became the specialist in French problems in the Wilhelmstrasse, rather as Ribbentrop was in British questions.

Two years later, his somewhat indiscreet knowledge of France earned him expulsion by Daladier, as head of the Fifth Column.

Laval had never met Abetz: he knew that he could meet him easily enough thanks to three French journalists, who were of somewhat doubtful reputation, but were on good terms with Abetz: Fontenoy, Brinon and Luchaire.

As soon as he heard of the Counsellor to the Embassy's arrival in Paris, he summoned this charming trio, received them separately and told each of them to inform Abetz of his desire for a conversation.

Of Laval's three emissaries, only one, Jean Fontenoy, who was the first to be received by Abetz, was personally disinterested. He was half mad and was always falling into political traps while thinking in all good faith that he was serving some incoherent ideal. A writer of some talent, he was noisy and impetuous, hare-brained and dynamic, fanatically anti-bourgeois and fiercely anti-Communist, though he at least had the courage of his convictions; having joined the Legion of French Volunteers against Bolshevism, he was killed in Berlin, during the street-fighting in 1945.

Luchaire had all his life manifested a devotion, which nothing could shake, to two things: an unconditional love of peace, that even the German victory did nothing to disturb, and an enduring attachment to the secret funds which Briand had been the first to begin paying over to him for the financing of inspired periodicals. Many successive governments furnished him with this odious but invisible manna which every political project seemed to impel towards his purse. In July, 1940, Luchaire was ready to fulfil the mission Laval desired: in two months it brought him in 150,000 Frs. (3 millions today),—without counting a "*cursus honorum*" and ulterior profits.[1]

Fernand de Brinon also remained true to himself. Since 1932, when Hubert de Polignac, a port wine merchant, had introduced him to Joachim von Ribbentrop, at that time a traveller in champagne, he had been a devoted Nazi.

At Vichy, Brinon was the object of universal scorn. Pétain, in spite of Laval's insistence, did not appoint him to succeed Léon Noël as Delegate-General to the occupied territories. Weygand publicly refused to shake him by the hand.

It was known that every word overheard by Brinon was reported to the Germans; in 1943, at Vichy, when he had become Secretary of State to the Presidency of the Council, he went from the Council of Ministers to the head of the Gestapo and gave him a faithful report of the Government's decisions concerning the organisation of forced labour.

There was only one thing to be said in his favour: Brinon used his relations with the Germans to intervene on behalf of arrested Frenchmen and thus saved many.

Such were the Three Musketeers of Treason whom Laval sent to Abetz.

On the 16th July, Vichy reverberated to a clap of thunder. Hitler, addressing himself to France no longer as to an independent nation, but rather to a satellite state, demanded that the French Fleet and Empire should join in the war against England: a *diktat* comparable to those to which the Führer's

[1] A few months later, his friendship with Abetz, the dispenser of German secret funds, was worth to him, among other payments, 480,000 Frs. (10 millions today) for the financing of his newspaper *Les Nouveaux Temps*.

previous victims had been subjected, the Austrian Chancellor, Schuschnigg and the Czech President, Hacha. From then on, there could be no illusions as to the manner in which the Nazis would respect the armistice.

Here is the beginning of the letter from Stülpnagel to Weygand, formulating the ultimatum.

"The High Command of the Army has commanded me to transmit the following demands from the Führer of the German Reich and Commander-in-Chief of the Army, that you may transmit them to the French Government.

"The Führer and Commander-in-Chief of the Army has made important concessions to the stipulations of the Armistice Convention in the matter of the free use of French territorial waters and in adjourning the disarmament of the French Forces to this end. HE EXPECTS THEREFORE THAT THE FRENCH GOVERNMENT WILL, ON ITS SIDE, ACCORD HIM THE SUPPORT HE JUDGES NECESSARY FOR THE EFFECTIVE CONDUCT OF THE WAR AGAINST ENGLAND."

This support consisted in placing at the disposal of the Wehrmacht eight Moroccan airfields, two meteorological stations, the railway from Tunis to Rabat, as well as the French ports on both the French and African coasts of the Mediterranean.

Faced with this *diktat*, the Ministers were unanimous in rejecting the ultimatum.

On the 17th July, a limited Council took place, which included Weygand, Darlan, Laval, Bouthillier and Baudouin, in order to draw up the terms of the reply to the Führer.

There were two proposals put forward:

The first, drafted by Charles-Roux and François-Poncet, representing the Quai d'Orsay, demonstrated that the German demands were juridically contrary to the armistice convention and rejected them categorically.

The second, drafted by Jacques Guérard, head of Baudouin's office, also emphasised the exorbitant character of the German demands, rejected them for the present, but left the door open for negotiations. This was its conclusion as put forward for Pétain's signature:

"I have therefore a basis for believing that the demands of the German Government place the French Government in an entirely new situation and present problems whose magnitude and gravity are beyond the competence of the Commission of Wiesbaden. I consider that a solution to these problems can only be found by new negotiations."

This second draft was adopted by the Council of Ministers after a discussion between Weygand and Baudouin. It was a revealing decision for it shows that Vichy, though unwilling to resist the Reich overtly, was determined, whatever it might cost, to preserve the Empire from seizure by the Nazis.

Three days after the arrival of Stülpnagel's letter, Laval left for Paris to see Otto Abetz.

On the 19th July, Fernand de Brinon, accompanied by the German Captain Meyer-Labastille, awaited him at the demarcation line.

It had taken a week for Berlin, to which Abetz had transmitted Pierre Laval's request, to authorise the Vice-President of the Council to go to Paris; but the conditions *sine qua non* which Laval had made for his stay—permission to take up his quarters in the Quai d'Orsay and to fly the French flag during his sojourn—were contemptuously refused.

The four meals he took in Paris were in the company of Nazis: for three of them, one of which was the first dinner he had in the capital, he was the guest of Abetz at the German Embassy in the Rue de Lille. The fourth gave him the opportunity of entertaining at the Hôtel Matignon a personality of the second rank, Lieutenant Weber, the Press Officer upon whom he no doubt counted to stop the vilification of himself by the Paris radio.

From his very first interview with Abetz, the conversations went much further than the limits the French Government had intended for these negotiations.

Burning all his boats, casting away all prudence and subtlety, Laval talked to this man whom he had never seen before and who but a few months earlier had been expelled from France for espionage, as openly as if he were talking to a friend.

"He began the conversation," Abetz reported, "by telling me that the journey he had just made had been the most painful of his whole life. It was not till he had passed the demarcation line that he had recognised the magnitude of the French defeat in seeing German soldiers on the soil of France. If he bore anyone a grudge for this situation, it was not towards the soldiers who occupied the country, but to the responsible politicians."

From confidences, he went on to give advice. Reversing their roles, he, as the Minister of a conquered country, lectured the conqueror on the policy to be pursued; in terms which were, moreover, both impressive and almost prophetic, he addressed the German as follows: "In the interests of his country," Abetz reported, "he wished to find on the soil of France the basis for collaboration with the Government of the Reich. Germany could do France much injury, but she could not annihilate her. Every abuse would one day return upon Germany herself, for all human achievement was but temporary. Germany did not as yet understand, as nor indeed did France, the importance of this historical hour; was it in the German interests to preserve an unconciliatory attitude when she was offered whole-hearted collaboration for the welfare of Europe?" It was at this meeting that, for the first time, the term "collaborate", used in a political sense, was applied to Franco-German relations.

Abetz maintained a prudent reserve: he was still in ignorance of the Führer's future intentions concerning France, and so limited himself to questioning his guest on a point which interested the Reich; what had Vichy decided in the matter of prosecuting the French statesmen responsible for the war?

In spite of his diplomatic prudence, the Counsellor of Embassy was won over by Laval. Abetz also thought how pleased his Nazi chiefs would be with him when he announced the French offer of collaboration in Berlin. His future career might even depend on it.

He immediately left to report to Berlin.

When, on the 22nd July, immediately on his return to Vichy, Laval made a report of his conversation with Abetz, he plunged the Government into consternation: "For two hours," wrote Baudouin, "Laval made an impassioned, detailed but disorganised account of his negotiations in Paris. He appears not to have negotiated, but to have conversed at large with Abetz, pledging himself very far.... He has promised a wide collaboration to the Germans without stating precisely what he understood by that word."

During the following fortnight there was no news from Abetz, and everything went from bad to worse.

On the 24th July, German Customs officers were placed along the crests of the Vosges on the old frontier of 1914: Alsace was officially re-annexed on the 29th July, and the German language alone was authorised.

French industry was increasingly subject to Nazi pressure.

The line of demarcation was hermetically closed; on the 22nd July, Hemmen obligingly recapitulated that "it could bring about the death of France, if France and Germany did not agree to collaborate."

The return of the Government to Paris was delayed on military pretexts. Pétain, standing on Article 3 of the Armistice Convention, decided nevertheless to proceed. Bouthillier was sent ahead as a scout and, on the 22nd July, installed himself in the Rue de Rivoli with the Ministry of Finance. The other technical Ministers, Belin, Caziot and Berthelot, were to join him on the 29th. On that day, General von Streccius, commanding the military administration in France, expelled Bouthillier from Paris. The Government therefore had to remain at Vichy.

On the 22nd July, the Germans seized the banks.

On the 23rd, they brought the courts under control by insisting that certain cases be submitted to them.

Were these to be the results of Pierre Laval's conversations with Otto Abetz, whose return was still delayed?

On the 30th–31st July, there were further dramatic events; these were of British origin and threw Vichy into confusion.

Within the space of two days, England made three aggressions. On the 30th July, a cruiser of the Royal Navy disembarked troops on French Colonial territory, at Duala, in the Cameroons, and the Commander of the English Fleet in the Far East sent an ultimatum to the Governor-General of Madagascar.

On the 31st, a decision was taken which was to have even more serious consequences: England included France, with the free zone and North Africa, in enemy territory, forbidding all trade between Metropolitan France and her overseas possessions.

This naval blockade thus joined the demarcation line in condemning the country to want and in strangling the colonies.

What could Pétain do?

Was he merely to await the results of the conversations with Abetz as Pierre Laval advised: "Nothing must be done until I have received Abetz's answer and seen him again"?

While Laval was left to play "sister Anne", Pétain no longer had confidence. On the 4th August he took two decisions.

In the first place, negotiations between France and Germany would be re-opened through the normal channels, by means of conversations between the two Ministers for Foreign Affairs. This was much to Baudouin's satisfaction, who was thus able to recapture the initiative Pierre Laval had usurped. He wrote to Ribbentrop, asking for an interview.

At the same time, Pétain made preparations for the eventual failure of the conversations. In the event of the Germans invading the free zone and occupying Vichy, he proposed to delegate his powers not to Laval but to Darlan: the latter would then leave for North Africa, while he himself would remain in France to protect the French people.

"It is definitely and precisely decided," records Baudouin, "that should Vichy receive a visit from the German army and the Marshal be placed in a position where it is impossible for him to govern independently, the Admiral will do his best to reach North Africa and there exercise the Government's authority in the name of the Marshal. The Navy, on an order from the Admiral, will sail to North Africa. Though we pressed for it, the Marshal, prudent as always, refuses to sign the commission I have drafted: 'I want no document, but you must consider my order as decisive. I shall not alter this decision. Furthermore, it must be understood that it remains strictly secret between the three of us. No one else must have knowledge of it.' "

On the 5th August, there was another unexpected event. It was learned at Vichy that Otto Abetz had been appointed Reich Ambassador to France.

Thus Baudouin was short-circuited in the most official way possible. The letter to Ribbentrop, which he had taken so much trouble to compose, would now never be sent. Laval, once more, was convinced that he had won the game.

From now on, he was but seldom seen in the provisional capital. Most of his time was spent in Paris. Now that he thought he had succeeded with Abetz, he wanted to meet Ribbentrop and win over the Minister as he imagined he had won over the Ambassador. That done, he would even gain access to Hitler and win him over too, persuading him that the interests of victorious Germany were to collaborate loyally with defeated France.

Laval, convinced of his infallibility, certain of playing a good hand, from now on would tolerate no opposition to his projects. To save France as a whole, which he was certain of being able to do, he was not prepared to refuse any concession of detail.

Did the Germans, for instance, wish to gain control of the Messageries Hachette? Without warning any of the directors of the business, Laval, declaring that he was acting in the name of the board, whom he had not even consulted, made over to the Germans an important proportion of the shares. The directors refused to ratify. Laval merely deplored the lack of patriotism and political sense of the Paris publishers.

The friendship of Otto Abetz was for Laval the necessary condition of Franco-German reconciliation. The confidence of the Ambassador was the basis on which he founded his policy.

In fact, whatever real sympathy may have existed between the two men, Abetz did not play a straight game and Pierre Laval was his dupe.

The instructions Ribbentrop gave Abetz, when he appointed him Ambassador, did not correspond with the illusions Laval cherished.

Indeed, here is a note Abetz distributed to the heads of departments in the Embassy on the 17th August, 1940:

"The interests of the Reich require on the one hand that France should be kept in a condition of interior weakness and on the other that she should be estranged from foreign powers hostile to the Reich. . . .

"Everything must be done on the German side to bring about the weakness and interior disunity of France. The Reich has therefore no interest in supporting the true popular or national movements in France. On the contrary, only those movements likely to create discord should be supported; sometimes these will be elements of the Left, sometimes of the Right."

This is evidence of the extent to which Pierre Laval was deceived in counting on the good faith and friendship of Otto Abetz. In reality, the Ambassador, in August, 1940, was then pursuing, under a diplomatic cloak, the manoeuvres which had led to his expulsion from France in 1939. With the arrival of Abetz, German pressure was not only transformed but increased: from being economic it became political; it was no longer only a question of pillaging France but of transforming her into a satellite of the Reich.

Abetz took the Press in hand, in accordance with Section 4 of Ribbentrop's instructions. Well before his arrival in Paris, a few newspapers had appeared under French titles, which had either been stolen from their legitimate owners or annexed by the creatures of the conquerors.

Immediately on the entry of the Wehrmacht, Gustave Hervé had, for two days, re-published his old paper, *La Victoire*, without even changing its name. Then had followed *le Matin*, edited by Bunau-Varilla, whose early editions, in both style and thought, seemed to have been translated from the German.

On the 22nd June, a counterfeit of Jean Prouvost's *Paris-Soir*, which had retreated into the free zone, appeared in Paris: it was edited by a German Lieutenant, Weber, and an ex-liftboy, Schisselé, the only member of the staff who had not abandoned the premises. On the 30th June appeared, for the first time, *La France au Travail*, the organ of the Nazi penetration into the working classes. Ill-edited and ill-conceived, it could deceive no one as to its true origin and ownership.

When Abetz took it in hand, his knowledge of French literary circles enabled him to give the Parisian Press a more Parisian flavour.

On the 10th September, 1940, he authorised two independent journalists, Henri Jeanson and Robert Perrier, to publish *Aujourd'hui*, in which they consistently refused to follow Nazi instructions: a curious, if only temporary, manifestation of German forbearance. After Montoire, Jeanson rejected an ultimatum from the Staffel Propaganda which gave him the choice of writing an article in favour of collaboration or resigning. On November 22nd, the names of Jeanson and Robert Perrier disappeared from the top of the paper and were replaced by that of Georges Suarez; and Jeanson was imprisoned. From then on the docility of *Aujourd'hui* was the more valuable to the occupying power for the fact of the independence previously permitted it.

On the 21st September, Abetz authorised Déat to re-issue *l'Oeuvre* in Paris: his non-conforming staff, partly reconstructed, was from now on in the service of Nazi policy. On the 8th October, the *Petit Parisien* reappeared with "its accustomed objectivity". On the 14th October, Doriot returned with the *Cri du Peuple*. On the 1st November, Jean Luchaire brought out

*Les Nouveaux Temps*, an evening paper designed to replace *Le Temps*, which had retreated into the southern zone.

Moreover, Otto Abetz, who knew how to live well himself, also knew how to help his journalist friends. Schleier, an attaché at the Embassy, interrogated after the end of hostilities by the American Secret Service, revealed that, from August 1940 onwards, the Ambassador paid over each month to Doriot and Déat 250,000 Frs., some 5 millions in the currency of today. Even the Communists frequented the Embassy in the Rue de Lille, seeking permission for *l'Humanité* to re-appear openly.[1] In the meantime, in the clandestine *l'Humanité*, they encouraged the French workman to fraternise with German soldiers. . . .

Thus the appointment of Otto Abetz to Paris allowed the Germans to bring a new threat to bear on the French Government by creating a centre of opposition in the capital.

August 1940 was a month of catastrophes, in which the tragic consequences of the defeat and the occupation were accentuated.

In economic matters the situation was extremely serious.

A certain Dr. Roos, representing in the occupied zone the Nazi Labour Front, was endeavouring to provoke a civil war. He was inciting the Trades Unions to demand the renewal of the collective conventions of before the defeat, that is to say to obtain the same advantages as in a period of full employment. He prevented the employers from satisfying these demands by requisitioning their factories and their stocks and by despatching their most modern machines across the Rhine. In the meantime, taking advantage of the unemployment which resulted from these contradictory measures, his organisation began to enlist workers for Germany.

Finally, in the French occupied zone, he officially set up Comités d'Organisation similar to those which, in Belgium, maintained the whole economy for the benefit of the occupying power.

In this instance, Vichy endeavoured to take steps by legislation. Two laws for the protection of French industry were promulgated: one, on the 16th August, 1940, created the Comités d'Organisation[2] which enabled French industry to shelter itself behind the State, and which forestalled the similar measures prepared by the occupying power.

[1] Cf., *supra*, p. 142.
[2] Cf., *supra*, p. 178.

The Germans were furious and took two reprisals: they demanded the creation of Comités de Repartition (Distribution) for all raw materials and reserved for themselves a right of inspection (the Law of 10th September); they also insisted that in future the *Journal Officiel*, since it had a Paris edition, should be submitted to their censorship. From then on Vichy could no longer appoint an official or promulgate a law without Nazi endorsement.

The second protective law re-established the measures in force before the war, which guaranteed French labour against an excessive influx of foreign workers. This time it was the Italians who were furious.

In financial matters the proceedings were scandalous: pillage pure and simple.

The only financial clause in the Armistice Convention, Article 18, stipulated, in accordance with International Law, that "the cost of maintaining occupying troops was to be a charge on the French Government." A perfectly clear and legal piece of drafting of which the Nazis were to make grossly excessive use.

On the 8th August, a certain Dr. Hemmen handed General Huntziger an ultimatum demanding, by virtue of Article 18, payments of at least 20 millions of Reichsmarks a day, approximately 400 million of francs then, and 8 billions today. In this exorbitant figure the cost of quartering German troops on French territory was not included and had to be paid in excess.

On the same day, Hemmen made another demand which Bouthillier called "an unprecedented claim".

He wished to make France sign a somewhat extraordinary clearing agreement which laid down that France would not have the right to limit her exports to the Reich; if these exports were greater than the total of imports, France would herself pay the bill for the exports. This was an extravagant demand, if one thinks that the word "exports" meant goods pillaged in France in order to be sent to Germany. France was to pay for the Nazi spoliations.

In both cases, Vichy tried to negotiate.

In connection with the daily indemnity, the Government produced, on the 12th August, a reasonable argument: the sum demanded corresponded, on the basis of the German official costs, to the maintenance of 18 million men, that is to say, infinitely more than all the troops of the Wehrmacht whether occupying France or operating elsewhere in the world.

The Germans not having even deigned to dispute the truth of the French remarks, Vichy protested again on the 19th and 21st August with legal arguments: the Reich was violating the Armistice.

Hemmen turned a deaf ear and, on the 28th August, the Exchequer had to pay over to the Germans 1,340 millions of Marks for arrears of occupation costs, including the 25th June.

The Government, compelled to yield, thought it inopportune to make its protest public.

In political matters, the unity of France was more and more gravely threatened: the situation became dramatic.

The most immediate threat was perhaps that created by the demarcation line which cut France into two. Vichy had been attempting to negotiate from the 15th July onwards; in exchange for the suppression of the line, it was prepared to accept that a cordon of German Customs officers should be established on the French frontiers of the Alps, the Mediterranean and the Pyrenees, doubling the French Customs officers. But, when, on the 22nd August, the Germans demanded to place, on the Swiss and Spanish frontiers alone, a force of 2,500 Customs officers in uniform, a far larger force than the French Customs, Vichy realised that it was not only a question of sharing the control of the frontiers with the occupying power, but one of surrendering them. And they stopped the negotiations for the suppression of the line.

They were equally helpless, alas, over Alsace-Lorraine, which, in fact, was annexed.

In August, two Gauleiters were appointed: Joseph Burckel for Lorraine, and Robert Wagner for Alsace. Measures for Germanisation were increasingly put into force: the educational curriculum was based on that practised beyond the Rhine. Persecution began: Mgr. Ruch, Bishop of Strasbourg, was forbidden to enter his diocese; a law based, so it was said, on liberty of conscience (what unexpected scrupulousness!) allowed children at the age of fourteen, by merely applying to the Registrar at the *Mairie*, to repudiate the religion to which they belonged: a quick method of removing them from the religious influence of their families.

On the 16th August, 1940, the Mayor of Thionville was expelled, as was Mgr. Heintz, Bishop of Metz.

The Marshal could not restrain his tears when he received

the Mayor of Metz: none of the Ministers resigned themselves to the annexation, with the possible exception of Pierre Laval who, in September, declared to the deputy, Fernand-Laurent:

"Alsace and Lorraine? Two children of divorced people who have always been torn between their parents, going constantly from one to the other. It's their fate, there is nothing we can do about it any more. The Nord and the Pas-de-Calais? . . . It's unfortunately probable that they will also be annexed . . . and more departments too. . . . If I can succeed in saving one or two, it won't be too bad. That's what I'm working for."

On the 3rd September, after a number of protests over details, the Government made an official protest drawn up in terms as impressive as those of the National Assembly of 1871:

"It is with the whole of France, within the frontiers of the State as they were in 1939, that Germany signed the Convention of the 22nd June.

"It was the integrity of the whole of France that Germany guaranteed in the Armistice Convention by laying it down that the French Government had the right to administer both the occupied and unoccupied territories, without territorial limitation whatsoever.

"Standing on its rights, the French Government solemnly protests against the measures taken, in violation of the Armistice Convention, concerning the departments of Alsace and Lorraine and their populations, which measures constitute a *de facto* annexation of those territories."

There was only one, but a considerable, difference between the declaration of 1871 and that of 1940: the latter was not made public. "The Germans are sadists," said the Marshal, "if I displease them, they'll pulverise the Alsatians. You don't know them!"

Weygand and Baudouin did not conceal their disapproval from Pétain: "This silence," they said, "makes us accomplices of the Germans."

And, indeed, many Alsatians then thought themselves abandoned by France.

All this was lamentable and manifested the powerlessness of the French Government.

Its attempts at resistance, when problems vital to the country arose, failed. Why then should it attempt resistance, when the questions were merely matters of honour and could have no practical consequences? On the level of honour and prestige, Vichy, having learned from experience, no longer made any attempt to resist.

Did the Germans express a wish that the mission of the Polish Chargé d'Affaires in France, whose Government, chased from its own country, had taken refuge in London, should be terminated? Vichy observed that this demand was an abuse of the Armistice Convention. Nevertheless, "the French Government, having decided to acknowledge the consequences of events" (singular periphrasis), did not restrict itself to expelling the diplomatist in question; Jacques Guérard, the director of Baudouin's office, forestalled further German demands by enquiring from the Nazis what attitude Vichy should adopt towards the representatives of other countries occupied by Germany, whose Governments had taken refuge in London: Holland, Belgium, Luxemburg and Norway.

Delighted with this piece of good luck, the Germans immediately advised that diplomatic relations should be broken off with all these countries. Paul Baudouin announced in person to the Belgian Ambassador, the Dutch Minister, the Norwegian Minister and the Luxemburg Chargé d'Affaires that their diplomatic missions to the French Government were at an end. A brief and cold official letter confirmed the decision.

The case of the German political refugees in France was still more painful, as well as being significant of French humiliation.

The only clause "against French honour" in the Rethondes document was, in fact, Article 19, which stipulated that the French Government must hand over, on the Nazi demand, all German nationals who had received asylum in France or her Empire.

Léon Noël had obtained from Keitel the verbal promise that the Reich would limit her demands to "those who had incited the war", which seemed narrowly to limit the Nazi claims, few of the refugees being sufficiently important to justify this designation.

It very soon appeared that the Nazis would not keep this verbal promise any better than they did their written engagements; the German Armistice Commission demanded the handing over of people who were totally unknown.

On the 27th July, the Government authorised a German Control Commission to visit the refugee camp at Vernet, in the Ariège, and to demand the list of Germans who had been interned there since the beginning of the war. The only one among them who had any political importance was the Rhenish Separatist, Niedermeyer, condemned to death by the Germans for having supported French policy at the time of the occupation of the left bank of the Rhine; three other refugees were agents of the French Deuxième Bureau. The Nazis demanded that they should be handed over immediately. General François, commanding the Region, asked Vichy if special measures could not be taken in favour of these Francophile Germans. Vichy telegraphed that Article 19 should be strictly applied. Fortunately, the Camp Commandant took it upon himself to disobey the order and allowed the prisoners to escape.

On the 27th August, in the free zone, fifty German nationals, ex-soldiers of the French Foreign Legion, were delivered up to the Nazis. On the 24th September, the same fate overtook forty of their comrades.

But these were only obscure victims; at the time of the armistice, there were three important German personalities who had taken refuge in France; they had all ceased political activity long before and could therefore not be charged with inciting to war. Breitscheid, an ex-Deputy of the Reichstag and a member of the Social Democratic Party; Hilferding, ex-Minister of Finance in the Republic of Weimar; and the industrialist, Karl Thyssen, who, having contributed to Hitler's success, had broken with the Nazis and expatriated himself.

Breitscheid and Hilferding, who were living in Marseilles, wished to go to America. Though they had not yet been the objects of German demands, Marquet, the Minister of the Interior, issued an order on the 30th August that they should be prevented from leaving; his successor, Peyrouton, on the 13th September, placed them under surveillance at Arles.

The same attitude was taken towards Thyssen and his wife, who were placed under similar surveillance at Nice before any German demand for them had been made.

They all later fell into the clutches of the Nazis.

The policy of Vichy with regard to the occupying power finally resolved itself into acceptance of accomplished fact and resignation to what appeared to be the inevitable.

The Empire was subject to other threats, against which France was in no better position to guard.

On the 2nd August, a Japanese ultimatum, presented to Admiral Decoux, Governor-General of Indo-China, demanded free passage through Tonkin for the Japanese troops engaged in the war against China, and the use of the French airfields.

According to Baudouin, resistance was impossible: the state of the French forces in Indo-China prohibited it.

The Americans, requested to come to the aid of Decoux, declared that they were in no position to do so.

In the opinion of the Marshal and Baudouin it was therefore necessary to negotiate and obtain an agreement by whose terms the Japanese Government would agree to respect the territorial integrity of Indo-China, while the French Government would recognise the predominating interests of Japan in the Far East. Under the cover of this agreement, France could grant Japan the military facilities she demanded.

Two Ministers opposed these negotiations. They were Weygand, Minister for War and Lémery, Minister for Colonies.

In its desire to put first things first, the Government decided in accordance with Baudouin's wishes. On the 29th August an Agreement was signed in Tokyo.

In the meantime, there were threats of dissidence in the Empire.

Since the middle of the month, the Gaullist broadcasts from London, *The French speaking to the French*, were conducting a violent verbal offensive, increasingly more virulent, against the Vichy Government. General de Gaulle inaugurated it on the 16th August. For the first time in his broadcasts, he accused Pétain of treason. On the 20th August, Churchill in his turn attacked the Pétain Government: "If France lies prostrate, it is the crime of this puppet government."

From the 27th–30th August, news from Africa flowed into Vichy, raising anger against England to new heights. It was successively learned that the Cameroons, Chad and Equatorial Africa had rallied to the dissidents. These events, which were in reality due to the initiative of French leaders whose names are still but little known, were attributed to the actions of British agents. On the 22nd August, Baudouin replied to Churchill on the radio. It was verbal fencing which, doubtless, resolved nothing but which did not envenom the situation. In any case it prevented two more serious eventualities: a reply by the Head of the State which would have been equivalent to a definitive rupture between the two countries, and the bombardment of Gibraltar, supported by Darlan.

But Laval, endeavouring to make use of these "favourable" circumstances to bring about the entry of France into the war against England, went on his own authority and without informing anyone to the headquarters of the occupying forces at Fontainebleau on the 26th August; he offered Marshal von Brauchitsch the co-operation of the French Air Force for the bombing of England. The German replied contemptuously that he had no use for the French aircraft and that, in any case, England was on the point of surrendering.

On the 30th August, after Chad, the Cameroons and Brazzaville had joined the dissidents, Laval suggested to the Council of Ministers that they should declare war on England. Pétain, Weygand and Baudouin opposed it, advancing, among other reasons, the increasingly Anglophile tendencies shown by public opinion.

No precise policy had therefore been determined on by the end of the month of August.

It was at this moment that the Marshal decided to take personal action.

His policy, as we have seen, excluded all extreme solutions: he neither wanted an alliance with Germany, as did Laval, nor open resistance, as did Weygand. He wished to protect the people of France by negotiation.

In order to achieve this, he first had to remove from the Government the two Ministers who held extreme opinions.

On the 6th September, he removed Weygand from all ministerial responsibility in order that he might devote himself to military and administrative matters, where his resistance to the Germans would be of the greatest value to the country, without creating immediate political consequences of an awkward kind. The General was appointed French Proconsul in North Africa; there he would maintain the sovereignty of France and increase, in spite of the Armistice Commissions, the power of the armed forces.

On the 8th September, Pétain tried similarly to diminish Pierre Laval's influence, but he did not succeed in doing so, at least for the moment. We know through Baudouin and Bouthillier of the conversation during the course of which the

Marshal informed Laval that he wished to abrogate the constitutional act which made him the "*dauphin*" and reduce him to the rank of Minister like the others.

A fortnight later, Constitutional Act No. 4 *bis*, published in the *Journal Officiel* on the 25th September, laid down the procedure to be adopted.

"In the case of M. Pierre Laval being for any reason unavailable, he will be replaced by a person appointed, on a majority of votes, by the Council of Ministers. Until the investiture of this person, the powers will be exercised by the Council of Ministers."

A clause which, without formally saying so, implicitly limited Laval's prerogatives, while admitting that another than he might be the "*dauphin*".

It was a complete victory over Weygand; with Laval a preliminary and indecisive skirmish. This semi-repulse did not prevent the Marshal from putting his own policy of prudence and waiting into execution.

In order to make the Nazi occupation less oppressive, the Marshal intended to use his personal prestige on Hitler: "I shall go and see the Führer as I went and saw the mutineers in 1917," he said to Charles-Roux. And on the 15th September, the Marshal ordered Admiral Fernet to write to Colonel Fonck, a French flying ace of the First World War and a personal friend of Goering's: "Please give me news of your parents in the Vosges." A harmless phrase, one might think, but in fact it was a code agreed between Pétain and Fonck a fortnight earlier: the Marshal charged Colonel Fonck to approach Goering in order to get the principle of an interview between Hitler and himself accepted.

To communicate with Churchill, his secret intermediary was Professor Louis Rougier. Rougier, a Professor of Political Economy, had taken part before the war in international conferences "for the resurgence of Liberalism". He had known Lionel Robbins, Professor at the London School of Economics.

In August, 1940, Rougier came to Vichy, where he met Baudouin, Weygand, Moysset and René Gillouin. They were all very concerned about the British blockade. Rougier decided to intervene; having obtained from Weygand an authorisation to go to Switzerland, he sent a telegram from Geneva to Lionel Robbins in which he deplored the blockade. On the 29th August, a reply came from Lionel Robbins inviting his colleague in economics to come to England.

Rougier returned to Vichy where he successively saw Baudouin, Weygand and Pétain. All three approved his action.

The Marshal received him on Friday, 20th September, on the recommendation of René Gillouin, the only other person present being Admiral Fernet. The interview had been arranged secretly and without going through the usual channels in order to avoid Rougier's name appearing in any register. The Marshal once again attacked Laval: "M. Laval is the man whom I despise most in the world, but I still have need of him; later, I shall get rid of him. You may tell the English so."

What was to be the result of these feelers put out to both camps? During the course of September, there were no results at all; in appearance, nothing had changed; they had, indeed, tended to grow worse.

On the German side, the Laval-Abetz negotiations seemed to be giving no results, except for the authorisation to correspond by postcard between the two zones; the return of the Government to Paris was indefinitely postponed; the demarcation line was more hermetically sealed than ever; and German pressure showed no lessening at any point.

At some points even, it was increasing: on the 15th September, 1940, the Nazis suppressed the French Customs on the Belgian frontier, thus officially marking the inclusion of the Nord and the Pas-de-Calais in the German administration of Belgium. The tension had reached a point where everyone was awaiting an early storm.

Bouthillier, feeling that the atmosphere was louring and believing a clash inevitable, stopped the payment of the occupation indemnities on his own authority.

In Indo-China, the concessions made to Japan did not prevent the Japanese Army from attacking the north of Tonkin and surrounding at Lang-Son a Franco-Annamite brigade which was too weak to resist successfully. On the 22nd September a convention was signed authorising the Japanese to use certain airfields, to garrison Tonkin with 6,000 men and to evacuate through Haiphong a division which was in a difficult position in Yunnan.

The British precipitated a new crisis almost as serious as that of Mers-el-Kebir. On the morning of the 23rd September, a British Fleet, carrying the Royal Marine Brigade and accompanied by a few Gaullist ships, appeared off Dakar in a thick fog, which was unusual at that season. The plan for the occupation of this great African port, proposed in the first instance by de Gaulle and adopted with enthusiasm by Churchill, would have had appreciable benefits for the British; French West Africa would have joined the dissidents and doubtless North Africa would have followed; the battle-cruiser, *Richelieu*, would have been seized in the harbour of Dakar, as would the Belgian and Polish gold which, confided to the Bank of France, had been placed by the latter for greater safety in the African capital. It was, however, understood that there would be no infringement of French sovereignty, which would be exercised by the Gaullist authorities.

The operation, which it was intended at first should be carried out by the Free French Forces alone, with 2,500 men in French ships, soon appeared impossible of success with such limited means.

A directive of Churchill's, dated 8th August, 1940, envisaged making available "an ample British naval force, both to dominate French warships in the neighbourhood and to cover the landing; a brigade of Poles, properly equipped; the Royal Marine Brigade which was being held available for the Atlantic Islands, but might well help to put de Gaulle ashore first, or alternatively commandos from Sir Roger Keyes's forces; proper air support, either by carrier or by machines working from a British West African colony." In spite of the use of British forces, Churchill specified this essential consideration from the French point of view: "It is not intended, after Dakar is taken, that we shall hold it with British Forces. General de Gaulle's administration would be set up, and would have to maintain itself. . . ."

The operation thus conceived failed owing to delays and also because of the stubborn defence of the French in Dakar, who were loyal to Pétain.

A squadron of ships which had remained faithful to Vichy and which was composed of three cruisers of the *Georges-Leygues* class, and three destroyers, passed through the Straits of Gibraltar on the 11th September without being intercepted and went to reinforce the defence of Dakar.

On the 23rd September in the morning, two launches laden with French members of Parliament detached themselves from the attacking fleet. On board one of them was Captain Thierry d'Argenlieu, who was carrying important communications to General Boisson and the military chiefs in Dakar.

The negro gunners serving the French coastal batteries did not realise that these were plenipotentiaries and opened fire. It was an involuntary violation of the rules of war to which fighting succeeded during the next three days, inflicting the loss of two submarines on the French Vichy forces, damage to the *Richelieu*, to the merchant ship, *Porthos*, and to two destroyers. On the British side, the *Resolution* was hit by a torpedo, which put her out of action for several months, while two destroyers were also seriously damaged. There were a few Gaullist casualties, among them Captain Bécourt-Foch, a grandson of the Marshal, who was gravely wounded during an attempt at landing.

As a result of this unforeseen resistance, Churchill sent the following telegram from London, dated 25th September, 1.27 p.m.: "We have decided that the enterprise against Dakar should be abandoned, the obvious evil consequences being faced." And the Prime Minister summed up the unhappy affair with the words: "Errors towards the enemy must be lightly judged: one cannot foresee everything."

It is a sad reflection that Frenchmen, believing that they were all equally fighting for the national interest, should find themselves, by force of circumstances, in two enemy camps.

The attackers were convinced that Dakar was full of Germans and that Boisson was a traitor; the defenders knew *de visu* that there were no Germans: they therefore considered de Gaulle in the pay of England and guilty of treason.

In spite of these bloody episodes, the conversations arranged by the Marshal were not postponed.

Rougier was on his way to England. Fonck had been able to see Goering and ask him to organise an interview between the two Heads of State.

Goering excused himself on the plea that he did not concern himself with politics and transmitted the Marshal's enquiry to Abetz, thus rendering useless all the precautions Pétain had taken to hold Laval's partner in ignorance of his personal *démarche*.

As soon as Abetz had been informed, he telegraphed to Berlin on the 8th October that Marshal Pétain had indicated his desire to meet the Führer.

Thus, Pétain on his side and Laval on his were both negotiating to meet their opposite numbers in the Reich. Laval wished to see Ribbentrop, Pétain to meet Hitler.

At this time Hitler also thought it necessary to meet Pétain. Until September, 1940, France had only taken a secondary place in the Führer's grandiose conceptions now that he was victorious in the West. His ultimate goal, his supreme ambition, which he had announced long before 1939 in conversations with Hermann Rauschning, was expansion towards the East and the acquisition of a vast "living space" at the expense of the U.S.S.R.

In September, 1940, the defeat of the Luftwaffe had persuaded the Führer that, before turning towards the East, he would have to pay further attention to the West.

His direct assault on England having failed, he therefore had to proceed to an indirect attack, for which Goering had made the plan, and which necessitated the collaboration both of Spain and France. First, he must take Gibraltar, an operation which everybody considered to be easy of realisation; then, he must cross North Africa and make for Suez. From there, moving south, he must take Dakar, which commanded the whole of the west coast of Africa, and from which British shipping on the Cape route might be intercepted. Because it had not been able to cross the twenty miles between Calais and Dover, the Wehrmacht was thus condemned to cross thousands of miles of the African continent.

It was a grandiose plan which necessitated, in the first instance, the consent of Spain to an attack on Gibraltar across Spanish territory and the consent of France to the crossing of North Africa. There could be no question of crossing it by force; that would have risked the whole French Empire going over to de Gaulle and the French Fleet entering the war again on the British side.

Hitler had, therefore, reached the conclusion, by the beginning of October, that he needed French collaboration in order to finish with England.

Circumstances were all the more convenient in that Hitler was to meet Franco on French territory, at Hendaye, on the 23rd October. He proposed taking advantage of this fact first to see Laval at Montoire, on the 22nd October, and then, on the 24th, to meet Pétain at a second interview. He expected that, during the course of these three days, he would obtain what he wanted both from the Spanish and the French.

What Hitler did not know, was that Pétain had been warned of his intentions and had informed Franco of them. During the second fortnight of September, the Japanese Ambassador at

Vichy, M. Renzo Sawada, had gone to Berlin to take part in the preliminaries of the Tripartite Pact between Germany, Italy and Japan. In the company of his Berlin colleague, he had seen Adolf Hitler who, "in the euphoria created by such an event," relates Admiral Fernet, confided to the two diplomats his plans concerning Spain and North Africa.

On his return to Vichy, Sawada, who was a sincere friend of France, told Fonck what he had heard. Fonck arranged an interview for the Ambassador with Pétain on the 27th September. The Marshal immediately sent for the Spanish Ambassador, Lequerica, and secretly asked him to inform Franco. The Ambassador left for Madrid and returned four days later; he thanked the French Head of the State in the name of the Caudillo and assured him that Spain would refuse or, rather, evade the passage of German troops.

On the 21st October, in the lobbies of the hotels and in the open spaces of the park, Vichy was in a state of effervescence. President Laval had just left for Paris, which was a fairly common occurrence; but there was a rumour to the effect that his luggage contained a top hat—a fact without precedent and even more surprising in his case than in that of anyone else: all Vichy was obsessed by the significance of this headgear.

It was certainly not in order to see Ambassador Otto Abetz, his usual host in Paris, that he had provided himself with such an object. There was only one conclusion to be drawn: the President of the Council, whose usual slovenly appearance was thus about to be transformed, was to meet someone in Paris of infinitely greater importance.

Who was it to be? Nobody knew, except perhaps Laval, and in any case it was not yet certain.

Indeed, here is the Théramène-like recital which Laval, on many occasions, delighted to repeat, and in which some people, including Charles-Roux, assert that he exaggerated the truth:

"I arrived at the Embassy at about 10 o'clock in the morning. I saw more uniforms than I have ever seen before, more cars, a coming and going which showed that something very important was happening.

"I got into the Ambassador's car and I said: 'Where are we going?' He said: 'I don't know. There's a pilot car in front, leading us.'

"When we reached Rambouillet, it was 11 or 11.30 in the morning. I said to the Ambassador: 'Are we going to the Château of Rambouillet?' He said: 'No, it's much further on.' 'But where are we going to have luncheon?' He said: 'At Tours.'

"We arrived at Tours. We had luncheon. I said: 'Where is M. de Ribbentrop?' The Ambassador replied: 'He is not here, but at 5 o'clock we shall drive on to another destination. I don't know where it is, but the pilot car will lead us there.'

"At about 6 or 6.30 the car drove off in a direction unknown to me. I did not know the district very well. But, after a certain time, I could see numerous sentries behind trees and, as we went on, they grew more numerous still.

"When we had crossed the bridge over the Loire, M. Abetz said to me: 'Do you know whom you are going to meet?'

" 'Of course: I'm going to meet M. de Ribbentrop.'

" 'Yes, but you're not only going to meet M. de Ribbentrop: you're also going to meet Chancellor Hitler.'

" '*Merde alors!*' "

After this last exclamation, Laval fell silent. The car continued to drive through the night.

It stopped by a little station whose name Laval did not know.

Accompanied by Abetz, he got out of the car, walked on to the platform and saw two armoured trains, those of Hitler and Ribbentrop, halted near a tunnel, which might serve as a refuge in case of an air-raid. Indeed, it was this shelter which predestined Montoire to play its part in history.

In front of the Führer's train, Laval was met by Ribbentrop and by Dr. Schmidt, Hitler's official interpreter. At sight of him, Laval showed some relief at seeing a face he knew: in 1931, Schmidt had been interpreter between Laval and Chancellor Brüning. A little later, during the course of his conversation with Hitler, Laval called upon Schmidt's memory to witness that, ten years before, he had already been trying to bring about a *rapprochement* between France and Germany.

In his book, *Hitler's Interpreter*, published in 1951, Dr. Schmidt says very little of the conversation between Hitler and Laval. He merely writes that it took place in a fairly cordial atmosphere.

Laval, in a report found four years later in his luggage, and of which Pétain never had knowledge, is much more categorical:

the atmosphere at this first meeting at Montoire was extremely amicable, indeed it was surprisingly so.

Hitler assured Laval that it formed no part of his intention to make a peace of vengeance, but a constructive one. "My interview with Chancellor Hitler at Montoire was a surprise to me, a delightful surprise. . . . We felt the same way and we ended by talking a new language: European."

On this day of the 22nd October, both for Hitler and for Laval, the interests of the two countries were momentarily in accord.

Laval, as convinced as ever that a British defeat was imminent, thought it essential to France that the Reich should accept her collaboration, first in the struggle against Great Britain, and then in the reconstruction of Europe. Entirely concentrated on this outcome, Laval did not suspect that in putting it forward he was doing no more than anticipating Hitler's secret wishes: the collaboration Laval wished him to accept was precisely what the Führer was concerned to obtain in view of his military plans. Hitler, thinking of his interview on the morrow with Franco, thought that an agreement with France was a necessary preliminary to the agreement he expected to make with the Spanish dictator.

When Laval stated that the only possible policy for defeated France was an understanding with Germany, Hitler eagerly approved: "It is in the interests of France, if she wishes England, rather than herself, to pay the costs of the war."

It was Laval's turn to outdo him: "As a Frenchman, I can only say that I desire with all my heart a British defeat."

Hitler gave him no guarantee for the future: the final settlement, the Führer said, could only be made after the end of the war; not only would the problem of Europe have to be considered, but also that of Africa; French interests would in all likelihood be safeguarded. . . . It was up to France to behave in such a way that any eventual loss of her colonies would be compensated by the gift of a British colony. . . . Nigeria, for instance, might compensate France for the loss of Tunisia.

Hitler had asked to see Pétain two days later; it was up to Laval to persuade the Marshal to agree. But Laval had no doubt that Pétain had long wished for nothing better.

Accompanied by Brinon and the German Counsellor to the Embassy, Achenbach, Laval returned to Vichy in the afternoon of the 23rd October.

His report to the Council of Ministers, which took place at 5 p.m., was so vague, so weighted with reticences, that it put the final touch to the latent discord between Laval and his colleagues and between Laval and Pétain.

Having made his Théramène-like recital, down to the final exclamation, for the first time—a recital which the Ministers listened to with a certain scepticism—Laval showed himself extremely optimistic: "My impression is a favourable one. . . . Hitler is a great man, who knows what he's doing and where he's going. . . . The Führer has offered France collaboration. . . . I have entered into no engagements, but it would be a crime against France to refuse his offer. . . ."

This "collaboration", which was now mentioned for the first time in the Council of Ministers, and concerning which Laval gave no details, was to consist in what? That was the question Belin asked.

Laval paid no attention. . . .

"France has reached the cross-roads. . . . If certain people criticise me and attack me, I don't care a damn. I have the certainty of doing my best for my country."

A few hours later, when Pétain declared his wish that his Minister for Foreign Affairs should accompany him to the second meeting at Montoire, Laval grew angry: "If Baudouin were to make the journey and if he, Laval, was not to be the only member of the Government at the side of the Head of the State for the interview with Hitler, the meeting would not take place." It was an ultimatum to which Pétain yielded: on the 24th October, Baudouin did not accompany the Marshal as his position required and, immediately after Montoire, he abandoned the Ministry of Foreign Affairs to Laval.

Very early, on Thursday 24th October, the Head of the State left Vichy. He did not conceal his great satisfaction at meeting the Führer.

Pétain was accompanied by Laval, Brinon, du Moulin, Ménétrel and Achenbach. They went in two cars. Laval and Ménétrel got into the first one with the Marshal; there were motor-cyclist out-riders in white gloves.

Nothing could have differed more from Laval's journey of two days before than did Pétain's. While, on the 22nd October, every precaution had been taken to assure that the journey of the

Vice-President of the Council and Abetz should pass unperceived, Pétain, on the 24th October, was received with considerable ceremony when he entered the territory occupied by the Wehrmacht.

Towards 10 o'clock, when the convoy had arrived at the Madeleine bridge, near Moulins, it halted at the demarcation line, which Pétain now crossed for the first time; the honours done him only made this first contact with the occupied zone the more painful.

Three German Generals, in full dress, saluted the Marshal: their embroidered uniforms contrasted strangely with the clothes of the French. Pétain, in a simple undress uniform, wore on his Verdun tunic as his only decoration the Medaille Militaire, which is the award for ordinary soldiers or Commanders-in-Chief. In his suite there was but one uniform, that of Dr. Ménétrel who, after considerable thought, had put on his uniform of a major in the Medical Corps.

A company of the Wehrmacht presented arms. The Marshal walked slowly along the lines of victorious youth who stood still as statues beneath their helmets.

On the further side of the bridge, they stopped again. General Schmidt, the Commander of a Panzer Division, the hero of the two *blitzkriegs* on Poland and on France, joined the convoy.

A German car now led the way, but at such a speed that the French motor-cyclists, trained merely to escort officials from the Élysée to the Étoile, were out-distanced. The convoy had to stop and wait for them. Laval took the opportunity to change places with Brinon: in the Marshal's car he was not allowed to smoke.

Every fifty or sixty kilometres they stopped in order to allow the commander of another German sector to pay his respects, introduce himself and take his place in the convoy with his car until the next sector was reached, where the whole performance was gone through again.

They lunched at Tours with the Préfet of Indre-et-Loire. At 4.30 p.m., they set off again. At the outskirts of Montoire, the Marshal's car drove between two or three companies of the Wehrmacht who presented arms in absolute immobility.

When Pétain left his car, he was received by a huge German, Graf von Doernberg, Chef de Protocole of the Reich.

The Guard of Honour consisted of a battalion of the Führer's Guard. Doernberg led the Marshal through the station building.

The Marshal briskly crossed the line and was met by Hitler on the centre platform, where he was waiting with Ribbentrop and Marshal Keitel. The Führer left the group, and walked forward towards Pétain. The two men shook hands. Hitler said: "I am glad to shake the hand of a Frenchman who is not responsible for this war." Pétain, for whom the words were not translated, thought the Führer had asked him about his journey, and limited himself to replying: "Thank you, thank you, very pleasant."

Magnesium flash-lights were going off in all directions: the handshake must be preserved for posterity as a symbol of Franco-German reconciliation. A few years later, Pétain was to say that he had given his hand only with the tips of his fingers, a mere simulacrum. This reticence was not visible at the time; the handshake, which was published all over the press by the Staffel Propaganda and distributed to cinemas, plunged France into stupefaction.

The conversation that followed bore little relation to that between Hitler and Laval. A difference which, with an interval of only two days, was due to three causes.

In the first place, Hitler had returned weary and disappointed from his interview with Franco. For nine hours, the two men had discussed the conditions for Spain's entry into the war. Franco, forewarned by Pétain, and determined not to yield, put forward demands which made agreement impossible. He asked for the whole of French Morocco and part of Algeria. For all their polite words, Franco inflicted a complete defeat on Hitler on the 23rd October. On the 24th, when he met Pétain, the Führer was still suffering from his disappointment: he had none of that dynamism which, two days before, had so impressed Laval.

A second difference between the interview of the 22nd and 24th was that the principal negotiator with the Chancellor had changed. Instead of it being Laval, whose attitude was precise and who was ready to take his stand at the side of Germany, it was now the Marshal who, having decided to refuse military collaboration with the Reich, avoided making any precise promises.

Resolved not to yield on the essential points, Pétain was led to make a concession on a matter which he judged to be of secondary importance, without realising its gravity. It consisted, on Hitler's demand, of making a broadcast extolling collaboration.

Hitler opened the interview with one of his customary monologues.

"I am certain of winning the war, but I must finish it as soon as possible, for nothing is more ruinous than war. England will have to pay the greater part of the cost. But every European country will suffer from its prolongation.

"It is therefore in their interest to form a continental community with the object of shortening the duration of hostilities.

"What position does the French Government propose to adopt?"

Pétain saw in this an excellent opportunity for replying vaguely: certainly, he was prepared to accept collaboration in principle, but he could not immediately specify to what extent France could participate; ways and means must be studied by his Government.

Hitler was not taken in by this climbing down: it was from Pétain, and from Pétain alone, that he desired an assurance of French collaboration. And he pursued the matter with greater precision: "Will France continue to defend her Colonial Empire, as at Dakar, against all attacks? Is she prepared to reconquer the dissident territories?"

As Pétain delayed answering, Hitler demanded with renewed insistence what France would do if England were to attack her again.

The Marshal, with his back to the wall, did not hesitate to side-track this question: "My country has suffered too much, both morally and materially, to engage herself in a new conflict."

Hitler was displeased: "If France will not defend herself and still has sympathy for England, she'll lose her Colonial Empire at the end of the war and will be subjected to peace terms as onerous as England's."

"No peace of reprisal has ever lasted in history," replied Pétain curtly, thus putting the Chancellor into a fury.

"I don't want a peace of reprisal," exclaimed Hitler, "on the contrary, I am prepared to favour France. What I want, is a peace founded on mutual agreement, guaranteeing the peace of Europe for several centuries. But I cannot bring it about unless France will make up her mind to help me defeat the British."

Pétain cleverly took the opportunity of making a diversion: since the Führer had spoken of peace, would he state in what terms he envisaged the final treaty, "in order that France might know her fate and the two million prisoners return as soon as possible to their families"?

As, no doubt, the Marshal expected, Hitler avoided answering: the final treaty could only be considered after the ultimate defeat of England. Pétain then observed that, while waiting upon events, measures must be taken to assure the early return of the prisoners at least, to ameliorate the situation with regard to the demarcation line, which was creating an intolerable situation, and to reduce the indemnity for the occupation.

To these questions, which for Pétain were the real object of the interview, Hitler did not reply with an immediate refusal: he agreed to study them.

The fate of the prisoners was, he knew, one of the means of exerting pressure to which Pétain was most sensitive. Hitler, also, by this shift, re-introduced the problem of collaboration and put the deal squarely before the Marshal: "If France and Germany achieve an agreement on collaboration, France may expect concessions on all the points the Marshal has mentioned."

At this point, Laval intervened: "Thanks to the Führer's offer, France is no longer face to face with a blank wall. . . . However, in spite of my own personal desire to do so, I recognise that there are difficulties in declaring war on England. . . . Public opinion must grow accustomed to the idea and then, in accordance with constitutional law, we need the consent of the National Assembly."

There followed a long speech by Laval, who repeated almost word for word his declarations of two days before and reaffirmed his desire to collaborate. Pétain listened without saying a word and only spoke again to demand the return to France of the departments in the north which had been attached to the military government in Belgium; he was less precise over Alsace-Lorraine.

Hitler finally promised to make known in writing his position on the various points raised; the Marshal, for lack of any more concrete promises, would make a radio appeal inviting the French to collaborate with Germany and thus, for lack of the reality, content himself with words. So the interview came to an end. Pétain, throughout, had been extremely reticent. Having obtained from Marshal Keitel the freeing of General Laure and an authorisation to visit a Prisoners' Camp near Amboise, the Marshal left for Vichy, where he arrived on the evening of the 25th and, on the 26th October, informed the Council of Ministers of the results of the interview. The impression he gave them was very different from that given by Laval in the Council of the 23rd after the first meeting at Montoire.

For Pétain, there was no question of military collaboration with Germany: Montoire had merely been an opportunity to make contact. The Marshal had not gone beyond the limits he had set himself.

On the very day of the first meeting at Montoire, the 22nd October, the negotiations Pétain had undertaken with England through the intermediary of Rougier seemed to be coming to a head. Rougier had arrived in London.

Received in turn by Sir Alexander Cadogan, Permanent Under-Secretary to the Foreign Office, who laid it down as a preliminary condition to all conversations that Rougier should have no contact with the Gaullists, by Lord Halifax, the Foreign Secretary, and then by Winston Churchill, he seems to have made two successive impressions. In the first place, there was considerable interest concerning the mission of the first emissary of the Pétain Government and satisfaction at learning the anti-German attitude which, according to Rougier, was manifest in Vichy. But soon there was a feeling that, in order to conduct real secret negotiations between France and England, Louis Rougier was not perhaps of sufficient standing. To read the history of his mission, it would seem that Louis Rougier, led by circumstances into a provisional employment which was disproportionate to his political position, persuaded himself more and more that he was playing an historical role, while, on his side, Churchill summed him up and gradually withdrew to the point where he only used him as a source of information and no longer as a diplomatist. From this arises the difference, which can be read between the lines in the records themselves, between Rougier's interpretation and Winston Churchill's. Rougier claims to have established, in agreement with Churchill and in accordance with manuscript corrections in Churchill's own hand, a protocol between the Government in London and the Government in Vichy: a protocol in which were to be found all the desiderata which it was Rougier's mission to transmit to Great Britain. England engaged herself to restore France in her integrity and her sovereignty, if she did nothing to assist the victory of the totalitarian states. She would authorise the transfer of colonial produce to France. She engaged herself to make no attempt to invade or turn towards dissidence those French colonies which had remained loyal to the Government of Vichy. Great Britain would cease her radio attacks on Marshal Pétain. On her side, France would engage herself not to recapture by force those colonies which had gone over to de Gaulle, to cede no bases or ports to the Axis powers, and finally to bring the Empire back into the war on the day that the British and their eventual allies were in a position to disembark a sufficiency of troops and to supply the French colonial troops with enough arms. She would engage herself to scuttle the Fleet rather than let it fall into the hands of the Germans or Italians.

Such was the outline of the protocol which Rougier supposedly brought back to Vichy to be ratified by Pétain.

The telegram received by the British Consul-General in Geneva on the 21st November, in which the British Government confirmed the results of the conversations, is infinitely less detailed than the supposed protocol of Louis Rougier.

The British official version differs from the assertions of Rougier by one addition, by several omissions and by alterations in emphasis.

The addition was the paragraph concerning the support the British reserved the right to give French Colonies which rallied to de Gaulle.

The suppressions were: the engagement to raise the blockade between France and her Empire; the engagement to cease attacking Pétain on the British radio; and that concerning the eventuality of the French Empire entering into the war.

The alterations in emphasis were that it was no protocol, but an announcement of conditions which might constitute a preliminary arrangement for a *modus vivendi*.

Louis Rougier's mission, in the eyes of the British, was purely one of exchanging information and views.

Pétain, on the other hand, attached great importance to Rougier's conversations with Churchill: he saw in them a possibility of putting an end to the blockade which threatened to starve out Metropolitan France.

Three engagements which the English, according to Rougier, had demanded of him, corresponded to his policy: not to allow the Germans to penetrate into the Empire, not to cede them bases, and not to recapture by force the Gaullist colonies.

The only person who saw the document was Flandin. In

December, 1940, Pétain, in order to persuade him to enter the Government and replace Pierre Laval as Minister for Foreign Affairs, took from his safe the only two papers that were in it and gave them to the Minister to read: one was the report on Montoire, the other Rougier's protocol. Flandin was thus made aware of the two documents which determined the Marshal's policy; for Pétain, the engagements he had made with England were more substantial and precise than those outlined at Montoire.

The Marshal's interview with Hitler at Montoire engaged him to nothing.

Laval and the Germans, on the other hand, thought that Montoire marked an important date in French policy.

This can be seen by Laval's speech in the Council of Ministers on the 26th October, as recorded by Admiral Fernet in manuscript notes taken at the time.

"This remarkable fact must be taken into account: the conqueror coming to offer collaboration to the conquered. Weather conditions have not as yet permitted a landing. But victory over England is achieved. The Germans are making a gigantic effort. Time is in their favour. But the war will cost dear. The defeated will pay. 'FRANCE WILL PAY,' said the Chancellor, 'UNLESS SHE DECIDES TO COLLABORATE WITH US.' . . . 'WE DO NOT WANT A PEACE OF VENGEANCE,' said the Chancellor. 'The destruction of Great Britain opens up new possibilities. I HAVE ALREADY TRIED TO MAKE PEACE WITH FRANCE,' he added. The Franco-German relations will therefore depend upon the outcome of the war. All will depend upon the attitude of France: a positive attitude or an attitude of waiting. The reorganisation of Africa will be subordinate to the reorganisation of Europe. France will be well treated in Africa: it is stated that Africa is a prolongation of Europe. The choice is there to be made."

The Germans shared Laval's point of view.

On the 12th November, in top secret instructions to Marshal Jodl, Hitler defined "the object of my policy concerning France: it is to co-operate with France in the most effective manner for the future prosecution of the war against England. For the moment, France will play the part of a non-belligerent power. She must accept the measures the Germans have taken in her territory, notably in the African Colonies, and support them as much as possible, using her own means of defence; the most important duty of the French is to protect the French possessions (West and Equatorial Africa) against England and against General de Gaulle's movement. From this initial duty there may result complete participation by France in the war against England."

It suffices to modify the introductory phrase and to substitute "the Führer demands that France . . ." for "the object of my policy concerning France . . ." to discover, almost word for word, the statements made by Laval at Vichy on the 26th October.

Thus, the Montoire interview aggravated and lent precision to the initial disagreements which, since the 25th June, 1940, had separated Pétain and Laval.

For the Marshal, the armistice was not and could not be more than a pause, which allowed France to exist provisionally, while awaiting the outcome of the war between England and the Axis; Montoire, looked at from his point of view, was but an episode and made no change in his policy towards Germany.

For Laval, on the other hand, the armistice permitted of a reversal of alliances, of which Montoire, in the most definite way, was to mark the beginning.

It is clear that Montoire was the origin of a triple misunderstanding whose consequences were to weigh heavily upon the whole Vichy drama.

Misunderstandings between Pétain and Laval, which were soon to come to a head in the clash of the 13th December; misunderstandings between Hitler and the Marshal on the exact meanings of "collaboration" and Franco-German relations, which would bring in their train the occupation of the free zone in November, 1942, the scuttling of the Fleet and, in August, 1944, the removal of Pétain by the Germans.

But there was also another misunderstanding, more grievous and more eventful in its dramatic and long term consequences for France, more complex and profound, though perhaps involuntary, between Pétain and public opinion. The majority of Frenchmen did not and could not understand what Pétain's real attitude, after Montoire, was towards the occupying power.

They did not know that by his secret message to Franco, Pétain had tried to torpedo the interview before even going to it.

They did not know that at Montoire he had not agreed to the proposals put forward by Hitler and Laval.

They did not know that, at the same time, he was carrying on negotiations with London.

They only knew of his spectacular statements on the French radio in which he extolled in words the collaboration he had been constrained to accept, but which he had decided never to allow to become military engagements.

Certain words have a terrifying and injurious power, when the head of a vanquished State, after an interview with the conqueror, expresses himself as did Pétain on the 30th October:

"It is in all honour and in order to maintain the unity of France—a unity of ten centuries within the framework of the constructive activity of the new European Order—that I am today pursuing the path of collaboration. . . . This collaboration must be sincere. It must bring with it patient and confident effort. An armistice, after all, is not peace. France is constrained by the many engagements she has taken towards the conqueror. At least, she remains sovereign. This sovereignty imposes upon her the duty of defending her soil, to extinguish divergency of opinion and to diminish the number of dissidents in her colonies. This policy is mine. The Ministers are only responsible to me. It is I alone whom history will judge.

"Until today I have spoken to you the language of a father. Today I speak to you in the language of a leader. Follow me. Put your faith in France eternal."

These words, even admitting that they were only words, were fateful in their consequences.

Montoire is perhaps the principal cause of the appalling crises of conscience that Vichy imposes on public opinion.

It explains why, for instance, certain patriots, who were originally loyal to Pétain, now tore up their photographs of the Marshal, who had, during the first months, been the object of their veneration and in whom they had placed their hopes. At Vichy itself, it brought about the resignation of the Secretary-General of the Ministry of Foreign Affairs, François Charles-Roux.

Conversely, it justified to some extent the actions of all those who believed that, by collaborating, they were obeying the Marshal and serving the country. This speech of the 30th October incited many Frenchmen to take a path that was to be fatal to them.

## CHAPTER 6

# THE ARREST OF PIERRE LAVAL

### (22nd October, 1940–13th December, 1940)

SIX weeks after the interview at Montoire, the French statesman whose wishes and policy seemed to be crowned by this event—the man who had seen the Führer first and been Pétain's companion at the historic encounter—was turned out of the Government and arrested. How did such a reversal of fortune come about?

On the evening of Wednesday, 30th October, at Vichy, Baudouin, taking care not to be seen by Pierre Laval, introduced a visitor into the Marshal's room with all the precautions of a conspirator: it was M. Gama Ochoa, the representative of Portugal in France.

In the presence of this diplomatist, the Marshal made a formal engagement, which was to be transmitted to Churchill: the interview at Montoire would result in no military collaboration with the Reich. Pétain would never authorise a hostile act against Great Britain. The next day, Thursday 31st October, in Paris, another remarkable scene took place, in striking contrast to the former. Accompanied by the Minister of Finance, Bouthillier, who was somewhat embarrassed by being present, Pierre Laval had luncheon at the German Embassy. After the meal, he had a conversation with his hosts:

"Pierre Laval spoke like a proud man. It was impossible to be wrong with greater fervour and sincerity. He did not say: 'Let us march forward together, you will see how useful we will be to you,' but 'The Führer is a great man because he has understood that he cannot build a Europe without France.' "

In the presence of all the civil and military heads of the departments of the Embassy, Laval envisaged, in particular, armed action against Great Britain: ". . . The Chancellor of the Reich has not asked us to declare war on England. He has asked us to enter into a European coalition against England and that, in the first place, within the framework of such a coalition, we should take action to collaborate militarily in Africa."

Thus, Pétain at Vichy and Pierre Laval in Paris drew opposite conclusions from the interview which had taken place less than eight days before. The differences between them were increasing; the misunderstanding was all the more evident from the fact that Montoire, to all appearances, had been of no service to France.

Indeed, the interview at Montoire brought no amelioration to Franco-German relations.

The first person to recognise this was Bouthillier, when, on the 31st October, taking his stand on the "collaboration" announced after Montoire, he suggested to Hemmen that the costs of the occupation should be reduced; he also asked that the exchange rate of the Mark should be lowered to between 12 and 15 francs; and that the departments of the Nord and Pas-de-Calais should be attached once more to the French administration. His opposite number paid no attention. Moreover, Hemmen insisted on obtaining satisfaction on another point under dispute: the remitting to the Reich of the Belgian gold which had been confided to France.

Far from minimising the effects of the demarcation line, the Germans used it to put pressure on the French Government to sign, on the 14th November, the export-import treaty[1] which was the second point in the financial ultimatum of the 8th August. This "agreement" was legally to bring the Reich in 164 billions of francs, at the 1939 value, in four years.

It was also after Montoire that the collective expulsions of Alsatians began. The transfer of population had been announced by Gauleiter Burckel at the end of November, 1940, as having been decided on in agreement with the French Government: another lie to the credit of the Nazis!

Between the 12th and 22nd November 66 thousand inhabitants of Lorraine and 120 thousand Alsatians were expelled into the free zone: 66 trains of refugees arrived at Lyon.

[1] Hemmen threatened Bousanger in these terms: "If you refuse to sign the agreement about payments, there is nothing to be done but to stop everything. I shall inform the Führer and you will have no facilities whatever over the demarcation line."

The Head of the State made no formal protest, but limited himself to uttering a few words of sympathy on the radio. Only Alibert, who met the trains at the Perrache station, uttered a few unofficial words against this violation of the armistice.

On the 30th November—five weeks after Montoire—Burckel officially declared that the Moselle was annexed to the Reich. Lorraine and the Sarre would form the Gau Westmark with Sarrebruck as capital. As for Alsace, it was attached to Baden.

In the occupied zone, German economic pressure was not diminished. To counteract the measures taken to re-absorb the unemployed and in particular the law inaugurating short time, the Germans increased to forty, forty-eight and fifty-four per week the obligatory hours of work in the mines.

There was no section of French activity which escaped the Germans. In November, 1940, Goebbels, in agreement with Dr. Ley, ordered that French predominance in fashion should not be revived: elegant women in the future must go to the Berlin *couturiers* and not to those of Paris; the Führer had decided it.

On the 28th November, a month after Montoire, wider and more detailed instructions were issued with the object of doing no less than ravaging France of her artistic and intellectual prestige: "the result of our victorious struggle should be to break the predominance of French propaganda in Europe and in the world. After having taken possession of Paris, the centre of French cultural propaganda, it is now possible to give this propaganda a final blow. Any support given it or tolerance shown it will be a crime against the nation."

Though all these confirmations or aggravations of German pressure on France might give the lie to his personal interpretation of Montoire, Pierre Laval was not perturbed.

He was convinced that he had achieved at Montoire, as he had expected, an international success comparable to his parliamentary triumph of the 10th July.

He showed nothing but contempt for the Government: he did not even bother to attend two out of three Councils of Ministers; he omitted, when he did attend, to report on his interviews in Paris with the German authorities. It even happened that, when a Minister had the impertinence to insist on an explanation of his policy, Laval gave him without comment an official file marked "Foreign Affairs: Franco-German Relations", which contained nothing but a sheet of blank paper.

Though he was not officially head of the Government, he acted as such, re-distributing ministerial departments and interfering indiscriminately in the work of the Ministries.

Thus Laval created an atmosphere of hostility about himself, which increased the prejudice that Pétain had for a long time felt against him.

"There's only one thing to do," said Laval in his homely way, "and that is to be nice to the Germans." Two demands by the occupying power, one concerning the Bor mines and the other concerning the Belgian gold in the Bank of France, gave the Government the opportunity of judging the consequences of this "niceness".

A French company, the Compagnie des Mines de Bor, had important copper mines in Yugoslavia and Bulgaria. Only a month after the armistice, the Germans had decided to seize these mines which were of value to their armaments production.

On the 26th July, the seizing of these French interests began with the expulsion of the directors whom the Nazis replaced by two German administrators, Dr. Hans Kuntze and Consul-General Neuhausen. Vichy, refusing to yield to this first *diktat*, protested on the formal advice of Baudouin.

In September and October, the Germans tried to persuade the directors of this French Company, MM. Champin, Vice-President of the Board, and Mirabaud, a director of the bank which financed the Company, to yield them the shares against some of the millions extorted under the pretext of refunding the costs of military occupation. They received a formal refusal from both men.

This was at the moment when Laval returned from Montoire, exalted by the great project of European collaboration with the Reich. What, in his opinion, did it matter to the country whether a few packets of shares remained in French hands or passed into those of France's new allies? On his own authority, he enjoined the directors of the Bor mines to yield to the German demands: "The French Government is not aware of my intentions," he said to Champin, who pleaded the contrary instructions given him by Baudouin.

"But that is of no importance: it is a matter of policy of which I am the only judge."

The deal went through on the 6th November. In order not to be held responsible, the directors merely demanded that the French Government should give them a letter stating that the deal had been made on its orders.

He adopted the same attitude and employed the same tactics over the question of the Belgian gold. It consisted of two hundred tons of gold confided to the Bank of France during the first days of the invasion and deposited, for greater security, at Dakar. On the 12th September, the Reich demanded that the ingots should be brought back to occupied territory, to Belgium or at least to Paris.

At Wiesbaden, on the orders of Vichy, Boisanger tried to negotiate: "In order to give proof of our spirit of conciliation towards the German Government" (a curious enough euphemism!), the French Government would be prepared to bring the gold, which belonged to her ally, back to Paris in exchange for a concession from which it would itself benefit: it asked that the exchange rate of the mark should be modified in its favour. It was not a very honourable deal and it did not succeed.

It was then, on the 29th November, that Bouthillier, on a visit to Paris, was called to the telephone by Laval and had a somewhat curious conversation with him:

Laval: "Is there still difficulty over the German gold?"

Bouthillier: "Yes, and the German position is indefensible."

Laval: "It is not a question of whether their position is defensible, but of whether my policy demands that I give them satisfaction. I am not telling you that it will be done. I am telling you that it is done."

Bouthillier: "I've got something to say about that. And I don't see what the hurry is. It's now several days since M. Hemmen. . . ."

Laval: "M. Hemmen is here. I am telephoning to you in his presence."

Astounded by this extraordinary behaviour on the part of the Vice-President of the Council of telephoning a Minister in the presence of an important German official, Bouthillier rushed round to Pierre Laval's office and there, in the presence of Hemmen, who had not yet left, he heard Laval reiterate his orders: "I am leaving for Berlin, it's a great thing. . . . What does your gold matter to me? I am thinking of the prisoners, of the French, of the future of my country. . . . Ribbentrop demands the gold, I am giving it to him. . . ."

Bouthillier was compelled to deduct from the French stocks of gold a quantity equivalent to the Belgian deposit, and transfer it to the Institut de Bruxelles. The law which, on the 18th October, regularised this payment was not published in the *Journal Officiel*.

At the same time, Franco-German negotiations on the subject of the prisoners of war had some success.

At the time of the armistice, the duty of protecting these million and a half men, fell to the United States who, since the declaration of war, had represented French interests in Germany. But when the armistice entailed the repatriating to Germany of the prisoners taken by the French army, a new situation was created which deprived the U.S.A. of any valid means of bringing pressure to bear on the Reich, and the French Government itself undertook the protection of the prisoners.

In a letter, dated 31st July, 1940, which did not reach its destination until the 20th August, the Marshal confided to Scapini, President of the Association for the War Blinded and an ex-President of the Franco-German Committee, a task which was in the first instance somewhat imprecise.

"I ask you to be good enough to lend your assistance to the organisation for the prisoners of war which has just been set up.

"Your mission will consist in intervening whenever necessary with the occupation authorities or the German Government in order to smooth out any difficulties which may affect the fate of our prisoners."

In November, 1940, the Government of the Reich informed the French Government that it proposed that France should play the part of protecting power for her own prisoners. Vichy accepted and informed Scapini that he was to assume this mission with the title and prerogatives of Ambassador.

His appointment was followed, on the 16th November, 1940, by the agreement of the German Government to the first measures in favour of the prisoners:

The discharging from captivity of the fathers of four children and the elder brothers of four children, who supported their families.

The liberation of French prisoners interned in Switzerland and the repatriation of the seriously wounded or sick.

The setting up in Berlin of a branch of the French prisoners' organisation.

An authorisation for every prisoner to send two letters and two postcards home each month.

The sending of three train loads of presents for Christmas.

This agreement, of the 16th November, 1940, entailed the liberation of fifty thousand prisoners: if five thousand dead, and sixty thousand natives of Alsace and Lorraine, considered as German subjects and in that capacity returned to their homes, are taken into account, the number of prisoners of war, by the end of 1940, amounted to 1,490,000 men.

At the beginning of November, a succession of political events increased still more the hostility Pierre Laval had provoked.

On the 9th November, three days after the agreement over the Bor mines, Reichsmarshall Goering, as a manifestation of gratitude, agreed to see him.

From the somewhat confused conversations between Goering and Laval, it nevertheless clearly emerged that the Reich would only show consideration towards France if she co-operated, by a military effort, in the defeat of England. An eventuality which Laval, one may suppose, did not reject.

On the following day, in the Council of Ministers, at which, exceptionally, Laval was present, the Marshal was explicit: he would never agree to France's participation in the Anglo-German conflict.

Nevertheless, in the middle of November, during the course of a Council of Ministers, Laval openly proposed a Franco-German military operation against the colonies in French Equatorial Africa which had gone over to the dissidents.

On the 23rd November, the Wehrmacht having reacted favourably, the project seemed to be taking shape: General Huntziger informed Peyrouton that the Germans were contemplating an attack against these territories. On the same day, Berthelot announced that they had bought 5,000 maps of the French African possessions.

On the 25th November, Laval left for Paris in order to meet Ribbentrop, whom he did not in fact see; on the 28th, he urgently summoned the Ministers of War and Marine, General Huntziger and Admiral Darlan, on whom, on the French side, the projected operations depended.

On the 29th November, at the German Embassy, a military conference took place during the course of which the Germans asked for French co-operation in recovering French territories occupied by the Gaullists. Darlan was silent. Huntziger, in order to delay the beginning of operations, advanced the fact that it was the rainy season. Laval gave his agreement.

On the 2nd December, in the absence of Laval who was still in Paris, there was a counter-offensive at Vichy. In the morning, Bouthillier, on his return from the capital, had informed the Marshal of Laval's negotiations. In the afternoon, at 4 p.m., there was a Council of Ministers which soon took on the aspect of an indictment of the Vice-President of the Council; Bouthillier told of the cession of the Bor mines, Huntziger of the military conference of the 29th. Laval was also charged with the use he made for his own political ends of the press and the radio.

Three Ministers, Baudouin, Peyrouton and Bouthillier met after the Council and decided to bring pressure on Pétain to dismiss Laval.

The following day, Peyrouton accompanied the Marshal on a journey to Marseille. The day after that, Bouthillier joined them at Toulon; and, during the journey back, the two Ministers discussed the matter with Pétain, as well as with Darlan who had joined them, and made certain of their co-operation. They demanded the dismissal of Pierre Laval whom Bouthillier suggested should be replaced by Pierre-Étienne Flandin.

Laval, returning from Paris on the 5th December, announced that his decisive meeting with Ribbentrop would take place before Christmas and that the second military conference was fixed for 10th December in Paris. General Valrimont, of the General Staff of the Wehrmacht, would attend in order to discuss with Darlan and Huntziger a plan of action. On the 9th, at Vichy, there was a preliminary conference at which Pétain enjoined on Huntziger to delay as much as possible the recovery of the Gaullist colonies and to evade a German demand to attack British colonies. Furthermore, the Council agreed to proceed to the arrest in Paris of Marcel Déat, who had written an inflammatory article against the Ministers of Vichy who did not agree with Laval, and informed General de la Laurencie that he was to make the arrest on receiving the password: "The Marshal's wife has crossed the line."

Completely unaware of the plot which was being hatched against him, Laval, on the 6th December, put forward a claim to be nominated Head of the Government. On the 8th December, the Marshal confided to Baudouin that he had his reply ready: "Agreed, but, as far as I am concerned, I'm leaving."

The dismissal of Laval was arranged for the morning of the 9th; at the last moment, Pétain ordered that the letter announcing it to Chancellor Hitler should be withheld. The Führer would thus be faced with the accomplished fact.

While waiting to get rid of Laval, Pétain pursued his negotiations with the British.

On Tuesday, 3rd December, 1940, at 5 p.m., M. Jacques Chevalier, recently promoted Secretary-General to the Ministry of Education, received in his office in the Hôtel Plaza Admiral Auphan, Deputy Chief of Staff in the French Admiralty and in charge of Merchant Marine. Neither of them had any idea of Rougier's conversations. The Admiral, whose great anxiety was the provisioning of Metropolitan France, talked of the straits to which France was in danger of being reduced by the lack of oil and the impossibility of importing it. Since the armistice, not one single ship-load of any form of mineral oil had entered France or her African possessions; stocks, on condition that the consumption was reduced to a tenth of the peace-time level, would last for eight months. After that, the whole French economy would starve to death. The only hope was to import from America or Rumania, neither of which could be done without British consent. . . . In spite of the horror he felt, as did all French sailors, at the Mers-el-Kebir attack, Auphan, from patriotism or perhaps more precisely from an instinctive desire to preserve his country, had come to the conclusion that it was necessary to treat with England.

The following morning, 4th December, at 10.45 a.m., once more in his office, Jacques Chevalier was given an unhoped for and providential opportunity. Pierre Dupuy, the Canadian Chargé d'Affaires at Vichy, a shrewd diplomatist, came to give Jacques Chevalier greetings from Lord Halifax, who had been his most intimate friend since, as young men, they had known each other at Oxford. The following is the verbal message transmitted by Pierre Dupuy:

"Tell our French friends that we are in an extremely delicate position. We cannot be openly friendly. We must maintain a state of artificial tension between us. If Germany suspected our friendship, Article 10 of the Armistice Convention would be immediately applied. But behind a façade of misunderstanding, we must understand each other."

Chevalier, who was thinking of oil, immediately saw the importance of this unofficial overture. He agreed and at once summoned Auphan for a technical discussion. On one point, the Admiral angrily disagreed: it was when Dupuy made one preliminary condition: England would support the French dissident colonies who wished to continue the war at her side. And Auphan had another grievance: the English had stopped without notice ships laden with corn and cod as well as those which were transporting demobilised soldiers back from the Antilles. . . . Dupuy who, in the circumstances, felt himself to be almost as much a Frenchman as he was a subject of His Majesty, spoke freely: "I promise you," he said, "to do something about: (1) seeing that it does not happen again; (2) petroleum, fuel and lubricating oils and coal, which could be obtained, I think, on condition that you promise they shall remain in the free zone and will not be transferred to the territory occupied by the Germans. As for your Gaullist colonies you must try and get them back on the quiet. The essential thing is to save the unity of the country and Christian civilisation."

On this basis, indirect negotiations could be put in train between Halifax and Chevalier.

On the 5th December, Jacques Chevalier reported on his interviews with Auphan and Dupuy to the Marshal. In the message the latter had transmitted to the French Minister, there was one word which disquieted Pétain and which he immediately altered. To say "artificial tension" would be playing with fire. It would be better to say "artificial coolness".

On the 6th December, at 11 a.m., Chevalier, who had prepared a personal and confidential memorandum on affairs with England and had made a draft of the agreement, took Pierre Dupuy to see the Marshal. The latter, who insisted that secrecy was essential to the success of the negotiations, declared his agreement to the memorandum drawn up by Chevalier and gave it to Pierre Dupuy.

The next day, the 7th December, the Canadian diplomat went back to London by Madrid and Lisbon.

The clauses of the document he handed Halifax were as follows:

1. It is agreed between France and England that a state of

"artificial coolness" rather than "artificial tension" should be maintained.

2. Concerning the colonies which have decided to continue to fight at the side of England, it was agreed that the actual situation should be provisionally maintained and that there should be an endeavour, when the time came, to arrive at some agreement, on the basis that these colonies should be ultimately returned to the French Government by a simple substitution of the police and armed forces.

3. Concerning the Fleet and the Colonies, Marshal Pétain renewed his formal assurance not at any price nor on any pretext to deliver them to the Axis powers. The fleet would scuttle itself rather than fall into the hands of the Germans or the Italians. The English, on their side, would agree to give all the support which was both necessary and within their power in the requisite form and at the required time.

4. English broadcasts would abstain from interfering in the internal affairs of France.

5. The British Government would treat in the same way as they did coasting trade the transport by sea of necessary supplies between the French North African ports and the French Mediterranean coast on the condition that these products would not be transferred to territory occupied by the Axis powers. On the vital question of petroleum and lubricating oil, the Agreement being made only in principle, technicians would consider the ways and means at Madrid.

French troops stationed in the Colonies and French possessions would oppose all attempts at invasion by whoever made.

Finally, the contracting parties agreed to hold the clauses of the Agreement, and the fact of the Agreement itself, rigorously secret.

On the 9th December, Pierre Dupuy sent Jacques Chevalier a telegram which read: "All is going well." Did this signify the definite agreement of the British Government? Or did it, as London later maintained, merely confirm the receipt of the text?

For London, the distinction had some importance; it had less for the Marshal who, considering himself already pledged by Louis Rougier's document, had no need of a supplementary one to confirm the accord.[1]

[1] The Chevalier agreement confirmed most of the points in Rougier's protocol without, however, making any allusion to the eventual re-entry of France into the war.

On the following day, in Paris, a military conference was held at the German Embassy. The Germans were no longer content with an attack on Chad: they were contemplating an expedition against a British colony: the Gold Coast or Nigeria. The delaying tactics of Huntziger, who asserted that nothing could be undertaken before October, 1941, did not prevent the Germans demanding the commencement of operations before the rainy season, that is to say, in the very near future.

Such an eventuality was incompatible with the engagements which the Marshal had just transmitted to Churchill.

In these circumstances, the dismissal of Laval seemed to become more and more necessary.

On the 11th December, a dramatic event occurred at Vichy.

Conversations had been going on for a long time, with Brinon as intermediary, in order that the Marshal, in default of the Government returning to Paris, might be authorised to make a stay in the capital.

On the morning of December 11th, the German reply arrived: the Marshal might stay at the Hôtel Trianon-Palace at Versailles. But, Brinon said over the telephone, this authorisation was only for the Marshal himself; no Minister might accompany him. This curious restriction determined the Head of the State to refuse the Nazi offer: "It's another little plot of Pierre Laval's," Pétain said.

The Marshal had not had time to make his refusal known, when Brinon from Paris got Vichy on the telephone a second time. The Germans had made a new proposal which replaced the first. This one came directly from the Führer; and it was sensational.

Hitler, taking up an idea which had been suggested to Ribbentrop in 1934 by Benoist-Méchin, had decided that, on the 15th December, the anniversary of the day on which Napoleon I's ashes had been returned to the Invalides, he would return to Paris the ashes of the Duke of Reichstadt, which had been buried since 1832 in the crypt of the Capuchins at Vienna. Thus the son would rest beside the father. Thus victorious Germany would restore to defeated France the remains of an unhappy Prince by a chivalrous gesture whose implications Hitler thought all Frenchmen would appreciate.

Such was the proposal of the Chancellor of the Reich. Unfortunately, the French were less appreciative of this funeral ceremony. The man in the street, whose acclamations Hitler was already savouring, was grumbling during this rigorous winter: "We need coal; 'they' make us a present of ashes."

The Marshal, for his part, did not appreciate Hitler's invitation at all. He did not take kindly to being given only four days' notice, to being treated thus at his age and in his position and to being offered the prospect, on his first return to "his" capital, of reviewing two German battalions, one at the station where he would be received, and the other on the Place Vendôme. . . . Supported in his attitude by Baudouin, General Laure and du Moulin de Labarthète, he told the latter, on the 12th December, to telephone Laval, who was still in Paris, and inform him of his refusal.

Abetz immediately went to the Hôtel Matignon to talk to Laval: "If the Marshal does not come, having been invited by the Chancellor, the Chancellor will take it as a personal insult."

To avoid this risk, it merely remained for Pierre Laval to bring his influence directly to bear upon the Marshal; accompanied by Brinon, he took the 11 p.m. train and arrived at Vichy the following day, Friday, 13th December.

This day's time-table is easy to establish from the records made of it by the various participants.

At 10 o'clock Bouthillier was received by the Marshal, who showed himself firmly decided not to go to Paris. He repeated his reasons: his determination not to return for the first time to the capital in order to preside over a Franco-German ceremony.

Towards 11 o'clock, Laval and Brinon had an audience with the Head of the State; Laval, rather casually, only stayed for a moment as he was in a hurry to go to Châteldon to have luncheon with his family. It was up to Brinon to make the first attempt to persuade the Marshal to change his mind. He gave him Hitler's letter containing the personal invitation. He talked to the old man of the pleasures of the journey, while stating strongly the drawbacks of a refusal. Little by little, so it seemed to him, Pétain began to waver and his resistance weaken. They soon got to the point of planning the route; leaning over a Michelin map, the conqueror of Verdun selected his route and his halts. He would go from Paris to Rouen, and then return by Orléans and Bourges. With regard to his lodging, he refused to sleep at the Élysée, which he disliked, and preferred to go to the Hôtel Trianon at Versailles. In the end, for reasons of heating, the Hôtel Matignon was selected.

The afternoon at Vichy began by a chance meeting between Peyrouton and Bouthillier. After luncheon, the two Ministers met in the narrow passage which separated the Hôtel du Parc and the Hôtel Majestic, and exchanged the latest news, which proved the necessity of making a quick decision. Bouthillier had received from Admiral Darlan a report on the military conference held in Paris on the 10th December. There was not a moment to be lost.

Peyrouton informed Bouthillier of the most recent events in Vichy. He told him of the Marshal's apparent change of mind, brought about by Brinon: "It's all on again," he said. "The Marshal's going to Paris. Brinon and Laval have persuaded him. There is even a possibility of his going as far as Rouen. The Marshal will go alone with Laval."

After a moment's thought, Bouthillier said: "It must take place tonight." It was during this conversation that the idea of arresting Laval was for the first time seriously contemplated.

"I shall arrest him," Peyrouton, the Minister of the Interior, suddenly decided. "He must not be given the opportunity of warning Abetz and his people."

"Let's go and tell the others. Inform the Marshal that you are going to arrest Laval."

At 3 o'clock, having returned from Châteldon, Pierre Laval went to see the Marshal. The latter once again mentioned the journey to Paris, but discussed ways and means rather than the principle itself. The question of lodgings and meals was spoken of. Laval gave the Marshal every possible encouragement. He left him, certain of having gained his point. Before the Conseil de Cabinet, over which he was to preside, at 5 p.m., he received Ambassador Lequerica, who came to discuss Franco-Spanish problems. Then he gave instructions to his staff concerning the journalists who were to travel to Paris. They were to wear formal clothes for the ceremonies, one at the Invalides for the delivery of the ashes, the other at the German Embassy, where there was to be a reception. Two cars, furnished with collective *ausweis* would enable them to go to Paris and return.

During this time, Bouthillier and Peyrouton had summoned such Ministers as they knew would support their action. The meeting took place, a little after 3 p.m., at the Hôtel du Parc in the office of du Moulin de Labarthète; Darlan, Huntziger and Baudouin took part. At 4 o'clock, the five Ministers, joined at the last moment by Alibert, had an audience of the Marshal. He received them in silence.

The risks, of which they were all conscious, did not prevent the Ministers from suggesting, nor the Marshal from taking, the necessary decision. It was agreed that the Conseil de Cabinet, which was fixed for 5 p.m., under the chairmanship of Laval, should take place as usual: nothing would be said. But at 8 o'clock, there would be an impromptu Council of Ministers, presided over by the Marshal, during which the Head of the State would announce the resignation of the Government. When it was over, Peyrouton would proceed to the arrest of Laval which would be carried out with the greatest possible consideration: he would be placed under house-arrest in his Château de Châteldon.

The Conseil de Cabinet, held at 5 o'clock, was devoted to a study of current problems, and then to a discussion on the proposed Labour Charter which was being prepared by Belin's Ministry. Laval showed himself hostile to it in its present form; besides, circumstances had been such that he had not been able to study it with care. Supported by Bouthillier, who on this particular point agreed with him, he postponed a decision and, at 7 p.m., the meeting broke up without any agreement having been reached.

All the Ministers, with the exception of Alibert, were present at this meeting. He was playing a part in the conspiracy which could not wait. In the first place, he had to arrange for the arrest in Paris of Marcel Déat, whose articles in *l'Oeuvre* were exasperating both the Ministers and the Marshal. Alibert told his Chef de Cabinet, M. de Font-Réaulx, to telephone at 8 o'clock, when the decisive Council of Ministers would be in session, to tell General de la Laurencie to proceed.

Alibert, encroaching on the prerogatives of Peyrouton who, in his capacity as Minister of the Interior, should have been alone responsible for the arrest of Laval, gave secret instructions to Colonel Groussard. He warned him that, at a sign from himself, which in the event was never given, he would have to arrest Laval when he came out of the Conseil de Cabinet which was held at 5 o'clock. Later, at about 8.30 p.m., when the Marshal's decision had been made known to Laval, he was to order him to place a guard on the Hôtel du Parc composed of his "Protection Groups".

Having taken this decision, Alibert, so it is said, went and knelt in the Church of Saint-Louis and prayed for the success of the plot. A recourse to the supernatural with which Peyrouton felt able to dispense, since his astrologer had told him that Friday, 13th December, would be a particularly lucky day.

At 8 o'clock, Laval, summoned a few minutes before by General Laure, and unaware of the reasons for holding this impromptu Council of Ministers (he thought the Marshal wanted to announce his journey to Paris), joined the other Ministers who were waiting for the Head of the State. The Marshal came in, rather nervous, accompanied by Baudouin and Admiral Fernet. He asked all the Ministers to sign a letter of resignation which had been previously prepared. Laval hesitated a moment: did his particular situation, as successor to the Marshal, guaranteed by a Constitutional Act, and the accolade conferred on him by the Assembly of the 10th July, allow of his resigning like an ordinary Minister? But, persuaded that in his case it was only a formality, thinking that the Marshal's intention was to get rid of Belin, whose ideas on the Labour Charter he did not share, Laval appended his signature at the same time as his colleagues.

The Marshal withdrew; then, a few instants later, re-appeared, very pale, and said only: "The resignations of MM. Laval and Ripert are accepted." Ripert, Minister of Education, who much wanted to go, raised no protest. Five years later he was to learn the reasons for his dismissal: his hostility to the National Revolution and Pétain's wish to give a post in the Government to Chevalier in order to permit the latter to negotiate with Lord Halifax on an equal footing. But Laval reacted with his accustomed vigour and vitality.

Standing behind a chair, his strong hands seeming to crush its back, he addressed the Marshal in vehement phrases, on whose sense all witnesses agree, even though they differ over the exact words.

He first asked a question: "What has happened, Monsieur le Maréchal? You received me this afternoon and said no word."

In his reply, the Marshal could not give all the reasons which had decided him to take action. He wished to be in a position, after Laval's dismissal, to write a letter to Hitler in which, while refusing the invitation to go to Paris, he could affirm that the ministerial change implied no modification of foreign policy—which assurance bore, moreover, if the Chevalier negotiations are taken into consideration, a double meaning to say the least. He therefore needed to declare his will rather than give reasons, proceed more by assertion than by explanation. And the old man, less clever at improvisation than the other, did not cut a very good figure in his dialogue with Laval.

He brought forward arguments which had little relevance: the Parisian Press, which applauded Laval's policy while attacking his Government's. Laval had no difficulty in replying that it was no responsibility of his, which was indeed true, and that the Paris journalists were not under his command.

He also brought forward the secrecy with which Laval surrounded his negotiations in the capital: "Every time you went to Paris,"—and these are the Marshal's own words—"I wondered what brick was to fall on our heads next." But here again, Laval found it easy to defend himself: he had his own methods of working; only the results mattered. He had never refused the Marshal personally an explanation. But he was suspicious of certain of his Ministers.

But it was a counter-attack which miscarried: the Marshal was accustomed to defensive battles. Aware that he might be over-run, he put a stop to it by saying simply, in a dead, precise voice: "You have lost my confidence! You have lost my confidence!"

Laval felt, at the firmness of these words, that he could no longer argue. Responding to the authority that at this moment emanated from the sovereign and imperious bearing of the Marshal with the only sort of grandeur he himself knew, the grandeur deriving from his convictions and his patriotism, authentic if wayward, he drew himself up proudly and, looking his judge, who was condemning him without appeal, straight in the face, said: "I have had no thought but of the interests of France. I hope, Monsieur le Maréchal, that your decision will not do too much harm to my country."

Then he asked the Head of the State to shake his hand. Pétain did so. Then, without a word to his colleagues, Laval went to his office to put his files in order, as he had done before the war, whenever Parliament had placed him in a minority.

"I began to put my papers together, I'm accustomed to leaving Ministries and to coming back again. I know that one has to pack up. I have done so."

CHAPTER 7

# THE FLANDIN INTERLUDE

## (13th December, 1940 – 9th February, 1941)

DURING the night of 13th–14th September, immediately after the Council of Ministers at which Pierre Laval had been dismissed, the provisional capital was to all intents and purposes in a state of siege.

All telephone communications with the outside world were cut, trains prevented from running, and the roads barred on the outskirts of the town. It was hoped at the Hôtel du Parc that Ambassador Abetz would thus not hear the news before the Government announced it to him officially.

Guards were placed in the corridor of the hotel: an American journalist, Heinzen, succeeded in outflanking them. It was the first successful professional exploit of the press that day. He found Pierre Laval and told him of the arrest of his chauffeur, to whom Laval had given the files he wished to take with him: the police were eager to read these confidential documents but found them to be of no interest in the event.

Pierre Laval, thus warned, complained to everyone who came to make sure that he was in his office, to Peyrouton and du Moulin, who manifested surprise and said they knew nothing of it, and to General Laure, whom he asked to demand on his behalf an audience with the Head of the State. Laure returned with a refusal.

"I shook his hand," said Pétain, "it's all I can do."

At 9.30, the professional policeman, who specialised in the arrests of Ministers and ex-Ministers, arrived: M. Mondanel, Director of the Sûreté Nationale, who, four months earlier, had arrested Georges Mandel, and was, tonight, a prey to serious scruples; for indeed the law forbade arrests after 9 o'clock, and it was now 9.30. Was he to take Laval away?

Dr. Martin, head of the Groupes de Protection, put an end to his hesitation: "Damn it," he said, "there's a state of siege; and when it's a question of taking revolutionary measures, one doesn't worry about the time."

Encouraged by these words, the policeman carried out his duty. "Monsieur le Président," he said, "I am charged with the duty of taking you to Châteldon."

During the journey, Mondanel, courteous as usual, thought he should warn Laval that a policeman would be sleeping in his room. The arrested man protested, and the policeman conceded the point: Laval might be alone in his room, but three Inspectors would be permanently posted outside his door.

While his political associate was being subjected to this treatment, Abetz in Paris still knew nothing of it.

During the night there was a grotesque episode when a second journalist succeeded in giving him the information. In spite of the orders and the state of siege, the correspondent at Vichy of the German press agency D.N.B. (Deutsch Nachrichlen Buro) succeeded in slipping out of the town. He crossed the demarcation line and, from Moulins in the occupied zone, telephoned the sensational news, of which everyone had until then been in ignorance, to Paris.

On this 14th December, at 7 o'clock in the morning, on orders transmitted by General Laure to General de la Laurencie, an event similar to the Châteldon episode took place in Paris, thus raising the German Ambassador's fury to the highest pitch. Four French Police Inspectors went to the Rue Villiers-de-l'Isle-Adam, to Marcel Déat's house, bearing a warrant for his arrest.

Déat was in pyjamas. His wife had hysterics; he himself remained calm. His first words, which are significant, were to ask: "Has the German Ambassador been informed?" On being given a negative reply, he dressed, packed a suitcase and went with the four policemen. "As soon as they had gone," one of the collaborationist leader's assistants recalled later, "Hélène Déat told a German friend, Dr. Grosse. Dr. Grosse informed the Ambassador."

Thus was Abetz informed almost simultaneously of the arrest of his two principal associates. His indignation flowed out immediately both upon Vichy and upon Paris. In spite of the interruption of communications, he managed to telephone Vichy through Wiesbaden, from whence the line to the Allier had alone been kept open. Abetz demanded the immediate freeing of Déat. Moreover, he insisted angrily that everything that had happened the evening before should be kept secret, and that Laval should be reinstated in the Government. He asked indignantly whether the Marshal thought he could revoke, without German consent, Constitutional Act No. 4, which determined his successor. This was the first open interference with the internal policy of Vichy.

Having fulminated against Vichy, he now thundered over Paris. General de la Laurencie, who knew nothing of Laval's arrest, was urgently summoned to the Embassy. When, at 11 a.m., accompanied by his Secretary-General, he entered Abetz's office, he found himself in the presence of the fine flower of Nazi diplomacy in France: Abetz was awaiting him, flanked by his two Councillors to the Embassy, Schleier and Achenbach.

Abetz was clearly in a flaming rage. He gave his visitor no opportunity to speak, but followed the Nazi custom inaugurated by Adolf Hitler of shouting and gesticulating: "Are you going to free M. Déat?" "I arrested him on my Government's orders." "I order you to free him." "I can only accept orders from my Government." "If you don't free him immediately, I shall hold you responsible, I shall have you arrested and hold you as a hostage." "I have never been afraid of threats." Abetz banged the desk with his fist and went into a neighbouring room.

With great dignity, la Laurencie concluded: "I think, Messieurs, that there is nothing left for me but to take my leave, not however before remarking that diplomatic conversations are today being conducted in a peculiar tone."

At Vichy, to which General de la Laurencie telephoned Abetz' reactions, there was considerable uneasiness.

Admiral Darlan and General Laure were ordered to go to the capital for the ceremony which, as we shall see, somewhat lacked conviction.

In the middle of all this confusion, Pierre-Étienne Flandin arrived in Vichy. He had never intrigued for Pierre Laval's position; but he had received the evening before, at 5 p.m., on the 13th December, a telephone call from the Préfet of Versailles, who had been told by du Moulin de Labarthète to summon him to Vichy that very night: "I told him," said Flandin not unhumorously, "that there existed such a thing as a demarcation line, and that I could not reach Vichy before the following afternoon."

He arrived there at 2.30 p.m. on the 14th December, having waited for two hours in the snow at the demarcation line, and thus contracted a quinsy which, according to him, was soon to become "celebrated". Still ignorant of everything that had happened, he asked the porter of the Hôtel Majestic the news; the latter, looking scared, refused at first to answer; then, on the President's insistence, he told him, with much hesitation, that the telephone in the town was cut, that trains no longer arrived from Paris, that Laval had been arrested . . . and that Mussolini was in flight!

Thus informed, Flandin went to see the Marshal who, without a word of greeting, pulled a letter from his pocket and said: "Read this."

It was the copy of a letter addressed to Chancellor Hitler.

In it, the Marshal expressed his regrets not to be able to be in Paris to receive the ashes of the Duke of Reichstadt.

It went on to announce the dismissal of Pierre Laval and ended by informing him of the appointment of Pierre-Étienne Flandin as Foreign Minister.

When Flandin had finished reading it, Pétain informed him that no comment was necessary. "This letter was handed last night by General Doyen to the Armistice Commission at Wiesbaden and, either last night or this morning, by General de la Laurencie to the authorities in Paris."

Flandin nevertheless expressed his astonishment at being faced with an accomplished fact. "I had neither the time nor the means of consulting you," said the Marshal. "Do you think that I was consulted when I was made Head of a defeated State? Moreover, you cannot refuse to succeed Laval in the present circumstances. Laval's negotiations in Paris risked leading us into a declaration of war on England. I will not tolerate these activities."

And Pétain, without further delay, introduced Flandin to his new duties by giving him two confidential documents to read: the reports on Montoire and on Rougier's mission.

On the 15th December, the atmosphere at Vichy was still thundery.

The news from Paris was far from reassuring, the return of l'Aiglon's ashes, which was to have been a great manifestation of Franco-German friendship, took place in the worst possible circumstances: seldom has an official ceremony gone so ill.

To begin with there was no one there to play the leading part, no Marshal, no Hitler, no Ribbentrop, nor indeed a Laval. On the French side, there were Darlan, Laure and, naturally, Brinon.

Hitler had detailed General von Stülpnagel and Abetz, to whom Counsellor Achenbach was added as a makeweight. There was but a paltry attendance to receive the unfortunate son of the Eagle back to his native city. It was a pitiful return, which General Laure described as follows:

"At half an hour after midnight I went to the gates in the Place Vauban. It was a lugubrious, almost sinister ceremony, at which no French but officials were present.

"The coffin was handed over by the Germans to the Paris Municipal Guard. It was carried across the threshold between two rows of torches.

"Admiral Darlan thought it his duty to greet General von Stülpnagel and Abetz, but they received him coldly."

Abetz was more than cold: he was haughty and insolent.

"Wait at your hotel," he said to Darlan and Laure, "I have a very important message to give you."

At 4 o'clock in the morning, the Admiral was in bed, having left Laure to await the message. A messenger from Abetz brought the following demand: "The Government of Vichy is absolutely forbidden to make any announcement whatever concerning the events of the 13th December." Laure rushed to Darlan and tried to awaken him. "Fix it yourself," said the Admiral. "I went to the telephone," Laure records, "I got du Moulin de Labarthète at Vichy on the line. . . . He said: 'The newspapers have gone out, there is nothing to be done.' "

That same morning, the 16th December, at 9 a.m., the ceremonies in honour of the King of Rome began once more with a mass in the chapel of the Invalides. There were the same representatives from both sides. And the same atmosphere of lack of courtesy. When the mass was over, Darlan vainly tried once more to greet Stülpnagel, who declined to be called upon, and similarly Abetz, who said: "I expect you at once in the Rue de Lille."

"We were received," Laure records, "with a diatribe, an hysterical diatribe of invective from Abetz concerning the events of the day before. . . . He addressed his remarks to me because in his eyes I represented the person of Marshal Pétain. In his view, I was responsible for what had occurred. It went on for a long time; I said nothing.

"He then turned to Admiral Darlan and overwhelmed him with encomiums: the undefeated Fleet, the place a man of his quality and stature might take in the reorganised Europe of the future. I needn't go on. I took my leave and left them talking."

During the day of the 16th December, first General Laure and then Admiral Darlan returned to Vichy; the Admiral brought with him from Abetz two important proposals for resolving the crisis: to take Laval back into the Government and constitute a triumvirate, in which Laval would hold, if not the first place, at least a place equivalent to that of his two colleagues.

Moreover, Abetz announced his own arrival during the course of the night.

And the unfortunate General Laure, hardly recovered from his Paris journey, had to set out once again for the demarcation line, accompanied by the Chef du Protocole and by the heads of the Marshal's civil and military offices.

In the freezing cold, he awaited the Ambassador for two hours and finally saw him arrive at the Moulins bridge in a singular convoy for an Ambassador: his car was escorted by two German armoured cars.

"I pointed out to him," Laure records, "that it was incorrect for him to assure his own protection on French territory when it was our responsibility. He did not reply. He quickly got back into his car and slammed the door in my face. He went off at full speed down the Vichy road between his two armoured cars.

"When I accompanied him into the Hôtel Majestic, I was jostled by his bodyguard, who prevented my entering the lift with him, for he had to take his bodyguard with him. Nevertheless, when I went into his suite with him, I persuaded him to dismiss his bodyguard so that they should not be in evidence in the Free French zone."

But, with or without his guardian angels, Abetz was determined to force the return of Laval to the Government.

His first action was to go to Pierre-Étienne Flandin who, ill with his quinsy, saw him suddenly erupt into his room. Abetz embarked on another monologue: "I shall have no dealings with you," he said, "if you accept the Ministry for Foreign Affairs. M. Laval has begun extremely important diplomatic negotiations with us and it is essential that he should conduct these negotiations to their conclusion. I make no objections," conceded Abetz, speaking as the master, "to your entering the Government in some other ministerial post; but certainly not in that of Foreign Affairs. M. Laval must return to the Government."

Flandin, in spite of his sore throat, replied firmly: "As far as I know, Marshal Pétain is free to choose his own colleagues."

On the morning of the 17th, Abetz was received by the Marshal in the presence of Darlan and Achenbach. He demanded the freeing of Pierre Laval,[1] the formation within the Government of a controlling committee of which Laval would form part with a standing equal to that of the other two members, the dismissal of several Ministers who were hostile to the policy of collaboration and presumed responsible for the 13th December (Belin, Caziot, Peyrouton, Alibert), the dissolving of the Groupes de Protection, the dismissal of la Laurencie and his replacement by Fernand de Brinon.

On the first point, Pétain yielded and, after the interview, told du Moulin de Labarthète to bring the prisoner back from Châteldon. The second point he evaded and tried to gain time: he could not recall Laval to the Government before there had been an enquiry into his activities: he proposed to give him a ministerial post of secondary importance: Agriculture or Production. Abetz accepted the principle of an enquiry on the condition that it was understood to be only a matter of form. Pétain declared that he could not make the decision alone, but must consult the Council of Ministers, whom he would summon for this purpose early in the afternoon.

Thus the interview came to an end on a misunderstanding between Pétain and Abetz. The Ambassador was convinced that he had won his case: the enquiry would be no more than a formality. Pétain, on the other hand, believed he had gained time.

In agreement with the proposed procedure, the Ambassador became more friendly and accepted an invitation to luncheon with the Marshal.

After luncheon, Pétain, who was suspicious of his guest, told Laure to chaperon him while the Council was in session: "I don't want Abetz to be left alone, because he might get wind of what goes on. He's got spies everywhere. Go with him to his room and stay with him as long as you can. Tell him anything you like."

A precaution which was, however, soon to reveal itself as useless. For Laval returned from Châteldon, having burst his chains as much morally as physically. In the presence of Abetz,

[1] Déat had been released, on an order from Abetz to the Prefect of Police, a few hours after his arrest.

he spoke so violently to the Marshal that the Ambassador was flabbergasted, and Laure, who heard them from the next room, couldn't believe his ears.

"The interest of France," said Laval to the Head of the State, "is to be on good terms with her conquerors in all honour and dignity, but you trifle with honour and dignity! You are no more than a marionette, a spinning jenny, a weather-cock turning to every wind."

When the scene was over, Pétain summoned Laure: "Draw up the report." Laure, loyal as he was, thought this an opportune moment to conceal the truth. "I can't draw up the report, I didn't hear anything." "Never mind," replied Pétain, "say that we have had a conversation about Government policy and that I have proposed to M. Abetz to give M. Laval a place in the Government, but one which will not entail his being part of the triumvirate, a place of secondary rank: Production or Agriculture." To all appearance a harmless report, it was nevertheless to bring about a complete rupture between Pétain and Laval and between Laval and the French Government.

Later in the day, all Vichy saw Laval dining at the Chantecler Restaurant with Abetz and Achenbach, wearing Nazi uniforms; and coming down the steps of the Ministry between two ranks of German soldiers armed with sub-machine-guns.

Above all, he was seen leaving for Paris with Abetz and Achenbach in a convoy of German vehicles.

General Laure, as always, was sent to accompany them as far as the demarcation line by the road with which he was by now all too familiar. He travelled in Abetz's car, Laval in that of Achenbach. At Moulins, Laure left them: Laval went on his way without getting out of his car, without even taking leave of the French representative.

As an epilogue to the drama, Laure could not help but remember the appalling phrase he had heard Pierre Laval utter in the presence of the Nazis through the partition-wall: "It's no longer on the French side I must look for friends; it's on the German side."[1]

Laval went on his way, accompanied by the Nazis, down the main road into the occupied zone.

As soon as he reached the capital, Laval installed himself at

[1] On this point du Moulin de Labarthète confirms General Laure's evidence.

the Matignon, as if he were still Head of the Government. He stayed there for two days, until Brinon, on the express orders of Vichy, turned him out of the palace. The following day, he wrote a really insane letter to the Führer, placing himself at his orders.

It showed that Laval counted more on the Führer than on the Marshal to help him save France.

"Monsieur le Chancelier du Reich,

"I wish in this letter to express to you my gratitude.

"As the victim of an absurd aggression on the part of the police, I heard on the radio, in the place to which I was sent with my family, the declaration Monsieur l'Ambassadeur made to the press with the deepest joy.

"From that moment, I no longer felt I was alone.

"The following day, I heard that your Ambassador was coming to Vichy, and that he would later visit me at Châteldon. I concluded that my liberation was near and that I would owe it to you.

"By its action, the French Government has committed a grave fault, but I hope with all my heart that my country will not have to suffer for it. France cannot be held responsible for it, for France will disapprove such behaviour as soon as it learns of it.

"The policy of collaboration with Germany is approved by the great majority of the people of France. The number of those who understand that it is the only path for us to take is increasing every day.

"This collaboration must be loyal, wholehearted and without equivocation. It is thus that I understand it and have always practised it. Nothing great or durable can be achieved through duplicity.

"I love my country and I know that it can find a place worthy of its past in the New Europe you are constructing.

"I believe I may conclude from your attitude, Monsieur le Chancelier du Reich, that you have faith in the sincerity of my efforts. You have been no less correct in this belief than I have been confident of the magnanimity and greatness you have shown in offering France collaboration on the morrow of your victory.

"Please accept, Monsieur le Chancelier du Reich, the assurance of my highest consideration and believe in my loyalty."

An extravagant communication, in which the author appears in the round, with all his ingenuousness and his knavery, his cynicism in his choice of method and his errors concerning the end to be attained. A treasonable letter which he thought was inspired by patriotism alone.

It gave Otto Abetz an important trump card in his game against Vichy.

For the German Ambassador, the dismissal of Laval was a real catastrophe: it might well bring in its train the failure of his policy, if not his own disgrace.

If Abetz, acting on his own initiative and doubtless forestalling instructions from Berlin, had achieved on the 17th December the return of Laval to power, his personal position would have been immediately restored and he would no longer have had to fear the Führer's displeasure. But his raid on Vichy had failed: a return to Paris bringing Laval with him was neither a decisive result nor a sufficient prize. He had, therefore, after the 18th December, to think out his policy anew, at least to re-formulate it in order to persuade Hitler that Laval's dismissal did not portend an irremediable defeat; he might endeavour even to show that it was a favourable event which would allow of the Nazis increasing their pressure on the Vichy Government.

On the 18th December, in the report he sent his Government on his return to Paris, he wrote: "The Government crisis which took place on the 13th December . . . allows us to interfere directly in French foreign policy"; and he suggested that all previous means of coercion should be brought to bear "without any consideration, in order to show these rash people what an indescribable folly they committed on the 13th December."

Moreover, from this time on, Abetz, the "Francophile", never ceased inciting the Führer against France. In a note of the 26th December, addressed to Ribbentrop, he put the interpretation on French policy which was designed to irritate Adolf Hitler the most: if Laval had been dismissed, it was because at Vichy they thought him not sufficiently favourable towards England. If Flandin, in spite of Abetz's pressure, remained in power, it was because the Ministers thought that the Ambassador was not supported by his own Government when he demanded the return of Pierre Laval. Finally, Abetz told Ribbentrop that, if Germany accepted the events of the 13th December without reacting sharply, it would be an avowal of weakness and an encouragement to the Marshal's Government to lean more and more towards the United States. It would also be abandoning the

French collaborators who would be delivered up defenceless to the terror organised against them by their own Government (Telegram: 1st January, 1941).

How can one be surprised that German pressure increased?

The demarcation line was closed to all French officials, with the exception of the P.T.T. and railway employees, whose services were necessary to the occupying power. No exception was made for the Government Secretary-Generals and Ministers on any pretext whatever.

In spite of the fact that Baudouin had received on the 17th December an invitation from Abetz himself to dine at the Embassy on the 20th, he was refused the *ausweis* which would have enabled him to keep the appointment, while Bouthillier, wishing to go to Paris on the 18th December, as he was accustomed regularly to do in order to see that his office in the capital was functioning properly, was expelled *manu militari* from his compartment on Moulins station.

"A Minister?" a German Customs official asked him.

"Yes."

"A Minister of Vichy?"

"Yes."

"*Heraus!*"

And, adding injury to insult, Hitler's subordinate threw the French Minister's luggage on to the platform. Only Brinon was still able to go from one zone to the other, while Flandin's representative in Paris was expelled from the northern zone.

But there was another means of pressure, of blackmail almost, used by the Nazis: the prisoners. All negotiations concerning them were broken off. When Jacques Benoist-Méchin, representing Ambassador Scapini, the Vichy delegate to the Stalags and Oflags, arrived in Berlin on the 14th December, he found that he was face to face with a veritable Iron Curtain: the German administration decided to ignore his mission. He was forbidden to establish any contact with the prisoners, visit the camps or study the possibilities of repatriation, even in the cases of the fathers of four or more children which had been already agreed.

There was another *diktat*: on the 18th December, four days after he had been appointed Secretary of State for Education, Jacques Chevalier received, at 1.55 a.m., an ultimatum from Paris. The Germans demanded that within twenty-four hours all schoolmasters from Alsace-Lorraine, who had taken refuge in the free zone, should be delivered up to them: if this were not done, they would cross the demarcation line.

Another means of pressure was that the Paris press, in the pay of the Embassy in the Rue de Lille, began a violent campaign against those responsible for Pierre Laval's arrest and demanded his return to the Government.

It was in these conditions that the Government was obliged to determine its policy: open resistance to Abetz's demands—the armistice in principle gave the Germans no rights whatsoever over Government policy—or negotiations in order to ameliorate the Nazi pressure.

After Laval's departure, there was no longer any fundamental disagreement between Pétain and the Ministers. They were all agreed in refusing to accept the return of the ex-*dauphin* or any form of military collaboration with the Reich.

The existence of a triumvirate in the Government was in accordance with the Marshal's hierarchical conceptions. Within the Government there now existed a controlling committee composed of three members: Admiral Darlan, President; Flandin, in charge of Foreign Affairs; and General Huntziger, in charge of National Defence.

Apparently nothing now threatened the Government's unity.

In fact, personal discord very quickly arose between Flandin on the one hand and the Marshal and the members of the triumvirate on the other. Pétain had received Pierre-Étienne Flandin with a feeling of confidence and relief as great as the hostility he felt towards Laval. He recognised the uprightness of his character, his intelligence, his education and his charm: from their very first meeting, he did not for an instant hesitate to show him secret documents which he had always kept hidden from Laval.

But it seems that very shortly this esteem and sympathy were counteracted by the prejudices Pétain had always felt against parliamentarians.

Flandin, and Pétain was unable to forget it, had been one of the most considerable figures of the Third Republic; he was also, at Vichy, one of the few for whom the fallen regime still had a certain prestige. "He's a parliamentarian," said Pétain.

On his side, Flandin was shocked by the casualness with which the Marshal often treated his colleagues.

What separated the two men most of all was that they had not the same kind of intelligence.

Among contemporary politicians, Flandin was one of the few who deserved the name of statesman. His policy consisted not only in dealing with current affairs in accordance with events as they occurred; he had a largeness of vision as well as principles on which to base his actions; he was one of those men who, behind the events of every day, most clearly recognised their historical implications: but Flandin was also sometimes hampered by the very loftiness of his views when engaged in the daily round of political life.

Before the war, his most lucid conceptions had often come to nothing through his inability to adapt himself.

For instance, the letter he sent Hitler after Munich, thinking that by so doing he was balancing and complementing those he sent Chamberlain and Daladier: intellectually, he was emphasising the fact that peace was indivisible and must be sought by the concerted action of everyone involved. But practically, humanly speaking, the letters sent to the ravisher of Czechoslovakia constituted in the eyes of public opinion so considerable a provocation that it eclipsed the other two; and Flandin remained, through this error of judgment, the man who wrote a letter to Hitler rather than the man who wrote letters to all three. Such blunders, which derived from a certain faculty of abstract thought, distinguished Flandin from the Marshal, who was less concerned with the wide issues of statesmanship, was more empirical, more of a realist and sometimes more of an opportunist.

And the difference between the two men was such that, though they could agree on essential points—a refusal to collaborate militarily with the Reich or to permit Laval to return to power—they were to end by adopting irreconcilable attitudes.

Flandin was of the opinion that they should play for the highest stakes even if it meant that Nazi pressure would be temporarily increased. He seems to have understood Otto Abetz's policy much better than did Pierre Laval or even the Marshal: far from seeing in him a friend of France, who would endeavour to restrain Hitler's demands, it seemed to him certain that the Ambassador was much more anxious than Hitler for military collaboration with France, for which the occasion or the pretext would be the re-conquest of Chad. Abetz made a personal affair of it and saw in it the goal of his whole policy, while to Ribbentrop or Hitler it was no more than a more or less important detail in the total situation.

Similarly, on the 17th December, after Laval's dismissal, Flandin was persuaded that Abetz had gone much further than the instructions from his chiefs had laid down.

Also, in order to avoid the danger of military collaboration with the Reich and Laval's return to power, he thought it necessary to oppose systematically negative replies to all Abetz's demands; faced with successive snubs inflicted on their Ambassador, surely Berlin would recall him. It might then be possible to establish a direct understanding with Chancellor Hitler on the basis of the armistice.

In the case of failure, it would be the destruction of the armistice, which, in Flandin's view, was preferable to the uncertainty that must weigh on France while Abetz had the right to interfere in its policy.

This conception of Flandin's was certainly coherent and extremely ingenious but it pre-supposed a trial of strength between the German Ambassador and Vichy.

But the Marshal did not want to risk a trial of strength; and this was the true reason of Flandin's failure. Obsessed by the Nazi pressure, Pétain desired above all things to diminish the sufferings of the population. Moreover, he was prepared to consider every German demand with the exception always of military collaboration with the Reich.

On the 19th December, Pétain sent a note to the Germans in reply to Abetz's ultimatum.

The first point (on which his determination coincided with Flandin's, who had threatened to resign if it did not) was that in no circumstances would he take Laval back.

Abetz had suggested the formation of a controlling triumvirate within the Government: Pétain accepted the idea, while proposing triumvirs other than those Abetz desired: they were to be Admiral Darlan, General Huntziger and Flandin. The first two names were favourably received by the Ambassador.

Abetz had also demanded the dismissal of those responsible for the 13th December, or of the Ministers whom he considered hostile to collaboration: Alibert, Peyrouton, la Laurencie, Belin and Xavier Vallat, Secretary-General of the Légion des Combattants, seemed to him undesirable.

Pétain gave him satisfaction in two cases instead of in five. He eliminated Alibert, a scapegoat, and replaced Vallat at the head of the Légion by General Laure. As far as Peyrouton was concerned, he asserted that he had taken no part in Laval's dismissal. As for la Laurencie and Belin, he maintained that on enquiry it was clear that their attitude towards collaboration had always been most loyal.

In concluding this note of the 19th December, which for the first time implicitly recognised the Ambassador's right to intervene in the actions of the Government, though it did not entirely satisfy his demands, the Head of the State reaffirmed his willingness to continue collaborating, and asked Abetz's agreement to the eventual publication of the measures envisaged in the newspapers of the occupied zone.

It was in fact a bargain that he was making between the Germans and himself, a bargain which, its principle having been once accepted, continued without interruption till the end of the regime.

But Abetz was not the man to be content with partial concessions: what he wanted was the return of Laval to Vichy.

On the 22nd December, Ribbentrop reacted violently, a reaction that no doubt Abetz had inspired and which he was happy to communicate to Pétain: "The Government of the Reich expresses extreme surprise at the fact that Marshal Pétain has not fulfilled the engagements entered into during the conversation (on the 17th December) and that M. Laval has not been recalled to the Cabinet."

Thus, ten days after the arrest of Laval, the situation had not improved.

Before this unremitting German pressure, the French Government did not adopt a uniform attitude: certain Ministers resisted, others yielded on individual points; all wished to avoid military collaboration and the return of Laval.

Among the first category, Jacques Chevalier, in spite of the ultimatum from Abetz, refused to deliver up the Alsace-Lorraine schoolmasters. Yves Bouthillier, on the other hand, decided to recommence the payments of the occupation costs, which he had suspended on his own initiative since the 6th September.

Pétain, for his part, taking up a position between the two, proposed to try finesse: unknown to Flandin, he began a new intrigue with Darlan as intermediary. Without asking the advice of his Minister for Foreign Affairs, he allowed the Admiral to ask for an audience with the Führer in order to give him a personal message from the Head of the State.

On the 25th December, Darlan met Hitler at Ferrière-sur-Epte. The prognosis of the results of the interview were so alarming that, at the moment of leaving Vichy, Darlan, in agreement with Flandin and Bergeret, decided to warn the Air Force to be ready to leave for Africa.

Was the armistice to be destroyed?

The reception Darlan received in the Führer's railway coach, drawn up near the inevitable tunnel forty kilometres south west of Beauvais, inspired him, when it was all over, to give this picturesque account: "Never," he confided to Admiral Docteur, "have I scolded one of my officers as I was scolded, and even then the interpreter can only have translated part of the vituperations of a demoniacal Hitler."

And, indeed, the Adolf Hitler who thus attacked him had nothing of the politeness, the self-control, he had manifested when, posing for posterity, he had received Pétain at the interview at Montoire. It was a passionate Hitler, a Hitler as he was on his worst days, as he must have been when he received Schuschnigg or Hacha at Berchtesgaden, as he always was when he intended the worst for his visitor.

Hitler, all the more exasperated by the fact that, through an accident, the German pilot car which was leading the Admiral had lost its way so that the latter arrived three quarters of an hour late, read the Marshal's two letters with indifference.

The first contained thanks for the return of the ashes of the Duke of Reichstadt, the second concerned the dismissal of Pierre Laval.

The Marshal ended the second letter with an assurance which, so he thought, must touch Hitler's heart: "I am a soldier, I do not understand the tricks of politicians."

It was wasted effort: "It's a dishonest letter!" foamed the Führer.

Without consideration for the author of the letter, he went off into a monologue, "his voice harsh, almost violent."

To begin with he recalled the concessions he had made to

France, and which had been taken for signs of weakness: nevertheless the war, he smirked, had shown that the weakness was not on his side.

He accused Pétain of duplicity, because he had replied to the offer of collaboration by suspecting Hitler's sincerity, when the latter had made the unforgettable gesture of restoring to France the ashes of the Duke of Reichstadt: "It's unprecedentedly infamous," exclaimed the Führer "to have suspected me of wishing to retain the Marshal in occupied territory on the occasion of so moving a European commemoration." Finally, he explained his reactions to the 13th December, in terms which, moreover, justified Flandin's hypothesis: "the form of the French Government and the men who compose it are profoundly indifferent, or could be indifferent, to me. . . .

". . . M. Laval was not among those before the war who were inveterate opponents of a policy of Franco-German understanding. It was with him, therefore, when he came to see me, that I wished to make a new attempt.

"The complaints made against him today were, so it appears, largely known before I met him. Therefore, at the very least, I must consider it a want of tact to have sent him. I might have been spared that meeting and he might have been dismissed before it."

Having thus confirmed that, unlike Abetz, he did not consider Laval as a necessary partner in the work of collaboration, the Führer, having promised to reply to the Marshal, brought his monologue to a close.

"I declare solemnly that, for the last time, I offer a policy of collaboration to France. But I fear that the French Government will engage itself once more in the same path that has led it to Vichy. I regret it, and I believe that sooner or later France will realise, if she refuses collaboration, that she has taken one of the most regrettable decisions in her history."

During the week which followed the interview at Ferrière-sur-Epte, the Vichy Government waited in vain for a reply from Hitler to the Marshal's letter.

It was at this moment that occurred a particularly painful episode due to the Nazi pressure on France: yielding to the menaces of Kriminal Kommissar Gessler, who was on a mission to Vichy, Peyrouton agreed to hand over to the Germans

Thyssen, the industrialist, who, having contributed powerfully to Hitler's accession to power, had broken with the Nazis and taken refuge in France.

Here, in all the simplicity of an official document, is the police report in which Divisional Commissar Broix announced the arrest of Thyssen and his wife and their handing over to the Nazis:

"On the 23rd December, I went to Nice with Inspectors X and Y, to transfer to Vichy M. and Mme. Fritz Thyssen, an industrialist of German nationality. Kriminal Kommissar Desterling accompanied me. M. and Mme. Thyssen were at the headquarters of the 18th Brigade of Mobile Police at Nice. They had seven suitcases containing their papers and their clothes.

"As we left Nice, on the 24th December, I said to M. and Mme. Thyssen that I was taking them to Vichy for the investigation of their foreign status.

"During the course of the journey, M. Thyssen, talking of his political activities in Germany, told me that he had parted with National Socialism when it began to make preparations for war. As for Mme. Thyssen, who approved of her husband's political decision, she expressed a fear of meeting Germans from the Armistice Commission at Vichy. Her fears subsided, and the journey took place without incident.

"Having arrived in Vichy, they were taken to the Inspection Criminelle. From that moment onwards, having understood the real reasons for their journey to Vichy, they preserved a calm and dignified attitude. M. Thyssen merely said that, if he had thought that France would hand him over to the German authorities, he would have written to his friend, President Roosevelt, and informed the Pope. He voiced the fear that the Germans would not allow him the time to do so.

"On the 26th December, still accompanied by the German Kriminal Kommissar, I took M. and Mme. Thyssen to the Madeleine Bridge at Moulins, at midday, German time. Two German cars arrived at the Madeleine from Paris. The Kriminal Kommissar made contact with his colleagues who took possession of M. and Mme. Thyssen's luggage and made M. Thyssen get into one car and Mme. Thyssen into another. The cars left again for Paris."

In its very soberness it is an appalling story, for it shows in almost every line the confidence that the two refugees had in

France: Thyssen, during the course of the journey, expressing his political ideas to a dumb listener, whom he did not suspect of being a Nazi police officer; his wife, fearing to meet Germans at Vichy. They did not for one instant believe that France would hand them over.

The Reich openly maintained its refusal to recognise Flandin as Minister for Foreign Affairs. An attitude which was manifest in, among other ways, an exchange of telegrams as unprecedented in diplomatic history as it is in the expression of good wishes for the New Year.

As was the custom, Flandin, on the 28th December, sent a note to Brinon in the following terms: "Please transmit through M. Abetz the Marshal's best wishes to the Führer for the New Year and add my own personal best wishes for M. de Ribbentrop."

Forty-eight hours later, the German Embassy communicated to Brinon the reply which had come by telephone from the Reich Ministry for Foreign Affairs: "The Führer has been much touched by Marshal Pétain's good wishes and thanks him for them. As for M. Flandin's message, no reply is necessary."

On the 5th January, Admiral Leahy, the new American Ambassador, arrived in Vichy, instructed by President Roosevelt to "gain the confidence of Marshal Pétain, who at the moment constitutes the only powerful element in the French Government firmly resolved not to go over to Germany." When he presented his letters of credence, the Head of the State, who attached much importance to American friendship, did not conceal his satisfaction.

"I had a very precise impression," Leahy recalls, "that by sending a fully accredited Ambassador to Vichy, Roosevelt had raised Pétain's morale."

This diplomatic event was clearly not likely to calm Abetz's fury.

Moreover, Flandin had wounded Abetz by certain contemptuous terms which he had one day used on the telephone about the Ambassador. The telephone was tapped and the words were reported to Abetz. "The silly little man in the Rue de Lille," he had called him. Flandin's attempt, which failed, to negotiate directly with Goering had also been a cause of annoyance.

Abetz's cleverness consisted in sending Pétain numerous French emissaries who were charged with explaining to him how the consequences of the 13th December weighed heavily on the population of the occupied zone and on the prisoners and that he must, in the interests of the country, be reconciled to Laval.

The first Frenchman to intervene in this way was hardly the most respectable: it was Brinon.

"All the ameliorations of our condition which might have been expected in the near future are wiped out. . . ." the Head of the State read in a threatening report sent him by his Ambassador Brinon from Paris on the 11th January, 1941.

"Our country today is placed in a dilemma: collaboration according to the German views or annihilation . . . this is the Führer's personal decision and, therefore, the decision of the whole of Germany. . . .

"The choice is therefore precise. The decision is naturally yours. But no half measures are possible, that is to say a policy of waiting is impossible.

"The Germans must be convinced that the policy of collaboration is being pursued by people who sincerely and energetically desire it and not by opportunists or adversaries. . . .

"Then, after a certain delay, Pierre Laval's return must be prepared."

In this report the threat is still veiled and conceived in general terms, which could still mask from the Marshal both its gravity and its imminence. Nevertheless, at about the same time, it became clearer by the return to Vichy of Jacques Benoist-Méchin, permanent delegate in Berlin of the Ambassador to the Prisoners, Scapini, to whom Abetz had given a pass that he might go to the provisional capital. Abetz asked him to negotiate an interview between Pétain and Laval. A mission which Benoist-Méchin says he refused.

At his interview with the Marshal, for whom the prisoners were a major anxiety (he called them "my children"), Benoist-Méchin found him very anxious about the consequences of Laval's dismissal: "The *coup d'état* of the 13th December," the Marshal declared, "has turned into a trial of strength between France and Germany." A trial of strength in which the Marshal felt himself not only incapable of influencing Flandin's intransigence, but also reluctant to await, without making some effort, the long-term result of the conflict, particularly when Benoist-Méchin described to him, in somewhat literary terms, the worsening situation of the prisoners following upon the 13th December: "We, the members of the delegation, opened our arms to them, but were unable to embrace them."

The argument had its effect on the old man: Benoist-Méchin persuaded him that to see Laval would not commit him to anything, but would merely allow of the erasing of certain too poignant memories. Once Laval was pacified, perhaps Abetz would cease demanding that he should return to the Government. On the 11th January, obviously without saying anything to Flandin, the Marshal was to decide to do a little finessing on his own account and enter into relations with Laval, of which only Darlan and Benoist-Méchin would have knowledge.

A few days later, on Saturday, 18th January, unknown to the Minister for Foreign Affairs, Pétain and Laval met at Ferté-Hauterive.

On that day, when Pétain, accompanied by du Moulin, left Vichy by car in the early afternoon, all his *entourage* thought he was merely going for his daily drive.

But five or six kilometres from the town, right in the open country, the Marshal, still followed by du Moulin, left the car on the road, painfully climbed the railway embankment and met Berthelot, Minister of Communications, who was walking up and down like a sentry by the Head of the State's special train, which was in waiting.

Berthelot, though he had been told nothing, suspected that these arrangements were not for an ordinary journey: "I hope you are not going to bring us back Laval, Monsieur le Maréchal." "No, my friend, don't worry."

The Head of the State, along with du Moulin, got into his carriage; the train left, and twenty minutes later stopped at the station of Ferté-Hauterive where, with a walking stick in his hand, Laval was waiting on the platform.

Pétain did not budge an inch on what seemed to him to be the essentials. All his old man's stubbornness, all his reserves of strength, were employed in holding firm on what he considered to be of capital importance; on this he gave no ground. But, in other matters, allowing his principal position to be turned and harassed by his failure to defend minor ones, he yielded concessions on less important points, without realising that he was thus diminishing or annulling the effects of his success.

Pétain was determined, absolutely determined, not to take

Laval back. He had told Benoist-Méchin so, he repeated it on the morning of the 18th to Bouthillier: "I shall enter into no arrangement concerning M. Laval; the meeting is a gesture, nothing but a gesture." Finally, to Laval, in the secrecy of a meeting which was only attended by du Moulin, he announced his decision in terms of which the only witness, who can hardly be suspected of indulgence, could not help saying: "I was taken aback by the force of such a reply."

But—and this conjunction always played a part in the old man's successes—once he had achieved the result he had set himself, Pétain allowed himself to be engaged in a discussion with Laval, in which the latter used all his cunning and from which, ultimately, he was able to gain an advantage:

"But why did you have me arrested, Monsieur le Maréchal?"

"Because you never told me anything."

"I did nothing else during the whole five months."

"Oh! Oh! You occasionally gave me information, about once in ten times, at some hasty interview. You merely told me what you wanted me to know and the proof of it is . . . ."

"The proof?"

"That you never gave me any reports."

"Reports?"

"Yes, written reports. What I want are written reports. I am a soldier. It's the way I work and you never gave me any written reports."

Laval then began to argue and blame the Marshal's *entourage*:

"Any reports I gave you would have been taken from your desk within forty-eight hours and communicated to Churchill. M. Gillouin has permission to enter your office and is in contact with Rougier the agent with the British."

This was a blow to the Marshal. He was disconcerted by the allusion to negotiations of which Laval (and the Germans) were supposed to be ignorant and he replied feebly by implicitly admitting the fact of the secret conversations:

"That is no reason. If you had given me reports, I would have had a safe put in my office and we alone would have had the keys."

Seeing that Pétain was put out of countenance, Laval launched into a long monologue. In a tone that was almost threatening, he advised Pétain to "liquidate" Flandin, the Marquess of Londonderry's man, a politician without greatness with whom the Germans "will always refuse to negotiate". He also advised him to get rid of all the "Anglo-Gaullists" at Vichy, Gillouin, Laure, Fernet, who would create great difficulties for him.

But this last tirade had put the Marshal back on the terrain he knew and on which his answer was ready. With great firmness and even spirit, he reproached Laval with having conducted a personal policy, of having, without consulting him, embarked on collaboration, and of leading France to war against England. He energetically defended Laure, Fernet and even Flandin. And, when Laval tried to interrupt him, Pétain cut him short with:

"Let me finish. I have come here to say what is in my mind; and I shall say it."

Laval realised the uselessness of a frontal attack. Provisionally accepting the fact that he was not to return to power, he changed his tone, made an oblique approach and thus succeeded, by cajolery, in partially repairing the defeat his excesses had earned him.

"Why should we quarrel, Monsieur le Maréchal, when we share the same point of view about many men and many things?"

"Do you think so?"

"But, of course, Monsieur le Maréchal, and since, at bottom, nothing serious divides us, I cannot see why we should not take advantage of the fact to agree on a few concrete points, for instance the terms of a short declaration, a *communiqué* to the Press, for example."

"That is an idea," Pétain conceded, doubtless thinking that after the snub he had inflicted on Laval, he owed him some reparation.

Du Moulin, seeing the trap, then tried to intervene. But first Laval, and then Pétain, indicated that he was not there to join in the discussions but simply to take notes.

Laval then took from his coat pocket a crumpled piece of paper, covered with erasions in pencil. He read it. It was the *communiqué*, prepared in advance, of the meeting at Ferté-Hauterive.

"Marshal Pétain, Head of the State, has met President Laval. They had a long conversation during the course of which the misunderstandings, which led to the disagreements of the 13th December, were dissipated."

Pétain, on the suggestion of du Moulin, made one alteration which in no way changed its import: "disagreements" was replaced by "misapprehensions".

Laval then left Pétain and the train returned to Vichy.

Abetz, when he read the *communiqué*, was able to "express the hope . . . that Laval would be recalled to the Government as Minister of the Interior and member of the Directory, and that those who had been responsible for the 13th December, 1940, would be punished and dismissed."

But there was one man who, after Pétain's return, at last learned of the journey and, when he read the *communiqué*, realised its importance and grasped the fact that, even if there was nothing in it corresponding to Laval's hopes, it was yet only a question of time before he returned to power—and that man was Pierre-Étienne Flandin.

He immediately counter-attacked, not hesitating for a second to burn his boats. The report of the conversation which du Moulin gave him to read furnished him with a sufficiency of facts to contradict the *communiqué* or, at least, limit the damage it could do.

He at once summoned all the foreign correspondents to his office. He informed them that they should pay no attention to the *communiqué* which was about to be published; but that the report drawn up by du Moulin showed on the contrary the Marshal's unshakable determination not to recall, for the moment at least, M. Laval to power. And in order to make sure that the news should reach the allied powers and be published as soon as possible in foreign papers, Flandin removed the censorship for their Vichy correspondents. By this rapid and vigorous counter-attack in face of a threat he had not been able to foresee but whose consequences he parried, Flandin made Laval's recall impossible and once again avoided the danger of a renewal of negotiations concerning the Chad operation. But at the same time, politically speaking, he was signing his death warrant.

The German reaction was immediate and severe: on the day after the interview, barely a few hours after the press conference, the demarcation line already closed to all Ministers and officials was now rendered impassable to all men between the ages of 18 and 45, whoever they might be. The Prefect of the Paris police, Langeron, who had been summoned to Vichy, was unable to get there.

The Paris press let itself go, particularly against Flandin, whom it accused of treason: "The news from Vichy emphasises that

Monsieur Flandin has latterly been playing a double game and that he is considered completely discredited in diplomatic circles."

The Germans took measures to make the food situation in Paris worse than ever, and the Parisian press blamed Vichy. They took advantage of the situation to attack the Minister for Food, Achard, with extreme violence.

Otto Abetz took measures to increase the political role of the collaborationist parties in Paris which were under his control: meeting after meeting denounced the treachery of Vichy. On the 1st February, Alphonse de Chateaubriant denounced the politicians of the Allier, and Jean Fontenoy imitated him on many occasions. It was now that Déat founded a new party, the R.N.P. (Rassemblement National Populaire), against the reactionary tendencies of Vichy and for collaboration with the Reich. In order to short-circuit Déat, a Comité du Rassemblement for the National Revolution was created in the free zone, on the suggestion of du Moulin de Labarthète: among others, Tixier-Vignancour, Frédéric Dupont, Charles Trochu, Vice-President of the Municipal Council of Paris, Thierry Maulnier and Antoine de Saint-Exupéry became members.

There was another political threat which Abetz directed at Vichy: he tried to create a French Government in Paris. He was even sufficiently naïve to send Charles Bedaux to suggest to Weygand that he should take part in it. He did not know the General, who wrote immediately and indignantly to Pétain: "It is hardly necessary, Monsieur le Maréchal, that I should inform you of my absolute determination, should the case arise, of never accepting a position in a government set up under German auspices."

At Vichy, Flandin saw a vacuum gradually forming about him. Most Ministers were beginning to think that relations must be restored with Abetz at all costs. Admiral Darlan asked to be sent to Paris to make contact with Abetz, implying thereby that he proposed substituting himself for the Minister for Foreign Affairs in essential diplomatic relations.

General Huntziger, intervening for the first time in political discussions, supported the Admiral: under the Armistice regime, France could not run the risk of a sharp conflict with the Reich.

The other members of the Government, even Bouthillier, ceased to support Flandin.

Repudiated by his colleagues, Flandin found no support from the Marshal.

The differences between the two men became accentuated over the creation of a new institution called the Conseil National.

Charged by the Marshal with organising this "emanation of the vital forces of the nation, of those forces which, beyond groups, parties and trusts, represent the essential elements of the national life",[1] Flandin was reproached by the Marshal for having completely betrayed his idea: had he not dared introduce seventy-one members of Parliament—twenty-seven Senators and forty-four Deputies—among the 188 Metropolitan members of the new Assembly?

On the 30th January, a decisive letter arrived in Vichy: Brinon transmitted a veritable ultimatum from Abetz, who was sheltering behind the Führer, whose answer had not arrived and indeed never would.

The French Ambassador informed the Head of the State that the Chancellor of the Reich was resolved to put a term to collaboration if the present Government team remained in power and that therefore an increase of German pressure was to be expected.

"The Führer has envisaged the cessation of all passes and the more rigorous closing of the demarcation line, the refusal to allow the last Constitutional Acts and Decrees of the Government to be applied in the occupied zone, and a refusal to give passes for the free zone to the members of the Conseil National."

On the other hand, if Vichy yielded to the German demands and the situation were restored to what it had been before the 13th December, in other words if a military collaboration were contemplated once more, the Führer would be prepared to make numerous concessions.

Consulted by Pétain, Darlan was explicit: the interests of France made it imperative that "collaboration" be accepted in the political and economic spheres and in the defence of the Empire by French forces alone, while "excluding war with our old allies".

With the Marshal's agreement, Darlan telephoned Brinon. He told him to inform the German Ambassador that: "The Marshal

[1] The law of the 24th January, 1941, which created the Conseil National, specified that this Assembly of Notables would only have a consultative role.

intends bringing President Laval into the Government of which Admiral Darlan will be Vice-President.

"Before making this decision official, the Marshal deems it essential that the Admiral should have an interview with President Laval and with Ambassador Abetz."

And Pétain summoned Flandin to inform him of his decision: Admiral Darlan would leave for Paris to study with the Germans the constitution of a government with which they would be prepared to negotiate.

For the last time, Flandin produced his arguments: he advised once more that Hitler's answer should be awaited, persuaded that the latter could not help recognising the Marshal's right to appoint his own ministers: at all costs French policy must be defended against interference by the occupying power.

On the 2nd February, General Laure made a similar protest to the Marshal.

On the 3rd and 4th February, Darlan was in Paris.

He first saw Laval, who set unacceptable conditions to his return to Vichy:[1] the Marshal would limit himself to exercising the functions of a Head of the State; Laval would be nominated, by a Constitutional Act, Head of the Government with practically total powers, while the Ministers would be responsible to him alone; Laval also demanded the Ministry of the Interior in order that he might be certain that the 13th December would not occur again.

Darlan grew angry. "And what happens to the Marshal under your proposals?" Laval replied cynically: "He's a decorative china vase, I shall put him on the chimney piece."

Darlan, who could only offer Laval subaltern posts, Public Works, P.T.T., or Minister of State, had the less difficulty in making Abetz understand that an agreement was impossible since the Germans no longer desired Laval's return to the Government. On the 5th February, 1941, Ribbentrop had made his intentions on this subject clear to the Ambassador in an instruction: "I pray you to arrange matters in such a way that Laval remains in the occupied zone and that the Laval affair be dealt with in relation to Vichy in such a manner that no understanding can, for the moment, take place between Laval and Vichy.' The

[1] Unacceptable at this moment, since Laval was to impose them in November, 1942.

head of German diplomacy no doubt found threats more efficacious than putting them into execution: whenever Darlan, in the future, was tempted to cease collaborating, Abetz frightened him with Laval's return to Vichy or with the creation of a Laval government in Paris.

The very day on which Ribbentrop wrote to Abetz, a Council of Ministers met in Vichy to hear Darlan report on his mission. Each Minister in turn gave his opinion on the Laval case. Flandin spoke with peculiar vigour: "Not only is the return of Laval inconceivable," he said, "but also all negotiations with Abetz concerning the construction of a French Government." A declaration of principle to which the Marshal listened in silence.

Faced with this tacit disagreement, it only remained for Flandin to see the Marshal after the Council and hand him his resignation, for Pétain had decided to negotiate with Abetz on a problem which was strictly one of internal policy.

On the 7th February, Darlan, who was at this date still the only Vichy Minister to be in possession of an *ausweis*, was once more in Paris, from which he returned the following day to be present at the last Council of Ministers in which Flandin took part. Darlan read a note: he enumerated the advantages of a policy of collaboration, but did not refer to its disadvantages. On the contrary, he gave an appalling picture of all the ills which would fall upon France if Pétain refused to collaborate: "The hour, Messieurs, is as grave as was that in which the decision had to be taken to ask for an armistice.

"If we cease collaborating, we shall lose all the advantages that we may expect from that armistice.

"For my part, I have made my choice, I am for collaboration."

This document reveals Darlan's illusions: he thought he could obtain from the Germans all the advantages they had promised Laval without giving them the counterpart offered by the ex-President of the Council: military collaboration.

On the following day, 9th February, Flandin sent the Marshal his letter of resignation.

The Paris press sang a hymn of triumph and, on the 10th February, the *Journal Officiel*, with the consent of the Germans, published Constitutional Act No. 4, *ter*, which gave Admiral Darlan the prerogatives of a *dauphin* and the Vice-Presidency of the Council was re-established for his benefit.

It was thus that the crisis begun by the dismissal of Laval on the 13th December came finally to an end.

After the National Assembly of July, 1940, two statesmen had successively attempted to make Vichy embark on far-reaching policies which entailed making a definite choice. For Laval, it had been a question of playing the German game to the utmost and of integrating France with the new European order; for Flandin, it had been resistance to the Germans and the maintaining of French independence in accordance with the guarantee under the Armistice.

These two policies, which were in opposition to each other but had in common a breadth and precision of outlook and implied making a choice, failed for the same reason: the hostility of the Marshal, who refused to pursue them and sought to gain time. Laval disquieted him, Flandin seemed to him too abstract in thought: to them both he opposed the same desire to wait and the same opportunism, which without yielding on essentials allowed him to negotiate wherever it seemed to him possible to do so.

In compelling Flandin to resign after having dismissed Pierre Laval, the Marshal showed precisely what his attitude was to be: he had chosen not to choose: he would neither collaborate militarily with the Reich nor resist openly.

His policy was to be one of expediency: he would never give the Reich a military alliance, but he would make the necessary concessions to avoid a rupture.

If the period between the 13th December and the 9th February saw the avoidance of the worst, it was also the period in which Vichy missed the only chance of rising to events.

Thus General Laure was right in his judgment that the 9th February, 1941, marked the decisive turning-point in the history of Vichy.

# Vichy, the Second Period

(9th February, 1941–18th April, 1942)

## CHAPTER 1

# DARLAN AND HIS MINISTERS

ON the 21st February, 1941, eleven days after the promulgation of Constitutional Act No. 4, which made of him the eventual successor to the Marshal, Admiral Darlan was charged with the formation of a new government. He gave himself the four key ministries: the Vice-Presidency of the Council, Foreign Affairs, Internal Affairs and Information. He came into political life with the prestige of the chief of an undefeated Navy. But the fate which awaited him in politics was most disconcerting: from the day of his accession to power, the Admiral became, according to a contemporary, "the great enigma of the War", as well as the scapegoat for every discontent.

Damaging nicknames, given him by every political party both in France and abroad, brought him into dishonour and turned him to ridicule.

Cruel and libellous stories about him were disseminated in every political camp to which he became successively affiliated, both in Vichy and in Algiers.

Two years after his accession to power, having been officially deprived of French nationality by Pétain and accused of dishonourable conduct by de Gaulle, Darlan was subjected to the same vehement accusations from both camps, sometimes even in identical terms. On the 25th December, 1942, François Darlan fell to the shots of a young fanatical patriot, Fernand Bonnier de la Chapelle, who thought he was serving France.

When France declared war in 1939, her Fleet, both in ships and crews, was one of the most splendid fighting forces the country had ever known. When Pétain had visited the Naval Headquarters at Maintenon on the 5th May, 1940, he had voiced his admiration: "At last, I've seen something that's really functioning properly. I congratulate you, Admiral."

And the Fleet was Darlan's work.

Born into a family of sailors and shipowners, he was a brilliant sailor and had always passionately loved the sea.

Besides his qualities both as a sailor and as a man, Darlan was endowed with clarity of intellect, a capacity for work and a quite exceptional gift for organisation.

But despite these talents, which attracted his intimate colleagues, Darlan had also obvious eccentricities. He was apt to display them to excess, almost provocatively: his vanity, for instance, which was sometimes childish. Although by his position and rank entitled to the highest decorations, he one day demanded two new ribbons, the Order of Malta and the Medal of Public Health!

People knew how to play upon his vanity. When, at Vichy, he talked of dissolving the Légion des Combattants and replacing it by a single party, General Laure, who was far indeed from being a Machiavelli, found an immediate answer. At the first meeting of the Légion, he arranged an ovation for Darlan. With spontaneous acclamations ringing in his ears, the Légion had nothing further to fear: it would continue to exist.

His journeys were not unnoticed. He had to have a special train which left, with a splendid disregard for time-tables, at the precise moment which happened to suit him, invariably disorganising normal traffic. He also required the attendance in his various residences of the resounding presence of his eighty musicians, the old-fashioned Navy band: it was to be heard playing distant music when Darlan received the Marshal at Nérac, his family home; it dispensed waves of harmony at Luchon, while the Admiral was taking a three weeks' cure.

There was another aspect of his character which, less serious, was nevertheless extremely irritating: like a schoolboy, Darlan could not help making a joke of everything. In words at least, he showed no respect for any subject, however painful it might be.

These eccentricities, however notorious they may have been, are not sufficient to explain the hatred in which the Admiral was held. Moreover, this hatred is surprising since Darlan's patriotism was incontestable: the narrative will show that, during the fourteen months of his Government, the Admiral abandoned no essential point, neither the Empire nor the Fleet; he stood up to the Germans on many points on which, as we shall see, Laval yielded.

Indeed, what has really exposed Darlan to general execration is the fact that he escapes all normal definition and, consequently, disconcerts.

We are inclined today, after three centuries of Cartesianism, psychological novels and historical biography, to place people in categories or subject them to precise labels: the virtuous or wicked man, the good or bad Frenchman, the man of the Right or the man of the Left; and one is inclined to suspect anyone who escapes these classifications or appears to distort their precision.

And Darlan can be placed in no category: was he pro- or anti-collaborationist, did he approve of the National Revolution or was he, as he sometimes said, a "Republican of the Left"? These were questions to which Darlan gave no answer, though they seemed essential to his contemporaries.

What Darlan really wanted was to achieve results: he was a realist who was contemptuous of political or intellectual labels, who was concerned only with the goals to be attained, and this sometimes gave him an appearance of opportunism.

François Darlan was a plain man, "who did not know Latin", "who had no University degree, nor *baccalauréat*, nor even a certificate of primary studies." Such were the portraits that, not without humour, nor indeed a certain vanity, Darlan liked to present of himself.

He believed in the Fleet, in France and in Darlan. To serve these three, whatever the political or partisan storms, was his dominant anxiety. He navigated the waters of public life as if at the head of a squadron which had to be brought to port by using, or cheating, the currents.

The arrival of Darlan in the Government coincided with the moment when real power was beginning to escape the Marshal.

The Head of the State was increasingly feeling the effects of his age; in 1941 he was 85. If he was still physically remarkable, his mental lucidity was beginning to suffer eclipses.

Grouped about the old Marshal, the new Government team had a heterogeneous appearance.

Indeed, it was drawn from two different sources. On the one hand, elderly men, humanists, often even Liberals who had known their best years under the Third Republic: important members of universities, members of the Institut, writers, such as Barthélemy, Carcopino, Moysset and Romier, who were all anti-German and anti-totalitarian. Never had a government had so many intellectuals, indeed Academicians, in its ranks.

They were men who had "arrived" long before July, 1940, who had nothing to complain of in their treatment by the old regime, that is to say, the defunct Third Republic. Joseph Barthélemy had attained the summit of Republican honours: Professor at the Faculty of Law and at the School of Political Sciences, a member of the Institut to which he had been elected by a majority never before achieved, he had been the French delegate to the League of Nations. Jérôme Carcopino, a Professor at the Sorbonne, Director of the French School at Rome, was also a member of the Institut. Romier was a bourgeois intellectual who edited *le Figaro* and whose book, *Explications de Notre Temps*, was the breviary of generations of students of political science. Moysset, the historian of French Socialism in the nineteenth century, was Professor at the Senior Naval School, where Darlan had appreciated his services.

They none of them felt that systematic hostility to the Republic which was the fashion at Vichy. Barthélemy before the war had published a book extolling the Constitution of 1875 as compared to those of the totalitarian regimes. At the Institut, his Republicanism had even one day created a scandal: during the course of a solemn meeting of the five Academies, at which General Weygand had pronounced an eulogy of Vauban, had he not dared to praise the French Revolution? They were people of note who, when in power under an authoritarian regime, preserved the intellectual independence and the freedom of speech inculcated by their training. If they gave their adherence to the Vichy Government, it was not that they approved all its decisions. Two of them were given charge of important ministerial departments: Barthélemy, at the Ministry of Justice, was often to be torn between his concern as a lawyer and the arbitrary decisions the occupying power compelled him to take. Carcopino, at the Ministry of Education, diminished the force of the discriminatory measures to the point where the Paris press called him "a protector of Jews and Freemasons."

Romier and Moysset had not in theory such heavy responsibilities: in the Government team they were "spare horses": Ministers of State without portfolio, who had their offices on the top storey of the Hôtel du Parc, called "the Storey of the Philosophers". Sitting above the battle, their function was not to act, but to comment on, and make appreciations of, events and the actions of the Government.

Never losing an opportunity to show his anti-German sentiments, nor his hatred for the totalitarian spirit, we shall see Romier frequently intervening in constitutional projects, and trying to advise Pucheu at the time of the execution of hostages. Moysset, in conversation with Marion, attacked the totalitarian propaganda he was diffusing over the country: "The French people are sane," he said, "and the proof is that your propaganda makes them vomit." On many occasions, Moysset was to warn Darlan against the dangers of a military collaboration with the Reich. He used almost prophetic terms in warning Pétain of the fate which awaited him if he allowed Laval to return to the Government in April, 1942.

In contrast to these distinguished men, there were new arrivals, young men in a hurry, of whom Marion, Benoist-Méchin and Pucheu were particularly noteworthy. They were certainly not Nazis, nor for the most part Fascists. They were indubitably patriotic but, faced with the totalitarian regimes, they had not that particular intolerance, one might almost say disgust, felt by the "old Romans". By temperament and training, they inclined towards dictatorship, or at least accepted it. Their accession to power marked the beginning of a new generation for whom the Republic was dead, if it had ever counted at all, and for whom France must adapt herself to the New European Order.

Marion, Benoist-Méchin and Pucheu, who would never have been Ministers under the Third Republic, came from quite different backgrounds and classes. Marion, who was of the lower middle-class, came from the extreme Left, Benoist-Méchin, who had aristocratic pretensions, came from the literary world and Pucheu, from a working-class family, had been brought up to the humanities in the École Normale, but belied his education in order to become a director in the iron and steel industry. But, in their very different careers, they had had one episode in common: before the war they had been members of Jacques Doriot's Parti Populaire Français, which they had all three joined in the hope of seeing a political movement come to birth which would be at once national and revolutionary; but they had all left it at about the same time in disgust at discovering that Doriot was receiving secret funds from abroad.

When they came to power, all three were approximately the same age: Marion and Pucheu were forty-two, Benoist-Méchin thirty-nine. They were a new generation, vigorous and in mid-career. They each had a very distinctive personality.

On the 23rd February, 1941, Marion was first appointed Deputy-Secretary-General to the Vice-Presidency of the Council for Information—an appointment which was designed to satisfy Abetz—then, on the 11th August, 1941, Secretary-General for Information and Propaganda. On the 18th April, 1942, when Laval returned, he became Secretary of State for Information, until the 5th January, 1944, on which date he was replaced by Philippe Henriot. From then on he remained in the Government as Secretary of State until the Marshal and Laval were compelled to leave for Germany; having followed them across the Rhine, he refused to take part in the "government" which Brinon wished to set up.

His life had been a very extraordinary one, filled as it was with successive and contradictory adherences. In 1922, he joined the Communist Party and became one of its leaders in France. In this capacity, he was received at Moscow, came back disillusioned and, in 1929, resigned.

A few years later, filled with enthusiasm once more, he joined Jacques Doriot's Parti Populaire Français, which declared itself to be both anti-capitalist and anti-Marxist. In 1939, he broke his political affiliations once again. Taking Doriot to task for his errors and mistakes, his profound amorality and above all his equivocal attitude towards the national interest, Marion left the P.P.F.

In 1940, like so many other people, he was a prisoner in Germany. Otto Abetz continuously intervened in his favour, pointing out that the "ideas (of M. Paul Marion) were very similar to those of National Socialism. . . . It might be of advantage to release Marion in view of the political situation."

Hardly had Marion been freed, when he was summoned to Vichy, where he became the *enfant terrible*.

He was one of the few French ministers openly to declare themselves Fascist. He wanted to save France by adopting a totalitarian ideology.

Superficially Benoist-Méchin and Marion seemed to have

nothing in common. While the second proclaimed his working-class origins, manifested a certain untidiness of dress, vehemence of tone and cynicism of speech which made of him a character for the stage and the popular novel, the other, who prided himself on his aristocratic background, calling himself a Baron of the Empire, was precise, neat, somewhat stiff and always seemed to be reserved in the expression of his feelings. The exact opposite of the demagogue and the orator, he was a secretive man who held himself aloof, but was capable of surprising. While creating an impression by the austerity and precision of his dialectic, imposing himself by his undeniable courage and dignity, he was not made to charm or carry people off their feet.

Benoist-Méchin was above all a man of letters, with all the qualities and artifice that the term implies.

He was a man of letters in his books, in his speech, in his life. Before the war he had published a monumental *History of the German Army*, which was republished in 1943 without one word of the criticisms he had made of the Wehrmacht and the Nazi regime being altered. It was a proof of intellectual independence.

Benoist-Méchin's mind was never so much at ease as when he was relating the history of the past or inventing the history of the future:

"A defeated country can take up three positions," he wrote on the 17th November, 1941, "*against* its conqueror, *for* its conqueror, or *with* its conqueror.

"I am against, as indeed France has shown herself to be against, the first position, because in a whole succession of circumstances she has not reacted.

"On the other hand, France is not agreed to be *for* the conquering power. I am a partisan of the third formula: *with* the conqueror."

The third of this team was Pucheu, perhaps the strongest personality of the three, or at least the one whose strength was most apparent. It was he who, in 1941–1942, aroused, according to party and circumstance, the most lively feelings of fear, admiration or hatred. Ultimately, he was the first of the men of Vichy to be tried and executed.

Coming from the people, his intelligence and his capacity for work won him scholarships to the École Normale. He was also an athlete, a champion footballer and a fighter who knew how to make himself respected with his fists.

He was not attracted by schoolmastering, since it did not satisfy his desire for action: one day, half ironically, half seriously, he told his comrades that he was leaving the Faculty and had delivered himself over to the "deux cents familles". His industrial career had been brilliant: having done extremely well in various enterprises, he was appointed, when still very young, to be managing director of a very important tool-making concern, Japy.

Extremely patriotic, he wished to see France governed as if she were an industrial concern; he hated inefficiency, despised democracy and thought that the police should be one of the bases of the new regime. Very ambitious, he could see himself playing the part of a dictator, and was persuaded that always and under all regimes his qualities would make him indispensable. Outspoken to the point of provocation, either brutal or cynical, he behaved like a man who had no reservations, and felt himself strong enough to have nothing to hide; in his way he was unique, a machine geared to success, which might, however, according to circumstances, beat all records or run off the rails.

And Pucheu was successively to know both these fates in their last excess and ultimate extreme: at Vichy he was the most dynamic and ambitious of young Ministers. Before the Tribunal in Algiers and face to face with his executioners, he was of all the condemned the most contemptuous of his judges, the most faithful to himself, the most assured in his patriotism, and as unyielding and authoritarian in the presence of death as he had been in his life.

Pucheu is no longer here to defend himself: he tried to do so in writings to be published posthumously, in which he asserted that the part he played had been to reduce the number of executions demanded by the Germans. Arithmetically, he is correct on this point. At the time of the Châteaubriant executions, his intervention succeeded in reducing the number of hostages shot from 150 to 50. In 1942, he threatened to resign if he were not immediately granted the liberation of 150 political prisoners held in the camps of the southern zone. Undoubtedly, therefore, his actions while in the Government reduced the number of victims.

His sin was not the shedding of French blood since, thanks to him, there were fewer deaths and more survivors. But his fault was to have brought a sort of statistical calculation to what should not be reduced to figures, the life and the death of men to whom he was united by the link of the national community. His sin was perhaps that he accepted without protest, if he did not deliberately engineer, that the Germans should select their victims among chosen categories of Frenchmen; his major fault was that the life of a Communist, fighting the same battle as other Frenchmen in the Resistance Movement, seemed to him less precious and less worthy of being defended.

Pucheu's fault was therefore not so much political as moral and metaphysical. He inspires the sort of sacred horror which a Pascal would have felt at seeing the gravest of human problems, those involving the life and death of human beings, treated geometrically.

## CHAPTER 2

# FRANCE IN THE TIME OF THE TWO ZONES

## The Divorce between Vichy and Public Opinion

THE fourteen months of Darlan's Government coincided with the greatest reversals of fortune of the world war.

On the 22nd June, 1941, came the sudden shock which marked the first massive extension of hostilities: Germany invaded the U.S.S.R. Six months later, on the 7th December, there was another event of the first importance: attacked at Pearl Harbour by Japan, the U.S.A. entered the war. From now on, the conflict took on the aspect of an ideological war: no country in the world was to know tranquillity.

The outcome of the war was still in suspense.

The only thing at this period which was sure was that no country, not even France, could come out of this world-wide violence unscathed: bombing from the air began to devastate French towns, for the British were attacking the factories working for Germany. In the occupied zone, on the 14th April, 1941, Brest had 76 dead; on the 3rd March, 1942, Boulogne-Billancourt had no less than 623 dead and 1,500 wounded.

What irritated the French, besides the equivocal relations between Vichy and the occupying power, was above all the difference between the official life they could see and the real life they had to lead. They watched France being inundated with photographs of the Marshal: official announcements interpreted as a "veritable plebiscite" the fact, and a most improbable one, that in Paris there had been as many photographs sold as there were inhabitants, young children included.

Official life seemed to consist of loyal ceremonies, the taking of oaths, and official speeches.

Real life, for the most part, was dominated by hunger and the lack of freedom.

As to hunger, these were the rations which were to suffice the French.

In May, 1941, adults received 240 grms. (approx. 8½ oz.) of bread a day, 250 grms. (approx. 8¾ oz.) of meat and 75 grms. (approx. 2½ oz.) of cheese a week, 550 grms. (approx. 19 oz.) of fat, 500 grms. (approx. 17½ oz.) of sugar, 200 grms. (approx. 7 oz.) of rice, 250 grms. (approx. 8¾ oz.) of flour a month, two packets of cigarettes every ten days and a litre of wine.

This under-nourishment encouraged the Academy of Medicine to suggest the turning of seaweed into ersatz cod-liver oil and to recommend the cessation—or at least the reduction—of physical culture in schools, all physical effort being bad for under-nourished children.

After hunger, the second dominant factor at this period was lack of liberty.

At all times, for good reason or bad, individual liberty was threatened, even that of the most famous of the great writers.

André Gide, who had retired to Nice, was to deliver a lecture on the poet Henry Michaux on the 21st May, 1941. On the very morning of the lecture, he received from the local head of the Légion Française des Combattants a letter in which the following was the most significant passage.

". . . It is hardly admissible, at the very hour when the Marshal is endeavouring to develop a spirit of sacrifice among the youth of France, that a man who has made himself the triumphant champion of the spirit of pleasure should deliver a public speech. . . .

"In the hope that this call to order, to tact and good taste, will be heard, pray accept this expression of our most distinguished sentiments.

"Légion Française des Combattants Alpes-Maritimes."

The prisons were crowded. While in March, 1940, the total number of prisoners had been 18,000, by 1942 there were 50,000, without counting the 30,000 government internees in the concentration camps: one Frenchman in fifty had been deprived of his liberty. The Santé prison, built to hold a thousand prisoners, contained four thousand.

Who were these prisoners and what was their life like?

Clearly, for the most part, they were "enemies of the regime".

In the occupied zone, where the prisoners were controlled by the Nazi authorities, they consisted of Jews, Communists and Gaullists. In the free zone, they were Communists, Gaullists and a few trades unionists and members of Parliament representing the Third Republic. Moreover, until November, 1942, the Vichy Government, which preserved a certain independence in its own zone, made 373 arrests for treason committed on behalf of the Germans. Of this number, 29 were condemned to death and executed. The others, for the most part, were freed when Laval returned to power.

The conditions of life in the prisons were appalling: at the Centrale at Riom, where in normal times the mortality was between three and four a year, 120 died every six months during 1941–1942.

Life in the Metropolitan prisons, however hard it might be, was nevertheless less intolerable than in the North African camps. By a denial of justice, more appalling than a good many others, foreigners who had enlisted as volunteers in the Foreign Legion during the campaign of France were, at the armistice, shut up in labour camps and put to the construction of the Trans-Sahara railway between the Niger and the Mediterranean.

Here follows, taken from official documents, an account of the life of these men who had been condemned for having served France.

"No. 6 Group of foreign labourers very soon took on all the appearance of a convicts' camp in which the interned were not treated as human beings. . . . The camp was literally starving; some ate anything they could lay their hands on and from this fact contracted serious illness. Others died from this state of things. In spite of their physical weakness, the men were subjected to particularly hard labour. . . . The overseers, armed with sticks, shamelessly beat the labourers, without reason, merely for the sake of beating them. . . . Those undergoing punishment were crowded into cells and compelled to perform their natural functions in their mess tins. . . . They were forbidden to fetch water to wash them. Their food consisted solely of very salt soup, deliberately salted to make it intolerable. . . . Sometimes the doctors were forbidden to dress the wounds of their comrades who were no more than living sores from being flogged by the guards. . . ."

In this world of concentration camps, there were however

certain privileged people: the important men of the Third Republic, who were shown a certain consideration in gaol.

Daladier, when he was appearing before the Court of Riom, was astonished to find that bugs were interfering with the preparation of his defence and sent the President of the High Court his visiting card in an envelope with a few of the insects pinned to it.

There was another characteristic of this period: the beginning of the assassinations.

The first victims were three politicians of diametrically opposed camps. On the 26th July, 1941, the ex-Minister of the Interior of the Popular Front, Marx Dormoy, was killed by the explosion of a bomb which had been placed in his room at Montélimar, where he was under house arrest.

The press, on strict Government orders, attributed the crime to anarchists, even insinuating that its authors were *agents provocateurs* of the extreme Left, who would not hesitate to assassinate one of their own people in order to rouse public opinion against the regime.

In fact, the authors of the crime were four extremists of the Right, members of the Parti Populaire Français, three young men, Vaillant, Meynier and Guichard, accompanied by an adventuress, Annie Mouraille, who was half woman of letters and half actress; they thought they were "heroes of the National Revolution".

They were none the less arrested by Vichy and the process of the law followed its natural course until January, 1943, when the Germans took over the prison of Largentières and liberated them by force.

A month after Dormoy's death, Laval himself was the victim of attempted assassination.

On the 27th August, 1941, for the purpose of presenting a French flag to the first contingent of the L.V.F. (Legion of French Volunteers against Bolshevism), a parade was held in the Borgnis-Desbordes barracks at Versailles.

In a fraternal group at the head of the procession marched the German Minister Plenipotentiary, Schleier, the French Ambassador, de Brinon, and the Prefect of Seine-et-Oise. Immediately behind them were Laval and Déat.

Pierre Laval and Marcel Déat were wounded: the first very

slightly, the second more seriously. The assassin, Colette, was the following day extolled as a hero by the London radio. Nevertheless, Colette soon returned to the obscurity from which, thanks to his gesture, he had momentarily emerged. Laval, unwilling to make a martyr of him, obtained his reprieve after he had been condemned to death.

Both the wounded, Laval and Déat, quickly recovered.

But soon the atmosphere of the Terror began to weigh over France due to the executions of hostages by the Germans as reprisals for attacks on their troops.

The entry of Russia into the war had thrown the Communist party, since the 21st June, openly into the struggle against the occupying power: on the 21st August, 1941, Midshipman Mozer, of the Kriegsmarine, was shot in the Barbès-Rochechouart Métro by Colonel Fabien of the Francs-Tireurs et Partisans. This first assassination was followed by many others. The Germans reacted by shooting hostages, of which the most unpleasantly notorious incident during this period took place at Châteaubriant.

Over and above the repressive measures taken against the Communists, the Parisians were at this time beginning to become aware of the red and black posters, written in German and French, announcing the execution of "terrorists". The first, posted on the 29th August, announced the shooting of three Gaullist agents, Naval Lieutenant d'Estienne d'Orves, who had been sent from London to organise the Resistance, and two members of his team:

*Bekanntmachung—Avis*

1. Naval Lieutenant Henri-Louis Honoré, Comte d'ESTIENNES d'ORVES, French, born 5th June, 1901, at Verrières,

2. Business agent Maurice-Charles-Émile BARLIER, French, born 9th September, 1905, at Saint-Dié,

3. Merchant Jean-Louis-Guillaume DOORNIK, Dutch, born 26th June, 1905, at Paris,

have been condemned to death for espionage. They were shot today.

Paris, 29th August, 1941,
*Der Militarbefehlshaber in Frankreich.*

This atmosphere of terror, as it spread across the occupied

zone, turned public opinion almost unanimously against the Germans. The only exceptions were a few stray Frenchmen who in politics or the press, had a personal interest in playing the Nazi game.

The Paris press, subject to German control and the political parties artificially created on the orders of the Embassy, thus constituted an official Fifth Column which was in process of committing treason.

The occupation had brought unexpected prosperity to those few parties which, before the war, had supported Fascist theories. Such, in the first place, was the P.P.F. of Jacques Doriot, whose pretensions increased in proportion as the authority of Vichy diminished. The meetings of the P.P.F. in Paris were for the Germans a sword of Damocles suspended over the head of the French Government, whenever the latter showed signs of lacking in docility. In the free zone, the followers of Doriot played the part of hired roughs and supplementary police.

Such also was the Francisme of Bucard.

The most important political organisation of the collaborationists in Paris came into existence in January, 1941. It was the R.N.P. (Rassemblement National Populaire), whose directing committee of five members consisted of three stars and two utility men.

In the first place there was Déat, the founder of Neo-Socialism, the unsuccessful supporter of the single party at Vichy who, since his return from the free zone, had led the opposition to the Marshal's Government. Beside him was Eugène Deloncle, the ex-leader of the Cagoule, recently converted to Franco-German *rapprochement* and to collaboration. The third leader was a reactionary, the President-General of the Union Nationale des Combattants, who had been one of the inspirers of the days of February, 1934, Jean Goy.

Besides them, there was Jean Fontenoy, a talented writer, but unstable of intellect, whom we have already met as Laval's emissary, and an unknown, Jean Vanor, who had been secretary-general of a similarly composite movement.

Within the R.N.P., Deloncle had tried, under the name of M.S.R. (Mouvement Social Révolutionnaire), to reconstitute the Cagoule. He also controlled the Légion, the shock troops of the movement. It was therefore the elements of the Right who formed the most militant part of this so-called popular movement.

There were also a few individuals who profited by the general misery to grow rich, Szokolnikow for instance, whose extremely profitable *cursus honorum* deserves mention.

Szokolnikow was a displaced Russian, who had been a refugee in France since 1933, and, before the war, had specialised in bankrupt stock. He had had trouble in the courts for issuing dud cheques.

The occupation brought him success: in 1943 he was official buyer for the S.S.

It was, apparently, a lucrative employment: a year later he owned a château in Saône-et-Loire and was the proprietor of several hotels on the Mediterranean coast.

This gentleman's mistress—a German refugee, Hélène Samson—dumbfounded Paris with her clothes. Her two fur coats, one of beaver, the other of mink, were worth three million francs. She bought fifty dresses a year from the greatest dress-makers, the cheapest of which cost 15,000 Frs. (approximately £300 today). She also possessed the finest jewels in Paris, worth one hundred millions of francs, and three cars of which one was an American Ford.

For one man who profiteered out of misery and a few politicians in the pay of the enemy, there were millions of Frenchmen who reacted against the occupation.

At Marseilles, on the 27th March, 1941, there was a popular demonstration in the Place de la Bourse in front of the commemorative tablet erected after the assassination of Alexander of Yugoslavia, in favour of the young King, Peter II, who had just turned out the Regent Paul and declared war on Germany.

At the other end of France, in the departments of the Nord and the Pas-de-Calais, which were attached to the German administration of Belgium, a strike broke out, on the 27th May, at the Dourges mines near Béthune, which spread quickly: by the 31st May, all the Courrières mines had followed suit and so, by the 7th June, had the rest of the mining basin.

The strikers, who basically wanted higher pay and better food, resumed work without conditions on Monday, 9th June, but their action had not been without effect. For fear of labour unrest, the occupying power and the Government satisfied, at least in part, the miners' demands.

It was at about the same period that, almost everywhere in

both the zones, walls began to bear the V sign. The V sign was invented in London, on the 14th January, 1941, by the B.B.C., as the symbol of future victory, on the suggestion of a Belgian speaker.

The French immediately adopted it and showed great ingenuity in their use of the symbol. They took cardboard V's to the cinema and hooked them on German backs. They cut V's from their métro tickets and dropped them at the exit. They chalked up V's on official buildings.

A much more important factor was that the Resistance Movements were beginning to be organised.

Two of the principal organisations, Liberté, founded by Henri Frenay, and the Mouvement de Libération Nationale, founded by François de Menthon, amalgamated to form the Combat Movement, which was to play an important part in clandestine activities and in the distribution of the clandestine press.

In October, 1941, appeared the first number of *Combat*, soon to be followed by *Franc-Tireur*, the organ of a movement which was recruited particularly from the Left and was soon to found groups for direct action.

In January, 1942, Franc-Tireur created the first *maquis* in France near Grenoble, where some fifty young technical workers, who refused to go to Germany, took refuge in a farm. In March, 1942, a second *maquis* was organised in the Ain, near Génissiat. While, in the Vercors, the first concentration of military resistance began to take shape.

It was also at this period that contacts, both exterior and interior, began to mark the growing importance of the Resistance.

In July, 1941, Henri Frenay, of Combat, made contact with both British and Americans in the free zone. In January, 1942, liaison was established with London, which began to help the Resistance financially.

A great turning point in the Resistance movement took place when Germany attacked Russia. Until then, the least that can be said of the French Communist attitude was that it was equivocal.

In a manifesto of May, 1941, the Communist party recommended, over and above their traditional friendship for the U.S.S.R., "the establishment of fraternal relations between the French and the German people in memory of the action taken by the Communists and by the French people against the Treaty of Versailles, against the occupation of the Ruhr basin and against the oppression of the people by another people."

A month later, following upon the invasion of Russia by the Wehrmacht, the "fraternal relations" were replaced by hostile acts. The Communist organisation of the F.T.P. (Francs-Tireurs et Partisans) joined in the secret war.

In the Autumn of 1941 it created its special organisation (O.S.), whose duty was to carry out acts of violence against the enemy: it was then that the assassinations began, to be followed by acts of sabotage.

Little by little, the country began to mobilise new forces for the struggle. The breach began to widen between the legislative processes, desired by the Marshal, the spectacular manifestations, the optimistic speeches—and true public opinion.

Vichy began to look like a Government divorced from the country, as if it no longer had the unanimity nor the impetus of its first months.

CHAPTER 3

# THE DECLINE OF THE NATIONAL REVOLUTION

THE National Revolution, during the first months following upon the Admiral's coming to power, still carried on, asserting itself by further *Words to the French People* from the Marshal.

On the 1st March, 1941, at Saint-Étienne, on the 1st May, 1941, at Commentry, and on the 4th June, 1941, in a speech at the Comité d'Organisation Professionelle, the Marshal dealt with the labour question.

On the 20th April, 1941, at Pau, in a speech intended for the rural population, he described the functioning of the Agricultural Corporation and its relations with the public authorities.

On the 8th July, he made a speech to the Conseil National on the Constitution.

All in all, these speeches conformed with the broad principles of the National Revolution. It still existed in words; and was trying at this moment to become manifest in institutions.

Among the latter, the Labour Charter was one of the basic documents of the National Revolution. It had for object the organising of labour relations between employers and employed so as to avoid a class war. It was the result of a compromise between two important social tendencies which were represented within the Government: Trades Unionism on the one hand, Corporatism on the other.

The point of difference between the Trades Unionists and the Corporatists was whether the workers' and employers' organisations, which represented class interests, should be maintained as autonomist formations, or whether workers and employers, abandoning their own organisations, should meet in corporative organisations which would represent, without distinction of class, such and such a branch of production.

The struggle continued for several months and gave rise to several grotesque episodes. Since the definitive text, before its promulgation in the *Journal Officiel* in Paris, had to be accepted by the German authorities, the Trades Unions Minister, Belin, suspected that the members of the Marshal's office, who had Corporatist sympathies, had submitted to the occupying authorities a text that did not correspond to the directives he himself had drawn up. Having accomplices among the typographers of the Imprimerie Nationale, he unofficially secured a copy of the proofs of the final text and discovered that in fact the part to be played by the Trades Unions had been considerably reduced; exhibit in hand, he made such a fuss at Vichy that he succeeded in obtaining a compromise. This consisted of "a free trade union within an organised profession".

The Trades Unions were retained, but with the innovation that there could only be one union to include every level and every category.

The Corporatist principle was safeguarded because, in the last resort, the decisions were taken by mixed professional organisations.

In order to abolish the class war, the right to strike was refused the workers, while the right of lock-out was withdrawn from the employers.

Finally, there was one incontestible advantage given the workers: for the first time the notion of a minimum living wage appeared in a law.

The Labour Charter was a hybrid in that it had not been able to choose between Trades Unionism and Corporatism and also because it made a compromise between professional independence and State control.

The State fixed the minimum living wage, thus reserving to itself the most consequential decision for the social life of the country.

Moreover, it provisionally reserved to itself the right of "nominating the first members of the Councils of Administration of the Professional Organisations".

This institution, which was but a rough and ready compromise between two opposite tendencies, was characteristic of the ambiguity of the National Revolution under Darlan.

The Conseil National came to birth in a quite different atmosphere.

On the 22nd March, the Marshal signed the decree applying the law of the 24th January, 1941. In accordance with his taste for small assemblies, Pétain had determined that the 192 councillors should meet but rarely in plenary session, but that the work should be done by specialised committees composed of a maximum of 25 members.

One after the other, a commission of administrative reorganisation, a commission to study municipal law and a commission to study the Constitution either adjourned without coming to any conclusion or decided on courses which were too theoretical ever to be applied.

Then a new commission was created, a Commission of General Information, so called, which ended by having as members more than a third of the Councillors (76 in March–April 1942) and which met three times. The atmosphere soon became more lively than that of the other commissions; the Ministers acquired the habit of attending in order to defend their policies as if before an elected assembly. But though more lively, its meetings were equally ineffective.

In April, 1942, the Conseil National ceased meeting without having ever, during the eleven months it functioned, succeeded in re-establishing contact between the country and Vichy.

Thus, under Darlan's Government, the National Revolution showed signs of decline.

The only novelty of this period appeared unexpectedly in dictatorial measures, which suddenly belied the inspiration of its beginning.

On the 12th August, 1941, there was a special performance of *Boris Godounov* in the Grand Casino at Vichy. During the last interval, a message from the Marshal was broadcast to an audience which included all the Vichy notables; they were startled by its tone of authoritarianism. It marked a sharp turning point in Vichy's policy.

"Frenchmen,

"I have grave things to say to you. I have felt during the last three weeks that an ill-wind was blowing from several regions of France. Anxiety is gaining on people's minds, doubt weighing on their souls. The authority of my Government is challenged, orders are often ill-carried out.

". . . It will take a long time to overcome the resistance of all the adversaries of the New Order, but we must set to at once to break up their organisations and destroy their leaders. If France does not realise that she is condemned by the force of circumstances to change her regime, she will see before her the abyss into which Spain almost disappeared in 1936 and from which she was only saved by faith, youth and sacrifice."

This undisguised tribute to Fascism preceded a number of dictatorial measures that Pétain proceeded to enumerate:

1. The suspension of all activity by political parties and groups of political origin;

2. The suspension of parliamentary indemnity from the 30th September;

3. Disciplinary sanctions against civil servants who were guilty of making false declarations concerning their membership of secret societies: "the names of these civil servants and the members of the higher ranks of Freemasonry were published in the last number of the *Journal Officiel*";

4. The Légion des Combattants was subordinated to the Government on all levels;

5. The powers of the police were doubled;

6 and 7. The creation of Commissaires au Pouvoir with the duty of breaking all opposition to the National Revolution and giving increased powers to the Regional Prefects;

8. The Labour Charter was to be promulgated immediately;

9. A re-modelling of the organisation of the economy in which small businesses and artisans would be better represented;

10. Reorganisation of the National Food Offices.

And, finally, two authoritarian clauses whose complete text must be quoted:

"11. I have decided to use the powers conferred on me by Constitutional Act No. 7 to bring to trial those responsible for our disaster. A Council of Political Justice will be set up to this effect: its report will be submitted to me before the 15th October.

"12. In the application of this Constitutional Act, all the Ministers and high officials must make an oath to me of loyalty and that they will exercise their functions for the good of the State in accordance with the laws of honour and probity."

In the hall, where members of the Government and diplomatists were gathered, this announcement provoked general stupefaction: the Garde des Sceaux, Joseph Barthélemy, was astonished to learn of the existence of a Council of Political

Justice of which no one had informed him. The United States Ambassador, Admiral Leahy, felt that Hitler might have written the phrases the Marshal had used: "This speech," he wrote, "had all the tone of a funeral service for the Third Republic."

Two measures, in particular, impressed public opinion.

"In the first place, the obligation of taking an oath, which Constitutional Act No. 7, of the 27th January, 1941, had limited to Secretaries of State, high functionaries and important Civil Servants, was now to be extended, on the 14th April, 1941, by Constitutional Acts Nos. 8 and 9, to the Army and the Magistracy:

"No one may serve in the army, if he has not sworn an oath of loyalty to the Head of the State. . . .

"No one may exercise the functions of Magistrate if he has not taken an oath to the Head of the State. . . ."

Five months later, on the 4th October, 1941, a new Constitutional Act (No. 10), extended this formula to "civil servants of all grades, and to the administrative personnel of the Public Services."

But the gravest aspect of these laws was that Vichy, from now on, wished to subject to its will the great professional bodies in the nation, in particular the magistracy and the courts, whose independence only ceases on the threshold of dictatorship.

Government intervention in the field of justice was to become manifest in two prosecutions which were peculiarly significant: in the free zone, the trial of the statesmen of the Third Republic; and, in Paris, that of the Communists, who became hostages after the first assassinations of occupying troops.

The statesmen of the Third Republic had no very good press immediately after the armistice. During the first months of the regime there was an almost unanimous feeling against them, from Alibert, for whom in July, 1940, their trial "would be the touchstone of the new regime," to the Communists, imprisoned by Daladier, who, in letters to the Marshal from Billoux and seven other Communist Deputies, demanded to be summoned as witnesses at the Supreme Court at Riom.

The accused were known, and their selection for prosecution easy, but it was less easy to select the charge on which they were to be tried. They were proclaimed responsible; but responsible for what?

The Germans had no doubts; they must be charged with having declared or provoked war: in this way, the conquerors hoped to get a French Tribunal to produce proof that the responsibility for the war could be imputed to France.

The French had no doubts either. But it was not for having provoked the war but for having lost it that the principal accused would have to answer. It was the direct responsibility of those who had been in the Government or in other important posts between September, 1939, and June, 1940, such as Daladier, Reynaud and Gamelin. It was a more remote responsibility for the members of previous governments, who were accused of having weakened or failed to prepare France: in particular, Léon Blum. Among those more remotely responsible should be included, so certain evil-intentioned adversaries of the regime went so far as to suggest, the person of the Marshal of France, who had been Minister of National Defence and had presided over the Conseil Supérieur de la Guerre during the last years of the Third Republic.

It was clearly difficult to adopt the German thesis, but it was not much easier to accept the French one. In the ensuing perplexity, a somewhat ambiguous formula was evolved, which could be applied either in a limited form or with the utmost rigour. The following were to be indicted: "The Ministers, under-Secretaries of State and their immediate colleagues, who had betrayed the duties of their position in acts which had contributed to a state of peace becoming a state of war, and in acts which had later aggravated the consequences of the situation thus created." A confused definition which, in fact, left a great deal of latitude to judges, counsel, and even on occasion to the accused, to turn the arguments in whatever direction might suit them.

The trial of the statesmen of the Third Republic, owing to the fact that the Government had been unable to choose between two opposite conceptions, was to open in ambiguity, continue in ambiguity and end in ambiguity.

It was no longer justice untrammelled, but it was not yet an entirely totalitarian trial.

The defence was embarrassed by certain inadmissible handicaps: on his first visit to President Caous, Bâtonnier Ribet, Daladier's counsel, stated that the defence counsel were being refused the right to assist their clients during their examinations. They were given no copy of the depositions of witnesses and had to content themselves with having them read out to them. They were not allowed to summon witnesses either during the enquiry or during the hearing.

There was another anomaly: the Supreme Court of Justice, created by the Government to deal with a new crime, "betraying the duties of their position", ought not to have tried indictable acts under this head unless they had been committed after the Law had been promulgated. The retroactive effect was, however, admitted as one of the bases of the trial.

But the most scandalous thing to lawyers was the arbitrary verdict pronounced against the accused *before* the opening of the trial by the Marshal himself. It was a condemnation uttered before the pleadings. In a message of the 15th October, 1941, Pétain, leaning on the opinion of a Council of Political Justice, whose members he had himself appointed, condemned the accused of Riom on suspicion. After that, they were to be tried.

"Frenchmen,

"The Council of Political Justice has submitted to me the conclusions on the precise date I fixed in my speech of the 12th April. Its conclusions are clear, complete and well-founded.

"Composed of ex-soldiers and of the best servants of the State, the Council of Justice has unanimously concluded that detention in a fortress—the maximum penalty under Constitutional Act No. 7—should be imposed on MM. Edouard Daladier and Léon Blum, as also on General Gamelin.

"I therefore order the detention of these three persons in the Fort du Pourtalet. . . .

"But the Council of Political Justice has asked me to preserve the judicial power from encroachment by the political power. A respect for the separation of these powers is already part of our customary law. It is therefore most willingly that I have replied to this appeal which corresponds with my own innate feelings.

"As a result, the Court of Riom retains its jurisdiction. . . . The trials are about to begin. . . ."

In the preliminary declaration addressed to the accused, President Caous disavowed the verdicts brought against them by Pétain before the opening of the trial:

"Messieurs, the decisions which have been taken concerning some among you and the motives for these decisions which have been published are, for this Court, as if they had never existed."

An assertion of independence to which the proceedings were to conform: faced with the ambiguity of the charge, the trial took on the orientation that French public opinion desired rather than that desired by the Germans: it was, indeed, for their part in the military preparation for the war, and not for their part in its outbreak, that the accused had to answer. They had the advantage in defending themselves of complete liberty of expression, even to the extent of criticising the Marshal, the Head of the State.

On the 15th March, 1942, in a public speech, Hitler did not conceal his displeasure at the way in which the trials were being conducted: "What we expected from the Court of Riom was a precise declaration on the responsibility for the fact of the war itself." It was a rebuke following on two Nazi demands made to the Marshal. On the 21st March, Ambassador Abetz telegraphed a demand that the trial should be suspended. At the same time, a legal adviser to the Führer, Grimm, asked for an audience with Pétain to confirm this demand. The Führer, he said, having decided solemnly to try in Berlin the Polish Jew, Grinzpahn, guilty of having assassinated the Counsellor to the German Embassy, von Rath, in Paris in 1938, wished on this occasion to demonstrate the responsibility of international Jewry for the declaration of war in 1939, and feared that the Riom trials would constitute a diversion.

Thus, on Nazi demand, the hearings of the Supreme Court came to an end on the 15th April, 1942. Nevertheless, the interrupted trial had shown that the political pressure brought to bear on the courts in the free zone had not entirely deprived judges of their traditional independence.

This independence, however, was impossible to maintain in the occupied zone.

The months of July, August and September, 1941, formed one of the first dramatic periods of the occupation in Paris. Following on the entry of Germany into war with the U.S.S.R., the Communist Party had gone over to the Resistance: it organised the first acts of sabotage and the first assassinations.

On the 21st August, for the first time, a German serviceman, Midshipman Mozer of the Kriegsmarine, was killed in Paris on the platform of the métro at Barbès-Rochechouart, without the assassin being arrested.

The Germans reacted with extreme violence. Hitler, informed at the General Headquarters of the Wehrmacht, demanded pitiless reprisals. The day after the assassination, M. Ingrand, head of the Administrative Department of the Ministry of the Interior at Paris, was summoned to an interview by a German Major, the Liaison Officer of the Wehrmacht to the Délégation Générale.

"He told me," Ingrand was later to record, "that the German High Command had reacted extremely violently to the announcement of the assassination, that General Headquarters had been informed and that Hitler himself had considered the matter, and that the German authorities had decided to take severe measures of reprisal. A hundred hostages would be selected at once, and a first batch of fifty executed immediately.

"And he made known the appalling decision that their bodies were to be exposed in the Place de la Concorde in order to impress the population."

The Germans were prepared to reprieve the first fifty hostages, provided French justice would be submissive to their demands; they made three conditions:

1. The immediate promulgation by the French Government of a law, which was already under consideration, against Communist plots, which law was to have retroactive effect;

2. The setting up of an Extraordinary French Tribunal;

3. The condemning to death, by this Tribunal, by virtue of the Law's retroactive effect, of six Communists, who had been imprisoned before the assassination and who, in consequence, could not have taken part in it. The execution was to take place no later than the 28th August, the day of the funeral of the murdered German.

One may imagine the tragic discussions that these demands gave rise to between the French judges and civil servants in Paris and the Ministers in Vichy. They were the more appalling for the fact that the conversations had to take place over telephone lines that were known to be tapped by the Germans.

On the 23rd August, Vichy began to give way and agreed to study the Nazi demands. But it had also to obtain the co-operation of the Paris judges. Ingrand summoned to his office, in the Rue de Grenelle, the deputy of the First President of the

Court of Appeal of Paris, who was then on holiday, the deputy of the Procureur Général of the Court, who was also away from Paris, the Prefect of Police, Admiral Bard, and the Procureur of the Republic, M. Gabolde. A high ranking officer, unaccustomed to matters of this kind, an important judge and two deputies had, in this month of August, when judicial life is normally at a minimum, to decide one of the most appalling cases that the bench had ever known.

As soon as the meeting opened, Ingrand announced that he had received orders from Vichy to draw up the text of a Law, which had been under consideration for twelve days, to repress anarchist and communist crimes and to draft it in such a way that it was given a retroactive effect and would allow of the execution of men who had been in prison before the assassination which was now to be punished. He pointed out the extreme urgency: it was necessary, within five days, to draw up the Law, have it promulgated by the Government, try and shoot the six Communists, with whom the Nazis would be content as an alternative to the fifty hostages.

The blackmail, indeed, presented an appalling equation: 6 men executed "legally" by a French Tribunal equalled 100 men shot without trial by the occupying power.

The Committee, which met on the 23rd August in the Rue de Grenelle, had on their agenda the accomplishment of the first act, that is to say the preparation of a draft which would give the law retroactive effect. The two deputies refused. But Gabolde, full of his own authority as being the only judge who was fulfilling his high functions in person, drafted the following lines, like a juridical Tartuffe: "Prosecution under the law is barred after ten years from the perpetration of the crime, even if the latter was anterior to the promulgation of the law." This, under pretext of allowing of the abandonment of a prosecution after ten years, was to stipulate that prosecutions could nevertheless be brought for crimes committed before the promulgation of the law.

On the following day, 24th August, 1941, the *Journal Officiel* of Vichy published the Law which had been drawn up the day before: it was dated 14th August, 1941, so that it might appear to be previous to the assassination which it was a question of avenging. This was another Tartuffe-like piece of trickery which was done on German demand.

For the second act, that is to say the actual membership of the Tribunal, things did not go so easily. Dayras, Secretary-General to the Ministry of Justice, informed by his delegate in Paris, Rousseau, that no Judge would agree to do the Nazis' dirty work, came urgently to the capital. The situation seemed to him so grave that he telephoned to Vichy, asking that the Garde des Sceaux should join him as soon as possible. Barthélemy arrived on the 25th August, to live through hours that were perhaps the most tragic that a French Garde des Sceaux had ever lived.

Barthélemy had decided to reject the German demand: he told Dayras so. But two conversations with Brinon were to make him change his mind. During the course of the first, Brinon said:

"It is essential to act at once, for if we do not act at once, we are taking the risk of having 100 hostages shot." Shaken by this blackmail, Barthélemy agreed to a second interview, which Pucheu, the Minister of the Interior, who was coming specially to Paris, would also attend.

After this meeting of the three, Barthélemy, death in his heart, appointed Cournet, the judge, to preside over the special session of the Tribunal. Summoned by the Minister, Cournet refused.

Dayras, who was present, rose from his chair, went over to another judge, the First President Villette, and exchanged a few words with him in a low voice. Villette then said: "But, Monsieur le Garde des Sceaux, one might perhaps ask for other opinions." "Very well."

And thus it was that a somewhat eccentric judge, M. Benon, was introduced into the office of the Garde des Sceaux. During the summer months, he was accustomed to haunt the lobbies of the Palace of Justice in search of a deputising job. No sooner had he come into the room, even before Barthélemy had explained to him what was required of him, than he said: "It's agreed, M. le Garde des Sceaux, you can count on my loyalty, and I accept." The President of the new Tribunal immediately summoned four judges to act as assistants. In order to avoid the risk of their refusing, he waited until the very last moment to tell them what it was all about. At the very second they were going into Court, he said, his hand on the door-handle: "We have got to pronounce six sentences of death." Then he passed into the Court, followed by the four judges who were thus *in extremis* before the accomplished fact.

During the course of this simulacrum of a trial, three of the accused were at once condemned to death as had been intended: the two first were ordinary criminals, whose misdeeds in neither case justified the penalty of death. Bastard had been condemned by an inferior court to two years' imprisonment and had, as well, eight previous convictions, of which one was for living on the immoral earnings of a woman, one for theft and six for disobeying the court's order as to residence. The second, Kebrouki, had been condemned to prison for five years for similar crimes.

The third, a man called Préchet, who had not yet come up for trial, nevertheless suffered the same fate as the other two.

When it came to the turn of the fourth, the judges came to themselves. The accused was a Communist journalist, named Sampaix, against whom there were no charges other than his political opinions. The judges condemned him to hard labour in perpetuity and Sampaix thanked the court for this relative clemency.

After Sampaix's appearance in court, the judges deliberated and came to the unanimous conclusion that they would refuse to pronounce further sentences of death. The two remaining cases, Woog and Guyot, were therefore withdrawn.

Before the sentences had even been pronounced, it was known what they were to be, and the public executioner had been summoned and warned that there would be work for him on the following day.

The counsel to the three condemned men put in a plea for mercy. In order that no time should be lost in useless formalities, the plea was transmitted by telephone to Pucheu, who refused it from Vichy.

The executions took place on the date arranged. As for the three survivors, the Germans having protested on the 3rd September, 1941, against the respite accorded them, the *Journal Officiel* published a new law setting up a Tribunal of State "to try plots, acts or activities of a nature to disturb public order, internal peace, public tranquillity, international relations, or of a general nature prejudicial to the French people." The survivors of the first trial appeared before this new Tribunal on the 20th September and were condemned to death.

There was a similar increase in the dictatorial tendencies of anti-Jewish legislation.

A new Jewish statute, signed on the 2nd June, 1941, was published in the *Journal Officiel* of the 14th June. Basing itself on the Nazi measures taken in the occupied zone, it did not take into account the promises made at the time of the first statute in October, 1940.

It had then been stipulated that the Jews would not be persecuted either with regard to their life or their property. But the measures of June 1941 allowed of "aryanising" businesses which belonged to Jews by taking them from their owners and appointing, in their place, provisional managers. In most cases, the Commissariat Général aux Questions Juives refused, on more or less false pretexts, or even without pretext at all, to give any compensation to the victims.

The Law of the 22nd July, 1941, in so far as it concerned "aryanisation", merely brought French legislation into line with the German ordinance of the 20th May, 1940, promulgated in the occupied zone. Contrary to the promise of Xavier Vallat, the French law made no exception in favour of ex-Servicemen.

The second statute instituted a "*numerus clausus*" in the liberal professions which were not *a priori* closed to Jews. For lawyers, civil servants and doctors, it was fixed at 2 per cent. For students, at 3 per cent.

A Law of the 29th November, 1941, organised Jews into a national minority by the creation of the U.G.I.F. (General Union of French Israelites). A census of Jews was ordered.

Finally, a *communiqué* from Vichy, dated 9th December, 1941, permitted the collecting into labour companies or concentration camps of foreign Jews who had entered France since the 1st January, 1936.

Xavier Vallat opposed the introduction into the free zone of the yellow star and the special curfew which were in effect in the northern zone. He even, from time to time, unofficially warned Parisian Jews of the dates on which he knew the Nazis intended rounding them up. On the 20th February, 1942, the Germans, annoyed by his lack of docility, refused him an *ausweis* to enter the occupied zone: he had to resign.

The Freemasons, another category of the excommunicated, were also subjected to new authoritarian decrees, though they were much less harsh than those applied to the Jews. The only innovations concerning them were formulated in a law of the 14th August which laid it down that the names of ex-office holders of secret societies should be published in the *Journal Officiel*. Article 2 extended to the ex-office holders similar prohibitions concerning the holding of public office or authority as was laid down in the second statute for the Jews.

Another domain in which totalitarian tendencies showed themselves was the press.

Paul Marion, as soon as he reached power, was in control of publicity: he issued instructions, notes on political orientations and schemes for articles, drawn up by his Ministry, to the newspapers. His instructions can be divided into two categories:

1. Permanent instructions: nothing must appear in the press which would imperil the policy of Franco-German collaboration as pursued by the Marshal's Government.

2. Daily instructions: some were negative and forbade the mention of a certain event. Others were positive, ordering the publication of an article, even detailing its position in the paper and its typography.

The Légion Française des Combattants, under Darlan's Ministry, was also beginning to suffer from the totalitarian contagion.

Pucheu, in spite of the opposition of François Valentin, Chairman of the Légion, decided to recruit within the organisation a more active minority, which was to be called the "Service d'Ordre Légionnaire".

The S.O.L. played a somewhat similar part in France to the role of the Nazi S.S. Shock troops, they were put in charge of one of the Légion's most authoritarian and dynamic leaders, Joseph Darnand.

The oath of the S.O.L. was as follows:

"I swear to fight against democracy, against Gaullist dissidents and against the Jewish leprosy."

Politics are one thing, administration another: in politics, Darlan's Government had suffered, willy-nilly, an encroachment of dictatorial methods. But at the same time, it supported its administration in resisting the Germans.

There was open non-co-operation when Caziot, the Minister of Agriculture, replied to the Germans, who were demanding the power to requisition such horses as remained in the southern zone, with a refusal. The Germans then decided to get round the difficulty by calling in unlicensed dealers to buy the animals for them. Two of these horse-copers, having been reported to the Minister, were arrested at Chartres railway station, having acquired twenty horses in the department of the Indre. Caziot had them fined 750,000 Frs. and impounded the horses.

In industry, resistance was manifest sometimes by the Government refusing to yield in similar ways, sometimes by the intervention of the Comités d'Organisation, which had indeed been specially created to protect businesses.

Charbin, Secretary of State to the Ministry of Food, played a considerable part in this battle. He took two kinds of measures: the first was to protect French agriculture against the Nazi requisitions by prohibiting the controllers of departments making deliveries without a Government order, and also by preventing the creation of stocks in the towns, which would have formed tempting prizes for the occupying power. At the same time, he had the ingenious idea of organising a method of supply which would escape German control: on the 23rd October, 1941, he instituted the "Family Parcels", which created a parallel market against which the Germans could do nothing but make continual protests: similarly, he delivered to the Germans barely half the quantities demanded.

Of all the various Ministries, it was that of Finance which, under the direction of Bouthillier, did most to curb German demands.

A special service, known as "the service of foreign interests in France", had, as its principal object, the opposing of German participation in French businesses.

Using the enormous sums of money they received in payment of the daily indemnities for the occupation, the Nazis had in fact a legal means, which was strictly in accordance with capitalist usage, of taking over French companies: it consisted in buying 51 per cent. of the shares. This they tried to do with some of the best industrial firms: the Compagnie des Batignolles, which built locomotives, Freins Westinghouse, Rhône-Poulenc, the Ateliers et Chantiers de la Loire, the Compagnie Générale de Construction Métallique, the Comptoir de l'Industrie du Sel, the Établissements Hutchinson, and certain subsidiaries of Kuhlmann, of the Compagnie Saint-Gobain and of the Automobiles Peugeot. All these were in turn the objects of their covetousness.

The ability and tenacity of French officials succeeded in limiting the Nazis to gaining financial control over three companies only.

The first was a new company, Francolor, formed with a majority of German capital (51 per cent.) to control French dye factories: but even then the French negotiators succeeded in obtaining that the President-Director-General should be a Frenchman, and that the French and German Directors should be equal in number.

A similar company was created for the textile industry: France-Rayonne was allowed to keep all the French factories, which employed 700,000 workmen, in production and to clothe the French people. In this association, the French industry benefited from German patents for the production of certain kinds of fibres.

Finally, a company, called Carburants Français, was founded in 1941 with a minority of German capital which was fixed at first at a third and then at a seventh.

## CHAPTER 4

# DARLAN, MINISTER FOR FOREIGN AFFAIRS

### 1. Military collaboration with the Reich? (9th February, 1941—June-July, 1941)

DURING the fourteen months of Darlan's Ministry, the Government found itself face to face with a dilemma: on the one hand, co-belligerency with Germany and, on the other, the "Polandisation" of France: that is to say, loss of independence and the population delivered up defenceless to the invader. The Marshal thought that military collaboration with the "Boches" (he never said Germans) would be dishonourable. We have seen the energy with which he asserted to Chancellor Hitler, at Montoire, that France would never become the ally of the Reich.

In April, 1941, he once more declared publicly: "Honour demands that we should undertake nothing against our old allies." Moreover, from May, 1941, Pétain was becoming more and more sceptical of a Nazi victory.

Darlan's attitude was less clear-cut than that of the Head of the State: he, too, most certainly, did not wish for military collaboration—on several occasions he reiterated that, he had promised Lord Alexander on the 18th June, 1940, not to be a party to any act of hostility against Great Britain—but Darlan, at least at the start, still believed in a German victory and wished France to be associated as quickly as possible with the New Europe that the Führer was creating. He also shared with several of his colleagues the fantastic belief that France would assume the first place in a Europe organised by the Führer.

Moreover, since Mers-el-Kebir, Darlan did not like the English and he sometimes went so far as to hope for a German victory: "Great Britain," he said to the American Chargé d'Affaires, Matthews, on the 14th December, 1940, "would ask too much, probably Madagascar and Dakar, whereas Germany would content herself with Alsace-Lorraine, which is lost in any case."

At the beginning of his Ministry, Darlan found himself in a similar position to that occupied by Laval after the vote in the National Assembly: all diplomatic relations were broken off with the Reich, while *diktats* and Nazi pressure increased.

In the field of economic pressure, the French Government received from Wiesbaden an "order" (a charming euphemism) for war materials, aircraft, aircraft engines, shells, explosives, wireless-sets and trucks. . . . In the occupied zone, Hemmen demanded the greater part of the French production of aluminium and copper stocks and, from overseas, Morocco cobalt. The demarcation line was closed, the *Ostland* was created: in the Ardennes, the Meuse, the Meurthe-et-Moselle, in the Aisne and the Vosges, German farmers seized 170,000 hectares and turned out 20,000 agriculturists, while Germany introduced forced labour into Alsace and Lorraine.

Pétain and Darlan tried to negotiate, each on his own level, as Pétain and Laval had done after the armistice.

Darlan used Benoist-Méchin as intermediary to establish contact with Ribbentrop and Keitel. But Keitel said to the French emissary:

"If France does not give Germany the control she demands in North Africa, she will be treated like Yugoslavia."

And, a fortnight before, between the 6th and 8th April, the Luftwaffe had bombed Belgrade, even though the capital of Yugoslavia had been declared an open town; it had caused 12,000 casualties.

Pétain had recourse to the good offices of a certain German art historian, Erckmann, a confidant of Hitler's, in order to get a letter to the Führer in which he complained in violent terms of the German proceedings in France. This letter remained unanswered.

At the same time, Pétain made a speech over the radio in which he was categorical: "Honour," he said on the 11th April, "demands that we should not undertake anything against our old allies."

Similarly, on the 14th February, he had assured the Caudillo, during the course of an interview at Montpellier, that he would never let the Germans enter North Africa.

During these days, between the 18th–26th February, 1941, there were conversations between General Weygand and Murphy, American Consul-General in Algiers. They reached certain agreements which Weygand brought to Vichy at the beginning of March and which were ratified by the French Government. With British consent, American ships would supply North Africa with primary necessities and, in particular, with oil. Twelve American consular officials would be appointed to furnish their government with the necessary information concerning these deliveries. On the other hand, Weygand reaffirmed his decision to oppose by every means in his power any attack against North Africa from wherever it might come.

But neither Darlan nor Pétain, by their different methods, succeeded in re-establishing relations with the Nazis: throughout the month of April no reply reached Vichy.

Suddenly, at the end of April, everything changed. Unexpected political circumstances obliged the Germans once more to take France into consideration.

A rebellion, fomented by Axis agents, began in Iraq, which to the whole Mohammedan world took on the appearance of being a Holy War against England: particularly in Damascus, where the windows of the British Consulate were broken.

This operation in Iraq was part of a great German strategic plan. Having given up their intention of making a landing in England and having failed in their air offensive, they proposed launching a pincer movement aimed at Mosul and Suez. The northern branch would be directed at the Levant, across the Balkans, where the Wehrmacht occupied Yugoslavia; while the southern branch would be aimed at the same objective via Tripolitania and Egypt. By the end of April, the Nazi forces were in readiness to launch the ultimate offensive. Greece and Crete had been occupied; Rommel had crossed the Egyptian frontier. Sollum was taken. If Iraq also fell, the British position would become untenable.

On the 2nd May, war was declared between Great Britain and Iraq. In order to support her new allies at this decisive point, the Reich had to pass through Syria; French collaboration had become indispensable to her.

On the 3rd May, Darlan was summoned to Paris by Abetz. The Germans offered him of their own accord the resumption of relations which he had been vainly endeavouring to bring about ever since his accession to power. The Ambassador let it be understood that, though he must not expect such an opportunity as had been offered at Montoire, he might perhaps in the near future be able to obtain an audience with the Führer and some concessions. In order to bring this about France must offer a *quid pro quo*.

"It might, for instance," continued Abetz, "take the form of help to Iraq over the arms she needs in her struggle against England. France might eventually permit the landing in Syria of German aircraft in transit to Iraq."

And on the 6th May, an agreement was concluded between Darlan and General Vogl.

The French Government agreed to furnish the rebels with arms, including aircraft, which were being held in reserve in Syria, and also to assist the transport of new supplies across the mandated territory. France would contribute to the refuelling and maintenance of German aircraft in transit, the airfield of Aleppo, in north eastern Syria, being placed at their disposal.

French administrators, whose loyalty could not be completely guaranteed, would be recalled from Syria and North Africa.

The French High Command and the German High Command would make a mutual exchange of all information on the forces and plans of the British in the Middle East. Finally, French officers would instruct the Iraqis in the use of the French arms given them.

The agreement also took into account the eventuality of a campaign against the Gaullists.

In exchange for this beginning of military collaboration, Darlan was granted:

1. An amelioration of the conditions at the demarcation line to consist in the free circulation of securities and produce between the two zones, the granting of *ausweis* in case of serious illness or the decease of near relations, the replacement of inter-zonal postcards, which bore only a few printed phrases, by ordinary postcards;

2. The rearmament of six destroyers and seven torpedo-boats;

3. The reduction of the costs of occupation from 400 to 300 millions a day;

4. The freeing of certain prisoners of war: non-commissioned officers and private soldiers who had served in the 1914–1918 war, amounting to approximately 83,000 men.

Over and above these concessions, the first important ones France had obtained since July, 1940, Darlan was at last to be received by the Führer.

On the 9th May, the first German aircraft arrived at Aleppo. They were three Messerschmitts. At the same time, a Junkers 52 landed at Damascus with a team of technical experts whose duty it was to study the question of refuelling the aircraft in transit.

All these aircraft were modestly camouflaged in Iraqi colours.

In order to facilitate the German use of the airfields and to assure the transmission to Iraq of the armaments Darlan had promised, a Franco-German mission arrived in Aleppo on the 9th May. It, also, was partially camouflaged: together with Jacques Guérard, Secretary-General to the Presidency of the Council, it included a certain French civil servant, Renoir, who was in fact no more French and whose name was no more Renoir than the aircraft with Iraqi colours were Iraqi. He was an attaché of the Wilhelmstrasse, a specialist in French problems and Eastern affairs and a collaborator of Abetz; he spoke French perfectly, but his real name was Rahn and his nationality German. As the Pétain Government had on several occasions promised both the Americans and the British not to let Germans, other than members of the Armistice Commissions, enter the French Empire, Rahn had become Renoir by a convenient process of false identity, known only too well to the victims of the Nazis in all countries, but which the Nazis now employed themselves.

The mission was not inactive; a hundred German aircraft, twenty-two Iraqi aircraft and four train loads of munitions crossed Syria.

It seemed indeed that, in order to avoid "Polandisation", the Government had been won over to military collaboration and had accepted it.

Darlan, of course, denied it: according to him, it was possible for France to help Germany win the war without being in a state of co-belligerency with her, nor in a state of hostility against Great Britain.

In order to give some basis to his argument, Darlan pleaded Article 10 of the Convention of Armistice, which made, so he said, an obligation of this collaboration. It is only necessary to read the Article in question to be convinced that this interpretation is erroneous: "The French Government undertakes not to mount any hostile action against the German Reich with any part of the armed forces which remain to it, nor in any other manner."

There was, indeed, a considerable difference between abstaining from hostile acts and effectively helping the Germans; Darlan pretended not to see it.

On the 11th and 12th May, Darlan conferred with the Führer and Ribbentrop at Berchtesgaden.

The Führer's attitude had nothing in common with his behaviour at preceding interviews. He was more brutal and more authoritarian, as a result, perhaps, of his concern at a surprising piece of news: the day before, the 10th May, one of his oldest colleagues, Rudolf Hess, Chief of the Party, who had been designated, after Goering, as the Führer's second successor, had left in his own aircraft for Scotland where, on his own initiative, he proposed suggesting to the British that they should conclude a separate peace.

Besides, Hitler no longer thought, as he had done in October, 1940, that France was a possible ally in his future plans: in May, 1941, there was no question of association.

"I have nothing in view but the protection of German interests. Collaboration is not an end in itself."

From now on, the principle of "give or I take" was to be the basis of all negotiations.

"If I have no confidence in France, I shall keep permanently those regions which are forbidden zones today, the Channel ports, the Nord, the Pas-de-Calais, and, also, a tract of territory on the Belgian frontier, part of the Meuse and of the department of Meurthe-et-Moselle, not to speak, of course, of the three departments which make up Alsace-Lorraine (Moselle, Haut-Rhin, Bas-Rhin). Moreover, even though Italy should make exaggerated demands, I shall satisfy them.

"But, if I have confidence in France, I shall reduce these territorial sacrifices on the continent to the minimum. I am not fanatically greedy for territory ('kein Raumfanatiker') and I am convinced that in war the gains never equal the losses. And, as compensation for the loss of Alsace-Lorraine, France might receive Wallonia and French Switzerland. As to the French Empire, Germany has no claims on it. Doubtless some concessions will have to be made to Italy; but France will receive in compensation certain spoils from the British Empire."

Almost as brutally as Keitel had done to Benoist-Méchin, Hitler placed Darlan before the dilemma: military collaboration or annihilation.

"It is high time France prepared her peace. She must decide whether she wishes to collaborate or not."

And the Führer concluded with his "classic" monologue: he stated that Germany could not possibly do other than win the war.

On the 12th May, Hitler had a new argument to prove his invincibility:

"As for Russia, she can be only held in contempt. Since the reform of the army, thirty thousand officers have been executed, so that the Russian army now lacks trained personnel: the officers can neither read nor write.

"Russia will have to withdraw very soon from the Baltic provinces. She will realise the necessity. If she does not realise it, she will be defeated in three weeks!"

What was the Admiral to reply? He still believed in a German victory: Hitler had indicated that there was soon to be war between the Reich and Russia; Darlan thus hoped that Hitler, soon to be busy in the East, would no longer need France's effective aid in the West: therefore to accept Hitler's proposals today, was perhaps to make promises that need not be kept, and obtain, as a result of these promises, immediate advantages. He also hated the British. All these considerations caused him to reply categorically to the Führer that "France was completely willing to help Germany win the war." A statement which Pétain would never have made six months earlier at Montoire.

"France," Darlan went on, "has already manifested her desire to collaborate with the Reich economically and militarily by lending her effective support in Syria.

"France will continue to pursue this policy, but it would be opportune if certain concessions were made from the German side."

Finally, not neglecting his personal interests, and desirous of obtaining for himself a confirmation of the investiture Hitler had conferred on him at Ferrière-sur-Epte, Darlan once more explained his position:

"I make a formal promise to direct French policy towards an integration with the New European Order, to tolerate no longer a policy of vacillation between the rival groups of powers who are at war, and to assure the continuity of this line of policy."

On the 14th May, the day after Darlan's return to Vichy, there was held a Council of Ministers of exceptional importance: it provides an opportunity of determining the sense in which the Darlan Government understood collaboration.

Together with the Marshal and the Admiral, there were present only the four Secretaries of State who had the prerogative, Bouthillier, Huntziger, Caziot, Barthélemy.

Darlan reported the essentials of his conversation with Hitler. It was a plea in favour of collaboration:

"1. It's the last chance we shall have of a *rapprochement* with Germany.

"2. If we favour the policy of England, France will be crushed, dismembered and cease to be a nation. . . .

"3. If we endeavour to maintain a policy of vacillation between the two adversaries, Germany will create many difficulties for us in the exercise of our sovereignty and will foment unrest. In any case, the peace will be a disastrous one.

"4. If we collaborate with Germany, without going so far as to place ourselves at her side for the purpose of making deliberate war on England, that is to say work for her in our factories, if we give her certain facilities, we can save the French nation, reduce our territorial losses to a minimum, both Metropolitan and Colonial, and play an honourable part, if not an important one, in the Europe of the future.

"My choice is made, and I would not allow myself to be deterred from it by the unconditional offer of a ship-load of wheat or a ship-load of oil."

For Laval collaboration had been an end in itself: thanks to him France had obtained an unexpected opportunity. It was a whole which had to be accepted without argument or prevarication. When asking the Ministers to approve the policy he wished to pursue, he gave them no basis for judgment; he demanded from them a complete and blind confidence which only his faith in his own infallibility could justify.

Darlan's case was quite different. For the Admiral, collaboration was a lesser evil, an inevitable deal, the means of avoiding the worst, that is to say both a military alliance and annihilation: it had therefore nothing absolute or eternal about it; it was a provisional expedient which corresponded to the circumstances.

Having therefore, to all appearance, been won over to military collaboration in order to avoid annihilation, the Marshal and the Admiral gave their decision all possible publicity in order that France might eventually benefit from it.

There were three broadcast speeches, one by Pétain on the 15th May, and the others by Darlan on the 23rd and 31st, informing the public of the choice they had made in its name: "In a triumphant Anglo-Saxon world, France would only be a dominion of the second importance. . . . It is a question of choosing between life and death. The Marshal and the Government have chosen life."

Ten days after the Berchtesgaden interview, on the 21st May, negotiations opened in Paris at the German Embassy. On the French side they were conducted by Darlan and Huntziger, with the assistance of Benoist-Méchin and Brinon; on the German by General Warlimont who, in December, 1940, had studied with Laval and Huntziger the possibility of a Franco-German military collaboration for the re-conquest of Chad.

On the 27th May, three agreements were signed by Darlan and Warlimont. These documents, known as the "Protocoles de Paris", dealt essentially with military questions. They mark the nearest point reached by the Vichy Government to entering the war.

The first protocol concerned the use of the airfield at Aleppo, the ports and lines of communication in the Levant to be used by the Reich for her military aid to Iraq, and the cession to the rebels of Iraq of three quarters of the stocks of munitions at present in Syria.

The second conceded to the Germans the use of the port of Bizerta and the right of passage through Tunisia to help Rommel's army; the use of the railway lines between Bizerta and Gabes; while transport vehicles and French guns from the African stocks were to be sold to the Germans.

The third envisaged the eventual organisation of a submarine base at Dakar and certain measures to be taken to drive the Gaullists out of French Equatorial Africa.

In exchange for this gradually increasing military collaboration, France received a variety of facilities for rearming her Empire.

But these did not suffice Darlan as a recompense for the advantages he was conceding the Germans. On the 26th May, after some violent interviews with General Warlimont, he obtained that the application of the three military protocols should be subordinated to a political agreement of which the following is the conclusion: "The great dangers implicit in the granting by France of the facilities contained in the Agreement on French West Africa and French Equatorial Africa make it essential that their being put into practical execution should be subordinated to the following conditions:

"1. The German Government will, as a preliminary, agree to necessary reinforcements for the improvement of the West African state of defence.

"2. The German Government will furnish the French Government, by means of political and economic concessions, means of justifying to French public opinion the possibility of an armed conflict with England and the United States."

In order that this collaboration, agreed in Paris between Darlan and Abetz, should become effective, there was but one small step to take, one minor obstacle to surmount: the ratification of the agreements by the Marshal. A mere formality, it might be supposed, if Pétain's attitude during the second fortnight of May is taken into consideration.

In fact, he would have nothing to do with them.

On the 2nd June, Weygand arrived in Vichy, having been summoned by the Marshal, as also were Governor-General Boisson and Admiral Estéva; the official reason for their journey was to be informed of the protocols which concerned North Africa and French West Africa. Upon his arrival in Vichy, Weygand was received by the Marshal, but was not even allowed to develop his arguments against military collaboration. The Marshal was of his opinion: a stop must be put to it. On the 3rd June, a first Ministerial meeting took place at 11 o'clock to which Weygand was summoned. It was not, properly speaking, a Council of Ministers, since the Secretaries of State were present.

Nor was it a Cabinet meeting, since it was presided over by the Marshal.

Weygand, having just arrived from Africa, seemed to his colleagues tired and anxious: his face was drawn. Could it be that on the 3rd June, 1941, the General was suffering from one of the worst problems of conscience with which he had ever been faced? A loyal and disciplined soldier, all his inclinations were *a priori* not to oppose the Marshal nor even the Prime Minister and to put into execution the policies formulated by the Government. But this policy was one of military collaboration: and Weygand hated the Germans. From the very morrow of the armistice, he had begun to prepare an army for revenge.

He took no account of Nazi threats. All that counted for him, was to hold to the armistice and above all see that the Germans did so too. He was convinced that the only way of keeping North Africa intact was to gain time. If the Government opened up North Africa to the Germans, he feared that it would be his duty to lead Africa into dissidence, though such a decision seemed to him premature.

On the 3rd June, while the Admiral explained matters, Weygand maintained his reserve.

As soon as the meeting opened, Darlan recapitulated his declaration of the 15th May and expounded the dilemma to the Government: collaboration or annihilation. Then he announced that, following upon a recent meeting in Paris, a protocol had been signed between himself and General Warlimont. Without reading the document, he commented upon it and explained the reasons for it: the policy of vacillation, which consisted in playing off one side against the other, would culminate for France in the loss of her coast and the territories demanded by the Axis.

Weygand then spoke in an atmosphere which he himself described as "unbreathable".

As soon as Weygand went into action he recovered all his vitality. He said that before he knew of the Government's intentions, he had written a letter which he now asked permission to read.

"Not only is it essential to refuse military collaboration, but we must at all costs refuse to allow ourselves to be drawn on to the slippery slope of an imprecisely formulated military collaboration, which runs the inevitable risk of becoming a fact through acts of provocation which must be prevented. For my part, I see no other means of preventing it but by affirming once more in public that the Government holds to the principles which are the foundation of French African confidence and which I state in this letter: no base in Africa must be put at the disposal of the Germans or Italians; French Africa will defend herself against all comers with completely French forces; and France will not enter deliberately into war against her old ally."

The Marshal until then had sat silent, now he intervened. He put a stop to the discussion. During the course of the afternoon he would examine the protocols with General Huntziger and General Weygand.

After Weygand had left the meeting, the Marshal spoke at last. And the few words he said make him appear in an unusual light —as President of the Council playing the political game according to parliamentary rules.

"The Marshal observes that the policy of the Admiral and himself is the object of lively criticism; and he asks Ministers present to express their opinions in turn."

This was a new language for the Head of the State, who had accustomed his Ministers to less consideration.

Three Ministers thereupon took up precise positions.

Chevalier energetically opposed the acceptance of the Paris Protocols and pointed out how catastrophic the dismissal of Weygand would be; Huntziger declared simply: "I haven't the army to make war on England," and Bergeret said: "The Air Force is only a façade, I have no means of defending the free zone, Africa and Syria."

Though these three men took up definite positions, none of their colleagues would say yes or no to putting the protocols into execution.

Pétain and Darlan listened to the Ministers, but said no word.

A few hours later, the Marshal received Weygand in the presence of Generals Huntziger and Laure and Admiral Platon.

Weygand suggested to the Marshal a manoeuvre which would permit of his not applying the protocols even though they had been signed. Without knowing it, Weygand appeared to be anticipating Pétain's secret plans.

The German Government had promised to furnish the French Government "by means of political and economic concessions" arguments to justify the protocols to public opinion. Why not therefore ask the German Government, in exchange for the considerable military advantages they obtained under the protocols, for even more considerable political advantages which would also be guaranteed by officially ratified documents?

For instance, a solemn engagement to respect, in the eventual treaty of peace, the integrity of French territory, both Metropolitan and Colonial; the liberation of all prisoners of war; the discontinuance of the indemnity charged for the occupation costs; and the suppression of the demarcation line? Why not purely and simply ask the Nazis to renounce all the consequences of their victory in June, 1940, in exchange for a military collaboration which would make France their ally?

Weygand was doubtless going a bit too far, so far indeed that there was no chance of the Germans allowing themselves to be caught in that trap. But the proposed manoeuvre furnished Pétain the means of refusing military collaboration without having to take the initiative of interrupting the negotiations again or of having to disavow Darlan.

During the morning of the 4th, Weygand had reason to believe that his point of view had gained the day: "At 11 o'clock (in the morning)," he wrote, "I saw Admiral Darlan. He told me that he had already been working on the draft of a communication to the German Government in the sense I had suggested to the Marshal the day before."

From then on everything contributed to make Weygand's intervention successful: on the one hand, he found much support among the French; on the other, the Germans, by breaking their word, destroyed all the arguments for collaboration.

Among Weygand's allies, the most important were Governor-General Boisson and the Minister, Chevalier. The former, who arrived in Vichy on the 4th June, was told of the situation as soon as he got out of his aircraft and decided to support Weygand with the Marshal and Darlan. The second wrote a still unpublished letter to Pétain, which began with the peremptory statement: "Darlan's deluding you."

At the same time, Jacques Benoist-Méchin, who had remained in Paris after the signature of the protocols, reported that the Germans were not keeping their promises: he told Abetz "that the reduction of the occupation costs, promised on the 6th May, was still under discussion and, except for the older prisoners of war, the figure for whom had moreover been considerably reduced, nothing substantial had been done in France's favour."

Owing to Weygand's energetic action and the bad faith of the Germans, the situation had considerably developed between the 3rd and 6th June, on which date there was a new meeting of Ministers to discuss the protocols, and which Weygand and the Governors-General Boisson and Estéva attended.

Darlan explained what he intended demanding from the German Government before giving them bases.

His note to the German Government had already been drawn up; he read it to the Ministers:

To begin with it recapitulated the risks that the application of the protocols carried for France.

"It is therefore necessary that substantial, tangible and durable advantages should compensate in advance for the loss and damage which are not only probable, but certain.

". . . The political and economic concessions the French Government consider indispensable to the pursuance of the projected policy are as follows:

"(a) The total restoration of French sovereignty over the whole of Metropolitan territory, including the Nord, the Pas-de-Calais and the Italian zone, and, account being taken of the military necessities of the army in operations, the demarcation line to be no more than the limit of military occupation, all French citizens being free to move from one side of the line to the other;

"(b) A special statute for Alsace-Lorraine until the treaty of peace;

"(c) Total suppression of the occupation costs and the appropriations by the Wehrmacht from all branches of French production;

"(d) Suppression of all activity by the organisation 'Ostland' and the return to their lands of dispossessed proprietors and farmers;

"(e) The return to their homes of all non-Jewish Frenchmen;

"(f) The staggered liberation of all prisoners; prisoners necessary to the economy of the Reich being made free workers engaged under contract;

"(g) A public assurance to be given by the Axis Governments that they make no demands on North Africa, French West

Africa and Syria [only the territories mentioned in the Protocols were named];

"(h) The suppression or considerable reduction of the Commissions of Control, particularly in Africa;

"(i) The cessation of all anti-French propaganda in Africa;

"(j) The handing back of all armament factories of every kind and assistance from Germany by the supply of raw materials, materials of all kinds, munitions and all varieties of fuel;

"(k) Anti-aircraft rearmament to assure necessary security."

How is this hardening on Darlan's part, indeed this sudden reversal, to be explained?

On the 11th May, when he had met the Führer, there is no doubt that Darlan had been completely dominated by Hitler's authority and had been sufficiently impressed by him to contemplate military collaboration.

Until the 27th May, the date on which the protocols were signed, the Admiral had not dared refuse outright the North African bases to the Germans. But hardly had he agreed to them when, during the night 27th–28th May, in spite of Warlimont's fury, he demanded that to the military engagements should be added a political protocol guaranteeing France important concessions. This addition of political conditions to military conditions was therefore much earlier than the General's intervention: it was the result of Darlan being easily swayed and of his habitual oscillations.

Thus, on the evening of the 28th, Darlan was hesitating to apply the protocols which had been signed twenty-four hours earlier. What was to be done? There were two possible solutions: the Marshal could refuse to sign the protocols and disavow the Admiral, which would entail the resignation of the Government and the risk of its being replaced by a Laval or Déat government under the orders of the occupying power; or the Government could take advantage of the political protocol to make the military agreements dependent on conditions which were unacceptable to the Germans.

It was as if, by summoning Weygand to Vichy, Pétain and Darlan were agreed to acquire the intervention of the only man who they knew would force their hands and oppose their designs, the only man whose authority was sufficient to allow them to contest or minimise the extent of their agreements. Weygand's intervention had moreover the advantage of shielding Darlan from the Germans. Darlan could throw on to the General the responsibility for non-ratification and continue to call himself a "collaborator": Weygand would be his scapegoat.

Two days after Weygand's departure, the problem of co-belligerency with the Axis, which might have been considered resolved, was to take a dramatic turn. The war in Syria began: for the first time Frenchmen, who a year before had been fighting the same enemy, were to oppose each other in pitched battles in a fratricidal war.

As a result of the landing of German aircraft on the Syrian airfields on the 8th June, British forces under the command of General Sir Maitland Wilson and French Gaullist forces under the command of General Legentilhomme crossed the Syrian frontier.

On the same day, General Catroux of the Free French Forces issued a proclamation to the populations of the Levant: he declared that France's mandate over Syria and the Lebanon was abolished and proclaimed that the two peoples were "free and independent".

"If the Free French Forces cross your frontiers, it is not to destroy your liberty, but to assure it. It is to chase Hitler's forces out of Syria and enforce respect for your rights as well as those of France."

From the 8th June onwards French partisans of General de Gaulle were fighting against their compatriots who were loyal to Marshal Pétain. The Vichy troops consisted of thirty thousand French and about fifteen thousand natives. The invaders were approximately of the same number, but among them the French were in a minority: they consisted of one division which was to fight side by side with a strong Australian division and an Indian brigade, reinforced by elements of the Trans-Jordan Frontier Force and the Arab Legion.

For most of the officers and soldiers who were loyal to the Marshal, de Gaulle was a rebel: Pétain was the uncontested leader who would sooner or later set them to fight the Germans again. Catroux learned of this state of mind with astonishment:

"They were persuaded that they had done their duty in obeying Marshal Pétain to whom they had sworn loyalty. The Marshal could not have made a mistake, nor have led them astray. If he had allowed German aircraft into the Levant, which they however denied, it was with good reason, and because international interests, whose guardian he was, demanded it. Truth was with Pétain and error's name was de Gaulle."

Dentz shared this loyalty to the Marshal who had ordered him to defend Syria against attack from whatever source it might come.

The Syrian campaign was to last six weeks during which General Dentz was a prey to an appalling moral conflict: his loyalty towards the Government obliged him to defend Syria, his patriotism impelled him in the first place to avoid spilling French blood and secondly gave him the hope of taking up the war against the Germans again later on.

Dentz, an irreproachable soldier, a convinced patriot and fundamentally anti-German, was one of the officers who, by remaining loyal to Vichy, suffered most from the circumstances of the period.

His troops having been driven back and decimated by the British fire, the German Rahn and the Frenchman Guérard suggested to him that, in order to stop the massacre, he should accept the help of the Luftwaffe. If the German bombers were to bomb the British Fleet, the result of the campaign would be very different. There would be a French victory and Syria would remain under French mandate.

At first Dentz refused: Rahn's arguments had the contrary effect on him. What a German suggested was *a priori* suspect. Unhappily, there was also a French military leader who for quite different reasons suggested the intervention of the Stukas. Admiral Gouton, commanding the Naval Division of the Levant, realising that his ships would be sacrificed to the superiority of the British Fleet, refused to consider the political problems; he merely kept to the military needs within his purview. Desiring to save his ships and, as was natural, to fight on equal terms, he insisted that Dentz should accept the Luftwaffe's intervention. And Dentz, who could understand this point of view, accorded Gouton what he had refused Rahn.

On the 12th June, somewhat against the grain, he telegraphed Vichy withdrawing his refusal of German intervention. The telegram astounded the Government: in the same way that they had sheltered behind Weygand to prevent the Germans entering Africa, Pétain and Darlan wanted to be able to say to the

Armistice Commission at Wiesbaden that General Dentz insisted on defending Syria alone.

Disappointed and embarrassed, Vichy replied to Dentz by a telegram which showed but little enthusiasm for German intervention and gave the High Commissioner of the Levant an opportunity to withdraw his demand.

"Assistance from Stukas may have serious repercussions on general political situation. It must not be asked for unless it can be prompt, massive and continuous."

Delighted with the chance, Dentz seized the opportunity of sending another telegram, on the 12th June at 9.55 a.m., declaring that he renounced the help of Stukas. And for the next three days hostilities continued without the question being reopened.

But on the 15th June, the situation of the Vichy troops was once more dangerous: Rahn became more and more persuasive: Gouton more and more anxious to spare French casualties:

"I am at this moment," Dentz was compelled to telegraph, "in a most unstable situation, particularly at Damascus where this morning I found the troops very exhausted. . . . A threat from the desert is confirmed. . . .

"In these circumstances, immediate intervention by Stukas based on Syria and taking action both by land and against the Fleet would be decisive.

"Rahn thinks that the visitors would depart as soon as the affair was over."

Darlan felt that Dentz had been overborne; making a decision, which proves that at this period he no longer had any intention of taking military action on the side of the Axis, he sent, on the 17th June, General Bergeret to Beirut, with the mission of preventing the Stukas from intervening in Syria. By this date, therefore, the Admiral, in agreement with Pétain, no longer wanted military collaboration. Supported by General Jeannekeyn, Commanding the Air Force in the Levant, Bergeret had no difficulty in convincing Dentz that, however painful the consequences might be, it was better to fail against the British than call the Germans in to help. Bergeret and Dentz, in complete agreement, now set themselves to multiply technical obstacles to the arrival of the Stukas and to make their participation in the Syrian war impossible.

The refusal of German aid had as its necessary corollary that Dentz should endeavour to stop the war as soon as possible.

On the 20th June, on his own initiative, he ordered his Director of Political Affairs to make contact with the American Consul-General, who was in charge of British interests and to ask him for armistice conditions. On the 26th June, he sent his military personal assistant to Vichy in order to explain the impossibility of continuing the fight.

An armistice, concluded at Saint-Jean-d'Acre on the 14th July, put an end to hostilities: it was a purely military convention, which made no reference to the political problems of the Levant.

It was signed in the name of Great Britain by General Wilson, in the name of the Free French Forces by General Catroux, and in the name of the Vichy Forces by General de Verdillac. All three being supported by large delegations.

Between Wilson and Verdillac agreement was reached on the following points: General Dentz's troops would be awarded the honours of war, the Allies recognising thereby not only their fine conduct but the absurdity of the rumours which accused them of playing the German game. During this campaign, neither in Syria nor in the Lebanon, did the Allies find one single soldier or servant of the Axis against them. And the Germans, at that moment, no longer had bases or ports in the Levant.

The Vichy troops were repatriated with their personal arms, which, in spite of express orders from his Government, General Wilson allowed on his own responsibility. Other arms were collected by General Catroux's forces; in spite of Vichy's orders, and to the anger of the Italian Armistice Commission and Rahn, they had not been destroyed. Similarly, there was no destruction of the industrial or economic life of the country. Dentz, in spite of German pressure, had refused to destroy the pipeline and petrol depots in Tripoli.

Such Vichy soldiers who chose to continue the war with the Free French Forces were allowed to do so. In fact, about two thousand out of twenty thousand went over to de Gaulle.

Among the Vichy troops there were 1,038 killed, of which 76 were officers and 256 non-commissioned officers. The Air Force had 7 officers killed and 13 missing, 23 non-commissioned officers killed and 13 missing. The Gaullist losses were estimated at 800 men.

"The dead," wrote Catroux, "lie in the cemetery of Damascus to which I had them brought. They will not lie there alone. Their graves lie next door to those who were their adversaries.

They are all alike and carry the same epitaph in these words: 'Died for France'."

Thus, during the first four months of Darlan's Government, France, faced with the alternatives of military collaboration or "Polandisation", seemed to have chosen the first: on several occasions she drew near to entering the war. But having never made up her mind to it, having always, when *in extremis*, managed to avoid the worst, she now found herself, after four months, exposed to the opposite danger: was Keitel's threat to be realised? Was France to suffer the same destiny as Poland?

CHAPTER 5

# DARLAN, MINISTER FOR FOREIGN AFFAIRS

## 2. Rupture with the Reich
## (July, 1941–December, 1941)

WHILE the Syrian war was going on, two quite other events had an effect on French policy.

On the 21st June, the Wehrmacht invaded the U.S.S.R. At Vichy, the French Government of its own accord broke off diplomatic relations with Russia and expelled Bogomolov.

At the end of July, a more limited conflict greatly shook Vichy. As a result of conversations between Darlan and Abetz, the Admiral openly took up a position against General Weygand. In a still unpublished letter of the 27th July, in which he summoned the Head of the State to choose between the General and himself, Darlan wrote: "There is a smell of Gaullism about the General's wake."

Thus the bridges were cut between two men upon whom the Marshal relied equally to resist the Germans.

On the 1st August, 1941, it became certain that military collaboration between France and Germany had been avoided. Was it to be "Polandisation"?

On the one hand, diplomatic relations had once more been broken off. The German Embassy was closed to representatives of the French Government. Soundly scolded by Ribbentrop, Abetz left Paris: he was "going to take a holiday".

Coincident with Abetz's departure, the arrival in Paris of General Otto von Stülpnagel seemed to indicate that from now on Franco-German relations would be dealt with exclusively on a military level: in spite of the Russian campaign, forty German divisions were concentrated at that time in the occupied zone: was the invasion of the free zone imminent?

At the headquarters of the Armistice Commissions there was a similar hostility towards France.

At the same time, in Rome, Italy began to make demands upon Tunisia and Corsica.

The French Government could see no help anywhere.

In the Far East, France had to yield to a new Japanese ultimatum. The agreement of the 21st July, 1941, gave the Imperial Japanese Forces access to all parts of Indo-China and admitted the principle of "joint defence of Indo-China against all external aggression". This Franco-Japanese Alliance lost the Vichy Government most of the sympathy it still had in Washington.

The result of these American suspicions, was that the Murphy-Weygand agreements, so scrupulously respected by the French, were to all intents and purposes not observed by the Americans. By the 1st July, America had sent only two tankers bringing oil or oil products to North Africa.

In England, since the events in Syria, there was no longer any sympathy for Vichy. The London radio never missed an opportunity of stigmatising the treason of the French Government. It no longer spared the Head of the State.

The Paris press, for quite other reasons, was equally hard on the "Vichy traitors". Cleverly organised by the Propaganda Abteilung, a violent campaign was let loose in the Paris papers in August, 1941. It asserted that the Vichy Government was responsible for all the ills that afflicted France.

There were further threats, more direct and more deadly, which were soon to weigh upon the French people.

The beginning of the war between Germany and Russia intensified action by the Resistance because from now on the Communist Party took part in it.

At the beginning of July, acts of sabotage took place in the coal mines of the Nord and the Pas-de-Calais, and also on the railways. On the 21st August, as we have seen, occurred the first assassination of a German officer in Paris.

The Germans replied by threatening to shoot hostages and demanding the creation of special Courts which would condemn to death on Nazi orders.

In order to try and pacify the Germans, while remaining faithful in fact to the political line defined on the 6th June, Darlan used two complementary methods: on the one hand, the continued assertion of his willingness to collaborate: a purely verbal manifestation which he himself practised and enjoined his Ministers to practise; on the other hand, to give the Germans concessions of secondary importance. Among these latter, Darlan wished to include Weygand's dismissal, unaware, because of his personal animosity, of its political significance.

"Everything," Darlan said to the Marshal, "must be said and done in order that the Germans may never have an excuse to lay their hands on Africa, the Fleet and the African Army."

All in all, the French Government had never protested its pro-German sympathies to the extent it did in August, 1941, when diplomatic relations had been broken off with the Reich.

Darlan hoped thus to dissuade the Germans from seizing French African territory.

At the same time, in order to preserve the Empire, the Marshal, on the 12th August, read the most vehement and most authoritarian speech he had ever produced.

This speech, which, of all Pétain's official utterances, provoked most hostility in France and abroad, did not contribute in the least to diminishing the Nazi pressure. The only possible reference to the Nazis' bad faith lay in the Marshal's daring to criticise the Paris press with which, however, he associated "the misdeeds of the London radio and certain French papers."

The second method adopted by Darlan to put an end to the state of tension between France and the Reich had also unfortunate consequences without having any ameliorating effect on Nazi pressure.

It consisted in granting the Germans minor concessions with which they could not possibly be satisfied.

Darlan, who still refused to put the essential part of the protocols into effect by yielding Bizerta to the Axis, decided to put into execution one of the minor measures which appeared in the appendix to the protocol concerning Bizerta.

In order to curry favour with the German army, he authorised them, at the beginning of August, to transport four hundred vehicles from Metropolitan France to North Africa, and use these trucks to transport to Libya merchandise bought by the Control Commission in Tunisia; he also authorised them to raise the personnel of the Commission to forty-one persons.

This concession on a secondary point had no effect: the state of tension persisted.

Moreover, by merely satisfying a limited German demand concerning one small point in order to be able to resist on the essential ones, the Admiral did not realise that, in practice, his concession over a detail ran the risk of nullifying the total effect of his resistance.

General Weygand pointed this out with considerable force in a letter, which he himself admitted was written in fairly strong terms. He denounced to the Government "the German manoeuvre which is a pretty blatant trick.

"To recapitulate: the buying of the trucks has allowed the Germans to install in North Africa a supplementary mission. Their journey has been the basis for a line of communications across Tunisia. Their being loaded with food supplies bought in North Africa has opened up a line of supply for the German troops in Libya. Cargoes arriving at Bizerta will be the origin of a Navy supply base. They are trying to obtain the transport of these cargoes towards the south by railway. And thus railway communications, which they have asked for for a long time, will be established.

"German methods are always the same: characterised by perseverance and bad faith. The Government has in principle been resisting the German demands for a base at Bizerta and the creation of a line of communications by land to supply their army in Tripolitania. The concessions of detail have doubtless been granted by reason of the little importance attributed to them; but we have been tricked and caught in the meshes of the German net. For my part, I cannot understand how a series of concessions should have been made without the addition being made of their sum and their results foreseen, that is to say military collaboration in the form of help given to Germany against our old ally. We have just seen in Syria the consequences of acts of this kind. Once more I am uttering a cry of alarm. . . ."

Thus the General stated his opposition to the policy of the Head of the Government, which gave Darlan new reasons for wishing to get rid of him. It was now that Darlan for the first time tried to dismiss Weygand: he thought that he could thus not only satisfy his personal animosity but temporarily appease the Germans who, for months past, had not concealed their hostility to Weygand.

In order to get rid of Weygand, Darlan first acted indirectly through the Government by demanding increased military powers which would make the General his subordinate and allow of his later dismissing him. He needed to become Commander in Chief of all the French armed forces: land, sea and air. And he suggested to Pétain that this supreme promotion, which would allow of his gradually ousting the ex-Generalissimo, should be conferred on him.

The month of September brought no amelioration to Franco-German relations.

In spite of the creation of special Tribunals, the Nazis continued to shoot the hostages themselves: on the 3rd September, in Paris, a German was killed: three hostages were executed. On the 12th September for one German assassinated, twelve Frenchmen were shot.

The collaborationist speeches had produced no relaxation of tension.

On the 25th September, 1941, Abetz, returning from a stay at the Führer's headquarters, presented the Marshal with an ultimatum: "The functions of General Weygand in North Africa are considered as constituting an insurmountable obstacle to the organisation of a constructive policy between Germany and France."

In North Africa, in spite of Weygand's resistance, the Germans demanded and obtained the opening of consulates at Casablanca and Algiers.

For the first time, a representative of the Reich came permanently to Vichy. Until then, a press attaché had been the only German living in the provisional capital; from now on a Consul-General, Krug von Nidda, accompanied by fifteen observers, would be there to watch and threaten.

Everything combined to show the Marshal that, unless Weygand were dismissed, nothing could pacify the Germans or make the political atmosphere in France more breathable.

Thus menaced with asphyxia, the Vichy Government used all its ingenuity in devising means to persuade the General to allow himself to be eliminated.

On the 16th October, hastily summoned by the Admiral to Vichy, the General was offered by Pétain, in exchange for his departure from North Africa, which the Germans had demanded by an ultimatum, the post of Minister of State charged with preparing "the constitution of the Empire". Weygand refused to abandon millions of French and natives: if the Government were prepared to take the responsibility of dismissing him, he would accept nothing in compensation. Besides, what good would it be to confer upon him civilian authority after having deprived him of his military command?

A few days after Weygand's departure from Vichy, Pétain received a snub from the Führer. The latter replied to the good wishes that Pétain had sent him on the anniversary of Montoire with unprecedented violence.

To the Marshal's fine phrases, which were designed to flatter him—"The victory of your arms over Bolshevism offers our collaboration, more now even than a year ago, the opportunity of becoming confirmed in peaceful work for the construction of a transformed Europe"—Hitler replied with furious recriminations against French deceitfulness: all the old grievances were recapitulated with bitterness; the Führer even went so far as to mention the 16,000 German women who were said to have been raped by the Senegalese in 1919.

But, above all, in this month of October, the German pressure took on a more dramatic character. It was now that the appalling episode of Châteaubriant took place.

On Monday, 20th October, towards 8 o'clock in the morning, Lieutenant-Colonel Holz, Feld-Kommandant of Nantes, was killed by unknown persons not far from the cathedral. General von Stülpnagel decided on the execution of fifty hostages as a reprisal.

On the 21st October, 16 hostages were executed at Nantes; on the 22nd October, 27 political detainees, interned in the camp at Châteaubriant, were shot. Among them was a student aged 16, Guy Mocquet, who was guilty of having distributed Gaullist pamphlets and above all of being the son of a Communist leader.

The same day, in Paris, five hostages were similarly shot, bringing the number of victims up to 48.

General von Stülpnagel then announced that 50 more hostages would be shot, unless the assassins of Colonel Holz were discovered within the next 48 hours.

The whole world became indignant at such cruelty.

On the 25th October, 1941, Roosevelt and Churchill denounced these "proceedings . . . which are revolting to a world however hardened already to suffering and brutality."

Upon learning of the shooting of the hostages at Châteaubriant, the Marshal conceived the idea of giving himself up to the Germans in place of one of the victims. A few hours later, when everything had been arranged for the Marshal's departure,[1] du Moulin learned that they were not going.

The Ministers, almost unanimously, according to du Moulin, laid siege to the Head of the State during the whole day. They told him that, if he gave himself up as a hostage, he would be failing in the mission he had undertaken of protecting the people of France, that a Gauleiter would be appointed on the morrow and that the prisoners—the eternal blackmail of the prisoners!—would not be liberated.

Thus Pétain yielded. He did not make the gesture which, according to some, would have made of him a legendary figure and, according to others, would have brought about still worse disasters. Was there not a risk that the Germans would keep the Marshal prisoner and, taking advantage of his isolation and his age, make him append his signature to laws they had themselves conceived?

In order not to run the risk of still greater reprisals, the Marshal confined himself, in a radio talk on the 27th October, to condemning the assassinations, without even saying a word to stigmatise the executions of hostages.

On the 29th October, the newspapers announced that the Führer had granted a reprieve *sine die* to the 50 hostages who were still to be executed as a reprisal for the assassination of Feld-Kommandant Holz.

But French opinion was indignant that the Marshal had not protested publicly.

On the 12th November, General Huntziger, the Minister for War, returning from an inspection in North Africa, was killed in an aircraft accident at Mont Aigoual.

Ambassador Abetz, having come to Vichy for the funeral, brought pressure to bear on the Marshal to dismiss Weygand.

[1] Du Moulin de Labarthète, Roger de Saivre, his deputy, Charles Vallin, Deputy for Paris, and Charles Trochu, Vice-President of the Municipal Council, were to accompany the Marshal and present themselves with him as voluntary hostages to the Germans.

Pétain replied firmly: "The German Government shows no consideration in its policy towards France; when it requires something, it seizes it brutally: as long as things are like this, no collaboration is possible."

Abetz was not abashed by the snub: he suggested that the Marshal might himself, by using his prestige with some Nazi personality, obtain some amelioration of Franco-German relations.

Unfortunately no German leader would agree to see the Marshal as long as Weygand was in Africa.

Abetz had found the blackmail to which the Marshal was bound to respond.

Weygand was summoned to Vichy. He arrived there on the 16th November.

The Marshal suggested once again that he might give the General some political compensation for the loss of his military command. Weygand, naturally, refused.

On the 18th November, in Pétain's office, the decisive interview took place in the presence of two Ministers of State, Romier and Moysset, as well as Admiral Darlan. The latter showed Weygand the notes containing the latest German blackmail. Having read them, the General said simply: "I've read them: there are only two possible alternatives: either take up my defence with the Germans and leave me where I am, or dismiss me." The four men remained silent.

"I want to know which it is to be," Weygand went on, "before I leave Vichy."

"It's settled," replied the Admiral.

There was another silence. No one dared break it. Weygand went on: "The Weygand case has been dealt with. Let's deal with Africa." He then reiterated in a few phrases how important he thought it was that all senior personnel, as well as the permanent secretariat general, should remain in office. The Marshal asked Weygand to write a memorandum on the subject. "Your testament will be put into execution."

As a counterpart to the dismissal of Weygand, the Government had asked that the Marshal might have a meeting with some high German military personality; that he should be authorised to cross into the occupied zone; that North Africa might be reinforced militarily; and that North African prisoners should be repatriated.

Of these four demands, only the first was granted. And it did not lead to any practical results.

On the 1st December, at Saint-Florentin-en-Bourgogne, Marshal Pétain, escorted by Admiral Darlan, met Reichsmarschall Goering.

But the interview came to nothing, since it was based on a misunderstanding.

Pétain thought to use his prestige to obtain the cessation of the executions of hostages, the return of the prisoners and an amelioration of the demarcation line. As for Goering, he had but one idea: to compel France into military collaboration at last and to acquire North African bases.

Pétain, in agreement with Darlan, who accompanied him to the interview, had prepared a memorandum which contained the French demands: "The Marshal," said the text, "reminds Chancellor Hitler that during the course of the interview at Montoire it was agreed that the prisoners should be freed, the demarcation line suppressed, the appropriations by the German army reduced and that, to some extent, the French army as it stood at the Armistice, and in particular the army of North Africa, should be rearmed." Pétain took care not to say that France had never performed the corresponding clauses to these promises, one of which was co-belligerence.

Goering then enumerated all the Reich's grievances: he complained that French agriculture was not at maximum production.

"Send us back the 800,000 agricultural labourers who are prisoners," replied Pétain.

Another complaint: "The transport of goods in France is working badly," declared Goering.

"Give us back the railway trucks that France has loaned Germany and which have never been returned."

"French industry is not producing enough," said the Nazi leader.

"You should give us coal and raw materials, we're still waiting for them."

And Pétain continued with demands and complaints. "The food appropriations by the Wehrmacht in France are scandalous. While the number of effectives have been reduced from two and a half millions to five hundred thousand, the German army quartered on our soil continues to appropriate a third of the tinned meat and fish supplies as well as food products of all kinds. . . ."

The interview became stormy. Goering shouted: "I should like to know who is the conqueror and who the conquered. The language you are using is unacceptable, you have handed me a note which I do not even dare transmit to the Chancellor."

To which Pétain replied with great dignity: "I have never so much felt the completeness of France's defeat as I have at this interview."

"I am confident," Pétain went on, "in the destiny of France and in her resurgence. As for myself, personally, you can well imagine that, for a man of my age, there is a very easy escape: that from life into death."

And as Goering had twice refused to take Pétain's memorandum, the latter in the end simply slipped it into Goering's pocket where it remained.

In this hostile climate, the interview of Saint-Florentin brought about no amelioration of Franco-German relations. The reprisals increased. In Paris, between the 8th and 14th December, the curfew was fixed at 6 p.m., a hundred hostages were executed and a fine of a billion francs was imposed upon the Jews.

The question of military collaboration remained static during December, 1941. Rommel's army was retreating in Tripolitania and it looked as if it would be forced to retire into Tunisia.

Darlan was summoned on the 9th December to Turin.

The interview between Darlan and Ciano was limited to generalities.

The position of the Axis armies in Africa grew worse: on the 10th December, the great retreat of the Afrika Korps began.

At this moment, Darlan no longer believed in a German victory. The United States had entered the war on the 7th December. On the 13th December, 1941, Darlan explained his uncertainties and his refusal to agree to military collaboration.

The Admiral gave the American Ambassador his solemn assurance that the Germans would never penetrate into the Empire: it was the first time that Darlan had made such a promise.

On the 15th December, Marshal Goering summoned General Juin, who had replaced Weygand at the head of the African army, to Berlin.

On the 20th December, Goering gave Juin an ultimatum: if the Marshal's Government desired to obtain some amelioration of the occupation, it must reply definitely to the two following questions:

1. An agreement over camouflaged supply through Bizerta.
2. An agreement on the principle of joint resistance in case Rommel's army retreated into southern Tunisia.

Juin limited himself to replying that he would transmit these questions to his Government: Vichy was faced once more with the dilemma of "Polandisation" or military collaboration.

On the 22nd December, the French Government sent its reply to the German Embassy. It still manifested the same tactics: while admitting the principle of collaboration, it subordinated it to the granting of unacceptable concessions: indeed, they amounted to an abrogation of the armistice as far as concerned North Africa:

". . . The French Government gives an affirmative reply to the two questions; it however makes the following conditions which will enable it to deal with the inevitable British reaction:

"(a) Complete liberty for the army, navy and air force in Africa and the western Mediterranean;

"(b) The liberation of essential cadres for the organisation of native troops;

"(c) Remilitarisation of southern Tunisia;

"(d) The provision, according to need, by Germany of fuel and lubricating oils of all kinds required for every variety of transport, and protection by the Luftwaffe for merchant ships in the eastern part of the western Mediterranean."

The Germans realised that the French Government did not want military collaboration.

And thus, the interview at Saint-Florentin was shown to be useless: there was, once again, a breaking off of relations.

## CHAPTER 6

# THE ELIMINATION OF DARLAN

## (January, 1942–April, 1942)

THE last three months, which had brought about the rupture between Darlan and the Reich, corresponded with one of those periods in which Vichy showed itself at its most firm towards the Germans. However, owing to a diplomatic imbroglio which it is difficult to unravel, this period also furnishes Pétain's adversaries with their most telling arguments: if certain of Abetz's documents are literally interpreted, Vichy, though it openly appeared to be resisting, had in fact decided to enter the war on the side of the Axis.

This is an apparent contradiction whose elements must be analysed and, if possible, some solution arrived at.

This mysterious episode of a pretended entry into the war began on the 5th January, 1942, with an interview between Hitler, his Minister for Foreign Affairs, Ribbentrop, and his Ambassador in Paris, Abetz.

The Axis forces had been undergoing a serious reversal in Africa. During the week of the 17th–24th December, the German armour had been surrounded by the British army. On the 24th December, Benghazi had fallen. The Afrika Korps were in some danger of being driven back to the Tunisian frontier.

After Christmas, the situation was restored: but, nevertheless, the crisis had once more brought the problem of Franco-German relations to the fore.

The Führer, when he received his two collaborators at his headquarters, had moreover just received, on the 30th December, a pressing demand from Mussolini to clear up the French intentions: "The question of the French bases in Tunisia is becoming absolutely fundamental. . . ."

And, on the 5th January, the Führer did not mince his words to Abetz who, as the initiator of the policy of collaboration, was partly responsible: "This collaboration is a unilateral business since the French appear to understand it in such a way that we are to give them every kind of concession without their being prepared to give us concrete returns."

This was a state of affairs that the Chancellor deplored: he was well aware of the important part that France could play in the evolution of the war: if France ranged herself unequivocally beside the Reich, the fundamental military problems of the conflict would be radically altered.

But, however much he wished to control the French Fleet and bases, the Führer, in January 1942, was under no illusion concerning the support he might hope for from France.

Hitler concluded the interview by postponing all definite decision till later: "In principle," related Abetz, "he was prepared for political conversations without any engagements to be begun with France and that Darlan should be received by the Reich Minister for Foreign Affairs and, later, by the Führer himself. However, before making any decision, he wished to await the return of the Minister for Foreign Affairs and have a conversation with him, which I was also to attend."

That was all, and indeed it was not much. Anyone else but Abetz, any career diplomat, would have adopted in the meantime an attitude of prudent reserve, but Abetz was decidedly not like other ambassadors: it was sufficient that the Führer should vaguely have adumbrated in his presence an interview in which he was to take part with Hitler and Ribbentrop for his imagination to run riot. Had he not been, before 1940, the only man to prophesy to the Führer the military collapse of France, when all the German Generals considered her as strong as before the previous war? Was he not the man who had brought drama, and, indeed, the intrigues of the stage into politics?

The great goal of his Embassy—to achieve by daring negotiation the co-operation of the French Fleet with his country, to provoke in the interests of both parties the co-belligerency of France by creating an incident in Africa which would allow of the Germans sending reinforcements—seemed to him nearer realisation than ever. His hypotheses took on the appearance of certainty, his desires that of reality. Abetz already saw himself triumphantly announcing in a few weeks time to the Führer and Ribbentrop that the policy of collaboration, of which he had unceasingly been the advocate and instigator, was bearing sensational fruit: that the French Government was ready to engage itself militarily. He thought that by his cleverness he could turn Hitler's inclinations into a triumphant success and bring the Chancellor a diplomatic victory for which he had ceased to hope.

As the intermediary between two parties separated by a no-man's land of silence and incomprehension, Abetz, in his vacuum, allowed his illusions to grow and his contrivances to take shape. When he returned to Paris on the 6th or 7th January, 1942, he had lost all sense of reality.

It was in these circumstances that, on the 9th January, 1942, he summoned the French Secretary of State, Benoist-Méchin, to the Rue de Lille.

Benoist-Méchin, with no self-doubts amid the European maelstrom, was pursuing a parallel dream to Abetz: he also wanted, against all the political winds and military tides, to be the artisan of Franco-German reconciliation.

But they each wanted it in the interests of their own countries: Abetz in order that the Reich might have the use of the French Fleet and Empire, Benoist-Méchin in order that France should benefit by important political concessions, and should henceforward be on an equal footing with the Reich.

In the conversation which took place on the 9th January, both men allowed themselves to be carried away by their dreams and tried to orientate Franco-German relations, which to say the least were already in jeopardy, in the direction of their own ideal.

The wish to negotiate, which the Führer had expressed somewhat confusedly and with considerable reserve, Abetz immediately exaggerated into a desire on Hitler's part to examine thoroughly the whole French problem and, if France showed herself worthy, bring it to an extremely generous solution. He told Benoist-Méchin that he must be able to take back to the Führer a satisfactory reply to the following question: "Was France prepared to associate herself with him?" And, in order to cajole Benoist-Méchin, Abetz continued: "The Führer does not demand a categorical reply which commits you: this is a sounding. I've got to take back an answer in principle."

These proposals, which the Führer had never mentioned to Abetz in January, 1942, filled Benoist-Méchin with enthusiasm. In order to make sure that he understood the Ambassador's thought on so essential a point, he recapitulated to Abetz the proposals he had just heard in a more systematic, a clearer and more French way than the other had done. As he formulated them he also interpreted them in the sense he desired, taking co-belligerency to be a distant eventuality but political negotiation, on the other hand, to be an immediate one.

In order to understand the implications of his interpretation, here is "the Führer's offer" as Benoist-Méchin transmitted it to Darlan in the report he sent him on the evening of the 9th January. It is essential to understand the parts Abetz and Benoist-Méchin played in transforming the Führer's words.

"Should France be prepared to march with me," the Führer is supposed to have said, "to the end of the conflict from which a new world will evolve, it is understood that the four following problems will have been discussed and will have been given a solution satisfactory to both parties:

"1. A profound modification of the Franco-German Statute;

"2. A definition in its broad lines of the future Treaty of Peace;

"3. An exhaustive study of France's military and economic needs for the successful undertaking of her new obligations;

"4. The best means of presenting this to French public opinion."

This offer compared in no way with anything the Führer had said. It was not even pure Abetz: it was corrected, denuded, rationalised, Gallicised, re-thought Abetz by Benoist-Méchin.

Benoist-Méchin, furnished with this message of which he was both bearer and co-author, arrived in Vichy on the 10th January in a state of exaltation which was only comparable to that of Abetz on Benoist-Méchin's return to Paris a few days later. Benoist-Méchin also felt that he was in a position to play a historic role and to resolve the Franco-German problem in accordance with his own policy. He had an interview with Darlan the same day.

At this meeting with Benoist-Méchin, who thought his great hour had come, the Admiral followed the same line which he had pursued for months: the conveying of a profusion of verbal good wishes to Abetz through the intermediary of his French opposite number.

The views of Benoist-Méchin were no more in accordance with the policy of the French Government than were the imaginings of Abetz with the wishes or fundamental designs of Hitler.

The Admiral considered the information brought by Benoist-Méchin to be merely one element among many others. After so many failures, he attached but little importance to it. And, if there had been any chance of negotiations, it would not have been Abetz's overtures but those of the Wehrmacht which would have attracted his attention.

It is probable that various meetings and conversations took place between the Ministers that day, and perhaps some of them included Benoist-Méchin, as Darlan sought advice here and there as to the demands that should be presented eventually to the Reich.

In any case, it appears certain that Benoist-Méchin was received on this visit by Pétain in the presence of Romier, who was continually assisting the Marshal at this period.

To reply to a question from Hitler with a negative seemed to Pétain to be probably incurring grave consequences: putting his tactics of delay into practice once again, tactics which over the months had proved themselves, particularly in having allowed him to deny Bizerta to the Germans without their fulfilling their threat of appointing a Gauleiter, Pétain was once more ready to accept the principle of eventual negotiations while laying it down that he was not prepared to consider co-belligerency in any circumstances.

On Monday, 12th January, Benoist-Méchin, leaving once more for Paris, was the bearer to Abetz of the Marshal's reply to a question the Führer had not put. The affair seemed to be prospering since, somewhat naturally, the reply was partially favourable: it envisaged, if certain political conditions—which in the event were never realised—were fulfilled, the opening of negotiations. But Benoist-Méchin very probably feared that the assurances were not solemn enough. He thought that a report of mere unofficial conversations would not impress the Germans sufficiently to determine them to open negotiations.

Thus, in the report he made to Abetz concerning his conversations in Vichy, he gave them, so great was his desire to see the decisive negotiations take place, the importance which he attributed to them himself. The private conversation with a few Ministers assumed an official character it had never possessed. If he were to be believed, it was a solemn and extraordinary meeting of the Council of Ministers which had decided to open negotiations. It was an unlikely assertion, for Benoist-Méchin had not taken into account the fact that his Government colleagues were tired and bored by the eternally renewed possibility of these supposedly capital negotiations with the Third Reich. The meeting at Saint-Florentin, the last in date, had been significant.

As the result of this report, which interpreted, or rather transformed, the dull reality, the German Ambassador and the Vichy diplomatic delegate drew up the text of a telegram which was to give the Führer the answer (to a question he had never asked) of the French Government (which had never seriously discussed the subject).

During the drafting of the telegram, Benoist-Méchin, who remained loyal to the Marshal's instructions, stipulated that any agreement must be subordinated to a satisfactory solution to the political negotiations.

Abetz then began to manifest a certain reserve. To every advance the Frenchman made, Abetz retreated, continually repeating that no undue haste must be shown in the matter.

Benoist-Méchin became aware of this and, in the report he sent Darlan on the evening of the 12th, stated sadly that perhaps the proposition (imaginary) made by the Chancellor for the opening of negotiations was no more than a manoeuvre to sound the real intentions of the French Government: rapid developments must not be expected.

The telegram which had been drafted with Benoist-Méchin's collaboration seemed to Abetz unsuitable for sending to the Chancellor. Unsuitable for two reasons: in the first place because the text drawn up with Benoist-Méchin was a reply to a question that Hitler had never asked (the report of the 5th January is the proof); and, also, because it must be realised that, if Abetz and Benoist-Méchin were to some extent in association, their points of view were radically different; for Benoist-Méchin, there was no question of dragging France into the war: his intention, in January, 1942, was, as it had been in June, 1941, to obtain the conditions France had demanded from Germany, while Abetz's intention, in January, 1942, as in May, 1941, the autumn of 1940 and indeed as it was to be ten months later in November, 1942, was on the contrary to lead France away from the armistice and into a position from which would emerge the co-belligerency he had so often forecast (the which had contributed not a little to his progressively diminishing credit). Therefore Benoist-Méchin's draft did not suit Abetz, who indeed could not send it.

Since he was unable to reveal the truth without provoking the Führer's anger, Abetz was reduced to inventing a report which might have the advantage of satisfying Hitler: the French, he said, were ready to engage their Fleet and their Empire in the war without making preliminary conditions with Germany.

Having to make a choice between truth and the Chancellor's displeasure, or invention, Abetz lied.

He therefore awaited Benoist-Méchin's departure, on the 12th January, 1942, in order to do what he had done several times before. He composed a telegram which merely recapitulated his fixed idea once again, but now adorned, thanks to Benoist-Méchin, though without his knowledge, with a number of new details.

"On the 11th January," cabled Abetz, "there was a meeting of the Ministers Darlan, Moysset, Romier, Bouthillier, Pucheu and Benoist-Méchin with Marshal Pétain. This meeting, which was of a solemn character, closed with a unanimous decision to declare war on England and the United States, after a clarification of the preliminary questions I mentioned to Benoist-Méchin; the war will be conducted side by side with Germany without reservation until victory is won.

"The Marshal, the Admiral and the other Ministers look upon this declaration of principle as a logical consequence of the policy of collaboration which is both desired by them and was offered by the Government of the Reich at Montoire.

". . . The persons who took part in this meeting agreed to keep it absolutely secret."

This incredible document certainly reached Berlin, since it was found in the archives of the Wilhelmstrasse. But what reception did it get? So far, no trace of a reaction from Hitler or Ribbentrop has been discovered: perhaps, having other sources of information than the Paris Embassy, and having had opportunities already of appreciating Abetz's capacity for distorting the truth, they were waiting for the French Government to give some overt manifestation of its intention of coming in on their side. But, though the telegram was not taken seriously by its recipients, it was, after the Liberation, so taken by the Judges of the High Court.

It is, therefore, Abetz's lies, assisted in the first instance by Benoist-Méchin, though ultimately without his knowledge, which have created the belief that Vichy agreed, in January, 1942, to unconditional co-belligerency.

Weygand's dismissal, the meeting at Saint-Florentin, the conversation between Abetz and the Führer and the manoeuvring which followed were none of them to bring any amelioration to Franco-German relations.

Tired of the repeated failures in negotiation with the Reich and no longer believing in a German victory, Vichy, for the first time since the armistice, made open and public protests against the Nazi pressure.

The Marshal, in his broadcast of the 31st December, denounced for the first time in public the German pressure and took to task both the collaborators in Paris and the Gaullists in London.

"It is my duty to call deserters all those who, in the press or on the radio, either in London or in Paris, sow the abject seeds of disunion. . . .

"In the partial exile to which I am constrained, in the half liberty which remains to me, I endeavour to do all my duty. Every day, I try to relieve this country from the strangle-hold which threatens it and from the disasters which lie in wait for it. Give me your help."

This message swayed French popular opinion towards the Marshal once more. On the other hand, he scandalised the Germans and the Paris press. *L'Oeuvre* wrote that "France is running probably a greater danger than at the time of the armistice. Our upholders of the policy of waiting (*attentisme*) are suffering from utter lunacy and the words of Admiral Leahy are now the daily Gospel of Vichy."

In the economic field, the Government openly resisted the Germans during the first quarter of 1942.

Bouthillier denounced on his own initiative the *diktat* concerning the occupation costs and published, in the *Journal Officiel* of the 1st January, 1942, a report addressed to the Head of the State which was bound to displease the occupying power.

On the 29th January, 1942, Bouthillier protested to the Reich Minister of Finance. On the 27th February, since the German Minister had not replied, Bouthillier asked Darlan to confirm his letter by an official note at Wiesbaden. Darlan agreed.

The French Government's protest was presented at Wiesbaden on the 4th March: the Germans contemptuously refused to reply, and the French, in spite of their protest, continued to pay.

The Government also refused to take action in another field and this time they were as good as their word.

At a Franco-German meeting, held on 14th January, 1942, Dr. Michel demanded from the Government an official declaration encouraging the departure of French workers to Germany.

Far from agreeing, Lehideux, Secretary of State to the Ministry of Production, sent through the Comités d'Organisation a circular dated 26th March, 1942, to the heads of businesses: it reminded them that they must observe absolute neutrality in the matter.

The Nazis increased their pressure: the Germans demanded that Vichy should agree to the departure of 150,000 workers. Darlan refused.

There were other examples of open resistance during the course of the first quarter of 1942: a refusal to reduce the normal number of trains in order to facilitate German transport; a refusal to agree to German demands concerning railway stock; a refusal to place at the disposal of the Reich 9,000 skilled railway workers; the prosecution of German agents, who were secretly transferring road transport from the free to the occupied zones; further protests at Wiesbaden against the annexation of Alsace-Lorraine and Ostland; and the cutting off of electric power to aluminium factories in order to slow up production earmarked for the Germans.

A few days later, Darlan protested officially against new anti-Semitic measures proposed by the Germans (orders issued to all Jews to wear the star of David).

In March 1942 there was a new Franco-German incident; Abetz invited the Marshal and the Admiral to come to Paris in order to attend the funeral of the victims of the bombing by the Royal Air Force of the Renault factories at Boulogne-Billancourt. They both refused. The ceremony was reduced to a mass at Notre-Dame attended by Joseph Barthélemy, Garde des Sceaux, representing Vichy, and Abetz, representing the Reich. It was arranged that the two men should enter the cathedral side by side behind Cardinal Suhard. But, at the last moment, the prelate pretended that he was tired or ill and required the support of Barthélemy's arm; Abetz, discomfited, had to walk alone in the second rank.

Thus, at the beginning of 1942, it looked as if Darlan had chosen open resistance to the Nazis. It was to compromise the very existence of his Government.

The Admiral's new policy indeed constituted a serious rebuff to the Reich Ambassador, Otto Abetz, who, for months past, had continually promised the Führer the collaboration of the French Empire and Fleet.

Moreover, Abetz had personal reasons for disliking Darlan. The Admiral in general openly refused to deal with him, preferring to have to do with General von Stülpnagel, whom he felt to be—and rightly—an opponent of Nazism.

Abetz had another grievance against Darlan: he had never resigned himself to the plot of the 13th December against Pierre Laval, the man who, from July, 1940, had staked everything on him rather than on the military chiefs and had thus assured his diplomatic career. Between Laval and himself there was a strong political bond.

All the Embassy's satellites in the Paris press or the collaborationist parties were openly pro-Laval and could not forgive Darlan the contempt he showed for them.

On his side, Laval passionately desired to play a political part once more: he was obsessed by the longing for some startling revenge for the 13th December; he was also convinced that he was the only man who could bring about some easing of Franco-German relations.

Already, in July, 1941, he would have liked Pucheu to refuse the Ministry of the Interior in order that he, Laval, might succeed to it: Pucheu had not lent himself to this manoeuvre.

Were Laval and Abetz to be rebuffed once more in January, 1942? How were they to persuade the Marshal to take back into the Government the man who had insulted him on the 17th December in the presence of the representative of the Reich?

In February, 1942, the Germans reopened the question of Laval's return for the first time for a year.

On the 24th February, the Counsellor to the Embassy, Achenbach, took his place in the weekly train which, for the benefit of ministers and important officials, ran to and fro between the two capitals. He went to Vichy "as a private person". During the course of the three days he stayed in the Allier, he never left the side of Dr. Ménétrel, the head of the Marshal's private office and, thanks to him, was invited four times to meals with the Marshal.

He explained to the Head of the State that, if Laval were not brought back, a Gauleiter would be appointed.

From this time on, Pétain was subjected to a siege which was to last two months.

On the 18th March, there was a second German offensive over Laval. The Führer's personal envoy, Councillor Grimm, who had come to demand that the Riom trials should be terminated, also told the Marshal that only the creation of a government under Laval could appease the Chancellor.

In Paris, Laval was far from inactive. In March, 1942, through Marquet, he had met Colonel Knochen, Deputy to the Chief of the S.S., to whom he announced his "astonishment at seeing our relations with Germany grow worse and the restrictive measures taken against France increasing." "I regret," he added, "not to have the opportunity of saying it to some important German personality." Knochen then offered to arrange a meeting between him and Goering, who was to arrive in Paris two days later.

Two days later then, on a Saturday, introduced by Knochen and by a nephew of Goering's, he went to the Quai d'Orsay to the minister's office, which he had so often occupied himself, where were Goering and General Hanesse, who had once been Air Attaché in Paris and was to act as interpreter. Knochen did not attend the meeting.

To begin with, Goering demanded that the interview should remain confidential and that Abetz, in particular, should never be told of it. On Laval's demand, he agreed that Pétain, but only Pétain, should be informed. In a state of angry excitement, he then proceeded to a violent indictment of France: "We made a mistake," he said in substance, "when we thought we could expect sincere collaboration from your country. We have now revised our policy and shall from now on treat France on the basis of the enmity which she ceaselessly shows us." Goering was doubtless not threatening France's "Polandisation" in so many words, but Laval understood that this was what he meant. "France," Goering went on, "shall be treated as she deserves." And, a still more alarming sign in Laval's opinion, Goering advised him personally to stand aloof from politics: "If the Marshal offers to take you back into power, refuse. For you, it will be either much too late or much too early. You have been an honourable enemy to us. Perhaps we shall meet again one day after the war, when peace has been signed, and then you will be able to uphold the interests of your country."

Laval decided to warn the Marshal of the dangers with which France was threatened and of the necessity of putting an end to the policy of waiting.

On the 25th March, René de Chambrun, Laval's son-in-law, arrived in Vichy.

He told Pétain that Laval must speak to him on a subject of the first importance for France. He and Ménétrel would organise, if the Marshal agreed, an interview to be held in the greatest secrecy: Laval wished to see the Marshal alone.

On the 26th March, Pétain met Laval in the Forest of Randan.

Laval informed the Marshal of Goering's statement and pointed out the seriousness of the situation for which Darlan's foolish policy was responsible.

Thus everything was set in motion for Laval's return to the Government; and, indeed, less than three weeks after the interview, he had become head of it.

This was, apparently, due to an extraordinary change of mind on the part of Pétain, which must now be explained.

Since June, 1940, Pétain had been obsessed by his anxiety to protect the population against the excesses of the occupation. But now, in April, 1942, his mission appeared to be somewhat compromised, for it had been announced that the German military administration in France was to be replaced by the S.S. Oberg, the S.S. General, who had repressed the Czechs, was to be appointed to Paris, and the shooting of hostages would increase.

It was a tragic situation before which Pétain felt powerless. And, in the meantime, everyone was telling him that the only way to avoid the "Polandisation" of France was that Laval should return to the Government.

Pétain was therefore torn between his suspicions of Laval and his dislike for the policy he had pursued up to the 1st December on the one hand, and his obsession with sparing the population as much suffering as possible on the other. From this arose the curious vicissitudes which followed; as well as Pétain's final decision and his lassitude and grief when the irremediable had taken place.

The news of the meeting between the Marshal and Laval had the effect of a bomb in Vichy. Admiral Darlan declared furiously that he had been faced with an accomplished fact.

On the 28th March, Laval, in an interview given to the Press, prophesied his return to the Government.

At Vichy, however, the days which immediately followed upon the meeting in the Forest of Randan passed quietly enough. Most of the Ministers still refused to believe that Pétain could bring Laval back into the Government.

On the 30th March, the Marshal saw Admiral Leahy, who handed him an ultimatum from President Roosevelt: if Laval returned to power, the United States would break off diplomatic relations with France.

Pétain reassured Leahy, telling him of his formal intention not to allow Laval to play any political role.

On the 2nd April, in the morning, Pétain received Laval at the Pavillon Sévigné. He told him firmly that he could not contemplate his presence in the Government. The Marshal used the same terms to the German Consul-General, Krug von Nidda.

The next day, 3rd April, Good Friday, the majority of Ministers left Vichy for the Easter holidays. The Laval question seemed to have been resolved: it had been decided that the ex-President of the Council could not return to Vichy.

It was then that two monumental blunders, one committed by Pétain, the other by Darlan, re-opened the whole question.

The Marshal, under the influence of du Moulin de Labarthète and Colonel Fonck, charged the latter with sounding out Goering concerning a ministerial reorganisation. There was doubtless no intention of bringing Laval back, but of substituting Barthélemy for Darlan. Nevertheless this *démarche* showed the Germans—and this was the essential point—that the Marshal was prepared to sacrifice the Admiral.

Darlan on the very same day, the 3rd April, committed the worst possible tactical error. In order to warn Krug von Nidda that all attempts to reinstate Laval in the Government were bound to fail, he told the Nazi diplomat of the American ultimatum and explained to him that Pétain would never accept Laval's return for fear of disobliging the Americans.

No more was needed to transform, in the eyes of the Nazis, Laval's return into a trial of strength between themselves and the U.S.A.

On the 10th April, the catastrophe occurred.

Krug von Nidda came to warn Darlan that the Führer, on hearing of the American ultimatum, had declared: "According to whether the Marshal charges M. Laval or not with the formation of a government, I shall know whether France prefers the friendship of the United States or that of Germany."

Moreover, Krug von Nidda gave Darlan a copy of the letter which Pétain had given Fonck eight days before.

Nevertheless, Laval had not yet won. On the afternoon of the 10th April, a Friday, Pétain, Darlan, Moysset and Bouthillier decided to counter-attack.

Darlan would offer Laval the Ministry for Foreign Affairs, while himself remaining Vice-President of the Council.

Laval was to answer merely "yes" or "no".

Under these conditions, his refusal could not be in doubt. Pétain could then inform the Germans, and the Laval business would be over.

Contrary to the Marshal's hope, Laval, on the 11th April, during his conversation with Darlan, did not fall into the trap; he certainly refused the Ministry for Foreign Affairs, but he demanded to be Head of the Government.

The Admiral, startled by the horrifying picture Laval drew for him of Franco-German relations and profoundly hurt by the Fonck affair, on his return to Vichy wrote a note to the Head of the State: he suggested that Laval should form a new government without further delay; while, for himself, he asked an exclusively military post.

Pétain was dumbfounded. Bouthillier, Moysset and Auphan did not as yet wish to admit Laval's victory.

On Sunday, 12th April, Bouthillier succeeded in making Darlan alter his decision.

He persuaded him to remain in the Government and go to Paris on the following day, Monday, 13th April, to inform General von Stülpnagel officially of the following points:

1. That Laval had refused to accept the Ministry for Foreign Affairs;

2. That the Marshal had decided to suspend indefinitely all negotiations with Laval.

Darlan made one condition to the carrying out of this mission: the Marshal would give him two letters; one would resume for the benefit of the German authorities the French position concerning Laval, the other would be a letter in which the Marshal would confirm his confidence in the Admiral.

As soon as Bouthillier transmitted Darlan's wishes to the

Marshal, they were fulfilled. Pétain sent the Admiral a letter which exceeded his hopes: far from limiting himself to disavowing Fonck, Pétain wrote:

"You know that you have all my confidence and that I cannot contemplate the idea of your not continuing to direct the Government."

To seal the reconciliation, Pétain signed a decree that Darlan had been demanding for a long time; it maintained the Admiral as Commander-in-Chief on the active list without any retiring age.

As soon as he had read these documents, Darlan gave orders to prepare for his journey on the morrow, Monday 13th, since he proposed leaving early in the morning. Moysset would accompany him. Bouthillier would remain in Vichy in order to mount guard over the Marshal who would be assailed by the supporters of Laval.

On the 12th April, therefore, Laval's return seemed very unlikely.

But Consul-General Krug von Nidda learned of the Admiral's imminent departure: he warned Abetz. The latter took the astounding decision to forbid Darlan access to the capital.

Abetz wished to avoid at all costs a meeting between the Admiral and Stülpnagel. The game might be won in Vichy: one moment's weakness on the part of the old Marshal would suffice. In Paris there was a risk of its being lost. To allow himself to be notified of an official and formal decision of the Marshal's would have been the greatest mistake. During the night of the 12th–13th, Abetz telegraphed Vichy that the Admiral would not be allowed to cross the demarcation line so long as the Laval question had not been settled.

Pétain and Darlan refused as yet to admit defeat. Since the Admiral could not explain the French position to Stülpnagel, the Marshal proposed to inform Chancellor Hitler that Laval had refused to become Minister of Foreign Affairs and that, in the circumstances, he himself refused to continue negotiations with Laval.

The message was to be telegraphed to Wiesbaden at midday.

But, during the morning, Ménétrel returned from Paris where he had spent the last twenty-four hours. He had seen Abetz several times and now transmitted once again the usual blackmail: either Laval returned to power, or a Gauleiter would be appointed. In any case, Ménétrel suggested, it would be better to await the arrival of Brinon.

Pétain yielded; he cancelled the order to send his message to the Führer.

Brinon saw Pétain at 2 p.m., warned him that the Germans would refuse all negotiations as long as Laval was not Head of the Government.

He then left for Châteldon to confer with Laval. A few hours later, Laval received Krug von Nidda and announced his victory: he would form a government from which would be eliminated all the Ministers responsible for the 13th December.

On the 14th April, Laval was received by the Marshal. An official *communiqué* indicated the formation of a government by Laval.

But was the game entirely over? On the 15th, there was a last offensive by Moysset, Bouthillier, Romier and Darlan.

The Marshal was still visibly hesitating to recall Laval.

"If I envisage his return, it is in order to spare the French misfortune and suffering, but I wonder how much truth there is in the threats professed: I was told that the departure of General Weygand would bring us great advantages, but the situation was never worse than it has been since then. . . ."

His colleagues one after the other, opposed Laval's return. Their arguments were impressive and lucid. Moysset, indeed, concluded with this prophetic warning: "Germany has lost the war. She will drag into the abyss all those who have marched or have seemed to march in her wake. Take care, Monsieur le Maréchal, not to survive your glory."

The Marshal then decided upon the tactics he would adopt to break with Laval once more. He proposed, on the following day, to ask him a series of precise questions on his political intentions: it appeared evident that the two men had not one single idea in common and, faced with the impossibility of adopting a joint programme, the Marshal would finally refuse to have Laval in the Government.

Thus, at 10 o'clock in the evening of the 15th April, all was not over, at least in theory. But, in fact, Pétain had not the stature to argue with Laval: the interview at Ferté-Hauterive had shown it. The following day he would give way.

On Thursday, 16th April, towards the end of the morning, the Marshal received Laval. He capitulated completely. He accepted all his proposals and nominated him Head of the Government. He only held out on one point: Benoist-Méchin was not to be Minister for Foreign Affairs.

On Friday, 17th April, at the Pavillon Sévigné, was held the last Council of Ministers of Darlan's Government. The Marshal circulated the collective letter of resignation: "Gentlemen, I am acting under constraint."

From now on, because he had yielded to the intrigues of a few Frenchmen and to the German blackmail, the Marshal would be compelled to cover Laval's policy with his authority, without being able either to modify it or put an end to it. It was a tragic situation. . . .

On Monday, 20th, when he received some of the resigning Ministers of Darlan's Government, Pétain said: ". . . You should be sorry for me, for, you know, I am now no more than a man adrift."

# Vichy, the Third Period

(18th April, 1942–22nd November, 1942)

CHAPTER 1

# LAVAL IN POWER

FROM now on Pierre Laval was, in fact if not in title, the real head of the State.

Constitutional Act No. 11, signed by Pétain under German pressure, laid it down that:

"The effective direction of the internal and external policy of France is assumed by the Head of the Government, appointed by the Head of the State and responsible to him.

"The Head of the Government will present the list of Ministers for agreement by the Head of the State; he will report to him concerning his plans and his actions."

The appointment of the new Head of the Government entailed the departure of nearly all the politicians recruited by Pétain since July.

Most of the Ministers, Bouthillier, Belin, Caziot, Carcopino, Berthelot, and Lehideux, resigned without waiting for Laval to dismiss them.

Pucheu also left the Government, but for quite other reasons; Laval removed him from the Ministry of the Interior and kept the appointment for himself.

The only survivors of the Darlan Ministry were Admiral Platon, who, in October, 1940, had approved the expedition to Chad, and Joseph Barthélemy, who had arrived in Vichy in January, 1941, and whose hostility to Darlan was publicly known.

The greater part of the Marshal's personal staff were also to leave Vichy. The Germans demanded the dismissal of du Moulin de Labarthète and of General Laure, whom the Marshal allowed to go without evincing the least regret.

In spite of his hatred for the "men of the 13th December", Laval had nevertheless to tolerate the most important of them:

the Marshal, the Head of the State, and his eventual successor, Admiral Darlan.

It is true that this tolerance did not cost Laval dear. Constitutional Act No. 11 reduced, indeed, Pétain to that role of decorative "china vase" to which, since 1940, Laval had wished him to be limited. Indeed, the Marshal, besides his constitutional and legislative powers, preserved in theory the right to dismiss Laval. But in reality the latter had given him clearly to understand that the Germans would consider any renewal of the 13th December as a sufficient motive to occupy the free zone. As an extra precaution, Laval had assumed the position of Minister of the Interior: he was thus in a position not to arrest himself.

Every morning Laval undertook a duty which was not altogether disinterested: in order to avoid giving the Marshal any excuse to blame him for keeping him in the dark, he went every day to ask Pétain "to approve" his policy. The Marshal allowed himself to be impressed by Laval's experience and nearly always finished by giving his authorisation. "Just let me do it, Monsieur le Maréchal, I've been Minister for Foreign Affairs, I know the ropes."

And Laval badgered Pétain till he had got what he wanted. Often, upon Laval's leaving him, Pétain would realise what had happened: "How could I have told him that I agreed? Jardel, go and tell him that I've made a mistake. . . ."

Jardel would go down to Laval's floor: and the Head of the Government would say mockingly: "Oh, so he's changed his mind again!" And, more often than not, he would cavalierly send Pétain's emissary away with: "For God's sake, don't bother me!"

Nor did Darlan give his successor much trouble.

He remained the *dauphin* of course; but if, in this capacity, he was to succeed the Marshal, he would inherit a supreme position which was more or less that of a figurehead. He had, too, been appointed, on the 17th April, Commander-in-Chief of the Army, Navy and Air Force, having finally obtained the position Weygand had prevented Pétain creating for him. But, this promotion notwithstanding, he had no real political power: he no longer attended the Council of Ministers unless summoned to discuss strictly military questions.

There was another sign of a total political re-orientation: the replacement of undesirable ministers by men who had never been part of the first ministerial teams of the National Revolution.

The new ministers were creatures of Laval: instead of the technicians or notable figures, strangers to political life, with whom the Marshal had liked to surround himself, Laval often chose his colleagues from among the political personnel of the Third Republic: many of them, like himself, came from the Left: such, as we shall see, were Cathala, Bonnafous and Grasset.

But, though they had the title of Minister, did they really have the power?

"None of my colleagues," said Barthélemy, "is a Minister in the sense that this function implies a political role. Only Monsieur Laval is a Minister. We are no more than his clerks, his secretaries. We carry out his orders. . . ."

Two of his favourites, Bonnard and Bichelonne, were certainly very curious individuals. Bonnard was "*l'académicien de choc*", Bichelonne "*l'intellectuel de main*". What a contrast they presented to the well-known figures Pétain had recruited in July, 1940!

Abel Bonnard was a typical intellectual dilettante, as well as being a pervert and a masochist; and Laval had the curious idea of selecting him as Grand Master of the University. This appointment, which he opposed in vain, made the Marshal indignant: "It's a scandal to entrust the young to that '*Gestapette!*'."

In the exercise of his ministerial functions, Abel Bonnard had one merit at least in a period when the French had but little to laugh at; he was the involuntary cause of a good deal of amusement. Here, for instance, is an extract from his message to "the young people of France" which, in May, 1942, on the occasion of the Feast of Joan of Arc, was to be read by the teachers in every class in every *lycée* and college in France: "Remember that this girl was continually among licentious soldiery but was always respected by them. Young men of renascent France, you must show constant respect to the girls who are the new springtime of France!"

For Bonnard, the strength of the Reich was the incarnation of virility, and he became a Nazi. He was no longer satisfied with his reputation as a frequenter of salons. He had had enough of being called the "charming" or the "subtle" Bonnard. He wanted to be "the formidable Bonnard" or the "*académicien de choc*". And Laval was delighted to have acquired such a recruit.

Bichelonne, on the other hand, was a mathematician of genius, and his mind was almost abnormal in its power of work and its exceptional memory; he was astray in politics, lived out of the world and had no contact with reality. One day, seeing a new-born child, he was concerned at the fact that it had not as yet any teeth.

During the occupation, he was sincerely convinced that the future of France could only be assured by collaboration with the Reich. The certainty of a German victory, which he preserved to the very end (in August, 1944, when leaving for Sigmaringen, he advised his colleagues "not to compromise themselves with the Allies. We shall be back in a few weeks."), did not prevent his making great efforts at certain times to preserve the industrial heritage of France. In 1940, he was even arrested by the Germans for his energetic opposition to the despatch of machine tools across the Rhine. At other times, however, he yielded to them with alacrity. In 1943, he showed great zeal in sending workmen to work in Germany.

How can these two irreconcilable attitudes within a period of three years be explained?

On the one hand, it is clear that in 1943, Bichelonne, when ordering the departure of workers for Germany, thought he was protecting French industry. "It must be done. We shall perhaps be shot. We shall not be understood. It is our duty. Otherwise, the Germans will requisition the whole of the labour force." But it was also because Bichelonne was a sort of calculating machine for whom human problems took on an abstract character: the more difficult they were to resolve, the better Bichelonne was pleased: "It's incredible how difficult it is to satisfy the German demands. It's passionately interesting!"

Thus, Laval could count on the exceptional intelligence of Bichelonne rather as he might have relied on the physical strength of a bodyguard.

Besides these two stars, Laval's Government included a curious mixture of men of the Left and of technicians, recruited in almost equal proportions from partisans and adversaries of the Right.

There was one Radical Socialist, an ex-Deputy and ex-Minister, Cathala, who believed in a Nazi victory. There were three Socialists, Brévié, Lagardelle and Bonnafous. Brévié, who called himself a Marxist, was the first Colonial Civil Servant to become Minister of the Colonies since 1885; Lagardelle, a

Revolutionary Syndacalist and a disciple of Georges Sorel, became Minister of Labour, where his impractical intellectualism was confronted with the painful problem of the S.T.O.; and Bonnafous put his degree in philosophy to good use by presiding over the destinies of the Ministry of Food.

Once again, there were two Radicals, one a senior man and one "a young Turk". The first was Dr. Grasset, Secretary of State to the Ministry of Health, who defended the Freemasons, the Jews and the *maquisards*. The other was Bousquet, Secretary-General for the Police who, in 1940, at the age of thirty-one, had been the youngest Prefect in France and was to be deported by the Germans in 1944.

Among the technicians, Gibrat, a first-rate engineer, accepted the Ministry of Communications, after having consulted one of his friends, Robert Lepercq, of whose Gaullist contacts he knew. After the Liberation, Lepercq was to be first Minister of Finance. General Jannekeyn agreed to go to the Air Ministry on the advice of General Bergeret, who was vacating it, and who said: "A collaborationist might be appointed in your stead."

Admiral Auphan's case was similar. He only agreed to become Minister of Marine because, except for Darlan, he was the only guarantor of the Agreement made with the British, on the 18th June, 1940, never to give up the Fleet.

Jacques Leroy-Ladurie, Secretary of State for Agriculture, resigned as soon as he discovered that the Germans were interfering in his province.

General Bridoux, Secretary of State for War, the only exception among the technical Ministers, was a protégé of Abetz and Brinon.

Besides these "new men" of whom most were shortly to be suspect to the occupying power, Laval, an expert in the management of proportions, summoned four others to power whose collaborationist sympathies were well known: these were Brinon, the Ambassador now promoted Minister, Marion, who was given the Ministry of Information, Admiral Platon and Benoist-Méchin. Laval wished to make the latter a Secretary of State to the Ministry of Foreign Affairs, but Pétain refused to sign the appointment. Laval finally arranged that Benoist-Méchin should be attached to him personally.

Finally, two Ministers remained in the positions they had occupied in 1941: Joseph Barthélemy, Gardes des Sceaux, and

Lucien Romier, Minister of State, practically the only two in whom Pétain could still have confidence.

On a general view of the world conflict, this Government of Laval's coincided with the period at which it became reasonable to believe in a Nazi defeat.

On the Russian front, the German advance was halted for several weeks in front of Voronezh and then came to a stop before Stalingrad where desperate battles began on the 4th September. In October, street fighting started. French public opinion was delighted: "Having fought for towns, indeed whole countries, the Germans are now reduced to fighting for houses."

In the Pacific and the Far East, the Japanese Army had their last successes in the Philippines and the Aleutian Islands. But the Japanese Fleet suffered its first reverses; in two naval battles it lost twenty-four warships, four aircraft carriers, and ten other ships temporarily put out of action.

In Libya, the summer ended by the halting of Rommel's offensive on the 2nd September, and by the German defeat of the 3rd November which left 40,000 prisoners in British hands.

At the same time, the R.A.F. was making its first destructive raids on German towns; on the 30th May, Cologne was bombed by a thousand British aircraft; on 1st June, Essen by 1,036; Hamburg was subjected to attacks by 300 and then 500 aircraft.

Finally, for the first time since 1940, France became a battlefield. The Canadians landed at Dieppe on the 19th August.[1] Rouen was bombed on the 5th September, le Creusot on the 17th October and, by August 1942, the French were beginning to wonder when the allied landing, which until then everyone had looked upon as an Utopian idea, would take place.

Two new facts characterised this period in which the French suffered more and more cruelly from hunger and lack of liberty: the first concerned official life, the second the real life of the country.

In official circles melancholy avowals of failure were succeeding to the complacent and irritating optimism of Darlan's time. To the enthusiastic speeches on the National Revolution succeeded appeals in favour of the "Relève", that is to say work in Germany.

On the 17th July, 1942, when making a speech on the occasion

[1] Cf. *infra*, p. 386.

of the second anniversary of the armistice, the Marshal, who till then had been so proud of the National Revolution, almost recognised the failure of his labours.

"Responsible as I am for the physical and moral life of France, I do not conceal from myself the weakness of the response encountered by my appeals.

"Certainly, the Government of this country has not been free from errors . . . in this period of hopes, failures, sacrifices and disappointments which mark the two first years of the armistice. . . ."

And Pétain concluded with a plea *pro domo*, which contrasted with the tone of his previous messages.

"Cast doubt from your minds, my dear friends, if you can, and the acerbity of criticism. Think of your leader who loves you and who is still standing upright in the storm for your sakes. He would like to do yet more for you. He can at least, on this second anniversary of one of the cruellest dates in our history, ask you to share the great hope which still animates him for the salvation of our country and which he prays God may be realised even after his death."

To his private visitors, Pétain gave the same pathetic impression. He did not conceal his discouragement from Jérôme Carcopino: "Carcopino, I've never given you my photograph. It's a piece of forgetfulness I should like to repair. But to you, Carcopino, I should not like to offer the picture of the Pétain of 1942. It's the picture of the Pétain of 1919 that I would like you to keep as a memento of me." And Pétain gave his ex-Minister a photograph showing him on horseback beneath the Arc de Triomphe on the 14th July, 1919, his glory still intact.

After Laval's return to office, except on particular occasions—the Feast of Joan of Arc, the Feast of Mothers or a meeting of the Peasant Corporation—there was no longer any question of the National Revolution. It was the "Relève" which had taken first place.

There was not a week in which the French did not either hear or read exhortations to go and work in Germany.

On the 22nd June, Laval, in his notorious speech in which he hoped "for a German victory without which Bolshevism will shortly be dominant everywhere," was the first to call upon French workers to go voluntarily to Germany in order, so he said, that the prisoners might return.

On the 11th August: the first train-load of repatriated prisoners due to the "Relève" arrived at Compiègne station, where they crossed a convoy of volunteers on their way to Germany. Laval was there to meet them.

As the months passed without the French being convinced of the attractions of working in Germany, the tone changed once more: enticements were succeeded by threats. On the 20th October, Laval adjured the workers to go in order not to be deported:

"Consider the two alternatives with which you are faced.

"On one side an engagement under contract with all the material advantages it will bring with it and above all with a clear vision of all the consequences, even the most distant ones, of your action which gives it its value; on the other, forced labour from which only Germany will benefit; a humiliating compulsion for you who will be its victims, but certainly more humiliating and more serious for France."

Later on, there was even an announcement threatening the arrest of the families of workers who did not leave for Germany.

After the official life, let us deal with the real life of the country.

There was one dominating factor during this period: the progressive bringing into line of the free zone with the occupied zone.

Until April, 1942, refugees fleeing the Germans had always felt, upon their arrival in the southern zone, an extraordinary and complete feeling of deliverance.

After Laval's return this feeling diminished.

Swiss newspapers were forbidden, as they were the other side of the demarcation line; English films—however harmless they might be—were withdrawn.

The assassinations which were continuing in the occupied zone —on the 2nd May in the Clichy métro, on 20th September in the Rex cinema, and in the Marbeuf métro station—now began in the free zone: on the 4th September, a bomb burst in the "Relève" office at Montluçon.

German police scoured the free zone in search of members of the Resistance.

In the prisons of the southern zone, Germans interned for espionage or Frenchmen for treason with the Reich were released on the orders of the Head of the Government.

The Nazi oppression of the enemies of the regime was exercised in the free zone by the Militia. François de Menthon, Professor of Law at the Faculty of Aix, had never concealed his hostility to Pétain's Government. In order to punish him, the S.O.L. threw him into the Lake of Annecy. There were considerable repercussions; the members of the S.O.L. were brought before the Courts, Darnand intervened and Laval gave the order to stop the prosecutions.

But, above all, and this was a much more serious matter, equally atrocious scenes now began to take place in both zones. It was known that the Nazis were capable of tearing children from their mothers; but no one had imagined that Frenchmen could be contaminated by such barbarity: had not the Marshal on many occasions in his speeches invoked the traditions of Christian humanity which, according to him, inspired his Government?

But here, from official documents, is how children, whose only fault was to be born of foreign Jewish parents, were treated both in the occupied and the free zones.

In the first place in Paris: "In the second half of August, 1942, 4,000 children without parents were taken to Drancy. These children had been arrested on 16th July with their parents. Two days later, the parents and the children were sent from Paris to the camp at Pithiviers. There the children were separated from their parents. These children were aged between 2 and 12 years. . . .

"The children got out of the buses and the older ones immediately took the little ones by the hand and did not leave them while they walked the short distance to the huts. . . .

". . . Every night, from the other side of the camp, could be heard the continuous crying of the desperate children and, from time to time, the shouts and screams of children who had gone out of their minds.

". . . On the day of their deportation, the children were awakened at five o'clock in the morning. . . . It sometimes happened that a whole hut of 100 children, as if seized with a sort of panic-stricken and uncontrollable madness, would not listen to the calming words of the adults. . . . Then the police would be called and the children, screaming with terror, would be carried down in their arms. . . ."

There were similar scenes in the free zone when several thousand foreign Jews were arrested and handed over to the Germans.

Here are some lines from a report sent to the President of Cahors for the Regional Prefect Cheyneau de Leyritz by Captain of Gendarmerie Annou, commanding a convoy of 960 "transferred Jews" which left the camp of Gurs, on the 1st September, for the occupied zone: ". . . The special train of the 1st September transported a mixed group of men, women, children, old men, sick and disabled, who were abandoned to their fate from the moment of departure.

". . . The whole crowd lay on straw soaked in urine. The women were in despair not to be able to perform their natural functions without being gazed at by strangers. There were many who fainted from the heat and from the stench and who could not be attended to. . . .

"The spectacle this train presented made a very unfavourable impression on the non-Jewish French people who saw it, particularly in the stations."

At Nice, where in spite of the regular police, Darnand's S.O.L. sacked the synagogue (another Nazi proceeding!) there were also scenes of horror: in order to prevent the police separating her from her child, whom she was in process of suckling, a Jewish woman asked for and obtained a temporary delay: when the police returned the baby had been strangled and the mother had committed suicide after killing her child.

What did the population think of a Government which tolerated such infamies?

The Marshal, during his journeys, was always cheered, but his *entourage* had no illusions: criticism broke out again as soon as he had gone.

From now on, the vast majority of the country was hostile to the Government.

The methods employed against the foreign Jews in the southern zone aroused general indignation. The Church openly condemned this aspect of Vichy's policy.

On Sunday, 6th September, a letter from Cardinal Gerlier, Archbishop of Lyon, was read in every church in the diocese:

"The putting into execution of the measures of deportation which are actually taking place at this moment against the Jews is giving rise all over the country to such dreadful scenes that we have the imperative and painful duty of recording the protest of our conscience. We are in the presence of a cruel dispersal of families where no one is spared, neither the aged, nor the sick. . . ."

The Third Republic, which had been so much criticised in July, 1940, was now beginning to be regretted. On the 14th July, 1942, obeying a Gaullist order, the French more or less everywhere manifested their nostalgia for freedom.

On this day, 14th July, at Vichy, there took place a ceremony at which the Marshal and President Laval took part with several Ministers. But, also on this day, another ceremony, which had not been foreseen in the programme, took place in the provisional capital. Five hundred people demonstrated before the statue of the Republic against the Government and the regime. . . .

It was a silent demonstration no doubt, but it was significant.

For many French people, who had been Pétainists in July, 1940, de Gaulle had now become what the Marshal had been at first: the symbol of renascent France.

## CHAPTER 2

# PIERRE LAVAL'S TWO HUNDRED DAYS

(Internal policy—External policy)
(18th April, 1942–8th November, 1942)

IN 1942, Laval believed, even more firmly than he had in 1940, if that were possible, that he was the man predestined to save France.

He was persuaded that in 1941 Colette's bullet should have killed him: if he were still in this world, it was because "Providence had not wished him to die because he had to save France."

Still convinced of his infallibility, he thought it possible to offer Germany the collaboration of France for the destruction of Bolshevism and, at the same time, to maintain cordial relations with the United States. He expected a German victory in the east, and in the west a compromise peace signed between the United States and the Reich with himself as intermediary. Thus France would be no one's satellite and would find in the New Europe the rank and place she deserved.

In foreign policy, this was the extravagant mission Laval thought himself destined to fulfil: but it was far from exhausting his ambitions.

In internal politics, he imagined himself chosen to perform a complementary task: the promoting of new institutions giving the country the political framework necessary to its regeneration.

Laval denied that he was Nazi or Fascist. He was, nevertheless, the supporter of an authoritarian regime, which was not without affinities with those of Hitler and, above all, of Mussolini, a man of the Left who had gone over to dictatorship. Laval had wished "to construct Socialism in order to destroy unemployment, poverty and disorder". His authoritarian regime would be as popular.

"The individuality of nations," he declared on 5th June, 1942, in a broadcast, "must be respected. No country will be able to impose its customs, religion or regime on other countries. But, make no mistake, every regime will have one characteristic in common. They will be fundamentally popular, labour will everywhere have the priority it deserves, for without this every political institution would be in vain since it would lack the basic adherence of the masses."

Here again he agreed with Hitler and above all Mussolini for whom every regime had in principle to be based on the priority of labour. He talked of "a humanised National Socialism" or of "a new Republic, stronger, more muscular, more truly humane". The Paris weekly *Je suis Partout* from then on always derisively referred to Laval as the "muscular Republican".

Everything seemed set on preventing Pierre Laval's realising his ambitions.

In his internal policy, Laval was subjected to the constant opposition of the Marshal and his *entourage*. There was an irreducible divergence between Pétain's National Revolution and the muscular Republic.

Laval very soon realised that he could not create—except possibly after the end of the war—the "Republican" and authoritarian regime he desired.

"Internal politics are your affair, Monsieur le Maréchal."

Laval limited himself therefore to putting a brake on the National Revolution: on the pretext of remedying its defects, he forbade meetings of the Conseil National; he fought against the anti-Masonic measures. In spite of the zeal displayed by Admiral Platon, who was in charge of Masonic affairs, Laval stopped the prosecutions for false declarations, multiplied exceptions, and set up a "Commission des Dérogations".

As far as anti-Semitic measures were concerned, Laval did not adopt so positive an attitude: the dismissal of Xavier Vallat having been demanded by the Germans, Laval, on a suggestion from Abetz, appointed as Commissaire of Jewish Questions a shady lawyer, Darquier de Pellepoix: the Germans could count on his fanatical anti-Semitism: they knew that Darquier de Pellepoix satisfied his considerable monetary requirements by the clever management of funds realised on sequestrated Jewish property. Laval doubtless became somewhat concerned at having appointed Darquier de Pellepoix and, wishing to add an honest man to his office, he appointed Monier, a Councillor of State. But Monier refused to have anything to do with it.

During these two hundred days of Laval, Pétain made no great innovations in internal policy. A few laws concerning the family, which are still in force, were promulgated.

On the 25th August, 1942, a decree of the Marshal's, countersigned by Laval, put an end to the functions of the offices of the Parliamentary Assemblies to date from the 31st August.

Herriot and Jeanneney officially protested against this violation of the Agreements made on the 10th June, 1940, with the National Assembly.

Being unable to realise his internal policy, would Laval have better success during his "two hundred days" in his foreign policy?

Laval's first act on his arrival at Vichy was to inform Admiral Leahy that he was ready to serve as mediator between Roosevelt and Hitler, while Germany in the east devoted itself to the annihilation of Bolshevism.

On the 27th April, the American Ambassador saw the new Head of the Government.

"My policy," Laval declared, "is founded on reconciliation with Germany. Without this reconciliation, I can see no hope of peace, whether for Europe, France or even the world. I am certain that the Germans will be victorious but, even if they were to be defeated, my policy towards them would be the same, because it is the only one which is in the interests of ultimate peace."

Laval, pursuing his fixed idea of a compromise peace in the west and the annihilation of Russia in the east, proceeded to an indictment of what he called Anglo-Soviet Bolshevism, but told Leahy that he would never undertake any action against American interests, but that "it was no use counting on him for the triumph of Communism."

And he continued in these words, which some may find prophetic though, in 1942, they were profoundly shocking: he took no account either of the German occupation of France, nor of the danger the Nazi regime held for Europe.

"This war is a civil war of which Stalin will be the only victor if the democracies continue to fight the Reich. It is in the interests of the United States, as it is in that of Europe, that it should come to an end as soon as possible. . . . Among the heads of non-belligerent Governments, I am," Laval went on, "the only one with the exception of General Franco who during the war has had an interview with the Chancellor. I am in the best position to renew personal contacts with the Chancellor."

Laval was calling his suit: at least he thought so; he did not realise that his conversation with Leahy was a dialogue between the deaf. Or, at least, between people who were not speaking the same language.

That Roosevelt would ever agree to sign a compromise peace with the Reich with Pierre Laval as intermediary and engage in an anti-Bolshevist crusade was an eventuality so far from Leahy's mind, one that seemed to him so extravagant, that the following was the conclusion he drew from his conversations with the Head of the Government.

"Pierre Laval is not on our side in the war. . . . He is convinced that the interests of France are irremediably linked with those of Germany.

"His Government will go as far as it can in collaboration with Germany to assist in the defeat of what he calls Anglo-Soviet Bolshevism."

The results of this interview were that, in order to protest against the return of Laval to Vichy, Roosevelt, carrying out the terms of the Note of the 31st March, recalled his Ambassador; a snub which Laval had certainly not foreseen.

On the German side, Laval was no more fortunate, very much to the contrary indeed. He had persuaded the Marshal that, notwithstanding what Goering had said, his return to Vichy would save France from "Polandisation". But, on the 28th April, less than a fortnight after his appointment as Head of the Government, the Führer notified Pétain that a senior Commander of the S.S. was being sent to France, General Karl Oberg: "The French Government must immediately give the necessary orders to the French administration to collaborate effectively with the German administration under pain of the most serious sanctions."

Before this decision had even been implemented, the shooting of hostages increased: from the 20th April to the 24th May, there were 201 executions.

Moreover, on the 17th April, 1942, a romantic event occurred which put the Germans in the worst of tempers and thwarted Laval's policy still further. General Giraud, who was a prisoner with a hundred other generals and admirals in the Fortress of

Koenigstein, a veritable eagle's nest dominating the Elbe, escaped. In spite of his sixty-three years, his wounds and his height (he was well over six foot), Giraud, thanks to a rope some fifty yards long, which he had made with the assistance of another prisoner, climbed down the wall.

As soon as the escape was known, the whole of Germany was warned. In the towns and on the neighbouring roads, police posts were immediately set up to stop all passers-by over six foot. After the Statute of the Jews, there now seemed to have been promulgated a Statute of Giants. While the police stations and the party headquarters were being filled with tall men, Giraud, quietly sitting in a train to disguise his height, was carrying on a conversation with an S.S. officer covered with decorations. Talking fluent German, he was able to pass himself off as a Nazi: the Gestapo, who were carefully checking all papers, did not dare to interrupt a conversation with such a hero. Giraud succeeded so well that, on 24th April, having covered 500 miles, he arrived in Switzerland and could at last deploy his full height without further concern.

The German anger was limitless: the ex-Military Governor of Metz rejoiced in having incomparable prestige with the Führer and, though it was not unmerited, it was in fact based on mistaken identity. For Hitler, indeed, took him for General de Gaulle in his capacity as an author, having been much impressed by the latter's book before the war: *Vers une Armée de Métier*. Having discovered that de Gaulle had been serving as a Colonel under Giraud, he confused the two. Believing Giraud to be the author of the work, he screamed in fury: "That man is alone worth thirty divisions!"

Violating the Hague Convention, he announced collective reprisals against all French prisoners of war. There were to be no more negotiations on their behalf: none was to be repatriated, not even for reasons of health. There were even individual sanctions such as, in certain Oflags and for certain prisoners, the deprivation of the right to go to the library. The generals were subjected to special treatment; apart from those who had declared themselves fervent collaborationists, they were all placed in fortresses and shut up in casemates.

Were these the things Pierre Laval had in his gift: the S.S. in France, a diplomatic rupture with the United States and a worsening of the prisoners' fate?

Then Laval counter-attacked.

On the 30th April, he suggested to Giraud that he should return to prison in Germany.

Giraud was firm: "I told the President of the Council that his views were mistaken and that I refused."

Abetz came to the rescue. Giraud agreed to meet the Ambassador on the 2nd May at Moulins in the occupied zone, escorted by Darlan and Laval. "History," he said as reason for his refusal, "only offers one example of a general who voluntarily returned to captivity: that of the Roman Regulus. It's an unfortunate precedent. A barrel spiked with nails awaited him in Carthage." Instead of a barrel, Abetz promised him a luxurious suite in the Adlon Hotel in Berlin. It was wasted effort, Giraud refused. The most he would agree to was to return to Germany if the Germans freed all the French married prisoners, approximately 500,000 men.

Abetz thought the demand exorbitant and the interview came abruptly to an end.

Finally, Giraud agreed, on the 4th May, to write a letter to the Head of the State guaranteeing his loyalty:

"Monsieur le Maréchal,

"As a result of our recent interviews, and to remove any doubts there may be about my attitude, I wish to express to you my complete loyalty.

"You have been good enough to explain to me, as has the Head of the Government, the policy that you propose following towards Germany.

"I am in total agreement with you. I give you my word as an officer that I will do nothing in any way to hinder our relations with the German Government or to impede the labours with which, under your high authority, Admiral Darlan and President Pierre Laval are charged with accomplishing.

"My past is a guarantee of my loyalty.

"I pray you, Monsieur le Maréchal, to accept the assurance of my utter devotion."

On reading this letter, Laval declared himself satisfied: "I shall be able to pacify the Germans."

As for the Marshal, he must have thought how vain promises could be when, six months later, after the allied landings in North Africa, he received from Giraud a still unpublished letter with, on the envelope, the postmark "Marseille, 9th November, 1942."

"Monsieur le Maréchal,

"I promised you to defend the policy which you personally explained to me. I have kept this promise with my relations and my friends, without giving any sign in spite of the attacks which have been made upon me.

"I consider that today the hour is too grave to remain a spectator. I believe that there is an unhoped for chance for our country to come out of the war with honour. I have no doubts about your real thought, but, freer than you, I can go to prepare in Africa what you yourself will achieve in France.

"I have no other ambition than to see the resurrection of my country. I shall dedicate all my remaining strength and possessions to this task. I hope you will preserve your esteem for me and consider me always as one of your most devoted and respectful subordinates."

Reading the two letters together creates an oddly comic impression. In any case it shows that all Laval's efforts to minimise the General's escape in German eyes had in fact had only temporary results.

During this romantic episode, an appalling menace hung over France.

On the 6th May, the "Polandisation" of France seemed inevitable: General Heydrich, Supreme head of the Security Police, arrived in Paris to apply Hitler's instructions of the 28th April: he was "the Protector of Czechoslovakia", and had subjected that country to a reign of terror. His arrival in France was therefore a most sinister augury.

Moreover, he refused in threatening terms to receive Laval: "I am not here to negotiate, the French must obey."

He summoned the Secretary-General of Police to give him his orders:

"1. General Oberg is responsible for everything concerning public order and internal security in the occupied zone. He will carry out his duties with the assistance of the German police and the S.S. divisions.

"The French administration will obey the orders given them by the German authorities in conformity with the rights appertaining to the occupying power.

"2. The German police is organised in such a way that permanent collaboration may be established with the French administration.

"In order to fulfil the task expected of it, the French police must be reorganised. . . .

"Men must be appointed to the head of the Police force who have given evidence of their sincere adherence to a policy of Franco-German collaboration. They must be chosen from outside the administration and recruited, as must the personnel under their command, either from the political parties who have given their support to this end, or from a single party created from the various existing groups as has been successfully done in Germany."

Thus Heydrich demanded that the maintenance of order should be entrusted to the Parisian political parties who had sold themselves to the Germans: it was "Polandisation"!

Bousquet did not conceal his indignation:

"I do not know why I have been summoned at all, for it seems to me that the communication which has been made to me puts an end to the exercise of my functions."

Realising that Heydrich was in France for the first time, he did not hesitate to attack the German occupation.

"I am not a collaborator, I do not approve of your regime, I am a French official, who can be nothing but a French official and defend the Armistice Convention, and I tell you that you are making it impossible for us to remain in our posts. Why do you ask us to do things, why do you impose things on us which you Germans would not do yourselves? . . ."

With one of those somewhat spectacular gestures which the Germans affect, the S.S. General rose to his feet and stood to attention before Bousquet who couldn't believe his eyes, saying: "Monsieur Bousquet, I have learned a lot. You are courageous. You have spoken to me in a most moving way of the question of hostages and reprisals. I believe, indeed, that an end must be put to hostages and reprisals. But I cannot myself make that undertaking.

"All that I can say is this: that having come to Paris in order to put into execution an order of the Chancellor of Germany, I accept the fact that it should be deferred. I shall go and report to Berlin."

Thus the danger of "Polandisation" was temporarily delayed. For once, a representative of the Vichy Government had openly resisted: the German recognised that fact.

However, Laval found himself face to face with another difficulty which, it is true, was not due to the Germans but to the Allies.

On the 5th May, the British attacked Diego-Suarez, a dependency of Madagascar, so suddenly that the French Naval captain in command of a squadron, thought at first that it was a Japanese invasion.

The British, ill-informed, had feared a Japanese occupation of Madagascar. In fact, there was not a single Japanese in the whole island, with the exception of an old woman who had arrived there in 1902 and a woodcutter who had been living there for twenty years: an inoffensive couple one might suppose, who, indeed, did not even know each other.

The British Expedition was a fairly strong force: two troopships, a cruiser, four destroyers, twenty-three other ships, four squadrons of twelve aircraft each and assault troops to the number of 20,000.

Diego-Suarez resisted for forty-eight hours: it was a defence without hope, a fight merely for honour but which, alas, was bloody enough. On the 6th May, the Navy had 114 dead and missing; the Army and the Air Force 180 killed of which 56 were Europeans. The town was destroyed by bombing.

In spite of the delay Bousquet had obtained from Heydrich, everything went from bad to worse in Laval's relations with the Germans.

On the 11th May, Laval arrived in Paris in the hope of seeing Goering. After five days of waiting, he had to return disappointed to Vichy, convinced that the service chiefs were hostile to him and that Hitler was under their influence.

Refusing however to be beaten, he wrote to Ribbentrop, on the 12th May, a letter in which one passage is positively scandalous.

"In order to protect Europe from Bolshevism, which will destroy our culture to its very roots, Germany is prepared for a gigantic struggle—the blood of her youth will flow. I would like you to know that the French Government is not indifferent to the immense extent of the sacrifices to which your country has voluntarily consented, and, in your misfortunes, I should like to tell you, simply and spontaneously, that France is prepared, as far as she can and without any delay, to contribute her part to your efforts.

"Germany has mobilised the youngest and most active members of her population for the greatest battle in history, in consequence she needs men. I understand these necessities and I am ready to put my assistance at your disposal.

"Consequently, it is my desire that Frenchmen, and as many of them as possible, should take the place in your factories of those who are leaving for the Eastern front.

"The French are linked to their soil, but I know that they will be prepared to leave it for a task whose historical and national significance has been explained to them.

"I shall do my best in this direction and I ask you to help me to create a psychological atmosphere which will facilitate my action."

It was an extravagant letter, which paid no more heed to the Reich's attitude towards France, as it had been expressed, two months before, by Goering to Laval himself,[1] than had the verbal offer to Leahy taken the American attitude into consideration. Above all, it took no heed of one undeniable fact: the French dislike of working for the Reich. In disposing of his compatriots in this manner, Laval was betraying his duty as Head of the Government.

Ribbentrop's reply soon arrived: he appreciated "your good will as is proper" and concluded: "the Government of the Reich cannot naturally let itself be influenced in the future by hopes and assurances, but only by the deeds of French policy."

The German demands increased in every sphere:

"A doubling of the deliveries of food supplies, a transfer to Germany of a supplementary 30,000 railway trucks and 1,000 locomotives; the removal of 1,500 miles of railway lines, points and other accessories to Germany.

"A new programme for the production of high explosive which, in the unoccupied zone alone, required 35,000 new workers; the seizing of 200,000 tons of French and neutral merchant ships which were anchored in French Mediterranean ports."

At the same time, there was an increase in anti-Semitic measures. An ordinance of the 29th May, 1942, ordered all Jews over six years of age in the occupied zone to wear a yellow cloth star: this decision, against which Darlan had protested, provoked considerable feeling throughout France.

The French living in the east were also penalised. Forced labour was promulgated in Alsace-Lorraine on the 30th May.

[1] Cf. *supra*, p. 350.

And, above all, the S.S. were a continual and serious threat over the whole of France.

Heydrich, having been killed in Czechoslovakia on the 27th May, before his return to France (the S.S., by way of reprisal, blotted out two Czech villages), the Sturmbahnführer Boemelburg, assistant to General Oberg, went to Vichy at the end of May: since Heydrich was dead, the conversation he had had with Bousquet was null and void.

Boemelburg notified Laval of the instructions which Bousquet had persuaded Heydrich should not be immediately applied: that policing should be handed over to the militants of the Paris parties and that a Ministry of Police should be created which was also to be under their control, etc.

Finally he organised in Paris a violent campaign against Vichy. Doriot, supported by the S.S., organised meeting after meeting criticising the "*attentisme*" of Laval, and attacked Bousquet as guilty of protecting Freemasons, Jews and Gaullists. He openly put himself forward as a candidate for the Presidency of the Council.

To complicate the situation still further, the Fascist leaders renewed their action of June, 1940, and, taking advantage of the hardening German attitude towards France, loudly proclaimed their demands for Nice, Corsica, Savoy and Tunisia. Agitators in their pay created incidents in Nice between French and Italians.

In June, this catastrophic situation grew still worse: Sauckel arrived in France. His title of Gauleiter alone evoked the ordeals suffered by Czechoslovakia and Poland which had both been annexed to the Third Reich. Originally a stevedore in the port of Hamburg and a member, since its foundation, of the Nazi party, of which he was one of the high dignitaries, ex-Gauleiter of Thuringia, he had been for the last three months general plenipotentiary for the organisation of labour. An arrogant and inhuman brute, his functions were to recruit in the countries occupied by Germany millions of foreign workers to replace the workers who had left for the front in the factories of the Reich. In the first instance, he demanded immediately from France 350,000 workers, of whom 150,000 were to be metal workers: if the French Government gave him no satisfaction, he would help himself.

Laval refused to protest openly against the Nazi demands, but was always ready to negotiate.

He wanted France to take a more active part in the fight against Communism and went so far as to envisage the raising of an army of volunteers against the Russians in the prisoners-of-war camps. This project came to nothing and Laval contented himself with creating the Légion Tricolore, which was to take the place of the L.V.F., a private organisation.

Fearing, on the one hand, that Sauckel would requisition the labour of the occupied zone and desiring, on the other, that France should participate in the Reich's war effort, Laval encouraged French workers to expatriate themselves voluntarily to Germany.

On the 10th June, 1942, a confidential note was sent by the Secretary of State for Labour to the Divisional Labour Inspectors and Prefects, asking these officials to facilitate the creation of German recruiting offices, to collaborate with the German organisation, and to give the Germans, in strict confidence, a list of skilled workers with a note of their professional speciality and of their address in order to facilitate individual propaganda at their homes.

Sauckel was not satisfied with these measures. During the course of a disagreeable conversation which lasted several hours, he threatened Laval with a general requisition of the labour force. Nervously exhausted, Laval felt ill. Then, feeling better again, he had "an ingenious idea", the inauguration of the "Relève", that is to say that one prisoner should be returned for every three workers who left for Germany. This proportion was too small, for nothing prevented the Germans from including among those freed on account of the "Relève" the sick, whom they should in any case have sent back to France.

Laval believed, once he had persuaded Sauckel to accept the principle of the "Relève", that he had achieved a considerable success. The prisoners' Ambassador, Scapini, who was not included in the negotiations (he learned of the "Relève" on the wireless), considered that Laval was making a fool's bargain and that, unless there were sufficient guarantees, he was making the Government an accomplice of the Germans. Scapini protested to Laval against the "Relève", but without effect.

In order to announce to France that, thanks to his policy and *his* "Relève", prisoners would now be freed, and to appease Sauckel, Laval decided to make a speech which would be his political manifesto: his words brought him into general execration at least as much as did his actions.

Some of the few intimate friends to whom Laval showed the text of his speech were disquieted. Rochat, in particular, the only one who was not favourable to the Nazis, warned Laval: "You cannot make a speech like that without submitting it to the Marshal."

Laval, accompanied by Rochat, showed his speech to Pétain, who made but one remark: "You have no right to say: 'I believe in a German victory.' "

Rochat sighed with relief: the Marshal would forbid Laval to utter the phrase which the French must look upon as sacrilegious.

Alas, Pétain then proceeded to explain his objection: "No, you have no right to say 'I believe', you're not a soldier, so you can't make prophecies concerning the results of the war, you don't know anything about it!"

Laval, in obedience to Pétain, suppressed the tendentious verb: he would not *believe* in Nazi victory, he would merely *hope* for it. A civilian has the right to express his hopes. Pétain did not protest at what was, in fact, an aggravation of the scandal.

Here are the essential passages of the speech of the 22nd June, 1942, which was to create considerable feeling in France and incline public opinion to believe that Laval was an agent of the Reich:

"I want to restore normal and confident relations with Germany and Italy.

"A new Europe will inevitably arise from this war. We often talk of Europe. It is a word to which we are not yet very accustomed in France. We love our country because we love our village. As for me, a Frenchman, I could wish that tomorrow we should be able to love a Europe in which France will have a worthy place.

"In order to construct this Europe, Germany is in the process of fighting immense battles. She is compelled, with others, to make enormous sacrifices and she is not sparing of the blood of her youth: in order to throw her youth into the battle she must seek for it in factory and in field."

Then follows the phrase which French public opinion interpreted as a provocation:

"I hope for a German victory without which Bolshevism will shortly be dominant everywhere.

". . . When I tell you that this policy is the only one which can assure the status of France and guarantee her development in a peaceful future, you must believe me and follow me. . . ."

". . . I have been in power for two months. Events have not been in my favour . . . My presence in the Government may be taken as an earnest that there will be a considerable amelioration in our relations with Germany and that this will make the consequences of our defeat less hard for France during this period of armistice.

"My first thought was for our prisoners. . . ."

And Laval let it be understood that, owing to the folly of Darlan's Government, "the moment, when liberations in mass might have been made, was allowed to pass"; through Giraud's fault, and though he did not name him the allusion was obvious, Hitler had decided to suspend all facilities granted the prisoners. He naturally did not utter a word of protest against the fact that these reprisals were a violation of the Hague Convention.

"During this time," Laval went on, "in France . . . unemployment has been increasing. Many workers are without work while Germany is in urgent need of labour. In this situation there is a new hope for our prisoners."

Having explained the material advantages which would be given the volunteers to Germany, Laval concluded:

"Thus the process of the 'Relève' will begin. And so from now on between the most important human groups in our country a deep bond of sympathy will be established upon which our new society will be founded.

"Workers of France! It is to free the prisoners that you are going to work in Germany! It is for our country that you will go in great numbers! It is to allow France to find her place in the New Europe that you will respond to my appeal.

". . . You will receive the gratitude of the nation.

"This war, as I have already said, is not a war like other wars. It is a revolution from which a new world must emerge. You will have nothing to fear but everything to hope for in the regime which will be instituted here. A Republic younger, more human, stronger, will be born; Socialism will flourish all over Europe, and the form it will take in France will be shaped by our national character.

"Frenchmen, a great soldier, whose whole life is an example of sacrifice and discipline, presides over the destiny of our country. I am speaking to you this evening in his name. The Marshal would say to you that France has never allowed history to shape itself without her. And that one can only climb from the abyss of misfortune by the path of courage."

In spite of this last phrase, Pétain, horrified by the disastrous effects of Laval's speech on public opinion, refused his patronage to the "Relève". On the 26th June, the Marshal's office stopped the printing of a propaganda poster for the recruiting of workers for Germany which bore, without his authorisation, a phrase of Pétain's as a slogan.

Laval was assailed by new German menaces. In the first instance, they concerned the shooting of hostages. Stülpnagel decreed "the code of hostages". . . .

About the 25th June, the Germans demanded that full powers should be given to Darquier de Pellepoix; they demanded the handing over of all foreign Jews in the free zone, and concerted action against all the Jews in both zones whether French or not.

Darquier de Pellepoix energetically supported the German demands: as far as the Jews living in the occupied zone were concerned, Nazi hypocrisy asserted that the Reich wished once and for all to settle their position under acceptable conditions. Being unable, for military reasons, to leave the Jews in the occupied territories, the Nazis proposed to create a Jewish state in the region of Cracow. When anyone talked to them of the deportation or arrest of Jews, their philanthropic souls revolted: the only words they would use were "transfer" or "re-grouping". These were admirably chosen euphemisms to describe the extermination camps and the cremation furnaces.

On the 1st July a German conference was held in Paris at which the Supreme Chief of the Berlin anti-Semitic Police attended. It was to discuss the resistance of the French Government and Administration to the Nazi demands and to discover means of making them yield.

On Thursday, 2nd July, 1942, at Vichy, the Council of Ministers, much concerned at the German threat, immediately decided, with Pétain's approval, to make a distinction in the free zone between French Jews and foreign Jews; the former would remain under the sovereignty and protection of the French Government. As for the others, they decided to contest the figures that Darquier de Pellepoix had given the Germans and according to which these victims, who were to be abandoned to Nazi law, were of the number of 54,000.

Darquier de Pellepoix informed Dannecker of the "falseness" of Vichy. The Minister of the Interior had had the audacity to state that there were only 12,000 foreign Jews in the free zone, the statistics had been falsified on the orders of the Government.

On the 8th July, there was a new ordinance separating the Parisian Jews from their co-citizens: they had the right to enter shops during only one hour of the day, between eleven and twelve o'clock, which to all intents and purposes made the buying of food impossible; the "Aryan" housewives were forming queues in front of the shops from six till ten in the morning, and all the goods were sold. Most public places were forbidden them.

On the 12th July, Dannecker gave the order to arrest all French Jews in the occupied zone, which created consternation in Vichy.

On the 23rd July, Laval succeeded in making a "deal" with Dannecker: the Germans would not deport the French Jews from the occupied zone, but Laval would give the order to the French police to arrest all the foreign Jews in Paris. Furthermore, he agreed to deliver to the Germans 3,000 foreign Jews from the free zone, besides all German Jews.

When he was told of this agreement, Pétain was indignant: "This disgrace," he said to Laval on the 24th July, "must be stopped," and, in public, he referred to Darquier de Pellepoix in sorrowful tones as "Monsieur the Executioner. . . ."

These interventions by the Marshal did not, however, prevent 20,000 Jews being arrested by the French Police in Paris on the 21st–22nd July and being taken to Drancy, from where they were deported, nor, during the months of August and September, 10,410 Jews, refugees in the free zone (the majority being German), being handed over to the Germans.

Mathematically speaking, Laval may perhaps have saved human lives, but he associated the Vichy Government with a disgraceful business. "Our aim," said Abetz on the 8th August, 1940, "is to sow division in France." The indignation aroused in both zones by the atrocious scenes we have described contributed more to fulfil the Ambassador's wish than all the propaganda of the Paris press.

Amid all this, what had become of Pierre Laval's "mission"?

Suddenly, on the 19th August, without any previous indication, the war, for the first time since 1940, came to the soil of Metropolitan France.

Anglo-Canadian Forces made a landing at Dieppe.

It was a failure. The operation, called "Jubilee", did not succeed in reaching its objective. It failed temporarily to occupy Dieppe, establish a bridge-head for effecting demolitions, attack the airfield of Saint-Aubin, three miles from the town, and to silence the coastal battery of Arques-la-Bataille.

Nevertheless, the attack was not without practical results. It furnished the Allies with information concerning the technique of landings, which they found useful in June, 1944. Politically, it placed a new obstacle in Pierre Laval's way.

Two days after the attack on Dieppe, a telegram was sent from Vichy to M. de Grosville, who was a member of Benoist-Méchin's staff in Paris, with instructions to transmit it to Hitler.

Here is the text:

"Vichy 21st August 1942

"Monsieur le Chancelier du Reich,

"Following upon a conversation which I have had with President Laval and the latest British attack which has this time taken place upon our soil, I propose that France should participate in her own defence.

"If you approve in principle, I am prepared to examine in detail the form this participation should take.

"I pray you, Monsieur le Chancelier du Reich, to consider this initiative as the sincere expression of our wish to see France contribute to the protection of Europe."

Signed: "Pétain."

This extravagant telegram, which was contrary to the whole attitude adopted by the Marshal, may not really have been sent by him. Opinions on this point differ.

Every member of the Marshal's *entourage* denies having drafted this telegram. The Post Office official, who transmitted it, is a witness to its existence. The people in Paris confirm having received it.

The only possible hypothesis is that a spurious telegram, bearing the forged signature of the Marshal, was taken, unknown to his staff, to the Post Office at Vichy, which is not unlikely.

It is a fact that at this period the fanatical collaborators on several occasions did not hesitate to take the Marshal's name in vain as the facts show. A first example: at the beginning of

August, Commandant Lacroix, of the L.V.F., came to Vichy; the Marshal refused to receive him. Lacroix, furious, went away uttering threats. The day after his return to the capital, he published in a Paris newspaper an interview with the Marshal, who had in fact not exchanged a word with him, under the title: "Two hours with the Marshal". One need hardly say that Commandant Lacroix made Pétain utter extremely Germanophile phrases.

Another example, again concerning the Dieppe affair: the Paris newspapers published a congratulatory telegram from Pétain to Hitler. The members of the Marshal's staff were flabbergasted when they read it: who had extorted it from Pétain?

Following on the Dieppe affair, and in order to recompense the population of Dieppe for their behaviour, the Führer decided to liberate the 340 prisoners who were natives of that region.

Thus was due to the British, though extremely indirectly, the only concession Hitler gave in August, 1942.

Indeed, during that month, Franco-German relations became no better. In spite of the declaration made by Oberg to Bousquet, in spite of the agreements made between the two men recognising the independence of the courts, the police and the French administration, and the cessation of executions, 93 hostages were shot on the 12th August.

"Polandisation" still seemed threatening. On the 25th August, military service was instituted in Alsace and Lorraine for "young men of German race." On the 28th August, the classes 1940–1944 were called up and the families of defaulters arrested.

Sauckel had reason to be very displeased with the "Relève": instead of the 350,000 men whom he had asked for immediately, 12,000 volunteers left in June, 23,000 in July and 18,000 in August.

On the 29th August, Dr. Michel, Chief of Staff to the Administration of the Military Command, presented an ultimatum to the Delegate-General to Franco-German Economic Relations demanding that the French Government should take a number of police measures to compel the "volunteers" to sign engagements and, eventually, to mobilise them by force.

On the 1st September, the Germans threatened to apply to occupied France, where the great majority of the labour was, Saukel's ordinance of the 22nd August, which covered all the invaded countries and allowed the mobilisation of all male and female labour to be decreed, and a census to be made of the whole population between 18 and 55 years of age. It was a question "of obtaining the maximum yield for the war necessities of the Reich".

Faced with these violations of international law, Laval, as always, proposed negotiating.

On the insistence of Pétain he agreed nevertheless to protest officially against the institution of military service in Alsace. On the 3rd September, 1942, he handed Abetz an inclusive protest against: "the deportations, the colonisation of Lorraine, the incorporation of the inhabitants of Alsace and Lorraine in National Socialist formations and in the Army, the granting of German nationality to the inhabitants of Alsace and Lorraine and the violation of the religious status of Alsace and Lorraine."

But Laval absolutely refused to allow this protest to be made public: he only authorised the insertion of a paragraph containing two lines on this subject in a newspaper of the free zone, the *Nouvelliste de Lyon*. "We must not irritate the Germans at this moment. The negotiations concerning workers going to Germany are so difficult."

Faced with Sauckel's *diktat*, Laval, once again, neither wishing to oppose it nor admit himself beaten, thought he would get out of the difficulty by a process of evasion: instead of allowing Sauckel's ordinance to be applied in France, the French Government promulgated a law, on the 4th September, 1942, which reproduced the principal demands and, though it mitigated a few, compromised Vichy and rendered the Government in the eyes of public opinion accomplices of the occupying power.

This new legislation affected all men between the ages of 18 and 50, and all unmarried women between 21 and 35, making them subject to mobilisation for forced labour. To facilitate recruiting, it laid it down that the men had to prove that they were employed on essential work but that, in most cases, the employing and dismissing of workers should be subject to the previous authorisation of the Inspectors of Labour. On the other hand, the Government guaranteed certain advantages to the victims; on their return from Germany, they would have the right to go back to the employment they had had on their departure. For those who agreed to go voluntarily under the

"Relève" scheme, their families would continue to receive from their French employers half their salary over and above the pay they earned in Germany.

Before this law of the 4th September was promulgated, there was so violent an attack on it by four Ministers that Laval was compelled to take some account of it. Leroy-Ladurie, Admiral Auphan, Bonnafous and Gibrat declared: "Even if the danger of 'Polandisation' exists, we have no right to 'Polandise' ourselves."

In the end, Laval obtained the signature of the opposers in exchange for three promises:

1. The law would not be published so long as Germany had not officially declared that Sauckel's ordinance was applicable to France.

2. It would not be published so long as it was uncertain whether it applied to the departments of the Nord and the Pas-de-Calais as to the other departments.

3. No sanctions, however light, would be applied to the defaulters without another debate in the Council of Ministers.

Finally, Gibrat, to make this guarantee the more precise, succeeded in obtaining that all methods of enforcing the labour law could only take place as a result of decrees made by the Council of Ministers.

Thus Laval was caught between the unexpected resistance of four of his colleagues and the German pressure, pressure that was all the more effective for the fact that the Nazis knew everything that went on in the Council. On the evening of the 4th September, Krug von Nidda sent a telegram to Abetz informing him of the opposition which had arisen among the French Ministers. Who had given him the information?

In September, there was another catastrophe due to the British.

On the 10th September, the British, renewing their operations in Madagascar, landed at Majunga in order to take over the island. The French had but one aircraft and five battalions officered by officials. Laval authorised Governor-General Annet to negotiate. But the Germans, informed of the conversations, demanded that they be broken off. Laval yielded.

During the two months of fighting which followed, the French had but two killed. The British warned the French of where they were going to attack and the latter politely gave way.

The armistice was signed on the 6th November. Governor-General Annet obtained from the British a clause formally guaranteeing the maintenance of French sovereignty over the whole island.

At the same time, the French Government yielded to two German demands which would, before Laval's return, have been inconceivable.

A German observer was authorised to go on an intelligence mission on Empire territory to Dakar. A German control mission was authorised to enter the free zone to search out secret radio posts. Two infringements of French sovereignty which Vichy had been trying to protect for the last two years.

The peculiar observer, who arrived in French West Africa on the 21st September, 1942, with false French papers in the name of René Martin, was really a certain Moellhausen, "auxiliary scientific collaborator" to Rahn. Born in Smyrna in 1913 of a French mother and a German father, he thought more of filling his pockets than he did of his mission.

Boisson, realising at once what sort of man had been sent him by some anti-Nazi Providence, regaled him with false information and other gifts for which the observer was grateful though not necessarily their dupe.

As a result, Moellhausen, delighted with the tangible results René Martin had obtained, reported the success of his researches as follows:

"It is not worth while sending a Control Commission to Dakar; all is quiet. I have returned with the certainty that France will defend herself and also with the certainty that there is no landing to fear."

The German Control Commission in the free zone was a more serious matter.

Darlan and Bridoux, Secretaries of State at the Ministry for War, negotiated, in July, 1942, an increase of 50,000 men for the Army of the Armistice in exchange for giving the Nazis facilities for sending their Police, furnished with French identity cards, to search for secret wireless transmitters.

Bousquet, whose duty it was to furnish the necessary false papers, delayed until the end of August. But then Laval received an ultimatum from Rahn (the demarcation line would be crossed unless the documents were immediately received). "I demand that it should be done at once," he said to Bousquet. "There's nothing either I or you can do about it. So let's have a little peace."

On the 28th September, 280 German police, under the command of Boemelburg, crossed into the free zone. If a few were obstructed or delayed in the execution of their mission, most of them unfortunately succeeded only too well. In the Lyon region they discovered five secret wireless posts and made eleven arrests. At Marseille they found two posts and arrested ten men. At Toulouse they discovered two posts, arrested seven men and executed one on the spot.

CHAPTER 3

# FROM THE LANDINGS IN AFRICA TO THE SCUTTLING OF THE FLEET

(8th November, 1942–27th November, 1942)

On the 8th November, 1942, in spite of the surrenders to the Germans to which Laval had had to agree, Vichy was still, in principle at least, a sovereign Government. Did it not enjoy two of the essential attributes: an army and a free territory? Did it not possess two trump cards, of which all the belligerents agreed in recognising the importance: the Empire and the Fleet? Did it not maintain diplomatic relations with the majority of countries, both neutral and belligerent, allies or enemies of the Axis?

By the 27th November, 1942, there was no free zone any more, the Army had been disbanded, the Fleet scuttled and the Empire become dissident. How had such a reversal of fortune taken place in less than three weeks?

On the morrow of the armistice, North Africa had appeared to many Frenchmen, who would not admit of a German victory, as the base from which the army of revenge would set forth.

The African troops, commanded until November, 1941, by Weygand, to whom Juin succeeded, were profoundly anti-German and loyal to Pétain.

However desirous they might be of chasing out the invader, the one point on which the great majority of the High Command was in agreement was that no premature action should be undertaken, that the French forces destroyed in 1940 should be patiently reconstructed, and that the few troops left to France under the Armistice Convention should be secretly re-armed and thrown into the battle only when the allies were in a position to give France adequate support. This was what Weygand meant when he said: "If the Americans come with one division, I shall throw them into the sea; if they come with twenty divisions, I shall embrace them."

Nevertheless, a few men who disapproved of this official view, because they judged it too timorous, and who could not believe that Pétain, having desired an armistice in 1940, would now give the signal for revenge, set about plotting.

At the beginning of 1941, in Algiers, a first secret association, composed of Staff-Captain Beaufre, Commandant Faye and Lieutenant-Colonel Jousse, had made contact with Murphy, the American Consul. With the assistance of the U.S.A., they wished to build up secret armaments in order, if the eventuality arose, to be in a position to oppose an Axis attack in violation of the armistice. The plot was soon discovered. Beaufre was arrested and then released, having in the meantime innoculated with his conspiratorial virus Achiary, the police officer who, in fact, interrogated him.

The second plot was more considerable in scope; and was to have an undoubted influence on the preparations for the allied landing.

But it was a hazardous enterprise for a few Frenchmen, lacking all official standing, attached neither to Pétain nor to de Gaulle, to decide on their own initiative to negotiate with the American Government and make an alliance whose object was to assist in driving the Germans from France.

The first conspirator was Lemaigre-Dubreuil, a rich industrialist, who had always had a taste for financing political enterprises outside the big parties.

Before the war, he had been the leading spirit of a Ligue des Contribuables which, though touching the French at the sensitive point of their pocket-books, had nevertheless been unable to persuade them to reform either their institutions or their customs.

The second conspirator was Jean Rigault. In character a cold, didactic man, he had for long past inspired the actions of Lemaigre-Dubreuil and had always preferred to play the part of a Grey Eminence rather than take the leading role. He had always been loath to accept office under the government.

In Algiers, on the 25th November, 1941, Lemaigre-Dubreuil met Police Officer Achiary, who introduced him to one of the earlier conspirators, Lieutenant-Colonel Jousse. The latter, worried at having already burnt his fingers, nevertheless consented in the end to reconstitute the arms programme originally elaborated by Beaufre.

A month later, on the 20th December, Jean Rigault arrived in Algiers.

"Everything has still to be done, but everything is possible." That was his first conclusion. And, in the preliminary note he sent the American Consul, Murphy, he did not exaggerate the means at his disposal for the realisation of ambitions that appeared excessive: "We have nothing. We represent nothing. We shall gather our forces, and we shall work. Until then, we ask for nothing, except for one assurance: when everything is ready, you will come to help us."

On their side, the Americans, since December, 1941, had been considering a landing in North Africa. On the 11th January, 1942, in Washington, there was a staff conference at which the American Colonel, Solberg, an intelligence expert on French Africa, and a French Colonel of the Reserve, Aumeran, provided essential information for the success of the operation.

From now on, Lemaigre-Dubreuil's and Rigaut's programme was to bring Africa into the war by means of an exclusively French operation, the allies limiting themselves to sending reinforcements on D day, and to work with anyone who wished to chase the Germans from France, whatever their political opinions might be.

Unlike de Gaulle's policy, they had no intention, *a priori*, of rejecting Vichy. Their attitude towards the Government would depend on its reaction when faced with an eventual German aggression or with the success of the plot.

Murphy, without committing himself, approved their proceedings; Lemaigre-Dubreuil and Rigault set to work without a moment's delay.

At Easter, 1942, the directing committee of the plot, the "Group of Five", was set up. Besides Lemaigre-Dubreuil and Rigault, it included a diplomatist, Jacques Tarbé de Saint-Hardouin, Deputy-Secretary for Economic Affairs to Weygand's Delegation, who was familiar with all the administrative personnel in North Africa and was in Murphy's confidence, and Van Heck, the head of the Youth Camps in all North Africa, who had considerable opportunities for intelligence work and recruiting.

Finally, the fifth and most picturesque conspirator was Henri d'Astier de la Vigerie, a fervent Catholic who began every day with prayer but more often than not continued it with actions that were a somewhat liberal commentary on these pious preliminaries. An adventurer in the noble sense of the Italian Renaissance, quite unsuited to modern times, except perhaps for the exposure of its faults and the underlining of its inconsistencies, he was a man of energetic action. When he joined the "Group", he had already formed a secret commando in the neighbourhood of Oran. Later, in June, 1944, he was the first man to land on the south coast of France in command of an official troop of this nature.

Finally, the "Group of Five" had the assistance of a military adviser, Colonel Jousse.

In order to prepare for the liberation, the Five decided to proceed by stages and came to the conclusion that three successive phases were necessary: a phase of intelligence which involved a detailed study of military and administrative organisations; a phase of recruitment to make certain that there would be sufficient support for the conspiracy in Africa where, to all intents and purposes, no resistance movements existed; and a phase of operations.

In less than six months, the team had acquired impressive support. In April, General Béthouart, commanding the Casablanca Division, and Colonel Lorber, commanding the Bone Sub-Division came over to their side; in August, General Mast, Chief of Staff to the Xth Corps, who was a member of the conspiracy, was appointed to the command of the Algiers Division, a position in which he could render them inestimable service. The Five created a network of accomplices all over North Africa, which fact the Americans came in the end to appreciate.

But who was to be leader of the conspiracy? De Gaulle? It was impossible: the army was loyal to Pétain and had not forgotten the Syrian war. Weygand? He would be ideal: the troops would rally to him with enthusiasm; the English would be prepared to treat with him; had not Churchill, in December 1940, encouraged him to "raise the standard of rebellion"? Unfortunately, Weygand did not respond to the arguments of the Americans and the conspirators. To Lemaigre-Dubreuil, and later to the diplomatic envoy MacArthur, who gave him a letter from Roosevelt offering to collaborate in the liberation of

France, Weygand gave a categorical refusal: "I'm too old," he said, "to become a rebel."

Giraud's escape got the conspirators out of their difficulties. The ex-Military Governor of Metz enjoyed considerable prestige, which it was believed would assure him the obedience of the army.

Sounded by Lemaigre-Dubreuil, then by Rigault in May, 1942, Giraud did not conceal his longing to take up the struggle against the Germans once more.

The Five's plan did not commend itself to Giraud because it entailed the abandonment of Metropolitan France. Moreover, so the General declared, the Americans had no business to intervene in North Africa where the Germans had not set foot; they should limit themselves to assisting the French Army to re-arm. According to Giraud, it was in Metropolitan France itself that the army of revenge must rise; France must enter the war with her own forces: at the most, one Anglo-Saxon corps might land to help her.

In spite of his reservations, Giraud accepted the command of the operation, whether it was to be limited to North Africa, as the Americans desired, or whether it comprised Metropolitan France as he himself wished.

In June, 1942, the Americans, impressed by the adherence of Giraud, consented to negotiate with the Group of Five. Colonel Solberg, Roosevelt's personal envoy, told the conspirators that America had now decided to take action and recognised them as the only people who were in a position to treat with America on all questions relevant to an intervention in North Africa.

But, in spite of Solberg's definite attitude, there is much evidence to show that the Americans, fearing indiscretions, only placed a very limited trust in the French conspirators.

It was thus that, when Roosevelt and Churchill decided in July on a landing in North Africa, which was to be called Operation "Torch", the French were only told some three months later.

Moreover, though the Five had been assured that the only allied forces to take part in the landing would be American, Roosevelt had finally agreed that "Torch" was to be a combined Anglo-American operation with British contingents.

Another allied decision which showed their lack of consideration for the French conspirators was that, though Giraud had made it a condition *sine qua non* of his taking part in the plans of the Five that he should be appointed to the supreme command of the troops engaged in the operation, this post was given to General Eisenhower. Giraud was limited to commanding the French troops.

During September, the Americans maintained their reserve. The French still did not know that "Torch" was in preparation. In spite of their promises, the Americans did not send arms to the irregular formations organised by d'Astier de la Vigerie.

On September 22nd, Roosevelt gave Murphy precise and confidential instructions on the attitude to be adopted towards the Five. Murphy was to present the Five with the accomplished fact. He confirmed that the landing was to be an operation mounted by the Americans: only sovereignty and civil administration would be guaranteed to the French. All military resistance would be destroyed. Conversely, the eventual assistance of French forces would be accepted. The United States would provide the necessary financial support. It was made clear that the expedition would be strictly American and would not include any participation by General de Gaulle's forces. The French would be given twenty-four hours' warning and, at Murphy's discretion, be informed of the approximate sites of the landings.

In October, Murphy, on his return from Washington with instructions, told Lemaigre-Dubreuil that the landing had been definitely decided on and, as evidence of its importance, quoted figures which, however, turned out to be incorrect. He did not reveal the points on which Roosevelt's instructions differed from the French demands.

On the 22nd October, there was a secret meeting at Cherchell, in a villa by the sea, between American officers, who had arrived by submarine, and the French soldiers who had joined the conspiracy: on the American side were General Clark, head of the delegation, General Lemnitzer, Colonel Holmes, Captain Wright of the Navy, and two other officers of the Navy and Air Force. There was one civilian, Murphy.

On the French side were General Mast, head of the delegation, Colonel Jousse, Commandant Dartois of the Air Force, and Captain Barjot of the Navy. There was one civilian, Rigault.

It was a melodramatic meeting, interrupted by alarms. In

spite of Murphy's personal friendship with the conspirators, the Americans did not play an entirely frank game.

Ten days after the meeting at Cherchell, the conspirators learned that the landing was to take place during the night of the 7th–8th November. The Five were furious, for it gave them insufficient time to mobilise their resources for the neutralising of resistance by the army and the administration.

Giraud was also indignant, for not only was he expecting to take command of the operation, but counted on a bridgehead being established in the free zone at the same time as the landings in Africa.

Nevertheless Giraud agreed to go to Algeria but, first, he insisted on passing by Gibraltar in order to see Roosevelt and decide the question of the command to which he could not believe that he would not be appointed.

During the night of the 4th–5th November, a British submarine stood off Le Lavandou to pick him up. Before leaving France, Giraud did not omit the curious courtesy of assuring the Marshal of his loyalty. A storm prevented the submarine surfacing. It was only twenty-four hours later that Giraud was able to embark. Owing to the detour by Gibraltar, it was impossible for him to be in Algiers to rally the French Army by H hour.

On the 5th November, at 8 o'clock in the morning, Admiral Darlan left Vichy by air for Algiers because his only son, Alain, had been suffering from poliomyelitis since the 13th October and seemed to be dying.

Two days later, contrary to the doctor's expectations, Alain Darlan was out of danger. The Admiral intended sending him to Paris, where he would be better looked after than in Algiers. He himself intended to return to Vichy on the 9th or 10th November.

He had no idea whatever of the imminent landings.[1]

During the night of the 7th–8th November, 290 British and American ships, divided into three groups, transporting 110,000 men, reached the coast of North Africa.

The conspirators prepared to go into action, taking no account

[1] The evidence of all those who saw Darlan during these days is precise on this point.

of Darlan's presence who, like Juin, was to be faced with the accomplished fact.

In Morocco, General Béthouart, commanding the Casablanca Division, had been warned that the landing would take place at 2 o'clock in the morning; the Americans lacked the grace to tell him that it had been postponed till 5 o'clock. Moreover, the American plan, which had not been revealed to Béthouart, was exactly the opposite to what the General expected.

The Americans, paying no attention to the French proposals, chose to attack Casablanca and Fédala frontally without taking into account the possibilities of peaceful penetration afforded them by the conspirators.

Kept in complete ignorance of the American decision and the postponement of the time of landing, Béthouart, at midnight, announced the imminent arrival of the Americans to Noguès, Resident-General in Morocco, who refused to obey Giraud. Being unable to convince the Resident-General, Béthouart arrested him, and ordered the troops to help the Americans. Unfortunately, Noguès had a private telephone; he called Admiral Michelier at Casablanca and ordered him to resist.

At 5 o'clock in the morning, the Americans had still not arrived; troops, loyal to Vichy, warned by Michelier, arrived at Rabat and arrested Béthouart.

At the very moment the Americans were beginning to land, Noguès was back in his command and the conspirators in prison.

At Casablanca, General Destrée, another conspirator, learning of the mishap, summoned his officers: "We have had a splendid dream, Gentlemen, now we must forget it."

The troops loyal to Nogués, therefore, resisted the Americans. In two days, thirteen French ships were sunk, while 15,000 French and nearly as many Americans were killed.

At Oran, there was a similar setback to the conspirators, who were not even able to make efficient or complete use of their forces. There, the setback was not due to the lateness of the Americans, or to their casualness, but to the "initiative" of one of the conspirators. On the 6th November, without telling his "accomplices", he had approached General Boisson, who put him in close arrest.

There, too, the troops resisted the Americans.

At Algiers, during the night of the 7th–8th, at half an hour after midnight, the conspirators set in motion their plans to neutralise resistance to the landings: volunteers, much less numerous than the Five had hoped, seized the tactical points in the town: the Central Commissariat, the Préfecture and the Post Office. . . . They arrested General Koeltz, commanding the corps, and isolated the principal military commanders in their houses.

By 2 o'clock in the morning, the operation was over: they awaited the Americans. Unfortunately, the latter had landed at Sidi-Ferruch an hour late, at 1.30. They could not reach Algiers in time to reinforce the conspirators.

At 3.30 in the morning, a platoon of Gardes Mobiles attacked the headquarters of the conspirators. Was the *putsch* to fail?

Owing to this fact, the Americans were obliged to treat with the Vichy representatives.

Since the French forces remained loyal to Pétain, it was Darlan alone, by chance in Algiers, but the representative of the Marshal and Supreme Military Commander, whom the army would obey: it was therefore necessary for the Americans to obtain an order from the Commander-in-Chief to cease all resistance.

In General Juin's drawing-room, Murphy, at the last moment before the landings of the allied troops, informed the Admiral of what was going forward.

At that decisive moment, when it depended on him, and him alone, whether the Americans were received as allies or invaders, Darlan did not conceal his fury at not having been informed of the American plan.

"I thought the Americans were less stupid than their British friends, I see I made a mistake!" he cried, scarlet with anger. Then, having walked up and down the room for a quarter of an hour without a word, the Admiral refused to issue the orders Murphy and Juin required. "I have given my oath to Marshal Pétain and, for the last two years, I have been telling my sailors and the country to unite behind the Marshal. I cannot break my oath."

The most Murphy could obtain was that Darlan would telegraph Pétain and ask for instructions.

At Vichy, the news of the landings was received on the radio at two o'clock in the morning. At four o'clock, the American chargé d'affaires, Tuck, handed in at the Hôtel du Parc a letter to Marshal Pétain from President Roosevelt. Roosevelt stated in it that the American landings in Africa had, as their aim, to prevent an Axis aggression against the French Empire. Then the President of the United States went on to assure Pétain, whom he styled Head of the State of the "French Republic", that: "I do not need to tell you that the ultimate and most important aim is the liberation of France and her Empire from the Axis yoke. . . . I do not need to reaffirm that the United States of America have no ambitions of conquest over any territories whatever."

It was not until seven o'clock that Dr. Ménétrel awakened the Marshal to give him the letter and announce the landings. "I dreamed about it during the night," replied Pétain imperturbably.

Having read Roosevelt's letter, he approved, with similar calm, the reply Ménétrel submitted to him.

"It is with surprise and distress that I have learned this night of the aggression of your troops against North Africa. I have read your message. You put forward pretexts which there is nothing to justify. You attribute to your enemies intentions which have never been transformed into action. . . .

"I have always declared that we would defend our Empire if it were attacked. . . . We are being attacked, we shall defend ourselves. This is the order I am giving."

Were the dice thrown? Had Pétain chosen to resist the allies whatever the consequences?

Less than an hour after having sent Roosevelt this negative reply, Pétain, at 8.45 a.m., telegraphed the Admiral the instructions for which he had asked on Murphy's suggestion. They were in a very different tone.

"I have received your message through the Admiralty and am glad you are on the spot. Take what action you like and keep me informed. You know that you have my complete confidence."

There was no longer any question of opposing the Americans. Darlan had been given a blank cheque and could use it as he judged best.

There was a striking difference between the two messages, the official reply to Roosevelt and the orders sent Darlan. The Marshal wished to appear to the Germans, to whom naturally the first communication would be made known, as having decided to oppose the aggressors. On the other hand, the telegram to Darlan left the latter free to negotiate with the Americans without having to deny his oath of loyalty.

Thus, faced with the extraordinary event of the American landings, Pétain continued to finesse.

During the whole of this day, he took only one action. He summoned Weygand to Vichy; but it did not alter the situation since Weygand advised strong measures which the Marshal refused to take: leave for North Africa, sign an armistice with the Americans, declare war on the Axis and give orders to the Army of the Armistice to resist the Germans if they crossed the demarcation line.

The Marshal, still obsessed by the idea that it was his duty to protect the population of Metropolitan France against the occupying power, would not take such decisive action.

Laval pursued the same policy of waiting but for other reasons: the Americans might well have landed, the Vichy Government might well be in process of losing its principal trump card, the Empire, but Laval, always the same, continued to negotiate; he showed no alacrity to satisfy the German demands whether military or political.

Early in the morning, Krug von Nidda demanded that he should sever diplomatic relations with the United States.

Laval showed no willingness to yield to this ultimatum: how could he obtain his supreme goal of serving as mediator between Hitler and Roosevelt, if he broke with America?

Then, turning to his own account the tactics which had so often served Darlan, he decided to put a condition *sine qua non*, which the Germans were bound to consider unacceptable, to the breaking off of relations: as Roosevelt, in his letter to the Marshal, had promised to maintain the integrity of the French Empire, Laval told the Germans that, as a condition of breaking with America, the French Government demanded a similar guarantee from them.

It was a demand which would clearly present Hitler, as the Duce's ally, with many problems. It was certainly one which France was in no position to put forward on the 8th November. Laval, doubtless, had no illusions concerning the granting of this guarantee.

And, indeed, the Germans did not even reply to the untimely demand.

But, at 2.50 p.m., Krug von Nidda came back to the charge with stronger arguments; he brought Laval a message from the Führer, offering France a total alliance with the Reich and demanding that she should enter the war: "Faced with the Anglo-Saxon aggression, the breaking off of diplomatic relations cannot be considered as sufficient and it is necessary to proceed to a declaration of war against the British and Americans. If the French Government are prepared to take up so strong a position, Germany is ready to march at its side for better or for worse (*Durch Dick und Dünn*)."

After consulting Pétain, Laval, that same day, refused, which much surprised the Nazi diplomatist. The latter then informed the President that the Führer was expecting him at Munich the next day at 11 p.m., and that Otto Abetz had also been summoned.

At 6.15 p.m., a Council of Ministers limited itself to declaring that America, by carrying the war to French territory, had by that very fact broken off diplomatic relations.

While Laval was manoeuvring at Vichy, Darlan in Algiers was trying as usual to reconcile the irreconcilable, to play off the Americans against the Germans.

Early in the morning, the Germans had proposed to Laval that they should put the Luftwaffe at the disposal of the French to repel the invaders.

Laval, far from anxious to accept the offer, which ran the risk of entailing a declaration of war against America, took refuge behind Darlan, whose competence could not be questioned and who was, moreover, on the spot.

Darlan certainly took care not to refuse, but his consent, in fact, amounted to a refusal: he agreed that the Luftwaffe should come into action, but on condition that the Axis aircraft should remain based in Sicily and Sardinia. These bases, however, were so far from the new theatre of operations that, in practice, they were useless. Moreover, Darlan, to minimise still further, if it were possible, this illusory concession, stipulated that the German aircraft should only attack the transports and Naval forces outside Algiers, thus forbidding them to take action against the troops who had landed.

The Germans were certainly not taken in by so obvious a manoeuvre. At 2 p.m., they replied angrily: "The affair presents an analogy with Syria where the French Government desired the collaboration of the German Air Force with the limitation that it remained based in Greece or Crete. . . . Collaboration can only be really effective if German aircraft are based in North Africa."

At midnight came an ultimatum: "O.K.W. deem support of Axis air forces from Sicily and Sardinia lacking in effect. They judge it necessary to base these forces at Constantine and Tunis. They consider that by putting limitations to their offer the French Government does not appear desirous of opposing the American attack with the requisite resistance. O.K.W. expect agreement within one hour from the French Government to base aircraft at Constantine and Tunis. If this agreement is not received within the time indicated, O.K.W. will take such measures as are deemed necessary."

A quarter of the permitted delay had barely elapsed when, at a quarter past midnight, Laval, on his own authority, accepted the *diktat*.

Thus, twenty-four hours after the allied landing, the Vichy Government, faithful to its tactics of delay, had still not taken up a definite position: it had certainly broken off diplomatic relations with America; and it had officially ordered resistance to the invaders; while the German aircraft come to help the French repel the aggressors had begun to land on the Tunisian airfields. By the evening of the 9th November, in spite of the protests of Admiral Estéva, Resident-General in Tunisia, one hundred bombers of the Luftwaffe had landed in Africa.

But, conversely, and parallel with these decisions which were favourable to the Germans, Admiral Darlan, heir-presumptive to the Marshal, had signed an armistice with the Americans for Algiers, where the French could easily have continued to defend themselves; and Laval, Head of the Government, had refused "the generous offer" of the Führer to enter into a definitive and total alliance with France.

Wishing to play off the two belligerents against each other—the invaders of the Empire and the occupiers of Metropolitan France—Vichy succeeded in arousing equal dissatisfaction in both camps.

Hitler decided to tolerate French equivocations no longer. Since even Laval had rejected the offers of an alliance, the Führer took irrevocable decisions: the total occupation of France, a landing in Corsica and a bridgehead in Tunisia.

At Algiers, in the meantime, the American General Ryder warned Darlan that, if the French did not immediately cease all resistance, an "extremely severe" armistice would be imposed on them.

On the 9th November, the invasion of the free zone appeared imminent.

The Army of the Armistice, however, was preparing to fight again. But its strength was much reduced: it had never succeeded in recruiting the 100,000 men authorised by the Armistice Convention: the eight divisions of which it was composed, with their horse-drawn artillery and their infantry who could only move on foot, were anachronistic, capable only of keeping internal order. No doubt, the general staff of the army had secretly prepared a plan of mobilisation which, when the time came, would allow of tripling the number of divisions and improving to some extent their armament.

But these efforts and expedients did not suffice, on the 9th November, 1942, to make the Army of the Armistice capable of acting alone and on its own resources against the Wehrmacht. The most it could hope to do was to serve eventually as the spearhead to an allied landing in France. Moreover, the staff was anxiously waiting for Giraud to persuade the Americans to make this second landing on the Mediterranean coast.

For this eventuality, everything had been foreseen: movement orders for French formations to proceed to mountainous zones which would constitute natural strong points for defence: the Jura, the Massif Central, the Alps, Montagne Noire, the Pyrenees. The staff would have its headquarters at Mende, which would be tactically central. Camouflaged depots of war materials were prepared near the centres of resistance; the recall of the reservists had been arranged, which would allow of reinforcing the formations already in existence and the creation of new ones.

This plan began to be put into execution during the night of the 8th–9th November. Believing that the African landings would be accompanied by the arrival of allied troops in the free zone, General Verneau, Chief of the General Staff, sent to every Divisional Commander, in secret code and unknown to the Germans, a signal ordering the troops to march. The Deuxième Bureau expected the Germans to cross the demarcation line at midnight on the 9th November. The 9th November was the last day of quiet before the storm.

At Vichy, Pétain took no initiative except for his telegram to Darlan. Laval had left for Berchtesgaden in answer to Hitler's summons.

He had an appalling journey. . . . "During the long hours spent crossing the Black Forest, my mind was continually concerned with one question: what reprisals would the Germans take?"

Laval now decided to refuse at all costs the co-belligerency he had so much desired in 1940 and was prepared for the worst. Would he ever return to France? Fearing that Hitler had in reserve for him the fate of Chancellor Schuschnigg, he had provided himself with a phial of cyanide of potassium, the very one he was to use four years later in his determination to avoid a French firing squad.

In spite of all he had personally at stake, Laval was determined to fight to the end to avoid the total occupation of France. . . . In this determination he showed no lack of courage.

In Algeria, Darlan, in agreement with Pétain, continued to finesse. Without breaking with the Americans, he wished to give the Germans no excuse to occupy the free zone.

Throughout the day there was a continual exchange of telegrams between Algiers and Vichy of which the least that can be said is that they were not of a nature to encourage the taking of decisions.

Pétain neither approved nor disapproved the surrender of Algiers. To Darlan's telegram announcing it, he replied, at 6.30 p.m., that, in the absence of Laval, who had been summoned to Berchtesgaden, "No negotiations had been envisaged," and that "the orders given . . . remain in force." This was far from taking energetic measures to prevent armistice negotiations. Darlan entered into the game: "My intention," he cabled, "is not to negotiate, but to listen and report, with the one exception however of the particular case of Algiers."

At the same time, he sent the Marshal a report which was also a masterpiece of prevarication.

With his accustomed clarity, Darlan succeeded in sowing confusion in ten paragraphs.

A few hours after sending his report to Vichy, the Admiral was asked by General Ryder to sign a general armistice. The General did not know Darlan: on this occasion, to gain time, he sent the Marshal a telegram of eighteen paragraphs submitting the American conditions and a second telegram of three paragraphs formulating his own advice: twenty-one paragraphs, of which this was the conclusion:

"We can do no other than refer to the Marshal and assure him that his orders will be carried out."

To make things still simpler, Giraud landed in Algiers on the 9th.

The circumstances of his arrival underlined the failure of the Five conspiracy of which he was the leader: instead of making the expected triumphal entry into the town from the first moment of his arrival in Africa on Blida airport, where his aircraft landed, he was baffled and almost insulted by the commander of the base.

During the night of the 9th–10th November, the French troops in the free zone began to march: the first stage of their advance to their battle positions.

The staff left Vichy and established its provisional headquarters at Rapine Farm, near Leroux, a little town thirty kilometres from the Allier.

General Verneau spent the night there, waiting for the two pieces of information that would justify his operations: the entry of the Wehrmacht into the southern zone and the landing of the allies on the Mediterranean coast.

The following morning there was still nothing except for an unexpected piece of news from Vichy: General Bridoux, Minister for War, in a violent rage, vituperated against "the seditious officers" who had led the army into dissidence, threatened to attack Rapine with the Garde Mobile and demanded the immediate evacuation of the new headquarters.

The 10th November was the decisive day, the last moment at which Vichy still had the power of choice. In twenty-four hours it would be too late: the total occupation of France by the Wehrmacht would put an end to her independence.

"I have lived," said an important witness, Admiral Auphan, "few such dramatic hours as during that morning of the 10th

November, with, on the one hand, Darlan and the Americans negotiating in Algiers, on the other, Laval at grips with Hitler in Munich, and in the middle, at Vichy, an old Marshal, beset with telegrams and objurgations, seeking a solution."

What could the Head of the State do? He might have joined Darlan immediately, become head of the dissident movement and taken command of the French armies who were renewing the struggle. The Marshal was not lacking in advice to do this from his intimate friends and colleagues. Successively, General Héring, General Serigny, Trochu, General Georges, Lehideux, Colonel de Gorostarzu, Robert Gibrat, Bouthillier and General Weygand pressed him to leave for Africa. An aircraft was ready waiting, guaranteeing him a quick and safe journey that would have been followed by what an apotheosis! But the Marshal replied to everyone that, having taken an oath to the French people not to abandon them, he would never quit Metropolitan soil: "A pilot must stay at the helm during the storm. He cannot leave the helm. If I had left, France would have suffered the same regime as Poland. . . . You do not know what the Polish regime was like. France would have died of it."

Apart from Algiers, there were two possible choices open to the Marshal, if he did not wish to be merely the hostage of the occupying power. Either he could do what, in his eyes, would have amounted to an almost similar defection as going to Africa: that was to renounce power, put an end to the Government and retire to a château where he would have been virtually a prisoner like the King of the Belgians, while confiding to the Secretary-Generals of the Ministries the administrative life of the nation. But in Pétain's view this solution would inevitably lead to the Nazis constituting a government in the pay of the Germans and presided over by Déat or Doriot.

With both departure for Africa and abdication set aside, the only solution was to remain where he was and openly resist the Germans. But this was an attitude which, for two and half years, Pétain had never adopted: could he, in this final hour, in these critical circumstances, cross such a Rubicon?

He tried to—at least during the day of the 10th November.

On the 10th November, at 10 o'clock in the morning, Clark, Darlan and Juin met in Algiers. The American demanded the signature of a general armistice valid for the whole of North

Africa. Darlan was at first evasive, then said that he could not make a decision without knowing the Marshal's intentions.

"What the Marshal thinks doesn't matter a damn to me," said Clark. "You know very well that forty-eight hours ago Vichy broke off diplomatic relations with the U.S.A. If you won't sign, Giraud is prepared to."

"The army doesn't recognise General Giraud. If I won't sign, no one will sign."

"Very well, we shall arrest you," said Clark, "that's my last word."

"I don't care a damn," Darlan replied.

General Juin realised that a conversation carried on in this tone would get nowhere. He took Darlan aside and lectured him: "What will happen," he said, "if, in a few hours' time, as is quite likely, an official message arrives from the Marshal who, either of his own accord or under German pressure, disavows you for having signed an armistice at Algiers? In that case, you will represent no one, either in the view of the Americans or in that of the French in Africa. And Giraud will have carried the day. Sign, sign, sign quickly before the danger materialises."

Convinced by this argument *ad hominem*, Darlan quickly signed. Within a few minutes everything had been arranged. It was a purely military agreement without any political clauses. Juin, continuing to play the part of a *deus ex machina*, took advantage of this first successful manoeuvre to attempt a second: interpreting the clauses of the agreement in the widest sense, he immediately gave the order to all the French troops in Africa to make ready to resist the Germans.

Alas for the Admiral of the Fleet, the ink was hardly dry when there arrived from Vichy a message from the Marshal enjoining him to continue the struggle: "I gave the order to defend Africa. I maintain this order, Philippe Pétain."

It was a hard blow. "I'm a lost man," cried Darlan. There was another conference with Juin: the two officers decided that the Admiral should reply to the Head of the State that he would give himself up in person as a hostage to the Americans, which in fact signified nothing, but might furnish the Marshal with an argument against the Germans.

"I have received your message. I have countermanded the order [he did nothing of the kind] and have given myself up as a prisoner."

Having thus also made the gift of his person, Darlan awaited the German reaction, and also Pétain's.

It was then that the Marshal, in a conspiratorial manner, unveiled his real intentions and showed, somewhat late in the day, that he was making preparations to resist.

On signature of the armistice, the Germans had demanded that they should be given all the secret codes used by the Government and the French Army. But one of them had been concealed: it was a personal code of Darlan's, established after the armistice, and which the Admiral, anxious not to reveal its existence, only used on very rare occasions. This top secret code was known only to two officers: at Vichy by Captain Joannin of the Navy, at Algiers by Admiral Battet.

On the 10th November, Captain Joannin considered the circumstances grave enough to allow of his revealing the existence of this secret code to Admiral Auphan. The latter saw a providential means of establishing communications with Darlan which would be secret from both the Germans and Laval; he immediately informed the Head of the State; and that very day, at 3.15 p.m., a singular conspiratorial meeting took place in the Marshal's office. The head of his office, Jardel, his medical attendant and secretary, Ménétrel, as well as Admiral Auphan, were present. A message was sent to Darlan:

"You have all my confidence. Act for the best. I entrust to you the interests of the Empire."

There was an immediate reply from Darlan: "I understand and I am happy," which was transmitted by the same means.

From then on, the situation at Algiers was clear: Darlan knew that the Marshal approved his changing sides in favour of the Americans.

Vichy also seemed to be becoming anti-German. Laval might well telephone, demanding that no definite attitude be adopted before his return from Germany, but the Marshal, taking advantage of the absence of his Prime Minister, was preparing to make decisions.

Resistance could be shown openly in two different ways: by the political gesture of dismissing Laval, a new 13th December, or by military measures: the French Army of the Armistice opposing the entry of the Wehrmacht into the free zone, the Fleet sailing for North Africa. The Marshal considered both these plans during the course of the 10th November.

It was thus that, on the evening of the 10th November, the last on which he still exercised power over a free territory, the Marshal at last determined to take energetic measures and endeavour to make use of his last chance to rally French public opinon unanimously to his side. With no intention of either leaving France or renouncing power, he set about taking the leadership of the Resistance. All those about him, who had agreed to serve him out of patriotism, from Weygand to Admiral Auphan, from Robert Gibrat to Jardel and Lavagne, anxiously awaited the gesture that would justify their choice.

Though Laval kept on telephoning, Rochat, who transmitted the messages, did not shake the Marshal.

At Berchtesgaden, however, a decisive transformation was taking place which was to reduce the Marshal's plans to nothing.

At the very moment when, on the morning of the 10th November, Laval was waiting to be received by Hitler, Goering, Ribbentrop and Ciano, Abetz handed him without a word the intercept containing the news of the armistice Darlan had signed in Africa. Laval had no other resource but that of telephoning to Vichy and demanding that no decision should be taken in his absence.

"Hitler," related Count Ciano, "treated him with glacial politeness. The conversation was of short duration. The Führer spoke first and asked in a few words whether France was prepared to guarantee us landing places in Tunisia. Laval, as a good Frenchman, tried to gain time and wished to take advantage of the opportunity to get an assurance from Italy that she would renounce all claims to Tunisia."

Hitler, refusing to enter into a discussion, declared that he considered the Italian demands extremely modest. Laval, feeling that the game was lost, then merely tried to get out of the scrape. He could not "take the responsibility upon himself of ceding Tunisia and Bizerta to the Axis." But, as Hitler said that he was determined to intervene in Tunisia, Laval thought to play Pontius Pilate: "Go there," he said, "but without our authorisation."

On the 11th November at 8 a.m., as Laval was leaving for Vichy, Ribbentrop informed him that, in consequence of decisions taken before his arrival, the Wehrmacht were on the march to occupy the southern zone.

During the night of the 10th–11th December, at 11.50 p.m.,

the decisive ultimatum concerning Tunisia arrived in Vichy: "The German and Italian Governments consider themselves obliged to address a formal demand to the French Government to take all measures possible to assist the immediate disembarkation of contingents of Germans and Italians at Tunis and Bizerta, in order to oppose from those places the American occupation of North Africa, free those territories and supplement the French armed forces. . . ."

At 2 o'clock in the morning, the French Government was informed by a verbal note of the entry of German troops into Tunisia.

"The German and Italian Governments declare that, by taking this action, they merely have the intention of defending themselves and have none whatever of departing from the spirit of the Armistice Conventions as long as the French Government gives them no motive for doing so."

This respect for signed agreements was given the lie three hours later by further German communications.

At 5.30 a.m., the Secretary-General to the Ministry of Foreign Affairs, Rochat, received for transmission to the Marshal, Hitler's letter announcing the entry of German troops into the southern zone: at the same moment, in Munich, Laval, on the point of leaving for Vichy, was given a similar communication.

In the text of this communication the Führer, as always, was playing the innocent victim: he had unceasingly respected the armistice conditions with the utmost scrupulosity; he had not profited "by France's weakness to take advantage of her". However, knowing "that the next objectives of the Anglo-American invasion were Corsica and the south of France," he had to forestall them. He was not responsible for this decision: it was "the behaviour of a French General" which had compelled him to act as he was doing. "This General, during the course of his imprisonment, had pretended to be ill and, on this account, had been granted certain facilities of which he had taken advantage to escape. Contrary to the assurance which was given me of his word of honour to you, Monsieur le Maréchal, he has decided, not only from now on to fight against Germany in the service of the Anglo-Saxon powers, who are the authors of the aggression, but even against his own country."

It was therefore Giraud who was responsible for the total occupation! Moreover, the Führer's generosity extended so far as to offer Pétain a concession which had been refused for the last two years: "I wish to . . . assure you . . . Monsieur le Maréchal, that you and your Government may freely and without hindrance move from now on wherever you like in France."

Hardly had this savage and hypocritical letter been received than it was followed by action.

Before 7 o'clock in the morning, the frontier posts on the demarcation line reported the passage of units of the Wehrmacht: thus, from Bourg-en-Bresse and from the region of Toulouse, General de Lattre de Tassigny, commanding the Montpellier Division, was informed of the enemy movements, and prepared to put Order 128 into execution.

At 8.30, General Bridoux, Minister for War, telephoned the Divisional Generals to cancel the order to leave their garrisons. De Lattre alone refused to obey; he tried in vain to reach the Corbières plateau and was imprisoned the following day in the military prison at Toulouse. It was the only attempt to resist made by the Army of the Armistice.

As soon as he heard of the events of the night, General Weygand went to see the Marshal at 8 a.m., in order to persuade him to protest. He was joined there by Admiral Auphan, who on his side was trying to get the Head of the State to send a message to Algiers, before Laval's return, to order a suspension of hostilities. There were two extremely violent scenes between 8.25 and 8.50, then between 9.30 and 9.55, in the Marshal's office with Auphan and Weygand on one side, Platon and Rochat on the other. The last, by repeating to the Marshal Laval's threat over the telephone, which made him fear that there would be appalling reprisals taken against the population if the French Government appeared to support the dissidents, finally decided Pétain to "take no measure of a political character in Africa before the return of M. Laval".

However, continuing officially to disavow Darlan, Pétain nominated General Noguès as his only representative in North Africa. A measure which, as soon as it was sent, was unofficially contradicted by a secret telegram from Admiral Auphan informing Darlan that he still had the Marshal's confidence: "Inform Admiral Darlan that the Marshal's decision . . . has only been taken because Admiral Darlan is a prisoner."

At 10.30 a.m., Marshal von Rundstedt, in full dress, arrived at the Hôtel du Parc. Pétain was dressed in his Verdun uniform and wore as his single decoration the Croix de Guerre.

Having listened to Rundstedt notify him of the occupation of the free zone, the Marshal read his protest.

"I have received during the night a letter from the Führer announcing that for military reasons, he was obliged to take measures which in fact abolish all the principles and fundamentals of the armistice.

"I solemnly protest against these decisions which are incompatible with the Armistice Conventions."

Pétain then handed the protest to Rundstedt and told him that he was going to have it announced on the radio. The German Marshal made no opposition to this proposal but Renthe-Fink did not conceal his displeasure.

When Rundstedt had left, Marion, Secretary of State for Information, refused to broadcast the protest for fear of displeasing Hitler and Laval. He had however to bow to Pétain's express orders and the protest was repeated several times on the air. Towards midday a new proclamation of Pétain's was broadcast:

"To Frenchmen of France and the Empire,

"Frenchmen, I thought I had lived through the darkest days of my life; the situation today reminds me of the bad memories of 1940.

"I salute with sorrow the soldiers, sailors, airmen and all those who have fallen for the honour of the Empire and the safety of the Fatherland. Frenchmen of Metropolitan France and of the Empire, put your faith in your Marshal who is thinking only of France.

"Philippe Pétain."

Early in the afternoon, the Germans seized the wireless stations and forbade the further broadcasting of the protest.

At 2 p.m., the arrival of Pierre Laval, accompanied by Otto Abetz, put an end to Pétain's initiative. If the German Ambassador was silent when he learned of the Head of the State's intention to order a cessation of hostilities in North Africa, Laval reacted violently. "We must be able to say that we have exhausted all possibilities of resistance. If we cease fighting, the Germans will take vengeance on Metropolitan France. An Empire can be rebuilt, France cannot. In a few weeks, the Germans will have reconquered Africa. If we do not help them, they will keep it. . . ."

At 5 p.m., this thesis was to triumph in the Council of Ministers. Auphan was the only member to demand the cessation of hostilities. The Marshal gave way, and Laval was accorded a vote to order all troops in Africa to continue fighting "to the limits of their strength".

Thus, on this day of November 11th, the Marshal lost his last chance of reconciling all French public opinion under the aegis of his name.

And this day of November 11th, which marks the beginning of Vichy's death agony, saw the beginning of an appalling drama in Tunisia and the death of several thousand patriotic Frenchmen who, because they had not been able to make out Pétain's policy beneath the orders and counter-orders issuing from Vichy, involuntarily played the German game.

During the first hours of the day, General Barré received from General Bridoux, Minister for War at Vichy, a telegram informing him that the Germans were authorised to land in Tunisia, but that they must be prevented from having all contact with French troops and that the latter, without leaving Tunisian soil, should be concentrated in certain areas.

At midday, Admiral Derrien learned from General Juin, at Algiers, that German troops had crossed the demarcation line, that the terms of the armistice were broken and that, in consequence, the Germans had once again become the enemies of France. Furthermore, Juin telephoned Derrien at 5 p.m. that, "everything has changed, we fight the Axis." "Can I tell my troops this?" asked Derrien. And, receiving an affirmative answer, Derrien immediately drew up in definite terms the following order, which seemed to be without appeal: "After two days of discussion and confusion, I have received the formal and precise order which designates the enemy against whom you will fight. That enemy is the German and the Italian! Soldiers, sailors, airmen of the defence force of Bizerta, you know what you have to do: go to it heart and soul against the adversaries of 1940. We have a revenge to take. Long live France!"

This order which, when read to the troops, was received with great enthusiasm, did not unfortunately remain in force for long. For, at 7 p.m., Estéva, too subservient to the orders received in the morning from Vichy, called Derrien to order, telling him to withdraw his proclamation and maintain strict neutrality. But, alas, even this did not put an end to the day's peripeteia, for, a quarter of an hour later, at 7.15 p.m. precisely, it was no longer a question of neutrality but of fighting against the Allies: the Council of Ministers held after Laval's return had decided to continue to fight against the Allies and to let the Axis troops land while avoiding all contact between them and the French troops. "Obey the Marshal's orders!"

The Axis troops began to disembark on the following day, Thursday 12th. Owing to the confusion created by this extraordinary series of orders and counter-orders, they had complete freedom to occupy Bizerta, Tunis and the Régence littoral from which it took six months of fighting to dislodge them.

The last episode to take place on the 11th November was in Morocco, where Noguès signed an armistice with the Americans after three days of fighting that had annihilated French naval power in the area. French troops suffered two thousand dead and wounded.

Despite the Führer's promises, the occupation of the free zone put a practical end to the sovereignty of the Vichy Government.

Hardly had the Germans and Italians arrived in the provisional capital of the French state, than they behaved as if in conquered territory.

A German General installed himself in Vichy while an Italian General, Daverna, requisitioned Darlan's personal chalet for himself. The Hôtel du Parc, isolated and guarded by a cordon of police, constituted, according to a witness, a veritable forbidden zone. The Gestapo, under the command of Captain Gessler, took up its quarters in the Boulevard des États-Unis near the Turkish Embassy, and did not waste a day before making arrests as it had done in the occupied zone. Paul Reynaud and Georges Mandel, interned in the Fort du Portalet, wrote to Pétain saying that if, in face of the enemy invasion, they were not freed, he would bear before history the responsibility for their fate.

On the 12th November, there was a new proof of the subjection to which Vichy was reduced: General Weygand was arrested in spite of the opposition of the French Government.

Early in the morning, General Oberg telephoned Reichführer Himmler's instructions to Bousquet: the French police were to arrest the General.

Bousquet refused: "I only take orders from the Marshal." He informed Pétain and Laval of this new threat.

It was decided that Weygand should not return to his house in Provence, where it would be too easy for the Germans to seize him, but should take shelter in the Préfecture of Guéret.

Bousquet gave him the exceptional escort of three police inspectors to protect him on the journey, for which one of the Marshal's cars was used.

These precautions, however, did not prevent the French car, after it had been on the road but a quarter of an hour, from being trapped by two German armoured cars, manned by S.S. and armed police. Under the threat of sub-machine guns, the General, "armed only with his umbrella", was obliged to submit to the company of an S.S. Captain who took him first to Moulins and then on to Germany.

On the night of the 12th–13th November, in Algiers, General Noguès telegraphed the Marshal to inform him officially that a general armistice could be concluded with the Americans and to propose that Darlan, his powers now restored, should be charged with its application. On the 13th November, at 2 p.m., a third secret telegram was sent from Vichy dissipating all ambiguity: addressed this time to Noguès, it contained the usual formula: "Pay no attention to the official decision," and stated: "confidential agreement of the Marshal and President Laval. But official decision submitted to occupying power."

This "confidential agreement" of Vichy concerned the following stipulations made at Algiers between the French and the Americans: Darlan, under the title of High Commissioner in North Africa, was to resume the political powers handed back to him by Noguès; Giraud was to become Commander-in-Chief; Juin Commander of the land forces; North Africa was to proclaim temporary independence and total collaboration with the Allies. Thus, officially, the Empire had begun the struggle against the Germans once again.

The following day, at 10.15 p.m., Abetz's verbal message was confirmed by a letter to the Marshal which demanded that he should disavow Darlan. An ultimatum to which Pétain agreed without much discussion. What was the use of refusing the Germans this sterile satisfaction, when secret telegrams had brought about the desired result, and the armistice with the Americans had been signed?

Towards 6 p.m., the situation grew worse: there was a new German ultimatum. Brinon arrived in Vichy bearing a telegram from Ribbentrop which demanded that France should declare war within twenty-four hours: if she did not, she would be treated as Poland had been.

On the 15th November, there was a Cabinet meeting attended by Jacques Barnaud, Delegate-General to Franco-German Economic Relations.

Hardly had Laval announced the German ultimatum, than there was a flock of resignations.

In turn, Admiral Auphan, Gibrat and Barnaud declared that, owing to the total occupation of France, the existence of a government at Vichy seemed to them unthinkable.

On the 16th November, during the course of a meeting which was only attended by a few Ministers, Laval proposed a compromise solution between the demands in the ultimatum and the majority opinion held by the Ministers: there was no question, he said, of declaring war on America, but simply of announcing that, from the very fact of the American aggression, a state of war existed between France and the United States.

As soon as the meeting was over, Laval telephoned Brinon that the proposal had not been accepted, and that he himself now considered it out of date.

On the 17th November, the Germans, coming back to the charge, once more demanded from Laval a declaration of war. Replying to Abetz, who transmitted the demand, Laval tried to gain time: on the one hand, repeating Barthélemy's arguments, he pointed out that the constitution forbade the taking of such a decision without the assent of the Chambers and slyly proposed to Ribbentrop that they should be convened; on the other, he asked that, before making any promises, he should be received by the Führer, knowing perfectly well that the latter would refuse the interview.

Laval now tried to make use of the circumstances to obtain, for his own advantage, the Marshal's abdication.

He used every variety of argument to this end. Sometimes persuasive and considerate, he pointed out to the Head of the State that to continue in the exercise of his powers, after the occupation of the free zone, would disqualify him in the eyes of Frenchmen: "You must not be tainted, Monsieur le Maréchal: I am here to be compromised." Sometimes threatening, he warned the Marshal that the only way of avoiding "Polandisation" was to reinforce the authority of the only man in whom the Germans had confidence—a periphrasis which, obviously, referred to himself.

Subjected to blackmail of this kind, feeling that he had come to the end of his strength, Pétain did not resist for long.

On the 18th November, he agreed to sign Constitutional Act No. 12 which Laval had prepared.

Its single clause stipulated that:

"Except for Constitutional Laws, the Head of the Government may, under his signature, promulgate both Laws and Decrees."

It was conferring full powers on Laval: it was reducing the Marshal to the purely formal role of Head of the State, in comparison with which a President of the Republic, before 1940, would have looked like a dictator.

Its Head dethroned under pressure from the occupying power, the French State was nevertheless not spared by the Nazis; demands and *diktats* succeeded each other.

On the 18th, the Germans in exasperation presented another ultimatum. The Government was "to declare war immediately on America and to raise Imperial legions to fight in Africa... The Government has a time limit of twenty-four hours in which to reply. If this time limit expires without a favourable reply... the armistice may be broken and France administered like Poland."

It was the classic blackmail to which Laval replied on the 20th November by a broadcast in which he explained in his own way the events in Africa. Pretending to believe that America had "invaded" North Africa to compensate for the losses inflicted on her by Japan, he concluded proudly:

"France does not admit herself beaten. A day will come when the French flag will fly alone over Algiers. . . ." Then he announced the formation of a new Legion of Volunteers to defend the Empire.

However, the diplomatic isolation of Vichy became disastrous. The American Embassy had taken up temporary residence in the foot-hills of the Pyrenees. The countries of Latin-America one by one broke off diplomatic relations with France.

Except for the Papal Nuncio and the Swiss Minister, there only remained in Vichy the representatives of those countries which were either allies or satellites of Germany.

Even Abetz had been recalled on the 19th November. Abetz, who was always endeavouring to restore negotiations with Laval, received a brutal snub from Ribbentrop who told him to cease playing any active role: "I pray you to cease all activity concerning questions of political development in France and relations between Germany and France and to take no personal initiative. Communications and proposals made by the French Government are simply to be received by the Ambassador without his taking up any position with regard to them, and immediately transmitted here. I pray you to give confidential instructions to this effect to Consul-General Krug von Nidda."

At the same time, Vichy lost her last African territory: French West Africa rallied to the dissidents.

On the 14th November, Governor-General Boisson, whose anti-German feelings were known, had received a visit from General Bergeret, who came to inform him that the agreements signed in Algiers with the Americans had been approved by a secret telegram from the Marshal.

Nothing now prevented Boisson's adherence. On the 15th November, he summoned the Generals and Admirals of French West Africa, to inform them of the news from Algiers. On the 23rd, the last African territory went officially over to the dissidents.

On the same day, Boisson received a telegram from the Marshal officially disapproving the re-orientation, which would not however have taken place but for the secret agreement with Darlan.

Vichy no longer had an Empire. It had but one trump card left: the Fleet.

The ships concentrated in Toulon, in November 1942, belonged to two different organisations: the High Seas Fleet, under the command of Admiral Count Jean de Laborde, which comprised nineteen vessels, one of which was a modern battle cruiser, the

*Strasbourg*, five cruisers, one aircraft-carrier, ten destroyers and three sloops. This Fleet was intact and ready to get under way, while its tonnage corresponded to approximately one quarter of the French warships still afloat, and constituted the most modern and best trained naval force at the disposal of France. Beside it, under the command of Admiral Marquis, Commander-in-Chief of Toulon, was a somewhat heterogeneous collection of one hundred and thirty-five ships, consisting of the warships "on guard duty under the armistice" or under repair, such as the battle cruiser, *Dunkerque*, which were not seaworthy, a multitude of small craft which served the harbour or the necessities of the High Seas Fleet. Of these all that were intact and had any military value were two destroyers, two torpedo-boats, seventeen patrol ships and four submarines which, if the Fleet sailed, were to go to sea under the command of Laborde.

These two Commanders were under the orders of the Secretary of State of Marine, that is to say, Admiral Auphan, until his resignation on the 18th November, and then under Admiral Abrial, who succeeded him.

For both Marquis and Laborde, who together were responsible for the French Fleet of Toulon, discipline was the supreme virtue in anyone who wore a sailor's uniform.

Moreover, Laborde, who was profoundly anti-British, did not for one moment consider sailing to join Darlan.

The Admirals responsible for the Fleet were not, therefore, prepared to make any decision that was not the Government's. It was therefore at Vichy and not at Toulon that the future of the Fleet was decided.

The orders Auphan gave the two Admirals at Toulon on the 11th November were as follows:

"1. To oppose without bloodshed the entry of foreign troops into the establishments, air bases and workshops of the Navy;

"2. To oppose similarly—that is to say without bloodshed—the entry of foreign troops on board ships of the Fleet; and to endeavour to arrive at an agreement by local negotiations;

"3. In case the above is impossible, to scuttle the ships."

Instructions which Marquis and Laborde scrupulously obeyed.

On the following day, 12th November, in the morning, both Admirals summoned to their headquarters their immediate subordinates and made them individually take an oath of loyalty and obedience, the text of which, having been typed during the night, had previously been distributed to them. Only one among them, Captain Pothuau who, under Laborde was in command of a squadron of destroyers, declared he could not take the oath. He was immediately relieved of his command. The same thing happened to a senior Army officer who was in command of the defences of the entrenched camp of Toulon, Colonel Humbert, commanding a half brigade of Chasseurs Alpins, and whose Gaullist sympathies were well known.

On the 13th and 14th November, when the German and Italian forces had invested the Toulon camp, staff conferences took place between Admirals Laborde and Marquis on the one hand, and the German Generals von Neubronn, von Fischer, von Kosper and Admiral Weber on the other. They eventuated in an agreement concerning the defence of the beaches: the French obtained permission for twenty extra battalions, approximately twenty thousand men, with arms and guns, under the orders of General Hanoteau, to reinforce the two battalions of Marines which had until then been the defence of Toulon. They also obtained agreement to the re-arming of thirty or forty ships, which were part of the Fleet under the command of Marquis: thanks to the extra crews which they received during the course of this re-arming, these ships were able to scuttle themselves twelve days later with the rest of the Fleet.

The 15th November seemed thus to mark the climax of Vichy's last illusion concerning the maintenance of a free zone round Toulon and the safeguarding of the Fleet. On that date, Admiral de Laborde, in an order of the day to the ships under his command, could still show an optimism to which forthcoming events were cruelly to give the lie:

"In spite of absurd rumours spread by foreign agents, the stronghold of Toulon has not been occupied and remains, as does the High Seas Fleet, entirely under the control of the French Navy.

"This situation is entirely due to the feeling of admiration inspired in the high Axis authorities by the conduct of our sailors."

On the 17th, following on the arrival in Toulon of Admiral Raeder, coming from Berlin, alarming symptoms gradually transformed this atmosphere of confidence.

On the 17th, the Germans forbade all French aircraft to fly over the Toulon region: what troop movements did they thereby wish to conceal?

On the 18th, they gave orders to the twenty French battalions, whom they had authorised to enter the entrenched camp, to return to their bases.

On the 24th and 25th November, trustworthy information came in that there was feverish activity among the German staffs, though there was no apparent reason for it.

On the 26th, the German liaison officers at Toulon disappeared without any explanation being given.

On the same day, a large concentration of German troops was noted on the western perimeter of the entrenched camp: the airfield at La Pascalette, near Hyères, in the French zone, was occupied.

None of this information sufficed to damp the optimism of the Commanders who were confident of the Führer's word of honour.

"On the evening of the 26th," said Laborde, "I was on board the *Strasbourg*. It had been agreed with Marquis, during the afternoon, since the situation seemed stable, that a certain number of married men might be given leave to sleep ashore. I was completely unconcerned when at ten minutes to five in the morning I was woken up by my Chief-of-Staff, Admiral Guérin, who told me that Admiral Dornon, whose post was in the arsenal, had just received information from Admiral Robin, Chief-of-Staff to Admiral Marquis, and who, with Marquis, had his headquarters in Lamalgue Fort, that the latter had been invaded without a fight by German tanks and that Marquis had been taken prisoner."

Laborde immediately gave orders to his Chief-of-Staff to wake the crew of the *Strasbourg*, to raise steam and cut all communication between ship and shore by hoisting in the brows. Then he telephoned Admiral Robin, Chief-of-Staff to Marquis, and exchanged a few words with him which were tragically cut short: "Admiral Robin, here. . . . Hang up, don't telephone any more: they're coming into my office." It was the Germans arriving.

By direct line to the arsenal, which allowed of free communication so long as the arsenal was not invaded, Laborde called Admiral Dornon, who was to replace Marquis in case the latter should be unable to exercise his command. Dornon asked: "Are you scuttling?" "I'm making preparations to do so," replied Laborde, "I advise you to do the same. I shall keep you informed of my actions."

Laborde asked Dornon to keep him informed by the direct line of the progress of the Germans. And he said: "We shall be compelled to scuttle. Warn me, as soon as they try to force the gates of the arsenal."

Five minutes later, at 5.25 a.m. precisely, Admiral Dornon telephoned that the Germans were in process of forcing one of the great gates of the arsenal. Laborde immediately said: "I am giving the order to scuttle; do the same."

The scuttling of the Fleet began; it was a double operation, which consisted on the one hand in opening the sea cocks in every compartment and, on the other, in rendering useless certain essential pieces of machinery for the working of the ships. Once begun, it was impossible to stop it. Only two sloops, which had no crews on board, could not be scuttled.

Shortly after the decisive order had been given, at approximately 5.45, the quays were invaded by German soldiers, who had been intended to take possession of the ships. All they could do was to be present at the sinking, at 8.30, of the *Strasbourg*, which settled perfectly upright, the officers' cabins remaining above the water line.

This was not the only misfortune which, on this tragic day, befell France: at approximately the same time that, in Toulon, Marquis and Laborde were awakened by the German aggression, at Vichy, Rochat, Secretary-General for Foreign Affairs, was awakened by the German Consul-General, Krug von Nidda: "I have a letter from Chancellor Hitler which I must give President Laval at 4.30 a.m." Rochat got up and, in the cold darkness, left with the German for Châteldon, where the President was spending the night.

Laval, having read the Führer's letter, returned with Rochat to the Hôtel du Parc, where he summoned the Minister of Marine, Abrial, the Minister of War, Bridoux, as well as Admiral Platon and Admiral le Luc. It was 5.30 a.m., the hour at which Laborde, in Toulon, was giving the order to scuttle. Gathered round the table, the Ministers listened to Rochat reading the essential passages of the Chancellor's letter, translating the German text as he went along: it intimated that the Wehrmacht were immediately proceeding, not only to immobilise the Fleet at Toulon, but to disarm the Army.

The Army of the Armistice had been shut into its garrisons for the last fortnight, having, under Bridoux's orders, given up all intention of resisting. During this night of the 27th November, while the Germans were flinging themselves into the assault on the barracks, the soldiers were asleep in bed and the officers at home in the towns. It was child's play for the aggressors to turn the French soldiers out in their shirts and seize their arms.

# Vichy, the Fourth Period

(27th November, 1942–25th August, 1944)

CHAPTER 1

# FRANCE UNDER TOTAL OCCUPATION

GERMANY'S defeat was becoming more certain. The Axis troops were reduced to the defensive on all fronts. In the U.S.S.R. the Germans were retreating and the first Russian counter-offensives, of November 1942 to March 1943, ended in the capitulation of the German Sixth Army: at Stalingrad, Marshal von Paulus, twenty-four Generals and 91,000 men were taken prisoner. The Japanese were retreating in the Far East where the Americans had landed on the Solomon Islands, recapturing New Georgia, and had reoccupied one of the Aleutians. The Axis was also retreating in North Africa where, on the 13th May, 1943, Tunisia was liberated; three hundred thousand Germans and Italians surrendered to the British, American and French troops, the latter under the command of General Juin: for the first time since May 1940 a French Command had to organise the equivalents of the Stalags and Oflags in which a million and a half Frenchmen were held captive in Germany. There was also a retreat in Italy: in July 1943 allied troops under the command of General Eisenhower landed in Sicily: on the 17th August Messina was taken. On the 3rd September the Italians capitulated at Syracuse and signed an armistice.

The enslaved country was increasingly expecting liberation.

The Atlantic Wall, constructed by the Germans round the coasts of France, played the same part in their illusions and in those of their collaborators that the Maginot Line had played four years earlier for M. Edouard Daladier. They boasted that it was impregnable and took journalists to visit it.

On the 3rd July, 1943, Hérold Paquis prophesied on Radio Paris: "A landing on the Atlantic coast or in the Channel would suffer a most bloody defeat."

Where was the landing, which was now becoming an obsession and at moments appeared to take on an ubiquitous character, to take place? The prophets spoke with equal assurance of Bordeaux, Sète, Nice. . . .

Life to all appearance went on, if not as it had been before the war, at least as it had been since the beginning of the occupation.

As in 1940–1941, literary and artistic activities flourished, particularly in Paris, to an extent that calmer periods might well have envied. The literary and theatrical "seasons" of 1943 and 1944 were among the richest that the capital had known: for the New Year holidays of 1943, there was the *Reine Morte* by Henri de Montherlant. In June, *Les Mouches* of Jean-Paul Sartre was produced at the Cité Theatre. In August, while the Germans were bringing out their Panther tank, Simone de Beauvoir published her novel *L'Invitée*, and Noël-Noël came back to the screen with *Adémai, Bandit d'Honneur*. There was one important first night after another: Giraudoux's *Sodome et Gomorrhe* and Claudel's *Le Soulier de Satin*.

As in 1940–1941, but even more than in those years which now seemed already so long ago, this intellectual life of rarified pleasures and entertainments was accompanied by a precarious physical existence. . . .

The enemy was appropriating greater and greater quantities of food-stuffs in France. It was essential that the German people should suffer as little as possible from restrictions, even when the Wehrmacht's "strategic retreats" obliged them to abandon the rich lands of the Ukraine.

In June, 1943, Laval declared that the occupying power had seized 28,000 head of beef cattle out of the 140,000 requisitioned by the Government, 20 per cent. But this was an underestimate: in fact, they took 90,000 head, 64 per cent. of the total, for the German slaughterhouses.

Adults were badly off: but the situation of very young children during the winter of 1943–1944 was tragic. Undernourished young mothers could not feed their children: fresh milk arrived irregularly. Condensed milk, from February 1943, was seized by the Germans and could only be had on a medical certificate: in the hospitals which had the power to give these permits there took place "dramatic scenes upon which depended the lives of thousands of babies".

Between the autumn of 1940 and February 1944, the cost of

living increased by 166 per cent. and the daily rations fell by 850 calories.

The mortality rate which, in 1937, had been 12 per 1,000 reached 17·8 per 1,000 in 1943; there was 30 per cent. more tuberculosis than in 1939. "Undernourishment", declared M. Gerthoffer, representing France at the Nuremberg trials, "was the immediate cause of the death of 150,000 French people, and the indirect cause of thousands more. . . . The growth of children and adolescents was seriously impaired and the future of the race is a source of grave anxiety."

This also had mental repercussions: "The population suffered from a debility which showed itself in many forms, accompanied often by mental depression which manifested itself in pessimistic speech."

The customers of the black market obviously escaped these misfortunes; they were often Germans themselves or Frenchmen who were hangers-on of the Germans. In order to supply these few privileged persons, in spite of the economic control which became more and more strict, the profiteers had recourse to the most fantastic frauds. In the month of March 1944, false coffins were discovered containing meat and salted provisions. In August, vans belonging to the Bank of France were discovered between Paris and Poitiers carrying sugar instead of notes and gold. The vans were not demeaning themselves by being loaded with such precious goods: 2 lb. of sugar cost 150 francs, meat 300 to 400 francs, butter 600 to 800 francs. These food-stuffs flowed into the black market restaurants, where the basic price varied between 500 and 1,000 francs. Wine cost 300 francs a bottle, and champagne 800 francs.[1]

But there was a new factor: France was in the grip of civil war.

In reaction to the German requisitions, in a desire to escape forced labour, for love of freedom and from anxiety to see national independence restored, the country little by little mobilised itself against the occupying power once more.

It ranged itself against the Nazis, but also against the Vichy Government in its submission to the demands and wishes of the Germans. Thus, in certain aspects, the Resistance movement

[1] To find the equivalent in the currency of today, the figures should be multiplied by approximately 15.

formed part of the world war and enrolled Frenchmen in a foreign war once again; on the other hand, it created between its members and the leaders of the French State that appalling form of struggle which is civil war.

It was in the spring of 1943 that the Resistance really became organised: in April, the three big movements, which had spontaneously come to birth in 1940 and which functioned often on a "trade" basis, Combat, Franc-Tireur, Libération, became co-ordinated: the M.U.R. (United Resistance Movements) combined their *maquis* and their fighting groups. On the 27th May, 1943, in Paris, at 48, rue de Four, there took place the first meeting of the directing organisation, the Conseil National de la Résistance, under the chairmanship of Jean Moulin. In the following month, at Caluire, near Lyon, Moulin held a meeting of senior officers to form the secret army: the Gestapo surrounded the house and arrested him: he died a fortnight later under torture at Metz.

The *maquis*, embryonic to begin with, gradually increased in numbers and acquired more arms, either by parachute drops, or by attacks on German or Government depots. The *maquis* of the Franc-Tireur movement embodied 29,000 men. The secret members of the Combat movement amounted to 800 to 1,000 fighting men; in the regular groups trained for sabotage there were 25,000 to 30,000 men in a secret army which was to act in contact with the allied troops after the landing. There were also *maquis* formed by young men who refused to go and work in Germany.

Besides its military formations, the Resistance had its political side, the N.A.P., (infiltration into political administration) and the Super N.A.P., (infiltration into the Vichy Ministries). It had its intelligence services, its study groups, of which some were directed by well-known intellectuals such as Mounier or André Philip. It had its Press which soon reached a considerable public. *Franc-Tireur* had a circulation of 165,000, and *Résistance* 70,000. *Combat* required three tons of paper a month which its secret manager cleverly succeeded in having supplied from Germany; at the same time, the Government newspapers had to restrict the size of their editions and reduce their format. The clandestine Press had its own printers, often changing from one edition to the next, but who did not limit themselves to publishing newspapers: some of them were experts at forging false identity papers. *Franc-Tireur* alone used the services of twelve different printers.

The Resistance had also its own periodicals: it had its own reviews, the *Lettres Françaises* which, at the end of the occupation, published an Almanac of 5,000 copies and a special number on Oradour, which had an edition of 20,000. There were also the *Cahiers de la Libération*, in which, under a pseudonym, Jean Paulhan made implacable use of his brilliant irony against the occupying power.

"Had we been occupied (as one politely calls it) by Swedes, we should at least have learned a dance step or a taste for blue and yellow ribbons; by the Javanese, a certain manner of moving the fingers; by the Swiss, the Italians or the Hungarians, we should have retained a song, a smile, some new gesture of the head. . . .

"But from these, we all know that we shall retain nothing. Not a song, not a facial expression. Even the child in the street does not think of imitating the goosestep. In the métro, which has become, with the grocers', our common meeting place, they never jostle anyone, as, alas, we still sometimes do. They even pick up the paper some careless person drops. And yet, they make us feel no inclination to pick up papers. They are not animate. They will pass like a great void. As if they were already dead. The only thing is that they spread death about them. Indeed, it's the only thing they know how to do."

The Resistance also published books: the *Editions de Minuit* put 33 works in their secret catalogue among which was the *Silence de la Mer* by Vercors.

Finally, the Resistance also had its medical services for the combatants in the *maquis*.

With this kind of structure and with its variety of organisations, the Resistance was the real country which, little by little, grew up beside the legal country which was on its death bed: a real country which, like every country in the world, consisted not only of heroes, of acts of the highest morality, the greatest courage and purest patriotism. There existed among them disreputable people, black sheep who disfigured organisations which were based on faith and ideals. It is clear that, under cover of the Resistance, acts of banditry were committed. There were thefts of jewellery, public and private funds, and sometimes a paying off of old scores which had nothing whatever to do with politics.

Nevertheless, the Resistance at this period constituted the country's great adventure, the Frenchman's great hope, and the only means he had of fighting the occupying power.

Attacks and demonstrations against the Germans and the Vichy Government grew increasingly frequent.

At this time, many Frenchmen, either collaborators of the Germans, or presumed to be so, received parcels containing miniature coffins: this was to inform them that they would be executed at the Liberation.

Sentences pronounced by the Resistance movements were also announced in broadcasts from London. Sometimes sentences were communicated direct to the accused.

It was at this period that Philippe Henriot, Secretary of State for Information, and one of the best known speakers on Radio France at Vichy, was assassinated.

Such acts increased all over France, and created a feeling of panic among the Germans and their collaborators. In May, 1943, the Resistance executed members of Doriot's Parti Populaire Français. In August, 1943, there were assassinations in the Paris region: in one of them Marshal von Rundstedt was very nearly killed. In July, 1943, there were assassinations of Trades Unionists who had gone over to the Government camp. On the 11th November, 1943, there were strikes and demonstrations which led to acts of repression. There were numerous attacks on centres of distribution of ration cards and tickets, in order to provide supplies for the *maquis*. There were others against offices of the Forced Labour Organisation which were responsible for the despatch of workers to Germany: in October, 1943, a group of irregulars entered one of these offices in the Rue des Francs-Bourgeois in Paris, bound the *concierge*, and seized sixty thousand card indexes which they threw into the Seine. Similarly in the spring of 1944, a group from the University Resistance movement invaded the offices of the Sorbonne where the particulars of students who were to be sent to Germany were being prepared. They seized all the dossiers. "A few days later," recalls Pierre Audiat, "those concerned received their personal dossiers through the post: attached to the dossier was a note drawing the recipient's attention to the fact that he had been saved from deportation. The Resistance showed itself intelligent and witty."

The Resistance began to play a more and more important military part. The first parachute drops of arms took place at the end of 1943 in the Cantal. In December there were attacks on saw-mills and factories working for Germany. Bronze statues, which were to be requisitioned by the Wehrmacht, were removed. Soon there were pitched battles; at Auteroche, near Murat, twelve Germans were killed and several wounded. In June, 1944, there was something approaching general mobilisation: battles took place at Margeride, Chaudes-Aigues, Le Lioran and Saint-Flour. . . . At the time of the landings, twenty thousand Germans were held up in the Cantal who should have been sent to Normandy. The Army Intelligence Services had established and communicated to the allies an accurate map of the locations of German forces before the landings. This was a sensational exploit, which was achieved in a methodical and unexpected way. The Intelligence Services started a laundry business with branches all over France and succeeded, by charging low prices, in getting the custom of the Wehrmacht. They were able to tabulate the distinguishing marks of every German unit from its linen and clothes.

In order to combat the general secret mobilisation of the country, which no longer admitted either defeat or occupation, the Germans did not hesitate to violate all the rules of war.

In an order issued to German formations in France on the 6th May, 1944, General Jodl, second-in-command to General Keitel, Supreme Commander of the Armies of Occupation, laid it down that "collective measures against the inhabitants of whole villages including the burning of the villages may only be ordered by the Commanders of Divisions or the Commanders of the S.S., and of the police."

Another general order, issued on the 27th August, 1944, clarified the policy concerning atrocities for the soldiers: "It is to be noted that the action taken is never sufficiently severe. There must be no fear of shootings, hangings and the burning of houses. The Division will take note in each case whether the responsible commander has acted in a sufficiently brutal manner. Therefore, to make an end, act brutally and with no consideration whatever; for instance, place women in the front of vehicles when crossing country infested with bands."

Frenchmen disappeared every day, without the occupying power giving any reasons: they had been arrested.

The Jews were naturally the first to suffer.

From November, 1942 onwards, in the southern zone as in the northern, Frenchmen of Jewish religion were arrested by the Nazis in exactly the same way as foreigners. The conditions at Drancy, where the condemned were concentrated before being sent to the extermination camps in Germany, grew worse in June, 1943. Having been administered by the French authorities until then, it now passed into the control of "a fanatical brute, the Hauptsturmführer S.S. Brünner with, as assistant, another brute, called Broeltke". There were bullying, violence, flogging, cells; letters and parcels were forbidden. From whatever sickness they might be suffering, the inmates were forbidden to be sent to hospitals outside the camp. Deaths and births took place behind the barbed wire in this tragic threshold to the deportation, torture and extermination, which the hundreds of thousands sent to Auschwitz or Ravensbruck were to know.

Children were spared no more than adults. Towards the end of the occupation, the orphanages of Montreuil, Varenne and Neuilly were emptied by the S.S. On the 31st July, four hundred orphans were deported to the east.

There came a climax of horror, of which the Jews until then had had the melancholy privilege, but which was soon to fall on "Aryans" as well.

In 1943, there were a dozen torture chambers in Paris in the centre of the town: the screams which came from them made the neighbours tremble. Some were Parisian agencies of the Gestapo, in which, alas, unworthy Frenchmen savagely maltreated their compatriots; or again in the Rue des Saussaies, on the premises of the Sûreté Générale, the headquarters of the German police, who neglected no means of making their victims talk. To begin with, informers: before the interrogation, stool pigeons were shut in among the unhappy crowd, the victims of round-ups or police raids. Passing themselves off as members of the Resistance, they endeavoured to acquire information. Whatever they heard was immediately repeated to the police, thus rendering all further interrogation superfluous and ruining all chance of the accused being set free.

This was followed by torture. The Gestapo and the Militia practised "as in the Middle Ages" two degrees of the "question": the "question ordinary" and the "question extraordinary". Among the tortures in the first degree was that of the bath, in which the victim had his head held under cold water to the point of suffocation, was then pulled out again, and then re-submerged and so on till he confessed. Among those of the second degree were blows with the hand and fist, kicks, beatings with clubs and whips. There were also more refined tortures: hanging by the feet over a tub full of water, which compelled the victim to double up as best he could in order to escape drowning, the crushing of fingers and toes, pricking with needles in the most sensitive parts, hot irons, electric shocks.

As the foreign war became complemented by civil war, the Germans were not alone in contributing to the dramatic and catastrophic atmosphere of these pitiless times: wearing the same uniforms as the Germans, or dark blue ones, there were Frenchmen whom they had enlisted in their support, militiamen, who also tortured their compatriots.

At night, the soldiers of the Militia, often assisted by the Gestapo, surrounded towns and villages to search out and execute suspects. At Saint-Amand they seized the whole Jewish population, 26 men, 35 women and 9 children. After the Liberation 24 bodies of men, appallingly mutilated, were found in the well of a farm: in another well, there were 8 bodies of women of which one had the hands cut off and the stomach slit open.

Here is another exploit of the Militia: the political prisoners in the prison at Eysses mutinied and made the Governor, Chivot, a militiaman appointed by Darnand, prisoner. The mutiny failed and Chivot was released on a formal promise that there would be no reprisals.

Darnand arrived, learned of the promise made to the mutineers, and said: "I don't care a damn; what we need are executions." A court-martial was set up on the spot, at 6 a.m. At 11 a.m., twelve mutineers selected at hazard were shot, without having been given an opportunity to defend themselves and without any of them having been recognised as having borne arms.

There were also assassinations that could be placed to the score of the occupying power, or to its French accomplices. On the 12th January, 1944, at Neyron, some fifteen kilometres from Lyon, were found the bodies of Victor Basch, President of the League of the Rights of Man and of his wife. Pinned to the clothes of the ex-political leader was a card bearing the words: "Terror against Terror". Other cases, which occurred later, were the assassinations of Georges Mandel and Jean Zay.

But soon, mere cruelty towards individuals was no longer sufficient to assuage the rage and fear of the Nazis. Collective reprisals increased continually, falling apparently at hazard in widely separated localities.

As we shall see, great numbers of villages were sacked, depopulated and burnt; some of them remain practically unknown against the huge background of the tragedy, while others acquired a pathetic notoriety.

Such was the case with Oradour-sur-Glane on the 10th June, 1944, where the S.S. Division, *Das Reich*, burnt alive more than six hundred women and children in the church. The crime was all the more appalling for the fact that it was committed against a perfectly peaceable village which was enjoying a sunny holiday season. Here, in all its simplicity, is the account of a transport driver who was by chance in Oradour that day, where his four children, between the ages of five and twelve, were on holiday: "... The next day at dawn, six men, of whom I was one, went to the village in the hope of obtaining news of the missing.

"We were faced with an indescribable sight.

"The house which the day before had been the Command Post had been completely burnt down. On the outskirts, there were numbers of cartridge cases and a heap of bicycles of which most were smashed.

"A little further on, we entered the main part of the village which we crossed from end to end. All the buildings, including the church, the schools, the Mairie, the Post Office and the hotel in which my family had been staying, were no more than smoking ruins. Only two houses had been spared, one at the entrance to the village and the other at its exit. . . .

"... It was then that I learned . . . that the bodies of women and children had been found in the church.

"There are no words to describe such an abomination.

"Though the superstructure of the church and the steeple had been completely burnt down, the vaulting of the nave had resisted the fire.

"Most of the bodies were burnt. But some, though burnt to the point of being reduced to ashes, had nevertheless preserved human shape.

"In the sacristy, two little boys of twelve or thirteen years of age, were clasped in each other's arms in a last spasm of terror. In the confessional, a small boy was sitting with his head bent forward. The remains of a baby of eight or ten months of age were in a pram. . . .

"I could bear no more and, reeling like a drunken man, I returned to Les Bordes.

"The next day, I returned to Limoges on foot by a circuitous route."

This unhappy man's nightmare obsessed the whole of France: during the last months of the occupation there were terrifying rumours and hideous omens all over the country.

There was talk of the Vlassov army, recruited by the Germans in the occupied Russian territories, and which committed excesses in the Seine-Inférieure and the Somme which recalled the ancient barbarian invasions. Almost every day there could be read in the papers announcements, within black rules, of executions of Frenchmen by the German authorities, or incitements to traitors to denounce their compatriots.

"During these last days some criminals have committed, on the pretext of political orders, acts of terrorism: sabotage of railway lines, the placing of bombs, acts of brigandage, arson. The majority of the victims of these activities have been Frenchmen.

"In consequence, the more reflective elements of the population are invited to transmit without delay any information which might lead to the arrest of these terrorists either to the German authorities or to the French authorities. Absolute secrecy is guaranteed.

"Furthermore, the Kommando of the Sicherheits Polizei S.D. at Lyon offer a reward of 100,000 francs for every discovery and arrest of terrorists made possible by information given to the German authorities by members of the population.

"Frenchmen, who in any way assist the terrorists or who fail to report the terrorists' plans of sabotage or any other suspect circumstances within their knowledge, will be considered the accomplices of these individuals and be liable to severe penalties.

Lyon, November, 1943."

To this appalling civil war were added additional sufferings. These were the allied air raids made in preparation for the landings. A ransom of blood for the Liberation, they might perhaps have been carried out with fewer casualties.

The bombings by night, carried out from high altitudes, increased from year to year and, towards the end, from month to month. In 1941 there was a single raid on Brest. In 1942, three. In 1943, twenty, of which one on Nantes inflicted 2,000 casualties. For the first time, in September, Paris was the objective of a raid, which resulted in 105 dead and 205 wounded. In 1944 there were nearly a hundred. In two days, the 26th and 27th May, Lyon suffered 600 dead and 500 wounded, Saint-Étienne 870 dead and 1,400 wounded, Marseille 1,976 dead and 1,323 wounded, while there were also raids on Grenoble, Nice, Chambéry, Amiens, Avignon, Nîmes, Rouen and the Paris region. That was the price France had to pay for the imminent landings. Total casualties from 1941–1944, based on unofficial statistics, were 67,078 dead and 75,660 wounded.

The horror of the martyred towns and the mourning of the survivors were given expression in funeral ceremonies by which Déat and Henriot endeavoured to arouse anger against the Allies.

At Vichy, the atmosphere in 1943–1944 was quite changed, it only remotely resembled that of 1940.

In the provisional capital, where four years earlier Pétain and Laval had moved about without protection among a crowd of the enthusiastic, the ambitious and the intriguing, there was now no one apart from officials.

All over the deserted capital Gardes Mobiles, armed with submachine guns, watched over the security of the leaders of the French State. By night, the Hôtel du Parc was transformed into a fortress.

In 1944, the enthusiasm of 1940 had been succeeded by fear. It reigned over Vichy.

For some, it was fear of the Germans who in these last months did not hesitate to arrest even the most initimate colleagues of the Marshal and Laval. Jean Jardin, the head of the latter's office, who had certain contraventions of collaboration on his conscience, feared that he might be arrested at his house one morning by the Gestapo. To which fact was due a recrudescence of piety which took him each day, at dawn, to one of the Vichy churches.

For others, it was fear of the *maquisards*. Laval took every precaution to see that the attempted assassination by Colette should not be repeated.

"At Vichy," wrote Maurice Martin du Gard, in September, 1943, "everyone was preparing his dossier." "I," would say a Minister, "have saved so many workers!" "I," would say a Chief of Police, "placed the sons of Gaullist Generals in a police school." "I," would say another, "have saved so many Jews."

Others made their plans to leave the sinking ship physically. Missions abroad were never so sought after as in 1944; particularly to Spain and Italy, from which people hoped to get comfortably to Algiers. Even among Pétain's friends, there were some who did not resist the temptation. Roger de Saivre and Estèbe went to North Africa, where indeed they behaved courageously.

Ménétrel found it increasingly difficult to suppress his pro-allied sympathies: he would show off his rucksack which he kept always ready and with which, if need were, he could go to join the *maquis*. He warned the *maquis* of German and Militia plans for attacking them. He even proposed the installation of a secret wireless set in the Marshal's office on which the Head of the State could launch an appeal to insurrection.

These turnings of coats had, morally speaking, very unequal value.

There were very respectable ones, soundly based and for which their authors were prepared to run risks. For instance, the manifesto issued by François Valentin, ex-Director-General of the Légion Française des Combattants which was widely but secretly distributed for the third anniversary of the association he had founded and which he now saw degenerating.

He expressed his disillusion in terms whose sincerity cannot be doubted:

"Somewhere in France, August, 1943.

"On the 29th August, the Legion will commemorate the third anniversary of its foundation.

"Until the return of Pierre Laval to power, I was the Director-General of the Legion. In that position, and whatever my intentions may have been, I may have contributed to misleading good Frenchmen, whether Legionaries or not, as to their duty. It is particularly to them that I wish to address this appeal in order at last to free my conscience. And since my past actions were committed in France and publicly, it is in France and publicly that I take my stand today.

"A cry of anger rises from our hearts when we gaze back along the road we have travelled for the last three years and, remembering the experiences through which we have passed, we realise the reality of the situation to which we have been led by disaster after disaster, conspiracy after conspiracy, lies after lies, betrayals after betrayals.

"But it could not be otherwise: our mistake was in believing that it was possible to raise a country up once more before liberating it. One cannot reconstruct a house while it is still burning. . . ."

Another example, at the same period, was a courageous article by Drieu la Rochelle, editor of the N.R.F. under the occupation, which he tried to publish in order to indicate to the Germans, upon whom he depended, his disappointment at seeing them betray the rash confidence he had thought fit to place in them; the article was censored; but its text remains as a memory of an honest but ingenuous writer, who became pro-Hitler through intellectual illusion and not through interest or sectarianism, was misled into intellectual collaboration and was to pay for his error with suicide.

"We have placed our hope not in Germany but in Hitlerian Socialism. We hoped in 1940 and in 1941 that Hitlerian Socialism, roused by a wonderful opportunity, would become stronger and spread in the two directions of European social economy and an internationalisation of nationalisms. But the war in Russia has absorbed all the thoughts, all the virtues and all the activity of the Hitlerian movement. We have seen no indications of those audacious, startling and transforming measures which as Frenchmen, accustomed to taking a world view, we awaited."

CHAPTER 2

# LAVAL, HEAD OF A SATELLITE STATE

(December, 1942–November, 1943)

IN December, 1942, France had become in fact a satellite state of the Reich: the whole of Metropolitan France was occupied by German troops, and the French army was no longer in existence.

Moreover, Vichy had lost the two trump cards which still gave her some influence with the Nazis: the Empire and the Fleet.

Pétain and Laval, however, continued to maintain the fiction of an independent Government, while pursuing the same policy as before the 11th November.

The Marshal wished to continue protecting the population against the rigours of the occupation. His continuing ambition was to serve as a protecting screen between the French and the Nazis.

The Head of the Government, on the other hand, was not content that the Government should merely be in being. Always convinced of being right in all circumstances, he wanted to assure the future of France in the eventuality of the German victory he desired: in order to achieve this, it was necessary that France should take part in the struggle against Communism.

On the 15th December, Laval learned from Hemmen that the occupation costs would be raised from 400 to 500 millions a day: apart from the total occupation of France, the number of troops garrisoning French territory had been increased. It was not sufficient that France should have been invaded in her entirety; she had also to finance the invasion.

Moreover, Hemmen decided to change his headquarters: he proposed leaving the Hôtel Majestic in Paris, from which he had been organising the pillage of French economy for the last two years, and go to Vichy: he would thus be in a position to exercise direct control over the activities of the Minister of Finance. Cathala submitted. The Secretary-General to the Ministry, Deroy, resigned, as did a number of Inspectors of Finance.

Soon after this blow to the Ministry of Finance, Laval left for the Führer's headquarters, to which he had managed to get himself summoned. He arrived there on the 19th December.

There are several accounts of the interview between Laval and Hitler, which took place in the presence of Ribbentrop, Goering and Count Ciano.

The Reichmarschall delivered a diatribe against the black market in France: the Parisians, he said, were gorging themselves while German soldiers were at the front. And what was more, and this was a much more serious complaint, had not French shops had the audacity to make him, Goering, pay 4,000 francs for a pair of shoes and 2,000 francs for a fountain pen?

The Führer's accusations were of a different order: if he still preserved his personal esteem for Laval, he had nevertheless to state that, through France's fault and that of the Vichy Government, Germans and Italians would have to spill their blood to reconquer North Africa. Moreover, the French Government had taken no measures against the families of the dissidents.

It was then that Laval learned the Führer's two new ultimatums.

Sauckel was to make new requisitions of French labour; and the French police were to be re-organised, that is to say subordinated to the Paris Collaboration Parties.

Compliments followed upon threats: "I have confidence in you," the Führer said to Laval. "I shall never deal with anyone but you. You are the last French Government. After you, there will be a Gauleiter."

At the moment of leaving the French statesman, the Chancellor could not resist making a spectacular gesture: he gave him a long handshake: "With you," he promised, "we shall always be in agreement!"

Encouraged by these kind words, Laval, on his return to France, cherished new illusions. The German demands certainly posed a number of delicate problems, but was not the essential that, in spite of the dissidence of the Empire and the scuttling of the Fleet, the Führer should agree to discuss matters with him, Laval?

A *communiqué* from the Wilhelmstrasse, on the 2nd January, 1943, supported Laval's illusions. Though worded in threatening tones, it left the door open for the belief that the Reich was offering France one last chance:

"France today is at the crossroads. She must choose between complete adherence to Europe and total disappearance from the world scene."

In fact, and Laval was not in doubt of it, the Führer had made his choice. Sauckel, whose job it was to recruit in France a new batch of 250,000 workers, was told on the 4th January, during a telephone conversation with Minister Speer, that, "following upon the Führer's decision, it is not necessary in future . . . to have any particular consideration for the French."

Furnished with these instructions, which were far from displeasing him, Sauckel arrived in Paris on the 11th January. He summoned to the military headquarters all the officials responsible for labour. He told them that new measures were to be taken.

Here are extracts from the official report of the conference:

"Gauleiter Sauckel thanked the various organisations for the success achieved in the first campaign. But now, at the beginning of the New Year, he was obliged to announce new and severe measures; there was a great need of labour both in France and in the armament industry of the Reich. . . .

". . . For the second recruiting campaign in France, it was necessary that, before the middle of March, 150,000 skilled and 100,000 unskilled workers, both men and women, should be transferred to Germany."

These were the German demands which Sauckel placed before Laval on the 14th January. It was no longer a question of volunteers nor of the "Relève".

Laval found himself faced with the following alternatives: either to leave Sauckel to recruit 250,000 workers himself, or undertake to furnish him with them.

On the 17th February, after a month of negotiations, during which the French Ministers infuriated Sauckel by their "temporising", the Service du Travail Obligatoire was instituted for young people born in 1920, 1921 and 1922.

The duration of the S.T.O. was to be two years. Apart from agricultural workers, who were placed in a special category, it entailed the total mobilisation of these three classes.

Eight days later, in exchange for the promulgation of the S.T.O., the Germans granted Laval the necessary concessions for rallying "French hearts" to the prospect of working beyond the Rhine.

These were: the subordinating of the departments of the Nord and the Pas-de-Calais to the German administration in Paris instead of to Brussels; the suppression of the demarcation line which, since the total occupation of France, no longer had any justification (only Jews and undesirables were still forbidden to cross it); freedom of postal correspondence throughout France; and the transformation of the prisoners of war into "free" workers.

"Germany," declared Pierre Laval, when announcing these concessions to the French, "has made great efforts at understanding . . . I am certain that we could obtain more important results yet if I were not impeded and prevented by the sort of collective folly which is encouraged by foreign propaganda and supported by the illusory hopes of too many Frenchmen.

"This is a clear, firm warning. I hope with all my heart that it will be heard while there is still time."

In spite of the "understanding" shown by the Nazis and the fiction of sovereignty preserved by Laval, France was being gradually transformed into a satellite state.

The Militia was joined to the regular police.

During his interview with the Head of the French Government, the Führer had demanded the creation of a supplementary police force on which he could count to maintain order in France and fight against the dissidents.

A law of the 30th January 1943, published the following day in the *Journal Officiel*, created the Militia, defining its objects and its recruitment, which though based on the Service d'Ordre Légionnaire, was not however limited to it.

It has "as object the grouping of Frenchmen who are resolved to take an active part in the political, social, economic, intellectual and moral recovery of France. . . ."

It was to be "composed of volunteers who are morally and physically suitable, not only to support the new State by their actions, but also to assist in the maintenance of internal order".

A ceremony was held in Vichy, on the 1st February, to mark the foundation of the new organisation and appoint its leader, Darnand. Laval spoke. Stressing once again the appalling danger which, according to him, Bolshevism was to Europe, he went on: "We must do everything we can and use every means at our disposal to prevent our country suffering this misfortune.

"I want France to understand that she must be at one with Germany in order to prevent it."

Apart from a few fools and adventurers, who joined the ranks of the Militia by chance as they might have joined anything else, apart from a few cunning people, who thought it clever to join in order to avoid the S.T.O., the Militia, this élite of Pierre Laval's "friends", soon consisted of mercenary roughs, whose lust for loot encouraged violence of the worst kind.

Here is an extract from the report of a Commissaire of Police who, in August, 1944, arrested a leading member of the Militia, Rousseau, who was guilty of using violence against an old man of seventy: "The interrogation revealed that Rousseau earned 10,000 francs a month (approximately 200,000 francs today), that he benefited from a special allowance of 350 francs a day and that he received, over and above this, 10,000 francs for every deserter or suspect he arrested.

"An examination of his police record revealed that he had been convicted eight times and that his sentences amounted to thirty-five years of imprisonment, and twenty years interdiction of residence."

In August, 1944, the Marshal devoted one of his last acts as Head of the State to protesting against the atrocities committed by the Militia.

"The Militia," he said, "has gained the hideous reputation of using methods which I knew well when they were used by the Reds in Spain. I cannot pass over in silence the tortures inflicted on victims who are often innocent, in places which, even in Vichy, are less like French State Prisons than Bolshevik Chekas.

"By these methods, the Militia has succeeded in establishing an atmosphere of police terror which has been unknown in our country till today."

At this period, there were many indications of the fact that France had become a German satellite:[1] the arrest of a judge in

[1] During this time, there were eight French departments in the South East which seemed to have been miraculously preserved from these excesses: Alpes-Maritimes, Var, Hautes-Alpes, Basses-Alpes, Isère, Drôme, Savoie and Haute-Savoie, which constituted the Italian zone of occupation.

The more humane Italians not only failed to make the discriminatory measures, the office of the Garde des Sceaux by the Gestapo in Vichy and a circular sent to the Governors of prisons ordering them to hand over to the Germans any prisoners for whom they made a demand.

More spectacular still was the destruction of the Vieux-Port at Marseille.

On the 3rd January, 1943, an attack was made in this populous district on a brothel frequented by soldiers of the Wehrmacht. There were several wounded and several dead, as many French as Germans, moreover. A report, much exaggerating the importance of the affair, was sent to Hitler by the local German authorities. Hitler flew into one of his rages and got into touch with Himmler, saying:

"The city of Marseille is a haunt of gangsters. It has always been so; but, today, it is Germany who has to put up with the consequences. There is only one possible step to take: from the information given me, all the gangsters are concentrated in the Vieux-Port district. There are underground vaults in this district; it provides special opportunities. I am informed that a large number of German deserters are hidden there. There is, therefore, only one solution: I order the Vieux-Port to be razed to the ground."

Himmler, on receipt of the order, got into contact with Oberg and reproached him with not doing his duty: why did he not know what the Führer had described? He threatened to dismiss him if he did not immediately put Hitler's instructions into execution.

---

which were in accordance with Vichy legislation, more severe, but frequently prevented the French authorities from applying them.

The Jews, so savagely treated in the rest of France, were surprised to find themselves protected by Italian troops; on the 3rd January, 1943, the Italian Delegation at Nice made the position of the Fascist authorities clear:

"The local French authorities who, upon instructions from Vichy (instructions probably dictated to the French Government by Germany), were on the point of taking in the Alpes-Maritimes measures similar to those which have been taken in the zones not occupied by our troops, have been informed, both by this Delegation and by the Italian Military Authorities, that they must annul all measures of this nature.

"This has been done, not, however, without encountering a certain resistance dictated once again by the French desire to confirm their sovereignty.

"Our attitude has awakened feelings of lively gratitude among those Jews resident in the department of Alpes-Maritimes."

This protection which, had it been prolonged, might have saved many lives, was terminated at the Italian surrender by the entry of Nazi troops into the eight departments.

Thus rebuked, Oberg dashed to Marseille. On the 13th, he had a meeting with Bousquet, Secretary-General of the French Police and Lemoine, the Regional Préfet. He informed them that the German police would undertake the operation. The whole first *arrondissement* of the city would be surrounded at three o'clock in the morning. All resistance would be crushed with tanks. Fifty thousand Marseillais would be sent to concentration camps. After which, German engineers would blow up all the houses, leaving it to the French Government to indemnify their proprietors.

Bousquet and Lemoine fought inch by inch to prevent the tragedy. All they could achieve was that the French police should be substituted for the German police and that the operation should be carried out according to plans drawn up by themselves.

Thus, from January, 1943, onwards, no French town could be sure that it was safe from destruction ordered by the Nazis.

After the dissolution of the French Army of the Armistice, the problem of military collaboration with France presented itself under a very different guise to the Germans. It was no longer a question of persuading France by political means to engage such forces as she still possessed on the German side: it was a question of authorising France to create new forces destined for no other purpose than to fight for the Reich.

The new units in which Frenchmen could fight for the Germans were the L.V.F. (Legion of French Volunteers against Bolshevism), the Légion Tricolore, the Premier Régiment de France, the French Waffen S.S. and the Phalange Africaine.

Between the L.V.F. and the Légion Tricolore, there was but this difference, the former fought in German uniforms and the latter in French. The L.V.F., created in July, 1941 on the initiative of the Germans, was recruited in the northern zone by the collaborationist parties and particularly by the P.P.F. For the French Government it had no official existence. At its head was an unofficial directing committee under the chairmanship of Benoist-Méchin, as if it were some charity or sporting society. For the Germans, it simply took its place in the registers of the Wehrmacht as Regiment No. 638.

Besides the L.V.F., which continued to be recruited in the northern zone, General Bridoux, in July, 1942, decided to form the Légion Tricolore, which became effective in January, 1943: the new legionaries were to be recruited in both zones and attached to the French army whose uniform they would wear.

Both the L.V.F. and the Légion Tricolore had difficulty in getting recruits: an attempt was made to incorporate elements of the disbanded Army of the Armistice. Recruiting offices were opened all over France. Official propaganda, in the form of speeches and circulars, praised the merits of the volunteers. Nevertheless, even in the German view, the results were very far from what had been expected: the organisation had counted on 50,000 men, but there were barely, all told, some 10,000 to 20,000.

To renew enthusiasm, it was then decided to create a new formation, the Phalange Africaine, which was to fight in Tunisia against the allied forces, and for which 10,000 men were required. The results were even more pitiful. The most optimistic figures only gave the Phalange 300 effectives, of whom most were recruited by Colonel Cristofini. Having once commanded the 43rd Regiment of Colonial Infantry, Cristofini endeavoured to recruit his old subordinates: he made contact with his old Lieutenant-Colonel, Perinelli, who opposed the project. Not a man signed on. As a last resort, Cristofini picked up 150 of the scum of Tunis, syphilitics and disease-ridden of all kinds, whom he attracted by offering them good meals and money: half his recruits were natives.

Before going to the front, this crack regiment took part in two ceremonies: the first was to swear an oath of loyalty to the Marshal and promise to obey the orders of the Führer, chief of the armies in which it was to fight. The second was to be reviewed by a German General: he proclaimed "his joy at seeing part of the glorious French army on the battle-field, shoulder to shoulder with German formations".

At the front, however, the behaviour of the volunteers hardly justified his eulogies: during the course of a single skirmish with a British patrol, sixty out of a hundred and twenty-five Phalangists deserted. Fourteen Frenchmen, who were among the survivors of this battle, were later taken prisoner by Commandant Bourguin, of Juin's army, who was fighting to liberate Tunisia: they were immediately shot as traitors to their country.

To continue the honourable list, the French Waffen S.S. was another of the fighting units open to French volunteers.

Formed in July, 1942, and furnished a year later with a Comité des Amis de la Waffen S.S., under the chairmanship of Marion, it was to owe a certain increase in its activities to the circumstances of November, 1942. It then decided to recruit volunteers, who would serve in German uniform and take an oath of loyalty to the Führer, among the Paris collaborators and also among the prisoners, whose manifest boredom might be exploited.

The last unit which came to birth during this period was the Premier Régiment de France. For once, the intended numbers, which indeed were modest enough (82 officers and 2,657 men), were reached: it was true that this regiment was not intended to fight outside France; in the occupied territory, its role would be at the most to guard communications and protect the population against the attacks of dissidents. At the time of the Liberation, it went over, arms, bag and baggage to the side of the allied troops.

Besides this military collaboration, the Service du Travail Obligatoire, created under German pressure, was not long in becoming one of the essential pre-occupations of the Vichy Government. There were a whole number of official edicts issued with the intention of hastening its application.

On the 4th June, Laval demanded the assistance of all the Prefects: "Give the Prefects all powers to organise operations necessary for the Service Obligatoire . . . The Government has undertaken to despatch 220,000 workers before the 1st July. This undertaking must be fulfilled. I count upon your devotion and your sense of authority. Success depends on your efforts."

But, at the same time that he was issuing orders such as this and openly addressing the Prefects in order to stimulate their zeal, Laval, if the evidence of many of them is to be believed, summoned them to a meeting and spoke to them in private in very different terms.

"We have the choice," he said in February, 1943, "between letting Sauckel organise the seizing of men, women and young people and the possibility of losing men in administrative chaos."

This appeal, by the administration itself, to sabotage the Government's orders did not fall upon deaf ears.

At the start, for the two first batches of workers, each of 250,000 men, demanded by Sauckel in June, 1942 and in January, 1943, the dilatory procedure employed by the French had very little appreciable effect. By the spring of 1943, 500,750 workers had in fact left.

But for the following batch, demanded by Sauckel in May, 1943, the Government and Administration having no doubt in the meantime perfected their methods, the delays began to bear fruit. Of the 220,000 workers demanded in May, 1943, only 170,000 had gone by July. In August, Sauckel presented a new demand for 500,000 men and the calling up of the 50,000 of which the previous batch had been deficient. Laval gave him no satisfaction and, from the 16th October onwards, all departures for Germany were suspended till the end. The Reich had no other resource than to seize, by police raids, the men with whom the French Government no longer consented to furnish them.

Laval thus appears as a sort of Penelope who destroyed by underhand methods the effect of the public agreements he had made with Sauckel.

But, at the same time, he continued, in the field of high policy, to try to re-establish more normal relations with the Germans. He was continuously dominated by one thought: to have an interview with the Führer and "chat" with him. He remained persuaded that he was the only French statesman in whom the Führer had confidence. In April, two events came to support him in this conviction. On the one hand, Hitler granted him an audience, and on the other, a letter from Ribbentrop to Pétain on the 23rd let it be known that in no circumstances would the Führer "allow" the departure of Laval from the Government.

On the 30th April, 1943, Laval reached Berchtesgaden to have a conversation with Hitler, which he hoped once again might prove decisive.

In fact, there was no other result of this meeting between the two statesmen than a *communiqué*, drawn up in imprecise terms, which "recognised the place of France in Europe".

Laval had no illusions about the results of this last meeting. On his return to Paris, when dining at the German Embassy, he recalled his first interview with Chancellor Brüning, at the period when France was still victorious and the dominating power in Europe. Brüning, leaving with empty hands, as now Laval had done, had uttered words which the Frenchman could now repeat on his own account: "Is there some fatality between our two people which prevents our uttering the same words at the same time?"

In May, the war in Tunisia came to an end with the victory of the Allies who, on the 7th, reached Tunis: they found the Residency empty. At 2 o'clock in the morning, German police had removed by force the Resident-General, Admiral Estéva, and put him into a German aircraft. On the evening of the 7th, at 9.15, the aircraft landed at Vichy: Estéva, received by Krug von Nidda, who forbade Jardel, representing the Marshal, to come on to the airfield, was handed an order to leave immediately for Paris.

Estéva protested: "I do not accept orders from Berlin, I am a French official." None the less, on the morning of the 9th, he was put into a German car which drove him to Paris. He remained there twelve days, shut up in the Ritz Hotel by the occupation authorities.

In August, two new Nazi offensives, one against the Jews, and the other in favour of the S.T.O., made it possible to determine the real game Laval was playing.

Darquier de Pellepoix, obeying German instructions, drafted a law for the denaturalisation of all French Jews, their wives and their children, which would automatically entail their arrest. Bousquet, who was the first to hear of it in Paris, obtained from the Germans that Jews in certain exceptional categories should be excluded from these measures.

At Vichy, Laval was dilatory, sheltered himself behind the Marshal's authority, and finally refused to give the French Government's agreement: the Nazis were therefore reduced to having the arrests made by the "Schutzpolizei", when they would have much preferred to leave this privilege to the French police.

At the same time, General de la Porte du Theil, head of the Youth Camps, was presented with a demand from the Germans to deport to Germany for the benefit of the S.T.O., ten thousand young men from the camps. With Laval's approval, General de la Porte du Theil, during the course of an angry scene with Krug von Nidda, formally refused. He did not hesitate to predict a Nazi defeat and threatened him with the camps going over to the dissidents. On the 20th September, the Germans replied that the despatch of men from the camps should be suspended until the 31st December.

Thus Laval continued his double game, not this time out of any love of duplicity, but because he believed that the equivocal position in which France found herself obliged him to take apparently contradictory measures.

CHAPTER 3

# THE MARSHAL'S LAST MOVES

## (November, 1943–March, 1944)

ON the 13th November, 1943, almost three years after Laval's arrest, the Marshal attempted a new *coup d'état* against the Head of the Government.

It was no longer a question of preventing military collaboration with the Reich.

The objectives of Pétain and his advisers were more complicated: in the first place they wished to preserve what still remained of the Marshal's prestige by sundering it from the reputation of a statesman who was hated by the majority of Frenchmen.

In the second place, they wished openly to assert hostility to a policy of collaboration.

In the third, they wished to restore Republican law so that when General de Gaulle arrived in France he would not be able to act as a dictator.

Circumstances were certainly less favourable to the Marshal in 1943 than they had been in 1940. The Germans were on their guard, as a warning from Hitler himself shows:

"The Government of the Reich will not permit the repetition of incidents such as those of the 13th December, 1940, and will not allow any re-opening of the question of the continuity of political development between France and the Axis powers."

The victims of the previous *coup d'état* were warned. Déat, in an editorial in *l'Oeuvre*, took those who were to be responsible for the new 13th December to task.

Laval was also alert to the situation but, supported by the Germans and sure of the loyalty of the police who, as Minister of the Interior, were under his orders, he was unafraid.

"During the course of the day," wrote Pierre Nicolle on the 1st November, 1943, "I was received by President Laval. I found him perfectly calm and well aware of all the intrigues which are going on around him. The President was not concerned about them but regretted these cabals which made his task the more difficult."

Another difference from the 13th December was that the number of the Marshal's "accomplices" had singularly increased. To a few Ministers of the National Revolution, who had wished to prevent military collaboration with the Reich, had succeeded a number of members of Parliament of the Third Republic.

They wished to prevent General de Gaulle taking power in France at the Liberation. Had he not announced a general excommunication against the deputies and senators who had voted the Marshal full powers? In order to eliminate de Gaulle, it was necessary, so they believed, that Pétain should break with Laval and, having in consequence been white-washed of all taint of collaboration, should restore Republican laws: the vote of the National Assembly of July, 1940, permitted him to do so constitutionally.

Ghosts from the *ancien régime* reappeared and became active.

During the forty-eight hours after the collapse of Fascism, Georges Bonnet and Chichery arrived in Vichy.

It was rumoured that a hundred Radical members of Parliament, meeting secretly in Lyon, had proceeded to an examination of the support the Marshal was likely to receive from the elected members of the party.

Frossard, ex-Minister for Labour, talked in October of convening the National Assembly. Anatole de Monzie, who had also held many ministerial posts, sent a denunciatory letter to the Marshal.

Moderate elements rallied unofficially to Vichy, persuaded that the only means of escaping Communism, for which Algiers passed as the precursor, was to break with Laval and to forestall General de Gaulle by re-establishing the Republican Assemblies: such, among others, was Bouthillier, who soon paid for his audacity by being arrested by the Nazis.

Faced with such a consensus of opinion, there were many indications to show that Pétain would modify his old anti-parliamentary prejudice.

There was everything to encourage Pétain to break with Laval.

In September, 1943, in agreement with the Ministers Moysset and Romier—the latter was to replace Laval at the head of the

Government—with the members of his own staff and with Bouthillier, who had returned to Vichy to play the part of an adviser, the Marshal prepared the constitutional instrument for the *coup d'état* he had in mind by drafting a new clause to Constitutional Act No. 4. This Act, in its fifth version, assured the succession to Pierre Laval, who was to replace Pétain in case of the latter's incapacity. In September, the Marshal, no longer wishing to have him as successor, prepared a new draft, the sixth, which was preceded by an explanation of his reasons.

Constitutional Act No. 4 (sixth version) appointed a Directoire of seven members as successors to Pétain until the convening of Parliament.

This new Constitutional Act was kept secret by the Marshal and his immediate *entourage*: they were waiting for circumstances to ripen and the conflict between Laval and Pétain to come to a head.

At the end of October, the moment seemed to have arrived: on the 25th, during the course of a stormy interview, the Marshal indicated to Laval "that he was no longer the man the situation required, that he was incapable of maintaining order in the country, that abroad he was suspected by the Germans whom he had indeed deceived."

In order to proceed stage by stage, Pétain began by asking Laval to replace three Ministers, of whom Bonnard was one and to whom he wished General de la Porte du Theil, who had just resisted the Germans over the Youth Camps, to succeed, Marion "whom he had never been able to take" and Gabolde, the Garde des Sceaux, who was too collaborationist for his liking.

Laval refused and retired, if not to the Aventine Hill, at least to the lower storey of the Parc, where for a whole week he remained, unwilling to climb the Marshal's stairs.

The latter, placed thus in quarantine, nevertheless lost no time; with the assistance of his Brains Trust, he drafted three new documents; in the first place a letter to Laval, which formulated their conversation in writing; it reached the President on the 8th November. There followed a new version of the famous Act No. 4 (sixth version). There was now no longer any question of a Directoire, which must include personalities as notoriously hostile to the occupying power as Weygand and Auphan. The duty of appointing a successor to the Marshal was now placed directly on the National Assembly.

Finally, the new Act was preceded by an appeal to the country, which was intended to be read over the radio on the eve of the Act's publication. Pétain forcefully reminded his listeners of the legitimacy of the power he held from the National Assembly, and that he alone was legally entitled to transmit it.

"Vichy, 12th November, 1943.

"Frenchmen,

"On the 10th July, 1940, the National Assembly reposed in me the power of promulgating by one or several acts a new Constitution for the French State.

"I am completing this Constitution. It reconciles the principle of National Sovereignty and the right of free suffrage with the necessity to assure the stability and authority of the State.

"But I am concerned at what might happen if I were to disappear before having accomplished to the end the task the Nation confided to me.

"It is respect for legitimacy which conditions the stability of a country. Unless there is legitimacy, there can only be adventures, rivalries of factions, anarchy and fratricidal struggles.

"I embody today French legitimacy. I intend to preserve it as a sacred trust and that it shall, upon my decease, return to the National Assembly from whom I received it, if the new Constitution has not by then been ratified.

"Thus, whatever appalling events France may suffer, political power will always be assured in conformity with the law.

"I do not wish my disappearance to open the way to a period of disorder which would place the unity of France in peril.

"This is the object of the Constitutional Act which will be promulgated in the *Journal Officiel* tomorrow.

"Frenchmen, let us continue to work together for the establishment of the new regime whose basis I shall shortly explain to you and which alone can restore to France her grandeur."

In the afternoon of the 12th, the Marshal's office sent to the radio, in preparation for translation and foreign broadcasts, the text of the speech which had already been recorded. The secret had been well kept: Laval knew nothing. At the last moment, an official of the radio, out of respect for the hierarchy, thought it irregular that there should be direct contact between the producer and the consumer without it passing through the necessary middleman, who was the Head of the Government.

Laval, having been warned, once again went upstairs to the Marshal's storey. At first he was amiable: he approved the Head of the State's initiative: it was not an old parliamentary hand like himself who would protest against Government being brought back into the political arena: the suppression of the succession was moreover indifferent to him: why should he wish to be Head of the State one day?

"But indeed, Monsieur le Maréchal, I was but recently reading some of your speeches, some of the messages which are in a little book. You have been rather hard on members of Parliament. And today, it's you who are calling them to your aid. As for me, I know members of Parliament, I've seen them, I'm accustomed to dealing with them, I know how to manage them. You seem to be in a great hurry, but we are not on our own. There is the occupying power, we ought to ask the Germans for their opinion, for courtesy's sake at least."

Faced with this "advice", the Marshal could do no other than yield: towards the end of the afternoon he summoned Krug von Nidda in order to communicate to him the message he intended broadcasting the following day. "If you please, Monsieur le Maréchal," the Consul-General objected, "I must refer to Paris."

Paris consisted of the Minister Schleier of the German Embassy. As soon as he was informed, he telephoned the message to Berlin and awaited instructions.

The following day, a few minutes before the hour fixed for the broadcast, Krug von Nidda entered the Hôtel du Parc. The Marshal received him with but little cordiality: he alluded to a recent defeat of the Wehrmacht on the Russian Front and protested that the Germans had no right to interfere: "This business has nothing to do with you," he said, "do I ask you why you have evacuated Jitomir?"

The argument did not convince the diplomat, who asked for the broadcast to be delayed. It might even be said that he demanded it: if the Marshal persisted, von Nidda had received the order to make "the Director of the Radiodiffusion Nationale personally responsible".

The Marshal had to yield. The radio, at the last minute, broadcast, instead of the message which all France was awaiting, selections from *Dédé*.

As for the Head of the State, he was furious, in the grip of an anger he had no wish to control; he proclaimed that henceforth he considered himself a prisoner.

Deprived of the opportunity of officially broadcasting his message, the Marshal set about spreading it unofficially. An official of the Ministry of Information read it to the representatives of the French and foreign press. The latter spread it across the world; the London radio announced the resignation of the Head of the State. False rumours went the rounds in Paris: the Marshal had made himself a prisoner, Laval had been arrested and Doriot was in power. The Bourse collapsed. "The directors of big banks made open propaganda against the Government."

The Deputy Frossard wrote to the Marshal: "You have saved France for the third time."

The dissidents, fearing this rallying of members of Parliament about the Head of the State, broadcast a message from Brazzaville, informing deputies and senators that the Council of the Resistance forbade them to take any part in any Assembly whatever.

Brinon, "Ambassador of France" and a creature of the Nazis, informed Pétain that the Germans were furious: a French Minister had told them of a remark made by the Marshal on the 13th November and which revealed his certainty that the Reich would lose the war.

On the 4th December, Otto Abetz reappeared on the scene, having been recalled from disgrace by Ribbentrop. He returned to a position similar to that of the 13th December, 1940, though a somewhat less satisfactory one. He arrived in Paris from Germany on the evening of the 27th November, as did Krug von Nidda, who was returning from Berlin where he had gone to receive orders. The Führer's two messengers found the French capital in a state of effervescence: deprived of official information on the results of the Marshal's initiative, public opinion was in a wild state of excitement.

Moreover, between Abetz's arrival in Paris and his departure for the Allier, there came news of an assassination which everyone believed to have a direct connection with the Vichy crisis. Maurice Sarraut, editor of the Radical newspaper, *La Dépêche de Toulouse*, had been murdered.

This might perhaps go some way to explain why Abetz, on his return to Vichy, on the 4th December, 1943, had recourse to the same police protection he had used as escort after the 13th December, 1940. Surrounded with a considerable armed force, the Ambassador reached the Hôtel du Parc at 11 a.m. Outside, there was an atmosphere of crisis: "The posts of the Gardes Mobiles had been re-inforced, there was a police cordon round the hotel: the Gestapo was there; it was even said that the environs of Vichy were occupied by numerous detachments of German police." Inside the hotel, the lobbies and ante-rooms were in a state of nervous agitation. It had just been learned that the whole personnel of the French Embassy at Berne, except for the Ambassador himself, had gone over to the dissidents. Marseille had been bombed, there had been a raid at Grenoble on barracks occupied by the Wehrmacht: these things did not create a particularly diplomatic atmosphere for the reception of the Ambassador and his armoured cars. Ménétrel did not conceal the fact that he expected to be arrested.

In an interview which lasted half an hour, the Ambassador gave the Marshal a letter from Ribbentrop dated 29th November. It was a long document, which took the Marshal to task for his permanent resistance to the occupying power.

Ribbentrop began by recapitulating the crisis of the 13th November: it denoted a state of mind "in open contradiction to the policy of collaboration between France and Germany." Then he transmitted, on behalf of the Führer, an ultimatum containing five points:

1. The Chancellor opposed all remitting of power to the National Assembly "which, in September, 1939, had declared war on Germany without any cause whatever, and of which a not negligible proportion of members are again fighting against Germany".

2. Since no election could take place in time of war, there existed, and could exist, "no legal body capable of exercising the functions which the proposed broadcast wished to confer on it, and which, for this purpose, could be recognised by Germany".

3. The Führer took the opportunity of declaring that the Marshal had not remained loyal to the spirit of collaboration envisaged at Montoire, but had on the contrary shown "permanent resistance". "The policy of the supreme controllers of the French State at Vichy has pursued a direction which the Government of the Reich cannot approve and which it will not accept in the future in its capacity as occupying power, in view of

the fact that it is responsible for the maintenance of order and public calm in France."

After these threats, here are the terms of the ultimatum:

"4. The Government of the Reich is compelled to demand that the supreme direction of the French State should in future submit all proposed modifications of laws to the agreement of the Government of the Reich [a statute for a Protectorate]; that, moreover, Monsieur Laval, should be charged with re-organising the French Cabinet without delay in a manner acceptable to the German Government as a guarantee of collaboration. This Cabinet must thereafter enjoy the unreserved support of the supreme directorate of the State.

"Finally, the supreme direction of the French State will be responsible for taking measures to eliminate immediately all elements obstructive to the important work of recovery in the influential posts of the administration and also for appointing persons worthy of confidence to these posts."

After this ultimatum, clause 5 was an insolent piece of blackmail.

"Today, the one and only guarantee for the maintenance of public calm and order in the interior of France and thereby the security of the French people and its regime against revolution and Bolshevik chaos is the German Wehrmacht . . . I pray you to take such action that Germany will be able to safeguard these interests in all circumstances by one means or another."

In conclusion, there was a formal recognition of the "freedom" left to the Marshal: "If however you do not consider that you are in a position to respond favourably to the German demands mentioned above, or if our rejection of your proposed law, directed against German interests, should decide you to consider yourself afterwards as before prevented from exercising your functions, I am to inform you, in the name of the Führer, that he leaves you entirely free to draw what conclusions you please. . . ."

It was an invitation, couched in barely diplomatic terms, to submit or resign.

Pétain's reaction was dignified. With his hands clasped, he replied: "I perfectly understand the meaning of this letter and as a soldier I cannot admit what you say. But it has taken three weeks to give me this answer. It raises extremely delicate questions which I want to consider. I would like to see you again tomorrow morning to give you my reply."

Abetz agreed to the delay, but not without inflicting two somewhat specious arguments on the Marshal. If Pétain refused, he was playing the game of the Communists. While the summoning of the National Assembly in the case of the Marshal's death placed a premium upon it. The "British Intelligence Service" would not fail to make use of it. "Do you think so?" said the Marshal.

"Yes, Monsieur le Maréchal, and we wish to preserve you."

All this did not unduly alarm the Head of the State; hardly had Abetz left when he openly took Romier for a little walk and confided in him as follows:

"Really the Germans are not clever politicians and Monsieur Laval is absurd to hang on to them. If he thinks that Churchill and the Americans will sit down at the same table as himself, he's making a big mistake. He'll prevent my welcoming them, and that's all he'll succeed in doing. If he was really intelligent, he would have taken the opportunity I gave him of flying to the Argentine or elsewhere."

By the morning of the 5th December, Pétain had not yet changed his mind. In a private conversation with some of his colleagues, Ménétrel, Jardel, Romier and Rochat, he was explicit: "I don't want Monsieur Laval. I have no confidence in him. Let him go away . . . I'm eighty-eight years old and I cannot allow this situation to continue any longer."

Half an hour later, Pétain received the German Ambassador and read him a note which contained three points: the first was equivalent to a capitulation except for the fact that a restriction limited its consequences. He was still using the methods of finesse to avoid precise solutions. Pétain began by saying that he agreed to take up once more the functions of the Head of the State "on condition that no publicity were given to his decision".

The second paragraph, in spite of later denials on the part of the Marshal, was aimed essentially at Laval. "The Marshal believes it only honest to observe that in the actual state of his powers his authority is extremely limited."

The Head of the Government, having been informed of this phrase, was not deluded. In the afternoon, he went and saw the Marshal: the Marshal went for him: he admitted that it was Laval who was aimed at in the note, but he wanted no more of him; Laval was unpopular and things could not go on as they were. Then he showed him the door.

Laval informed the Ambassador that he was prepared to resign unless the Marshal disavowed his intentions concerning him in writing. Abetz, having learned from the precedent of December, 1940, persuaded Laval not to give the Head of the State an opening by making a personal protest.

The *démarche* was made by Brinon. He went to see the Marshal and obtained from him in writing what was asked: "The Marshal confirms that the second point in the note remitted this morning to Monsieur the German Ambassador was aimed neither at the Wehrmacht nor at President Laval."

Abetz considered the incident definitely closed: the Marshal had yielded once again.

Two letters addressed by Marshal Pétain to Chancellor Hitler, on the 11th and 18th December, mark the stages towards his ultimate abdication.

The first, still in general terms, re-affirmed the Marshal's desire to pursue a policy of collaboration: a declaration of principle which might still have the effect of delaying the decisions demanded.

In the second letter to Hitler, dated 18th December, it appears that the vague and general protestations had not been sufficient to appease the occupying power. Pétain was obliged to draw the practical consequences of his capitulation.

"Monsieur le Chancellier,

"Further to my letter of the 11th December, and to the wishes you have expressed, I inform you that modifications to the law shall henceforth be submitted before publication to the occupying authorities."

In yielding to this Nazi demand, the Marshal took his place once and for all in the list of heads of vanquished states on whom Hitler had imposed his will before completely dispossessing them: after three years of shifts, the Führer behaved towards him as once, though it had taken less time, he had behaved towards Schuschnigg, the last Chancellor of Austria, and to Hacha, the last President of the Republic of Czechoslovakia.

On the 9th December, only four days after the arrival of Abetz, Pétain resumed the audiences which had been interrupted for three weeks.

On the 12th December, the ceremony of saluting the colours, which he had ignored since the crisis, took place for the first time with an official representative.

The following Sunday, 19th December, the day on which Renthe-Fink, the watch dog whom Hitler had insisted should be appointed to the Marshal's staff, arrived in Vichy. Pétain himself attended the ceremony of the colours.

Thus Abetz and Laval, plotting together, had won: they had torn from the Marshal a renunciation of the decisions taken after the 13th November.

Another object of their manoeuvres was now to obtain the dismissal of the ministers, high officials or intimates of the Marshal who had encouraged his rebellion and who were hostile to Laval.

On the 4th December, in his first ultimatum to the Marshal, Abetz, on the orders of Hitler, had demanded that three men should be brought into the Government who were favourable to collaboration, and who were among those now beginning to be nicknamed the "Ultras". These were Marcel Déat, Philippe Henriot and Joseph Darnand.

These three had earned the honour by different means. Déat came from the Left, where he had tried to renovate Socialism by a neo-Socialism with authoritarian tendencies. A supporter of the alignment of France to National Socialism, the unfortunate and misunderstood promoter of a single party in France, he was, as editor of *l'Oeuvre* and Chief of the Rassemblement National Populaire, one of the most vehement adversaries of the National Revolution in Paris, and one of the most dynamic and talented of Otto Abetz's recruits. His leading articles in *l'Oeuvre*, denouncing to the Germans Vichy's legitimate impulses towards resistance, had on several occasions over-stepped the limits, at that time so fluid and uncertain, of the crime of treason.

Henriot came from the Right: more damaging than Déat because his eloquence, less vicious and less intellectual than Déat's, was capable of arousing a response even in good Frenchmen, he attacked on the radio the damage done by the allied bombing of France, the operations of the *maquisards*, the plotting of the dissidents of London and Algiers with the foreigner which, so he maintained, would entail the handing over of the Empire to the Anglo-Saxons. Specious and tendentious though they were, his speeches had nevertheless more contact with reality than those of Déat.

As for Darnand, he was a sort of sergeant-major who believed himself to have been promoted Führer and statesman. Having fought magnificently in both wars—indeed France owed to him, in part, the reversal of the military situation on the 15th July, 1918, (as leader of a patrol, he had taken the German prisoners who revealed the imminence of the offensive)—in 1939, he had one of the rare successes of the "phoney" war by penetrating into German territory at the head of an irregular force. Anti-German, as long as he was ordered to be so, it had never even occurred to him, after Montoire, to question the policy of collaboration announced on the radio by his old chief of Verdun days. He had applied it strictly in its most odious manifestations and had made of the Légion, and then of the S.O.L., disciplined formations in the totalitarian manner.

Faced with this triple demand, Pétain decided to contest the appointment of Déat who seemed to him to be the least desirable, and to allow, under compulsion, his hand to be forced concerning the other two.

On the 18th December, a verbal message reached Vichy from the German Embassy in Paris announcing further German demands: two lists had been drawn up containing the names of the members of the Government and the Administration whom the occupying power considered undesirable.

Laval, who was in Paris, received these two documents from Abetz for transmission to Pétain: the first contained several hundred names of Prefects and administrative officials whom the Germans wished dismissed and, in some cases, deported. Laval reacted violently against a demand which, striking at so great a number of his civil servants, would decapitate the administration and make the country ungovernable. He persuaded Abetz that the lists should be reduced to forty names.

Faced with these German demands, a new discussion arose as to what attitude the Marshal should adopt. Laval, Abetz and Brinon brought pressure to bear on the Marshal to appoint the three "Ultras" to the Government: Déat, Darnand and Henriot. His *entourage*, among whom were Jardel, Ménétrel, General Campet and General de la Porte du Theil, insisted that he should refuse. In the end, the Marshal held out against Déat, but tolerated

Darnand and Philippe Henriot on the condition, however, that he should not have to sign the appointments himself; by doing this, Pétain managed to stand aloof from decisions he did not like, but at the same time he abandoned to Laval one of the last rights remaining to him: that of appointing members of the Government.

This new renunciation on the part of the Head of the State was accompanied and followed by a number of events which brought to a head its unfortunate consequences for the independence of France.

On the 27th December, General Laure was arrested by the Germans at his estate near Cannes.

On the 28th December, at 5 p.m., Abetz presented to the Marshal, Councillor von Renthe-Fink, Hitler's special envoy to assist and keep under surveillance the Head of the State.

On the 29th, Bousquet resigned from the position of Secretary-General of Police. He summoned his assistants to a meeting for the last time at 12.30 p.m.; most of them had already been appointed to other posts, while those who remained refused to accept the new Secretary-General, Darnand.

Two days later, Darnand and Henriot took up their duties.

Bousquet's Ministry had burnt a number of dossiers. The new Minister was received with scorched earth tactics: a void was created at the moment of handing over power. Darnand had to take over his office by himself.

The new Government, with few exceptions, included only partisans of Germany. Only Grasset and Jannekeyn had a definite anti-German attitude.

The Marshal never once presided over a meeting of this Government, whose coming to power marked the beginning of a series of dramatic events.

On the 5th January, the Nazis arrested General de la Porte du Theil and Bousquet. In the case of the first, the Germans accused him of, among other misdeeds, utterances made in private conversation with an intimate colleague of Laval's.

On the 6th, Bonnafous resigned: his extremely courageous letter to Laval, in which he attacked his policy, was published in the Paris Press and resulted in his being searched for by the Gestapo.

On the 10th January, 1944, Darnand received by decree, as a permanent delegation of power from the Head of the Government, the right "to exercise authority over all the police forces;

all bodies and formations which assure public security and the internal safety of the state".

Laval thus gave his new colleague full powers over the police. Ten days later, Darnand was authorised to set up courts-martial of three members to meet at the request of Commissioners of Police. This law, which was still in force on the 30th June, 1944, and later prolonged, suspended the judicial guarantees under Common Law. In case of flagrant crimes, the criminals were executed immediately and without trial.

When, on the 22nd January, 1944, Laval informed the Council of Ministers of the extraordinary powers conferred on Darnand, they were astounded. Laval himself admitted, in his speech to his colleagues, "that this law has no precedent in our annals. Even Fouché did not go so far."

Laval had at last reached his governmental objectives. He persuaded the Marshal never to attend these purely formal meetings.

"Let me do all the dirty work, Monsieur le Maréchal. You must remain above all that. Tracou will attend the Councils and give you a report. And besides," he said laughing, "when you're not there, I lead the Ministers along with flags flying and drums beating, and what's more I can smoke."

Only Marcel Déat was lacking to this assembly of dumb men in session in a smoking-room.

Laval wanted him to come into the Government in order to please the Germans and also to increase the appearance of "Left Republicanism" in the new Ministry. But he did not want him to have one of the leading Ministries desired by the editor of *l'Oeuvre*.

Two months of intrigue, in which Laval deployed all his old parliamentary tricks, succeeded in the end in limiting Déat to a secondary position in which the President of the R.N.P. would be the less embarrassing.

Originally, Déat had aimed at nothing less than the Presidency of the Council. During the course of the summer of 1943, a long note, which, drawn up with Luchaire, defined his policy, had doubtless seemed to him to be his future Government manifesto: in internal policy, he intended to take socialistic measures; in foreign policy, to increase collaboration.

But under compulsion, Déat eventually accepted the post of Minister of Labour, on condition that it was bracketed with a new

Ministry grouping all the activities designed to diminish the sufferings born of the war: National Assistance, Red Cross, prisoners, ex-Servicemen. . . .

Once again, Laval was not ready to take action and tried to gain time. German interference, whether provoked by Déat or not, compelled him to come to a decision.

In February, Berlin, suffering from growing man-power difficulties, demanded that Déat should be brought into the Government as Minister of Labour.

On the 22nd February, Laval told the Marshal of this Nazi demand which he thought it difficult not to obey.

On the 11th March there were two new assaults designed to make the Marshal yield. Laval, returning from Paris, informed the Head of the State of the limitations to the powers which would be given Déat. Abetz was in agreement that his Social Ministry should not include the ex-Servicemen. As for National Assistance, Déat could be given the assistance of a Commissaire Général, a "sensible man", who would neutralise him.

When Laval had left, Renthe-Fink was announced and followed up, in the most brutal manner, the diplomatic pressure which had been brought to bear by the President of the Council.

"I've got some unpleasant things to say to you today, Monsieur le Maréchal. The German Government attaches great importance to Déat's entry into the Government." Pétain tried to resist: "He is a man universally hated in France. If he comes into the Government, I shall resign."

As he left with Tracou, Renthe-Fink said, in order that it might be repeated to the Marshal: "You must know that no one will be concerned at his threat of resignation; we shall make no attempt to retain the Marshal."

The Marshal, having been informed, drew the appropriate lesson and the practical consequences for the struggle that was taking place. The lesson: "There may be far-reaching results," he declared. The practical consequences: the burning of all dangerous papers: the personal archives he could not allow to fall into German hands, if he were removed by force.

What courses were open to him? He might imitate the King of Denmark and remain under surveillance, playing no political part, and even forbidding the Ministers to retain their power: the Secretary-Generals would then administer the country alone. This possibility pleased Renthe-Fink: "Everything is so easy in

Denmark," he said, "there we don't have these constant and exhausting discussions on every point."

The Marshal considered this solution, but did not think it would last.

"If I withdraw, the Germans will not leave me free for long; they'll take me to Germany."

And then again, in his view, it would facilitate Nazi exactions.

Pétain, once again, had a tendency to avoid making extreme decisions. And on the 15th March, when Schleier gave Laval an ultimatum demanding that the Déat affair should be concluded within two days, Pétain had found a compromise.

He would not give his agreement or sign Déat's appointment, any more than he had done for those of Darnand and Henriot. Déat might be a Minister, but he would be an illegal Minister, whom Pétain could always ignore and disavow.

On the 16th March, at 8 p.m., a telephone message from Vichy informed the editor of *l'Oeuvre* that he was now Minister and Secretary of State for Labour and National Solidarity charged with "the control and co-ordination of Social organisations in the national interest".

Déat was delighted, perhaps not realising the successive abandonments of position that Laval had extorted from him during three months of negotiations: he accepted the Ministry of Labour which he had previously refused at any price. He agreed no longer to sign his articles in *l'Oeuvre*. His Ministry of National Solidarity had somewhat vague functions: National Assistance preserved its own autonomy; the Red Cross was protected by its international character; the prisoners and ex-Servicemen remained under the control of the Head of the Government. Finally, the decrees appointing him, which appeared in the *Journal Officiel*, of the 17th March, were not signed by Pétain.

Laval seemed satisfied, but did not show himself particularly generous: he stopped the subsidy to the Rassemblement National Populaire.

"I don't mind being scolded," he said, "but let it at least be gratis."

## CHAPTER 4

# THE DOWNFALL OF A REGIME

### 1. Before the Landings (March–June, 1944)

THE year 1944 saw total war spread all over French territory.

On the 15th February, the regime of the northern zone was extended to the coastal departments of the Mediterranean; it was a precaution against landings in the south which, on the 25th March, caused the three first convoys of evacuees to leave Marseille. It was a pathetic exodus which the Marshal deplored: "I understand and share their anxieties and their concern," but he did not protest against it.

At the same time, German reprisals took on an often atrocious form. There were arrests sparing no one. In the first place the *vulgum pecus*, if one may call it so, of the Resistance, of which only the numbers are important: it was recorded that in the month of March the Paris police made 4,746 arrests. Then they went for bigger game: in April, they arrested the families of "ex-General" Catroux, Florimond Bonte, François de Menthon, Louis Jacquinot, André le Troquer, Marc Rucart and Jacques Duclos. At the same time, the principal colleagues of Gastin, Secretary-General for National Defence, Generals Carayon and Lefort and Colonel Cornillon, were arrested for having used their high positions in the service of the Resistance. In May, thirteen Prefects were arrested.

Simultaneously with the arrests, executions increased, sometimes individual or sometimes in the form of collective slaughter. On the 6th May, as a reprisal for the execution of Colonel Cristofini, in Algiers, nine dissident leaders were condemned to death by a court-martial at Annecy: five of them were immediately executed. On the 8th May, twenty-eight "terrorists" were condemned to death by the German Tribunals.

As for the collective killings, they now surpassed all previous limits of horror and savagery: any pretext was good enough to annihilate villages and their populations: a shot fired at German troops, asylum given to members of the Resistance, were the reasons put forward for mass executions. Nevertheless, they quite often went by default: the "nervousness" of the occupying troops being the only possible explanation.

On the 1st April, at Ascq, near Lille, 86 inhabitants between the ages of 15 and 76 were massacred by a detachment of the S.S., following on the derailing of a military train coming from Russia.

At Rouffignac, in the Dordogne, on the 31st March, 1944, 66 hostages were taken of whom 16 were deported and 50 eventually freed.

At Sièges, in the Jura, on the 10th April, 1944, 29 houses out of 35 were burnt down, 8 people deported, and 5 shot after being tortured.

At Verjon, in the Ain, on the 16th April, 1944, 9 people were deported; on the 18th July, 1944, 47 houses were burnt down.

At Frayssinet-le-Gélat, in Lot, on the 21st March, 1944, 10 men were shot and 3 old women hanged.

At Ugines, in Savoie, on the 5th June, 1944, 28 hostages were shot and 6 houses blown up with dynamite.

While this murderous madness was spreading over France, Gauleiter Sauckel was making new demands for the despatch of ever increasing numbers of French workers to Germany. He was acting on Hitler's orders.

On the 4th January, 1944, at a conference held by the Führer at his headquarters, the industrial needs of the Reich in labour from occupied countries had been fixed at 4,000,000 men.

Of this total, France was to provide 1,000,000 between the 1st February and the 31st December, 1944—91,000 a month.

Faced with this hardening attitude of the occupying power, what was Pétain's and Laval's attitude to be?

During these last months at Vichy, the Marshal, while still the recipient of a certain deference, had no longer any power whatever in fact.

Pétain lived almost abandoned in the Hôtel du Parc or in the Pavillon Sévigné, surrounded by a smaller and smaller number of faithful followers among whom were Admiral Fernet, Commandant Tracou, Bernard Ménétrel and Louis-Dominique

Girard. . . . Such work as he did had now no further contact with reality; from time to time, the occupying power remembered his existence, put words into his mouth which did not correspond to his thought, or moved him from one residence to another.

It was a lamentable ending to the life of an old man of eighty-eight and particularly for a Head of a State of whom it had been said that he had greater powers than Louis XIV.

He was now the sovereign of a State that had no reality, a Principality of Gerolstein in the middle of a world drama. Since November, 1942, France no longer had an army: it was pitiful to see the victor of Verdun creating illusions for himself as he played at being a military leader with his personal guard (3,000 men) and with the only unit that had been re-constituted and was called "The First Regiment of France".

On the 1st January, 1944, the Colonel of this unit, who, by an obvious cumulative process, was also the Commander of "the Government's Armed Forces" (in fact they were co-extensive), drew up a proclamation in the purest of military styles: "With your help we shall hold our own. Be assured that in the difficult hours which are still in store for our Fatherland, we shall remain under your orders, the loyal soldiers of the Marshal." Then a battalion (a thousand men) went to Le Blanc (Indre) to parade in review order before General Caldairou, head of the office of the Secretary of State for Defence: a minor military parade which the Press turned into a triumph: "A brilliant march past followed: first came the motor-cyclists with their machine-guns aligned, their Commander standing up in a side-car, then the cyclists. The band followed, playing *Sambre-et-Meuse*; the infantry came last, marching in perfect order, their heads held high, their bearing proud, proving by their appearance that they were worthy to maintain the glorious traditions of the French Army."

What had glory to do with this derisory spectacle?

The history of Vichy at this period abounds in *trompe-l'oeil* of this nature.

There was another proof of the fantasies among which Pétain lived: the only matter in which the Marshal was still free to act, and might preserve the illusion of still possessing some influence, was a labour which the circumstances rendered purely theoretical: the giving of a Constitution to France.

On the 30th January, 1944, the Marshal signed this Constitution which was never put into effect, but whose very conception represented an astonishing innovation in the history of the French State.

In the first place, it was called "Projet de Constitution de la République Française", which thus marked some affiliation with the regime which one imagined had been abolished by the National Revolution. It comprised (who could have expected it?) a Parliament which was comparable in many ways to that of the Third Republic; a Senate, of whom 250 members were to be elected by the Councillors of the Departments and the delegates of the Municipal Councillors, while 50 were to be appointed by the Head of the State; a Chamber of Deputies of 500 members elected (who could have foreseen it?) by single, direct and universal suffrage.

The Assemblies were to vote the laws, and could pass votes of confidence or lack of confidence in the Government or in an individual Minister one clear day after the motion had been tabled (on this point the Constitution anticipated the Fourth Republic).

There was to be parliamentary immunity from arrest and a procedure for a constitutional revision which united the Senate and the Chamber in a National Assembly, all of which was in accordance with the best Republican traditions.

If these constitutional labours lacked reality, they at least contained nothing to which the population could take exception. Unfortunately, this was not equally true of certain phrases the Marshal uttered either spontaneously or under duress from the Germans.

His references to the collaborationists became at this time extremely ambiguous.

There were some whom he continued to encourage in words, such as Darnand, the Chief of the Militia, whom he did not hesitate to congratulate. "You are acting as I did with the mutineers in 1917."

There were others, on the other hand, who heard Pétain condemn and disavow the attitude which, in all good faith, they thought they had adopted with his agreement.

During this same period, the Marshal's messages or public speeches made his listeners indignant. The *Words to the French People*, to which he attached so much importance and whose authorship he so jealously claimed, were now either written under duress or altered before reproduction by the Nazi censorship.

It was duress in the case of the message the Marshal was compelled to prepare for the event of an allied landing in France. For three months, Renthe-Fink, armed with imperative letters from von Rundstedt and Ribbentrop, harried the Marshal to record in advance a speech which could be broadcast on the day of the "invasion". In the first instance, the Marshal refused outright but then was reduced to refusing in detail: he could not, in particular, contemplate the French authorities in France being replaced by Germans. Finally, on the 17th March, a text was agreed which Berlin thought "weak and indecisive" but which infuriated French opinion. In the presence of the head of his office, Jean Tracou, alone, the Marshal made the recording.

There was the same pressure, the same resistance and, in the end, the same yielding to the stronger will, over the message of the 24th April, 1944, which condemned terrorism: two passages demanded by the Germans were singularly provocative: "Frenchmen, whoever among you, whether civil servant, soldier, or simple citizen, takes part in the resistance groups, compromises the future of the country." And: "When the present tragedy comes to an end and, thanks to the defence of our continent by Germany and to the efforts of Europe, our civilisation is finally saved from the danger of Bolshevism, the hour will come when France will once more find and assert her position."

There was however one occasion on which the Marshal spoke freely to the population: it was on the 26th April in Paris, where he had gone, for the first time since his accession to power, in order to render homage to the victims of allied bombing in the Batignolles district.

As soon as it was known he was coming, the population rushed to give him an enthusiastic welcome. There was an official ceremony at Notre-Dame where the Head of the State was received by Cardinal Suhard. After the service, Pétain returned to the Hôtel de Ville through cheering crowds. From the balcony, he spoke a few improvised words to the huge, cheering throng.

"Mesdames, Messieurs,

"I have come to pay you a visit. I cannot talk to each one of you individually, it's impossible, there are too many of you, but I did not wish to visit Paris without greeting you, without recalling myself to your memory.

"Moreover, these are unhappy circumstances which have brought me here. I have come here to console you for all the misfortunes that reign over Paris. They make me very sad.

"But this is a first visit I am making you. I hope I shall be able to come easily to Paris, without having to warn my guardians. I shall come happily. But today I am not making an entrance into Paris, merely a little visit of gratitude. I think of you very often.

"I find Paris somewhat changed, for it is now four years since I have been here. But you can be sure that as soon as I can, I shall come back and, then, it will be an official visit. So I hope I shall see you again soon."

There was not a word against the allies, but an allusion to "all" the misfortunes that reigned over the capital, and an allusion to his "guardians", and an announcement of future liberty. It was enough to make the censors take a hand; and, without the slightest reference to the Marshal, recapitulating the business of the Ems telegram, they concocted a false speech which was made public in the Press:

"I did not think I should find myself in the presence of such a crowd and I shall not make a speech. I am concerned with the whole life of the country. If every day I receive a large number of people and take pleasure in conversing with them, I regret that owing to limited time I cannot do so today.

"In any case, I can say to you that I have much enjoyed being able to make you this short visit.

"I have come to pay homage to the dead, and console the living who are threatened with the attacks which are forecast for the whole country. As I went into Notre-Dame this morning, I was made very sad by the painful spectacle of families in mourning. I should like them to feel how much I share their sorrow.

"This is the first visit I have made you and it is a visit in particular circumstances in order to prove to you that the Government and the Head of the State have not forgotten you and are doing everything they can to help you in the grave hours through which you are living.

"But a day will come when peace restored will allow us to bring back to you the joy of living.

"Our pleasure will then be mutual, for I shall have to thank you for your attitude which has always been so understanding and so loyal.

"I rejoice merely at the thought that this moment will come; but until then, I ask you, in my name and in the name of President Laval, to do nothing that can compromise our actions and the future of France."

It was a very different version from the original: an allusion to Pierre Laval had been added; while the misfortunes which had fallen upon Paris seemed to consist merely of allied bombing, as if the Germans were not relentlessly persecuting the Paris population.

But, even thus sweetened, the speech said too much and the Germans wished to avoid further incidents of the same kind.

Pétain, therefore, had to be isolated more than ever: at Vichy, he still saw too many people, might say things and take action which the Nazis disapproved.

Moreover, the provisional capital lived in fear of some conspiracy or parachute drop to remove Pétain as Hitler had freed Mussolini.

From now on, the Marshal no longer could choose where he would live. He was transferred like a prisoner from château to château.

Renthe-Fink, on Ribbentrop's orders, brought pressure to bear on the Marshal in order to persuade him to go and live temporarily at Voisins, in a château of the Ile-de-France, where it would be easier to "protect" him.

On the 1st May, in a private conversation with the Swiss Minister, Stucki, Pétain expressed his distress: "Nervous and depressed, Pétain remarked to me that all his advisers had been taken away, that he had no political experience and that he had been the victim of intolerable pressure. . . . He had often yielded, too often, but on one point he would never yield, he would never voluntarily leave Vichy."

On the 4th May, Renthe-Fink told the Marshal that a landing was imminent, that he must be placed in safety, and demanded that he should leave for Voisins, near Rambouillet. The Marshal at first refused, then discussed the matter, and finally yielded, not without however having obtained permission to draw up a declaration, whose text was argued for hours with the Germans, to be handed to the Nuncio for the Diplomatic Corps.

"The German Government has informed the Head of the French State that it wishes temporarily to transfer his residence from Vichy to occupied France. The reason for this move is the safety of his person.

"The Marshal has many times declared that he intended remaining in Vichy, which he has made the legal seat of the Government ever since the armistice.

"However, faced with the demand that has been made, and in view of the circumstances, the Marshal will leave for the neighbourhood of Paris. But the seat of the Government remains in Vichy, to which the Marshal will return as soon as the circumstances which necessitate his departure shall have ceased to exist."

On Monday, 7th May, the Marshal left for Voisins in a convoy of nineteen cars, of which twelve were full of German police. He arrived at nightfall.

From Voisins, while he was living there, he went to Rouen. It was a most moving visit for the town had been heavily damaged by raids. The Marshal could not reach the cathedral which was surrounded by rubble. The Regional Prefect, who received him, was in plain clothes. He had lost his uniform in the last raid.

Very soon, on the 19th May, Renthe-Fink, fearing allied landings in the northern zone, suggested to the Marshal that he should return to central France, where another château would be made ready for him near Vichy. The Marshal submitted, but insisted that his return journey should be made by way of the bombed towns in the East.

On the 26th May, he left Voisins to visit Nancy, Épinal, Dijon, and Lyon. He was received with varying degrees of enthusiasm.

At Lyon, on the 6th June, the Marshal learned of the allied landings in Normandy. Laval telephoned from Vichy that the situation was serious and that he advised the Marshal to return immediately.

But the latter did not want to give up the last of his arranged visits, which was to Saint-Étienne. In this industrial town, which was profoundly perturbed by the events of the day, what reception would he receive from the population? An excited and enthusiastic crowd filled the square where the Marshal halted. Once more, and for the last time, the Marshal spoke to the French people. And once more he improvised: "Thanks to you," he said to the men who crowded round to listen to him, "I leave strengthened to accomplish my task." A rousing

*Marseillaise* answered him. It was his last contact with the country. The last popular ceremony in which the Head of the State took part.

On his return to Vichy, the Marshal was received by one of his "guardians", Böhland. The latter stated that on reliable information the *maquis* were about to attack the Hôtel du Parc. He insisted that the Marshal should that very night leave for a new residence, a luxurious and isolated house, the Château du Lonzat, seventeen kilometres from Vichy, where in future he was to spend his nights. It was a musical comedy décor for the growing drama.

During these two months in which Pétain was lamentably transferred from residence to residence, Pierre Laval had to carry the whole burden of the situation. During these dramatic hours, he remained astonishingly true to himself.

Come wind come high weather, he continued trying to play the political game on the grand scale: he also persisted in believing in a Nazi victory.

In February, 1944, in a conversation with the Swiss Minister, Stucki, he showed himself as being completely unimpressed with the German reverses which were growing more numerous. He took from his brief case two "documents" which proved that the Reich could not be defeated: "Having discreetly asked him," Stucki recalls, "who were the authors of these letters, I received the following astonishing reply: 'One is from a French General who is a prisoner in Germany and can only write through the German censorship, which proves that what he says is true: the other is a well-known French collaborator who at this moment is paying a visit to Germany.' I limited myself to remarking that one could really not place much reliance on such sources. Laval said goodbye to me with great goodwill."

If one is to judge by his actions, Laval's policy had two aspects.

On the one hand, he wished to continue giving the Germans satisfaction, believing as he did in their victory.

He passed such immoral laws as that of the 27th March, which authorised Frenchmen to enlist in the Waffen S.S. and made speeches of such deluded and erratic mysticism as that to a meeting of the leaders of the French Militia, those French torturers of other Frenchmen.

We will cite here, without making any attempt to place the examples in order, a few of the actions taken by the French Government against their compatriots who were rebelling against a foreign yoke. It was Guérard who, according to the documents produced at his trial, proposed using 80 mm. mortars against the *maquis*. It was the Vichy police who, in February, 1944, co-operated with the Germans in an attack against the *maquis* in Haute-Savoie. It was the Militia who, on the 25th March, collaborated with the Wehrmacht, twenty thousand men in all, to destroy the four hundred and sixty French on the plateau of Glières. The French Government agreed to the setting up of courts-martial, on the 20th January, 1944, which had no concern with justice; Laval prepared the law and forced Gabolde, Garde des Sceaux, to sign it: "Have the courage to sign." They immediately began functioning in the most abominable manner as two examples bear witness. At the Préfecture of Marseille, a court-martial was due to open when the Clerk of the Court remarked that there was no table on which to record the decisions. "There's no point," came the reply, "we don't write anything down." Andrieu, the Intendant of Police, sent in his resignation: on the 2nd February he was dismissed. In Paris, at the Santé, a court-martial pronounced sixteen death sentences, which were immediately put into execution. This time a record was made, but it is marked "illegible".

As if all this were not enough, a new law was promulgated in March punishing with death anyone who helped the *maquisards*.

The second aspect of Laval's policy, which he was pursuing at the same time, consisted in continuous efforts to reduce the effect of the German demands on France, in particular those concerning the S.T.O.

In order to protect the agricultural workers, Laval persuaded the German Minister of Agriculture to guarantee that all French agricultural workers should remain in France till the end of the harvest, that is to say, until the autumn.

For industrial workers, a similar manoeuvre was made by Bichelonne: he made an agreement with Speer, the Minister for Armaments, which stipulated that all French factories, engaged on war work, should be excluded from the necessity of providing workers for the Reich.

Sauckel complained that the French were making direct appeals to the German Government in order to dodge his demands. On the 17th March, 1944, he wrote to the Führer:

"The realisation of my plan is now meeting with serious difficulties which go beyond my competence and which I must submit to you and ask you respectfully to make a decision.

"At this actual moment, approximately five thousand nine hundred armament factories in France, employing eight hundred and thirty thousand people, and eight thousand five hundred civilian businesses, employing approximately five hundred and fifty thousand people, have been withdrawn from my control by being transformed into 'S' factories. . . .

". . . I must observe that besides these 'S' groups of factories mentioned above, the following groups are also protected:

| | | |
|---|---|---|
| "Railways and transportation: approx. | 450,000 | workers |
| Agriculture: | 2,750,000 | ,, |
| Todt organisation: | 150,000 | ,, |
| Construction for the Luftwaffe:<br>Construction for the Navy:<br>Armaments Section: | 200,000 | ,, |
| Wehrmacht services: | 140,000 | ,, |
| Public Works: | 250,000 | ,, |
| Police: | 130,000 | ,, |

As a declaration of his own failure drawn up by the purveyor of French labour to the Reich, the document constitutes an involuntary acknowledgement of the energy displayed by Laval in a particularly grave matter concerning which the Nazis were making continual demands.

In fact, the departures of workers suspended after October, 1943, only began again in the form of replacements for workers already in Germany by new batches sent from France; but only a small proportion were thus relieved.

Thus, in this essential matter of the S.T.O., it is incontestable that Laval resisted the Germans.

At the beginning of 1944, two of the important posts in the regime received new occupants: the Commissariat General for the Prisoners, to which at the end of January Pierre Moreau was appointed by Laval to succeed André Masson whose notoriously collaborationist policy and deplorable conduct of affairs had aroused unanimous disapproval; and the Commissariat for Jewish

Questions, in which Mercier du Paty de Clam replaced Darquier de Pellepoix.

Moreau, before accepting, asked the advice of the Resistance organisations which had been formed among the prisoners; they encouraged him to take the post, subject to three precise conditions: (1) to liquidate the "prisoners' movements", founded by Masson in support of the policy of collaboration; (2) to eliminate all politics from the central and local services under the Commissariat which should be purged of its worst elements; and (3) to assure as far as possible the protection of escaped prisoners or those who had joined the Resistance.

Moreau faithfully carried out this programme.

Mercier du Paty de Clam only accepted the post of Commissaire Général to Jewish Affairs, in February, 1944, on the advice of a cousin, d'Ursel, who was head of an allied secret network. The latter persuaded him that the Commissariat was an important listening post and that, moreover, he could do good work there by disorganising its administration.

As soon as he was in office, Mercier du Paty de Clam set about doing this with astonishing zeal. He liquidated, either by accepting their resignations or sending them on leave, a large number of officials who were never replaced: among them the Directors of the Services.

On the 1st June, 1944, du Paty de Clam was replaced by a less "benign" personage, Antignac. But the disorganisation of the administration persisted until the end.

No doubt, the deliberate action of the high officials could not prevent the abominable police methods either demanded or carried out by the "racialists", nor the mass arrests and the continually increasing deportations. But they did at least put a brake on some of these arbitrary measures and partially dissociated the French Government from these practices.

CHAPTER 5

# THE DOWNFALL OF A REGIME

## 2. From the Landings to the Liberation (6th June, 1944–25th August, 1944)

ON the 6th June, 1944, the allied landings took place and, on the 8th, the first French town, Bayeux, was liberated. In France there was almost unanimous enthusiasm.

The allies made a lightning advance.

On the 27th June, the Cotentin was entirely reconquered and Cherbourg liberated. On the 9th July, after some hard fighting, Caen was liberated in ruins. On the 30th July, the Americans made a decisive thrust in the Avranches sector which made a double movement possible, one to liberate Brittany, the other to advance on Paris.

The two offensives were mounted at the same time: the month of August brought in Brittany the liberation of Vannes, Saint-Brieuc, Morlaix, Quimper, Saint-Malo and, on the 11th August, Nantes. Only Brest was still occupied and this fell on the 17th September.

The march on Paris was broken by the taking of Alençon on the 14th August, Dreux, Chartres and Orléans on the 17th, Evreux, Meaux and Sens on the 23rd, and finally, on the 24th, at 9.30 p.m., the first tanks of Leclerc's Division entered the liberated capital.

On the 15th August, 1944, coming from North Africa, the army of de Lattre de Tassigny, which included French and American contingents, landed on the coast of Provence between Saint-Raphael and Cap Comarat. After the liberation of the nearest towns, Draguignan, Brignoles and Castellane, the allied troops thrust towards the west and north: Aix-en-Provence was taken on the 22nd August, Marseille and Grenoble on the 23rd. Taking both lines of advance into account, the end of the month saw the liberation of Cannes, Antibes and Toulon on the coast and, in the interior, Montpellier, Béziers, Narbonne and

Valence. The entry of the allies into Lyon on the 4th September, Mâcon on the 6th September, and Dijon on the 12th September was a prelude to the junction between the allied forces in the north and those in the south which took place on the 13th September in the region of Dijon for the American troops, and on the 14th September at Châtillon-sur-Seine for the Leclerc Division and de Lattre de Tassigny's Army.

At the same time, the last weeks of the Nazi occupation of France saw a recrudescence of horrors. On the 10th June, there took place the massacre of Oradour. In July, the French part of the village of Saint-Guingolph on the Swiss frontier was burnt down. On the 16th August, in Paris, thirty-four young men were executed near the Grande Cascade in the Bois de Boulogne. On the 20th August, the Gestapo massacred 100 men, women and children, whom they burnt alive with petrol, at Saint-Génis-Laval, near Lyon. On the 25th, 126 people were massacred at Maillé, in Indre-et-Loire, by the S.S.

These once again were collective killings and were accompanied in both camps by individual assassinations.

Philippe Henriot, Minister of Information, was assassinated on the 28th June.

On the 20th June, Jean Zay was assassinated. Three unknown people arrived at the Riom prison on the pretext of transferring him to Melun, and disappeared with him. Laval tried vainly to discover the murderers.

On the 8th July, Mandel was assassinated. The Germans, who were holding him prisoner with Reynaud and Léon Blum, handed him over to the French authorities in Paris. They took him to the Santé prison, but the Governor refused to keep him on the pretext that there were no regulations to cover his case. Handed over to the Militia, who were ordered to take him to Vichy for imprisonment in the Château des Brosses, the ex-Minister was assassinated by his French guards on the way, which was what the Nazis had hoped.

Besides these assassinations, June, 1944, saw an extension of fighting by the various *maquis*. They were by now well organised forces, having transport, commissariat and medical services at their disposal; sometimes they even had inter-allied missions with their forces.

In the Vercors, which had been chosen as the central stronghold of the French Resistance, several thousand *maquisards* had been concentrated to keep German troops from the Normandy front. Unfortunately, they had insufficient arms, no artillery, airborne troops or indeed air support. At the end of July, 1944, S.S. troops in gliders landed in the middle of their positions and took them by surprise. In spite of determined hand to hand resistance, they were wiped out. At the same time there were similar massacres at Mont Roucket and in the neighbourhood of Saint-Flour, where the Germans used tanks and aircraft. Among the victims of this heroic fighting, the name of Jean Prévost, the writer, must be recorded. He was killed as a Captain of F.F.I., on the 3rd August, in the Vercors.

In July, faced by the imminence of the total liberation of French territory, intrigues started both within and without France to prevent General de Gaulle from being triumphant, or at least to limit his triumph.

Pétain at first, somewhat ingenuously, began by reassuring General de Gaulle concerning the measures taken against him in 1940. "They will lapse as soon as all Frenchmen are reunited again; they were more spectacular than anything else." General de Gaulle need not be anxious: he would preserve his French nationality and would not be shot.

"You will also tell the General," said Pétain to a secret agent from Algiers, "that I have no intention of remaining in power; merely a few months with him in order to ensure the transition and consolidate the union which will come to birth through our mutual understanding. Then, as soon as possible, I want to go back and live in peace on my estate and finish my days in tranquillity."

Vichy anxiously awaited a reply to these overtures: there was none.

On the 3rd July, the Papal Nuncio declared that the Vatican offered to negotiate a reconciliation between Vichy and Algiers. The Marshal replied favourably. But on the 16th July, Monsignor Valerio Valeri, on being received by the Head of the State, had to admit his disappointment.

The Marshal was therefore prevented from playing any part in that reconciliation among Frenchmen which appeared to be his ultimate ambition.

Vichy was more and more cut off from the outside world: the roads were barred, the trains were not running. On the 6th

July, Abetz, asked by Laval to sound out the Führer about installing the Marshal in Paris, returned with a negative reply: Hitler "advised" that the Marshal should remain in the neighbourhood of Vichy.

For the Head of the State, it was the end of all his illusions.

There were extraordinary rumours concerning General de Gaulle's intentions.

As they were understood at Vichy, the General's intentions were to assume power contrary to the will of the Americans: that this might be achieved, it was necessary that Paris should be liberated by French troops, that de Gaulle should appear immediately in the capital and constitute a revolutionary government at the Hôtel de Ville: which meant that there could be no contact with the Marshal, for his absence would be an essential condition of the operation's success.

In order to eliminate de Gaulle, Laval decided that he must persuade the President of the Chamber of Deputies to forestall the General by immediately summoning the National Assembly. It was thus, curiously enough, on Herriot that he counted to put a spoke in de Gaulle's wheel. The President of the Chamber was comfortably shut up with his wife and cook in a lunatic asylum at Maréville, near Nancy, where he was simulating a form of madness, of peculiarly present relevance, whose falsity, according to the experts, it was impossible to discover: the fear of imprisonment.

While endeavouring to bring off this delicate piece of negotiation with Herriot, Laval was faced with a new threat, no longer from the Resistance, but from "the Paris collaborators". Still desiring a total alliance with the Reich, they were preparing a late offensive against Laval whom they accused of "*attentisme*": they wanted to substitute for him a Government in the pay of the Germans.

On the 9th July, Admiral Platon arrived in Vichy from the capital, bearing a "joint declaration on the political situation", signed by four Ministers, Déat, Bichelonne, Brinon and Bonnard, and by some thirty other well-known politicians and journalists, including Doriot, Platon himself and Luchaire.

This document demanded that the Government should take strong measures: an end to "*attentisme*", of which the "Ultras" accused Laval, the return of the Government to Paris, the entry into the Government of "incontestable elements", the participation of all Ministers in the general policies of the Cabinet and, finally, "severe sanctions to the extent of capital punishment for all those whose actions encourage civil war or compromise the European position of France".

This document, inspired by Déat, and drawn up by Dominique Sordet, aimed at transforming the Government into a Committee of Public Safety, which, unlike its great predecessor, would be in the service of the enemy. Renthe-Fink, the eventual beneficiary of the plot, had an interview with the Marshal who avoided all discussion by talking of his kitchen garden.

On the 12th July, at 4 p.m., Laval summoned the Council of Ministers at Vichy to examine the situation resulting from the "joint declaration". All the Ministers summoned were present except for Déat who still refused to come to Vichy.

This Council of Ministers, which took place in the presence of Guérard, Rochat and Commandant Tracou, is the only one during this period of which we have a report. Laval, with as much spirit as he had shown four years before while destroying the Republic, defended his prerogatives and denied all responsibility for the German atrocities.

He violently counter-attacked the conspirators, Bichelonne, Brinon, and Bonnard, who immediately collapsed. "I signed this document out of weariness," Bichelonne excused himself. And Brinon said: "I approved the ideas of this document but with certain reserves. I did not draw up the text; I took no part in drawing it up; I don't know the author." As for Bonnard, he said: "I have no responsibility for the drawing up of this document, but it expresses the general psychological outlook in Paris . . . Paris is feverish, and the fever of Paris is the fever of a giant."

Faced with these conspirators, their machinations now exposed, Laval defined his policy with so much authority that he succeeded in persuading the very people who wished to replace it to adopt it.

To begin with he opposed, in view of the assassinations of Jean Zay and Mandel, all further handing over of French politicians.

"Let anyone who disagrees with me say so (silence, lowered heads).

"I note the unanimous decision of the Council to refuse in future all handing over of hostages and all reprisals of this nature."

There was the same—spontaneous?—unanimity, when Laval refused to contemplate the return of the Government to Paris.

He succeeded in neutralising the signatories to the Declaration by two means. In the first place, by producing a letter that the bearer of the document, Platon, had been sufficiently imprudent to write to his brother a few days before. Laval had discovered the existence of the letter through his Intelligence Service. Here follows one of its paragraphs:

"At the moment when France is being invaded by the Anglo-Saxons, and when Normandy is ravaged, it seems to me most unfortunate that the Head of the Government should declare that we are not in the war. That man deserves not only to be shot, but hanged. He will be."

Furthermore, it asserted that among the signatories, there were "instigators and even assuredly Gaullists . . . ready to change sides".

This was an unexpected revelation which sowed dismay among the Ministers: who among them could be a Gaullist? A silence followed of which Laval took advantage to confirm his policy.

France would not enter into the war: if Déat wished to fight, "let him enlist, it's easy enough". Laval, supported by Chasseigne and Marion, profited by the advantage he had gained to get unanimously approved the following *communiqué*:

"The Head of the Government has presided over a meeting of Ministers in Council on the 12th July at 4 o'clock at the Hôtel du Parc at Vichy.

"President Laval recapitulated the principles upon which French policy is based and which have always guided the Government's actions. The Council unanimously approved his statement.

"He declared that France could have no other policy than that defined by the Head of the Government on the 6th June last.

"All the Ministers were present with the exception of M. Marcel Déat."

It was a day of illusion for the Paris "Ultras": but hardly was the Council over, when Brinon, taking vengeance for his discomfiture, went and informed the Germans.

"Do you know," Laval reported to the Marshal, "that that bastard Brinon went and told Struwe all that happened at the Council: he accused Bichelonne and Bonnard of having collapsed. Struwe has already been to see me to say that the German

Government will not permit Déat's dismissal. That's what we've come to."

The Council of Ministers held on the 12th July was to all intents and purposes the last. From then on, all Laval's activity was concentrated on his negotiations with Herriot; while Pétain's energies were devoted to preventing his departure for Germany.

Since the beginning of July, there had been a rumour that the German Government intended to transfer the seat of the French Government to eastern France.

Faced with these persistent rumours, the Marshal, on the 16th July, received the Papal Nuncio, Monsignor Valerio Valeri, and gave him a short note unknown both to the Germans and to Laval:

"Persistent rumours incline one to think that the Germans intend to move the French Government and the Marshal to the neighbourhood of Nancy.

"This transfer would take place if the German armies were obliged to abandon part of the territory of France and retire towards the east.

"The Marshal hereby declares to the Nuncio, as Doyen of the Diplomatic Corps, that he will oppose by every means at his disposal all displacement from Vichy to the east.

"The Marshal has remained on French soil since 1940. He is determined not to leave it now."

On the 22nd July, Pétain received Admiral Auphan at his house, Lonzat: the Admiral, whose loyalty and courage he well knew, and who had been forced from power in November, 1942, because of his anti-German views, seemed to the Marshal the proper person to negotiate, since he could not do it himself, with General de Gaulle.

Laval proposed to leave for Paris. He would see members of Parliament there. He would persuade the Germans to authorise the summoning of the National Assembly and to restore the Marshal's freedom of movement. Then he proposed going to Maréville to free Edouard Herriot.

On the 8th August, the President's plans were reinforced by an anguished appeal from the capital: the head of his Paris office, Guénier, came to Vichy and informed him that a meeting had been held on the 7th August at the Hôtel de Ville, in Taittinger's office, in the presence of Victor Constant, the Prefects of the

Seine and the Police, and Comte René de Chambrun, Laval's son-in-law. The Americans were approaching the city by forced marches: the Paris authorities asked that Laval and Pétain should be there to receive them.

But the Marshal was no longer free: he had to let Laval go to Paris alone. On the evening of the 8th, the President left Châteldon in a car with his wife and daughter. It was a sleepless night for Laval, during which his car was frequently stopped by the Germans; during the journey he perfected his plans for preventing the destruction of Paris and the triumph of "the mob".

As soon as he arrived in Paris, Laval began negotiations. From the Germans he tried to obtain the freeing of Herriot, liberty of action for the Marshal and the summoning of the National Assembly to Versailles, where it should be in session when the allied troops entered Paris.

Abetz agreed, telephoned to Ribbentrop, and immediately obtained the necessary authorisations for Herriot and the Assembly.

Nevertheless, Laval's plan became manifestly unrealisable. Anatole de Monzie, pursued by the Militia and the Gestapo, came secretly to see him in a safe place. He stated that he was speaking in the name of 255 members of Parliament: if it were Laval, he said, who was summoning the National Assembly, neither Senators nor Deputies would respond to his call. If it were the Marshal, they would come. And Monzie suggested that Herriot, after the Germans had departed, should be named President of the Constitutional Commission, and that de Gaulle should be head of a government of parliamentarians: with the assistance of his inexperience, they would be able to get rid of him within three months.

Laval sent two messengers to Vichy, Dr. Grasset, Minister of Health, and Loyer, Director of Handicrafts, to persuade the Marshal to come to Paris. But the Marshal refused on the pretext that his "guardians" forbade it: perhaps he also did not wish to link his fate to Laval's.

On the 12th August, early in the morning, Laval, accompanied by Enfière, left for Nancy, then for Maréville in order to liberate Herriot. There was a most moving scene: embraces and general effusiveness.

At 10 o'clock that night, Herriot, Mme. Herriot, Laval and Enfière left by car for Paris.

At 7 o'clock in the morning, the cars arrived at the Hôtel de Ville, where the Prefect of Police, Bouffet, had a moment of fear when he saw the civilians arrive: was it the Gestapo come to arrest him?

He was reassured: it was only Laval and Herriot. He received them with enthusiasm.

During the next three days, from the 13th to the 16th, Laval failed to obtain any of the help he required. There was nothing left for him to do but leave Herriot to return to his asylum, which must have seemed like a temple of reason after the three days he had spent in the Paris imbroglio. Laval himself had no alternative but to abandon power and let himself be removed to the east by the Germans.

During his stay in Paris, Herriot had taken his meals with the Prefect of Police, showing himself to be a dazzling and encyclopaedic conversationalist. But his attitude, taken as a whole, showed that he was not burning with zeal to prepare a meeting of the National Assembly.

Laval was no more fortunate with the Marshal. The latter, who had charged Auphan with informing the Provisional Government that he was ready to negotiate with it (an invitation which remained unanswered), sent Loyer back on the 15th July, with his reply to Laval. He refused to come to Paris without having previously received sufficient guarantees, among which were, the certainty of his being taken nowhere except to the capital—the escort of his personal guard during the journey and the stay—and an assurance that no German should take part in the arrangements made to assure his security in Paris.

And there was still more to come. "The Marshal," said Loyer to the President, "has asked me to tell you that in no circumstances can you be part of the Government."

The Germans were warned by the Paris collaborators, Brinon and Déat, who were not at all pleased to see Laval endeavouring to escape their common fate. By-passing Abetz, who was in semi-disgrace and who they knew had approved the President's designs, they warned General Oberg, the supreme head of the Gestapo. The latter was furious at the mere idea of the summoning of the National Assembly. He telephoned direct to Hitler and Himmler and demanded full powers.

On the 15th August, at 10.30 p.m., Laval received Abetz

who had come to give him a piece of "good news": Paris would not be defended. Laval was delighted. Hardly had Abetz left when the telephone rang. The French policeman charged with guarding Herriot announced that the Gestapo had arrived to arrest the President. Laval rushed round to the Hôtel de Ville and cursed the German officer.

It was no use: the Germans had their orders. Laval went to the Prefect's office and drew up a protest which he sent immediately to Abetz:

"Monsieur l'Ambassadeur,

"I was informed by you that I might tell President Herriot that he was free. I went to Nancy to tell him so and brought him back to Paris.

"The news of his arrest and his being transferred once more to Nancy or to Germany, which I have just learned, has profoundly shocked me.

"If this order remains in force, it will do me a great injury. I shall be accused of duplicity which, as you know, is no part of my character.

"I shall have to ask you to consider me a prisoner in the same way as is President Herriot and, in any case, you will have placed me in the position of having to renounce immediately the exercise of my functions.

"The relations I have had with Chancellor Hitler authorise me to address him directly through you to ask him to reverse this decision."

This message, written at 4 o'clock in the morning, was immediately transmitted to the Führer by Abetz, who had no illusions as to its reception.

On the following day, the 18th August, a definite reply arrived from Berlin. It was an order for Herriot, Laval and the other Ministers to leave for Belfort. It was the last journey, Abetz assured them: in any case, they would not have to leave French territory.

At 7 o'clock, the Council of Ministers met for the last time. Brinon, Déat and Darnand were already on the road to the east. General Bridoux and Admiral Bléhaut were at Vichy. There only remained Bichelonne, Gabolde, Bonnard, Grasset, Chasseigne, Cathala and Marion.

They unanimously approved Laval's reply.

"Monsieur l'Ambassadeur,

"The French Government does not agree to transfer its seat from Vichy to Belfort, whatever reasons you may put forward. In these circumstances, I and all the Ministers present cannot respond to your invitation."

At 10 p.m., there was a German ultimatum.

"The communication which I had the honour to make to you concerning the transfer of the members of the French Government to Belfort represents an irrevocable decision of the German Government. I therefore regret to have to reply to the French Government's protest that, in case of refusal, methods of coercion will inevitably have to be applied."

Laval immediately replied:

"I cannot but yield to threats of coercion, but you will understand that, in these circumstances, I cease to exercise the functions of Head of the Government."

Laval immediately summoned to the Hôtel Matignon Bouffet, Bussière, Taittinger and Constant, to whom he gave two letters and charged them with assuring the order and food supply of Paris.

Then he signed his last decree: "The Secretaries-General or, in their default, the most senior Directors are charged with assuring the interim working of the Ministries."

It was the end of the Vichy Government. The Gestapo invaded the Hôtel Matignon. Laval said goodbye to his colleagues.

"It is not the Head of the Government who is leaving, it is not Ministers who are accompanying him. It's a new batch of prisoners added to so many others."

While this drama was taking place in Paris, Vichy saw a similar one being enacted which was to end in the transfer under duress of the Marshal to Belfort.

After Laval's departure for Paris on the 9th August, and as the threat of an exodus towards the east became clearer, the Marshal invited the Swiss Minister, Stucki, to dinner at his Château du Lonzat. It was "an exceptionally silent and melancholy" meal. The Marshal said privately to his guest: "The situation is exceedingly strained, so strained that important decisions must be expected at any moment. My most intimate colleagues and myself are no longer sure of our lives. At the very least, we shall be arrested and interned somewhere for a long time. Our documents may be seized or destroyed by our external or internal enemies. They both have a tendency to strangle or pervert historical truth; but I attach the greatest importance to the world and history knowing one day, as exactly as possible, what has happened at Vichy during this stormy summer. That is why I wish the representative of a friendly State, which is both neutral and universally esteemed, and who is himself a warm friend of France, and is alone in having, I know, permanent communications with his Government, to be the historical witness to the events which are about to occur. I ask you to respond to my summons at any hour of the day or night and to be present at everything that happens. I ask you to listen and to look and one day to report objectively what you have heard and seen."

Stucki's agreement restored the Marshal's serenity.

He spent the final days before the threats were put into execution studying the last plans submitted by his *entourage* for attempting to escape an ineluctable fate.

Some advised him to send a secret emissary to General Eisenhower and ask for an interview with him. Others wished him to place himself in the hands of the F.F.I. Others again naturally wanted him to defer to Laval's demands and join him in Paris.

At times, the Marshal contemplated armed resistance: on the 14th August, he warned General Perré, commanding the Guard at Vichy, asking him to draw up a plan of mobilisation for his forces should the Germans attempt armed intervention.

The plan as drawn up received the Marshal's approval: General Perré prepared to put it into execution. He reported that everything was ready on the evening of the 15th. But the same day the allied landings in Provence took place: on the following day, the German preparations for evacuation became more precise. The Marshal was placed under a surveillance which forced him to abandon his plans. On the 17th August, at 7.30 p.m., the Nazis officially presented the expected demands: while Struwe, Chief of the Delegation to Vichy of the German Embassy in Paris, saw the head of Laval's private office, Renthe-Fink demanded to be received by the Marshal.

He officially notified him of the German Government's orders. On the pretext of the dangers to which the Marshal might be exposed if there were an attack on Vichy by the Resistance, he demanded that the Head of the State should transfer his residence to the northern zone. The members of the French Government who were in Vichy, Rochat, General Bridoux and

Admiral Bléhaut, were to accompany the Marshal in order to allow the Government to be reconstituted. The Diplomatic Corps were also authorised to follow the Head of the State: an authorisation of which, as soon as they learned of it, Stucki and Monsignor Valerio Valeri declared they had decided not to avail themselves.

According to Renthe-Fink, this change of residence was merely to be considered provisional and necessitated by military considerations.

To a question of the Marshal's, Renthe-Fink said that the seat of the Government would be in the east, probably at Nancy. He said that Laval was already there, giving the Marshal to understand that he had gone there voluntarily.

The Marshal replied, as he had already often done, that he had no wish to leave Vichy to go to the east, that if he were to leave, it would only be to install himself in Paris. He declared that Laval had promised him on leaving to remain in Paris and never go to the east. Since the President had not communicated with the Marshal, the latter took it for granted that his attitude had not altered: before coming to a decision, he required to know what had in fact happened in Paris: he proposed sending a messenger to Laval. Moreover, he asked Renthe-Fink to formulate the German demands in writing.

During Friday, 18th August, at midday and again at seven, Renthe-Fink had two more interviews with the Marshal to persuade him to leave: the latter replied that his position remained the same and that he was awaiting news from Laval. Renthe-Fink once more asserted that the President of the Council had already gone to Nancy, the seat of the Government.

The Marshal refused to give way.

On Saturday, 19th August, at 11.30 a.m., a new German joined in the game. General von Neubronn, representing the Wehrmacht at Vichy, was not a fanatical Nazi but an officer of the old German Army, who had a sense of honour and a respect for the Marshal. He came to warn him that his departure was formally ordered from Berlin, that as a soldier he could not question it and must put it into execution. The Marshal replied to Neubronn, who was obviously embarrassed by the part he had to play, that he would resist by all means in his power. At midday, a new attempt was made by Renthe-Fink, but it had no result except that the Marshal dismissed him.

Faced with this continued resistance, the Nazis had recourse to their accustomed procedure to which the Marshal always ended by yielding: they used blackmail and threatened the Head of the State with the shedding of French blood. They proposed to bombard Vichy.

The Marshal, informed by Stucki, replied simply: "I'm sorry for Neubronn," and added: "I have no right to let Vichy be bombarded merely to enter history with more glory."

Once again, blackmail was in a fair way to succeed.

At 6.30 p.m., Renthe-Fink demanded an audience with the Marshal for 7.30 p.m. The Head of the State was already engaged in arranging his papers and supervising the packing of his trunks.

At the hour arranged, the Marshal summoned to his office Generals Bridoux and Debeney and Admirals Fernet and Bléhaut.

Renthe-Fink and General von Neubronn had just arrived in the ante-room.

At the precise moment when they were to be shown in, at 7.57 p.m., Commandant Féat was brought to the Marshal's office by Ménétrel. He had that moment arrived from Paris bearing documents and information which proved Renthe-Fink's bad faith. He showed photostats of Laval's letters to Abetz, the Prefects of Police and the Seine, Taittinger and Constant: Laval had resigned, as had the rest of the Government, and had charged the Secretaries-General to carry on with current affairs. He was a prisoner of the Germans who, contrary to Renthe-Fink's statements, had carried him off against his will, as they had the majority of Ministers, to Belfort.

Having been enlightened at the last moment on the truth of the Nazi diplomat's statements, Pétain and his entourage summoned the two Germans into his office as Commandant Féat left it.

The German Minister was the bearer of two notes, one confirming the German Government's demands which he had presented orally on Thursday, the other being the list of the people who were to accompany the Marshal. These were General Debeney, Rochat, de Longueau, Ménétrel, General Bridoux and Admiral Bléhaut, with their orderly officers, Captain Destreleau and naval Lieutenant Sacy.

Renthe-Fink recapitulated his arguments: he stated for the first time that Laval and his Government were at Belfort rather than Nancy, but still allowed it to be supposed that they had gone there of their own free will: they were awaiting the

Marshal, who moreover could return to Vichy as soon as the necessary conditions for his safety should have been restored.

"All this business is nonsense, absolute nonsense," replied the Marshal. "I am in no danger at Vichy. President Laval is not in the east, he has resigned and is a prisoner of the Germans. I have just received proof of it. In these circumstances I refuse to leave and intend remaining at Vichy."

Admiral Bléhaut then spoke without having asked permission to do so. He could restrain himself no longer: Renthe-Fink's bad faith infuriated him: "Your arguments bear no relation to the truth. You lied to us when you said that President Laval had transferred the Government to the east. If I am compelled to go, I shall no longer have control of anything; if I leave Vichy, I no longer represent anything. I merely become a simple Rear-Admiral without any power at all."

Renthe-Fink protested, but Bléhaut silenced him.

The Marshal then asked what hour was proposed for the departure. (It was then 8.35 p.m.) Renthe-Fink replied: "10 p.m." As this gave too little time, Renthe-Fink turned to Neubronn who said: "5.30 tomorrow morning."

The Marshal said: "That's too early."

Neubronn said: "6 o'clock." Pétain did not reply. Neubronn made another concession: "7 o'clock."

At this moment there took place another dramatic scene, but one prepared by the Marshal.

The Head of the State's usher, Brochier, announced the Nuncio and the Swiss Minister. Since the beginning of the audience, Ménétrel had periodically been looking through the door from the neighbouring office to judge the right moment for the entry of the two diplomats.

The Germans reacted sharply to this unforeseen interruption: "But, Monsieur le Maréchal," protested Renthe-Fink vehemently, "this has nothing to do with foreigners. It's a strictly Franco-German affair." And Neubronn said: "It's really impossible...."

Monsignor Valeri and Stucki nevertheless came into the office. Bléhaut, turning to Renthe-Fink, said: "Monsieur le Ministre, will you repeat before these gentlemen the terms of the coercion you are imposing on us?"

Renthe-Fink, beside himself, "furious and shouting ... refused to prolong the discussion, took General von Neubronn by the arm and dragged him towards the door. Mannerless and undignified, without taking leave, the special plenipotentiary of the Führer left the Marshal's office for the last time."

After the Germans' departure, Pétain informed the two diplomats of the coercion to which he was subjected: "He would only yield to this coercion when it was pushed to extremes." He asked the Nuncio and the Minister to do all they could to make the truth known.

Between midnight and 1 o'clock in the morning, the Marshal drew up with Admiral Fernet and Rochat an "Appeal to the French" which he proposed to record the following morning, if that were still possible.

"Frenchmen,

"I have learned that owing to the measures of coercion that the German Government have exercised in Paris on the Head of the Government, he and the Ministers present have been compelled, in spite of their anxiety to fulfil their duty to the end, to yield to force. They have decided that, in such circumstances, they could do no other than resign.

"Faced with this situation, I have taken the decision of assuring the power of the Government henceforward through those Secretaries of State who are at my side. There can be no question of transferring elsewhere the seat of the Government which remains tied here, where the majority of the officials attached to the Government live.

"I annul Constitutional Acts 12 and 12 *bis* which delegate to the Head of the Government legislative powers.

"With regard to the relations which may be established in Paris with the leaders of the allied armies, I have nominated an individual who has my confidence to represent me.

"Lawful power cannot cease to be exercised."

This document was posted on the walls of Vichy and reproduced in the newspaper *l'Avenir du Puy-de-Dôme*.

At the same time, the Marshal revised the ultimate message to the French people which he had composed a few days before and which was disseminated by unofficial channels.

"Frenchmen,

"When this message reaches you, I shall no longer be free. . . .

". . . I have had but one object, to protect you from the worst. . . . On occasion, my words and my acts may have surprised you. You should know that they have given me more pain than they have given you. I have suffered for you and with you. . . .

"Once again I adjure you to be united. It is not difficult to do one's duty, even if it is sometimes difficult to know what it is. . . .

"I legitimately represent order . . . Obey those who will speak to you of social peace, without which there can be no order.

"Those who speak to you the language of reconciliation and the renewal of France through a mutual forgiveness of injuries and the love of all our countrymen, those are French leaders. . . . It is with joy that I accept my sacrifice, if it can help you to find once again the path of sacred union for the renascence of our Fatherland."

On Sunday, 20th August, the Marshal was taken away.

Men of the Feldgendarmerie and of the Security Police S.D., helmeted and wearing raincoats, took up their positions round the Hôtel du Parc, having come from the Boulevard des États-Unis where their vehicles were parked.

They isolated the block formed by the Hôtel du Parc and the Hôtel Majestic.

There were about a hundred of them, armed with rifles or sub-machine-guns: there was a machine-gun mounted ready to fire and another heavy machine-gun mounted for anti-aircraft defence.

A little further off, armoured cars were in position near Cusset: and still further away the division at Clermont was ready to intervene.

A few minutes later, General von Neubronn got out of his car in front of the entrance of the Hôtel du Parc. He went up to the Marshal's storey, followed by his orderly officer and Detering. Having arrived there, he said to Colonel Barré: "I must speak to the Marshal, please open the door." Barré refused with a shake of the head. Very politely, Neubronn asked all those present to move aside, which they did. He advanced to the door and tried to open it: it was locked. At a signal, a German non-commissioned officer smashed it in pieces with a kick. Neubronn entered followed by Barré. The same performance took place at another locked door, which was that of the Marshal's room. Neubronn tried to open it but the handle would not work. A German soldier tried to pick the lock but without success. Another took it off its hinges with steel levers. Neubronn went alone into the Marshal's room.

The Marshal "was sitting on a chair, clothed only in his shirt and trousers and was in process of tying his laces".

Neubronn retired and waited outside the door with a group of completely silent French. It was then 7.30 a.m.

At 7.45 the Marshal had not yet left his room: on the orders of Neubronn, his orderly officer, Luttiz, informed the Marshal that time was limited, and that he must hurry. Ménétrel, provoked, replied: "You know the Marshal's age. He has been suddenly awakened. He's got a long and tiring journey before him. Has he not the right to have his breakfast?"

Breakfast was ordered, prepared, and eaten by the Marshal and his wife.

At 7.50, the Marshal received the Nuncio and Stucki whom he took to witness the violence to which he was subjected: he read them his last declaration to the Führer, dated that very day, which concluded as follows: "I solemnly protest against this forcible act which makes it impossible for me to exercise my prerogatives as Head of the French State."

The members of the Marshal's entourage came to say goodbye to him. "I am compelled to depart for an unknown destination. You must remain and keep the administration going. Have confidence as I have. I shall come back, I do not know when, but perhaps it will be soon. I wish everything to continue here as before. . . . Have confidence."

It was the last expression of the Marshal's illusions. . . . Hardly had he uttered the words than the German soldiers were ordered to leave the ante-chamber; in their haste, they forgot their tools. They went down the stairs.

The Marshal came out. His face very pale, his expression utterly sad, he advanced slowly, silently shaking the hands of those who extended them to him for the last time.

The Marshal turned to salute the Nuncio and M. Stucki. He went into the lift, followed by his wife.

When the lift reached the ground floor, there was a sharp order: "Present arms." A company of the Marshal's personal guard, standing impeccably to attention in a square, did him the honours. The Marshal slowly walked down the front rank of the detachment and shook hands with the officer.

At 8.15, the Marshal got into his car with his wife and Dr. Ménétrel. A crowd of some hundreds of people, who had gathered in front of the Hôtel du Parc, in spite of the rain, cheered him for the last time and sang a moving, if discordant, *Marseillaise*.

Surrounded by German cars, escorted by six motor-cyclists of his Guard, who no longer wore his flag of Head of the State, the Marshal left Vichy for a destination selected by the Germans.

The week that followed Pétain's departure to Germany marked the total disappearance of everything concerned with the Vichy Government.

Admiral Auphan, whom the Marshal had told on the 11th August to get into contact with General de Gaulle or his qualified representative in Paris, tried vainly to fulfil this last mission. According to the instructions he had received from the ex-Head of the State, he went, on the 20th August, to see Monsieur Caous, Procureur Général près de la Cour de Cassation, and collected from him the sealed envelope containing Constitutional Act No. 3 *sextiès* of the 27th September, 1943: this was the Act which created a "directory of seven members (Admiral Auphan, MM. Bouthillier, Caous, Gidel, Porché, Noël and General Weygand) charged with exercising provisional power in case of the incapacity" of the Head of the State, and the summoning as soon as possible of the National Assembly. Among the seven people nominated, eleven months earlier, two were now German prisoners: Weygand and Bouthillier. Ambassador Noël had refused the honour and was not in Paris. There remained Gidel and Porché, whom Admiral Auphan and Caous decided to summon on the following day, 21st August, at 3.30 p.m., to Porché's office at the Conseil d'État.

At the appointed hour, no one came. Auphan and Caous could only record the absence of their presumed colleagues and the impossibility of fulfilling the mission confided to them by the Marshal.

As soon as the French troops entered Paris, Admiral Auphan endeavoured to establish contact with a qualified representative of General de Gaulle: on the 27th August, in the flat of General Lacaille, ex-Director of General Huntziger's office, he met General Juin, Chief of Staff to the French Army of the Liberation. He gave him a letter for General de Gaulle, and a memorandum stating the circumstances of the mission with which Pétain had charged him.

The letter contained an appeal for French unity.

The memorandum, dealing with "the necessity for a legitimate transmission of power", had as its object the avoidance of civil war and the regular transmission of authority from Marshal Pétain to General de Gaulle.

These two documents were transmitted to General de Gaulle, who made no reply, unless it was in a speech made to the Assemblée Consultative on the 2nd March, 1945:

"At the moment of my arrival in Paris . . . I received a communication from a representative of Marshal Pétain. The representative had by written orders, dated 11th August, all necessary powers to negotiate with us 'a solution of a nature to avoid a civil war'. I showed the representative the door. Messieurs, where is the civil war?"

On the day of the interview between Admiral Auphan and General Juin, the 27th August, 1944, the Marshal's message no longer had any relevance to events.

Vichy was liberated to delirious enthusiasm. A hundred men of the Forces Français de l'Intérieur (F.F.I.) had been sufficient to take possession of the town. The transmission of power from the representatives of Vichy to those of the Resistance had taken place at the Swiss Legation under the auspices of Minister Stucki. On the following day, nearly all the high officials of the Vichy Government, who had remained in the capital, were under arrest.

Paris was liberated and General de Gaulle proceeded down the Champs Élysées in triumph, escorted by his companions and members of the Conseil National de la Résistance.

At the Hôtel de Ville, the President of the Conseil National de la Résistance, Georges Bidault, asked the General to appear on the balcony and proclaim the Republic.

"No," replied the General, "the Republic has never ceased to exist."

It was a short but revealing reply: it refused not only all legitimacy but even all reality to the Government which, at Vichy, during the four years of the occupation, had asserted that it represented power.

EPILOGUE

# SIGMARINGEN

## (25th August, 1944–26th April, 1945)

AT Pétain's last halt on French soil, he was welcomed by the smallest of French Departments and the only tract of Alsatian country which, since 1871, the Germans had not claimed.

On the 21st August, towards the end of the afternoon, the Marshal was received at Belfort by Laval, who had come from Paris with Ministers Bichelonne, Gabolde and Marion, and by the Prefect Lalanne. Bonnard joined them.

Belfort was also the place chosen by Darnand for six thousand of his most compromised Militia who were accompanied by their wives and children, altogether some ten thousand people. Darnand needed money to support all this crowd. But there was no difficulty about that! There was a branch there of the Banque de France. The Militia surrounded it, sub-machine guns at the ready. With this escort, Darnand marched into the Manager's office with a Requisition Order, which he had taken the trouble to sign himself, for five hundred and thirty million Francs (ten billions today). The Manager protested that he had only three hundred million; Darnand graciously accepted it.

The leaders of the collaborationist parties Déat, Doriot, and the Führer of the Parisian Press, Luchaire, were at Nancy, where was also Ambassador Brinon: they were already intriguing with the German authorities for the formation of a satellite Government.

On the other hand, the Marshal and Laval rejected all political activity, wishing there to be no doubts concerning the freedom that had been left them.

"I am a prisoner," said the Marshal when refusing to receive Bichelonne and Gabolde, who asked for an audience, "a prisoner sees no one but his guard." Laval adopted the same attitude: "I wanted to hand you my resignation, Monsieur le Maréchal, but now that I know what has happened, I have changed my mind. I do not wish to allow Déat, Doriot, and Brinon to form a Government. I refuse to take any governmental action. But I shall not resign."

During these days, Pétain and Laval made their last public acts. The Head of the Government was in the Préfecture of a strip of Alsatian territory: the Head of the State lived in the château of a village, at Morvillars.

Laval learned that four hundred political prisoners were detained in a barracks in Belfort: he intervened, had two hundred freed, among whom was the Senator-Mayor of Nice, Médecin, and had food and clothes sent to the rest. On the 24th August, Hemmen, the organiser of the economic pillaging of all France, wished to continue his thieving in the eastern territories which were still temporarily under his control. He demanded that eight billions of francs, which were due on the occupation costs, should be immediately paid; he asked Laval to make the Banque de France at Nancy make valid new bank notes. The ex-Head of the Government replied that he no longer exercised power: "You took enough in Paris. That should suffice."

On the 25th August, there was a last intervention by the Nazis, a last piece of blackmail to persuade Laval to play a political part. The Führer himself invited the President to his headquarters to discuss Franco-German relations, a fact which the French statesman did not think augured well. He summoned the Ministers, who were present in Belfort, to the Council Room: an air raid warning obliged them to hold their discussions in the basement. It was there, in this last avatar of his political life, that Laval informed his colleagues of the negative reply he was sending Abetz.

Since Déat, Brinon and Darnand had accepted the invitation, Laval, in agreement with the Marshal, sent Marion to accompany them: his role was merely that of an observer; he would travel as a private individual and without official status.

Faced with Laval's refusal, Abetz was furious: "The Führer," he said, "will take your refusal as a personal insult. You still have two million Frenchmen in Germany: Hitler is capable of reacting in an appalling way."

In fact, the Frenchmen were not received with much cordiality. Hitler's headquarters at this period was still preserved from the realities of war. This gave it an extraordinary atmosphere which resulted in complete confidence in victory and in the secret weapons which guaranteed it in German eyes.

On arrival, the French notabilities, who, having been joined by Doriot, had travelled in the personal aircraft of Burckel, the Gauleiter of Alsace, were searched by the guards. Then, having been herded into a corner and watched over by S.S. men with pistols at their belts, they were received first by Ribbentrop and then by Hitler.

The Führer addressed them in the following terms: "Gentlemen, I have already defeated the British army on the Rhine. I have at my disposal secret weapons of which the V 1 and the V 2 can only give you a feeble idea; thanks to these weapons I shall again take the offensive, I shall throw the Anglo-Saxons into the sea."

Then, staring fixedly at them, he said: "It will be terrible because the battle will be fought over the body of your country; I ask your pardon, Gentlemen, and of France and of God."

Impressed by these threats, which in a few days' time were to be the background of all conversations of the French in exile, the collaborators obeyed the Chancellor's wishes. Brinon felt that he was called on to take the lead and he decided to constitute a "Governmental Commission for French Interest in Germany" whose President he would be "under the high authority of the Marshal".

Pétain, when Marion on his return made his report, disavowed the Government Commission, refused to receive Brinon and limited himself to informing him through General Debeney that the prisoners were protected by the Hague Convention, that the workers were protected by regular agreements between Vichy and Berlin, and that his so-called Government had therefore no reason for existing. Following the Marshal's example, Ambassador Scapini, who was in charge of relations with the prisoners, always ignored the Government Commission.

Furthermore, in an exchange of letters with Laval, the Head of the State declared categorically that there was an end to all French governmental action under German constraint:

"Having no longer any French territorial support," Laval wrote to the Marshal, "as you say in your letter, my position as Head of the Government has no further relevance.

"You have adopted the same attitude. My resignation in these circumstances would constitute a governmental action on my part of which you could not take cognisance, since you have yourself renounced the exercise of your functions as Head of the State.

"The situation is perfectly clear, clearer indeed than a resignation which could not be published in the *Journal Officiel.*"

In spite of the Führer's threats, it was abdication pure and simple.

In the meantime, Brinon was organising his Government Commission at Belfort, with the object, according to him, of protecting French interests in Germany and of assuring to French workers and prisoners the normal status of nationals of an allied Government. Three ex-Ministers formed part of it: General Bridoux, who was concerned with military affairs (they did not dare appoint him Minister of National Defence) and the prisoners; Déat, appointed to Labour and Social Solidarity; Darnand, to the Militia. Jean Luchaire was appointed to Information; but the latter, who was unlucky, didn't even then obtain the rank of Minister which he had always coveted: he had to content himself with being "Commissaire Général of Information and Propaganda".

On the 7th September the journey to Germany took place. The fighting was approaching Belfort: it was known that de Lattre's army was at Strasbourg. At 6.30 a.m., the convoy set out accompanied with considerable military strength.

As he got into his car, the Marshal gave Renthe-Fink a protest addressed to Hitler:

"To Monsieur le Chef de l'État Grand Allemand,

"The Government of the Reich gave me on the 19th August, 1944, an assurance that, whatever the circumstances, I should remain on French soil, when I was obliged under constraint and by force to leave Vichy where I had fixed, in the freedom accorded by the Armistice Conventions, the seat of the Government.

"Today, in spite of this solemn assurance, I am being taken into captivity in Germany. I take note of this new coercion which is added to so many others and I declare that it is impossible for me to exercise the functions of Head of the French State, with which I was invested by the National Assembly. I refuse to bow to this demand as I refused to leave France in 1940.

"Once again, I make the most solemn protest against this act of force which nothing can justify."

On his side, Laval, profoundly moved at the moment of leaving France, indeed scarcely able to speak, read a verbal note to Abetz:

"Last April I gave Prefects and officials orders to remain at their posts in case of landings. They obeyed me. Some have paid with their freedom and sometimes even with their lives for having obeyed this order. It seems to me that I have behaved badly, like the captain of a sinking ship who orders his crew to remain on board while he himself leaves. He has no right to say to his men: 'Stay here, while I go.' You will therefore the better understand my protest, which I reiterate today, at the moment when I am leaving the soil of my Fatherland.

"I knew the risks I was running. I accepted them with a sense of duty towards those who have always obeyed my orders. I accepted them in order to give all Frenchmen a new proof of the love in which I hold my country."

The Marshal crossed the Rhine at 11 a.m. They halted at Fribourg-en-Brisgau. Due to the emotions aroused by leaving, Laval had forgotten at Belfort the overcoat in whose lining, ever since November, 1942, had been kept the poison, which he used in prison a year later. A car retrieved it for him.

On the 8th September, in the morning, the Marshal resumed the journey; Laval resumed his on the morning of the 9th.

After a splendid drive through the Black Forest, the convoy arrived at Sigmaringen and found the population in a state of excitement. The little town on the banks of the Danube, which had been assigned as a residence for the French, was one of the places in Germany which had remained the most anti-Nazi, and was even attached to the old reigning dynasties. Dominated by the castle of the Hohenzollerns, Sigmaringen, a romantic old town to which each generation of princes had added colossal and complicated stone buildings, was still living on the periphery of the war.

The Marshal's car drew up at the foot of an enormous castle built on a crag of rock at a bend in the Danube. There was no reception ceremony. Pétain, accompanied by his suite, went up in the lift to the seventh storey where were the private apartments. He took up his residence there with his wife, Ménétrel, General Debeney, Admiral Bléhaut and naval Lieutenant Sacy.

On the 9th September, Laval arrived with his wife, and ex-Ministers, Bichelonne, Bonnard, Gabolde, Déat, Brinon, Bridoux, Darnand and Marion. There were also a few high officials such as

Rochat. Hundreds of Militiamen and hangers-on found room in the castle and its dependencies.

At Sigmaringen, the Marshal and Laval persisted in the attitude they had taken up at Belfort: they refused to play any political role or to have any relations with the Germans.

The Marshal even went so far as to ask that his own residence might be transferred outside Sigmaringen in order that he might avoid the neighbourhood of Brinon and his "Ministers".

He protested every time the broadcasts of Brinon or Darnand from Radio Stuttgart invoked his patronage.

He avoided the traps the Nazis set in order to try and compel him, in spite of himself, to make some authoritative act.

In their state apartments, which were next door to but separated from the rooms given to the Marshal and his suite, Pierre Laval and Mme. Laval adopted the same attitude of aloofness towards the Germans.

In his voluntary retirement, Laval was less canvassed than the Marshal. Hitler had forgiven him neither his refusal to obey his summons on the 25th August, nor his refusal to recognise Brinon's Government Commission. He decided to isolate him, to place him in a less luxurious habitation and one more easy to keep under surveillance. Laval was transferred to Wielflingen, in Württemberg, to a modest country house, where he might at least enjoy the rural atmosphere he loved.

The Vichy ex-Ministers in Sigmaringen behaved in a variety of ways.

Some, who might be called "passive", such as Gabolde, Marion and Bichelonne, also behaved as prisoners and refused to take any action so long as the Marshal was not free and had not resumed the exercise of the powers which had been conferred upon him by the National Assembly four years earlier. They had, moreover, no illusions about a German victory. Marion said that Germany had lost the war, that only a rupture between the U.S.S.R. and the U.S.A., which would allow of a reversal of alliances, could give the Reich the chance of winning the war with either Russia or America as her partner. This hypothesis was the subject of much talk and exercised idle minds: there were many discussions as to whether an alliance with Stalin was preferable to an alliance with Roosevelt: the exiles at

Sigmaringen declared themselves anti-capitalists or anti-Bolsheviks according to choice. That was the extent of their activity: to this their hopes were reduced.

Bonnard also maintained a reserve: in order to console himself for the inaction to which he was reduced, Sigmaringen gave him the opportunity, as Vichy and Paris had done in the past, of making witticisms some of which were brilliant though others were in more doubtful taste.

On the other hand, the members of the Government Commission were extremely active.

Luchaire, to mention but one of them, set up his organisation on a ministerial scale: his staff amounted to over two hundred people with a number of Directors General. . . . He created a radio station, "Ici la France", called "the Government Station", which broadcast every day for an hour and a half, from 7.30 to 9 p.m. He issued a daily paper called *la France*.

The ex-Commissaire for Prisoners, André Masson, who had given his adherence to the Government Commission, transformed himself into a recruiting agent for the Waffen S.S. in the camps.

Beside these so-called "officials", the political personnel of this simulacrum of a capital included the Paris organisations which had retreated to the Danube. The Militia had reformed itself at Ulm. Darnand had the honour of being summoned by Hitler who congratulated him on the attitude of the Militiamen who had "died for a great cause". Himmler then presented him with an ultimatum: he was prepared to allow a Franc-Garde of two thousand men to exist on condition that a third of the Militiamen enlisted in the Charlemagne Brigade to fight on the Russian front, and that another third worked for the benefit of the Reich. Darnand accepted: two thousand Militiamen, abandoned by their Chief, were enrolled more or less by force in the Charlemagne Brigade. Darnand (in the uniform of a Commandant of the Wehrmacht) inspected them.

Some of the militants of the R.N.P. had grouped themselves about Marcel Déat in the offices of the "Minister for Labour". Déat took his role of "future head of the State" extremely seriously, and assumed great airs of importance at Sigmaringen while waiting to rule in Paris. He became the patron of organisations which were still imaginary and created a "Centre Syndicaliste de Propagande", which was to recruit the cadres for the future Syndicalist and Socialist state of which he had always dreamed; a college of public instruction, of which Professor Lalouelle of Nancy was put in charge, already seeing himself as Director of the École des Sciences Politiques or Rector of the University; a centre of Études Sportives, which was confided to Cartonnat, and which was to assure the regeneration of French youth; and an organisation for leisure, which might have been of some use to the idle emigrants.

There was only one party which took any real action in exile, and this was Doriot's Parti Populaire Français. The fact was that Doriot, among the Déats, the Bucards and the Luchaires, among all the hirelings of Otto Abetz who had followed him from the banks of the Seine to the Danube, was the only one who had an effective force under his control, a taste for political action and a sense of organisation. Doriot also had the benefit of the complete support of one of the Nazi leaders, Burckel, the Gauleiter of Alsace.

Doriot, an ex-Communist leader who had gone over to Nationalism and had been subsidised even before the war by the Fascist Embassy, seemed, however paradoxical this may appear, to be imitating at Sigmaringen, de Gaulle's actions in London. He also considered himself a dissident who had abandoned France the better to reconquer her. He organised parachutings into France and had secret ways by which his secret agents could cross the frontier. From October, 1944, to March, 1945, the average number of secret agents crossing into France was between ten and fifteen a week, their losses amounting to 20 per cent. in October, 60 per cent. in November, 35 per cent. in December, 20 per cent. in January and February, and 45 per cent. in March. Those who were not caught remained in contact with the dissidents on the Danube by means of secret wireless messages to Radio-Patrie, which was set up at Landau on the 22nd October, 1944, and which relayed Radio Stuttgart. Doriot also had his paper *le Petit Parisien*, which now appeared in Germany. He set up his own Intelligence Services in the complementary formations by placing his creatures in good jobs in the Government Commission, the R.N.P., and the Militia. Finally, wishing to acquire similar laurels to the Comité Français de la Libération Nationale, which had prepared de Gaulle's return to Metropolitan France, he founded at the beginning of 1945 a Comité de Libération Française, of which he was the President and which was to transform itself into the French Government when he returned to France.

Doriot also maintained that he had his own secret *maquisards* in France.

Doriot, who thus stands out as the only authentic militant revolutionary in Sigmaringen was, moreover, the only French emigrant whose actions were directly supported by Hitler. He had an interview with him at the beginning of December at which Ribbentrop and Himmler were present: the Führer, after dinner, conferred on him a solemn investiture, which had more than purely moral advantages: "Doriot," he said, "I know that you are a brave soldier; I also believe that you are a really revolutionary politician. I believe in your success," and, turning to Himmler and Ribbentrop, he said to the former: "You will give M. Doriot the power and material means necessary to the success of his task," and to the latter: "Give him Reinebeck with the title and powers of Ambassador Extraordinary. That will facilitate M. Doriot's work."

Over a period of several days, the Führer, who must have had more urgent tasks in this month of December, 1944, conferred with Doriot and charged him with forming a Government for Franco-German collaboration.

Having returned to his headquarters at Landau in possession of money, motor cars, petrol, paper for his newspaper and accommodation for his staff, Hitler's newly elect tossed back the champagne at a wild orgy during which his companions and the young women of the P.P.F. sowed on German soil those morals which are reputed to be "Parisian". The "Chief" was in full euphoria. He would succeed in his activities which would bring him power when the Germans won the war: Déat, Luchaire and Brinon were no longer of any importance beside him.

The life of this charming crowd, which swarmed in the shadow of the lofty residence of the imprisoned Head of the State, falls into three periods: one of place-seeking in the expectation of victories to come; one of hope in which it seemed that the victories might soon be realised; and one of confusion and flight.

The first period dated from the arrival at Sigmaringen in September, 1944, to December, 1944. For the most part, it was a period of disappointment.

The emigrants at Sigmaringen somewhat naïvely imagined that they could soon make their return from Elba, and be received as liberators by the population of a France indignant at the excesses committed by the "Communists" of Algiers and by the invading troops. In fact, all the news coming from France was favourable to de Gaulle, depicting him as being everywhere acclaimed and recognised by all the Great Powers.

Nevertheless, the emigrants did not despair. They were busy over the quarrels between Doriot and Déat, while the Führer's summonses to the French leaders persuaded them that France would play a leading part in Nazi Europe. For they believed in a German victory and in their early return to France. Some, misquoting de Gaulle, asseverated that the Reich had lost the battle but would not lose the war. Had not the Wehrmacht terrible secret weapons? Fourteen V weapons, of which the V 3, to be fired from submarines, could reach New York. Then a liquid air bomb, an atomic bomb of course, an incandescent bomb which would give off thousands of degrees of heat, mauve gas, orange gas, human torpedoes against aircraft, pink clouds and the notorious death ray which would bring down the American Flying Fortresses in their dozens.

A mixture of disappointment and illusion created the bitter-sweet climate which reigned over Sigmaringen when von Rundstedt's offensive began in the Ardennes: it was the beginning of the second period, the period of hope.

This offensive, which for a few days made the populations of Belgium and France fear a return of the Nazis in force and a new occupation, was received by the majority of the French at Sigmaringen with a joy similar to that with which, seven months earlier, in June, 1944, the French of the occupied territories had learned of the allied landings. It was, too, according to the Germans, May, 1940 beginning all over again: a blitzkrieg in force against the hinge of the allied armies which would destroy them.

On the 16th December, when the news broke, a mad hope filled the hearts of all these misguided Frenchmen. For the most part, they had no doubt: they would all be back in Paris by the 1st January.

But Rundstedt's offensive failed: the people of Paris could celebrate the New Year in peace. In Germany, the Wehrmacht began to disband itself, while the Gestapo, the last bulwark of the regime, grew more and more inflexible. Soldiers travelled in the trains in groups of ten with false leave passes, their aspect perfectly normal, but they did not return to their regiments. At the front only the S.S. and the tanks were holding out and, in the rear, the police. Communications were cut by the bombing. The bread ration was reduced. After the occupation of Silesia, sugar disappeared. The news from all fronts was bad. Twilight was falling on Nazi Germany and on Sigmaringen.

Two months later, it was a question of flight.

The first man to grasp the imminence of the catastrophe and to succeed, while there was yet time, in getting comfortably away was Louis-Ferdinand Céline who, towards the middle of March, fled to Norway, thus preceding by more than a month his exiled fellow countrymen.

Céline, in this tragic spring, was the migratory bird who anticipates a change of weather by flying away first. A month later, at the end of April, the French at Sigmaringen realised that they had to go: Stuttgart was surrounded by the Americans, de Lattre's army was marching towards Lake Constance.

Like fish in a bow-net when it closes, the fugitives rushed despairingly to and fro in a frenzied search for refuge or escape. Some went to the Tyrol, where it was said the Wehrmacht was organising an impregnable redoubt: others towards the Italian frontier, as if a Customs post could stop the advance of Patton's tanks; others placed all their hopes in Swiss hospitality, and others still, of higher rank, who thought they would have an aircraft at their disposal, already saw themselves in Spain or in the New World.

Mingled with this atmosphere of panic were still a few of the illusions which had been nourished by the exiles. Some still believed in the secret weapons, which would bring victory at the last moment. Others awaited, in their more optimistic moments, the compromise peace which the Führer would "offer" the Anglo-Saxons in order to help them deal with the Russians. The P.P.F.—such of them as remained—arrived one day in Innsbrück, where they obtained passports to go to a new concentration area at Verona in Italy. Darnand's Militia followed them with their arms and baggage. But soon the frontier was closed: Brinon was seen in Innsbrück going from Consulate to Consulate without being able to obtain a visa. Déat and his wife disappeared during an excursion into the mountains. Luchaire suddenly discovered that he had another nationality: stating that he was an Italian, he wished to go to his country, Italy, to the land of his fathers. This new nationality was disallowed: he was compelled to call himself French.

Amid this collapse, what became of the ex-Head of the Government and the ex-Head of the State?

Laval had left Sigmaringen for the Swiss frontier with his wife and Gabolde. Having no official Nazi papers permitting him to pass the German Customs, and knowing that de Lattre's army was advancing towards Lake Constance, he telegraphed Ribbentrop asking for his authorisation. On the 4th April, the German Minister for Foreign Affairs replied: "Am prepared to give authorisation for Switzerland. But impossible make decision without agreement Chancellor Hitler." Laval sent another telegram to the Führer: which was answered at once: "Authorise departure on certain conditions which will be transmitted to you."

On the 15th April, Graf von Grussig arrived, bearing the Chancellor's conditions. They were unacceptable: Laval had to engage himself to make a declaration, on his arrival in Switzerland, that the German Government had always left complete autonomy to the Vichy Government and that Franco-German collaboration had had as its sole objective assistance to Germany in the defeat of Bolshevism.

Laval argued breathlessly, knowing well that time was short, but he refused to agree at least to the first part of the declaration. Nevertheless, the authorisation was in the end given. On the 16th April, Laval and his *entourage* appeared at the Swiss Frontier, asking for the right of asylum. There were conversations all day with a Swiss diplomatic agent, who that evening transmitted the reply of the Swiss Government: it was a refusal. Trapped, Laval the following day tried the Lichtenstein frontier. This tiny principality, normally so welcoming to business men in difficulties, also refused him access.

Laval, in a state of exhaustion, then sent a message to his friend Lequerica, ex-Spanish Ambassador to Vichy, and now Minister for Foreign Affairs at Madrid.

On the 28th April, Lequerica replied: Laval might come to Spain on condition that his stay did not exceed three months and that he consented, for his own personal security and for diplomatic reasons, to reside within the precincts of the fortress of Monjuich. He was given an assurance that he would not be handed over to the French authorities, should they demand him, but that he would be handed over to the allied authorities, if they so desired.

On the 2nd May, a Junkers 38, placed at Laval's disposal by the Wehrmacht, left one of the last airfields in the west still under German control; on board was Laval, his wife and Gabolde.

Laval remained in Spain for the agreed three months. On the 31st July, the Spaniards deported him against his will; he left the peninsula by air and was handed over to the allies at Linz.

Alone of all the survivors of Vichy, Pétain wished at all costs to return to France. The Marshal, while still at Sigmaringen, had learned on 5th April, by the radio, that his trial would begin in Paris on the 24th April. Far from wishing to avoid appearing, he desired to reply personally to the accusations.

"Monsieur le Chef de l'État Grand Allemand," he immediately wrote to Hitler, "I have just learned that the French authorities propose to put me on trial in my absence before the High Court of Justice. The trial will begin on the 24th April. This news imposes an obligation on me which I look on as imperative and I ask your Excellency to facilitate my accomplishing my duty.

"I received on the 10th July, 1940, from the National Assembly, a mandate which I have fulfilled to the best of my ability in the circumstances. As Head of the Government in June, 1940, at Bordeaux, I refused to leave France. As Head of the State, when grave hours once more faced my country, I decided to remain at my post in Vichy. The Government of the Reich compelled me to leave on the 20th August, 1944.

"I cannot, without forfeiting my honour, allow it to be believed, as some tendentious propaganda is insinuating, that I sought refuge in a foreign country in order to evade my responsibilities. It is only in France that I can answer for my actions and I am the only judge of the risks that this attitude may entail.

"I therefore have the honour of earnestly asking your Excellency to give me this opportunity. You will naturally understand the decision I have reached of defending my honour as Head of the State and of protecting by my presence all those who have followed me. It is my only object. No argument can make me abandon this decision.

"At my age, there is only one thing one still fears: it is not to have done all one's duty, and I wish to do mine."

This letter remained unanswered. On the morning of the 20th April, the Marshal received a visit from his Nazi guardian, Reinebeck.

"Monsieur le Maréchal, the military situation has become such that it is essential you should leave for the south-east."

"You know my position," replied the Marshal. "I want only one thing: to return to France as soon as possible. I have written a letter to this effect, but have received no reply. The journey you suggest would have the result of postponing my return to France. I refuse to go."

In spite of this protest, at 4 a.m., the following morning, the cars were drawn up in the courtyard of the castle. Boemelburg, in command of the S.S., who were to protect the convoy, said: "If it's necessary to handcuff the Marshal, I am prepared to do so."

Six cars full of police escorted the three cars containing the Marshal and his suite. The convoy made its way through the night along a road crowded with fleeing and disorganised troops, frequently threatened by low level attacks from allied aircraft.

Their first halt was at a little town, Wangen, where no preparations had been made and where the Mayor had to sound the air raid alarm in order to make the population take refuge in the shelters and free the streets about the Marshal's car.

The second halt was at Zell, further north, at a castle full of refugees: two religious communities from Cologne, an orphanage, people from Berlin, Silesians, and the treasures from the museum at Stuttgart. Three freezing rooms were put at the disposal of the French: the Marshal's guards, fearing he would be kidnapped, slept on mattresses at his door.

There was every indication of the early arrival of the allied armies: an uninterrupted flow of retreating German troops passing below the castle. The sound of bombing could be heard near at hand.

Tangstein, who had replaced Renthe-Fink, had permanent instructions never to allow the Marshal to fall into the hands of the allied troops. He would answer for it with his head.

Pétain, on the other hand, proposed to await at Zell the arrival of the Americans, who had already taken Ulm.

The American tanks were now no more than 20 kilometres from Zell. At 6 o'clock in the morning, Tangstein rushed into the Marshal's room. It was necessary to leave.

From his bed, the Marshal replied: "Leave me alone, I've had enough of this. At my age, one can't bear fatigue of this kind. . . . If I knew that you had the agreement of the Swiss to my entry in transit, I might believe you."

Tangstein saw a possible solution.

"The Swiss Minister is only twenty minutes away . . . I'll go and see him. We can ask Switzerland whether they will agree: you will see that I am acting in good faith."

"And then," said the Marshal, "I shall not leave unless a Swiss diplomat accompanies me to the frontier."

On the 24th April, in the morning, the agreement of the Swiss authorities having been received, the Marshal, whose eighty-ninth birthday it was, reached the Swiss frontier. The Germans took their leave of him.

"We have taken this upon ourselves," said Tangstein, "and I fear that it may not be very well received in high places."

The Swiss Government informed the provisional French Government of the Marshal's desire to surrender himself as a prisoner at the French frontier.

On the 25th April, the ex-Swiss Ambassador at Vichy, Stucki, came to spend the afternoon with the ex-Head of the State. At 4 p.m. he received a telephone call from Berne: it was to ask him to inform the Marshal that the French Government requested him to be at the frontier, at Vallorbe, on the following day, at 7 p.m.

At the agreed hour, a leading French official, the Commissaire de la République of Dijon, entered Swiss territory to meet Pétain and inform him that a warrant had been issued against him: the Marshal was to be placed under surveillance.

At the Frontier, the barrier rose; the cars entered France and stopped.

A few soldiers and policemen hesitated, uncertain whether they should present arms or not. A General came forward and asked the Marshal to get out of his car: it was General Koenig, whom Pétain did not know.

Having placed his foot to earth, the Marshal extended his hand. Koenig refused to take it.

# BIBLIOGRAPHY

THE complete bibliography for this book appears in the French Edition, published by the Librairie Arthème Fayard, Paris, and in the American edition in the French language, published in Montreal and New York by the Cercle du Livre de France. It consists of no less than eleven pages. In addition to the published works, it contains a great quantity of unpublished documents and oral evidence to which the English reader would find it difficult to refer.

For the latter's benefit, I have drawn up a shorter bibliography, containing only books published in France, most of which are still in print.

They are mostly personal memoirs of the period with which this book deals. Some few, written apologetically or defensively, lack impartiality. Others adopt a polemical tone unsuited to an historical work. They may, nevertheless, be useful to the English reader by providing him with direct knowledge of the principal actors in the drama and a better appreciation of the contrasting currents of the period. I should like to draw the attention of specialists in this historical field to the existence of the Bibliothèque de Documentation Internationale Contemporaine of the Académie de Paris, 5 Rue Auguste Vacquerie, Paris (16°), whose competence and understanding of historical research have been of great help to me in my work. The assistance of this specialised organisation is indispensable to the student.

## I PUBLISHED TRIALS

*Le Procès du Maréchal Pétain:* Shorthand report, 2 vol, Albin Michel, 1945, and *Journal Officiel.*

*Le Procès Laval:* Shorthand report, Albin Michel, 1946.

*Le Procès de Charles Maurras:* Shorthand report, Albin Michel, 1946.

*Les Procès de la Radio: Ferdonnet et Jean Hérold Paquis,* Shorthand report, Albin Michel, 1947.

*Les Procès de Collaboration:* Fernand de Brinon, Jean Luchaire, Joseph Darnand. Shorthand report, Albin Michel, 1948.

*Le Procès Benoist-Méchin* (29 mai-6 juin 1947). Shorthand report, edited by Jean Louis Aujol with some variations and suppressions. Albin Michel, 1948.

*Bâtonnier Paul Buttin: Le Procès Pucheu*, Amiot-Dumont, 1948. Maurice Ribet. *Le Procès de Riom*, Flammarion, 1945.

## II MEMOIRS

Paul Baudouin: *Neuf mois au gouvernement*, la Table Ronde, 1948.

Yves Bouthillier: *Le drame de Vichy*. Tome I *Face à l'ennemi, face à l'allié*, Plon, 1950–II *Finances sous la contrainte*, Plon, 1952.

Fernand de Brinon: *Mémoires L.L.C. . . .*, 1949.

François Charles-Roux: *Cinq mois tragiques aux Affaires Etrangères, 21 mai-1er novembre 1940*. Plon, 1949.

Pierre Cathala: *Face aux réalités. La Direction des finances françaises sous l'occupation*. Editions du Triolet, 1948.

Amiral Decoux: *A la barre de l'Indochine* (1940–1945) Plon, 1949.

Amiral Fernet: *Aux côtés du Maréchal Pétain. Souvenirs, 1940–1944*, Plon, 1953.

Comte Galeazzo Ciano: *Journal Politique (1939–1943)* 2 vol. la Baconnière, 1946.

Albert Kammerer: *La vérité sur l'armistice*. Ed. Médicis, décembre, 1944.

*Laval Parle:* (Notes and memoirs written by Pierre Laval in his prison cell together with a preface by his daughter and numerous unpublished documents.) A l'Enseigne du Cheval Ailé, Genève, 1948.

Albert Lebrun: *Témoignages*. Plon 1945.

Amiral William D. Leahy: *J'étais là*, Plon 1950.

Jean Montigny: *Toute la vérité sur un mois dramatique (15 juin, 15 juillet 1940)*. Editions Mont-Louis, Clermont-Ferrand, 1940.

Henri du Moulin de Labarthète: *Le temps des illusions, Souvenirs (juillet 1940–avril 1942)* Le Cheval Ailé Genève 1946.

Marcel Peyrouton: *Du service à la prison commune*. Plon 1950.

Pierre Pucheu: *Ma Vie*. Amiot-Dumont, 1948.

Paul Reynaud: *Au coeur de la mêlée (1930–1945)* Flammarion, 1951.

Rossi: *Les communistes français pendant la drôle de guerre*. Iles d'Or, 1951.

Louis Rougier: *Mission secrète à Londres. (les accords Pétain-Churchill)* Cheval Ailé, 1946. Genève. *Les accords secrets franco-britanniques. Histoire et imposture*. Grasset, 1954.

Jean Tracou: *Le Maréchal aux liens*. André Bonne, 1948.

Général Weygand: *Rappelé au service*. Flammarion, 1950.

## III STUDIES

Pierre Arnoult: *Les finances de la France et l'Occupation allemande (1940–1944)*. P.U.F., 1951.

Pierre Audiat: *Paris pendant la guerre.* Hachette, 1946.
Louis Baudin: *Esquisse de l'économie française sous l'occupation allemande.* Editions Politiques, Economiques et Sociales, 1945.
Prince Xavier de Bourbon: *Les accords secrets franco-anglais de décembre 1940.* Plon, 1949.
Chamine: *Suite Française. La Conspiration d'Alger.* Albin Michel, 1946. *La querelle des Généraux.* Albin Michel, 1952.
Adrien Dansette: *Histoire de la Libération de Paris.* Fayard, 1946.
Alain Darlan: *L'amiral Darlan parle.*
Louis Dominique Girard: *Montoire, Verdun diplomatique.* André Bonne, 1948.
*L'Appel de l'Ile d'Yeu.* André Bonne, 1951.
*La guerre franco-française.* André Bonne, 1950.
Mgr. Guerry: *L'Eglise catholique en France sous l'occupation.* Flammarion, 1947.
Albert Kammerer: *Du débarquement africain au meurtre de Darlan.* Flammarion, 1949.
*La passion de la flotte française.* Fayard, 1951.
J. Lubetzki: *La condition des Juifs en France sous l'occupation allemande, 1940–1944. La législation raciale.* Centre de documentation privé contemporaine, 1945.
Henri Massis: *Maurras et notre temps,* 2 vol.
Henri Michel: *Histoire de la Résistance.* P.U.F. 1950.
Rossi: *Physiologie du Parti communiste.* S.E.F.I. 1948.
*Une page d'histoire: les communistes française pendant la drôle de guerre.* Iles d'Or, 1951.
Pierre Varillon: *Mers-el-Kébir.* Paris, Amiot-Dumont 1949.

## IV BOOKS PUBLISHED SUBSEQUENTLY

Général De Gaulle: *Mémoires de guerre.*
Tome 1—*l'Appel* (1940–1942). Plon, 1954.
Tome 2—*L'Unité* (1942–1944). Plon, 1956.
Louis Noguères: (Ancien Président de la Haute Cour de Justice). *Le Véritable Procès du Maréchal Pétain.* Fayard, 1955.
Hoover Institute: *La vie de la France sous l'occupation* (1940–1944). 3 volumes of documents collected by Josée Laval and René de Chambrun. Plon, 1957.
Jacques Benoist-Méchin: *Soixante Jours qui ébranlèrent l'Occident.*
Tome 1 *La bataille du Nord* (10 mai–4 juin 1940).
Tome 2 *La bataille de France* (4 juin–25 juin 1940).
Tome 3 *La fin du régime* (26 juin–10 juillet 1940).
Albin Michel, 1956.

# INDEX





34

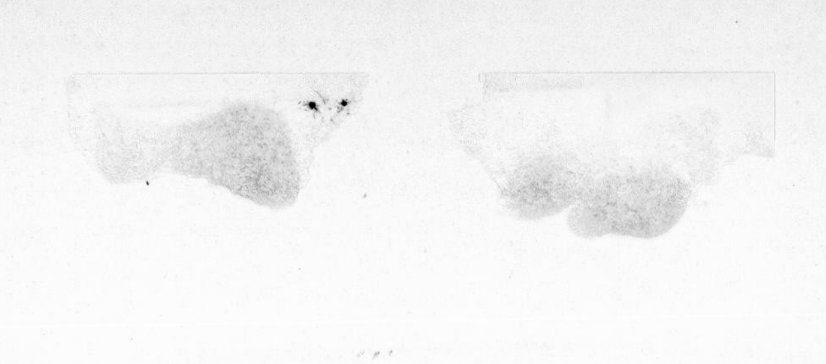